LITTLE
WILSON
and BIG
GOD

ALSO BY ANTHONY BURGESS

novels

The Long Day Wanes
   Time for a Tiger
   The Enemy in the Blanket
   Beds in the East
The Right to an Answer
The Doctor is Sick
The Worm and the Ring
Devil of a State
One Hand Clapping
A Clockwork Orange
The Waning Seed
Honey for the Bears
Inside Mr Enderby
Nothing like the Sun: A Story
   of Shakespeare's Love-Life
The Eve of Saint Venus
A Vision of Battlements
Tremor of Intent
Enderby Outside
MF
Napoleon Symphony
The Clockwork Testament
   or, Enderby's End
Beard's Roman Women
Abba Abba
Man of Nazareth
1985
Earthly Powers
The End of the World News
Enderby's Dark Lady
The Kingdom of the Wicked
The Pianoplayers

for children

A Long Trip to Teatime
The Land Where the
   Ice Cream Grows

verse

Moses

non-fiction

English Literature: A Survey
   for Students
They Wrote in English
Language Made Plain
Here Comes Everybody: An
   Introduction to James Joyce
   for the Ordinary Reader
The Novel Now: A Student's
   Guide to Contemporary
   Fiction
Urgent Copy: Literary Studies
Shakespeare
Joysprick: An Introduction to
   the Language of James Joyce
New York
Hemingway and His World
On Going to Bed
This Man and Music
Ninety-Nine Novels
Flame Into Being
   The Life and Works of
   D.H. Lawrence

translator

The New Aristocrats
The Olive Trees of Justice
The Man Who Robbed Poor
   Boxes
Cyrano de Bergerac
Oedipus the King

editor

The Grand Tour
Coaching Days of England
A Shorter Finnegans Wake

LITTLE
WILSON
and BIG
GOD

THE FIRST PART OF THE CONFESSIONS

ANTHONY BURGESS

GROVE WEIDENFELD

New York

Published by Grove Weidenfeld
A division of Grove Press, Inc.
841 Broadway
New York, NY 10003-4793

First published in Great Britain in 1987 by
William Heinemann Ltd., London

A signed first edition of this book has been privately printed by
The Franklin Library.

Library of Congress Cataloging-in-Publication Data

Burgess, Anthony, 1917–
    Little Wilson and big God.

    1. Burgess, Anthony, 1917–   —Biography.
    2. Authors, English—20th century—Biography.
    I. Title.
    PR6052.U638Z464   1986   823'.914   86-26721
    ISBN 1-55584-100-7
    ISBN 0-8021-3240-5 (pbk)

Manufactured in the United States of America
Printed on acid-free paper

First American Edition 1987
First Evergreen Edition 1991

10   9   8   7   6   5   4   3   2   1

Time, in fact, is rather vulgarly dramatic; it is the
sentimentalist of the dimensions.

Music Ho! Constant Lambert

Preface

A Foreword to a reader is a hindword to an author. The author
knows what has been written, the reader has yet to find out. The
author, when he does not use his foreword to acknowledge help
received in his completed labours, sometimes stands at the
threshold which the foreword is, biting his nails and wondering
whether a brief warning, an apology for inadequacy or excess, an
avowal of mediocrity where he had intended brilliance, might
not be a courteous gesture to the person who has had the kindness
at least to pick up his book.

As far as acknowledgments of help are concerned, I have none
to make. These memoirs, which chronicle my life from birth to
the age of forty-two, are pure memories, unratified by the
reminiscences of others or by documents other than maps and Sir
Richard Winstedt's remarkable English–Malay Dictionary
(Singapore, 1952). Memories sometimes lie in relation to facts,
but facts also lie in respect of memory. Sometimes a photograph,
which pretends to record fact but in fact does not (fact cannot be
removed from time and frozen into space), can at least seem to
tell a truth more pungently than words, and I regret that, unlike
many autobiographies, this has no supplement of visual records.
When I lived in the Far East from 1954 until 1959, termites and
damp heat destroyed any photographs I had of my family or
own early life. The same has to be said of letters, school and
army reports, newspaper clippings and the like. I know that the
human brain is an inadequate storage and retrieval system, and I
trust my own little, but still I trust it.

This first volume of what, following St Augustine and
Rousseau, I call my Confessions – without the promise of such

basic spiritual revelations as they provide — is longer than I intended, and I foresee that the projected second and last volume — whose title will probably be *You've Had Your Time* — will be as long, if not longer. The delineation of oneself at such length must look like egocentricity, but an autobiography has to be egocentric. On the other hand, what do we mean by the ego? It is an existential concept, I believe, and the ego I examine is multiple and somewhat different from the ego that is doing the examining. Even the ego that began the book in September 1985 is not the one that has completed it in 1986. In other words, the book is about somebody else, connected by the ligature of a common track in time and space to the writer of this last segment of it, which cheats and looks like the first.

I write about this somebody else because I think he may stand for a great number of my generation — those who were dimly aware of the muddled ethos of the twenties, were uneasy in the thirties, served their country in the forties, and had some difficulty in coming to terms with the postwar world — the peace or prolonged truce that is still with us. He may stand also, but far more so in the as yet unwritten second volume, for those who have tried to earn a living from writing. And, as a Catholic of the North of England with Irish blood, he may stand for many who are termed English but have always had a dubious relation with their country of birth. In other words, this is allegory in the original Greek sense of 'speaking otherwise', presenting others in the shape of myself.

I think I may predict, unless some miracle of renewed inspiration occurs, that the second volume of my memoirs will bring my writing career to an end. It started late, but there are many captious critics who think it has gone on too long. Such critics will, in this book, find a whole hockeyfield of sticks to beat me with. Those readers of my novels who are not paid to review them (although reviewing does not necessarily entail reading) may be interested in their genesis and the real-life materials out of which they were made. I suppose that a novelist who produces an autobiography has a right to expect that most of its readers will also be readers of his fiction. As a good deal of real life has got into my fiction, I forbear to unscramble it all into what has been fabled by the daughters of memory, though I have unscrambled some. If anyone requires an apology for ineptness or coarseness or self-indulgence before meeting these properties in my narrative, I gladly render it now. I have spent much of my life apologising, asking for pardon first and then deciding what I should be pardoned for afterwards. Apology, then, before apologos. Now, as Walther sings in *Die Meistersinger*, begin.

A.B.   Principauté de Monaco. 1986

ONE

IF YOU REQUIRE a sententious opening, here it is. Wedged as we are between two eternities of idleness, there is no excuse for being idle now. But sometimes idleness is forced upon us. This was my situation on the afternoon of Saturday, September 21, 1985, when I sat in the vestibule of the Plaza Hotel in New York with many hours to waste before taking a taxi to Kennedy Airport. There are only eight chairs in that vestibule and they are much contended for. Having found a seat, you had better keep it, despite the scowling of cripples and matrons. I had checked out of Room 1137 (with some relief, since it is above the fire escape level) and fancied neither a stroll down Fifth Avenue in the intense autumn heat nor the sharing of a bench with a mutterer in Central Park. I could have settled to a sequence of whisky sours in the Palm Court or the Oak Bar, but my drinking days are, I think, over. The human liver, unless it is Graham Greene's, can take so much and no more, as the ghost of my first wife, dead on March 20, 1968 of cirrhosis, continues to remind me. So I sat idle, looking with old man's regret at the elegant Manhattan nymphs who swung through the swing doors on their long American legs. There were three wedding parties that day at the Plaza, the brides dressed, perhaps cynically, in white. Life was being celebrated.

Death too. There were several New Yorkers who had caught salvatory flights out of Mexico City, which had been devastated by a series of earthquakes. Their interpretation of Mexico's woe was mostly financial. 'This,' said an evident tycoon, 'is their coo de grass.' What Thomas Malthus called natural checks were at their inadequate work, trying to defuse the demographic explosion. Besides earthquakes there was an ailment called Acquired Immunity Deficiency Syndrome, busy in those New York bathhouses where male homosexuals revelled in promiscuity. It had also been a bad year for air disasters. I was shortly – after five hours of idleness – to fly to London by British Airways, and statistically, having clocked up too many thousands of air miles, I was due at least to think it possible that I might die over or in the Atlantic. It was proper to think of death.

It is always proper to think of death, especially when one is a year or so off seventy. I had, a few days before, met young people in Minneapolis who were surprised to find me still alive. They had studied a book of mine in high school or college and assumed I was a classical author, meaning a dead one. But there I was, loud and smoking Schimmelpennincks, absurd in the British manner but clearly vigorous. I had given a lecture on the sin of censorship to honour the first centennial of the Minneapolis Public Library. I had also just published two books – my twenty-eighth novel and a short study of D. H. Lawrence, who had also, the day before my lecture, accomplished his first centenary. I was at work still, but I could see that I was fast sliding into the past. A large number of tattered paperbacks dating from the 1960s were brought for my signature. A week before in London a Canadian academic had approached me with a view to writing my biography. In New York I had received the same proposal from a well-regarded literary hack. Both men assumed, touchingly, that there was a life to write about. At my age, they supposed, there had to be. But they had no doubt that I belonged to the past and, with luck, my death might occur before they reached the last chapter. They had better get their facts straight from the subject before he joined the ultimate idleness.

Sitting idly in the Plaza vestibule, I considered that it might be a reasonable idea to pre-empt the work of these two would-be biographers. I might not necessarily do it better nor even more truthfully, but it would be easier to transfer my life to my own paper than to theirs. As for truth, I might, through sheer shame at the banality of my life, be forced to distort it more than they. But Pontius Pilate's question has still not been properly answered, though he may well have given the only possible answer with his other great dictum: 'What I have written I have written.' He is surely the patron saint of writers (I accept the story of his ultimate conversion). He even had the writer's gift of choosing an infelicitous time for important utterances. The truth is fabled by the daughters of memory. It is also a variable commodity. Neapolitans in courts of law know this, for they earnestly ask their judges which kind of truth they want. The *vera verità* is the only variety unavailable. God holds possession of that, though God knows what he does with it.

Is a negative motive, the desire to pre-empt, sufficient to fire the writing of an autobiography? It is the way of modesty, for, whatever value the biographer puts on his subject, nobody ought to think that he is worth writing about. This is especially true of professional writers. They are not remarkable people, and if they are novelists they are particularly lacking in interest. The novelist siphons his inner life into the work he has already published; his outer life may be summed up in the image of a man at a desk. The career of a taxi-driver or window-cleaner is far fuller of incident. But, since he is a human being, he is not unqualified to have his life set forth. As an allegory of all men's lives it may serve to reassure, comfort, thwart ambition, reconcile the reader to the pain and frustration he has previously believed were reserved for him alone. Few lives record large triumphs. Most are memorable for misery. Any life will serve as a type of all lives. The autobiographer can see himself as the only true historian in the sense that he is presenting the life of perennial humanity. In the narrower sense he provides the raw material for the social historian, demonstrating what it was like to be imprisoned in a particular segment of time.

The professional novelist will sometimes have a sly and perhaps unworthy reason for writing about himself. In a fallow time, when he does not have the energy to invent, he will be glad to fall back on reminiscence, though recognising that it is difficult to draw a boundary between the remembered and the imagined. Finding no other food, he becomes autophagous. An autobiography may be a substitute for the novel that cannot be written. Sitting in the Plaza vestibule, I thought about the novel I had spent the past year trying to compose. My last act before leaving home for America had been to tear up a hundred and seventy pages of typescript. I had got on to the wrong track, I had researched in vain, the style was wrong, the theme seemed trivial. I was now finishing a promotional tour of a couple of books that American critics did not like. My best work, such as it was, lay in the past. I perhaps had no future. At least two reviewers hinted that I had written enough and should give up writing for golf or gardening. But I have no garden and I sold my golf clubs twenty years ago. All I can do is write.

One goes on writing partly because it is the only available way of earning a living. It is a hard way and highly competitive. My

heart drops into my bowels when I enter a bookshop and see
how fierce the competition is. But one pushes on because one has
to pay bills. There is also a privier reason for pushing on, and
that is the hopeless hope that some day that intractable enemy
language will yield to the struggle to control it. I am often told
that I write badly, and I do not disagree. Even Shakespeare envied
this man's art and that man's scope. When I hear a journalist like
Malcolm Muggeridge praising God because he has mastered the
craft of writing, I feel a powerful nausea. It is not a thing to be
said. Mastery never comes, and one serves a lifelong apprentice-
ship. The writer cannot retire from the battle; he dies fighting.
This book is another battle.

With my mind made up to write it, I took my taxi to Kennedy. At the check-in desk of the British Airways terminal I
encountered a problem that was not new. Linguists would call
it a matter of onomastics. What is the name of the man writing
this story? The air ticket said one thing, the passport another.
Travelling under a false name smells of shady dealings and
arouses suspicion in the breasts of airline agents, who are deliberately chosen for their lack of literary knowledge. It is no
good explaining that Mark Twain was not Mark Twain and
Alberto Moravia is somebody quite different. I have been
interrogated by the police at Rome Airport about my double
identity, and at Luqa in Malta I was not allowed to board. My
passport calls me John Burgess Wilson and my books are written by Anthony Burgess. As Anthony Burgess is the public persona, it is his name that gets on to hotel bills and airline tickets.
United States immigration forms insist on first and last names
and destroy an explanatory link. They show the carapace of my
nominal shrimp, the head and tail I pull off to disclose the soft
edible body. I was christened John Burgess Wilson and was
confirmed in the name of Anthony. When I published my first
novel I was forced to do so in near-diguise. I was an official of
the Colonial Office at the time, and it was regarded as improper to publish fiction under one's own name. Monographs
on the *adat perpateh* of Negri Sembilan were a different matter.
So I pulled the cracker of my total name and unfolded the
paper hat of Anthony Burgess.

Those who called me Jack are all dead. Those who call me
John are getting old. I answer to Anthony and, in Italy, to
Antonio. In the United States the digraph *th* is given the full
value of a theta or else elided. Renaissance etymologists, despite

the evidence of the Roman origin of the name, liked to believe it derived from the Greek *anthos*, a flower, and I am stuck with a piece of bad philology. Franco Zeffirelli calls me Tony, which I resent; Anthony, being a confirmation name, never had to accept the erosion of daily use and it must stand unabbreviable. Lord Grade once called me Tone boy, which was too fantastic to be resented. Glad to discard the Wilson, since there were so many Wilsons about in the literary world, I learned that Burgess was doomed to have a connotation of treachery and defection. Careless journalists have sometimes confused Guy with Anthony. I have so far merely demanded a printed apology; soon I may get tough. The name is an international one – Bourgois, Borges, Borghese. Jorge Luis Borges had the kindnesss to say to Paul Theroux in Buenos Aires: 'Anthony Burgess is good – a very generous man, by the way. We are the same – Borges, Burgess. It's the same name.' A concept, that of high citizenship of a burg or borough, united us. Although, in joke, he once called himself the Burgess of Argentina, I have never dared to call myself the Borges of Great Britain.

Burgess was the maiden name of the mother I never knew. Elizabeth Burgess, a dancer and singer, was pleonastically named the Beautiful Belle Burgess on music hall posters. She married a Manchester Wilson but was right to insist that her slightly more distinguished surname get on to my baptismal certificate. There have always been too many plain Wilsons around. Of the Wilsons I belong to there are few historical records, and the family had always to rely on myth. I have always wished to believe that the Jacke Wilson of the Lord Chamberlain's Men was one of the family. He gets into a stage direction of the First Folio, with, in *Much Ado About Nothing*, 'Enter Prince, Leonato and Jacke Wilson.' He was a singer and, as Balthazar, sang 'Sigh no more, ladies'. A contradictory tradition has a John Wilson as an Elizabethan martyr for unreformed Christianity. He was executed for publicly refusing to acknowledge the Queen as head of the Church. A good many Catholics in Lancashire, that chief stronghold of recusancy, contrived to cling to the practice of the old faith without undue molestation, but my family has never been notable for quietness or discretion. The Wilsons, anyway, were obstinate in their adherence to Rome, and I seem to be their first apostate.

The great English Catholics of the age of toleration, from Cardinal Newman to Graham Greene, have all been converts. A cradle Catholic finds it hard to take them seriously. They missed out on the suffering, never gave a drop of blood to the cause, and yielded not one rood of land to the Henrican expropriators. Until the Emancipation Act of 1829, no British Catholic was permitted higher education. The iron door of the Test Act, which required willingness to take the eucharist in its emasculated Anglican form, shut them from the legislature and the other modes of public service. The converts can look back to a family history graced by the economic rewards of Protestantism and to the advantages of education provided by a Protestant establishment. They converted in a cool time. Families may have bitterly opposed their desertion of the national church – as, to his everlasting pain, with Gerard Manley Hopkins – but the state had ceased to care. The converted Catholics of modern literature seem to be concerned with a different faith from the one I was nurtured in – naively romantic, pedantically scrupulous. Novels like *The Heart of the Matter*, *The End of the Affair*, *Brideshead Revisited* and *Sword of Honour* falsify the faith by over-dramatising it. Waugh's fictional Catholicism is too snobbish to be true. It evidently hurt Waugh deeply that his typical fellow-worshipper should be an expatriated Irish labourer and that the typical minister of the Church should be a Maynooth priest with a brogue.

The Emancipation Act was intended to placate the Irish, and the British Catholics benefited from it adventitiously. It came too late to benefit most. The wealthier recusants already sent their sons to foreign universities. Emancipation meant the establishment of Catholic public schools. The older Catholic families have never been properly assimilated into the British way of life. Even Guy Fawkes Day worries firework-buying Catholic parents. Few Catholics can enter the great English cathedrals without unease and even resentment. Catholic patriotism is inevitably imperfect. To fight for England means to fight for a Protestant culture. The monarch seems to preside over a church whose incense is compromise; there is even a detectable whiff of ancient guilt. The English Reformation undoubtedly had to come: it was a gesture of insular rejection of the Continental System, it was a clearing of the ground for the mercantile imperialism of Cromwell. Martyrs like St Thomas More and that uncanonised John Wilson were fools for turning their backs on a necessary historical process, and they had to wait long or indefinitely for their posthumous reward from Rome. They are the idiots of English triumphalism. Nevertheless, that reform came out of concupiscence, cynicism, casuistry and greed. The Church of England began as the morganatic gift of a bleary monarch; it is ending as a cricket club in which nobody knows the rules.

Whatever land the Wilsons originally had they lost. Having no land, achieving no distinction in the public life which was barred to them, they merit the silence of history. All we have is shaky myths told by the fire. They did odd jobs, sang and danced, joined foreign armies and disappeared into Belgium, migrated to Dublin, came back again with Irish wives. There was a regular tradition of marrying into Ireland, which meant often into Irish families that had taken the boat from Queenstown to Liverpool and wandered inland to Manchester. I end up as more of a Celt than an Anglo-Saxon. My father broke the tradition by marrying a Protestant of mainly Scottish ancestry – Lowland, hence Anglo-Saxon – but he married her in church with a Maynooth priest officiating: she converted easily.

My great-grandfather is the first figure to emerge from the mists, though he is misty enough. He served in the British infantry, always spoke of the Rooshians and Prooshians, and swore that the Duke of Wellington, in iron old age, had spoken to him. He also swore that he was the one who, working backstage at the Free Trade Hall when Charles Dickens was giving one of his readings, told the great man that he could have been an ornament to the profession, meaning Manchester melodrama. He ended up with one of those pungent herb shops that no longer exist. My father and his brothers would drop in on their way home from school and say: 'Please, grandad, can we have a drink of water?' They were then given draughts of sarsaparilla or dandelion and burdock or even steel wine. There used to be a quip in the Manchester music hall: 'Ah've got blue blood in mah veins, ah 'ave.' – 'What der yer think ah've got in mahn – dandelion and burdock?' This would make no sense today.

My grandfather, Jack Wilson, kept a pub in north-east Manchester called the Derby Inn. There was a nominal irony in his being a Catholic landlord. He followed tradition in having an Irish wife – Mary Ann Finnegan from Tipperary. He had a large appetite for traditional Lancashire dishes – hotpot, steak and cowheel pie, Eccles cakes, black puddings. He was pointed at in the street as a man who could 'ate a tater pie as big as his yed'. I was brought up on the same diet, though I have always found black puddings (balls of fat and blood polished with oil) far too

rich for a naturally weak stomach. Some years ago, in a *Paris
Review* interview, I gave my American interlocutor the recipe
for Lancashire hotpot. Auberon Waugh, noticing the transcript
in the *Spectator*, found the recipe 'disgusting'. This expresses a
class division as much as a regional one. The dish is made by
alternating layers of trimmed best end of neck of mutton with
sliced onions and potatoes in a large earthenware dish. Stock is
added, and finally oysters. The whole is cooked slowly in an
oven and eaten with pickled red cabbage. It was a favourite dish
on New Year's Eve in Lancashire Catholic households – or rather
it was taken out of the oven just before the striking of midnight.
New Year's Eve, preceding as it does the Feast of the Circumcision, used to be a day of abstinence. To rush to eat meat as soon
as the vigil was over was seen as a jocular flirting with sin, and
the New Year hotpot was called the Devil's Supper.

I have, in the long voyage from childhood to a kind of retirement in a Catholic principality (a sort of homing, really),
tackled most of the cuisines of the world, but, as Lin Yu Tang
said, we are finally loyal to the food of our youth, and this is
perhaps what patriotism means. In exile I can cook dishes like
hotpot, meat and potato pie, steak pie with cowheel (a Bolton
speciality, as Jeanne Moreau, who has Bolton blood, reminded
me). I cannot get Eccles cakes, nor the pork sausages sold by
Seymour Meads on Princess Road, Manchester. Graham Greene,
exiled in Antibes, feels as I do about the British pork sausage,
which the French scorn as a mere ungarlicky *boudin*. Fish and
chips are everywhere now, but they are essentially a Lancashire
matter, not even a national one. There are none like those that
came out of the huge square seething vats of the Manchester
chip-shops. Lancashire used to be famous for shops which
provided an instant meal to take home – meat pies with gravy
poured in hot from a jug, tripe and cowheels, above all fish and
chips. Lancashire housewives worked in the cotton mills, where
their delicate fingers were preferred to the clumsier, and more
expensive, digits of men. They had no time to cook, except on
Sundays, the great day of the roast with potatoes under, rice
pudding with a brown skin on, rhubarb and custard. The shops
stood in for them.

My grandfather ate what Mary Ann Wilson from Tipperary
cooked, and she cooked in the Lancashire way, which is not
fundamentally too different from the Irish: drisheens and crubeens
are black puddings and trotters in disguise. He drank tay, not tea,

of a strength sustained in the family and very much by this sundered particle of it. He spoke a modified form of the Lancashire rural dialect, one suitable for the outskirts of a great city. I inherited the accent, if not the vocabulary, and had to work hard to lose it. It was not taken seriously outside Lancashire. London saw it or heard it as a wilful and comic deformation of Received Standard, suitable for George Formby Senior or Junior but to be despised as a medium for serious intercourse. My grandfather would say, if Mary Ann had a headache, 'Oo's getten 'eed-warch.' The 'oo' is Anglo-Saxon *heo* and the 'warch' is from *weorc*. He would translate this for foreigners as 'She's got a headache,' but the Lancashire phonemes would cling to the straight English. So, for a long time, with myself. I regret the death of the dialect, which was once a literary medium: *Sir Gawain and the Green Knight* comes from the Wirral peninsula and would have been intelligible to the mediaeval Wilsons. It was debased and sentimentalised in Edwin Waugh:

> Th'art welcome, little bonny brid,
> But that shouldn' 'a coom just when tha did:
> Times is bad.
> We've 'ardly pobbies for our Joe,
> But that of course tha didn't know,
> Did t'a, lad?

Since the provincial revolt of the 1950s, the Lancashire accent, especially in its Liverpool form, has become acceptable in the big world, but the dialect itself is nearly dead. It has no orthography, and there is no literary tradition to elevate it. D. H. Lawrence was bold enough to write verse in the Derbyshire dialect, which is not very different, but it was a rearguard action, not a revolutionary one. We take the extinction of the English dialects for granted, but I have lived long enough in Italy to know the power of the Roman and the Venetian and to admire the pertinacity of the poets who continue to publish in them. They are lucky to have a traditional orthography; we can only represent our dialects in deformed and inadequate versions of the standard language, which makes them automatically comic. Lancashire, like the others, is a victim of a centralising linguistic culture. Cradle-speakers of that south-eastern dialect which became the national language of the educated have never sufficiently realised the pain we provincials have suffered in forcing ourselves to conform. For conformity was once an economic and social necessity. The standard vowel in words like 'love' is still unnatural to my tongue. I had to train myself for years to differentiate between the back vowels in the following:

> Don't rush upon your butcher in a rash and bloody passion
> If he offers you blood puddings for the customary ration.
> Don't push your mother over, utter threats or even mutter
> If she puts no sugar in your cup or on your bread no butter.

The northern dialects have a sound – represented phonetically by an inverted *m* – which serves for both the *u* in 'push' and the *o* in 'mother'. They are historically right (Shakespeare pronounced 'love' like a Lancastrian) but history cut no ice when my generation sought jobs outside the native province.

My grandfather stayed where he was – in the Derby Inn, with the odd trip to Blackpool. He tapped the barrels, removed the bungs and hammered in the vent-peg; he ranged the bottles; he served. His customers had names like Charlie Hetherington, Joe Higginbottom, Alec Warburton, Jim Shufflebottom, Jack Bamber, Albert Preston, Fred Whittle. There was one heavy beer-drinker called Taypot. To these customers my grandfather would tell stories he handed on to my father and thus to me. They were brutal jokes in the Lancashire tradition, much possessed by death and deformity. A man in north-east Manchester visits a friend in south-west Manchester and misses the last tram home. Never mind, says the friend. You can sleep with our kid. The man does so and the following morning is asked if he slept well. Aye, but your kid's arse isn't half cold. Has to be, says the friend. He's been dead three days. There is the tale of the man seen digging a hole in the depths of Boggart Hole Clough. Another man comes along and asks him what the hole is for. For t'girl I'm knocking around with. What, are you going to kill her! Naw, fuck her. Then why the hole? Because, says the digger, she's a 'unchback. There was also the grim story of the widow who kept her husband's ashes and took them as snuff. Why? Bugger was up every other 'ole of me body when he was alive, he can 'ave these now he's dead. A gentler story about husbands' ashes concerned the woman who kept them in an eggtimer. Bugger did no work living so now's his chance.

The late celebrated poet and self-confessed swingeing reviewer Geoffrey Grigson noticed a volume of my essays and divined a personality behind them. 'Who,' he said, 'could possibly like so coarse and unattractive a character?' He, son of an Anglican country vicar, was acknowledging an alien culture gruffly subsisting outside the covenant of the Protestant establishment. The coarseness is in the Wilson family, and it is bound to be unattractive to southerners. Southerners, one of whose outposts was Blackpool, were not well regarded in brutish Lancashire. They used cut glass, it was said, and peed in the same pot. To them high tea was half a hard-boiled egg and a bit of lettuce. They spoke lahdy dah. They were all bloody Protestants.

My grandmother was illiterate and had to have the evening newspaper read out to her while she was ironing. My grandfather would often falsify the news – Duke of Clarence nicked for buggery in a back alley, Kaiser's gunboats halfway up the Irwell, price of ale to be doubled – and would reserve his simpler fantasies for the necrology columns. 'Tha knows Charlie Hetherington? Well, he's dead.' My grandmother would go glory be to God and put down the flatiron to cross herself. Charlie Hetherington would then walk into the pub, alive and ready. 'Tha knows Jackie Eccles that gets called Taypot? Well, he's dead.' Taypot had a stroke that night and got into the obituary columns next day. After that my grandfather gave up his falsifyings.

He rarely used the definite article. 'Shift cat,' he would order when it was sitting on his rocking chair. The shifting was never done unkindly. He loved household pets, which would include weasels, ferrets and even a little pig. The little pig he brought back drunk from market (a landlord was always sober on his own premises) and placed in the bed of my sleeping Uncle Jimmy, then five. Jimmy cried when he woke in the dark to the company of an incontinent grunter. There was always a singing bird in the house. When my grandfather and grandmother went to Southport for two days to see the sea, which nobody ever sees at Southport, leaving the pub in the hands of the barman, the hired girl neglected to feed the songster and it died. My grandfather never cared much for any of the hired girls, who were changed like bed linen. They were all stupid and also nitty or chatty. 'Look at bugger, scratching her bloody nut.' This delinquent he hit out at smartly, saying: 'Go on, clear off.' Her father came to protest, and he was hit out at too.

My grandfather had four sons and no daughters. The eldest, Jack, died recently in his nineties. Jimmy, Billy and my father, Joe, will greet me in purgatory as comparatively young men. Billy had the true Finnegan blood in him, for he fell from a roof drunk. His wake held no promise of resurrection. He had been working as a builder's labourer, having been dismissed from his post as an undertaker's assistant. The two stories told of him in this latter connection are probably apocryphal. Preparing a baldheaded body for its coffin, he had been told by the widow that her poor husband was to be buried in his wig. He found difficulty in affixing it. He called up to his employer: 'Mr Clegg, have you got a bit of glue?' And then: 'Never mind. I've found a nail.' He came into a pub, not the Derby Inn, ready to stand drinks all round with a bright sovereign. 'Where did t'a get that, lad?' – 'In the mouth of this Jewish bugger we just coffined.' – 'But that's to pay his fare across river Jordan.' Billy pocketed his change and said: 'Bugger'll have to swim.'

Jack and Jimmy became plumbers, specialising in the installation of lavatory systems in Catholic presbyteries. Jimmy always found it hard to interpret the incongruity of genuflecting before the Blessed Sacrament with the bloody petty on his shoulder. Jack became a master plumber, which Jimmy never did. He also became a Catholic communist and swore that if Jesus Christ were alive today he would be general secretary of the carpenters' union. He died staunch in the two faiths. My father, Joe, was destined for less tangible trades. He was even given piano lessons. Whatever he did during the day, in the evenings he was to be found in the orchestra pits of music halls, pounding the continuo for a cornet and a fiddle. He first met my mother by way of her ankles. She was in the chorus at the Ardwick Empire, but soon she was to be elevated to the status of soubrette. She also understudied for Josie Collins, the dark brooding star of *The Maid of the Mountains* and reputedly a bit of a bitch. My father took some classes in book-keeping and, during the day, kept people's books. There is a vague story I have never properly understood about his cheating a firm that sold encyclopaedias door to door and having to run off to Scotland. The firm itself was arraigned for financial irregularities, and he came back to Manchester married to Elizabeth Burgess, who had been performing at a music hall in Glasgow. He got a job as cashier at Swift's Beef Market and was later promoted to chief cashier. He rented a house in Carisbrook Street, Harpurhey, in north-east Manchester, and it was there that I was born.

I AM PROUD to be a Mancunian. I have, after a struggle with a people given to linguistic conservatism, even succeeded in importing the epithet *mancuniense* into the Italian language. Italians do not realise that the British are honorary Romans, and, lecturing in Rome, I have declared myself a *cittadino mancuniense, cioè romano*. At the time of my birth, Manchester was a great city, Cottonopolis, the mother of liberalism and the cradle of the entire industrial system. It had the greatest newspaper in the world, meaning the only independent one. The *Manchester Guardian* debased itself when it grew ashamed of its city of origin: a superb liberal organ was turned into an irritable rag dedicated, through a fog of regular typographical errors that would have appalled C. P. Scott, to the wrong kind of radicalism. Manchester's Free Trade Hall housed the Hallé Orchestra, one of the finest in Europe before the BBC stole its best players ('Amiable bandits!' cried Sir Hamilton Harty, its conductor at the time). Manchester was encircled by fine colliery brass bands and beefy choirs, and its musical acumen, of which Ernest Newman and later Neville Cardus were the critical voices, far surpassed that of London. Its cosmopolitan musical taste was kept sharp by the Italian and German Jewish colonies. It was, under Miss Horniman, the focus of a theatrical renascence that learned from Ibsen but expressed, in plays like *Hobson's Choice* and *Hindle Wakes*, the Lancashire soul. The response of Manchester audiences to new theatrical productions was found reliable by London managements, and even songs of Cole Porter had their first airings on the stage of the Manchester Opera House.

The economic substructure of a lively international culture was, as Marx and Engels had observed, founded on injustice. If the revolution was ever to be fomented in England, Manchester would be the hotbed. I remember a Manchester of frightful slums and hard-headed magnates and cotton brokers gorging red meat in chophouses. It was an ugly town and its proletariat could erupt in ugly violence. The Peterloo massacre was well remembered by my great-grandfather. My family had apparently been concerned with settling as far away from St Peter's Fields, which became St Peter's Square, as it could. This meant the north-east. But a walk

down Carisbrook Street on to Lathbury Road brought one to
Rochdale Road and its intersection with Queen's Road, great
arteries along which rattled the Manchester trams. Rochdale
Road led south to Shude Hill, where my father worked. Shude
Hill led through Withy Grove to Corporation Street and the
Royal Exchange. Then Cross Street carried one to Albert Square
and the assertive hideous Town Hall, all neogothic spires and
sprockets. Further west, the river Irwell marked the boundary
with the city of Salford, and the Irwell flowed into the Manchester Ship Canal, which turned an inland city into a port.
'Manchester Goods for Manchester Docks' was the slogan in the
Corporation trams. Trafford Park, south of the Canal, held the
Metropolitan Vickers Electrical Engineering Works, which
helped to bring Soviet Russia into the modern world. East of it
was the Manchester United Football Ground and, east again, the
cricket ground called Old Trafford. It was a large city, and
dwellers in Harpurhey were somewhat frightened by its energy
and sprawl. Queen's Road and Rochdale Road, the joint Harpurhey western boundary, formed a sufficient world of amenity.

My mother left the stage and became a shopping housewife on
these thoroughfares. Just before the War of 1914–18 began, she
gave birth to my sister Muriel. I had a photograph of the two of
them, long since eaten up by Malayan humidity and termites,
and it showed a firm-featured smiling woman of considerable
blonde beauty and a promise of similar beauty in the daughter.
My father did not rush to leave them when war broke out: the
Manchester Irish priests were not convinced of the righteousness
of the war, and the liberation of Ireland from the Protestant English yoke took precedence. This was an imperialist war, and it
was not right that British Catholics should slaughter Bavarian
Catholics. The Wilson patriotism was, of course, a highly qualified commodity: the king they were urged to fight for was of a
dynasty of Protestant usurpers: it had been passed down to my
father that the last legitimate British king was James II. The Wilsons had supported Prince Charles Stuart when he had come recruiting in their city, and his song 'Farewell, Manchester, sadly I
depart' could still bring tears to their eyes. My Uncle Jack, being
a plumber, reluctantly at length joined the Royal Engineers, and
my Uncle Jimmy had the bronchial complaint which is in the
family: he kept to his genuflecting with lavatory basins on his
shoulder. My father, being a cashier, joined the Royal Army Pay
Corps, jocularly known as the Apple Pie Core, and spent his

entire war career in barracks in Preston. It was honorable work
that he performed: soldiers save the sum of things for pay.

I was born when the war was at its grimmest, on February 25,
1917. Unrestricted submarine warfare had begun at the beginning
of the month, though food rationing was not to come in until
my first birthday. England was still stunned by the death of a
finger-pointing ikon: Lord Kitchener had been drowned on June
5, 1916, when the *Hampshire* struck a mine. The battle of the
Somme, which had begun a month later, had whimpered to an
end on November 13, with 420,000 British losses – a figure as
hard to visualise as great wealth. But the Americans declared war
on April 6, 1917, and on June 26 their first contingents arrived in
France. I was not quite a month old when the Leningraders re-
hearsed the October Revolution. My birth thus coincided with
that of the modern age – American world hegemony, the dissolution of Christendom. I yelled my Otto Rank anger at the
light just as the Sunday pubs were opening. A child of the Fishes,
I was thirsty as a fish: the lactal ducts could never refill fast
enough.

February 25 is the feast day of saints and martyrs not much
regarded – Victorinus and his companions, Caesarius of
Nazianzus, the virgin Walburga, the bishops Tarasius and Ger-
land, Ethelbert of Kent. In 1601 it was an Ash Wednesday and
the day of the execution of the Earl of Essex – one of those
historical dates I can never forget. It is the birthday of musicians
– Caruso, Myra Hess, of the impressionist painter Pierre Renoir,
above all of the dramatist Carlo Goldoni, with whom I have
always felt a faint affinity. The day before is the birthday of
George Moore and of Arnold Dolmetsch, the day before that of
George Frederick Handel. The day after honours Victor Hugo,
Honoré Daumier, and Buffalo Bill. How much truth there is in
astrology I do not know, but the first fortnight of Pisces certainly
presides over arts to which I was attracted about equally in my
youth. I spent too long deciding which art to follow – music,
writing, drawing, the popular stage. It was not until I was thirty-
seven that I became a writer. Certainly I had to be an artist of
some kind or other. My father breathed beer on me and said: 'He
may be a new Napoleon.' Not Wellington. The Catholic north-
west, like Ireland, had looked to the French being on the sea,
and the decay of the Orange.

One's first memories are often vicarious: one is told that one
did something or was involved in something; one dramatises it

and folds the image falsely into the annals of the truly remembered. So, less than two years old, I am sitting on a shoulder
in Manchester's Piccadilly while a flag-waving crowd cheers the
Armistice. Then the lights go out. In early 1919 my father, not
yet demobilised, came on one of his regular, probably irregular,
furloughs to Carisbrook Street to find both my mother and sister
dead. The Spanish influenza pandemic had struck Harpurhey.
There was no doubt of the existence of a God: only the supreme
being could contrive so brilliant an afterpiece to four years of
unprecedented suffering and devastation. I, apparently, was
chuckling in my cot while my mother and sister lay dead on a
bed in the same room. I should not have been chuckling; I should
have been howling for food; perhaps the visiting neighbour who
had herself just been stricken had provided me with a bottle of
Glaxo. My father's attitude to his son must now have become
too complicated for articulation. It would have been neater if all
three in that room had been obliterated. When I was old enough
to appreciate his mingled resentment and factitious gratitude at
my survial, I was able to understand his qualified affection, his
lack of interest in any future I might have, the ill-considered
second marriage which was a way of getting me off his hands.

Of my sister Muriel he passed on no memories. My mother
survived briefly in vague reminiscences of the Manchester music
hall – a voice that could ride over a restive audience, the shining
abundant hair, the neat ankles. When she herself became part of
an audience she was a comedian's gift: her laugh was loud and
primed general laughter. As a housewife she had no further duty
to the lissom shape that had been her professional pride. She took
to Guinness and boiled puddings. It would be easier to recreate
her in fiction, relating her to Molly Bloom and Rosie Driffield,
than to wrestle with a virtually non-existent reality. It is difficult
to know how far we have an obligation to the dead. I sometimes resent my father's failure to introduce me even to her insubstantial after-image, but he spoke little of her. She joined the
great boneyard of the war and its aftermath. My father went
back to Swift's Beef Market, bought a straw hat, took heavily to
draught Bass, and waited for the cleansing 1920s.

I come to full consciousness in a terraced house on Delauneys
Road, Higher Crumpsall, in the care of my mother's sister, Ann
Bromley. She was a war widow with two daughters, Elsie and
Betty. Opposite the house was a great infirmary where, I learned,
people were cut open. This gratuitous slashing and slitting seemed

reasonable to me, who must have absorbed by osmosis the ethos of the times. My father was a lodger, visible mainly on Friday evenings, when he brought home a prime joint from the beef market. For the rest of the time he drank or tried to cut down on his drinking by playing the piano in one of the local cinemas. He then combined both diversions by becoming the regular pianist at the Golden Eagle, a huge pub on Lodge Street, Miles Platting. There he met his second wife, who was the widowed landlady. In 1922 I was told that she was my new mother. Before then I called my aunt mother.

There is no magic in the word: it is the name a child will happily give to any woman who looks after him. It did not follow that Elsie and Betty were my sisters. I hear myself calling at the age of three and a half, with a Lancashire vowel: 'Mother, mother – there's a donkey on the road.' A workman had knocked on the door asking for hot water for his tea can. He said: 'You're a big baby, shouting for your mother because you see a donkey.' I did not know what he meant – fear of the donkey, wonder at it? How, anyway, did I know it was a donkey? Across the road, behind that gaunt façade of many windows, the cutting up of living bodies was calmly proceeding.

I slept alone in a cold room with one picture on the wall. It was of a gipsy woman looking balefully and pointing a finger. I was told that the legend beneath it was 'Beware'. When I thought I was asleep the picture would open on loud hinges and disclose the world of cutting up live but uncomplaining bodies. It was lighted by fire. I was given the choice of joining the bodies or else remaining where I was, in the big lumpy flock bed which was steadily filling with horse shit and turning into Delauneys Road. The turds were turning into aromatic serpents with teeth. I would scream and scream, and my aunt would come in her nightdress to see what the trouble was. The trouble was the picture, but it was not removed. I was never taken into her bed. After so much public horror, what was a mere child's nightmare?

The house was damp and looked out on a damp back garden which was full of slugs and, I feared, snakes. I was shown a picture of Christ being laid in his tomb. I asked what was happening. A male voice said: 'They're going on a journey.' It must have been the voice of a local boy named Stevie, who sometimes had dinner with us. Among the peas on his plate was a black one. He impaled it on his fork and said: 'My name is Stevie Blackpea.' Blackpea had to be some relation of Blackpool, where I must

sometime have been taken. I can remember only a railway
compartment with a black pool outside it: etymology was
drawing me slowly to a life of words. I had new dreams in
which Christ was laid in a black snaky pool in the back garden. I
did not know that he was Christ. He was merely a man inexplicably naked. Nakedness had something to do with going on
a journey.

There was a piano in the front room, as there seemed to be in
all the front rooms of that period, but I never heard my father
play it. Elsie did. There was a volume of popular songs that must
have been called the Star Folio, for there was a star on the cover
and a couple dancing. I would take the cat on my knee and sing
to it – a rigmarole about dancing on a star. I hear the vowel in
'dancing': the short front one of Manchester. I draw the external
world into senseless recitatives: couch dance star cat fire dinner.
One Friday my father brought with the weekend joint a large
new cash book and a thick-leaded pencil. I began to transfer the
external world to its pages in vigorous pictograms. It became a
matter of urgency, like going to the lavatory. I saw in some
newspaper a heart transfixed by a dart. I had to rush to the cash
book and scribble it in before it disappeared.

This early life of fragments has little meaning. There is murk
with occasional dull flashes of things and people. It is the lack of
continuity that disconcerts, as though one were perpetually dying
and being reborn to trivialities. My life as yet had no religion in
it. My aunt and cousins were Protestant but did not go to church.
My father had probably lost his faith. All his life long he said:
'When you're dead you're finished with.' Nobody taught me
how to pray. I do not remember visits from the other Wilsons,
who had nothing to mourn and retained a certain devoutness. In
1921 I was taken prematurely to school by little girls who lived
two or three doors down. One Friday afternoon I, or they,
showed up late. I knew it was Friday, because we had had shop
fish and chips for the midday meal, which we called dinner. 'Why
are you late, Jack Wilson?' the teacher asked. 'Too many chips,' I
said, wondering why I said it. Then we were set to draw a teacup,
and the teacher emphasised the slight tapering of its shape. One
boy, with modish logicality, drew a perfect inverted cone. I
crayoned a multicoloured jack-in-the-box. I think it was a
Protestant school, because I half-remember hearing a Protestant
hymn sung as the winter twilight settled down. It began 'Herb,
hide with me.' Childish religion was full of shadowy characters

like Herb. God was Harold on both sides of the fence. His brother Will was cooked till done.

But as yet I had no need of God. My nighttime world was terrifying enough without him. Snakes persisted. I remember a dream which may be a distortion of a memory of seeing a film with Mary Pickford in it: she, the young girl, sat on the knee of an old man in a white suit and hat in a garden. They looked calmly at a writhing mass of monsters which prefigured the pythons and hamadryads I was to know in Malaysia. They were all dead white. Where did they come from? I had not at that time been taken to the Belle Vue Zoo. My snakes may have been the Kundalini serpents of the collective unconscious – forms of white female flesh which lived in the base of the spine, already sexual, ready to be transformed into the *prana* or inner life force. They related to bleached dog turds on the road. They were garden worms terrifyingly magnified. A healthy human bowel movement, so I was later to be told in the Royal Army Medical Corps, went 'twice round the pan and was curly at both ends'. The snake as vitalised faeces is still a frightening presence of my dreams. Sometimes I dream that Sigmund Freud and Carl Jung are together, looking at my snakes and coming to no conclusion about them. They have no resemblance to real snakes, which I have found to be graceful, warm, and intelligent. They disappeared from my dreams in Delauneys Road when, after a bout of night hysteria, the picture of the gipsy was removed from my room by my father. But they came back later.

1922 was a key year in modern literature. It saw the publication of *The Waste Land* and *Ulysses* – a denial of life and a celebration of it. I got out of the waste land of my aunt-mother's house into the vital labyrinth of a huge pub. 1922 was the year of my father's marriage into the Dwyer family. The Dwyers were successful immigrants from Dublin. There was no Irish brogue left in them, and their speech was pure Manchester. The troubles of their native country – the heavy fighting in the capital, with the blowing up of the Four Courts, which followed on the setting up of the Irish Free State in 1921 – aroused little interest. One of the Dwyer women who had stayed behind cursed the curse of Cromwell on the Black and Tans but ended up marrying one of them. Other Dwyers crossed the water later on odd visits, with Irish Sweepstake tickets for illegal sale tucked in their bloomers. The Manchester Dwyers were adoptive Mancunians, though very Catholic in the Irish manner. The greatest member of the family is George Patrick Dwyer, who was to become Bishop of Leeds and then Archbishop of Birmingham. It was he who, in a television discussion, cured Malcolm Muggeridge of his atheism and initiated his long climb to sanctity. When George was installed as archbishop, the novelist Olivia Manning said to me: 'John, I did not realise you were so well connected.' When I told her that Birmingham was merely a Catholic archdiocese, she said: 'Oh, that explains it then.' The economic substructure of the Dwyer passion for turning sons and daughters into bishops and mother superiors was a flourishing greengrocery and poultry business. There was, however, a George Dwyer who went to Australia and became a millionaire. He was involved in sexual irregularities scandalous in a great Catholic family. His son Dan became aide de camp to General Blamey.

The woman my father married had herself married into the Dwyers and became one of them. She had been Maggie Byrne, again Manchester Irish, and her husband, Dan Dwyer, had been landlord of the Golden Eagle. She took over the licence when he died – not in the war and not of influenza. She had two grown daughters, Agnes and Madge, of exceptional beauty, though she herself had run to fat in the acceptable mode of pub landladies and suffered from spectacular pains in the feet and back. She was not, in other words, an attractive woman. She was also virtually illiterate and drew her name on a cheque as though from a memory of Egyptian hieroglyphics. Her marrying a Wilson entailed long instruction in the carving of new signs. She needed the strong arm of a husband, whom she called a 'usbint, in the management of a large and rowdy pub in a slum neighbourhood, but the licence was hers, and hers the name in the legal legend over the front door. She was to be boss. My father, once the wedding was over, was bold in rejecting the inferior status proposed and revealed that he had not resigned from Swift's Beef Market. I saw him now even less than previously, and my seclusion in a remote corridor of the labyrinth was perhaps what he sought. He played the piano in the huge music saloon in the evenings, accompanying performers like Tim Carlisle, whose sister Elsie became a famous radio crooner with Ambrose's band. I, as a minor, was not allowed in there, and I was always asleep when the pub closed.

The Golden Eagle of Miles Platting was well known, a boozer of Victorian amplitude, gleaming with brass. The brass sign with its spread wings on the façade was much coveted by local Protestant clergymen. There were three singing rooms, a vast spit-and-sawdust, and a number of snugs. The beer came from the Cornbrook Brewery, which owned the premises and rendered the title landlord or landlady a misnomer. An era of limited drinking hours had been initiated by the Defence of the Realm Act, represented in newspaper cartoons as Dora, a repressive dragon of a female in black, but before the war the pub had opened at six in the morning and did not shut until eleven at night. Workmen came in early for rum and coffee; some came in early and stayed till closing-time. One man died on the premises of delirium tremens, after several days of seeing snakes and Germans leering from the ceiling. There was a legend that an American soldier, not yet demobbed, had come in to boast: 'Waal, I guess and calculate your lil asshole of a country had to call on us to fight your goddam war for you,' and been stabbed to death, his body, by common consent, being deposited in the middle of the night in the middle of Queen's Road. There was a fearsome character known as Nancy Dickybird, whose violent approach was signalled by runners – 'Nancy's coming'. The main bar would clear on her entrance, and my stepmother would greet her with a truncheon and knuckledusters. There was an extensive armoury available for defence, including two army revolvers complete with ammunition. Nancy would sail into an ecstasy of foulness, urinate on the floor, and then leave.

Lodge Street was a tough street in a tough area. I had moved a short way south from my birthplace to the northern segment of Miles Platting, with Collyhurst to the west, but the Queen's Road where my mother had shopped was the tram-clanging artery which fed all these districts. I was in an ugly world with ramshackle houses and foul back alleys, not a tree or a flower to be seen, though Queen's Park and a general cemetery were available to the north-west if a breath of green was required. If the beer-intake of an urban area is an index of its prosperity, then Miles Platting was not badly off, but heavy patronage of the Golden Eagle often meant neglect of domestic responsibilities. A husband came into the public bar one evening in need of his pint. He was shaken. His wife, dead out from a debauch with her cronies, had left the bathing of the children to him. He conscientiously sluiced them all in a tin tub, dressed them for bed, then asked one girl: 'Where's your nightdress, love?' The girl said: 'I don't live here.' It was a district where the women did most of the fighting, usually because of suspected or discovered adultery. For a small transgression, it was enough to smash the delinquent's downstairs windows with a house key. But in bar or street or alley there could be hair-tearing and even breast-slashing. Children played barefoot not because they had no shoes but because they had grown out of them.

The old Lancashire mythology of clogs and shawls and morning knocker-up was to be looked for now more in towns like Rochdale than in Manchester districts like Miles Platting. The clatter of clogs was infrequent, but black shawls were plentiful. My stepmother and stepsisters put them on when they went shopping. The knocker-up was dying out because of the advent of cheap alarm-clocks. My Uncle Billy had once taunted an old woman knocker-up with her long pole that could tap at upper windows: 'Hallo, missis, art going fishing?' He was chased and swiped with 'I'll give you fishing, you young bugger.' It was he who had given the lying excuse for being late for work one summer morning: 'I slept with my pillow on the window sill. Knocker-up knocked pillow and I couldn't hear.'

I was brought to the Golden Eagle without warning of what was in store for me. There was no attempt to prepare me for a change of ménage. I was brought into the pub by my father between three o'clock closing and five-thirty reopening, trod sawdust and tried to take in brass beer engines and swabbing barmen, then toddled left down a corridor to a bright kitchen -living-room where the three females of my new life were waiting for me. They had not seen me before. I wanted my mother. 'This is your mother now, love, and these are your sisters. Her you called your mother is now your Auntie Annie.' I was thin, small, pale, undernourished. Annie, my new mother said, had done her best but it hadn't been good enough. As an earnest of a more nutritious régime she handed me a fairy cake. I knocked it out of her hand. The younger daughter, Madge, said, without rancour: 'You'll be buried with your hand sticking up out of the grave, and everybody that passes by will hit it and say: There lies the boy that knocked a fairy cake out of his mother's hand.' My stepmother should have swiped me but did not. She was pretty tolerant. The introduction of a snivelling lad into her household meant a new gratuitous responsibility, and she had a pub to run. I was to sleep in the little downstairs room of Harry the chief and resident barman, on a little trucklebed. Shortly afterwards a proper child's bed was bought for me, and it was placed in the corner of the master bedroom where my father and his new wife slept. I have no recollection of waking up to amorous noises.

I remember going to bed in the summer light, unable to sleep because of the downstairs racket. I wandered that upper floor, which, corresponding to the ground-floor drinking palace, was vast and had a huge drawing-room with eight windows looking down on Lodge Street and one of its slummy tributaries. I would go into all the bedrooms and micturate in all the chamberpots. I would return to the drawing-room and try to leave some residuary golden drops on the carpet. Then I would bang the piano. Nobody heard. Down below three pianos thumped and tinkled simultaneously, like something by Charles Ives. Across the road from the window by my bed a gramophone played 'Margie' or 'The Holy City'. I looked out of another window, which dominated an outdoor women's lavatory and its yard. One black-shawled crone said to another: 'He sent me this letter, the false bastard.' And she showed it before taking it into the closet to befoul.

My stepmother, whatever else she was, was a good plain cook, skilled at mutton stews, meat and potato pies, classical hotpots, fruit tarts, nutmeggy custards. My fattening began with butties spread with home-made damson jam. Breakfast was bacon and a fried egg, with bacon fat poured all over the plate: this was for the dipping of bread and was called dip. I ate but was perpetually angry. I expressed my anger in drawings of my stepmother wearing a chef's toque, beating a pudding batter, and displaying male genitals. These were the only genitals I knew about, and I always scrawled the penis as an ikon of foul insult. I lacked the comforting contact of female flesh, and when I was offered it by my stepsisters I was unwilling to accept it. I would be called into their bedroom in the morning while they were dressing and told to give them 'a kiss and a love', but I was shy of touching their exposed arms and backs. They noted the shyness and giggled at it. They were well-shaped girls with fine Irish creamy flesh, a year or so between them, in their very early twenties. Agnes was coal-haired and showed the blood of a wrecked Armada; Madge was prettily mousy. They were pure and deeply Catholic. They took me to mass, which was boring and incomprehensible, but the Gregorian line of a priest (the mass must have been high and sung) stuck in my head: *'Per omnia saecula saeculorum'*. A queer kind of English, a sort of code, the *orum* dangerous magic.

I was a fidgety child, and, as a revenge for my transplanting, fidgeted odd coins off the kitchen dresser into my pockets. I see myself, fidgety, being told to lie still on the kitchen sofa, the pub cat in my arms, while the two-minute silence of November 11, 1922 was observed. If I moved, I was told, the war would start again. I did not know what the war was, but one-legged drinkers in the public bar, men coughing their lungs up, black boozing widows were the war. War was a word like 'runcible' or a termination like *orum*. In November my stepmother started mixing her Christmas puddings. In December the greengrocer-poulterer Dwyers arrived with the colossal turkey. On Christmas Day, when the licensing hours imitated Sunday, the pub closed at two and Christmas dinner was eaten at three. The turkey stuffing was herbs and pork sausage meat. No Dwyers came for Christmas, nor any Byrnes. My stepmother and her brother had quarrelled, as always happens in families, over a family will. The Dwyers kept their own green Christmas over the greengrocer's shop, laden with all the unsold holly and mistletoe, but the Wilsons were welcome at the Golden Eagle. My stepmother approved of my two uncles – the master plumber Jack, who looked like Stanley Baldwin, the common plumber Jimmy, who looked like James Maxton and whose wife Lily, my apparent godmother, she considered a shiftless slut.

My grandfather was dead by 1922, and my grandmother kept to her bed in a rented house with an imported pair of Finnegan girls to look after her. My father had taken me to visit her by tram – a clean, smiling old Irish lady sitting up in a lace mobcap – and I had begun to learn to read on the outward and homeward journeys, my primer my father's packet of Three Castles with its citation from Thackeray's *The Virginians*: 'There's no sweeter tobacco than comes from Virginia, and no finer brand than the Three Castles.' I was seeing more of my father now. He had even lifted me from sleep to be shown to some visitors in that huge drawing-room. I remember crying: 'Bugger off, you buggers,' at the same time wondering where I had learned the word and its double usage. It came from nowhere, like the chef's toque and the genital obscenity.

The visiting Wilsons were two families. My Uncle Jack and Aunt Nell spoke grammatical Lancashire English, as befitted a master plumber and his wife, and their two daughters, Joan and Winifred (who was later to sign her name Wynné), were to be taught the piano. My Uncle Jimmy and Aunt Lily had the one daughter, named for my dead sister Muriel. She was to become a dancer with stage hopes, but she declined into being a hostess in a night club run by a former boxer. The Wilsons were revealed as a fair-haired family, except for Uncle Jimmy, who had picked up a Spanish swarthiness and Eskimo straight hair. My father and Uncle Jack were gingerish. My cousins were pale of eyelash and had translucent skins. I was to favour my Uncle Jimmy in a modified form – hair curly and dark brown, near-invisible eyebrows a halfhearted tribute to the family fairness. The family nose was assertive. *'Il est juif, sans doute,'* a French lady said of me in 1939, in a Luxembourg night club full of visiting Nazis.

These Christmas parties, beginning in the Golden Eagle, continued in the later locales to which we moved. After the afternoon torpor there was the powerful tea of my stepmother and rich iced volcanic-earth-coloured uneatable Christmas cake. The real festivities began after ten at night, when my cousins and myself were dropped food-drugged and bloated into the one double bed. There was a supper of cold turkey and ham and tongue with piccalilli, sherry trifle, charlotte russe, mince pies, the sullen reappearance of the Christmas cake, Moët et Chandon champagne. Then in the great drawing-room three pianists accompanied songs in turn – my father, my Aunt Nell, my stepsister Madge. The songs were 'Finnegan's Ball', 'Here's Another One Off to America', 'Coronation Day' (the correct version, not Buck Mulligan's), 'Pale Hands I Loved', 'Because', 'Dear Little Shamrock', numbers from *Little Nelly Kelly*, 'Ma, He's Making Eyes At Me', 'Avalon', 'Yes, We Have No Bananas'. When my cousins and I had grown, and another pair of cousins had been added to the master plumber's ménage, we too participated, and I sang 'The Golden Vanity' with, for some reason, my trousers falling down. Trousers were called kex, which properly means the dry hollow stalk of umbellifers like cow parsnip and wild chervil.

Clad in new short kex, I was taken to school in 1923, to St Edmund's RC Elementary at the corner of Monsall Road and Upper Monsall Street. I was still weak and unmuscular through having no proper mother, though I was no longer undernourished. In the school hall, Miss Sullivan, the headmistress, a dried spinster of a ferocious irritability now rarely seen in schools, ordered us to crawl in a phalanx like little mice, and I see myself still as a lone mouse laggard, all the others well ahead. There were, till the tropics ruined them, photographs of me at six, one of them as a melancholy pierrot, and the pallor under the straight fringe, the deficient vitality, the rejection of the external world were striking and terrible. But I could read fluently, apparently without much teaching. Miss O'Flaherty wrote THE CAT SAT ON THE MAT on the blackboard, and I was the only one in the class able to rattle it off, though, through a kind of surrealist perverseness more than ignorance, I transposed the nouns. Miss O'Flaherty had a short way with chatterers. She would make them stand in front of the class and paste over their mouths, using gloy from the conical gloypot, a neatly scissored strip of coloured paper. One boy, a sufferer from adenoid growths ('Dodt do it, biss, I cadt breathe') screamed at the prospect and fainted. Another boy, tall and with a courtly manner, accepted the punishment philosophically. When Miss O'Flaherty was not looking, he doffed the gag, smiled and bowed, then replaced it. It was better than the strap from Miss Sullivan.

I was now taught some Catholicism, which chiefly had to do with eternal punishment for trivial offences. We were told that each of us had a guardian angel, an invisible monitor even in the lavatory, and we sang a song to him or her or it:

> Guardian angel, from heaven so bright,
> Watching beside me to keep me aright,
> Fold thy wings round me and guard me with love,
> Softly sing songs to me of heav'n above.
> Beautiful angel, so tender and mild,
> Lovingly guard me, for I am thy child.

It was a harmless and charming fiction; it still is. But the Manichee in us all, even at the age of six, had to assume that there was another angel, a very bad one, hitting out at the pale epicene from heaven, and, since fighting was a sin, winning most of the rounds. One of our teachers, more Butlerian than was right for a Catholic, assured us that sins like nosepicking and incontinence of the bladder were really a disease that merited our being carted off to Monsall Isolation Hospital, which was just across the road. Presumably people were cut up there in isolation. I was sent there eventually, but it was for scarlet fever.

To be a Catholic meant primarily belonging to a minority faction which was despised by the scholars of St Augustine's C of E Elementary School, on the other side of Monsall Street. I was taught by my fellows to call them proddy dogs in response to their jeer of cat licks. The opposed canticles of abuse are still going strong in Northern Ireland.

Cat lick, cat lick, going to mass,
Riding to hell on the devil's ass

was answered by

Proddy dog, proddy dog on the wall,
A small raw spud will feed you all.
A ha'penny candle will give you light
To read the Bible of a Sunday night.

I did not know what the Bible was, but evidently it was a dirty book. It was confirmed for me later that not only was it dirty, it was dangerous. It was the prime cause of people losing their Catholic faith. This is, historically speaking, a sound enough judgment. There was perturbation at my secondary school when the Book of Job was a set book for the Higher School Certificate examination. My English teacher, a Xaverian brother who had not read it before, conceded that the style was sound even if the theology was shaky. Anyway, the Bible was mostly a foul book that had produced proddy dogs.

Across the street from the Golden Eagle was a little shop run by the Misses Hogan, a couple of witches in dusty black. After two days of constipation I was sent across there with a teacup to buy two pennyworth of California syrup of figs. This, the most saccharine thing, outside the films of Mary Pickford, that California ever produced, did not act at once but when it did act it acted relentlessly. I was taken short in afternoon school and bewrayed my kex shamefully. In the whole of a man's life there is no worse humiliation than the dropping of that heavy load clothed. I had to run home, accompanied by two girls, and was given by Madge for some reason a lace doyley for the tersive act. I was in a deep pit of shame, but my schoolfellows, when I went back next morning in fresh kex digesting a hardboiled egg, did not point the finger. It was the sort of thing that might happen to anyone, like being bust. 'You see that lad over there? Well, he's bust.' This meant that in the playground the one remaining button at the back of his kex had snapped off. One lad to whom it happened said: 'Told my bloody mother to sew the bloody thing on proper and she didn't bloody listen. Now my bloody kex is coming bloody down. Have to walk bloody home with my bloody hands in my bloody pockets, bloody it. And there goes the blooming bell.'

There were certain school clowns who, for a halfpenny fee, would guarantee to make you laugh. One boy had a continuing saga about a man with a dog called Bugger. The two were always travelling by rail. The guard would shout 'All change for Oldham,' and the man would say: 'Come on, Bugger, we're on the wrong train again.' On the way home from school, one little girl pointed me out to her friend as a boy that could make you laugh. I obliged with funny faces and no fee charged. The faces were funny only in the sense that they were the objective correlative of an exercise of the risor muscles. Nature was telling these children to laugh, and it would have been madness to laugh at nothing. There is nothing intrinsically funny in anything – certainly not in a man whose dog was named Bugger. One regular comedian of St Edmund's would exchange humour for cigarette cards, but he had to be given the cards first. The cards were his comic property. He would hold them up to the sun and say: 'You see them? Them's shit, them is. Ta-ta.' And he would amble off, his act finished, occasionally turning round with his tongue lolling as we collapsed in dutiful mirth. The performance was highly popular. Young learners about sex are told nowadays that an orgasm is a kind of sneeze. Laughter is the same kind of shocked release but it is less apocalyptical and, to most children, pleasurably controllable, like the action of the rectal sphyncter. When I published my first novel, I was surprised to be told it was comic. Those two little girls were making a proleptic judgment on my career.

At the age of six a social function was imposed upon me that had everything to do with entertainment, though not necessarily of the comic kind. On Queen's Road there were two cinemas – the Rex and the Electric. They faced each other, like the Globe and the Rose playhouses on the Elizabethan South Bank, but not in true rivalry. Going to one on a Monday and Thursday (the day the programme changed) did not prevent your going to the other on a Tuesday and Friday, if you could afford it. The cinemagoer's criteria had more to do with hygiene than with the quality of the entertainment offered. The Rex was called a bughouse and the Electric not. The Electric used a superior disinfectant like a grudging perfume; the Rex smelt of its patrons and its lavatories. With the Rex, it was said, you went in in a blouse and came out with a jumper. So it was to the Electric that the children of Lodge Street went, clutching their pennies, on a Saturday afternoon. Because I lived at the Golden Eagle I was called Jackie Eagle, and ten or twelve boys would, after midday dinner, cry out for Jackie Eagle from the verge of the public bar the law forbade them to enter. They would hold on to me in their redolent jerseys all the way down Lodge Street and left and over on Queen's Road. I was the only one of them who could read.

The manager of the Electric did not wish too many even of his front rows to be defiled by children, and so we were jammed three to a seat, with a gaping black auditorium behind us clean for the evening's two houses. So I began a lifetime's devotion to the cinema, a one-sided love affair in which I was more bruised than caressed. In those old silent days the art was almost an aspect of literature. I hear my little treble voice crying the text aloud for the benefit of even big louts whom the reading mystery had passed by. 'Kiss me, my fool', mouths the Spanish gipsy siren, and the caballero who proposed knifing her trembles so that his knife silently clatters to the floor. 'Came the dawn', a regular cliché. We saw Rudolph Valentino in *The Sheik* and Ben Turpin in *The Shriek*. There was *The Four Horsemen of the Apocalypse* ('What's that mean, kid?'), with artistic camera-masks that varied the shape of the frame. There was a Chester Conklin comedy which began with lovers kissing on a doorstep. 'The end', the legend said. There were roars of kids cheated. 'Of a perfect day.' That was all right, then, but the humour was too adult for relief: the buggers were clearly not to be trusted. There was one frightful shock for me. A character with dirty beard and gabardine spoke, and then the black screen filled with unintelligible letters. I know now it was Hebrew; I even remember a beth and a ghimel. To my illiterates it was all one, and there was bafflement and then anger at my failure to twang it off. 'Thought you said the bugger could read.' So I improvised a flight of suitable invective. No piano played in the pit: we were too cheap for music.

At Christmas 1923 my stepsisters took me to the pantomime at the Palace Theatre on Oxford Street in the heart of the city. It was *Dick Whittington* and Dorothy Ward was the principal boy. She sang 'Nothing could be finer than to be in Carolina in the mor-or-orning'. This was theatre, this was the real thing. The auditorium smelt of cigars and rustled with chocolate boxes. Dick and his cat soared over us in a balloon. When I got back to the family kitchen I was hysterical with wonder at the size of the proscenium arch. 'It stretched from there to there,' and I ran with trembling pointing arm from one end of the kitchen to the other. The mensuration was sound in a relative way: one kind of architectural extension was the figure of another. Dorothy Ward's song summed up the magic and still does. Where was Carolina? In America, like California. Where is America? Never mind. Carolina must have been better than California: it exported no bewraying syrup of figs. When I first went to Chapel Hill in North Carolina I found I remembered every word of the song and could even play it on the piano. 'If I had Aladdin's lamp for only a day, I'd make a wish, and here's what I'd say: Nothing could be finer than . . .'

The years become confused, obedient to Proust or Ford Madox Ford. Real time emerges with a vague chronology. I could not have been sitting in the front porch of the Golden Eagle in the enchanted days after seeing *Dick Whittington*, trying to draw a stage on a panel of a shoebox. ('What's that you're drawing, kid?' – 'A pantomime.' – 'You're bloody daft.') It must have been in the spring of 1924. But I get up from my work and toddle to the kitchen, where the women are discussing the scandal of Fatty Arbuckle, a muffled news items of 1923, which gave California a worse name than syrup of figs, or the wedding of the Duke and Duchess of York, which, as the Queen Mother will confirm, took place on April 26 of that year. I can recall no procession of the seasons, which Lodge Street could not manifest through flowery spring or russet autumn. I can remember no rain, and rain, according to the outsider's myth of Manchester, is the one thing I ought to remember. I seem to have spent a lot of time sitting in fine weather in the porch of the Golden Eagle, drawing or else playing with the sixpenny toys I could buy at the Misses Hogan's – metal fishes to be fished for with a magnetic rod, a fragile earthbound Sopwith Camel. Also reading.

The reading must have reached a fair stage of efficacy before the Saturday processions to the Electric. I had a weekly paper for children called *Chick's Own*, with Rupert the Chick as the front-page hero. This came out on Mondays. Madge said that *Tiger's Tim's Weekly*, out on Thursdays, was a nice paper too, and it sounded sympathetic. I was called a weakly child, and it was comforting to think of a tiger brought down to my level. I read the balloons in the cartoons about anthropomorphic animals, and assumed that the print récit under the coloured pictures would be beyond me. But it was not: I was merely lazy. Words were helpfully split with hyphens into their constituent morphemes. There was always a full-page story that did not so condescend.

This I found I could read too. 'Let us give this poor dog some of our hot soup.' 'Soup' I read as 'soap', not unreasonably, since that is how it is rendered in what Henry Higgins calls Broad Romic. The notion of comforting with hot soap was not unpleasant. Soap was at least wholesome – the whole of Miles Platting, said my stepmother, could do with more of it – and might be palatable hot.

The wicked press barons who put out these twopenny rations of kidfeed had sensible editors. The child's ideal companion would be a rational animal with his own weaknesses. Animals will take love without demanding it; they have teeth, but they will not bite with the vindictiveness of human adults. They are free and indifferent, but they will go into spasms of affection with a discontinuity the child understands. They demand no covenant and do not know the meaning of obligation. Dress them in jerseys and kex, give them a minimal vocabulary but no expressiveness in their masks, save the query marks of an occasional smile of triumph at some naughtiness, and they earn love without mawkishness. I look back at that anonymous sub-art with a genuine gratitude. I saw no implausibility in Porkyboy's eating sausages for Christmas breakfast or Tiger Tim making a stew out of bread and cheese. The gentle way out of the animal world into the human was through Marzipan the Magician, with his candy-striped wand, and the gnome Bushybeard. Stories about human adults would have been frightening, for human adults were irrational, gross, demanding. They also rejected magic, whose power had been confirmed by the child's distortion of religion. Certain features in both of my weaklies or weeklies encouraged, like a gentle laxative, activities which would have been too costively painful in school. You became numerate through linking digits with a pencil and ending with an angular cartoon sketch. You could paste a torso and sundered limbs on a piece of card, scissor them out and assemble them with paper fasteners, so that you had a flat marionette that could walk and gesture. These publications had an acceptable moral content. Naughtiness was behovely, but all would be well.

Incoming and outgoing customers must have noted something unhealthy in this thin-legged child drawing on ragged card or gaping over *Chick's Own*. I should have been throwing stones or kicking an old tennis ball about Lodge Street with its tougher urchins, or slopping in bare feet through the mud and horsemerds. Occasionally, to oblige, I would take off my shoes and half-heartedly slop, only to have my shoes stolen. That was naughty. My stepmother would take time off from the beer pumps to clout me. I would cry and be called, as D. H. Lawrence had been called, mardarse. The clouting would then be just enough, but there was a double clouting that was not. There was a hired girl named Bertha, who turned out to be mad. She came down the stairs that led from the private quarters to the sawdust concourse that was the public bar. It was a noble staircase, and she descended with the grace of a Tolstoy princess. But she was stark naked. She had to be taken back to her parents in Collyhurst. Clothed, of course. Before then she had played on me a trick of curious malice. Every Monday we children had to take to school a coin in an envelope, a contribution to an African mission for dragging black infants to the light. I took my wrapped penny, but it turned out to be a penny-sized watch crystal. I was clouted in class and then clouted when I took home a written complaint. Bertha eventually admitted with glee that she had been responsible for the pointless substitution, but by then it was too late. The great truth of the world's injustice had been established for me.

A strange collective naughtiness came over a group of us when we were going back to school one day after the dinner break. A ragged man appeared from an alley, which was called also an entry or a ginnel, with a battered straw hat set rakishly. He danced and played a tin whistle. He was a pied piper whom we had to follow. He also sang the songs of the day – 'Margie' and 'I'm Forever Blowing Bubbles'. We joined in, we capered, we followed him from street to street. Then he doffed his cady in farewell and disappeared down another entry. We were very late for school, but, because the piper was an undoubted adult, we had felt him somehow to be a representative of the establishment that regulated our education, a kind of demented school inspector. We were not walloped by Miss Sullivan: there were too many of us. There was also a sinister magic in the occasion which she must have recognised. There was a mystery to be considered: the cane did not meet the case.

My joining a group of peers, delinquent or not, was a rarity. I was grasped eagerly, even desperately, on Saturday afternoons, when the eccentricity of my being able to read was a blessing, but for the rest of the time I was either distractedly persecuted or ignored. On Saturday mornings I would stroll like a clubman down Lodge Street, turn right on Queen's Road and go into an ice cream parlour that served a penny vanilla ice in a glass dish. I was cut off from the halfpenny wafer-lickers. I was Jackie Eagle, who partook of the glory of the polished brass effigy with its spread pinions, of the wet wealth within. I was also one despised, mardarse.

In 1924 there was a change in my life. My stepmother grew tired of the stress of what she called the public business, and my father had had enough of Swift's Beef Market. It was time his book-keeping skills were employed to a more profitable end. The stock and goodwill of the Golden Eagle were sold to a new tenant, and we moved to a tobacconist's shop on Princess Road, Moss Side. This was a sizeable migration.

MOSS SIDE, WHICH was to become a Caribbean slum, was at that time a respectable district with decent houses, front gardens with trees in them, a bowling green, the scent of a coming seediness. It was a long way south from Queen's Road. The small boy who could reduce the stage of the Palace Theatre ('Butterflies will flutter up and kiss each little buttercup at daw-aw-awning') to the dimensions of the Golden Eagle kitchen could as easily expand a city to a world. Harpurhey and Miles Platting were now wrapped in north-eastern cold, and the bulk of Ancoats, the city centre itself, the University and Hulme kept off the Arctic winds. Moss Side is bounded by Moss Lane East and West to the north. Princess Road is to its east. In my boyhood it ran north through Hulme to the centre, as it does still, but to the south it stopped at Southern Cemetery. It was to move on to new housing estates like Wythenshawe and lead to the international airport at Ringway. Princess Road was like Queen's Road, a loud artery which fed quieter streets. These considered the impropriety of becoming slums before leafy Moss Lane East banished the thought. Trams clanged down and up Princess Road, and one of my first sights there was of an amorous dog caught in a cow-catcher. Our shop was Number 21, and Wilson's stood in gold paint over its window. The name did not represent my father's new assertiveness. It was also my stepmother's now, and M. Wilson was inked like an ideogram at the foot of cheques. Our shop was divided by a narrow alley or entry from a cinema called the Palace. On the other side of the shop was a barber, Louis Cohen. The cinema was run by Jakie Innerfield. Jews thus entered my life, admirably flamboyant ones. Innerfield had come south from Cheetham Hill, the Jewish quarter very well presented in Louis Golding's forgotten novel *Magnolia Street*. Innerfield's two daughters were Jewesses of a recognisably Cheetham Hill type – dark, scented, overdressed, dangerously erotic. Manchester Jewish speech seemed strongly adenoidal and always loud. Manchester Jews matched Manchester Catholics by getting on. They recognised an affinity.

The shop sold not only cigarettes and tobacco but boxes of chocolates: it was not a sweet shop in the sense that you could buy gobstoppers or Ogo-Pogo sticks there. Ogo-Pogo sticks were named for a mythical creature in a popular song:

> I'm looking for the Ogo-Pogo,
> The funny little Ogo–Pogo.
> His father was an earwig,
> His mother was a whale.
> I want to put a little bit of salt on his tail.

Though customers could come in for a packet of Player's or Gold Flake or Black Cat, the business was from the first trying to expand into a wholesale supply depot for smaller shops. Rough boys coming to buy their fathers a packet of Woodbines would see me proudly lifting the heavy wooden slab that was a continuation of the counter. 'You're not supposed to go in there, kid,' they would say. But I could say: 'I live here.' Beyond the shelves crammed with King George V and Gold Leaf chocolates, and cigarettes, some of them of brands now forgotten, lay the stockroom. Here parcels were made up for delivery by a straw-haired young man named Harold Smith. He taught me a song:

> I want to be alone,
> Yes, I want to be alone,
> I want to be alone with Mary Brown.
> Would I take her through the park?
> Yes, I'd kiss her in the dark
> And tell her she's the nicest girl in town.
> Is she a raving beauty?
> No, I wouldn't call her that.
> Has she a form like Venus?
> No, she's just a trifle fat.
> But she's got a lot of dough

And she's single now, you know.
So I want to be alone with Mary Brown.

The stockroom had a strong odour of the pinewood of Swan matches and it was full of huge cartons, some empty. Harold Smith shut me in one of these and then sat on the flaps. I learned fear of darkness and asphyxiation. I think of dying even now as being shut in an empty cardboard carton. It is the panic of not being able to breathe that effects many Mancunians. The damp air, admirable for cotton spinning, brings us up bronchial. One of my earliest medicines for a weak chest was Owbridge's Lung Tonic, which had once contained opium. There were other opiates, all from the North-West – Battley's Sedative Solution, Dover's Powder, Dr Collis Browne's Chlorodyne, Godfrey's Cordial, Mrs Winslow's Soothing Syrup, Atkinson's Infants' Preservative, Street's Infant's Quietness. We needed opium up there, but doctors' lobbyings had banned it. It was at 21 Princess Road that I first became aware of Manchester's damp. It had never rained on Lodge Street; it was all reserved for Moss Side.

Behind the stockroom was a small living-dining-room at whose table my father kept the books and looked after the orders. He always wore a bowler hat while working, and he had a fine heavy ebony ruler of the kind that Bob Cratchit raises to the Scrooge whose new benevolence looks like madness. It was a dark room looking on to Louis Cohen's backyard, and the electric light was always on. Beyond it was the kitchen where my step-mother cooked. I saw more of her now, and of my father, though it was mainly his waistcoated back and his bowler, which he called a pot. My stepmother watched him at his figure-totting as though he would cheat her. But he had only an actuarial control of the money: it was she who carried the account at Williams Deacon's Bank at the corner of Princess Road and Moss Lane East.

She revealed herself now as interested mainly in money, not so much the acquisition of it as the fear of losing it. Had she done the right thing in leaving the public? Was my father competent to conserve her capital? She had little to do now but cook and brood, teeing and laying as she put it while she lay sleepless in bed. Agnes and Madge were working, both of them at the Manchester offices of Famous Lasky, which organised the dis-tribution of Paramount pictures through the North-West. They were both courting, and soon they would marry, and there was the question of the cost of their weddings. My stepmother talked of little but her pains and apprehension about money. She was interested in other people's pains, though more pharmaceutically than compassionately, for she had a number of home-made remedies inherited from her misty Irish past. These were danger-ous and contained paregoric, ipecacuanha, and a substance she called ikey-pikey. My father, given a cloudy bottle for his cough, would hide it unopened in a drawer. She made me gargle with chloride of lime. To comb one's hair with water was good for it. After all, the hair was a plant, and plants throve on water. When, run down and weak as I was, I got blood-poisoning in my left leg through carrying a pen with a rusty nib in my stocking, she exacerbated the poison with hot fomentations. But she cooked well and gave us all a fine shop tea of tinned salmon, lettuce with Lazenby's dressing, and cream horns from Price's up the street. 'Eat hearty,' she would say. 'There's half a crown's worth of food on the table.'

Upstairs was the drawing-room, with a piano hardly touched by my father. The room was used for alternate courting by the two daughters. There was a portable gramophone up there, with Layton and Johnstone ready to sing 'It Ain't Gonna Rain No More' and 'Bye Bye, Blackbird'. There was also 'Me and Jane in a Plane', played by Jack Hilton's Orchestra, and, on the other side, 'I'm Going Back to Imazaz (Imazaz the pub next door)'. Why does one remember these vapidities so well?

> I'll be keeping my eye
> On the man in the moon.
> He's a dangerous guy
> When he starts to spoon.
> My kisses I'll shower
> A million an hour.
> No traffic cop
> Will ever stop
> Me and Jane in a plane.

Open on the piano was a new song which Madge played and sang. It was called 'When It's Nighttime In Italy It's Wednesday Over Here'. One of the lines ran: 'Oh, the onions in Sicily make people cry in California'. So they ought to cry, the bewraying buggers. I would take no more of their syrup of figs.

We had also a crystal set, a miracle never superseded by elec-

tronics, for music and speech of insuperable clarity came from a
cat's whisker tickling a tiny nugget of carborundum pyrites. 2ZY
was the Manchester call sign. We heard John Henry and Blossom.
And also 'If you speak to an Eskimo his breath will freeze your
ear. When it's nighttime in Italy –' And then the patch of crystal
would die and a new facet had to be tickled. My father was not
impressed by the wonder. The only entertainment he sought was
in the Alexandra Hotel, a pub opposite Williams Deacon's Bank.
There he drank draught Bass with new cronies, most of them
shopkeepers like himself – Lee and Aldridge, rival butchers; Price,
floury and vanilla-scented from the cake shop; Flynn, smelling of
fish; the manager of Seymour Meads, who looked like an
undertaker; an undertaker. I saw more of him, but not much.

Visits from the Wilsons were, as before, reserved for Christmas,
but the greengrocer Dwyers – Jack and Ima – came with a professional interest in the new shopkeeping venture. Other relatives,
and relatives of relatives, turned up for Sunday tea. There was
even a German relative of relatives named Wilhelm Froelich but
called Billy Fraylish, Catholic Bavarian and headmaster of a
Catholic elementary school. He told coarse jokes in a full-blooded
Manchester accent. 'Why does the sea roar?' – 'Wouldn't you
roar if you had crabs on your bottom?' I remained unsociable,
too much the silent reader of *Chick's Own* and *Tiger Tim's
Weekly*. A weakly child still, not enough devilment.

The school I was sent to was the Bishop Bilsborrow Memorial
Elementary up Princess Road, next to the tram depot. Because of
its religious liaison with the English Martyrs Church on Alexandra Road, which was the near parallel of Princess Road, it
was sometimes itself called the English Martyrs. Nobody knew
who Bishop Bilsborrow was, beside presumably being an English
martyr. I have never found out. Bilsborrow sounded like bilberry,
and the Protestant children called us Ripe English Tomaters: there
was a flavour of Dwyer greengrocery around. We were told
what martyrs were – Catholics mostly Irish unbelievably tortured
by the English proddy dogs. This was to habituate us to the
tortures meted out by Sister Ignatius, the headmistress. She raised
the strap back over her shoulder before smiting. She never missed.

I was too young for her. I was with Mother Andrea, who
looked after the juniors. I rose from the first class to the second in
half an hour, being the only one who could read, with noise and
fluency, the neat print script on the blackboard: 'Stop, stop, Mr
Pancake. But the pancake went spinning like a wheel down the

hill.' Mother Andrea had a sweet face and was kind and gentle. She taught us the Our Father and the Hail Mary and the Glory Be. We knew who Hail Mary was. There was a statue of her, in blue with a wreath of stars, in the school hall. There older boys, whose screams from the strap we could hear, were sent sobbing to kneel and beg forgiveness. We had to be satisfied with the promise of more apocalyptical punishments. Hell, gently explained by Mother Andrea, was all the more terrible for the gentleness. 'For ever, Mother Andrea?' – 'Yes, for ever and ever. I pray to Almighty God that none of you children will ever merit his eternal fire.' The End of the World might not be far off. It might come so swiftly that sinners would not have time to repent.

One summer's day the End of the World came. A sunny morning grew, in an instant, black. It was industrial fog, encouraged by the rare lack of a western wind to settle. The classroom lights were switched on: it was the middle of the night before dinnertime. It may also, said Mother Andrea gently, be the consummation of all things. Let us pray. The prayer was efficacious. God relented. A summer's day returned to sinful Manchester. But it had been a terrible moment.

I fell in love with a girl named Joan Price. She was dark, pretty, probably of Silurian stock, and she was seven years old like myself. I fell in love with her because she was talented. She could sing 'Felix Kept On Walking' with a stylised lope, hands joined behind in the manner of Pat Sullivan's cartoon character, whom we all knew and admired in both his animated and syndicated strip forms. She was sometimes asked to perform during one of the little dancing lessons we were given when Mother Andrea was oppressed by the tedium of Sums. My love of her was expressed through the urge to make her admire her admirer through skill in her own sphere. I offered to sing the whole of 'Me and Jane in a Plane' but did not get past these lines:

> In my two-seater
> What could be sweeter?
> I'll have St Peter
> Step inside
> And bless the bride.

They were considered blasphemous. 'Proddy dog,' jeered some classmates. Joan Price was our only star. I loved her without knowing what love was. Not having yet read William Blake, I told my love, though not to my love, and discovered that the rest of the boys knew what love was. Love was kissing. In the playground a gang tried to force us to kiss. The mask of fury of a girl can be terrifyingly adult. Joan Price beat me with her hard little fists. I learned, and have never unlearned, that falling in love is dangerous.

One humiliation followed another. I found that I was colour blind. That could be called a kind of unwilled patriotism, since John Dalton, after whom the complaint is named in most languages, discovered its existence while teaching at New College, Manchester. I was already known to be able to draw well, but my first trial with water paints had me making green leaves orange. My classmates saw first with awe and then with giggles, and they called on others to see and giggle. They were in the presence not of decent stupidity, like getting a sum wrong; this was a physical deformity. Mother Andrea was not teaching us; a Miss Clayton, later to be called Clayballs by her pupils, had come down from the upper school to give us what was called Art. The crowd around my desk attracted her. She came, saw, and hit. It was a response pedagogically unsound. She shook me before the class and held up my painting for derision. She, or I, got plenty of that.

They say that about one in fifty of males is daltonian. It is a defect of the optic nerve passed on from grandfather to grandson through the female, who is rarely colour blind herself. Apparently it is due to the absence of one of the photopigments in the foveal cones. The Ishihara test shows me to have a particularly full-blooded variety of the defect. There is a kind of *pointilliste* diagram crammed with polychrome dots: a large white 2 appears in it for the normally endowed; for the daltonians there is a large white unequivocal 5. But for me there is more than a dubiety about green and the various reds, or blue and violet. I am not sure how to name any colour; I am totally without a chromatic glossary. I recognise that there is a huge variety of colours in the world, but I am dubious about saying what they are. Women, who cannot understand the defect, like to test me with their gamboges and aubergines, and end in awe, as in the presence of genius. Women, anyway, have a wider colour vocabulary than men, and no man ought to turn his back on John Dalton as on the prophet of a breed of cripples. There is more colour blindness around than is recognised.

I make a plea for the daltonians to all organisations that use a colour taxonomy on the oppository lines of a phonemic system. At Charles de Gaulle airport in Paris, travellers to the United

States are split up for boarding on the basis of the issue of a card of a colour of perverse subtlety, as befits the capital of *haute couture* − violet, vermilion, kelly green. There are concert halls with green areas and brown areas. If the three colours of traffic signals were displaced I should be lost. There is sympathy for the blind, but not for the colour blind. There is also an epistemological problem. If a daltonian reads green as orange, what philosopher may say that he is wrong? The secondary realities, of which colour is one, are not to be decreed by a majority vote.

Clearly, daltonianism is a barrier to the writing of fiction (less, it would seem, to the painting of pictures, where the bizarrely idiosyncratic vision may be accepted. Turner? Cézanne?). Fiction deals with the external world, where things are coloured, and the fiction-writer has to get the colours right. My first wife not only used to check the colours of my sunsets and gladioli but also would equip me with detailed wardrobes for my fictional characters. Critics would sneer at my prose and psychology but often praise the dress-sense of my women. I was cheating, but there is no art without cheating. That is why Plato and Tolstoy condemned literature.

I naturally now became shy of painting lessons and, in compensation, concentrated more on line, but drawing, especially vicious caricature, became more and more of a private activity. At the same time there began slowly to germinate what might be termed a synaesthetic faculty − a capacity to interpret the visual as the gustatory, and, much later, the auditory as the visual. I mean that I responded to a colour as if it were something to taste: this colour, which might not be that of a lemon, stung the tongue like a lemon; what might be black or deep purple nauseated like undercooked liver. When my father took me to a Hallé concert, I heard what I was told was an oboe as silver-green lemon juice; the flute was light brown and cold veal gravy. The urge to write for an orchestra, which came much later, was a compensation for painting the pictures I could not paint. Whatever the music critics say, I orchestrate well; I am in control of the tonal palette, or palate. When the tonal colours do not flash out, or when the mixture sounds wrong, it is always the fault of the conductor. I do not find a chromatic or tastebud analogy in words. I doubt if anyone does. The famous sonnet of Rimbaud, in which the vowels are given colour qualities, has everything to do with alchemy and nothing at all with visual perception.

1924 was the year of the British Empire Exhibition at Wembley: I remember the commemorative postage stamp. What I most strongly remember is a newspaper photograph of the Prince of Wales sculpted in New Zealand butter. My imagination tasted the sailor prince. He smoked a pipe when he was not snapped smiling with a fag in his teeth, and the tobacco he smoked was called Baby's Bottom (smooth as a). We had this tobacco, its tin crawling with bare infants, on our shelves. My schoolmates doubted that such a proddy dog obscenity was possible. I brought five of them to the shop to prove that it was, but we happened to be out of stock at the time. This, like the colour blindness and the yearning for Joan Price, did me no good. I was a lone walker home – the tram depot, Bowes Road, Claremont Road (O claremont, O loving, O sweet Virgin Mary), Alison Street, Graeme Street, Great Western Street, Raby Street, 21 Princess Road, half a crown's worth of food on the tea table.

We had only one Christmas at 21 Princess Road. I was given fine presents – a conjurer's outfit, the *Chick's Own Annual* (my first book), a magic lantern with slides of jungle animals. I had been regularly patronising the cinema next door, and there was a regular subsidiary feature called *Wild Life Round the World*. The Wilsons and the two Dwyer daughters, torpid after turkey, were to be shown a still but coloured version of this, and a candle was placed inside the magic lantern and lighted. '*Wild Life Round the World*,' I announced, and shoved in my first slide. Nothing appeared on the wall. The candle was too long. We had to wait till it burned down to lens-level, and Uncle Jimmy said: 'Play us something, Joe, while we're waiting.' So my father hammered out Musetta's song from *La Bohème*. Eventually the candle shortened, and the wild life roved stately on the wall that was a buff-coloured screen. What I cannot understand to this day is why the entire family agreed to wait on the candle's convenience. What was to stop our chopping it down to size? Were we stupid or merely torpid? I put this event or non-event into my early novel *Inside Mr Enderby*. Like T. S. Eliot's gamblers under the vine-crowned lintel or the white horse galloping in the meadow, this has remained as a symbol of something profound but unknowable. The image is accompanied by my stepmother's belching in the corner. She had become a great and loud belcher. 'Let it come up,' she told us. 'That's what the doctor says. You can always say excuse me.' But she never said excuse me.

How did I know it was Musetta's song my father played? He told me. It was the printed title above the music in one volume of many that had appeared in the sitting-room, the total compendium called *The Music Lover's Portfolio*. There was also *Music Masterpieces*, which came out in fortnightly parts. I do not know why there was this sudden incursion of middlebrow music – Boccherini's Minuet, a selection from *Madam Butterfly*, Tchaikovsky's Fifth Symphony in molecular instalments, also chatty articles by Tetrazzini, Percy Pitt and even Ernest Newman. I think that it was a matter of shopkeeper's reciprocity – a heavy-smoking music dealer had to be encouraged to fuel himself at Wilson's, 21 Princess Road.

My father did not now go at once to the Alexandra Hotel, or Big Alec, in contradistinction to the Little Alec on Alexandra Road, at five-thirty when it opened. He played the piano for a while out of *The Music Lover's Portfolio*. He did more. He played a march of his own composition which he had intended for the Royal Flying Corps. Then he complained of pains at the base of his spine which could be alleviated only by standing at a bar and drinking draught Bass. I was partly or wholly responsible for these pains. Working in the shop back room in shirtsleeves and bowler, he had stood to reach over for the daybook on the windoward side of the table. I had pulled his chair away and he sat down heavily on the floor. There was no malice in the act: it was something I had seen in comic papers and comic films. He may, after loud shouts to heaven all round, have interpreted it as a gesture of my desire for more notice than I was getting. He gave me this notice, though not much of it. I was seven now, and hence had arrived at the age of reason: I had to become a rational son of the Church by making my first confession and by taking my first communion. I needed advice about this confession, to be made in a dark box to Father O'Reilly at the Church of the English Martyrs. I had committed sins, I knew, and that removal of my father's chair had been one of them, but I was vaguely aware of a frontier between true peccancy and mere unacceptable social behaviour. For instance, nose-picking and deliberate farting could not be regarded by God the Father and Son (though I could see them going into earnest discussion about it) as acts worthy of hell. But there was a little song that I had been singing to myself, and I felt it was obscene enough to be sinful. What was the song, my father wanted to know. With shame I sang it:

> There is a happy land far far away,
> Where little piggies run three times a day.
> Oh, you should see them run,

With their fingers up their bum,
Oh, you should see them run
Six times a day.

My father was grave about this, and said that I would have to
sing to an assembled congregation while the organ played the
tune. I did not, frankly, believe him. It struck me that, in the
manner of a proddy dog, he was poking fun at a holy sacrament.

I did not have to sing the song. Father O'Reilly accepted the
generalised package of dirty words and bad thoughts, and I
received my absolution, though with, I thought, a dispropor-
tionate penance of five Our Fathers and five Hail Marys. The
morning of my first communion should have been the happiest
moment of my life. It was, up to that point, the most terrifying.
I was given the body and blood of Jesus Christ in the form of a
thin wafer that cleaved to the roof of my mouth, and I came
away from the altar, hands joined, eyes closed, murmuring 'My
Lord and my God.' I could clean Christ from my palate with my
tongue, but hellfire awaited if my teeth touched him. If even a
morsel of food or a droplet of liquid had preceded his ingestion,
then heaven would rage and fresh coal be trundled in against my
sudden and unrepentant death. It became, from the moment of
being a full communicant, very important to put off death. I
made my first communion with Manchester rain beating down.
On my way to church I had opened my mouth to receive a few
drops. Was that liquid nourishment? From now on, I had to be
good. I had qualified for hell. My stepsister Madge was devout
and over-scrupulous, far more so than the priests. Father Fitzjames
at the Church of the Holy Name had thumped his evening paper
(open at the racing page) and told her not to be a little fool.
Father Myerscough had told her not to be disturbed at the incursion of some minuscule malice: the old boy, he said, had
merely been tickling her with his tail. She was not convinced,
and she passed on her fear of hell to me. It was all too easy to sin.
Life, indeed, seemed all sin. I bought a twopenny sausage roll at
Price's and then remembered it was Friday. I ate it nevertheless.
Still chewing, I ran to evening confession. Swallowing the last
flake, I began to whimper.

Both my stepsisters were courting, and presumably they
permitted kisses but nothing else. The agony of the long courtship, as Graham Greene's whisky priest puts it, before the relief
of marriage; the salty pretzels that exacerbate thirst for the

cocktail. Agnes's marriage was to come first, and her fiancé was Jack Tollitt. *The Music Lover's Portfolio* was rightly of folio size, with great virgin flyleaves that cried out for ravishment with a pencil, and at the end of Volume One I drew Jack Tollitt. I emphasised his Nipponese buck teeth. He was a small, wiry toothsucking Mancunian from Chorlton-on-Medlock, a follower of Manchester City football club, whose stadium at Maine Road was not far away from the shop, a Protestant undergoing slow instruction before being received into the Church, a condition of the impending marriage. He was now working in the shop, with the vigour and efficiency of one who foresaw a familial role in its running. My father was pleased to delegate responsibility. He had other interests than sitting bowler-hatted before cash books. He needed a longer lunchtime session in the Alec, where prolonged standing eased the pain at the base of his spine. In summer he liked to watch county cricket at Old Trafford; in winter he patronised the Manchester steeplechase meetings. Jack Tollitt had no time to shut me in a cardboard box, like Harold Smith. Harold Smith had left to emigrate to some corner of the Empire (the Wembley exhibition had, even at a Manchester remove, impressed him), and his successor had not lasted long: he had the habit of adding the date to the pounds, shillings and pence on the invoices. Jack and Agnes Tollitt were to set up their home at 21 Princess Road, which had three storeys and ample room for the breeding of a Catholic family. But residual Protestantism, as well as obstetric difficulties that were to oppress both my stepsisters, promoted an interest in Dr Marie Stopes's *Married Love*, and there was to be no philoprogenitiveness on the Irish pattern.

This proposed setting up of a new ménage at 21 Princess Road clinched the fulfilment of an enterprise that my stepmother had brooded on ever since the revelation that the new business was doing well. She was lonely without the noise, smoke and effluvia of drink and drama that had animated her life at the Golden Eagle. She wanted to be back, as she put it, in the public. A new pub was out of the question: it was unheard of to run one of those and a tobacco business as well. She compromised with a beer, wine and spirits store, an off-licence as it was termed, and there was one available at 261 Moss Lane East, a mere five minutes' walk from Princess Road. So she, who had so recently sold stock and goodwill in one place, now bought it in another. My father would not be concerned with the new venture. He would leave home for work in the morning like any other man, ready bowler-hatted, after his breakfast of a thick slice of pork pie and a pint of draught Bass, conveniently sleeping in its barrel on the premises. He would come home at three o'clock, when the Alec closed, for his lunch of grilled sweetbreads. He would fret in the house on Sundays over the *News of the World*, after the roast and the lemon pudding, his favourite, or only, dessert. The off-licence followed pub hours, and no evening family life was envisaged. Once more I was to see little of my father.

The off-licence was at the corner of Moss Lane East and Lincroft Street, where David Lloyd George had been born. A smaller and more radical politician lived on that street now, a man named Edwards, whose wife and chidren looked as if they had just served long stretches, for their heads were cropped to the limit. Their furniture was wooden boxes. Edwards had ambitions to bring communism to the City Corporation, but he was never elected, since he could never put up the deposit. He would get up on a soap box on the rec, or recreation ground, a grim black gritty expanse at the head of Lincroft Street, and rant about the wrongs of the times, with a peroration on polluted Corporation water. Moss Side was a respectable district, and Edwards let down the tone. On the other hand he was all we had in the way of eccentricity and he had to be ambiguously cherished.

Our new shop, which was to end as a Caribbean shebeen, was very well patronised by Moss Siders who preferred to do their drinking at home. Their respectability was sometimes suspect: one old man came every evening with a jug for the supper ale and could be seen going home down an entry, where he would drink off a portion and make up the volume by urinating in the jug. When he was too old for this regular errand, his family complained about a loss of strength in the beer. Prim old ladies would come for a quarter bottle of gin, known in those cheap days as mother's ruin, and complain about the growing presence of black men in the town. These were probably Indians who had come to learn about cotton and ways of undercutting our major industry. 'They ought to be kept in their own country' was the usual judgment. An off-licence madam had to tolerate the prejudices of her customers, just like a pub landlady, and my stepmother had no difficulty there, for she subscribed to all the current bigotries. She would even, for the benefit of trade, agree with anticatholics who blamed the Pope for the coming war with America or alleged that the Eucharist was rank cannibalism. Haters of the Irish, who were many, met no opposition in her. Her

Irishry was purely ancestral now, and she hid even that behind an English surname. England, she agreed with my father, was plagued by come-all-ye's and July barbers. A come-all-ye ('Come all ye good Irish and hark to my song / Of the butchers of England who did Ireland wrong') was an Irish immigrant rough, and a July barber was over to cut the harvest.

My stepmother did not improve as a character on the closer acquaintance now granted to me. She had few topics of talk beyond her days as a factory lass, an era of sweated freedom, when she and Katie 'Erbert got stuck in the works elevator or 'oist. This was not an anagram of Otis. She was rigorously consistent in her aitchlessness. When she said, as she regularly did, that she had a 'orrible 'eadache, she did not understand my father's wit when he said all she needed was a couple of aspirates. She picked her teeth with tram tickets and cleaned the wax out of her ears with hairclips. Her teeth ached, just as her bunions did, and she had jealously stolen from my father his pains in the base of the spine. I would, perversely fascinated, tick off an anatomical manifest – head, nose, neck, chest, stomach, legs – and conclude that she was a symptomologist's gift. It seemed impossible to me that anyone so afflicted should wish to survive, but she maintained a large vigour. Occasionally she would move out of the prison of pain, money and memory to speak of the world at large, which meant the royal family: the Old Queen, the Duke of Clarence who was really Jack the Ripper, King Teddy and the Jersey Lily (who dropped ice cream down King Teddy's back), Queen Mary's enamel maquillage. King Alphonsus and Queen Edna (sic, sic) of Spain once appeared on the margin. She recognised that foreign nations existed, since sherry had an Iberian provenance, and she had a respect for the Italians, of whom the Pope (dying from dropsy, she affirmed) was one. She was friendly with a Mrs Frascati, whose English was as aitchless as hers, and spoke once of seeing a woman in the street so beautiful and dark she had to be Italian. Gipsies frightened her, and she always bought their clothes pegs.

Her cooking remained good if plain, but she recognised no other arts. When we moved into 261 Moss Lane East, she gave Madge a handful of silver and told her to buy some second-hand pictures in the manner of buying oranges (no spotty or overripe ones allowed). So we had *The Light of the World* and *The Lady of Shalott* and *Dignity and Impudence* and even *The Stag at Bay*, as well as a few weeping moral anecdotes with bustles and Elgarian moustaches. In the bedrooms were pictures of the Pope blessing *urbem et orbem* and hagiographs straight from art-loving Dublin – the Sacred Heart, the Mater Dolorosa, St Anthony, St John the Baptist with an anachronistic infant Jesus. There were whatnots around, tenanted by a diminishing sequence of ebony elephants, a ringless ring tree, a ceramic girleen with her skirt wind-raised, a cloisonné dish bought in fear from a wandering Chinaman, a seashell ashtray (souvenir of Clevelys), empty tortoiseshell spectacle cases, the remains of a doll's tea service, a backscratcher penitentially unemployed: we all wore wool next to the skin. There were no books even as part of the décor. Books were timewasters or worse. When, in my teens, I came home with a 1683 chapbook bought for twopence, she shrieked at it and put it on the fire with the tongs: she had heard of the Great Plague and here was a paper bubonic rodent.

People, even stepmothers, are not to be condemned for lack of art or aitches. I had no claim on her love and only a minimal one on what must be called her duty. She had accepted me as a pale thin adjunct of my father, whom draught Bass was rendering neither pale nor thin, and had to see me fed, clothed and educated up to the age of ten – or fourteen, when she had been apprised of the law. She herself had left school at ten, and this explained her illiteracy. Education did not guarantee success in the world, as witness my father, who had even been given piano lessons and yet spent his working time as an employee of M. Wilson, quondam Dwyer, née Byrne, and his leisure time boozing. Education for the priesthood was a different matter: you needed Latin for the Sunday hocus pocus. She saw from the start that I was not cut out to be a priest, and priests anyway were reserved to the Dwyer dynasty. She was to frown later on my reading of books, but she was tolerant of *Comic Cuts* and *Funny Wonder* and *Film Fun*, which passed harmlessly through the system, did not have too many words, and could be used for lighting the kitchen fire. I had now graduated from the coloured nursery fodder of *Chick's Own* to the black and white vulgarity of Weary Willy and Tired Tim.

My Aunt Annie came sometimes to visit me, bringing on one occasion the gift of a half-crown gramophone which soon overwound. I should have conceived a nostalgia for the days when she seemed to be my first-hand mother, but, with a child's brutality, I rejected her as the president of damp, snakes, and a nightmare gipsy as well as, I now learned, an inadequate cuisine. She faded into her own greyness and died. Elsie and Betty, now called my cousins, occasionally wrote little letters. They were still writing them when I was a university student, and I objected to being addressed as Master Jack Wilson. But one of my fellow students said it sounded fine, like something Elizabethan. Elsie died single but Betty married after a long Lancashire courtship – twenty years, I believe. That was no record in Manchester. A lady named Miss Horrabin kept a newspaper and tobacco kiosk outside the Opera House on Quay Street, and she had been courted by a Mr Whittle for forty years. Of this couple the following was told, a typical Lancashire paring down to bare dialogue: 'Isn't it time we got wed, Jim?' – 'Ay, but who'd have us now?' I wrote to Betty congratulating her on her marriage and got a letter back telling me that, alas, her dear husband died on the wedding night. Excitement lethally exacerbated, said one of my pedantic friends, by excessive deferral. In Lancashire the comic and tragic easily mix.

A marriage with healthier omens was soon to be celebrated in high style. Jack Tollitt had at last been received into the Church and, after sessions of long burning kisses in the cold drawing-room of 261 Moss Lane East, which I, a mere household animal, had been permitted to witness, the otherwise chaste pair awaited the sanctification of delights hinted at in the films of the roaring twenties. The sacrament was to be celebrated in the Church of the Holy Name on Oxford Road. We were now in its parish.

THE HOLY NAME fills the block between Dover Street and Ackers Street, across from the University. Ackers Street specialised, in my youth, in theatrical lodgings, and my mother had stayed there before becoming a Mancunian. The church itself has theatrical associations. The Carl Rosa Opera Company would sing a flamboyant high mass with orchestral accompaniment. Leslie Stuart, before his fame as the composer of black-face songs and the musical comedy *Floradora*, was the regular organist. In the double quartet of *Floradora* – 'Tell me, pretty maiden, are there any more at home like you?' – he had invoked, to the shocked derision of the producer, the movements of the concelebrants at the highest mass possible. The priests of the Holy Name were Jesuits, hence men of the world, and they spoke the silver-veined English of Cardinal Newman. Any Irishman here had been absorbed into the British Jesuit establishment, and there was no room for Maynooth vowels. The church is large, far larger than the Birmingham cathedral where I saw George Patrick Dwyer installed as archbishop, and it asked of its preachers the professional vocal projection of a Henry Irving or, better, a Noël Coward. Father Bernard Vaughan had preached there with, as Joyce's Father Conmee remembers, droll eyes and Cockney intonation, though he was Welsh. 'Pilate, why don't you 'old back that 'owlin mob?' The preachers I remember frightened me with more patrician diction: religion was no longer the rollicking or folklorical leprechaun stuff of Ireland; in the Holy Name it attained the dignity and authority of imperial law. The priests were steely-eyed and blue-jawed and, by God, knew their theology. My father was to be frightened off the place. He entered for eleven o'clock mass one Sunday with his bowler hat on and Three Castles burning – sheer absentmindedness: he must have thought he was entering a pub – and was unlucky enough to meet the priest and his acolytes in the ceremony of the Asperges. His cigarette was fiercely doused with a well-aimed blast of holy water, and of his hat the priest hissed: 'This is not a synagogue.' Then he became the subject of a brilliant improvised sermon on wilful irreverence. He never went back, except for his one mass a year – Christmas, midnight, drunk. Like many Catholics, he made his own rules.

At Agnes's wedding he gave the bride away in hired morning clothes, somewhat sober, rather tubby. He behaved well. He had not behaved so well at other people's weddings. At one, not sober, he had wished the bride many happy returns and made her cry. At another, Wesleyan or Baptist, he had joined in with the singing of 'Tell Me the Old, Old Story' but roared, instead of 'of Jesus and his love', 'as you have done before'. My stepmother seemed to be counting the cost of the wedding, to which she had contributed with a hat like a cake from Duncan and Foster's, panached all round with nodding ostrich feathers. Madge was chief bridesmaid and looked lovely in lace and a Dutch cap (which at that time had no connection with birth control). The bride wore her white legitimately and was shyly ravishing. I was clumsily ravishing, since I wore a claret velvet suit as trainbearer. I dropped the train halfway down the aisle and had to run after it. This was the beginning of my great love of weddings, and I regret that both mine have been functional or hole-in-a-corner affairs. There is nothing like a wedding. Let the roaring organs loudly play, cried Edmund Spenser, who had a Lancashire connection (he uses 'mard' in *The Shepherd's Calendar*) but was married in a church in Cork where there is scarcely room for a barrel organ. 'Hear that?' my father whispered to me as we went up the aisle to Mendelssohn. 'That's the only bit of music I know that doesn't begin on a common chord.' True: the Wedding March for Theseus and his Amazon begins with a secondary seventh of the dominant key. It was a strange time to impart that titbit of musical education. Proleptic elation probably. Poure not by cuppes but by the belly full!

The wedding reception was held at Shorrocks's, a well-known dance hall of the time, often stained with blood, beer and semen on the University's rag night, as I was to learn later. The management catered for weddings and funerals alike and, this being Manchester, with equal gusto. There was a slippery ballroom and sitting-out areas with plush loveseats. There were ample lavatories for the overcome. I, and the Wilson and Dwyer young, slid along the dance floor before the little band struck up 'The Sheik of Araby', gorged on cake and ice cream and lemonade tempered by Big Tree Australian burgundy, then were duly sick. I was not sick over my claret velvet. That came some days later with artificial induction. I was sent to school in my trainbearer's outfit, which provoked worse persecution than the Joan Price affair. After the careful ruination I rejoined the lads with holed jersey and torn kex.

Mr and Mrs Tollitt honeymooned in Douglas on the Isle of Man and returned fulfilled and energetic to take over the top floors of 21 Princess Road. At 261 Moss Lane East, my father, Madge and myself settled to my stepmother's keening over the cost of the wedding. God was unjust in giving a woman two daughters marriageable at much the same time. There was a consequent delay in announcing the banns for Madge. She was affianced to Clifford Kemp, a son of Collyhurst and of a widow who ran a tobacconist's shop smaller than ours on Queen's Road. He was another Protestant undergoing instruction. He was said to look like the Prince of Wales. Strange that both girls had fallen for heathens when there were so many good Irish families around – the Fitzgeralds and Kilpatricks and Groarkes and, for all I knew, Dedaluses. Perhaps not so strange. There was a whif of incest in this too easy consolidation of the faith and blood. Nature, or Lévi-Strauss, was counselling healthful exogamy. God, or the Society for the Propagation of the Faith, was quietly urgent about the need to breed English

Catholics. Certainly, though Kemp Catholicism came to little, the Tollitts have become mainstays of a number of north-western parishes. Jack Tollitt became, like Greene and Waugh, a fierce and pedantic Catholic, shame and example to us all. God is love and works through tumescence.

Madge did not dream of marriage, since marriage was going to happen. She dreamed rather of a world above all our stations, glimpsed tantalisingly in women's magazines and fourpenny fiction. She met it too in the Paramount pictures which Famous Lasky, for whom she still stenographed, distributed. It was a world of wealth and refinement, not specifically American: we read the film subtitles in cisatlantic English. It was nevertheless the world of the illustrations to Scott Fitzgerald's stories in the *Saturday Evening Post*. There were cocktails in it but no boozing, intrigue but no fornication, short skirts but no indecency, fast cars without accidents, beaches with striped umbrellas and orangeade sipped through straws. Madge's mother regrettably blasphemed against this side of paradise with her belches and aitchlessness, but her daughter bore no grudge: honour thy father, though not necessarily thy stepfather, and the other one. It was I who let the dream down.

Madge become a kind of disciple of a Mrs Hopwood, who lived in a house not a shop and spoke refined. She said to me: 'Hello, Jackie, have you come home for lunch?' I corrected her. 'Dinner.' One day Madge prepared to invite the visiting Mrs Hopwood to stay to tea, and she covertly sent me out to buy a quarter of a pound of boiled ham. That this would not chime with Mrs Hopwood's conception of afternoon tea did not seem to occur to her. I came back to Madge's and Mrs Hopwood's chatting presence and plonked the moist package in Madge's hand. 'Here y'are, then.'

Mrs Hopwood did not stay to tea: she had to go home and supervise the preparation of dinner. Madge turned on me not angrily, since anger was a sin in those days, but with the damped frustration of a Norma Shearer.

'So you failed.'

'What yer mean, failed?'

'Failed to show me up. Putting a quarter of ham in my hand in the sitting-room. Mrs Hopwood didn't notice, because she could never imagine anyone being so coarse as to do anything like that. And I haven't forgotten the time you made her blush.'

'Me?'

'When she said lunch and you said dinner. You went out of your way to make her embarrassed.'

'Lunch is what you have at eleven. Dinner's what you have after that. Then you have tea. Then you have supper.'

'Not where Mrs Hopwood comes from. Go away. Your silly face makes me sick.'

Even I, young as I was, could see that Mrs Hopwood was shabby genteel, a shaker of her own mats at the front door. It was the accent that snared Madge, the fluty relic of some minor girls' school, with a plaintive tonal range and long ah's. Madge was never invited to Mrs Hopwood's for lunch or for soup of the evening, but she knew what good table manners were. What she imagined as proceeding at the Hopwood meals was a pedantic fulfilment of what *Modern Woman* laid down. The Irish have never had good table manners, since they have never had a good table. My stepmother would occasionally cut her meat with a pair of scissors if the knife-sharpener had been slow in trundling up his whetstone. There was a visiting Aunt Kate, one of the outer or Plutonic Dwyers who dressed as though in mourning for Prince Albert, and she would impale potatoes on her knife and mouth them in whole with much hot exhaling. I ate fast, my father alone. Madge was let down and sustained a disregarded solo of table decorum, even introducing a finger bowl for grape-eating, but she had a manducatory problem which kept her awake at night. She could not manage a chop or a chicken leg with her knife and fork. She did not believe that anybody could. Posh people, she was sure, left such items half-eaten, and *tête-à-tête* diners would wait till their partner temporarily left the room and then ravage their meaty bone with brutal swiftness. Staying at seaside hotels with Clifford Kemp, she would mourn, hungry with sea air while the dinner trio played 'Softly Awakes My Heart' from *Samson and Delilah*, over her browned drumstick. And then, with exemplary courage, she one evening picked it up openly and smilingly and set, as she thought, a new fashion. She never looked back. This was Manchester Irish grit.

There was an opportunity to touch the great world when George Dwyer the millionaire came from Australia on a family visit with his son Dan. He was bowed and penitent over the sexual scandal down under, but he brought few piacular gifts. Dan came to lunch with his Aunt Maggie, my stepmother, and was given a solitary feast on Madge's instructions, since none of us could be trusted to handle a knife and fork. The lunch was a displaced dinner, consisting of hors d'oeuvres, chicken soup, a steak of halibut, a whole chicken properly garnished, and a charlotte russe. I was brought in from my plate of hotpot in the kitchen for a brief introduction, and Dan Dwyer said, in a high-class pommy voice: 'He has a typical Lancashire accent, hasn't he?' Then I was shoved back to my cooling hotpot. The great George Dwyer gave a great dinner for his kin at the Midland Hotel. Madge could bring Clifford Kemp. 'But er, has he, er, a dinner jacket?' George Dwyer asked. 'Of course,' Madge replied in a bright reverse shot. George Dwyer, she said after, seemed surprised but also relieved, or it may have been the other way round. We saw less of Mrs Hopwood from then on, except, as we passed, shaking the mats or promising the rent-collector she would definitely pay her arrears next week. Australian Catholic snobbishness may have been a contradiction in terms, but it pulled back the curtain on a certain moral hollow in the high life.

Still, social mobility is built into women and may be an aspect of their biology. Madge remained refined, though ill-informed, and she dressed elegantly in the bosomless style of the day, going off to her stenography in a cloche hat and with exposed pretty knees. She was well informed only about the cinema, in which she had a professional stake. She fed me for a time with a dream of Hollywood, of which we were all learning more, not only from film magazines but from the screen itself. I had seen at Jakie Innerfield's cinema a movie with the title *Hollywood*, which memory confuses with another movie called *Sodom and Gomorrah*. The film capital was already cannibalising itself, and there was one expressionist scene in which this happened literally: a huge human head with HOLLYWOOD burnt into its brow swallowed pigmy aspirants to film fame. This did not impair our fascination with the place, which was more magical silent than talking. The first squawk on the Vitaphone disc was a great disillusionment. In 1925 Rudolph Valentino still had a year of life ahead of him, and he was lucky to die voiceless. There was nobody like Valentino, so Madge thought, and she was right. I remember a party of friends of hers, all knees and cigarettes and no bosoms, in the upstairs drawing-room, and they were discussing a film in which Valentino appeared in white wig with a beauty spot. I said knowledgeably: 'It's called Monsewer Bewcare.' I was corrected and left the room in humiliation, hearing Madge say: 'Poor kid.'

The poor kid, quite apart from school, was learning to be

better informed than his stepsister. I slept in the attic, which was narrow but long, and here there was a bookcase full of books long discarded by my father, who had concluded that education was a mug's game – a truth my stepmother had always known. Here there was a complete set of the *Manual of Freemasonry*, whatever that was. A secret society apparently, with passwords and obscure rites. Was my father a member? It was only when I got down seriously to the penny catechism that I discovered that the Church anathematised secret societies. A Catholic could not be a mason, but how did Catholic businessmen prosper without belonging to that congeries of reciprocal help? Smoking Masons bought from Mason smoke-shops. On the other hand, my father had his own rules of religious conduct, and I fancy he was a quiet low-degree apron-wearer without the ambition or the wealth to become Grand Master of a lodge. How else was I able to go to a Masonic children's party at Christmas 1925? There was a Masonic Felix the Cat, hot and irritable in jumping fur, who miaowed 'Those kids that don't line up proper for their presents from the tree don't gerrenny.' A Mason lady said of me to Father Mason Christmas: 'This little boy wants a ball.' This little boy didn't. He never wanted a ball. My father also belonged to the Ancient Order of Buffaloes: a framed certificate nested among the dusty attic junk. The rituals seemed less portentous, according to what he told me. 'Mr Primo, may I partake of weed? Mr Primo, may I partake of gatter?' These were respectively tobacco and beer. In 1953, in an Oxfordshire country pub, I saw one of these framed diplomas hanging on the wall of the public bar. I was shocked with a sense of the uncanny, not uncommon for me in that haunted county, when I saw that the name on it was Joseph Wilson. Somebody else, of course.

There was an illustrated set of Dickens and there were Ball's *Story of the Sun* and *Story of the Heavens*. In both these there were folded celestial maps which opened out to show fire, desperate blue, Pascalian emptiness. Seeing the heavens, for the first and last time in my life I fainted. I came to quickly enough but have never overcome the horror of maps unhumanised by roads and churches. I was a map-reading instructor in the army and was unfearful of tracts that could be covered in a day's march, but a world map terrifies me and visions of interstellar space bring on convulsions. This is more than agoraphobia: call it diastematophobia. I am poised till I die between fear of the cardboard darkness of the stockroom and the terror of space. I wanted the free limitations of my own skull and a world I could build with a pencil. I have not changed much since 1925.

Whatever I rooted out of the attic – Scott's *Marmion* illustrated, Rider Haggard's *She*, a French primer with Margaret Dwyer on the flyleaf (my stepmother? Of course not: her younger daughter. Some Catholic girls' high school. That explained her getting *Monsieur Beaucaire* approximately right), my shallower instruction proceeded at Bishop Bilsborrow Memorial School. Promotion from what was called the babies to the real kids was achieved by age, not attainment, and I found myself functioning as a teacher's help with mouth-breathing analphabetes. Some of them could not even cope with three-letter words. We would sit at a desk together and look at THE. I was too young to explain the mystery of the digraph even to myself. If only I had known that the Normans kicked out the Anglo-Saxon thorn and eth and substituted the Latin inadequacy for theta. But we were not ready for the illogicality of history. AND should have been easier but was not. I would plonk my hand on the stained primer and say: 'What's that?' I knew I would get the right answer. Outside of reading lessons I joined the instructed and was no better than anyone else.

We were now in the violent world of Sister Ignatius and her strap. She lorded it over laywomen who, like most of the ladies of Madge's hell of the unenlightened, had malodorous armpits, which my stepmother called oxters (the suggestion of oxtail soup was not inappropriate). Madge herself used a depilatory called Veet. Our teachers – Miss Clayton or Clayballs, Miss O'Rourke, Mrs Hampson – smelt of unredeemed female. We were taught the catechism and even scripture – not from the bible but from some deodorised redaction of it. We loved the name Esau, which provoked a folk-rhyme all ready and wrapped within the space of half an hour:

> I saw Esau
> Sitting on a seesaw
> Eating mouldy peas.

A kind of Lear limerick came out of an arithmetic lesson:

> Pounds shillings and pence
> A lady jumped over a fence
> The fence was sticky

It stuck in her dicky
Pounds shillings and pence.

Folk art bubbled away in parallel to official education. We
were still close enough to the Great War to have

Ar soldiers went to war
Ar soldiers fought
Ar soldiers stuck their bayonets
Up the Germans'
Ar soldiers went to war

And so on for ever. Aitch, which, despite our teachers' puffing
and sighing demonstrations, never got into the phonemic inventory, was to be heard only as a percussive device in

Hum. Hum.
Kiss my bum.
If I 'ave a party *you* won't come.
Bread without butter,
Tea without sugar.
Hum. Hum.
Kiss my bum.

Anyone heard reciting such nonsense was made to stand on his
desk with arms stretched sideways. Boys on the back row rather
liked this, because they could lean on the wall, gag, cross their
eyes, and pretend to be Christ crucified. Christ, whatever else he
was, was a popular hero: an exotic cat lick done in by the Roman
proddy dogs.

The crucifixion, and for that matter the spreading of the gospel
of love, which we were taught with some violence, apparently
proceeded in a hot robed land while the Ancient Britons were
running coldly around in woad, whatever that was. But one lad
swore that his dad had actually been out there in Punchus Pilot
territory, fighting the Turks or some similar buggers in the recent
war. We knew that was a lot of balls, because the war had been
fought at Ypres on the Somme, with barbed wire and tanks and
bayonets up the Germans' and so forth. We knew Ypres was
pronounced Eep and not Wipers, because another lad's dad had
been stuck in the mud there where the real war was. Eep was
what the natives called it. The late war never got into our cur-

riculum. It was left to the cinemas which were lavish with re-construction of the agonies of the tommies on the Marne and 'Ill Sixty. I was back to the old game of reading out the titles on Saturday afternoon. 'You've got a blighty one, you lucky beggar. Have a fag.'

The war was secular agony completed. The more serious pain was reserved to eternity, and there was the promise of it every morning, not in words but in the practical demonstration of Sister Ignatius's strap. Sister Ignatius was a sort of Lancashire fishwife got up as a nun. She conducted morning prayers as though crying fresh halibut. Prayers were lengthy and featured the Virgin Mary more than her son or the great fuming dyspeptic God who raged round his punishment laboratory. Mary was there, visibly sweet and forgiving of words like 'arse' and 'bum', though it was assumed she was too well brought up to know what they meant. She was surrounded by candles which, on a dull day in the assembly hall on to which the classrooms disembogued, gave off a pleasant Christmassy feeling. We recited 'Hail Holy Queen' and many decades of the rosary. Occasionally a boy, never a girl, would faint from the long standing. ''E's chucked a dummy' would get into the Hail Mary. The boy, terrified of the strap for lateness, would probably have missed breakfast. Punishment for lateness was immediate, fired by the resentment of a nun who had had a foredawn mass call, and meted out in the cloakroom or on the run: black skirt arustle, she saw no indignity in chasing the reluct-ant. The strap hurt damnably, as she knew, and there was a kind of sinful logic in running away from it. She never once strapped empty air. It was a relief to turn from her to the Virgin Mary, dumb, puzzled but forgiving. 'Hail, our life, our sweetness and our hope. To thee do we cry, poor banished children of Eve. To thee do we send up our sighs, mourning and weeping in this vale of tears. Turn then, most gracious advocate, thine eyes of mercy towards us, and after this our exile show unto us the blessed fruit of thy womb.' I still think that is good prose. It has two phrases — 'children of Eve' and 'after this our exile' — as good as anything produced by Pontius Pilate. I have used them frequently as titles for disregarded articles. I even won a prize for a story called 'Children of Eve'.

A priest would occasionally look in to see how Our Kay or RK or Religious Knowledge was getting on. Sometimes it would be a newly ordained priest whose holy hands we were bidden kiss: he would wipe them, all slobbered on, with a snowy handkerchief we would admire: ours were filthy snotrags when we had them at all; sleeves were mostly our line. In 1927 I got into an argument with one of these scrubbed magicians (what he did concealed at the altar had to be magic: turning bread into living meat, for God's sake). He spoke of the sacrifice of the mass. In a sacrifice there had to be a priest and a victim. We all knew who the victim was; who was the priest? He beamed in the expectation of the answer 'You, father'. But I said no, it wasn't him, it was Jesus Christ himself. The priest wasn't big enough to do the job, he was merely standing in for the master, who clearly couldn't be everywhere at once. Are you sure? I think I'm sure. He laughed merrily, and the issue was not resolved. Sister Ignatius escorted him out and then came in again, pointing the finger. 'Arguin' with a priest, mind yer.' But no action was taken. Perhaps they feared, out of the mouths of, I might consult the Jesuits at the Holy Name and be proved right.

The lasting secular things one learns at school are all matters of rote. 'Thirty days hath September' and the tables – once-one-is-one up to the twelve times. We each had a tables pamphlet, with, for some reason, advertisements in it. One was for Gilbey's Port, white and red, with a pretty lady asking 'Which will you have?' Another was of a fierce man saying 'Pain or Sloan's Liniment? You can't have both.' I confused these two and still believe that a taste for white port (which makes one drunk in a genteel buttonholing way) excludes a liking for the other, which merely makes one sick. As for the tables, I have never discounted their value. Children nowadays use pocket computers. When the battery dies they are put in the position of Beethoven, who never learned his tables and has left us a bill scrawled with '7 + 7 + 7 + 7 + 7 + 7 + 7 = 49'. Whatever else we learned, we all learned to rattle them off. At the end of the summer holiday we had to tell our teachers which masses we had been to, left to our parents' doubtful supervision. When I cried out 'Four elevens' the class immediately responded with 'Forty-four'. That was old-time strapped and thumped education.

1926 WAS NOTABLE for the death of Rudolph Valentino and the General Strike. The first struck my stepsisters the harder. We saw a newsreel of howling mourners and banks of arum lilies in New York or somewhere. For the first time, with no help from Valentino's ancestral religion, we pondered the mystery less of physical resurrection than of vital continuity. Valentino might be dead in the off-duty flesh, but we knew him only as an on-duty projection which was nobler than the life of crass subsistence. Marilyn Monroe and Humphrey Bogart have undergone the same transfiguration, dead but not really dead, more live in death than in life. Gore Vidal, in his novel *Duluth*, has pushed this eschatology to the democratic limit: when anyone dies in Duluth he or she is at once glorified into a character in a television series called *Duluth*. But Valentino's life-in-death seemed to us to teach that only the glamorous merited eternity, which would last till the emulsion dissolved and the celluloid cracked. That glamour was ours for threepence. When Valentino's will was published I felt a vague pique that he had not left me a tin of his favourite brilliantine. Admiring his sleekness I was using Woolworth's brilliantine myself. It smelt nicer than my teachers.

The General Strike should have smelt very nastily, but it did not. Uncle Jack, a master plumber on the side of lowlier operatives, wanted the red revolution to come. He claimed to know all about counter-revolutionary measures being prepared by the government. He remembered 1919, when Austen Chamberlain had said: 'We are in front of a situation here which may require all our forces. I am for holding the British coalfields rather than the Silesian ones.' Lord Birkenhead had cried: 'Howl on, you wolves of Moscow! We shall slit your soft white throats for you!' Tanks in Liverpool. A battleship anchored in the Mersey. Seven years later, it stood to reason, the government was better prepared. The lions of Moscow were watching. Uncle Jack was not pleased when strikers played football with policemen. 'Murder, rape and bloody arson when the red revolution comes.' That was sung at these matches derisively to the tune of 'John Brown's Body'. The British would never learn. The news sheet called *The British Worker* was a reactionary rag counselling calm and the upholding of the Constitution. Winston Churchill's *British Gazette* did the fire-eating; it should have been the other way round.

Wilson's of 21 Princess Road still sold fags and Baby's Bottom. Smoking did not come to an end. The real revolution operated in the sphere of communication. 'Look at this,' said my bowler-hatted father in disgust, holding a single sheet of newsprint. 'This is supposed to be the bloody paper.' We were getting our news from the British Broadcasting Corporation, no longer a mere company, and mainly at Pearson's the wireless shop, where there were valves and loudspeakers. Our crystal set seemed inadequate to the times. What grieved me most was the failure of *Comic Cuts, The Funny Wonder, Chips* and *The Boys' Magazine* to appear. When they came out again at the end of the strike they were all, I saw, predated to the strike's beginning and its continuation. They were not, after all, printed red hot like newspapers. They were myth, not news. I felt vaguely cheated, shunted into timelessness when, like the rest of the world, I wanted to feel that I was riding time. Jack Tollitt had the honour of rushing out from Pearson's to shout to the whole of Princess Road that the strike was over.

The intermission of my comic papers and *The Boys' Magazine*, which was far from comic and had a serial story about the End of the World (delayed because of the strike), impelled me into trying to make my own kidfeed. I had two talents. I could draw and I could put words together. A story of mine had already been displayed in the school hall tacked between somebody's crayoning of a tulip and somebody else's of a house on fire with stickmen refugees. It began '"Boom! Boom! Boom!" went the town clock. It was the hour of three.' My punctuation was sound. I had learned the more violent points from the comics and the quotations marks from magazine serials. I could do a neat small print script. I had a ruler for cartoon boxes, a penny bottle of ink and a J-nib. I could find no paper large enough for a *Chips*, but an ordinary exercise book, its cover removed, would serve as the ready-stapled body of a magazine. I was forced to move beyond the coarse hilarity of pies labelled PIE, sausages poking from mounds of mash, dominoed burglars with bags marked SWAG. The sophistication of *The Boys' Magazine* asked for emulation.

I admired *The Boys' Magazine* but had something against it. There was a joke page made out of what readers sent in. The best joke of the week was awarded a cricket bat and the runners-up a fountain-pen. I wanted a fountain-pen. I sent off a joke. 'Where did you get that swollen nose?' – 'Well, do you see that broken paving stone there?' – 'Yes.' – 'I didn't.' This won first prize and was given a rollicking illustration. I was not pleased with the cricket bat which, untreated with linseed oil, dried up and splintered. I had nothing against cricket, except that I did not play it. At school we were wholly in the hands of schoolmistresses, who taught us no games. Schoolmasters would come into our lives sometime, if we were not kicked out of the elementary scholarshipless at fourteen. For the moment they were only in the

Gem and the *Magnet*, which, not at all to the rancour of lads of our station, presented a gowned and bum-freezered world we would never attain. Anyway, I recognised a vocation and was angry at gaining first prize.

The magazine was called *Boy*, which I still consider a good title. It was, at that time, an avant-garde one. I must have been sick of teaching THE. Having engrossed the name, with a stylised juvenile under it, I came to the contents page, which I had to leave blank until I knew what the contents were to be. The contents were filched jokes with my own illustrations, serial stories which started but were never to finish, competitions with no one to compete, a 'Believe It Or Not' double spread stolen from the *Sunday Express*, riddles, even advertisements. The advertisements were careful copies of the real thing. My father, shown my Guinness and Veet, doubted their value – I was burking the issue of creation – but I sensed that I was on the right McLuhan track. During World War Two GIs were dissatisfied when they got condensed copies of *Time* and *Life* without advertisements. McLuhan saw why: the advertisements pointed outwards to the real world of the commodity market where life was lived, it was also usually better composed and illustrated than the contents of the magazine itself. I had, then, a sound journalistic instinct; as for creation, I was by no means ready for it.

Children are uncreative. They can only imitate. The closest I got to originality was in a blasphemous daydream about a comic strip called 'God the Creator', passing on the creative to someone else. I never devised its content, which was clearly to be gross and fundamental magic. In my novel *The Wanting Seed* there is a comic strip about a Mr Livedog, who palinlogically combines the Maker and the Unmaker, which points back to the fantasy. Mr Livedog fills the earth with unwanted life in the time of the great demographic explosion, but Mr Homo, who has sacrificed his balls to humanity, thwarts him with lethal sprays. My cartoons in *Boy* followed those of *Film Fun* in being about Charlie Chaplin, who puffed a cigarette and made the smoke come from his ear, Chester Conklin and Harold Lloyd. My serials had dialogue like 'Egad, Jack boy, I've seen grown men crying like babbies when made to walk the plank. You're dry-eyed like a hero.' There was a poem in galloping fourteeners about a train wreck: 'The fireman saw the twisted rails and sweat began to start. / The driver felt a feeling of despair rise in his heart.' The drawings were over-ambitious and crude. I scorned collaboration after a boy living at 255 Moss Lane

East, Eddie Mitchell, contributed a short story about some lads locking their schoolmaster in a lavatory and going off to live a life of riot. 'When they got back the master was dead so they threw him in the river.' No retribution. Eddie Mitchell was a proddy dog.

The Mitchell home was the first Protestant one I ever entered, except for my aunt's, which I did not so much enter as come to consciousness in. The Mitchell one was not much different from a Catholic home, except that there were no hagiographs, drying Whitsun palms, or empty holy water stoups. The father made water for a living, as he put it, meaning he worked for the Water Department. He said there was no God, a shocking but comforting assertion. He was punished for this when Eddie, at the age of nine, fell from the roof of the local Temperance Billiard Hall, where he had climbed to retrieve a ball, and was impaled on the surrounding railings. These had swordlike points which pierced his intestines. He crawled home, lay down on the family sofa, and said: 'Nobody knows what I've been through.' Then he died. So, I discovered, even the young can die. It seemed to me terrible that his agony should at once be eternally compounded by hellfire. It wasn't his fault that his father was an atheist. His sister Lily, who was thirteen, asked me to come in and see his laid-out body, which, she said, looked lovely. This was the more macabre because once, in a bedroom game while the family was out, she had taken most of her clothes off and lain down in a pretence of death. I was supposed to tickle her body back to life.

Sex was coming, and it was no comic paper. It began with my obsession with female breasts, which I had of course never consciously known in a maternal context. The breasts that fed had been removed from me. I had evidence from my classmates that mothers' breasts and, for that matter, sisters' genitalia could be accepted coolly and in an atmosphere of domestic fun. In genitalia I had no interest: when a girl in the school yard (not Joan Price) offered to show for a halfpenny and allow a brisk feel for a penny, I approved the commercial instinct but was no customer. But breasts outside the family filled me with hot delirium. Inside the family, a step-family after all, there was neither a Freudian current nor a clinical indifference. My stepmother's breasts, glimpsed swinging as in a belfry during one of her rare all-over washes (immersion weakened you), conveyed no current except vague disgust; Madge had, I supposed, cut hers off to conform to the fashion of flappers. It was the breasts of my younger teachers, outlined in yellow jumpers, that excited me. The other boys did not seem so excited. One teacher's breasts, unrestrained by a bust bodice, moved like live things when she strode from desk to blackboard and back again. One dull boy assured me they were her lungs; male lungs were different and well tucked away. But they were breasts all right.

I used to nurse a curious daydream. All my teachers, naked to the waist, were to be disposed on a film set, and I had to carry them, all light as air, to rostra where they formed a still décor. I was also the cameraman. A voice kept repeating: 'You'll get good money for this.'

It was now that strange women entered my life in circumstances of great intimacy. My stepmother needed what she had always had at the Golden Eagle: a hired girl or maid, twelve shillings and sixpence weekly, one afternoon off, all found. There were only three bedrooms – the master one where my father and stepmother slept, blessed by the Pope and the Little Flower; Madge's; the attic which had been wholly mine. In the attic were a big lumpy bed and a smaller one. I had had the space and the lumps; now I was to sleep straight and confined. None of the quick succession of maids we had raised any objection to sharing a room with a nine-year-old. If they had been used to privacy they would probably not have been candidates for the job.

But even the most deprived could not have found the room alluring. It was primarily an annexe for junk and a stepson. I had entered into the spirit of the place and scrawled all over the striped wallpaper. This was the old Delauneys Road custom of capturing what I had seen in rapid pictograms, but now I had substituted whole walls for the pages of a cash book. I had seen the first version of *The Wizard of Oz*, and there was Larry Semon as the Tin Man; there was a stylised owl from an eerie film about graveyard doings; there was the shameless declaration I LOVE BABY PEGGY (a child star, precursor of Shirley Temple, whom I used to pray to God to find installed in my bed the following morning). This avowal may have suggested to some of the hired girls that I was sexually more mature than I looked.

The first girl stayed one night only. She got up early, ostensibly to light the kitchen fire, then called upstairs: 'There's someone at the door.' We heard the door unbolted, then 'There's nobody there,' the door slam, then silence. She had absconded, taking the petty cash, a clock, two candlesticks, and my gollywog moneybox. The next girl, who brought more substantial luggage, stayed longer. She spent a lot of her free time taking baths, an unwonted luxury for her, so was at least clean. She not only showed me her breasts but insisted that I play with them. Perhaps many women have this dream of a small harmless male, a castrated dwarf, a penis that can do no harm. She granted me a total exhibition one night, flaunting mothernaked, and, like John Ruskin, I was shocked at my first view of female pubic hair. She was dismissed for taking baths when she should have been working.

Phyllis Cornthwaite, who stayed longer, carried on an ocular affair with a married man who lived opposite. There was a small attic window with a folding ladder beneath it; she would mount the ladder and look across, exchanging signs that grew nightly more amorous. At length, when signs were no longer enough, there was physical contact and street scandal, and she had to go. But before she went she taught me how to kiss. She did more. Like my stepmother, who had an Irish Catholic terror of it, she feared thunder, and I woke during a storm to find that she had got into my narrow bed for comfort. She was wearing a woollen nightdress she proved willing to take off. It was not a full seduction (who, anyway, was seducing whom?), but I remember shaking like a leaf and learning what heaven was. A heaven meriting hell: the devil's heaven. I now had to face confession.

I had got through it easily enough after the earlier occasions of concupiscence. I had had the good sense not to confess at the Holy Name, where the Jesuits would have probed relentlessly; I had gone to the English Martyrs, where a curate had not taken too seriously the unbidden sight of total nakedness and the breast-touching – regrettable but perhaps unavoidable in a large ill-housed family, probably like his own in County Cork or some-where. An easy absolution, and the maid, after her final bath, had left. I might have got away with the later encounter with that same priest, especially since Irish-style brontophobia came into it, but Madge, who might well have heard suspicious noises from her neighbouring bedroom, insisted that she and I go to con-fession together at the Holy Name. So we walked through the rain down Moss Lane East to the Number 44 tram stop outside the Alec, and we travelled, me sick with fright, to Oxford Road. To Father Fitzjames I made what is known as a clean breast of it (clean breast better applied to the bath-taking girl). I could see through the grille that he was reading the racing results in the *Evening Chronicle*. My revelation proved more interesting than the *Chronicle*, which he rolled into a tight staff to hit out at my engrilled image. Filth, deadly sin, one so young too, what's your name, where do you live? I knew all about the secrecy of the confessional and insisted on my right to anonymity. I was told to get out and then called back to be given weary absolution and a damnable penance – five decades of the rosary then and there in front of the main altar. Madge, who soon got through her regular one Our Father, one Hail Mary and one Glory be, had to wait a long time for me. What sins, she wanted to know. Fighting, disobedience, answering back. She did not seem convinced.

I lay straight in my narrow bed and kept my eyes shut. There had to be an invisible wall between Phyllis Cornthwaite and myself. The thunder obligingly kept off. I had been told, not by furious Father Fitzjames, to pay careful attention to the meaning of the words of the prayers I said and, in this phase of penitence, I did. It meant, for instance, taking the *Gloria* and breaking it into its constituent images: 'Glory be to the Father' (easy enough: a jamboree of angels around a sour greybeard on a throne) 'and to the Son' (enter Jesus, on whom God's back is turned as on the boy not prodigal) 'and to the Holy Ghost' (carrier pigeon belonging to Jack Brownlow opposite flutters over) 'as it was in the beginning' (now began the interesting part with a montage of brontosauruses and tyrannosauruses and pterodactyls) 'is now' (short skirts and Ford motorcars) 'and ever shall be' (the radiant future, all urban aircraft and skyscrapers) 'world without end' (future going on for ever, with bigger and better skyscrapers).

Madge and Clifford Kemp were duly married in the Holy Name with Father Fitzjames officiating. It was an almost exact duplicate of the wedding of Agnes and Jack Tollitt, except that I did not bear the train, which was entrusted to a small fair child from the outer reaches of the Dwyer family, Agnes was matron of honour, and the bride gave signs of breaking down during the ceremony: 'Courage, courage,' cried Father Fitzjames. The Kemps went to live in West Gorton or some similar leafy skirt of Manchester, and I now took over Madge's bedroom, with its Sacred Heart and Saint Anthony, whom, for want of knowing someone better, I was to adopt as my confirmation patron. It was the Saint Anthony who finds lost things, though never for me. Thoroughly robbed by Algerians in Avignon in 1968, I went to his own church in Padua and pointed out his duty, but he did not respond. Under his picture in my new room there was an unused gas jet that worked. I had rational intentions for that. I was, when Christmas brought me, as I intended, a chemistry outfit, to become quite the little scientist.

I was removed from fleshly temptation, since our new hired girl had the attic to herself and could, if she wished, lock the door. But she was a Welsh girl who, though of large stupidity, was of melting prettiness, abundant fair hair, and long legs in gunmetal artificial silk. Her stupidity was attested in various ways. The cat slept all night in the dutch oven and, when she lighted the morning fire, cried that it was baking. She opened the oven door, closed it again on the poor cat, and called us down to see its distress. When clothes set to air by the same fire caught alight and blazed to the ceiling, or rather to the laundry-rack full of underwear that was suspended near the ceiling, she cried only that the smoke was getting in her eyes. Her stupidity was accepted as a Welsh property, better than Welsh treachery (Taffy was a wicked Welshman and Taffy was a thief). The Irish and the Welsh have never got on. This girl, Glynis, was destined soon to be sent packing, but there was time for at least one visit to her room, where, in her marvellous nudity, she encouraged me to perform a shallow variety of the sin of Sodom. This was an ecstatic experience, as it had to be if it deserved God's brimstone. All I dared confess was a generalised sin of impurity – not at the Holy Name. My tolerant curate prescribed decades of the rosary in a cold bath if we had such a thing. The new maid, named Nelly, stayed long. She was bespectacled, leering, and deformed: like the character in *The Way of All Flesh*, she had a back that jutted out at opposed angles, like the outer notes of the chord of the augmented sixth. Jack Tollitt called her Awkward Bottom. I was no longer tempted.

Moreover, glasses were now put on me to make me look like a sexless swot. Never wish for anything for you will get it. I wanted to be Harold Lloyd but had always assumed, rightly, that his horn rims were plain-glassed décor. Now, after tests at the public eye clinic, I was given idiot-boy frames round corrective lenses and made to read a passage about a starling that I found later was from Sterne's *Sentimental Journey*. I was to be jeered at as Specky Four Eyes. The household situation was grotesque: everybody at 261 Moss Lane East now had glasses, including the maid, and even the cat, after its experience in the oven, was squinting. I taught myself to go through the world, though not to the cinema, with naked imperfect eyes. I would see the world I wanted to see: with so many diopters of correction the real thing looked gross and over-sharp. There was later to be a film cartoon which has never lost its appeal for me. A little mole saw every day a beautiful crystal palace until a pedlar rat came along and fitted him with spectacles: then the palace changed into a mass of broken bottles. The mole smashed the spectacles and brought back the old magic.

My myopia was intense, but it was a matter of pride, as well as vanity, to adjust phenomena to the limitations of the eye: see what you could and to hell with the rest. I had already been removed from what the world called colour; why should I have to submit to the world's view of the primary ocular reality? I was being drawn to a dangerous solipsism. I would accept only my own inner laws. Take bicycle-riding. Empson was to write: 'Johnson could see no bicycle would go: / "You bear yourself and the machine as well."' That was my belief too, despite streets whirring with cyclists. To ride a bicycle meant subscribing to nature's own legerdemain: there was a trick of balance that was beyond conscious control. So with swimming. A body in water sank, therefore I, though swimming, sank. I have had a lifelong difficulty in accepting physical laws. Aeroplanes fly, and I have read all the books which explain aerodynamics, but, flying, I have sometimes been fearful of the sudden exposure of the science of flight as untenable and, with a kind of satisfaction, of hearing the pilot announce that we were falling. Occasionally I see the impossibility of walking and have to stumble to a bench. There are without doubt easy somatic explanations for this madness – something malfunctioning in the inner ear – but my situation seems to me to be a metaphysical extension of daltonianism: if my brown can be your green, a whole universe of physical, mechanical and neural incompatibilities has to follow. Myopia compounded this withdrawal from Newtonian realities.

It has caused embarrassment and worse. Again, a cinema cartoon has provided the poetry for my condition: Mr Magoo bids the normally sighted, or the smug spectacle-wearers, laugh at uncorrected myopia. He shakes hands with a bear he takes to be Dr Milmoss, thinks a skyscraper scaffolding is a restaurant, believes the seabed to be a motorway, but he always comes through unscathed and disabused. My adventures have been less sensational. I once entered a bank in Stratford-on-Avon and ordered a drink. I have waved back at people waving at somebody else. There was an electric skysign in All Saints, Manchester, which said UPHOLSTERED FURNITURE and I read as UPROARIOUSLY

FUNNY. In the army I failed to salute officers and, fiercely rebuked, then saluted privates. I have spoken to women in the streets I thought I knew and thus got to know them. Clear sight can be switched on if necessary: the means is in one's top pocket. But switching on is submission to the public world. One has, anyway, a choice. The myopic eye is not lazy: it is too busy creating meanings out of vague *données*. Compensation for lifelong myopia comes in old age: presbyobia supervenes on the condition and cancels it. I am forced now into perfect sight and I am not sure I like it.

This boy, nine going on ten, was clearly abnormal. He needed a real mother, not a surrogate one, and a real-life male model, not a mostly absent drunk who called himself a father. I did not blame him altogether for evading evenings with my stepmother, teeth-picking and aitchless in the living-room until the clang of the shop bell summoned her to serve. I was not taken in by his apparent concern with my education, expressed in his subscribing, at one of the newsagents who bought cigarettes from him wholesale, to the fortnightly parts of Arthur Mee's *Children's Dictionary* (which seemed concerned with holding back vocabulary rather than building it) and *The Science of Life*, by H. G. Wells and his son and Julian Huxley. I was much on my own, pale, weedy but eating heartily – twenty pancakes on Shrove Tuesday, encouraged by the vulgar greed of *Comic Cuts*. I see myself very distinctly in oilskins and wellingtons, epicene to some of the shopkeepers, going to Mr King's on Moss Lane East through the Manchester monsoon to buy a pound of cheddar, then to the greengrocer's opposite and further down, past a garish poster for Eden Phillpotts's *The Farmer's Wife*, for lettuce, to the dairy for a jugful of milk. 'You're spillin' yer milk, Jim,' says a gormless policeman (all our policemen at the Moss Lane station were gormless. 'There's someone breakin' in at Grimshaw's. Get there quick.' – 'I'll just 'ave a drinker tay first.'). I would sometimes, though laden with shopping, cross Princess Road from the Public Library to the Alec, outside which stood the tram clock. The conductor would clock in with a key and, for any boys standing there, obligingly stamp their hands with its oily butt. This was, for some reason, worth having, like the ashes on the brow on Ash Wednesday which we tried to preserve all day; there was nothing like sacramental dirt.

Nearly friendless but not wholly. Across the road from our off-licence, on Lincroft Street, lived the Carters, Protestants with a long walled garden which faced the Princess Cinema. On that wall they permitted the cinema manager to paste his posters in exchange for a free pass. The grandmother never went out; the mother was hooked on spiritualistic séances; the father spent his evenings constructing bigger and better wireless sets; that left the son, Eddie. The pass admitted two, and I was his partner in exchange for last week's *Boys' Magazine*. The pass later fell to pieces and became his twiddling fingers at the *guichet*: they did as well. I was now going to the cinema six nights a week as well as on Saturday afternoons, when I had my thankless duty of title-reader. Mondays and Thursdays the Princess; Tuesdays and Fridays the Palace; Wednesdays and Saturdays the Claremont on Claremont Road. Hollywood was certainly churning the stuff out in those days. I saw it all.

Eddie Carter and I also made fireworks. At Christmas 1926 my father took me on the tram to Wiles's, which was next to Lewis's and probably anagrammatically the same firm. Wiles's sold kids' stuff and here I had my present of the Boy's Chemistry Outfit. My father grumbled at the outing, late Advent being a busy time, but he never let me believe that Christmas generosity was a monopoly of Santa Claus. I had to see my presents bought by him who was buying them, good silver shelled out under the shop's lights. Santa Claus, anyway, had played little part in my youth. Taken to see him at Lewis's when I was five, I asked for 'a large motor car' and then fiddled with some of the token packages in his sack. 'Leave them bleeding toys alone,' he told me. Therefore he did not exist. The Boy's Chemistry Outfit, augmented by a bigger model for my birthday, was to be the basis of a commercial pyrotechnic project. Eddie Carter and I were, of course, too ambitious.

But first I had to fix a rubber tube to the gas jet under St Anthony and attach it to a Bunsen burner. More loving parents would have been concerned or at least suspicious. But nobody came to visit me bending glass or boiling permanganate of potash solution in a retort. I distilled water and found it pretty tasteless. Chemistry laboratories, according to the *Gem* and the *Magnet*, were places where foul stinks gave off and there were unpremeditated explosions. Everything that happened on my marble-topped washstand was very mild: it confirmed the constitution of nature rather than offering ways of disrupting it. But if I mixed potassium nitrate, sulphur and charcoal I would get gunpowder. This had to be done in either the Carters' weedy garden or our own. Theirs was less bad, its jungle had clearings.

When I cleaned my stepmother's grossly stained ivory earrings with sulphur she exclaimed as at a miracle and rewarded me with a shilling. Carter and I could buy a lot of the ingredients of gunpowder with that.

We rolled cardboard tubes and made fuses; we mixed glue with strontium nitrate into balls which we hoped would explode luminously in the air. Our aim was not to compete with Brock's, whose fireworks filled the shops from October and were ceremonially destroyed on Bonfire Night, a great time for major injuries; it was rather to provide a firework service in the slack season after Christmas, when kids needed cheering up. Our fuses either refused to ignite or else wasted matches on a weak display of children's sparklers. We had to give a lot of pennies back. But we achieved one rocket that went off with professional panache, though at an angle, and broke an upper window of the Carter house. Nowadays we would have been building a nuclear missile. We were innocent and neolithic. But nothing is ever wasted. Twelve years later I wrote a story about children letting off their own fireworks and won a prize of five guineas which I spent on an engagement ring.

IN 1927 WE looked forward to the ultimate firework display. The End of the World, prefigured in a blanket of darkness in 1924, was to come as fiery destruction with the total eclipse of the sun. *The Boys' Magazine* had dealt vigorously with the End of the World, from which two jerseyed boys escaped on a rocket and landed in a garden suburb on Mars, and my father, struck by my excitement, which was close to hysteria, had thrown one issue on to the fire. But his own newspapers were becoming interested in the supposed instability of the solar system. Mars was said to be shifting out of its ancient orbit and nudging its way towards ours. The *Manchester Evening News* ran a competition for the best interplanetary greetings. 'Are those canals canals, O Mars, / Or merely parks for motor-cars?' 'Hallo, Mars! Our mars are out charlestoning.' It was about time, thought some, for the End of the World. Skirts were too short, and not in the epicene manner of the later miniskirt, a pageboy defuser of sexual allure. At the top of artificial silk stockings fancy garters were visible. There was the Black Bottom as well as the Charleston. The first *Great Gatsby* film had been seen at the Palace on Princess Road and it

sprouted a number of epigones – wealthy decadence with too
many silk shirts, necking in cars, liquor in hip-flasks, hot kisses on
black lips which were really crimson, flaming youth. Grown men,
including Clifford Kemp, tuned my-dog-has-fleas on the ukelele
and sang

> If you like-a ukelele lady,
> Ukelele lady like-a you.
> If you like-a linger where it's shady,
> Ukelele lady linger too.

In May Colonel Lindbergh flew the Atlantic solo. His triumph,
danced to the Lindy Hop, met retribution later in the kidnapping
and killing of his child. God was watching. There was even
Antichrist about. Horatio Bottomley, recruiting hero of the war,
philistine jingoist of *John Bull*, emerged from his sentence for
fraud and roared on posters: 'I Have Paid, But –'.

The *Sunday Express* had a double-page headline: THE NEXT BIG
END OF THE WORLD. Having read that and no more (it was the
title of a rather comforting article about millenarian cranks like
Bishop Wulfstan) I went out dithering on to the street and ran
for my life when a puff of smoke burst from an alley. That was
at the beginning of the week that brought total eclipse. There
was a pilgrimage from Moss Side on a 44 tram as far as Southern
Cemetery. I joined this, completing the journey on foot between
competing bands of hymn-singers to the crest of the hill where
we would see the sun snuffed out. Manchester weather was kind.
Through bits of smoked glass we watched the moon pass over
the fiery body and darkness come. There were terrified giggles.
There was a swift wind, angels speeding over. In Belle Vue Zoo,
we were to learn, the mammals panicked. And then light
returned. Disappointed, we relaxed to an acceptance that there
would be no End of the World, not anyway until 1999, when
the next total eclipse was due. We had a future, and it might be
like the one depicted in Fritz Lang's *Metropolis*.

This was the great film of 1927, already seen in Germany the
year before. It and the End of the World excited me about
equally. Thea von Harbou's book of the film was on sale for
sixpence in Woolworth's (it opened with 'Now the gigantic
organ rose to a mighty roar . . .'), and there were publicity leaflets
and COMING posters around. These showed a robot with a background of strictly European skyscrapers. UFA had spent a lot

of money on the film and come to near-ruin with Lang's extravagance: they were determined that everybody should see it. Seeing it at the age of ten remains one of the major artistic experiences of my life; I still list *Metropolis* among the best dozen films ever made. Its expressionism has dated, and it has a feeble political message; the futuristic décor is clearly of lath and glue; there is too much melodrama. But remove its faults and you kill its essence. The performance of Brigitte Helm, evangelist to the enslaved workers and later the outward shape of Rotwang's robot, remains a great one. The work itself has an oceanic quality: it touched depths in an age which was awaiting some apocalyptic revelation – the End of the World or the rise of the Nazi party. Weird snakes were waiting to slither up from the sewers and chew the fancy garters.

My mind, like that of any imaginative child at that time, was looking for myth. The mythology of Christianity did not intoxicate, though the Hebraic image of a thundering Jehovah, ready to unleash the End of the World on red sports cars and flaming youth, was frightening enough for a horror film. The myth of the Great War was still to be fashioned: it was too much a piecemeal memory, leaving behind rack like motheaten uniforms, a gasmask in the Carters' junk room, the blond blind man who would horrifyingly appear from the living quarters of Price's cake-shop and mumble nonsense at the customers before being led back. Popular sub-art, like *The Boys' Magazine*, or the genuine art of the cinema, was better equipped to satisfy myth-hunger in the young than reminiscences of the war or the Jesus Christ and Robin Hood of Bishop Bilsborrow Memorial School. The film version of Conan Doyle's *The Lost World* led some of us to prehistoric animals: the recent past and the remote past had known destructive monsters, but the brontosaurus snarling in Piccadilly was more compelling than Ludendorff or the Kaiser. The future of *Metropolis* terrified like prehistory, but the monsters were the Paternoster Building and the mysterious machines it housed. We needed terror in the age of the ukelele.

Jakie Innerfield called on my father to play the piano for the Saturday matinée of *Metropolis*. The regular pianist was ill, and he knew my father had performed that thankless work before. My father agreed and chainsmoked over the noisy keys. He improvised and tried to meet the challenge of the rapid film cuts. The evening orchestra – fiddle, cello, piano and percussion – had, as even I knew, been inadequate with its *Midsummer Night's Dream*

overture and selections from grand opera. My father, undoubtedly half-slewed, gave a performance alternately grim and rollicking, full of dissonant Stravinsky effects. In 1975, when I was
at the University of Iowa, there was a film festival organised by
the students and *Metropolis* was shown. I offered to accompany it
on the piano as a kind of memorial to my father and I sat down
to two hours and more of extemporisation. It was difficult and
exhausting – a more than Mahler symphony on the hoof – but it
was worth doing. I was a ten-year-old again, though now
equipped with muscularity and a certain musical skill. Impressed
students rewarded me with marihuana.

After the eclipse of the sun, my stepsister Agnes gave birth to
my step-nephew Dan. She came to 261 Moss Lane East for the
accouchement, and a bed was placed in the drawing-room. It
was a difficult birth and I listened all night to the moans and
screams. I did not know what precisely was happening. I had
some idea, knowing that the sexual act produced children, that
she was undergoing a very lengthy sexual act from Jack Tollitt
while the rest of the family looked on. In the morning she was
crunching toast happily and taking tea from a feeding-cup. The
shattering sexual act was over, and there was a blind scowling
child. He grew up to be a tobacconist and travel agent and to
marry the sister of one of my schoolmates (Father Michael
Brown, who turned into a genuine French *curé*). He begot many
children who in their turn begot many children. All have been
true to the faith. God knew what he was doing when he made
Agnes Dwyer fall in love with Jack Tollitt.

I rather liked the notion of a bed in that long drawing-room.
There was a fireplace there, and I had an image of myself sick but
also warm, staggering moaning to the lavatory on the same floor.
The true bedrooms were glacial in winter, but all houses in those
days had a core of heat in the kitchen and arctic extremities where
pipes froze and cracked and washbowls had a mantle of ice. You
had to be rich and decadent, worthy of the End of the World, if
you relished warmth everywhere. I was determined to be ill in
the drawing-room that year, and I was. I had not been really
well, I was outgrowing my strength, I had had blood-poisoning
which had failed to yield to my stepmother's hot fomentations. I
had even prayed: 'Please, God, make me fit as a fiddle.' God
responded by striking me down with rheumatic fever. He knew
that what I really wanted was to be ill in the drawing-room.

Every child destined to be bookish needs a month or so of

bedridden calm to read *She* and *The White Company* and an illustrated history of the British Empire. He even needs bound
volumes of *Punch* to leaf through straight-faced. I leafed through
straight-faced. But I still remember a double limerick signed APH
and I wonder why:

> There once was a girl with a flivver
> And a man with no reason to live.
> She sank with her car in a river.
> He filed off his head with a sieve.
> For her car wouldn't run,
> And his liver was bad,
> And it's really no fun
> To pretend to be glad
> When your liver's no good as a liver
> And your flivver refuses to fliv.

There is something desperately wrong with our remembering
mechanisms. The trivial, especially if it is in verse, sticks. Great
thoughts and great expression of great thoughts vanish. I have a
repertory of about a thousand popular songs and only one line of
Goethe. From one of the 'Little Tales' in *Punch* I remember this:
'He said I love you, and she said I love you too. Then they went
in to tea, and he made jokes about the jam sandwiches.' What the
hell is wrong with us? The greatness of James Joyce lies partly in
his recognition of the importance of the trivial, but it is not his
responsibility to explain the importance. Flaubert's Félicité dies
seeing a parrot flutter over her head. I shall die on the memory
of the HP Sauce bottle from which I first learned French: 'Setty
sauce, de premier choyks . . .'

My main reading achievement during what was dramatically
called Rheumatism of the Heart was to get through the whole of
Don Quixote in the two-volume Everyman edition. Auden said
that nobody had ever read the book through; here is one to say
he was wrong. I have read it four times, the second time in
Spanish. What worried me two years or so after first reading it
was that I chiefly remembered the meal Sancho and his master
have with some goatherds in a wood: cheese hard as a brick and
acorns, with draughts from the wineskin hanging from a tree.
There were better things to remember. Moreover, why does that
ghastly meal seem to be one of the most delicious in all literature?
Of *She* I remember the eponym, who was also Ayesha, and falling

in love with her. I remember Holly screaming: 'Look, she's turning into a monkey!' I had not only books; I had morning visits from my father in his nightshirt. I had white fish and boiled potatoes. I got up for Christmas. My Uncle Jack and Aunt Nell brought me a tie-press, which I thought to be a miniature trouser-press. I was in something of a daze. I saw Don Quixote, lean shanks exposed, sitting in the *retrete*.

I went back to school in the new year and had to join in singing in a strange language. '*Regina coeli . . .*' Funny words, I whispered. Sister Ignatius beat time with the strap. There came the word *meas* – attached to what feminine accusative plural I have not since discovered – and a boy singing it caught my eye. I collapsed: *arse* in an evidently holy song. The strap descended; the pain was unbelievable. I whined. I shivered in the wintry playground during physical training. We were divided into teams, and the leader wore a coloured sash. 'Who else is stupid among the greens?' called Clayballs. I put my hand up, the boy who had read *Don Quixote*. But the Don had been stupid too. I went into class shivering, wrote an exercise in tremulous cursive that looked like a new alphabet and was at once demoted from Standard Five to Standard Four. There they had not yet arrived at cursive and were still on print script. I had to unlearn cursive. But I sat with Joan Price at the back, and she not only kissed me: she put my hand up her skirt. I was disappointed: the star of 'Felix' was turning into a whore.

We had a class anthology of verse which, by some mischance or bold accession of genius was all modern. Not Eliot, not even Hopkins, but Harold Monroe and J. C. Squire's 'Lines to a Bulldog': 'We won't see Willy any more, Mamie,/He won't come home any more./He came back once and again, and again,/But he won't get leave any more.' There was a poem about allotments. We knew what those were: wretched plots where town labourers grew cabbages and rhubarb, 'While night,/As if to hide their misery from sight./Falls fold on fold from the cold catafalque of the sky.' In one poem a sinful soul came to heaven's gate and tirléd at the pin (good dialect English, though not Lancashire) and cried 'Let me in!' I mumbled a nonsense verse under its influence: 'My life began/In an old tin can./Now let me in/The old can tin.' A boy was sharp to raise his hand and cry: 'Please, miss, Jack Wilson says that Jesus Christ's cross was laid on an old tin can.' I denied this, but I was summoned out to be hit. I felt weary, lonely; I felt I was growing

beyond my coevals. We were asked which we preferred, day or
night. I specified: night, so long as it is dark, cold, and trafficky. I
was either going mad or preparing myself for entry to the adult
life of the city. One boy kept rubbing his thumb nail against his
incisors. He said it was lovely. I could believe him without
trying it myself. Another boy had a union jack handkerchief. I
blew my nose on it. I had blasphemed against Christ and now I
blasphemed against the Empire. Rheumatic fever in those days
ended in chorea or else delirium.

We trooped upstairs to the domain of Standards Seven and X-
Seven, of big-booted louts who were ready to leave and become
errand-boys on bikes. There was a stage up there, and they performed for us, under beefy Mrs Hampson's direction, the clown
scenes from *A Midsummer Night's Dream*. Then they danced a
bergomask. Then they sang a setting of John Masefield's 'Cargoes'.
My heart yearned towards them, achieved and mature, my true
unattainable models, especially the boy who played Bottom: his
hair flopped about as he grinned through the bergomask. I was
destined not to join them. In the spring I was to take many
examinations, all for Corporation scholarships. One for St Bede's,
one for the Xaverian College, other, lesser, ones for council
schools which threw you out, ripe for a minor clerkship, at fifteen. The big Catholic establishments, Bede's and Xav's, could
keep you for ever, or at least till you passed the School Certificate
examination. Any scholarship I gained but could not use would
go as a gift to one of the higher failures. I won them all; I scattered
largesse. I elected to go to the Xaverian College. My stepmother
was distressed when she learned I was to have a secondary education.

These passes could be the triumph of anyone with enough
brains. What required genius in an eleven-year-old was to be
published in the *Manchester Guardian*. There was a competition in
which children were invited to submit a drawing of one or other
of their parents. I had only one true parent, so him I drew in
Indian ink. He had come home for his three o'clock lunch of
grilled sweetbreads and then passed out in an armchair. He snored
the fumes of draught Bass at convalescent me, right hand in
trouser pocket, left hand supporting head. I genteelised him. I
gave him a small round table with a bottle of whisky and a
siphon and a copy of *Punch*, the supposed causes of his stupor. I
sent the drawing in without fanfares: if it won and were published
it would be a salutary surprise for him, to say nothing of money

for me. It appeared, all six square inches of it, and I was sent a cheque for five pounds, a lot of money in those days. The cheque was cashed solemnly at Williams Deacon's Bank, and I misspelt 'received'. I gained respect. I invested the money in radio equipment. My bedroom was already a stained chemistry laboratory, the saints looking blandly down, and now it was going to be a wireless shack.

I gained respect even at school. Going home, looking at the Easter display in a sweet shop, I heard the voice of Miss Clayton asking me if I would like her to buy me a small chocolate egg. I said no. We had enough chocolate eggs in our own window, and those were large. When I arrived late at school one morning, Sister Ignatius forbore to give me the strap. I registered another triumph. The *Daily Express* also ran a drawing competition for children, and I submitted a caricature of its editor, whom I had naturally never seen but whom I represented as a less refined drunk than my father, dead out at his desk while ten telephones rang. The drawing was paid for (two guineas) and published, and the term 'libellous' was good-humouredly used in the legend. I had to look the word up. When I began my career as a novelist I had to look it up more thoroughly. But at that time I thought my future might well lie in all that daltonianism had left me of the pictorial gift – strong line and a touch of fantasy. I studied the professional cartoonists. I even sent an illustrated joke to *Punch*. It was not accepted; I was not yet out of the kids' league.

I have the impression now of very mature classmates coming into my life, so mature that memory has turned them into grown men. One huge boy shook hands with me when we met and proposed that we collaborate on a magazine to be called *Chin Chin Chow*. He was fair-headed and I see him as grey. Another boy seemed to speak with an American accent, though it may have been displaced Plymouth, and he told dirty jokes of some sophistication, including the one about the man with the wooden testicle whose doctor gave him little time to live: 'You've got syph in one and death watch beetle in the other.' He had managed to sneak into an adults-only film about venereal disease (men one night, women the next) and was knowledgeable about gonorrhoea as John Donne might have been knowledgeable about specular stone. He was talkative about diseases in general, and when he helped me home rather ill from school he diagnosed appendicitis.

This was on a Monday. On the Sunday evening I had eaten

raw onion slices in vinegar and I thought they had given me a deadly disease of the stomach. Dr Sneddon was called in and saw at once that I had scarlet fever. He saw also that I had bitartrate of potassium among my chemicals and said that I could usefully drink that in solution. My stepmother, knowing my disease was damnably contagious, was more anxious to shoo me off the premises than solicitous about my headache and nausea. Dr Sneddon wound the handle of our extension telephone and told 21 Princess Road (Moss Side 1274) to call an ambulance. Agnes shrieked 'Me baby!' at the other end (I had played with the child the day before) but was calmed. I was taken back to where I started – north-east Manchester, Monsall Isolation Hospital, between Monsall Road and Northampton Road. There, while I desquamated, I completed my primary education.

I had been isolated before; now in an isolation hospital, I grew into society. I learned hate. Nurses, especially sisters, could be more vicious than schoolmistresses. I could never manage a bedpan, which, a kind of ceramic skillet with a hollow handle, must be the most inept of all the clinical inventions. You were supposed to reserve dry defecation for it, micturating into a chill pot bottle. Like most people, I performed both acts in the same vessel, which regularly overflowed. I was hit by the ward sister, who, when the matron came on her rounds, would say, pointing: 'As for that dirty little devil there –' My father and stepmother appeared at the window on a weekly visit, unpermitted to enter the ward, mouthing and waving from beyond the isolating glass. They brought eggs and motoring chocolate which the ward sister distributed to the other patients, rarely to me. In their lives before and beyond the hospital, those patients were deprived boys: let the cake be cut fairly and undeprived me get none. I developed a rudimentary political sense. I had never seen myself as one of the privileged, but now I was marked as such by my aspirates, which were mocked. There were two classes in the world, then, and they were bitterly opposed.

In one of those tedious after-lights-out discussions which enliven, with a circular deadness, both wards and barrack-rooms, everybody except me assumed we were living in the nineteenth century. Stood to reason, didn't it? This was 1928, and there was the 19 telling you what century it was. But, I said, we've already completed nineteen centuries. We're twenty-eight years into the twentieth. I was howled down. Look, I said, we've got 1927 years and a bit behind us. That means nineteen centuries

are over. This has to be – Get your 'ead down, and so on.
Think you know it all cause you've got a rich dad. A rich dad?
That was a new one. I convinced nobody that we were in the
twentieth century, even when I showed a picture of a train
called the Twentieth Century Special. That's for the next century, innit? Modern, innit? They 'ave to go one century over
like to show off. It was a fair anticipation of the army. It was
a good thing there was no Italian in the ward, ready to confirm
their ignorance by saying we were in the *novecento*. But they
would have mocked his lingo.

When desquamation was proceeding well and the infectious
phase was over, we were moved to a ward where some of the
nurses, including one who was alleged to have won a beauty
competition, kissed us good night. The beauty said to me: 'And
don't forget to say your rosary.' She knew I was Catholic and
that Catholics told beads. It was the one sentimental and discardable aspect of Catholicism that they knew. It was pretty,
something for a novelette. And then one day I was told I was
dying. 'A minister's come to see you,' very gravely. Oh God, the
last rites. But it was a rollicking Maynooth priest paying a pastoral
call. Still, my wardmates watched for my death. One of the privileged, privileged to die. I was treated better then. Treated better
also because I could draw. Draw a man in bed with a girl. Draw
my dick. There was a lot of dick-showing in the dayroom. A
nurse who supervised my bath told the ward that I had more
pubic hair than the others. Let's see your 'airs. There was an exhibition of masturbation by a fourteen-year-old in a dark suit.
He spurted and fainted. This was the great world. It grew tired
of watching for my death. I was permitted to join the living.

This meant, among other things, the meeting of the desquamated from the girls' wards in some neutral zone of the
grounds. The meeting was always collective, with spokesman and
spokeswoman. Our spokesman was nicknamed 'Angin Out because, crying for an urgent bedpan, he had said that was what the
faeces were doing. The spokeswoman was a serious girl, guarding
her flock as Maria did in *Metropolis* when she said to the privileged: 'These are your brothers and sisters.' The social ritual
featured male aggression, though it was purely verbal, and female
reasonableness. 'What wards are you lads in, then?' – 'Who wants
to know?' – 'That's not a nice way to speak.' – 'We're not 'ere to
be nice.' – 'What are you here for, then?' And so on. When I said
to 'Angin Out that the spokesgirl was not exactly pretty, he said

that there was more to a girl than prettiness. There was a good 'art and nice manners. He told me this with immense seriousness.

But it was with a pretty girl that I rolled naked on the grass behind the shrubbery. We had shed all our skin like snakes and were proud of our new bodies. So we showed our bodies to each other and to the Monsall sun; we embraced and rolled. We rolled to a concealed hollow and kissed and stroked and said we loved each other. We did not know each other's name: the situation was Laurentian though without the phallus entering like a slow sword of peace: we had entered a zone beneath personality. Somewhere from an open ward window voices sang:

> Mammy, daddy, take me 'ome
> From this convalescent 'ome.
> I've been 'ere a month or two,
> Now I want to be with you.
> In comes the nurse with a red 'ot poultice,
> Slaps it on and takes no notice.
> 'Ow,' says the patient, 'that's too 'ot.'
> 'No,' says the nurse, 'I'm sure it's not.'

'Put your hand there,' she said, so I did. I touched the soft outer doors of the infolded mystery. Her breasts were beginning to bud.

> Goodbye to all the doctors,
> Goodbye to all the sisters,
> Goodbye to all the nurses,
> And jolly old Monsall too.

The sole Catholic among Protestants, though as ready as any such heathen to roll naked behind the shrubbery, the sole aitched male of the ward, I saw now clearly for the first time my minority situation. I was among the privileged, and yet I was also among the beleaguered. The paradox could be resolved in a dream like *Brideshead Revisited*, but not in the life of a Manchester schoolboy. The Protestants had persecuted the Catholics, and yet the Protestants were the downtrodden. The Catholics and the Jews built businesses and became privileged, though not on the Marchmain level; the Protestants worked in factories and became unemployed. The coming depression was already a strengthening monsoon in our city of monsoons. My father spoke of bad debts, but we were to move to bigger premises – still on Princess Road, but at Number 47, on the corner of Raby Street. He and my stepmother came on their last visit to Monsall in an Austin saloon, driven by Jack Tollitt. I was to go to a posh Catholic school, where lay teachers wore gowns and there was a stinks laboratory, though no Greyfriars fags or bum-freezers. The very name of the school was an affront to my wardmates: it began with an X, it was unpronounceable, it was foreign. It was conceivably Jewish.

It was appropriate that, in my last week in hospital, a rabbi should come to visit me. Wrong ward, wrong name – still, I was one of the minority. To my fellow convalescents I became a Catholic Jew, an acceptable anomaly. I was not a Protestant and I had a rich dad. My nose, which had a spot on it my father called a beer blob, was big enough for a sheeny's.

> A Jew a Jew a smoggy Jew a Jew a Jew.
> I can no longer stay with you, stay with you.
> I'll 'ang my 'arp on a weepin' willer tree,
> And may the world go well with thee.

I would see how the world went. I left the hospital in the new Austin saloon, made a long confession at the English Martyrs, took (my Lord and my God) Christ's body on my tongue, and prepared to go on holiday with my stepmother.

We went south, to the Protestant world which had swallowed the Reformation whole, leaving no rockpools of dissent. Southwest, to be exact – Torquay in Devonshire. The hotel was of the kind that catered for youngish people – charlestoners, young men in Oxford bags and young women with last year's fancy garters. My stepmother had difficulty with the register and drew M. Wilson where she should have written her nationality. Normally, she said, her 'usbint saw to such things. She would not go up in the lift, which she called the 'oist, recounting to a bemused lobby what had happened to her and Katie 'Erbert. But she ate with her knife and fork and showed, as she should, knowledge of wines, ordering a tenpenny Médoc. We went to Torbay, where William of Orange landed to enforce Protestantism on a newly Catholic land and to drive our last king to exile after the battle of the Boyne. I wrote a little essay on the visit, and the *Daily Express* published it in their children's corner. One guinea – a couple of valves and a variable condensor. Every evening in the hotel there was an impromptu concert followed by a dance. The last dance of our stay was a fancy dress ball, and I stood too close to the adjudicatory march round. A button of my jacket caught in the webby swathings of a mock-gipsy. It took five minutes to disentangle. I was growing up now, and this had to be seen as Pooterish – not the epic comic of the bust in the playground of St Edmund's.

The world, as I could see back home at 261 Moss Lane East, was growing up too, or at least changing. There had been a magical winter hour at the lighting of the lamps, when a man in floury white came round with a bell and a baker's tray, crying hot muffins, crumpets and pikelets. He had disappeared, and the English muffin, diminished and mechanised, was to survive only on American breakfast tables. We were being encouraged to buy not warm anonymous loaves but wrapped Crusty Bread. We had run for our ice cream in wafers and cornets, with a dollop of raspberry vinegar, from Italian carts, but now the uniformed Wall's vendor, looking like a relaxed SS man, treadled his blue refrigerator on the streets, ringing his stop-me-and-buy-one bell and offering chill blocks in paper. The chickens I was sent to buy – from an old witch's backyard with a rank rural smell – had the taste of nature, but chilled lamb came from Canterbury, which is in New Zealand, no longer from the Welsh hills, and iced beef from Argentina. The old sharp tastes were disappearing. It is not nostalgia alone that makes old men say that food was better in the past.

We had no refrigerator. Fish became phosphorescent, bluebottles buzzed over the meat-mesh, butter ran in summer. But we had the Morris saloon, which took us on Sunday trips to Blackpool. On the evening road back we saw entire villages sitting on the green, watching the cars, their sole Sunday entertainment. Not everybody sat round the home loudspeaker, listening to Reithian religion and a Palm Court trio. We, the Wilsons, the Tollitts and the Kemps, had that amenity. The various tobacco companies were beginning to offer gifts in exchange for astronomic numbers of coupons in cigarette packets, and the wholesaler stored the gifts, which we kept for ourselves. One of them was a portable five-valve radio, which was fed with a hundred-volt dry battery and a rechargeable accumulator. Another was a portable gramophone. We had music in the home without benefit of the drawing-room piano, whose lid was now always down. We were into the modern age.

At the age of eleven and a half, ready for the Xaverian College,

I had, so literary biographers might say, amassed my basic emotional experiences and achieved a thin tracing of the pattern of my life. But what had I really learned? From school, little. I had reached literacy with no real help, and numeracy through drills and odd slaps. I knew that America existed, for I had seen it at the cinema, and America had a past of cowboys and Indians and a present of skyscrapers and bootleg liquor. Germany had shown me the future, which was to be first slavery and then a weak handshake of worker and monopolist. France was the language of the HP Sauce bottle. The rest of Europe did not exist, except for Rome where the Pope blessed and whence organ-grinders and ice-cream men were exported. There was a British Empire, but that was merely patches of red on the school map: it was as remote as London. Ireland was both a foreign country and part of my blood, but Ireland meant chiefly the reservoir that fed our Catholicism. If there were cities outside Manchester, they were Rome and Dublin, with Liverpool, our maritime rival which we despised (nature had made it a port; man had put Manchester on the sea), as a kind of overgrown embassy of the Irish Free State.

I had learned history of a kind through the illustrated volumes of my rheumatoid languor, but I knew it was Protestant history and mostly a lie. At school we had moved from Ancient Britons improvidently shivering in woad to Robin Hood, who was a Catholic and even had a resident priest named Friar Tuck (Try a Fuck to some of the boys; I did not understand), and then came Henry VIII, who had wantonly cut himself off, along with his kingdom, from the truth and grace of Rome. We, of the blood of the English Martyrs though refreshed in the faith from Ireland, kept a little light alive. We had suffered and would suffer again. We had at least to know what the suffering was about, and so we spent a lot of time on the penny Catechism of Christian Doctrine. What is God? God is the Supreme Being who alone exists of himself and is infinite in all perfections. Who made you? God made me. Why did God make you? God made me to love him and serve him in this world and to be happy with him for ever in the next.

The immense and shattering truth which England had, through stupidity, innate wickedness, and the urgent prompting of the devil, not merely abandoned but derided and derided still, was the Real Presence in the sacrament of the Eucharist. That Christ was really present on the altar, disguised as unleavened bread and sweet red wine, was the abiding reality which dwarfed the imi-

tation realities of gob-stoppers and pork sausages. Of this reality I
had no doubt at all. We had Christ's own words to confirm it,
and we heard them relayed by the priest at mass in universal
Latin. *Hoc est corpus meum.* In India, Siam, among the Australian
aborigines, those same words, though perhaps in varying accents,
presided over the divine mystery. That Protestants could, in their
blindness or deafness, interpret the sacrament as a mere commemoration was a sure sign that the devil had led them astray.
Here, and not in niceties of doctrine about limbo and purgatory,
lay the huge and irreparable fissure, the national wound beyond
healing, which denied English unity, a common past and a
common future. The Real Presence lay all over Manchester in its
squalid little Catholic churches, signalled by the red eye of a
lamp. Passing a church, one made the sign of the cross in reverent
greeting. The proddy dogs scoffed.

As for the imitation realities, including above all the appetites
of the flesh, some of these were neutral, uncovenanted powers,
though the devil could creep in when the hutch of tasty lust
admitted gluttony. Sexual crime seemed, in the Ten Commandments, limited to adultery, which was 'all sins of impurity
with another's wife or husband'. But the Commandments of the
Church expanded this enormity to enclose not merely fornication
but also 'immodest books, pictures and dances' (why not songs?
Why not swear words?). Rolling naked with a girl in the grounds
of Monsall Isolation Hospital, playing with the breasts of the
twelve-and-sixpenny maid in the attic, were undoubtedly sins,
but I could not help feeling that the red eye on the altar was, if
not wholly sympathetic, yet not as censorious as Father Fitzjames.
Food tasted good, and that was in order, God's gift; flesh felt
good, and that was wrong. But perhaps flesh was the devil's
work, unless God stepped in and somewhat arbitrarily sanctified
it in a wedding at the Holy Name: after all, we were warned off
the triad 'the world, the flesh and the devil'. That could lead to
Catharism or Manicheism or Jansenism, which we had not been
taught. There was, anyway, a contradiction hard to resolve. It is
still there.

I had learned no more and no less than other British Catholic
schoolchildren. At home there were things I would never learn.
One was the relationship between mother and son. I was dimly
aware of a deprivation when, one night in bed, entertaining
fantasies of wantonness, I excused myself to God by crying
aloud: 'I never had a mother.' I was not encouraged to express

tenderness. I was reared emotionally cold. I could embrace the cat, which squirmed away, associating a human touch with a hot oven. I could take my brief puppy for a walk, play with it, even, on one slapped occasion, crouch down to share its cold hotpot. But I held human flesh only in the promptings of precocious lust, which was very remote from true affection.

There was no Oedipal element in this childhood. I was not jealous of my father. He, anyway, was an absence who homed to the smoky sodality of the pubs. He did not even, despite unlimited opportunity, sin against the sexual bond of marriage. At least, there were no discoveries of infidelity and no blazing rows about it. He woke up once murmuring 'Poppy', and my stepmother heard him, but, outside of *Poppy's Paper* for girls, the name had no known referent. He was Irish in his indifference to sex: drink was the thing. He provided me with no model of aggression, industry, or erotic drive. He was not Humphrey Chimpden Earwicker; he was not even Leopold Bloom. He wasted his musical talent. When I became musical in my turn, I had to start alone with the elements. He was to offer me as I approached maturity a certain vindictiveness for displaying his own faults. If I was not much of a son, it was because there was nothing to be a son to.

My stepmother, as I have said, fulfilled a stepmother's duties, which did not include the bestowal of love. She was not a stepmother of the fairy stories: she lacked the tyrannical impulse which, with Cinderella, was powerful enough to call into being her opposite. I had a godmother, my Aunt Lily, but she brought no fairy pumpkin. If my stepmother demonstrated no affection, she was at least neutral, though there would be an occasional shaft of disaffection – sometimes gratuitous, sometimes in a transferral from father to son. She made a point frequently of telling me that her daughter Madge and I shared a natal Sabbath, but I had been born when the pubs were opening and she when the bells were ringing for vespers. My hair, she said, was coarse, not like that of her daughters. I was selfish. All I wanted was money to buy sweets and comics. I evaded work, meaning errands and 'filling up'. 'Filling up' was carrying bottles from the kitchen-stockroom to the shelves of the shop. I would end up like my father, a boozer. There was no evidence of this at the time, but it was a just prophecy.

We are right to hate malignancy, but not either indifference or stupidity. I resent nothing, and I feel no pity for the eleven-year-old who was now, with some reluctance, kitted out for the Xaverian College. I was not in rags and I did not starve. I was permitted an education. But I regret the emotional coldness that was established then and which, apart from other faults, has marred my work. I read of family relationships in other people's books and I envy equally the tranquillity and the turbulence. *Sons and Lovers* and *Fathers and Sons* are from an alien planet which I can visit only by stretching my imagination.

In the bigger family of the nation, which, as George Orwell said, was ruled by wicked uncles, I belonged to a gang of orphans, kids who could play in the yard so long as they kept quiet but were not admitted to the drawing-room. We were asked to be loyal to the disloyal. I was right to wipe my nose on the Union Jack. I was now going to give my schoolboy loyalty to an establishment named for the Apostle of the Indies, who had had different aims from the colonising British, a Spanish pillar of the Counter-Reformation, one of the seven founder members of the Society of Jesus. Nothing could be less English.

TWO

GOING TO SCHOOL now meant walking to the suburb of Rusholme or taking the tram there. The Number 53 passed down Great Western Street, one of the tributaries of Princess Road that opens on to Wilmslow Road. Wilmslow Road begins in the city centre as Oxford Street, becomes Oxford Road when it nears the University, and then undergoes its last change of name at Moss Lane East before passing through Rusholme and moving south to the refined suburbs of Fallowfield and Withington. The Number 53 tram was unique in that it was single-decked and had a rear platform laterally open to the air: there was a continental quality about it. I would as often as not walk down Moss Lane East, passing Whitworth Park with its pond, its meteorological station, and its highly regarded art gallery from which for some time I was banned: in the company of other kids I had sucked at the marble breast of a Greek goddess and been ejected by one of the curators. Later I was able to go and admire the original William Blakes. At the end of Moss Lane East I would turn right into Rusholme. This was a district with its own flavour – superior shops and tea rooms and the promise of green in four parks: an extremity of Whitworth, then Platt, Birchfields and Victoria. Victoria Park was a distinguished residential enclosure with a tollgate, and in it the Xaverian College stood.

Rusholme was nationally known for its repertory theatre – the Rusholme Rep – and became internationally known for having produced two remarkable film actors – Richard Donat and Wendy Hiller. The Manchester tradition of both local and experimental drama, which had begun with Miss Horniman at the old Gaiety (and been Hibernicised at the Abbey in Dublin), had developed here into post-Ibsen daring, with Ernst Toller and Elmer Rice, even audience-frighteners like *The Great God Brown* by Eugene O'Neill. A Xaverian schoolmate of mine played in this as somebody's son and was bewildered by the perpetual changing of masks. I saw the last days of the Rusholme Rep and its reduction to a cinema.

The Xaverian College was one of my early signposts towards the East: I met its namesake in Malacca, where the eponymous saint had ordered the torture of Malay Catholic backsliders and held off, by some miracle, the invading Buginese fleet. The Xaverian Brothers were men who dressed like priests but were little more than glorified laymen who knew they were a fair cut above Paddy Stink and Micky Mud of the Christian Brothers. Some were holy, some were very secular. Some had joined the Company of St Francis Xavier in order to be paid for a higher education: such were completing their studies at Manchester University while teaching us. The senior English master, Brother Andrew, brought southern patrician English into my life as a medium of instruction. Hitting his thumb or stubbing his toe he said 'Blaaahst.' He was to revert to his secular name of Gordon Baldwin and become Director of Education in a Caribbean colony. He bequeathed to me his *Beowulf* and *Sir Gawain*, both sedulously and excessively annotated. He was determined to get on. He admired John Galsworthy and wrote his thesis on Robert Browning.

The adopted holy names of the brothers followed no pattern of relevance to the co-founder of the Jesuit order. There was no Brother Ignatius (having had a Sister Ignatius with a strap, I personally did not need one), and the Brother Francis we had ineptly in the physics laboratory was probably named for him of Assisi. Brother Cajetan's name declared strong antilutheranism. Brother Alphonsus was the college cook, a West End chef who had responded to visions, and he was devoted to the Jesuit lay-brother Rodriguez who, as Hopkins's sonnet tells us, spent his life watching the door in Mallorca. Brother Campion's name was ambiguous. He taught French but was learned in English litera-ture, a heavy smoker with religious doubts probably more drawn to the poet Thomas Campion than to the saint Edmund. There were also Brother John Vianni, Brother Sebastian, Brother Anselm, among others. There were also a few laymen and lay-women, with and without graduate's gowns.

This staff worked in commodious premises. To the original ivy-grown manse-like structure, which one could reach from a leafy avenue and a drive sad with wet privet and laurel, there had been added a red-brick teaching block. The laboratories were conjoined outbuildings of which the chemistry lab soon fell into disuse – broken retorts and nesting swallows. A great green expanse called Marylands was for games and garden parties, and beyond it was a mansion named for its donor Grommé, where the teaching staff had bedroom-studies with gasfires. The majority of boys were day scholars, but there were boarders too, some of them foreign. The head boy when I arrived, and for some years after, was a grown Brazilian with a moustache and a marimba, an admirer of Villa-Lobos, with whom he shared the first name Heitor. Almost the first boy I saw when trembling through the gates was a hairy Latin in the uniform of Mussolini's young fascisti. He was greeted with 'Hello, Corradi, how's your daddy?' This was Adolf Corradi, ominously named, who was to be expelled from the fascists for declaring that it was better to live one day as a mouse than a lifetime as a lion. He later married Irene, a daughter of the estranged Byrnes, and became a great expert on dyes. The first boy I met stood at the gate as one deputed to ask for a password. 'Right, kid,' he said to a new one, 'say PUCK like this.' And he hooked his fingers into his mouth-corners and pulled. This was my first lesson in organic phonetics. Delabialisation produced a foul obscenity.

I had now met this foul obscenity in full flood, having been taken by Jack Tollitt to Maine Road football ground to see Manchester City play. He incautiously said: 'McCabe is the best centre-forward playing anywhere.' There was a derisory and even bitter response of *fuck off, is he fuck, is he fuckin' hell, what the fuck does this fucker think he fuckin' knows about it?* the answer being *fuck all.* I was now familiar with the word in all its declensions, which equally reduced a tender act into rottenness. I had not been expecting to have to say it in order to enter the Xaverian College. But there was already an unwilled obscenity in the school motto, which I had met in the prospectus: CONCORDIA RES PARVAE CRESCUNT. This was blazoned high over the stage in the school hall. Many a boy, inattentive or bemused at the music lessons held there, would I see shutting from his eyes with a finger all except the last four letters. It was like reading a banned book. And the meaning of the motto – small things grow big, etc. – had a complementary phallic overtone.

The big brother who ruled the school was Brother Martin. It was to be a disturbing name, like Adolf, for the greatest figure in reformed religion is Martin Luther. His true name was Eugene McCarthy, which, the secular state not acknowledging the nomenclature of sanctity, he had to sign on official documents. But he would sometimes use B. Martin, perhaps to cause confusion or doubt or delay, perhaps at the prompting of a double personality. He was, of course, Irish, with a long Irish head and a long Irish neck and bouts of Irish neurosis. To join the Xaverian order entailed a vow of celibacy but not one of temperance. Br Martin had bottles in his rooms and access to a very decently stocked cellar. I had already met him briefly and frighteningly when, having passed the written entrance examinations, I was summoned to the College for an oral test and a kind of social appraisal.

We lined up in tens with our curricula vitae. I did not understand Br Martin when he said, with a theatrical clarity of utterance and a distinction of delivery I was unaccustomed to, 'Give me your paper.' In my house we had not, despite Madge's tuition, the correct codes for requesting a repeat, so I said 'Mmmm?' This went down very badly but was not corrected. He spoke the words again like a headline, and then my Manchester twang was winced at in the recitation of a chunk of *Sesame and Lilies*. Then we were asked what was our favourite colour. Most said blue because it was Our Lady's colour. I said red because it was the colour of blood. The school had four houses – St Francis Xavier's, St Edmund's, St Cuthbert's and St Bernardine's. We were asked the impossible question which would we like to belong to, and one boy who brilliantly said the first, because it was the name of the school, was loudly commended with 'Very excellent'. I said St Bernardine's because I was dry-mouthed with fright and the house emblem was a chalice, but I did not give this reason.

Br Martin proved to be very keen on high-class phonemes and front vocal projection, but there were moods when he adopted the stage Irish of the first act of *John Bull's Other Island*, complete with 'may your shadder never grow less' and 'isn't it the truth I'm tellin ya?' If he had ever read, which is extremely doubtful, *A Portrait of the Artist as a Young Man*, he may have pondered Stephen Dedalus's unrest of spirit at hearing *Christ, home, ale* and *master* in the mouth of the prefect of studies at University College Dublin and (a more reasonable gloss than that of most of the Joyceans, who look for too much) finding his own pronunciation of those words too provincial. There was nothing provincial about Br Martin's vowels: he had beaten the upper-class bleaters at their own game. If he had never read Joyce, he was to claim to me, when I expressed admiration for the great Dubliner, a close personal acquaintance with him and spoke rollickingly of 'Jimmy Joyce'. But he spoke also of Bernard Shaw with familiar affection and called Sean O'Faolain 'Johnny Whelan', which was his abandoned British name.

Br Martin may, as some alleged, have tried to get to the bottoms of various of the more beautiful junior scholars, but we never got to the bottom of him. That he was given to homoerotic fancies, if not practices, was confirmed for me by Br John Vianni, whom I met in later life as a roving inspector of National Insurance irregularities. He would talk much of Christ and the beloved disciple and suggest that there were works hidden in the dust of the Vatican Library which countenanced, on the Christine example, carnal love between man and man. It was certain that Br Martin was no scholar, though he claimed to be a specialist in English History. He would occasionally, unnaturally bright-eyed and flushed of face, come into someone else's history lesson and give an impersonation of Henry VIII at table or of James I slobbering over Steenie. I suspected a failed theatrical background. He always left the classroom on a good line. When, in the Fourth Form, 'The Rime of the Ancient Mariner', a poem he did not seem to have met before, was apportioned among us for class recitation, he stopped the lesson and asked which line appealed to us most. We mostly said 'Water, water everywhere' or 'A painted ship upon a painted ocean', but he chose 'Heaven's mother, send us grace' and strode out, arms spread as to receive, or give, divine blessing, crying the phrase to the air.

He alone gave formal physical punishment. The masters, and the odd mistress, might slap, punch, or shake, but Br Martin made a ceremony of the cane on hands or bottom at the day's end and on the stage in the school assembly hall. A piece of paper came to each classroom in the morning, and this had the printed heading 'Names of boys who have not done their homework, or who have done it badly'. But other malefactions were permitted to go on the slip, as it was called, and we never considered this fair. Br Martin walked on to the stage for the farewell assembly of the day, slips in one hand, cane in the other, and, with a homily before or after the act, would swish and hurt. He naturally preferred the bottom to the hands, and once or twice hit at a rump protected only by underpants and shirt tail. This was when he got no yell of pain on the first stroke: he suspected, always rightly, that the miscreant had stuffed books in his trouser-seat. He enjoyed weaving a fantasy of reproach around the name of the unhappy boy, if it were at all possible. He could do little with mine, but he leaped gladly on Harry Hinderer with 'An inner devil hinders your moral sense, Mr Hinderer, but nothing hinders my driving him out, with God's grace and this not too weak right arm.' He was delighted to call up for thwacking a boy named Prince, with the announcement 'His Royal Highness Mr Prince.'

Quite often the school was not dismissed to its work after morning prayers but kept in the hall for as long as an hour to listen to some Irish rhapsody inspired by the morning's *Manchester Guardian*. He believed in the League of Nations and said there was not going to be another war. He spoke, clearly crapulous, on the dangers of drink, and cited a love of champagne as the worst of evils, in spite of the empty Moët and Chandon bottles outside his study door. Horatio Bottomley, whom he called Bumley, was the horrible example, and Br Martin gave us a powerful piece of acting, with a parched Bumley shaking his prison bars and crying out, like Dives, for some Lazarus to touch his tongue with a fingertip dipped in Mumm or Lanson. Sometimes Br Martin would discuss, at great length, his various bodily ailments, especially sciatica, and tell us that, with all his agonies, he some-times felt like throwing himself on his study fire. But then he would talk of health and fitness and prescribe a useful exercise for the lungs which consisted in turning oneself into a four-legged beast or table and singing 'Oft in the stilly night' to the floor.

He was mercurial, capricious, unpredictable and dangerous. The sadism of repression, sexual or thespian, led him to go the round of the classrooms with his cane and ask, interrupting a secular subject, the two worst questions of the catechism: 'What is the holy mass?' and 'What is the holy eucharist?' The difference between the answers is one of phraseology rather than essential distinction, and few could get them right. Then he would whack and swish and exclaim on the added agony we, through perverted ignorance, were heaping on the already yelling-with-human-torment divine Saviour, sending us back to seats that struck with the fire of another cane. He would, at closing assembly, entrust the leading of several decades of the rosary to the head boy, and, arms folded grimly, fix bitter Irish eyes on a student arbitrarily chosen, saying no word, letting the poor wretch go home to rack, rarely vainly, since he was young, his palpitant conscience. I was picked out for this treatment when I was in the fourth form, and I had a week of it. When, in middle age, I had a collie dog named Haji, Haji, white-collared and black-suited like Br Martin, would fix me in the same way, standing and groaning in front of the television set to do so, though with the clear motive of wanting a walk. I was back in the fourth form again.

Br Martin hit on a preliminary punishment for those who were, rosary over, to be publicly smitten, making them stand in a bunch before their innocent fellows with their hands held high in the air. This seemed to disrupt the blood supply to the higher centres and induce delirium. I was one day among these guilty, and it was on me that Br Martin started. He said: 'You know, Wilson, you're low. You do nothing for your house and nothing for your school. What excuse have you devised for not doing your homework?' I intended to say that I couldn't do it, but this came out as 'wouldn't'. When bellowed at to say that again, I amplified in my delirium with 'I didn't want to do it.' Then I was attacked with shillelagh fists and blindly impelled to the door with 'Get out. Go at once to the hell reserved for ye. Never darken the portals of the Xaverian College again.' This gave away the status of his probable theatrical background: you would never hear about darkening portals at the Gate or the Abbey. It seemed to me that I was expelled – the very word is like a knell. I staggered home, and my father, who was Irish enough to know the Irish (my stepmother said of the race: 'They cut your 'ead and then plaster it'), told me to take no notice: it would all be forgotten the following day. So I did my homework with trembling fist, went to the Princess and sobbed through Richard Dix in *Redskin*, hardly slept, then woke for school visibly ill. There was no sneaking in: Br Martin remembered. But he sent me home with almost a show of affability, saying that he wished to see my father. My father, grumbling with sharp insight about the treatment of scholarship boys, went to see Br Martin with cash in his pocket. The bribe caught, and I was told I could go back to school next day.

I went back and was hawked round the classrooms by Br Martin as the best boy in the school. I had guts, I was honest, he wished the rest of his students, a cowardly and hypocritical lot, had the same good Christian candour to speak God's truth. And God's truth had been that I didn't want to do my homework and I, God's truth's burnished vessel, had said so. At the end of the school year he signed my report with 'I wish I had three hundred John Wilsons.' I do not know how much my father had contributed to the college funds, but clearly money was an important consideration to Br Martin, despite his occasional histrionics about

Shylock and his dirty ducats. He kept a variable quantity of the lay
teachers' salaries in escrow, despite their having been decreed by
a national scale, and, when they complained, told them they did
not know his difficulties. He wanted all boys to stay for a midday
meal in the refectory, paying a fair sum for a scanty table d'hôte,
even if their mothers were laying the family table just round the
corner. He exclaimed on the injustice of too many boys living in
the city and environs, when, in a properly run world, they would
be foreigners like Adolf Corradi and Anton Bruckner and Ber-
nardo Fughetti, to say nothing of dear moustached Heitor with
his marimba, and be charged for sleeping in the school's dormitories. He may conceivably have been the treasurer, doubling
on the heavy roles, in some remote Irish repertory company. He
perhaps made speculative investments under the name B. Martin.

Being the head, he had the monopoly of showmanship, and
his staff felt little compunction to show competitive eccentricity.
Neurosis was a different matter, like that of Br Francis, who
wept at his lack of rule and taught us little physics. So was incompetence, displayed in Br Sebastian's supersessive teaching of
the same subject: he left much of it to one of our classmates,
Dowd, who grinned maniacally in the uniform of the British
Fascist Party. So was unnatural piety, as in Br Antoninus, who
beat his breast moaning in the darker corridors. The rest did such
work as they were paid for, and some of them rather more.

The classes were streamed into A and Alpha, nominally de-
noting equal learning ability, but we in the Alpha stream knew
better: did not the Greek alphabet take precedence over the
Roman? We began in Lower Three and then proceeded to Upper
Three, Four, Lower Five and Upper Five. Br Martin, who may
have been reading a confiscated *Gem* or *Magnet*, dreamed once in
a morning assembly of introducing a Remove and a Shell, but
nothing came of it. Promoted to the Sixth Form, boys became
men, could wear hats not caps and smoke between classes. In the
fine library of the Old Building they assembled, as at a board
meeting, around an oaken table, surrounded by Chinese vases
and books with the Ex Libris plate of Lady Gregory and other
lights of the old ascendancy. The library gave on to a beautiful
garden, an Eden only recoverable through adolescent sin. Sixth
Form men, though closer than before to the closets of power and
even sometimes stumbling over the empties, were less disturbed
than formerly by Br Martin's unannounced visits. The good name
of the school depended on the Higher School Certificate results,

and there might even be – though this was a dream like the Shell or Remove – a Corporation or even a State Scholarship. Frivolous interruptions of Livy or Sallust with a discussion of why one drank water from a glass and milk from a cup (did one?) were not really in order.

I began my career at the Xaverian College in a converted private house just within the school gates. This housed some junior boarders and a music room. A lower second violinist of the Hallé Orchestra, who was not backward in denouncing the classical music he had to play for a living, presided over daylong unresined squealings. Lower Three Alpha was allotted its desks and awaited its education. This came in a piecemeal manner. A Belgian brother, Urbain, would enter and say: 'Occupy yourselves.' Then I would draw and others would read their *William* books by Richmal Crompton. A Br Dempsey, burly and implying in his name a proleptic canonisation of the great boxer, would enter and make us repeat *amo, amas, amat* without telling us that this was Latin or, indeed, anything. Then he would disappear, not to be seen again. We would be thrust into a cellar, given wool-tufts and hooks, and told to make rugs. Then we would go back to the light for Speech Training under a Miss McManus.

Dorothy McManus, called Dolly, was the middle-aged remains of a superb figure of a woman. She, a kind of Fenian, was to teach us the King's English. She began by saying: 'A lady came up to me t'other day and asked me if I was Irish. I said I was and so she said Speak some Irish.' So I said Certainly: *Bhì sé dorcha amuigh, mar bhì na tràthnòinti ag dul i ngiorracht*. And she was much taken aback, expecting me to say Begorrah and Sure he's a broth of a bhoy. Irish is one thing and English is another. 'Tis the tongue of the Protestant oppressor, but under the oppressor we must live and speak his language. And speak it as well if not better than them who have thrust it upon us. So,' she warned, 'no begorrahs and may your shadder never grow less.' This, of course, encouraged us to say begorrah, an exoticism we had never heard before. And also to think of the King's English as a foreign language whose eccentricities must be approached with cunning – especially the unrounded back vowel in *love* and *mother*. My tongue muscles still have a memory of trying to master the unnatural phoneme. There was also aitch, acceptable as a Catholic consonant, but foreign to the Manchester phonemic inventory. It was Harry Hinderer, who believed he was Arry Inderer, who suffered most from trying to acquire it. Flash out the sign, and he at once interpreted it as a zero value. His brain was so programmed. He would suffer all his life from his name.

Then we had Kitty Masterson, who wore a graduate's gown the better to emphasise the femininity of her persona. She was a handsome woman, soon to marry and thus to engage us vicariously in her defloration. Her legs were superbly hosed and much on display. She had a dirty laugh and saw in our texts double-entendres before we did. Thus, in an essay by Washington Irving, there was a reference to 'Nature and her harmonious combinations'. Eliot's *The Waste Land* was only six years old, and the drying combinations of the typist home at teatime were not yet a matter of historical annotation. We read Charles Lamb's *Adventures of Ulysses* with Miss Masterson, and the narrative seemed to burst with concupiscence. One boy, Flaherty, summed it up: 'It's all fighting and fucking tarts stiff.' We also had Miss Gray, a Charlotte Brontë type who taught unerotic geography.

It was in Lower Three Alpha that I made two friends or cronies who, true to the etymology *khronios*, sustained friendship chronically or at least till the marriage of one and the shady disappearance of the other. These were James Burgess, who came from Openshaw, and Eric Williams, who lived in Chorlton-cum-Hardy. Burgess was the cleverest, and, when I began to publish under the name, it was assumed by some alumni that it was he who was the author. In class examinations he regularly came first, I second, Williams third. I pointed out how this was miraculously figured in the placing of the O in the names of our respective suburbs – Openshaw, Moss Side, Chorlton. But Burgess moved from Openshaw and the pattern was broken. Nobody, once having arrived there, ever moved from Chorlton-cum-Hardy.

James Burgess was more imaginative than I. He maintained a fantasy about his father, who lay in bed all day and traced apophthegms in the deep dust of the floor: he called this dust *erudita*. There was a maid called 'Er, and Burgess's father would say: 'Tell 'Er to bring the lunch up.' Burgess swore that there was a Latin word for *yes* unrecorded in Roman literature. This, he said, was *chut* and derived from the sneezing of Caligula. When Caligula sneezed at the games it was interpreted ambiguously – yes, let him die; yes, let him live. Because the meanings cancelled out, *chut* did not survive. Burgess read thirty times the opening pages of *Hard Times* with undiminished delight. He had literary ambitions that came to nothing. He was, in Five Alpha, already at work on a Laurentian novel which contained such gems as 'She laughed, and it was the sound of a pigeon pissing in a milk can'. A train wreck was the climax of the narrative. The leading character was in the train toilet when it happened, and 'the brown stump of a turd protruded from his arse as he lay prone and lifeless'. Burgess became a communist and would read aloud from *The Ragged-Trousered Philanthropists*.

Williams was fair-headed and had what was then known as the girl's parting. He broke a front tooth in a bicycle accident, and this was to be capped with gold. He scratched his head at difficulties. The broken tooth and the head-scratching were gifts for the caricatures I drew of him in the class magazine I started. He took piano lessons, his due as a child of Chorlton-cum-Hardy. Like a mule, he was unable to eat, and he drank a whole bottle of whisky at a wedding and could not void it. It emerged as rank odour and the windows had to be opened. He became a distinguished Catholic engineer.

My class magazine began in Upper Three Alpha, and it was predictably called *The Alpha*. The one copy had a circulation of thirty classmates and such of the staff as could get hold of it. Like any people in authority, especially Catholic authority, they were on the lookout for heresy and disaffection. They did not find any. I was discreet and specialised in fantasy. I had an *Alpha* zoo with beasts like the Wiggle Poof:

> Sometimes, in winter, just for fun,
>   It flies round and disturbs
> Poor youngsters who are trying hard
>   To swot up Latin verbs.
>
> The colour of the Wiggle Poof
>   Is green with purple spots.
> It's harmless as a chimpanzee:
>   I'm sure you'd love it lots.

When the prism came into our lessons on optics I wrote on that in the same mode:

> A prism is a useful thing:
>   Besides refracting light,
> When tied on to a piece of string,
>   It's useful in a fight.

> Warmed in a sauce or chilled with ice,
>   It makes a splendid meal,
> With prunes, asparagus or rice,
>   Or even candied peel.

All very harmless, and all my own work. The only outside contribution I accepted was a song by Burgess about French firemen:

> *La maison est en feu.*
> *Faites venir les sapeurs.*
> *Tout le mond cherchez*
> *Les sapeurs pompiers.*

Burgess could not write down his own tune, nor could anybody. I had to learn to do it myself, and this led me to a concern with musical notation.

IN THE DOMESTIC sphere, the late twenties were convulsed with the problems Madge had in giving birth to her only baby – a boy named David, probably because his father looked like the Prince of Wales. The complications of her confinement were epic – great Manchester obstetricians discussing her case in Latin, so that the patient would not understand; the threat of puerperal fever; her name on the daily list of the Dangerously Ill in the *Manchester Evening News*. She came through, but the boy David was held out to micturate by the nurse, instead of being allowed to wet a napkin, and sustained a rupture. Agnes produced, with no great difficulty, a daughter named Sheila Margaret. In those non-vernacular days she had to be baptised as Julia Margarita. So the Tollitt future was fixed, though the Kemp future was in some doubt. I remember praying fervently for both Madge and the sickly child, in perhaps the last phase of piety I was to know, and the prayers seemed to be answered. I prayed with my radio headphones on in my bedroom, to a background of Jack Payne and the BBC Dance Orchestra.

This bedroom still had its retort and test tubes, though I was becoming disillusioned with chemistry. This was partly the fault of school, where the subject was all valencies and no bangs and, through a more professional disillusionment, disappeared from the syllabus. I had turned myself into a radio engineer, and there

was a regular radio section in *The Alpha*. I kept a crystal set by
my bed, trying to use the wire mattress as an aerial but, perhaps
because it was choked with dust and fluff, it preferred to be an
earth. I bought aerials which festooned the ceiling, not only for
the crystal set – which I favoured for clarity of tone – but for the
valved contraptions which picked up all the stations of the earth.
In 1932, when the Baird television transmissions began, I heard
the audio element in one of my radios, and I can still hear the
voice of Stuart Hibbard announcing, lazily, a 'lazy dance'.
Readers of Aldous Huxley's *Brave New World* will notice that,
even in the remote future, sound and vision belong to different
systems. That was the situation he and I knew in the thirties.

But, in 1929, the fascination of radio was nothing to the great
innovation in the cinema. 'Have you heard *The Singing Fool* yet?'
Eric Williams asked me. That *heard* was operative; we took for
granted that we could see. My nearest talking cinema was the
Claremont, and my father, aware of the importance of the new
phenomenon, took me to see and hear Al Jolson. After an
eternity of titles in the old style, though with a canned score
moaning and bitching underneath, Jolson spoke: 'You ain't heard
nothin' yet, folks' (this, rightly, has got into the *Oxford Dictionary
of Quotations*). And then, to the night club pianist, 'This is a
ballad.' – 'You can't sing a ballad' (which I took to refer to the
form, not the singer's competence) and the revelation of throaty
American-Jewish melody: 'I can be humble, I can be proud,/I
can be just a man in the crowd:/It all depends on you.' And,
towards the end, the tinned orchestra pointed Jolson's *Pagliacci*
situation – going onstage blacked up though Sonny Boy was
dead – with *Vesti la giubba*. Finally, 'Friends may forsake me,/Let
them all forsake me –/I still have you, Sonny Boy.' It was a
great experience, but it had its sinister aspects. The pit orchestra
had disappeared; musicians were joining the industrial unemployed. Under the screen were pot plants on soap boxes.

Our local cinemas, the Princess and the Palace, were sullen and
kept to silence. Rewiring and installing the new equipment cost
dear, and the depression was on. The Princess showed a silent
version of *The Jazz Singer*, with amplified gramophone records
of Al Jolson's voice, very imperfectly synchronised. And then it
showed silent films with its own canned accompaniments: the
coming of the talkies seemed primarily a chance to fire the orchestra. Jakie Innerfield did not fire his. He even brought in the
dance band from one of his dance halls as an intervallar treat. The

band leader put a cap and muffler on and sang 'My wife is on a diet,/And since she's on a diet,/Home isn't home any more.' Innerfield, despite his shrinking audiences, wanted to believe that the innovation would not last. 'Never Mind the Talkies,' shouted his posters. 'We Will Make You Talk.'

Yet, like most cinema owners, Innerfield had difficulty with silent rentals. He brought in a large number of German films, of a strong expressionist tendency, including the early Freudian *Secrets of the Soul*. There were heavy comedy films about Vienna, full of brilliant montage effects. I was watching, without knowing it, the twilight phase of the art of the Weimar Republic. Nowadays aesthetic historians would flock to such showings. I dimly saw their significance – they were more subtle and serious than the all-talking, all-singing, all-dancing extravaganzas we got at the Claremont – but I despised Jakie Innerfield's parsimony, disguised as a reactionary conviction. It was not long before he yielded, as he had to, and his first talking film was *Broadway*, with Regis Toomey. I could hardly understand a word the characters were saying, or moaning, or nasalising: the Innerfield equipment was not good. Soon the Princess too succumbed to the talking age, and any Manchester cinema still silent was probably a locale for the fencing of stolen goods or the fixing of assignations.

The talking films gave us new heroes and heroines. One lad in Upper Three Alpha, MacKinnon, adored Maurice Chevalier in *Innocents of Paris*, dressed his hair in the Chevalier style, thrust out his lower lip, and spoke English with a French accent, though French with an English one. We loved Renate Muller in *Sunshine Susie* and worshipped Marlene Dietrich in *The Blue Angel*. The German language, which was not taught in school, took on an erotic glamour and some of us formed little groups to learn it. I remember Peter Rice murmuring, as we came out of morning prayers, *'Der Sommer ist warm, der Winter ist kalt.'* The urge to be educated sometimes has strange roots. I amassed a number of German primers, but most of them in the Gothic type that had disappeared with Weimar but would come back with Hitler. 'Translate into German: "One day three students were walking along the road and they saw ahead of them an old Jew. The first passed him, saying 'Good morning, Father Abraham.' The second passed him, saying 'Good morning, Father Jacob.' The third passed him, saying 'Good morning, Father Issac.' The old Jew threw up his hands, crying: 'Young gentlemen, I am none of those holy patriarchs. I am Rechab who was sent forth to look for his father's asses, and behold I have found them.'"' A nice balance of the antisemitic and the liberal. There was a time when I was able to translate that.

I have shameful total recall of all the theme songs of the time, no film, however non-musical, being considered an authentic talkie without such an appurtenance. Even *The Doctor's Secret*, with Ruth Chatterton, had a song entitled 'Half an Hour' (after the J. M. Barrie one-acter on which the film was based). *The Pagan*, with Ramon Novarro, had 'Pagan Love Song'; *Weary River*, with Richard Barthelmess, had 'Weary River'. But the great songs were from *The King of Jazz* ('The Song of the Dawn'), *Paramount on Parade* ('Painting the Clouds with Sunshine') and *The Fox Movietone Follies of 1929*. I bought a record of songs from this last, and I wore it out on our portable gramophone. Madge, not yet confined, or recovered, took down the words of 'Breakaway' in shorthand. I sang 'Walking with Susie':

> She leads me, she feeds me
> Beauty and charm.
> I'm goosey when Susie
> Touches my arm.

('Goosey' seems to have disappeared from Anglo-American demotic. There was a song that went 'How do you feel/When you've married your ideal?/Ever so goosey, goosey, goosey, goosey.' The death of a usage is another nail in the coffin of the past.)

Very few of these early talking films seem to have survived, even in the ever open cinematic museum which is American television. We never see *Gold Diggers of Broadway*, which had 'Tiptoe Through the Tulips', or *Syncopation*, with Morton Downey, or even *Broadway Melody*, with Charles King and Bessie Love and Anita Page and 'You Were Meant for Me'. Probably the Vitaphone process, sound-on-disc, was too primitive to be compatible with electronic techniques. Probably we would be appalled to revisit old delights. We all, young as we were, recognised that sound pushed back the art of film to the infantile. We missed the old biblical epics – *The Ten Commandments*, *Noah's Ark* (Cecil B. De Mille, like his master D. W. Griffith, knew the appeal, before James Joyce, of a compound of myth and contemporaneity) – and such apocrypha as *Moon of Israel*, *Ben-Hur* and *Quo Vadis?*

Some of these came back with talk and high colour, but speech killed the magic by over-localising. Gore Vidal has only to camp up Ann Bancroft saying, with flapping hands of dismissal, 'Oh, Moses, Moses,' for us to hear the impossibility of a talking Bible. And I have always taken the impossibility of a talking *Metropolis* for granted.

My generation was vaguely aware of being set upon by technological changes that were not matched by new aesthetic or moral certitudes. The radio receivers that crammed my bedroom were only there to demonstrate the wonders of themselves. I could range all Europe on the dials but not even in 1929 was Europe telling me anything. Our convictions were superficial and secondhand. Learning by heart 'It was a summer's evening, / Old Kaspar's work was done' induced no literary transport. The Catholic shibboleths took on a brief reality only when some visiting missionary spoke of teaching the doctrine of the Holy Ghost in the African bush (always difficult; they always had a Ghost of their own, and it was not holy). I, without knowing it, was waiting for a revelation.

There had been a major quarrel in the Alec – something to do with teasing a man by alleging that pickled walnuts did not exist – and my father was doing his evening drinking with members of the Hallé Orchestra in the pubs near the Free Trade Hall. It was an all-male orchestra in those days, except when a second harpist was needed for Richard Strauss or Debussy, and the players were mostly formidable boozers. Charlie Collier, first or only harpist, belied the traditional femininity of his calling by having the worst male faults: swilling, rioting, swearing. The brass section, red and burly, drank no more than the violins. My father was led back to seeing these new friends in musical action, and he thought it a good idea to take me along to a Hallé concert. I was getting drunk with sound and vision, and I needed to be sobered up with pure sound. I was dragged to a Wagner night.

Manchester was a Wagnerian city. Hans von Richter, conductor of the Hallé from 1899 to 1911, had established the tradition of throwing bleeding chunks from the music dramas to Mancunian audiences stiffened with German immigrants, and Michael Balling, another German and another Wagnerian, sustained the heavy meat diet from 1912 to the outbreak of the war. Under Sir Hamilton Harty Manchester had started to become a Berliozian city, but Wagner still packed them in. The Wagner night he conducted and I attended in early 1929 bored me, except for the glockenspiel in the Apprentices' Dance from *Die Meistersinger*. I had shown no aptitude for music. A half-term on the violin had taught me only to shudder at the smell of resin. Miss Masterson had once asked me in class what was the purpose or value of music, and she had mooed in horror when I said that singing was probably good for the lungs (a boy named Higgins did better: 'Music hath charms, miss'). I was impressed only by the smell of hot air from the heating grilles of the Free Trade Hall – a mustiness which I was to recall in Singapore in 1954 in the aroma of Frazer and Neave's tonic water. The Manchester cold came back in the tropical night: real past time cached and waiting for its Proustian release.

I was bored, I say, but a few days later I found a tune turning and turning in my head, whistled it to my father over his sweetbreads, and asked him what it was. It was, he told me, the main theme from the Overture to Wagner's *Rienzi*. It was not solely the melody that had adhered to my brain but the harmonies too. I could hear what later I was able to call a sixth suspended over a chord of the dominant seventh. There was, I had grudgingly to admit, something in what the lowbrows called classical music. A week or so later I prodded my carborundum pyrite crystal and heard a coughing silence. Then I heard a sinuous flute. I listened and went on listening. At the end of an eight-minute tissage of impressionistic colour I was told that I had been listening to Debussy's *Prélude à l'Après-Midi d'un Faune*. The fact that I knew enough French by now to understand the title was a kind of confirmation that music too could be intelligibile. And, of course, a truth that still astonishes when we care to remind ourselves of it, music transcended language. My impaired colour sense was already finding, in the quiet impact of Debussy's orchestra, an auditory compensation. There was a large palette there, and a delicate painting hand. But I was not satisfied with merely hearing the colour; I wanted to see it too.

I am all too alphabetic. I have never been able to pick up a language solely by ear. The International Phonetic Alphabet, in its narrowest possible form, was meant for people like me. I need even Zulu clicks to be annotated. I had an idea, which could not be fully articulated, that the reality of the Debussy piece lay not in any single performance – transient, insubstantial, lost on the air – but in the written notes. I could find out what instruments he used in his score, I could even look at them and handle them, but I had to see the notes they were playing (had played, would play again) as a primary reality, with the sounds as a mere consequence. I had neglected learning how to read music in my abortive violin classes. I could not now ask for a renewal of musical instruction that went beyond Mr Sandiford's sessions of 'appreciation' in the school hall. I would have to teach myself.

Musical notation, anyway, had become an aspect of my amateur journalism. James Burgess's song *'La Maison est en Feu'* had to appear in the next issue of *The Alpha*. I sang the song to my father as, bowlered and ready for an evening's heavy boozing, he came out of the lavatory. He nodded and led me the few steps to the drawing-room. On top of the piano were the four volumes of *The Music Lover's Portfolio*. Beethoven's Fifth Symphony, in a simple piano reduction, was distributed throughout Volume One. He found the slow movement and pointed to the mock-martial secondary theme. 'That's the tune,' he said, and, bowlered, he played it with a fag in his mouth. 'All you have to do is copy it out. That, by the way,' pointing with a nicotined index, 'is middle C. Under the treble stave or over the bass stave, it's still middle C. And here it is on the joanna.' He prodded and it sounded. 'Just to the right of the lock,' meaning the ward. And then, fresh fag glowing, he went off to the Alec. He had given me a music lesson of exemplary brevity, the only one he ever gave, the only one I needed.

I copied out, on a double page of the exercise book that was my magazine, the top line of the Beethoven, much in the manner of my stepmother drawing her signature on a cheque. I decorated the feature with a blazing home and a sleeping *pompier* (*'Il dort'*) and felt that I was presiding over a trinity of the arts. But my primary art still seemed to be that of the cartoonist, and Miss Masterson encouraged me to convert *Julius Caesar*, which we had just started to study, into a sort of *Ur-Astérix* comic book, complete with anachronisms and *fumetti*. She even gave me a beautiful volume of bound drawing sheets with a stiff cover. I was working on this while I was also working on the elements of music. It was a prediction of my professional life – doing too many things, and all of them different, and all at the same time. The mechanics of turning notes into sound on the drawing-room piano became a time-absorbing passion, and it interfered with homework. I dimly felt then, and feel very strongly now, that there is something wrong with an education system that takes no account of passion. Stamp-collecting, amateur ornithology, pulling a car engine to pieces are indulged as hobbies so long as they do not impair the learning of *fero, ferre, tuli, latum*. The passion that went into Englishmen's hobbies, and not into their learning of Latin verbs, fired the building of an empire. Singapore was made out of Stamford Raffles's hobbies: as a sideline he founded the London Zoo, fruit of an amateur passion for exotic animals. The things that counted for me had only a marginal connection with official education. When Br Martin said I was low and did nothing for my house or my school, he meant that I was preoccupied with hobbies.

I found at the bottom of the piano stool at home a ragged copy of some two-part pieces by Handel. Knowing where middle C was, I could learn to play the notes, but I did not know how to interpret crotchets and quavers. I could understand the vertical element in music but not yet the horizontal. But I listened to a performance of Tchaikovsky's Fifth Symphony on the radio, and I followed it with the reduced version in *The Music Lover's Portfolio*. At the end of fifty minutes of close attention, the notes began to yield their temporal secrets. I found it possible to figure out the meaning of the Handel note-values. I also admired the look of the music on the printed page. It was a kind of drawing. I wanted to be able to draw like that: I was sick of Brutus and Cassius in comic togas, hairy Roman legs peeping out beneath. I wanted to write my own music. At the age of thirteen I decided that I was to be a great composer, and I trained myself, pursuing an indulged hobby, to that end. It was an ambition that only really faded in my late thirties, and sometimes, in my late sixties, it is encouraged to re-emerge. I have just received (November 20, 1985) a letter from a stranger who heard my settings of four of D. H. Lawrence's poems, performed in Nottingham as part of the Lawrence centenary celebrations, and he declares that the songs are 'wonderful and original'. I was not present at that performance, and I did not particularly wish to be. The reality rests in the calligraphic score. Still, the appreciation of a musical stranger who was moved by the sound of my work disturbs me into worrying whether I was wrong in turning to literature and taming an old ambition into a diversion like knitting. I am receiving musical encouragement too late. Anyway, it is more than balanced by discouragement from critics. But I cannot live without proposing to myself some massive musical composition to end (I would never say 'crown') my artistic career. I am halfway through the writing of a libretto for an opera about Sigmund Freud.

At thirteen I had a vague idea of the music I wanted to write. It was to be 'modern', like Stravinsky or Schoenberg. I was finding my way about music through the simple tonalities of Handel and early Beethoven and the children's pieces by Robert Schumann (God bless his shade: he was a huge help). But I rather despised these diatonic harmonies and cadences all too easy to anticipate. Those composers were saying nothing about the modern world. Debussy, though dead in 1918, had said plenty about it: indeed, it seemed to me that he was the primal force that charged all musical innovation. There were no classical cadences in his work (except when, as in *Minstrels*, they were used ironically), and his harmonies were built on four notes, not the Beethovenian three. I heard this four-note harmony — added sixths and seconds — in the late-night dance music that beguiled me as I lay headphoned in bed. That music was trivial, but it was certainly modern as Debussy, though not Stravinsky, was modern. There seemed to be a little of Debussy in those saxophone chords but, at that time, there was no one who dared say so. There was a great gulf fixed between what was termed, wrongly in both cases, jazz and classical music. If you subscribed to the *Musical Times*, which had the flavour of the culture of the organ-loft, you had to read occasional sneering articles about the masturbatory or insipid qualities (qualities difficult to reconcile) of 'jazz'. And yet the works of George Dyson and E. J. Moeran are not now much heard, while Cole Porter and George Gershwin are as fresh as ever.

I felt guilty about enjoying Carroll Gibbons and his Orchestra, and Jack Payne and Ambrose and Geraldo and Harry Roy, when I had neglected to tune in to a Beethoven sonata. The guilt was resolved on November 12, 1929 (the date is in Grove's *Dictionary of Music and Musicians*), when Constant Lambert conducted at a Hallé concert the first performance of his *Rio Grande*. The rhythms of jazz were used wittily in this choral setting of a poem by Sacheverell Sitwell, and Sir Hamilton Harty, in the virtuoso solo part, had casually turned himself into a brilliant syncopated pianist. Lambert, who admired Duke Ellington and proclaimed his harmonic roots in Frederick Delius (who in his turn had taken them from Debussy), was a fearless reconciler of what the academies and Tin Pan Alley alike presumed to be eternally opposed. I was present at that first performance, and so was my father. And, in 1972, on a plane from New York to Toronto, I found myself sitting next to Duke Ellington, who spoke almost with tears of the stature of Lambert, admitted that he had learned much from both Delius and Debussy, and expressed scorn for the old musical division, which had been almost as vicious as a colour bar. He had lived to see it dissolve and jazz become a legitimate item in the academic curricula.

Once I had mastered the elements of Debussyan harmony, I found it easier to turn myself into an improvisatory player of popular music than a Beethoven recitalist. Wrong notes could be interpreted as 'blue' notes; chromatic sequences of ninths were in order; there were certain basic harmonic patterns – like the tonic, submediant, supertonic and dominant chords of 'Blue Moon'; the rhythms seemed to reconcile speech and physical movement in a way that Beethoven did not. I am still a player of 'standards' and could, at a pinch, find employment as a cocktail pianist. I have never yet played a Beethoven sonata without making gross errors. I learned the wrong way: I did not work on scales: my speciality is big chords. But I had never wished to become a true pianist. The piano was a useful device for learning how to compose – no more. From the age of seventeen on I did my composing away from the piano.

Learning the techniques of music meant buying the textbooks put out by Novello, though these were firmly fixed in the Mendelssohnian past. The harmony primer had not even heard of Wagner. Consecutive fifths? Horror of horrors. The orchestration manual assumed that horns had not yet been equipped with valves. For musical history I read Grove in the public library at the corner of Moss Lane East and Princess Road. It seemed to be the original edition, or at most the second, for it spoke of the new and dangerous school of Richard Wagner. I got my real instruction on musical culture from the *Radio Times*, as I got my listening experience from the BBC.

The *Radio Times* of that period was a substantial publication like a weekly *Blast*, only better printed, and all for twopence. Its tone was intellectual, its artwork highly contemporary; it abounded with gratuitous erudition. Its cover could sometimes startle – a woodcut of Beethoven in terminal agony, the huge stark legend *Morning Heroes* to herald the first performance of Arthur Bliss's choral symphony of that name, a tortured Wagnerian fantasia for the fiftieth anniversary of the composer's death in 1933, the announcement *The End of the World* to signal an expressionist drama on that subject. There were, until what James Joyce called the bairdbombardmentboard started up in 1932, only radio programmes to be covered, and there were only two radio channels – the national and the regional. 'This is the BBC National Programme' meant that we were hearing London; otherwise we heard, in Manchester, Manchester. Our regional station promoted local talent, put on dialect plays, dramatised local history or merely talked about it. I can hear dialogues still from one of the regional comedies: 'Give us another cuppa tay, lass – that tater pie tha made were a bit salty like.' – 'Aht else tha can find fault wi'?' – 'Nay, lass, what's coom over thee?' Such dialogue was meticulously articulated, as from an academic class in Lancastrian. The promotion of regional talent often meant bad accordion-players and screechy singers. The London Regional listeners did better: they got the cream of the capital. The *Radio Times* had the duty of telling us what was on and, by today's standards, this was not much. But it expanded the week's programmes with learned information conveyed in the style of the higher journalism. Thus, when a Sousa march appeared in a military band programme (there was a BBC Military Band in those days), there were a couple of paragraphs about Sousa's first visit to Paris and the strange fact that Debussy was the only classical columnist to notice the event. 'M. Sousa,' Debussy wrote, 'strikes a tennis ball into the bass tuba and catches a butterfly as it emerges from the first trombone.' That sort of thing.

There was a mock seventeenth-century diary written by 'Samuel Pepys, listener', and extracts from an updated life of Dr Johnson, in which the Grand Cham listened to the radio, frowning, and made caustic Augustan comments on Henry Hall and the BBC Dance Orchestra. There was a serial in Byronic *ottava rima* which dealt with a new Juan. The Christmas number was a feast, and it had one year (when Spike Hughes was editor) a coloured Nativity on its cover, specially commissioned from Frank Brangwyn. A man named Longstaff produced a radio pantomime, and this was hailed with

> Scriabin scoffs, Bill Bartok cocks an eyebrow.
> Lay on, Longstaff, and let who will be highbrow!

This was disingenuous: the BBC was brilliantly highbrow, and so was its popular organ. *The Listener*, which had a smaller public, was stratospheric in its intellectuality.

Sir John Reith intended that radio should educate us; it was, to use a term of the period, a 'social technique'. The educative was

fleeting, lost in the air, but the *Radio Times* and *The Listener* were
solid printed counterparts of the broadcast seed. I was certainly
educated. Sunday was more than educative; it was devotional,
and the channels palpitated with the silence of prayer until three
in the afternoon, when the Sabbath pleasures opened up with a
Bach cantata. The newspapers, tribunes of the people, had the
duty of demanding more popular entertainment for the day of
rest, but they never did. They wanted people to tune in to Radio
Luxembourg, which seethed with popular song and advertisements like 'We are the Ovalteenies, here to share your joys –

> At games and sports we're more than keen,
> No merrier children e'er were seen.
> Because we all drink Ovaltine,
> We're happy girls and boys.'

It was in the interest of the press tacitly to support its own adver-
tisers by praising the Reithian religiosity. Thus the *Daily Mail*
and the *Daily Express* may have helped, without intending to, the
cause of the five evangelists, the fifth being Bach.

The culture the BBC purveyed was not all classical and traditional. The BBC was very up to date. It put on the *Dreigroschenoper*, whose protagonist was Captain Macky, not Mack the
Knife, and a *Lehrstück* by Brecht and Hindemith, with the
comedian Harry Tate in the clown's role. It presented Hindemith's *News of the Day*, with a typewriter in the percussion
section, and Krenek's jazz opera *Johnny Spielt Auf*. The BBC's
programme directors knew what was going on in the Weimar
Republic. They commissioned plays which exploited the techniques of expressionism and Brechtian epic theatre – L. du Garde
Peach's *The Squirrel's Cage* and *The Flowers Are Not For You to
Pick* and Walter de la Mare's *Yes, and Back Again*. Everything
was 'live': there was an urgency of performance no longer available now that recordings are so much dead meat ready cut up
and waiting to be taken out of the refrigerator. Effects were all of
the 'spot' variety, contrived in the studio: there were no blatt-
nerphone libraries of storms at sea and train wrecks. Music came
from wind-up gramophones, and diminuendi and crescendi
relied on the shutting and opening of doors. This was the great
age of radio: it demonstrated that experimental art owes more to
the *bricoleur* than to the engineer.

There was light relief from this heady or heavy diet. Invisible variety shows featured comedians like Gillie Potter and Stainless Stephen, whom I never found funny, and Clapham and Dwyer and Ronald Frankau, whom I did. I tried to memorialise Ronald Frankau (Gilbert's brother, Pamela's uncle) in my novel *Earthly Powers*, where he is transformed into the brother of my hero-narrator – specialist in the comic deformation of Shakespeare who assumes a certain sophistication in his audience. Such sophistication is no longer to be found. Clapham and Dwyer were funny because they were low: they would break away from their script to see what subtle vulgarities they could get away with. When one of them said of a joke that misfired 'That fell on stony ground,' they were proscribed for blasphemy. There was a Jewish comedian, Izzy Bonn, who made fun of bar-mitzvah banquets: 'Vater flowed like vine. Vhen Mrs Tittlebaum vas full to bursting, she peeled an orange, put her false teeth on the table, and said, "*Iss, iss.* You eat, I can't."' Those were the innocent days when Jewish jokes were not antisemitic. And, invisible as the shows were, the BBC introduced a team of dancers called the Step Sisters, who tapped away on resonant boards and tinnily sang 'Happy Days Are Here Again'. That was the time of the depression.

But it was the BBC Symphony Orchestra, a superb instrument under Sir Adrian Boult, that gave me the food I wanted. I took in Beethoven and Brahms distractedly – there were no orchestral surprises: it was all line drawing with occasional wash – but devoured Stravinsky, Schoenberg, Hindemith and Honegger, who made horns leap and trumpets coruscate and me drunk with discords. The Hallé Orchestra provided no such thrills: its programmes were solid but unadventurous, like the cuisine of the city chophouses. We were always being promised *Le Sacre du Printemps*, but we never got it. Not even visiting Stravinsky could coax more than *L'Oiseau de Feu* out of that all-male hard-drinking body that regarded musical experiment as womanish frippery. Ernst Ansermet came and conducted Debussy's *Ibéria*; he had to stop and start again after the first three measures, to my referred shame. When Mossolov's piece of Soviet realism *Factory: the Music of Machines* was announced, I went eagerly: at last we were getting somewhere. But Sir Hamilton Harty, amiably tipsy, diluted the impact of the work by telling the audience beforehand that they were going to be shocked, and then letting us hear first strings, then wind, then percussion play their parts. The audience giggled, and giggled even more at the anticlimax of the totality.

The horns stood up to play a theme symbolising the dignity of labour, and this was considered a fine joke. Later the Hallé and Harty dared to give the first British performance of Shostakovich's First Symphony, but this was acceptable Tchaikovsky and water. We had to wait for a visit from the BBC Symphony Orchestra to hear unashamed modernity in the Free Trade Hall – Hindemith's *Philharmonic Concerto* and Ravel's *Boléro* – and also to see women playing quite as well as men. I fell in love with the first harpist, Sidonie Goossens.

At the age of fourteen I tried to compose modernistically, but it was either too easy or too difficult. Too easy to set down arbitrary discords; too hard to make a whole composition out of them. I compromised with diluted Debussy, but the only performance I achieved during my early schooldays was of a choral and piano setting of the shanty 'Let the Bulgine Run'. Still, I got my name in the programme just above that of Ralph Vaughan Williams, who had done an arrangement of 'The Golden Vanity'.

MY FRIEND ERIC WILLIAMS had been taught to play Beethoven's Minuet in G on the family piano in Chorlton-cum-Hardy, but this was a social achievement that had nothing to to with art. His father, an engineer at Trafford Park, despised music and passed on to his son certain of the shibboleths of the philistine: that people only went to concerts to be admired; that there were some folk so perverse that they liked to be bored; that Beethoven and Mozart were poseurs. I seemed to be surrounded by philistinism: my step-brother-in-law Clifford Kemp declared, to family applause, that Shakespeare was a flat-footed highbrow. James Burgess, composer of *'La Maison est en Feu'*, kept his own counsel but once turned up at the Free Trade Hall to hear Schnabel. In school essays I would refer to the Mozartian limpidity of Addison's prose or the Wagnerian richness of Thomas De Quincey's, always to find these similitudes questioned by the teacher and derided by the class. But I was the only one in a French lesson able to say what a *casse-noisette* was, thanks to' Tchaikovsky. I also knew the Faust legend, because of Gounod and Busoni, and could read Cyrillic, having studied in the Manchester Central Library the original score of *Le Sacre du Printemps*. Asked to compare the styles of Tennyson's 'Ulysses' and 'The Lotus Eaters', I said that one had the austerity of Sibelius and the other the sensuousness of the Venusberg music in *Tannhäuser*. What I should have said was that one was in blank verse and the other rhymed. The advantages of knowing something about music were minimal – knowing that *tanner* meant to bore, since, after the first Paris performance of *Tannhäuser*, Parisians said '*Wagner me tanne aux airs*' – and the main disadvantage was a kind of social ostracism. Br Martin once wove drunkenly into one of our classes to burble something about the heavenly message of Palestrina, but that was probably something he had picked up from the morning's *Manchester Guardian*. A new student joined us in Lower Five Alpha, and he was not unsympathetic to my musical enthusiasm, since it was in his own family. But he happened to be a Jew.

His name was Harold Foreman, and his family ran a draper's shop on Princess Road. Why a Jewish boy should be sent to, and accepted by, a school with an aggressively Catholic name was a mystery only to be unravelled by reference to Br Martin's interest in money. Young Foreman's parents probably paid extravagantly high fees. It was a pity that he should, in appearance, so blatantly anticipate the *Stürmer* caricatures. He was ugly and big-nosed, and he was a gift to my class magazine, one issue of which featured him as the beautiful Greta Foreman, glamorous star of *Passion and Polonies*, all nose and coyness. He was affronted on his own behalf, not that of his race, and he scrawled viciously over the libel with a greasy crayon. This was considered ungentlemanly and probably Jewish. When he refused to lend his spare fountain pen to Peter O'Brien, O'Brien said: 'You're a real Jew.' Foreman replied, with adenoidal ready wit: 'Well, I'm not an artificial one, am I?' Some inner tension, perhaps to do with insufficient love for his mother, made him gesticulate grotesquely. With a sudden arm spasm he would send his inkpot flying; his neck and jaw muscles would go rigid, and he would snap like a trout at an invisible fly. This gesture became his nickname: 'You know what old – did?', the space being filled with fly-snapping. I do not think modern linguistics is yet able to accommodate this intrusion of gesture into syntax. Chomsky has nothing to say about it.

Foreman helpfully tried to instruct Peter O'Brien, who had the face of an Irish wolfhound, into the mysteries of obstetrics, but this was regarded as dirty and Jewish. Even at sixteen O'Brien would not accept the phenomenon of natural birth. Asked where babies came from, he would say that the nurse brought them, and if asked where the nurse got them from, he would say they were a gift of the doctor. He was a model of stupidity on the peasant Irish pattern. He did a lot of thinking, he said, when lying in bed, and he thought especially of what the St Bernardine's house badge would look like if it borrowed the colour of the St Cuthbert's one. He desperately wanted a house badge, which was a reward for merit in work or games or, to be fair, notable eccentricity (I cannot think I received mine for any other quality), and, dreaming he had been awarded one, he awoke crying. He learned Warner and Martin's history book by heart and gained a distinction in the School Certificate examination. He was a good racial and religious foil to Harold Foreman.

It worried O'Brien that Foreman had not been baptised, and he tried to arrange for his head to be shoved under a washroom tap while he pronounced the *Ego te baptizo*. But he did not know the Latin equivalent of Harold. It awed him that here, at the next desk, was one of a damned race that had killed Christ. And then it worried him that Foreman knew all about Abraham and Isaac and Jacob, who, though pre-Christian, had been good Catholics. Foreman sneakily stayed in class during a Religious Knowledge session and put Br Campion right on the twelve tribes of Israel. All this was unfair.

I went to dinner at Foreman's house – which, like mine, was at the back of a shop – and expected Palestinian spiciness. What I got was blandly kosher. He taught me some Yiddish and lent me a gramophone record of comic songs in that language: one of them was called '*Men darf nit zein verschlufen*'. From his elder sister Rebecca I renewed the image of Oriental seductiveness which I had first met, at the distance proper to customer and cashier, in Jakie Innerfield's daughters. There be none of Beauty's daughters, as Byron put it. For me the feminine ideal has always been Mediterranean. I understand very well the desperation that Shakespeare felt for the dark lady. The musky presence of this girl, who must have been about seventeen, induced painful erections and no hope of detumescence. She was an occasion of sin. She forced me into sin, though not with her.

I was fifteen when I met a girl named Edith – a noble Anglo-Saxon name attached to a forward Manchester fourteen-year-old who was not Jewish, merely Protestant, but with the full Hebraic seductiveness I had found in Foreman's sister. I sat next to her on the back row of the Princess cinema, and it seemed to her natural to give me her hand to hold. She had been eating sweets, and it was a sticky hand. She was transformed into a Rebecca-surrogate, and I boldly put my arm around her and fondled her breast ('ripening', said Keats of Fanny Brawne's: there was, after all, a relevance to real life in school work). When the film was over she invited me home. Home was on Lincroft Street, no distance. Her parents? Her father had gone off with another woman; her mother would be drinking Guinness in the snug of the Little Alec till closing-time. We had been at the first-house film showing: there was time if no suitable space. Her two young brothers shared a bedroom with her: they had best not be disturbed. The front room was reserved for visitors and Christmas, but there was the floor of the regular living-room, very dusty. The house smelt of old cabbage and face powder: her mother was a bit of a slut. On the floor, totally naked at Edith's request, I was able to see debris under the one armchair, including a bloodied clout I was later to identify as a sanitary towel. She too stripped totally: it was like the day in the grass at Monsall Isolation Hospital, but dust and dark and my increased years and the burden of the image of Rebecca made impossible a recovery of that joyous innocence. This was deadly erotic. She asked me if I had a thing to put on, and I did not know what she meant. But almost at once it was too late anyway. Boys cannot make love. Nature is so eager to shoot young seed that she forgets what it is for. Premature climax: it sounds like a drama critic's rebuke. But there was no tristitia, though I could hear Catholic guilt creaking into position. The stale smell was the smell of stale incense; the dust was the dust of the confessional. And yet if this was not the ecstasy promised in heaven on condition that one forwent ecstasy on earth, what on earth was it? Surely this smooth tawny girl's body delivered spiritual transports to the caressing fingers? Surely the gratitude for her beauty and generosity was of a higher moral import than the belch (*eructavit cor meum*) of repletion? I could feel the promise of my becoming tougher within and being willing to answer the Church back. This might have had something to do with my having become an acolyte of a new spiritual complex, which did not merely promise heaven but actually gave it with nothing asked in return: I mean music. Heaven's harps, even if Sidonie Goossens was at the first desk, would be thin compared with Richard Strauss. And even music was nothing to the loving whispers of a naked girl of fourteen on a dusty floor. Love one another, children, and to hell with the apostles of love.

I knew that we would not meet again unclothed, or even in a context of back-row caresses. She had merely wanted to see what

I was like. She was very young and precocious, probably in her promiscuousness as well as her Protestant guiltlessness. I began to feel guilty about my own guilt. I had some idea, which would be put right later in my history classes, that the Reformation had something to do with the cancellation of original sin, which began with the nuzzling of a girl's ripening breast smooth as an apple and went on to acts in the dust of Eden unmentionable in Genesis. Contact with a Jewish family and a Protestant girl named Edith hinted that there were people in the world who got on healthily enough without having to confess their sins, which were not sins, since a sin could be defined as what was confessable. Nor did such people take hell seriously, though I was sensible enough to see that this did not necessarily invalidate the great grim doctrine. If God could send Spanish influenza as a gratuitous bestowal after the worst war in history, he was quite capable of capping the agony of terminal cancer with eternal torment. And, of course, he still is. If sex was a compelling reality, so was hell, and I went to confession at the Holy Name very much in two minds.

I confessed to Fr Clancy, who did not speak in a rollicking brogue but with the clipped phonemes of the BBC National Programme. It seemed to me unfair that the anonymity of the confessional prevented the priest from considering my past record and taking prolonged good conduct into account when assessing my present state of ungrace. I had been good for nearly a year: the *Radio Times* had ensured that. But now I was raved at as an inveterate fornicator. Fr Clancy would not give me absolution this time: I had better brood on my sin, realise its enormity in a cold bath, and come back next week. So I went next door to Fr Fitzjames, who was deep in the racing columns. I was conventionally roared at but distractedly absolved, with a penance of five Our Fathers, five Hail Marys, and five Glory Bes, with the *bonne bouche* of an ejaculation or so, such as 'Christ, have mercy; Mary, help.' I dared, absolved, to ask him what was wrong with sex. He said: nothing in the married state; sexual pleasure was a good and holy thing, so sanctified, since it produced souls which, with luck, would people God's wide acres. I said that I did not see how the *qualitas* of an experience could be modified by the purpose for which it was conducted, especially when nature took out of our hands the consciousness of that purpose. He then tried to have a close look at me through the grille before roaring again. I feared he might cancel the absolution, so I got the hell out.

I got the hell out in, I am sure, long trousers. A time comes in

the life of every Western male when the *toga virilis* of long kex
replaces short pants and filthy knees. It is always hard to remember when exactly the transformation took place. It is a crucial
transformation since it is long trousers that have to be taken down
for the sexual act, and there is something monstrous in the idea
of doffing shorts for it, unless, as happened to me much later, one
is serving the Empire, or the rump of the Empire, in the tropics.
At school one was initiated into long trousers when one played
cricket, but, walking to the playing field in whites, one did not
have to look apologetic for pretending to be a man. With the
first suit from the small men's department, there was an element
of pretension that could be overcome only with the first functional shave. Previous games with the razor merely sheared fuzz,
but, when blood welled on the upper lip and the neck was sore,
one was justly into virile trousers.

In Upper Five Alpha everyone was in these except, briefly,
James Burgess, whose inky knees let us all down and had to be
chastised with thwacks from rulers. Upper Five Alpha accommodated not merely the promoted Fourth but also boys with blue
jowls who had been there for a long time, vainly trying to pass
the School Certificate examination. The veterans were headed by
Michael Callaghan, a brilliant pianist and now a distinguished
chorus master, whose primary art at that time was the cribbing
one. In term tests he produced serially, ostensibly to see how the
time was going, six or seven broken wristwatches, behind whose
crystals were irregular Latin verbs minutely penned. He had geo-
metry theorems up his jacket cuffs. He had a coverless Warner
and Martin, reduced to its component signatures with the margins
shaved off, and this was distributed about his body. There were a
number of burly Irish cribbers around, but Callaghan was king,
though the art had to be considered as being practised for its own
sake, since he consistently failed his papers. The Irish thugs wished
to enter St Mary's Catholic Training College, called Simmary's,
at Strawberry Hill in Twickenham, there to be turned into
elementary school teachers. It frightened me to observe this
planning of lives so early, since I did not wish to be anything but
a great composer and cartoonist on the side, and I knew that this
was not a practical ambition.

Everybody talked about sex, but I kept quiet about my premature experience of it: one should not kiss and tell. Peter O'Brien
only talked of it negatively, in the sense that he did not believe it
existed, or, if it did exist, it was not necessary, since doctors and

nurses were responsible for babies. I knew it existed, more than ever before, since I was being instructed in it by a very mature woman. Br Andrew, our teacher of English, had taught us a poem by James Elroy Flecker – the 'War Song of the Saracens', from *Hassan*, in anapaestic hexameters – and he ordered me to fill in one of our free Wednesday afternoons by going to the Central Library, finding such information on Flecker as I could, and afterwards delivering a lecture on that minor poet. I went to the Central Library, at that time in Piccadilly, and had difficulty with the index system. It was all numbers, and I was looking for names. A woman of about forty put me right, a charming woman running acceptably to fat, dressed in a green skirt and a blue sweater, her hair prettily mousy, before getting down to her study of Engels. When I had gained enough information about Flecker (he married a Greek girl named Miss Skidaresse), she apparently had gained enough information about Engels, whoever he was. On the steps of the library she said I looked cold and asked if I would like tea. I thought she was proposing a Kardomah café, but she put myself and herself on a tram and took me to Ardwick, where she had a small flat over a confectioner's shop. It was a bookish flat, warmed by a gas fire, with bright rugs and pictures on the walls that were nothing like the anecdotal post-Millais horrors we had at home. These pictures were like what I painted in the elementary school before my daltonianism was painfully and hilariously discovered. But she told me they were by great artists, only reproductions of course: I needed, she said, to be educated.

She meant more than instruction in the visual arts. She was a widow whose husband had drowned at Southport (this seemed improbable: I had been to Southport and never even seen the sea), and she was earning a living by lecturing for the Workers' Educational Association. Marx and Engels, whoever they were, were among the subjects of her lectures. But she was not disposed to talk about them after our strong tea and ginger snaps. She took from a drawer under her shelves of economic history a packet of condoms. I had heard of these but never yet seen them. They were commonly called French letters, presumably because they let or hindered pregnancy. I knew that this term had to be a vulgarity unacceptable to, and perhaps unknown by, educated people, since I had seen one of Br Andrew's literary magazines, which had a section headed 'Our American Letter' and another headed 'Our French Letter', and this latter had been about people

writing poems in Paris. She now gave me detailed instructions
about love-making on the rug before the gas fire. She had fine
big bouncing breasts, ripe not ripening, and her skin had an acrid
smell as of woodsmoke. Now, protected by latex, I did the deed.
It was a totally anonymous undertaking, since she did not ask me
my name or divulge hers. It did not seem to be a sin, because the
tone was educative, as for a serious session of the Workers'
Educational Association, and the moans of fulfilment had an
appropriate decorum. She seemed a healthy woman, Protestant of
course, who had certain physical needs which needed to be regularly gratified. She gave me a little postcoital instruction in the
materialistic philosophy on which Marxist economic theory was
based. God was a fable designed to uphold the capitalist exploiters,
and sin was a fabrication intended to make the workers feel guilty
about demanding their rights. Then, as tumescence renewed itself,
that aspect of my new education was intermitted. I got home late
and weary. My stepmother, not normally given to commiseration, remarked on my tired eyes and said they was making
me study too 'ard. She gave me two fried eggs with my bacon.

I saw this woman twice again. I gave my rather tired lecture
on James Elroy Flecker, inscribing AMDG (Ad Maiorem Dei
Gloriam) on the blackboard before listing the vital statistics, and
volunteered to find out about Gerard Manley Hopkins, whose
'Pied Beauty' and 'The Starlight Night' were among the addenda
to Palgrave's *Golden Treasury*. That my using the Central Library
for an assignation was the beginning of a lifelong devotion to
Hopkins somehow still mitigates the sin that was no sin. She was
there, making notes on the *Communist Manifesto*, only too ready
to give me tea. The third occasion was after a Hallé concert.
How did she reconcile the spiritual transports of listening to
Brahms with a metaphysic that denied the non-material? Epi-
phenomenal, or something, she said; mere excitation of the nerves.
Like this. And then we were at it again. For the last time, she said
afterwards. No, no. Ah, yes. Ah, no. She was a woman incapable,
rightly, of being satisfied with mere schoolboys. (Were there
others? I was learning mature jealousy.) Where, if I had been
older, I would have been ready to speak of infidelity, she would
have said something about fidelity's being a very bourgeois notion.
She needed sex, but she needed various sex. I had been taught,
without fee, and she had known the creative joy of the teacher.
Now I could be on my way. It was so late that the trams had
stopped running.

I went to confession with some confidence, telling Fr Myerscough that I had taken tea with a Protestant widow who had instructed me, among other things, in the principles of materialism and affirmed that the whole Church structure was built on a fable. He did not ask about the other subjects of instruction; instead he railed about keeping bad company but concluded that I had been led by the devil to the coverts of Marx, and possibly Ibsen and other atheists. I must not see this person again. I promised not to. Who was Ibsen? There were several things I did not know. I did not know how to masturbate, and I did not know of the existence of lending libraries. I found out the first for myself belatedly, and James Burgess, long-trousered, told me about the second. He had *Hard Times* from the public library on quasi-permanent loan, though he read no further than the opening chapter, with Mr Gradgrind and Cissy Jupe. He would rub his hands and chortle over his fiftieth re-reading. Yes, he said, there was Ibsen there; also Björnsen. I ought to know Ibsen because of Grieg's music for *Peer Gynt*.

So I got a reader's ticket and read *The Wild Duck*. Then the BBC put on *The Wild Duck*, with Elisabeth Bergner in the role of Hedvig, and this confirmed that it was a great play, though Protestant. But, damn it, all our set books were Protestant – *Julius Caesar*, which was positively pagan, and *A Shorter Boswell*, and the poems of Tennyson and Browning. Br Andrew spoke of our getting ready to enter a Protestant society. In an essay, one Irish lout had written: 'When I got home from mass I read the Sunday papers.' Mass, said Br Andrew, would not do. Put that in an examination essay, and you might meet the prejudice of an examiner who would knock marks off. We were all sucklings of the Scarlet Woman. Write 'When I got home from church.' One lad, in a history essay, had referred to John Huss as 'a gross heretic', and this too was a dangerous confession of faith beleaguered. It was L. W. Dever who said that. Dever was a lay graduate of Liverpool University who joined the staff when we were in the Upper Fifth. Br Martin introduced him in a courtly manner, not without condescension, as though Dever, being new, lacked advantage. Dever was tall, fair-haired, with a head of Scandinavian shape: he probably had remote Dublin Danish ancestry. He did me a lot of good, especially in the Sixth Form. He introduced me to the work of James Joyce and Aldous Huxley. He also taught me to drink.

The most austere scholar on the staff was Br Cajetan, who had taken the name of one of the Vatican trouncers of Martin Luther.

We were not permitted instruction from him until we reached the Upper Fifth, since he was too learned to teach the elements of either Latin or mathematics, which were his specialities. He was an admirable pianist, and he also played football, turning out for the first eleven, since there was no staff team. I remember a town lout of a local side who observed to Br Cajetan that it was fucking parky today. Br Cajetan recoiled and agreed that it *was* rather cold. There was no tinge of the lubricious and not even a hint of the vulgar in his lessons. With him we studied the fourth book of the *Aeneid*, which is about Queen Dido of Carthage falling passionately for Aeneas, but he doused the flames in chill trickles of philology. He approved of my Latin prose exercises and went into a minor ecstasy at my phrase '*salvus pervenit*', which (pom-diddy pompom) had the echo of a Vergilian hexameter. When students had difficulties with accidence or syntax he put on a look of what James Burgess called puzzled pain. I let him down very badly when the school had a full-dress going-over from His Majesty's Inspectorate. The Latin inspector asked me for the dative singular of *genus*, and I could not remember it, though even the Irish louts did, calling out '*Genui*'. Br Cajetan writhed and moaned and gaped and nearly fell. These things will happen.

But Br Martin came in after the inspection and cried: 'Upper Five Alpha covered itself with glory.' This was because the history inspector, Dr Oast, who was dressed like an Edwardian cyclist, asked if anyone knew anything about Elizabethan music. I alone did, and I knew plenty. I threw Byrd and Weelkes and Orlando Gibbons at him, a composer for each of his supernumerary pockets, and informed him about the technique of the virginals. John Bull, Morley, Dowland: he got the lot. But he got nastily in with: 'And what precisely is the relevance of this superfluity of warbling and twanging to the graver aspects of your Elizabethan studies?' I replied to the effect that the history of a country was the history of its culture, and that the political and economic sides were a mere sustentive substructure. My Workers' Educational Association widow had not taught me that, but she had given me the vocabulary. Answering, I had a hard erection.

I gained my School Certificate in English Language and Literature, Latin, French, History, Art, Architecture, Mathematics, but not Physics. I blamed Br Sebastian for this, as well as his blackshirt pet Dowd. My interest in music had led me to at least a curiosity about Sound, but the Acoustics taught had been as shabby as the Heat and Light and Electricity. This was to be a problem later, since a qualification in physics was necessary for entry into the Manchester University Music Department. If I had passed in physics, I would probably have become a professional musician, instead of the doubtful amateur I still am. Still, I had gained passes in the five esssential subjects which officially matriculated me, and now my education could properly begin.

My father and stepmother naturally assumed it had ended. I was sixteen and I ought to be looking for a job, along with the other four million of Britain's unemployed. I had not been sheltered from the cries of the dispossessed in the greenery of Victoria Park. I regularly saw the undernourished beneficiaries of the dole and the means test, drab, thin, living on bread, and an egg every two days. The ravaged north-west was to become Orwell's world, matter for anger and idealistic programmes of reform, as well as terse hard prose. It seemed to me in my youth that the dole had to go far enough, since things were getting cheaper: canned Japanese salmon for a few pence, Indian cotton goods that competed murderously with the products of our own Lancashire mills, fags going down a halfpenny a packet. I did not realise that the dumping of cheap goods manufactured by unsyndicalised Oriental workers was one of our problems. I clearly needed more than the few pre- and postcoital lessons I had been given by my WEA widow. I saw the workers march, and they were not always the lantern-jawed troglodytes of *Metropolis*. They sometimes dressed in torn pierrot costumes and shambled over the cobbles in phalanxes, buzzing popular tunes through their kazoos or bazookas, with occasionally a tumbling girl student of a school of acrobatic dance doing the splits and flaunting her knickers in the van. We were safe in our wholesale tobacco store and our retail liquor shop. Drinking and smoking went on, a desperate solace. Men squatting at corners in Moss Side or Rusholme, shirtless, warmed by dirty scarves, shared a Wild Woodbine, clamping it at the end of the tunnel made by a loosely clenched fist, gasping in air as well as smoke and rendering the draw a stronger one.

The retail tobacconists we supplied were often cutting their prices, following what could be thought of as a healthy competitive urge. But this was not permitted by the city tobacconists' association, called the Raleigh Club. My father would send me, newly matriculated, to spy, armed with a shilling, demanding a packet of twenty Player's from some downhearted corner shop and getting as change not the legitimate halfpenny but three halfpence and sometimes twopence. The miscreant was reported, and a functionary of the Raleigh Club would issue the warning of a cessation of supplies. This was, I suppose, a dirty business, an officious interference with the free market. But any local left-wing politician, like Edwards of Lincroft Street, could argue against it only hypocritically, since the labour movement was committed to denouncing cheap goods.

The depression should have generated violence, but it did not. Ragged boys in gangs would pounce on the well-dressed, like myself, and grab ostentatious fountain pens. Their fathers did not have the energy for aggressive robbery, or even for loud protest. There seemed even to be a lack of sexual energy around. I remember a body of young women in their Sunday best high-heeling along Moss Lane East, singing 'Hold Your Hand Out, You Naughty Boy'. No naughty boys responded. Eddie Cantor pranced on the screens of the caverns of the dispirited afternoon cinemas, where the unemployed shared a Wild Woodbine and coughed. Other unemployed hired barrel organs as an accompaniment to a tired dancer who clacked the rickers or, in Chaplin bowler with stick, minced a trot or a corner brake. There were clog or molly (or morris) dancers, grim with their grimy festoons and bladder-bearing jester. Because of the lack of disorganised noise and the energy of rage, things looked less bad than they were. The Wilsons and the Tollitts and the Kemps did not suffer. They even took seaside holidays.

FOR LIFE WAS not all work and music and covert sex. Every year, almost as an act of discipline, I went to Blackpool or Cleveleys, Scarborough or Torquay. Sea air was therapy, and the sea air was most therapeutic on the northern coasts. Torquay and Bournemouth were posh and southern, but their breezes were relaxing and their hotel or boarding house dinner portions insufficient. Scarborough was fine, and occasionally the actor Charles Laughton served in his brother's hotel there; moreover it preserved with pride the wartime ruins of another hotel on the edge of the sea; the Germans had torpedoed it with gratuitous vindictiveness. But Scarborough was in Yorkshire, and my stepmother did not trust the people of the Ridings. 'If ever tha does aht for naht,' she would quote, 'do it for thisen.' That was the Yorkshireman's creed, along with 'Sup all and pay naht, 'ear all and say naht.' The Wars of the Roses went on, with an annual cricket battle at Old Trafford. The Lancashire coast was best, and there was no place like Blackpool.

True, and there never will be. As the Industrial Revolution began in Lancashire, so did the institution of the wakes week, when an entire mill or factory or even village would close down, the boilers cold and raked of their clinker, and the whole community go to Blackpool. It was, in one sense, not much of a change. You did not escape your regular co-workers and neighbours, but you saw them against a festive background, and that was change enough. The festive background was often provided by a pub, or a Yates's wine lodge, and that was little different from an evening back home, but there was more drinking and there were heartening fights with strangers, preferably slumming southerners. There were would be rows too with pub landlords over thinned beer or short measure. 'We've supped some stuff tonight' could be heard as feet stumbled up the boarding house stairs, and 'I did for the bugger'. Girls, too, got off with strangers in the Tower Ballroom. My stepmother had once got off, and her admirer had been ardent, but she dismissed the affair with 'It was only a seaside flirtation,' a literate not to say novelettish locution.

There was everything at Blackpool the holidaying heart could desire. There was sand with few pebbles, these being reserved to Cleveleys or Bispham a brief way up the coast, and the ozone raged like a Monsall ward sister. The sea was full of jellyfish, but the stinging and the screams were part of the fun. Vacationing workmen in full dark suits but no tie, handkerchiefs knotted on their scalps to ward off sunstroke, benevolently watched from deckchairs their kids demolish the sandcastles of other kids. They would ever and anon peer at ancestral turnip watches to see if the pubs were open yet. The men would meet in pubs men they met every day of the year in pubs less exotic; the women would sup port or sweet sherry in Yates's wine lodge, which made a real change. But there was much more to Blackpool than sandcastles for kids and booze for grown ups. There was Blackpool Tower, which was modelled on the Eiffel, and some could remember the Great Wheel, a revolving monster with benches that had proved unsafe and been demolished. At the base of the tower were a zoo and restaurants and bars and a ballroom. There was the Tower Cinema, where films were seen before they were seen in London, and there was the Tower Circus, complete with final aquacade. On the South Shore was an amusement park of large acreage,

with a Noah's Ark and Big Dipper. There were three piers, each
with a pierrot show at the end, and on the piers were slot
machines which gave a good return for a penny. One showed
the entire judgment, flogging and crucifixion of Jesus Christ,
though it omitted his resurrection. Lancashire pennies were hard-
earned and not to be spent lightly. At the box office of one pier
theatre or another could be heard: 'How much, missis? For two,
right, I can manage. What? *For bloody one?* You need your bloody
'eads seein' to.'

All along the landward side of the promenade were sideshows
and song booths. The music publishers – Lawrence Wright and
Connolly and Francis Day and Hunter – fought with each other,
seducing peeling holidaymakers in out of the sun to sing the
latest and buy the sheet music of what they had sung. Lawrence
Wright was the most energetic firm, and it was even in charge of
one of the pier shows, where evening dress was worn, not pierrot
pompoms, and love songs ended in burning kisses sustained till
the curtain fell. The songs sung were, of course, all published by
Lawrence Wright, who, under the name of Horatio Nicholls,
was also their composer. He composed 'Somewhere in Sahara'
and 'Deep in the Heart of the Sunset' and 'Shepherd of the Hills'
and 'Among My Souvenirs'. The ginger-haired master of cere-
monies, clad in a white coat as though song-plugging were a
surgical operation, would shout from his large fund of Lancashire
energy: 'And now – Colonel Barker's great song.' We giggled,
and then we seriously sang:

> WITH the parting OF the ways,
> You took ALL my happy days
> And left me lonely nights.
> Morning never comes too soon,
> I can FACE the afternoon –
> But oh THOSE lonely nights.

Colonel Barker was in the news at the time – the pseudonym of
a transvestite woman who had married an innocent girl. It was
assumed by an equally innocent public that there was a zero sexual
relationship, hence the lyric association. But we were all innocent
about lesbian sex. Radclyffe Hall's *The Well of Loneliness* had been
banned in 1929, but one of our fifth-form Anglo-Saxons swore
that his parents had a copy, and that the book was all about the
use of dildoes. (Joke of the period: Two maiden ladies ask a

greengrocer for two bananas. 'They're three for twopence, lady.'
– 'All right, we'll eat the other one.') It was assumed that, without
pseudo-penile penetration, lesbic nights were lonely.

Also in the news, though not at the same time, and to be seen
in person in a barrel on the promenade, was the Rector of Stiffkey
(which unfortunately was pronounced Stooky), who had been
involved in a sexual scandal that built up the circulation of the
News of the World to nine million. In the Rector's presbytery
were a number of girls who waited on him at table naked. One of
them was named Barbara Harris. In those days there was a
handsome coin called a half-crown (wantonly killed by the
decimal reformists of the 1970s), and it was serrated. There was
also a big penny which was not. A fifth-form quip was to ask
which one was Barbara Harris. The answer was the penny, because it had no nicks on. There was also a fifth-form rhyme:

> Under the spreading chestnut tree
> The Rector of Stiffkey sat,
> Amusing himself by abusing himself
> And watching it drip in his hat.

There was nothing to be seen in the Blackpool barrel but an
unfrocked clergyman reading the *Daily Express* and smoking a
cigar. Sacco the Starving Man did nothing either, but he had
clearly done, or neglected to do, something. There was also obscene art on display, in the shape of Epstein's *Genesis*. Epstein's
Rima in Regent's Park had been tarred and feathered, and the
same thing would have happened to his *Night and Day* on the
façade of the London Underground offices if anyone had been
able to get up there. *Genesis* was gaped at with awe as indecent art.
Indecency and vulgarity were all part of the Blackpool holiday.

But Blackpool was run by clever anonymous bodies which
were aware of their duty to at least a wisp of culture. The trams
were in the shape of beautiful Venetian gondolas, and they were
labelled, on one of my visits, with notices in Esperanto. At one
theatre you could see Somerset Maugham's *Rain*. The autumn
illuminations were lavish but tasteful. A lot of Blackpool's residents had posh accents, as though they were carpetbaggers from
the south, and there was a famous girls' school which promoted
the accent. The town was for Lancashire, but it constituted a sort
of extraterritorial enclave. There were even Jesuit priests in the
many Catholic churches, and they were intellectuals of the stamp

of the Holy Name. But they recognised that this was a pleasure resort, and they galloped their masses to get worshippers speedily on to the beach.

I never went to Blackpool alone. I was with one segment or other of the family – the Kemps or the Wilsons or the Tollitts (the Dwyer blood was there, if no longer the Dwyer name) – and sometimes two or more segments conjoined. We stayed at the smaller hotels, some termed 'private' since they served no drink, others with bars which were private in that they did not permit the public in. A private hotel really proclaimed in its title its conversion from a private residence to a lodging house that was too small to sustain the impersonality of a true hotel. You could tell it was really a house, since there was no reception desk and no elevator and, whether you wished it or not, you were involved in the family that ran it. I remember one in which the husband was a bearded patriarch who drove a tram, the conversion of which to a gondola he abhorred as a Scarlet Woman frippery. He could be seen praying deeply over his cooling dinner, and he would make cryptic remarks about sin in a hallway that had an odour of seaweed and stale breadcrumbs. When he was out steering his gondola the place was cosy and pally and rang with the clatter of buckets and spades and the yells of newly clouted overexcited kids. There was a front patio concreted over, with iron chairs on which you could sun and wait, rumbling, for the dinner gong. Meals were large in those days, and even breakfast had five courses – stewed fruit, porridge, fish, a mixed grill, and toast and marmalade. Still, one was always hungry. No air like Blackpool air. Sitting, one gave a penny to strolling entertainers dressed like Punchinello, who sang to a banjolele:

> Oh, Shinaniky Da,
> He play the guitar
> Outside the bazaar, bazaar, bazaar,
> While he strum his guitar,
> He puff a cigar
> And laugha da ha, ha ha, ha ha.

Lawrence Wright, or Horatio Nicholls, whose huge photograph blessed his booth like that of a pope of song, would have scorned to write that.

I was, though young, triply a step-uncle, and I had step-nephews and a step-niece to help watch over. Young Dan, I noted, made his beach castle by transporting sand from a spot many yards away from the structure, as though that were choice sand and the rest of an inferior quality. The kids yelled and pissed covertly in the sea and grew red and painful and ruined their milk teeth with Blackpool rock. I sat and read, progressively, *The Boys' Magazine, Radio Times, Lives of the Great Composers* (encouragingly unedifying), Ibsen's *Peer Gynt, Iphigenia* in the Thinker's Library, Schopenhauer. I would take the kids to South Shore and cool their terror by dissembling my own on the Big Dipper and through the Tunnel of Love, which, with its dangling skeletons and eldritch shrieks, proclaimed true Lancashire necrophilia. After dinner the kids subsided into a ten-hour death, and we elders went to dance in the cathedral called the Tower Ballroom. Here I would see rosy millgirls nudge each other at the prospect of getting off and, as smooth men approached, hear: "Ere they coom – watch thi haitches, lass.' Then we would go back to the Gradeleigh (for Gradely Folk) or the Alhambra or the Palms for a light meat supper and bed. My father, if he holidayed with us, would spend the evening at his usual pursuit. If the private hotel had a private bar, he would drink there and show a professional interest in the economy of the establishment. He foretold the end of one when he saw the head waiter pouring drinks with a fag in his mouth. Soft at the centre, couldn't last. Needless to say, this was not the place with the tram-driving patriarch.

My last family holiday on the Lancashire coast was, or could have been, disastrous. It was at a private hotel in Cleveleys, considered quieter and more refined than Blackpool, though only a mile or so away. I was with the Kemps and the Tollitts and, being seventeen, was probably too old for a family vacation. The cuisine was indifferent. The mistress of the house could not cook and served everything out of cans: there were not even fried eggs for breakfast. I smoked more than I ate: I was growing up now. At table we were waited on by a pretty blonde girl named Amy. Her, on her night out, I invited to the cinema and a sweet sherry or two after. We took the bus back (trams were disappearing) and kissed in my room, where two step-nephews lay like the sheeted dead. Amy was sweet and, I presumed, guileless. She smelled of vanilla and her mouth tasted of wallfruit. A girl's body in one's arms, its exciting nudity progressively disclosed: this has to be a figure of the male heaven. She invited me to spend the night in her room ('Come to me' was her phrase, like

Malvolio's) when the house stilled. I did, armed with the condom I now always carried in my wallet (a lesson learned from my WEA widow). I knew now how to delay climax: it was a matter of reciting Milton inly – 'High on a throne of royal state . . .' (*Paradise Lost*, Book Two). There is a Lancashire saying about physical love that beats all the poets: 'If God made owt better, he made it for hisself.' Her bed was narrow, cheap and creaking, bought from the same purse as the canned goods, apter for the placing of body on body than their companionable sundering. The act of love was renewed twice more, with interruption at climax, since no decent man or boy uses the same condom more than once. I crept from Amy's room at foredawn, naked, and met my host and her employer, a grey, dim man named Mr Clegg, coming from the toilet dressed and buttoning. I did not know why he was up so early: perhaps the Blackpool market operated a cut-price scheme for canned goods before the sun rose. We nodded at each other, he with vicarious balefulness: I was, after all, a paying guest; it was poor Amy who was going to suffer.

Amy was no virgin. Amy, who was two years older than I, had had her share of erotic experience. I had offered her nothing new: she was as well acquainted with the sexual repertory as my WEA widow. Still, I felt myself to be the seducer. To Mr Clegg, I said: 'I know what you're thinking. I got out of bed to go where you've just gone. But someone was in there, it was you as a matter of fact, so I was going back to bed. I went to the wrong room. Simple as that.'

'You're telling *me* you went to the wrong room, lad. And you're not the first. She's got to go.'

'But it was a mistake, I tell you.' Hands covering genitals.

'If it was a mistake, where's your pyjamas? Don't talk daft, lad. I'm not having no hanky panky here. She'll go quiet, and you'll keep quiet, and we'll get somebody else from t' Labour Exchange. Now get back to your bed. Your own bed, mind.' All this while, Amy, drugged with love, slept. I did not dare see her leave. I went out, clothed for seaside pleasure, as dawn came up to landward. The sea was bitter and writhing with jellyfish like outsize spermatozoa. I walked into Blackpool and breakfasted off tired fried eggs and a doorstep in a workman's caff. Having then no money for paid pleasures, I took free sun and freckled and peeled. I looked gloomily at the Donald McGill picture postcards: love ended up as this – fat red arses and henpecked men. At lunchtime I crept back to a canned lunch. Jack Tollitt was waiting for me. He knew all about it. Amy had been flaunting her shop window at him, he told me, meaning a low-cut bosom. It was a man she was after not a schoolkid. Clegg had got a cross-eyed duenna from the Labour Exchange: there would be no hanky panky there: she was serving the canned lunch at that very moment. But, Jack Tollitt added, I was not out of the wood, not by no manner of means. I would not be out of the wood for nine months, if I wanted plain speaking. Amy had packed her traps and buggered off, taking our address with her.

I got a love letter from Amy, and also a full-length studio photograph which made her look tarty and dumpy. In the thirties women were short-legged creatures, nothing like the postwar breed with, as vulgar men put it, legs going up to their arses. Only mannequins looked good in clothes, but they would be bicycles in bed. Naked, Amy had been ravishing. Her letter had what would later be termed a Barbara Cartland vocabulary. She apologised for her 'poisonous scrawl' and spoke of the 'estasy' of our encounter. On the back of her envelope she had lettered the conventional acronyms of passion: SWALK for 'sealed with a loving kiss'; ITALY for 'I trust and love you'; HOLLAND for 'hope our love lives and never dies'. Under her signature was a cross for a kiss, also BOLTOP: 'better on lips than on paper'. I was warned by my stepmother, who possessed vestigial wisdom in affairs of the heart, against writing back. But if I wrote back what could I say? I fearfully awaited other letters. Our postman came into our off-licence with his regular facetious 'Another Billy Ducks,' which my stepmother perverted in her turn to Tommy Duck's, the name of a well-known city pub. Another *billet doux* came from Amy, who was with her mother in Irlams o' th' Height (she apologised for the vulgarity of the toponym), and there was bitterness in it. I had taken advantage of her, sullied her purity and so on. There was no reference to the coming of a little stranger, thank God. I was ashamed. I was nostalgic for my WEA widow. There was a great divide between the joy of sex and its social implications. Eschatological too, Fr Myerscough would have added.

It was not to Fr Myerscough I confessed. It seemed appropriate to seek to be shriven in Blackpool, seat of the sin or very nearly, where I expected priests to be laxer in their judgment of seaside indiscretions. But I was thundered at in good Holy Name fashion and given a penance which ate up a great deal of the summer

evening. I found myself offering the penance to Amy, transformed for the purpose into the blue-clad, star-crowned Virgin
Mary. God, I was very nearly sure, did not care one way or the
other.

We do not learn our lesson. The priests would go out of business if we did. Sex is behovely, but no manner of thing shall be
well. The pleasure city of Blackpool, and even its refined annexes,
seethed with sex, as it had to. At eighteen it was thought better
that I should be sent alone for a holiday to the island of Anglesey,
off the coast of what is now called Gwynedd in North Wales. I,
with various members of the family and once, even, with my
Aunt Annie, had been to North Welsh seaside resorts and been
miserable in the rain while drinking in the health-giving ozone.
Llandudno, Colwyn Bay, Rhyl (where the beach had upright
wicker coffins instead of deck chairs) had made us long for
Blackpool and even Scarborough, but the dull clang of the bells
of the Welsh chapels reminded us that a vacation was a kind of
spiritual duty: we would be glad to get home again, starved,
oxygenated, sick of the lilting speech and the magicians' faces.
North Wales, or rather a steamer which sailed through the Menai
Straits, was the place where I had been vomited upon. I had seen
David Lloyd George on that steamer: Robert Graves was right
when he said he had the eyes of a sleepwalker. And then I leaned
over the taffrail to be sick, and a passenger on the upper deck was
sick all over my bowed head. A Welsh baptism. It was presumed
that I would celebrate no more pleasurable sacrament on the
island of Anglesey.

I was sent to a farm equidistant from Holyhead and Amlwch,
with no public transport available to either place of temptation.
The farm took in the odd holiday boarder, and I had a sitting-
room to myself as well as a double bed – a mockery really. The
farmer and his family spoke only the dialect of Welsh proper to
the north of the principality. The girl who waited on me was
named Selina. She was an intense, dark, handsome girl, or had
been before she lost all her front teeth in a motor-cycle accident.
She brought in whole joints of Welsh lamb and massive deep-
dish puddings, which I naturally assumed were all for me. In fact,
I was supposed to take my cut and send back the rest for the
family, but it was difficult to convey this in sign language. So I
ate monstrously, though not all: the family did not quite starve. I
needed solid nourishment to tackle Kant's *Critique of Pure Reason*
in a bad translation. I should have brought some poetry along to

sweeten the *a priori* categories, which I have never been able to swallow, but I was determined to write some poetry of my own. I achieved a sonnet which came, as I believed all poetry had to come, unbidden:

> I wrote on the beach, with a stick of salty wood,
>   'Our deeds are but as writings on the shore',
>   Believing it: I never thought them more
> Than prey for growling time: all ill, all good
> Were friable as sand. There where I stood,
>   The wild wind whistled, driving all before,
>   And the inexorable waves, with a damped roar,
> Strode on, like beasts that smell their living food.
>
> So I forgot. But, ages older grown,
>   Revisiting, I caught that distant day.
> The sands still stretched, without life and alone,
>   But from one spot the waves had sheered away,
> Fearful to touch it. There, as if on stone
>   Stark and clear-chiselled, that inscription lay.

A touch of Hopkins in the sprung rhythm of the first line, but the rest a mixture of Meredith and Shelley. I was doing my best, but it was not good enough. The intolerable wrestle with language, and so on, even though a lot of it was happening in the dark.

It was in the dark, among the sparse grass and sea holly, that Selina reminded me that language was not everything. She taught me to say *cariad*, which has a stronger impact on the Welsh nerves than 'sweetheart', and, armed with a whole set of six condoms, which she called *ffrens leters*, I sailed confidently into my first, but far from last, encounter with a Welsh girl. Selina held up all her fingers twice to show her age, as if to confirm that no crime against the state was to be committed. Her ardency was of an order not much found among the Anglo-Saxons. The lack of front teeth rendered her kisses softer, but, teeth or not, she could bite, probably with intact premolars. It was a warm night, and we were near enough naked, though not entirely. At the moment of the second climax I had some mad notion that this should properly be confessed in Welsh, but the only Welsh I knew was *cariad*. The Welsh are a different breed of Celt from the Irish and Scots. They have never learned to distil a spirituous liquor; they drink, when they drink at all, thin bitter beer. Their vice is sex, which the fuddled Scots and Irish practise only enough to keep the race going, and this vice is vigorously denounced in their chapels. The denunciations are enjoyed by sinning aficionados of the *hwyl*, or melody of rhetoric, especially when a woman taken in adultery is made to kneel in the aisle for a particularised attack. The male adulterer sits smug, virtually exonerated, since it is confirmed for him from the pulpit that sexual sin is Eve's monopoly. I knew nothing of this while I writhed with Selina, who could no longer bite an apple. But I sensed that I was meeting an alien culture. Selina would not be fired, nor would she write me letters. We were preaching to each other the unimportance of verbal communication.

I ANTICIPATE. THIS had not yet happened when, a matriculate, I looked vainly for a job. I was underqualified for everything higher than the post of errand boy, and for that, knowing some French and Latin and the difference between synecdoche and metonymy, I was overqualified. I did errands for Wilson's unpaid, so that was outside the job covenant, and I stacked bottles in our off-licence, which was a quasi-domestic chore, but I was officially idle. I was not one of the unemployed to be pitied, since I had never been employed. Fr George Dwyer came from Rome to visit us and told his Aunt Maggie that I ought to push on with my education. My Latin, he said, would be wasted unless it got beyond the *Gallic Wars*. He worried my stepmother because he smoked cigarettes stuck on a pin. This looked like the indigence of one who cannot afford to waste the last half-inch, but it was the fashion among priests in Rome, since it kept the sacramental fingers clean of tobacco tar. She did not know what the Gallic Wars were, but she was refreshed by Fr George in her sense of the magic of Latin, a sense which had been long in abeyance, for customers scoffed at my attainment in it and said: 'Let's see if he can draw some beeribus into that juggibus.' I was to go back to school, then, and enter the Sixth Form and learn more Latin. I would study for the Higher School Certificate and perhaps become a reporter for the *Manchester Evening News*. Latin would be useful when I went to report on inquests and post-mortems. My stepmother, like my stepsisters, believed that doctors were expert in Latin. They were a sort of counterpart of priests.

So I went back to school, though it was no longer quite like school. My classroom was the fine old library, all oak and Chinese vases, with wistaria tapping at the windows. It was an adult ambience, and we had to learn to adjust to it. Oswald Dewhurst, who had been one of the Fifth Form veterans and previously outside my social sphere, was slow in his adjustment. He pissed in one of the Chinese vases and, emptying it to applause on to the wistaria, broke its rim. This we all helped to mend laboriously with seccotine, fearful nevertheless that the sharp Irish eye of Br Martin would spot the fracture and even divine its history, though he was in America at the time, screwing Mae West as we said in our desperate innocence. There was also an unworthy search for ancient dirty books on the shelves of the library, but everything was clean and Irish. The real adjustment we had to make was in the matter of headgear. I had been waiting for the bus on Moss Lane East (the old 53 trams had disappeared) with my school cap on, and a little girl said in wonder: 'Fancy a man wearing a Blue Hat. I have never seen a man wearing a Blue Hat before.' From then on I knew I had to go bareheaded. Oswald Dewhurst, the pissing in the vase clearly his last adolescent fling, took to a grey trilby.

There were not many of us in the Sixth Form: there was plenty of room around the great oak table. Eric Williams and James Burgess were there, but they were not sure why. Burgess did not wish to study for the Higher School Certificate, but Br Martin, his bags packed for America, spoke loftily to him of the importance of General Culture, and Burgess put GC after his name. Michael Callaghan was there, waiting to become a student teacher and earning the odd shilling as organist at the Holy Name, but he had shot his academic bolt with the School Certificate. Asked to write an essay about Milton in terms of the quotation 'Thy soul was like a star and dwelt apart', he argued about Milton's being a recluse and concluded that he was not. He had, said Br Andrew, somehow missed the point. I did not do much better when told to discuss the Platonic content of Wordsworth's 'Ode on Intimations of Immortality'. I wrote about the irrelevance of analysis to the aesthetic experience and denied the validity of the task set.

I could not, however, deny that bald and stone-eyed Plato was entering our lives. He was there, on one of the bookcases, contemplating universals. Socrates was there too, just behind him. These philosophers had proved the immortality of the soul. One of the Platonic dialogues had foretold the coming of Christ, a man so good that he would appear bad and have to be scourged and crucified for it. Vergil too, so Br Cajetan told us, had prophesied the Messiah, and he read out the lines from the appropriate Eclogue. These classical prognostics were worrying to me, for I was beginning to lose my faith.

Loss of faith shows as a syndrome. Many symptoms come together and add up to it. One sympton may be sheer slugabed laziness, an unwillingness to get up early on Sunday and go to mass, an indication that sleep is more important than the renewal of the divine sacrifice. Another may be the putting off of confession because of the weariness of being railed at for sexual sin. My growing disillusionment with the Catholic Church had more to do with aesthetics than with doctrine. I had, on the previous May Sunday, attended the crowning of the statue of the Virgin Mary at the Holy Name. A highly intellectual Jesuit preached about the immorality of Liszt and Wagner and the incapacity of the glory of their music to redeem their habitual sinfulness – a sermon irrelevant to the occasion and not well understood by the congregation. They were met not to be preached at but to assist at a highly pagan ceremony, all spring flowers and candles. A little girl dressed as the May Queen placed a chaplet of daisies on the head of the Madonna. The women were wet-eyed and sang 'Daily, daily, sing to Mary, sing, my soul, her praises due', also 'Let us mingle together, voices joyful and glad, singing hymns to our Mother . . .' There was, after all, some point to that Sermon. God hated art. I had just read about Sir Edward Elgar's response to the atrocious first performance of *The Dream of Gerontius*. God had been against it, God had flattened the basses and sharpened the sopranos and made a *Schweinerei* of a great mystical tribute to his love and justice. Elgar, so Br Cajetan informed us, was not a good Catholic. But Elgar delivered the ecstatic goods, and good Catholics didn't.

Good Catholics sang an atrocious mass at St Edward's, the little church separated from the gates of the Xaverian College by walled ash trees, on the branches of one of which a white owl sometimes stared like Plato. The habit of taking the same bus six days a week (for Saturday had a working morning) induced the inertia of making the same trip on the seventh. Though not in the parish, I made St Edward's my mass centre. It was a detestable little church, in which people always seemed to be farting, especially on warm days. The frank loud fart was technically known as a 'bare foot un', while the more subdued variety was called a 'stocking-feeter'. An old man took the plate round at the offertory, and, if the contributions seemed too meagre, he would pass the plate along the pew once more. I detested equally the canon and his gormless curate. The canon would preach mainly about money, saying that he wanted to hear, at today's second collection for an unnamed cause, not the clink of coins but the rustle of banknotes. I went accidentally once to an early children's service, and he preached about God loving poor boys more than rich, with a meaningful glare or two in the direction of myself, who had but a bare penny in my kex pocket. His curate gave ridiculous sermons about Christ the bridegroom and us the brides, in a Cork accent thick as butter. He censored Holy Writ, which was too bold for him. 'Blessed be the womb that bore thee, and the paps that gave thee suck' was cleansed, though even then doubtfully, with 'breasts'.

It was laziness, not masochism, that sent me to the last mass, which was always a sung one. It was basely sentimental, stickily chromatic, and the only stop the organist knew was the vox humana. The girl who sang nasally the *Agnus Dei* – crooned it rather in Bing Crosby style – I could have punitively raped. I had been taught that the beautiful was an aspect of the divine nature, and here was beauty being denied. But I was a snob, and democratic God detested snobs. He liked the Men's Confraternity and the Knights of St Columba and the Children of Mary, who went to the altar rail with back tippets shaped like a V to show they were virgins. God liked his children to have a good innocent time with not too much thinking. Good taste was no aspect of ultimate reality. Vulgarity meant the vulgus, for whom St Jerome had prepared the Vulgate.

My way out was to attend regularly some austere early mass without trimmings, make my Easter duty, confess my sins and be stoical at sacerdotal abuse. But L. W. Dever was teaching us European History, and we were learning about the Reformation not from propagandist primers but from disinterested historians like H. A. L. Fisher. My heart warmed to Martin Luther, and I even began, some decades before John Osborne, to write a play about him. It was a verse play, and it was meant, on the technical level, to exemplify a theory I had that blank verse was really tetrametric with a supernumerary beat and three implied rests after it. Luther was clearly neither mad nor a fool, and he was right to thunder for reform. I also wanted reform. The basic Christian tenets were unassailable, but the superstructure had gone wrong. I could not become a Lutheran, since that would mean becoming a German, and I could not be a Calvinist or a Zwinglian either. I could not found a church solely for myself. I needed the Eucharist, and I had no power to transubstantiate. But perhaps transubstantiation was not necessary: Luther had established consubstantiation, and there were Christians around who denied that the sacrament was more than a ceremony of commemoration. But there were the words of Christ, boldly cannibalistic, and they were as unequivocal in the Vulgate as in the Douai New Testament. St Augustine seemed to offer a solution: *'Cur preparatis dentes ac ventrum? Credite et manducastis.'* Believe, and ye have eaten. Could I then take a sip of port and a morsel of Crusty Bread alone in my bedroom and, believing these were Christ, truly swallow his substance? Protestants confessed only to God; could I do that? Were the sacraments all that necessary?

I carried my worries to the Holy Name and a private interview with Fr Myerscough. I was innocent enough to expect his sympathy and even his blessing on my desire to be an extra-ecclesial Catholic. When I said that the sacraments seemed to me to be a superficial excrescence on the faith, which was essentially about love and right living, he blew up and cried 'Heresy'. He seriously enjoined me to give up for the moment my schoolwork and spend all my time praying for grace. Then he sent me away. Afterwards, I heard, he told somebody that it was a sad business, a matter of 'little Wilson and big God'. I prayed for grace, but big God was at some major archangelical conference and had no time for little Wilson. L. W. Dever was sympathetic but too discreet to proffer advice. He was young, he was lay, he was clearly worldly, he had betrayed tones of irony when presenting the case of the Church against Luther, but he could do no more than tell me to read. Read what? Well, for a start, read James Joyce's *A Portrait of the Artist as a Young Man.* So I bought this for three shillings and sixpence in the Jonathan Cape Traveller's Library edition and read it. The modernism did not deter me. It was not John Galsworthy; it was something better. I, who had read the score of *Le Sacre du Printemps*, was not likely to be put off by literary experiment. 'Once upon a time, and a very good time it was, there was a moocow coming down the road.' Brilliant: childhood direct. But when I came to the school retreat and the two sermons on hell I found myself outside literature. I was terrified. Ironically, against the aesthetic canons that were so eloquently expressed by Stephen Dedalus, I found the power of the novel was wholly didactic. I ran to the confessional, poured out my sins of doubt almost sobbing, and received kind absolution and a nugatory penance. I went to mass with my missal, reading the *Dies Irae* moaning, calling on Christ, *fons pietatis*, to drench me in his mercy. I do not know whether L. W. Dever intended my reading of Joyce to have this effect.

I suppose the pattern of apostasy usually runs in this manner. One doubts openly, is scared back to conformity, and then, at a purely unconscious level, is slowly divested of the peel of faith. I had conceived a devotion to the poetry of Gerard Manley Hopkins, and this was to help to hold the faith for me as a mere poetic *donnée*, its ontology carried in suspension, since it was the aesthetic transport that counted. Reading 'The Windhover', I both believed and did not believe, and belief anyway was irrelevant. I was not frightened of Hopkins's Jesuitry, since it was modified – and, I guessed, impaired – by the impulse of a poetic imagination too large to be enclosed by sectarianism. Soon I would be able to tiptoe back to *A Portrait* and take it entirely as a work of literature.

It seemed to me that we all, not just I, needed to think, and not in the way of the 'Think, boy, *think*' of the classroom. We had none of us got down to first principles; we knew no metaphysics. Br Cajetan, with rare jocosity, had recited a rhyme in some connection now forgotten:

> There once was a metaphysician
>   Who proved that he didn't exist.
> When others had learned his position,
>   They said that he wouldn't be missed.

If metaphysicians could even jocularly be thought of as demonstrating such fundamentals, they deserved to be looked at. We met names like Descartes, Spinoza, Leibniz and Hegel in our reading of literary criticism; now was the time to meet as much of their substance as our chained minds could take in. Perhaps we – I rather – would discover that the chains were a human necessity, or an illusion, or a metaphor for freedom. I put to Br Andrew, our form master, the proposal that we form an upper school philosophical society. He agreed, so long as it could be literary as well. I suggested it be called the Cosmos Society, not to be confused with the Kosmo Club, a shady confraternity in Pendleton which had recently been raided by the police. The poster for the first meeting had a quotation from *Henry VIII*:

> Only they
> Who come to hear a merry bawdy play,
> A noise of targets, or to see a fellow
> In a long motley coat guarded with yellow,
> Will be deceived . . .

It was typical of my orientation that I should take that not directly from Shakespeare but from Robert Schumann when he was announcing a new musical journal.

Br Andrew defused the project, which I had envisaged as radical and dangerous, by giving the opening talk, which was on John Galsworthy. It was a paper really, well prepared and expertly delivered, and it was unintentionally more dangerous than any argument for atheism would have been, since it confirmed for the intelligent that literature lay elsewhere than in Galsworthy – in sex-ridden Lawrence and Church-mocking Joyce and obscene Aldous Huxley. But a fortnight later I gave my lecture on basic metaphysics, and this had two effects: it made the superficial argue about the meanings of 'here' and 'there', thus in a manner foreshadowing the linguistic philosophers; it drove any religious waverers there might have been in the audience back into the arms of the faith. I opened the door to the howling wind of scepticism, and everybody called on God to shut it. They wanted Catholic cosiness, not metaphysical rigour. I had taken my facts and arguments from a primer in the Thinker's Library, and they were pretty elementary, suitable for the WEA. The trouble was that a first cause kept poking its great wet snout in, and once you had a first cause everything else followed – infant baptism, Limbo, Ember Days, Friday abstinence. During the course of my lecture I was astonished to hear myself saying – it was as involuntary as a belch – that the Church was the enemy of free thought. My apostasy had come out into the open. I would be in trouble when Br Martin got back from America.

Once you have made a public declaration it is very difficult for you to retreat from it. I had nailed not ninety-two theses to the church door but a simple statement capable of two interpretations. Free thought could be a bad thing, after all, even an absurd thing, and the Church was right to oppose it. Unfortunately I was misrepresented. I had, it was alleged, said that the Church was the enemy *tout court*. Not even James Burgess said that when, a few weeks later, he gave a talk on the necessity of communism, meaning the rather mild socialism of *The Ragged Trousered Philanthropists*. Later we had a debate in which, following the Oxford Union, the house refused under any circumstances to fight for its king and country. I proposed the motion, and it was heavily defeated by all those Irish Catholics. When the arguments from the floor degenerated into wrangles about the respective merits of the bands of Joe Loss and Harry Roy, I knew that nobody really wanted thought.

Everybody wanted sex, or jokes about it. 'What's the biggest drawback in the world? King Kong's foreskin.' Mae West made sex humorous, not intense:

> So you're Mr Hore-Belisha.
>   Your name's as famous as mine.
> If your balls are as big as your beacons,
>   You can come up and see me sometime.

Literature was full of humorous sex too, not like Galsworthy. I had a three-and-sixpenny collected Shakespeare, and it was not all like *Julius Caesar*. There was *Measure for Measure*, with Pompey Bum and 'What's he done?' – 'A woman' and 'groping for trout in a peculiar river'. Then James Burgess disappeared and came back, a visitor, to announce the Laurentian novel he was writing (the one with laughter that was like a pigeon pissing in a milk can), and a twenty-one-year-old named Frank Lundy used the Sixth Form as his daily club while awaiting admission to Strawberry Hill. Michael Callaghan reported on his student-teaching. A school inspector entered the classroom with his hat on and asked what he had done wrong. Nobody knew. Come, come, what's the first thing your father does when he comes home? Please, sir, he pees in the sink. One boy missed school because his mother had caught her titty in the mangle. It was a fine life of innocent bawdry, and we smoked between classes. Frank Lundy had a cigarette case in which dimps were ranged like organ pipes. That, he said, was the Simmary way. The poor Irish never smoked a fag to the limit. He was learning the *mores* in advance. Then Br Martin returned from America.

He was still a Xaverian brother, but he looked like an American Xaverian brother, whatever an American Xaverian brother looked like. His soutane was of a brisker cut, and his clerical collar was narrower. He had met Mae West, he said, and she was a fine woman. And then he said, with a steely American eye and a Hollywood British intonation: 'You, Wilson, are having religious difficulties. Come to my study, boy.' He offered me a tumbler of New York State champagne and burbled about the beauty of Christ's love. 'Read Renan,' he said. 'But,' he added, 'not yet.' And then, with disarming American frankness, 'First things first. Take your Higher School Certificate. Get high marks. Everything depends on you. It is a considerable experiment, and it has to work. The honour of the school depends on it. It is a two-year course, we know, but you are to sit at the end of one. And you are to gain a State Scholarship.' He had forgotten all about the religious difficulties. Time was money.

There was no hope of my winning a State Scholarship, nor a Manchester Corporation one either. He had a go-getting dream. The Xaverian College, despised because Catholic, would beat all the big educational establishments, including even Manchester Grammar School, by entering students with insolent prematurity for an examination the Protestant teaching establishment would say they had no hope of passing. If even one candidate got through it would prove some point or other – probably the eccentric brilliance of Br Martin CFX. It might also win a bet. If Fr Fitzjames, on the evidence of his confessional reading, was a punting man, why should not a man in minor orders be so too? Br Martin had told us, in morning assembly, that there was only one way of following horses with success, and he had gone into a mime of shovelling aromatic dung. But that had probably been the humorous despondency of one who had come a cropper in the Manchester November Handicap. He was backing me now, though at long odds. I had to go into heavy training, and the American hell with my religious problems. I did not think he could be serious about the State Scholarship – highly competitive; out of our, or my, league. But one had to allow for the extravagance of his Irish fancy.

So I ground away at Pliny's Letters and Vergil Book Six, at seventeenth-century English History and Modern European (meaning for me mostly the Reformation), at Shakespeare and the Romantics and the Book of Job. And in high hot summer, with the tar pure treacle on the streets of central Manchester, I went to the neutral territory of a school on Portland Street where all scholarship candidates had to go. The heat was equatorial. Manchester has a monsoon climate, and the rains break for the

Test Matches. I had been given money for two pork chops at a Lyons restaurant, but the lunchtime waitress implored me to have cold sausage and salad. The kitchen fires had been doused.

I was fired into vigorous writing by sexual bitterness. For our invigilatrix was my WEA widow, earning a little daytime money by giving out the papers and watching for cheaters. She shot me no glance of sexual complicity as I came in. She bestowed the Hopkinsian sake of her odour as she came by with English Literature I, but she did not seem to recognise her old pupil in love. I groaned over my erection and then subdued it with the Book of Job. 'Hast thou not poured me out like milk and curdled me like cheese?' represented a tradition of homely imagery rejected by the Romantics but revived by Hopkins. Compare the sonnet sestet beginning 'I am gall, I am heartburn.' But perhaps, like Br Andrew, the examiners did not know Hopkins.

With the examination over, it was time to bring out the school magazine. *The Alpha* had long folded. The final issue had been a cyclostyled one of thirty copies, and it had been both composed and processed on a single Wednesday afternoon and evening. It lacked panache and it betrayed hurry. I had scamped homework and was told by Miss Gray that a class magazine was a very secondary matter compared with Euclid. I was discouraged and gave up editorship. The school magazine was Br Andrew's responsibility, and it was full of group photographs and sports results. I contributed a triolet:

> The strain of waiting for results
> Is more than any man can stand;
> It ages children to adults,
> The strain of waiting for results.
> 'Mention? Or space that just insults?'
> Turns in the brain on hand and hand.
> The strain of waiting for results . . .

But there was a long time still to wait. We had the Sixth Form dinner, for which, as treasurer, I had been collecting money for a year. It was a great spread, and I wrote the menu in Latin, with coffee as *kupha*, a Modern Greek borrowing from the Turkish. Br Alphonsus, the former West End chef, poached a whole salmon or *salmo* in a classical sauce. There were *fraga* (no known singular) *cum flore lactis*. And there was *vinum merum Californiense* which got us drunk. Then we took the bus to the Palace Theatre to see and hear Harry Roy and his band and be rebuked by a soberer public. Then came the summer vacation.

My stepmother had been for a long time grumbling about work that was killing her and ending with the refrain: 'Never mind, Johnny, some day we shall 'ave our little 'ouse.' It was a prospect that seemed to exclude my father. I did not really believe that she proposed retiring from a business whose trials and gossip were her life, but in the summer of 1934 she proved that the refrain was not a mere canticle of hoped for deliverance. We left 261 Moss Lane East, handing over to a surprisingly arty bachelor with a boy friend and a grand piano. Nowadays we would have sighted at once the relationship, but we were innocent then about sexual inversion. This was in spite of the big Altrincham scandal, in which low working men wrote passionate letters to lipsticked lads. 'I love you, Frank, and when I pulled your nicks off satday night you was bloody wonderful.' This sort of thing got into the *News of the World*. We in the Sixth Form were incredulous, proving that the Xaverian College had preserved our innocence well: despite the boarders it clearly lay outside the British tradition. But Bernard Dunne had left school to become a policeman, and on his uniformed visits back to the Sixth Form he affirmed that things went on in Manchester, let along Altrincham, which would make our hair horrent. He was a highly literate policeman who was planning a novel called *Just A Copper*. He believed that I had a profound knowledge of professional football and, when I disavowed this, would laugh heartily and call me a bloody liar. He would sing with me, helmet on and hands in belt, a duet I had composed, a setting of the opening lines of Dryden's *Absalom and Achitophel*:

> In pious times, ere priestcraft did begin,
> Before polygamy was made a sin,
> When man on many multiplied his kind,
> Ere one to one was cursedly confined . . .

Polygamy? There was plenty of that around. Well, bigamy mostly. There was an old Colne custom of placing a broom outside the door when the husband was away, to show the wife was available for adultery, and this had been imported to eastern Manchester. Every father in Longsight shagged his daughters on the corner of the kitchen table at Saturday throwing-out time. Incest, that was called. As for buggery – one man had been had up on a charge of copulating with a pig. Dunne knew them all. He had been wavering in his belief in God, but he had been brought back to him through evidence of the existence of his opposite. His desk sergeant was a devout and bigoted Calvinistic Methodist. Law and order required eschatological sanctions, a kind of Erastianism. Theological wrangles in the nick. Dunne left the force and took orders. It was a logical move.

Anyway, we handed over the off-licence to the man with the boy friend and the grand piano (you can guess what they use that for, said Dunne later, darkly) and moved to a rented semi-detached red-brick box on Leabrook Road in Fallowfield. It was terribly suburban, horribly clean and quiet. It was like Chorlton-cum-Hardy, where Williams lived, but it did not have the *cachet* of that cut-glass *rus in urbe*. An abstract space had been imposed on the long fallow land. It you wanted trees, you had to plant your own, and they took a long time to grow. You could eat your dinner off the road. Here, in this unnatural salubrity, my stepmother and I sat and looked at each other, and neither much liked what the other saw. I planted rose bushes and manured them with pony dung. I tied them to their trellis and watched a gale, unimpeded by arboreal breaks, tear at them. I wrote:

> Wind, you may your gustiest blow.
> But never these weak knots undo.
> Though the land with leaves you strew . . .

I forget the rest. The theme was that man's soul was knotty and could not be disnoded by the winds of death. I had lost my Catholic faith but still wanted my immortality. I had to decide now what the immortality was to be filled with. It was probably a Platonic reality of which this world was a copy. Beauty was the reality, since truth was an ontological proposition without substance, and goodness was the essence of ethical relationships, which did not exist in eternity. I was learning all about beauty, though not from my stepmother.

I had a little library now. My stepmother had even agreed to my buying a ten-shilling bookcase. I had all my school texts, my Everyman *Don Quixote*, and certain book bargains connected with newspaper subscriptions. There were the collected plays of Bernard Shaw, and also a dozen sociological novels by H. G. Wells in rough red bindings. Among these was *The Soul of a Bishop*, which was about an Anglican cleric losing his faith. The bishop came to the decision to give up his church and his gaiters while standing in his club under a bust of John Wilson Croker. There was my name, and this was as good a directive as any to apostatise, though L. W. Dever said that was sheer superstition. My physical substance was not happy about the changes taking place in my soul, and I grew thin and had to be nourished with Glucose D. I developed an ulcerated throat, and my stepmother prescribed gargles with chloride of lime. I had migraine headaches, during which I saw visions of battlements or had the illusion that a ship's prow was cutting into my frontal lobes. Then I vomited.

I say that I lost my faith, but really I was no more than a lapsed Catholic, as boring a figure as the stage Irishman and sometimes the same figure. What makes him a bore is his lachrymosity, especially in drink, about being a bad son who has struck his mother and dare not go home. There is also the matter, also in his cups, of claiming to belong to an international club to which he will not pay his subscription (this, in the form of obligatory communion, falls due every Easter). Yet the claim is not entirely false; indeed, it does not go far enough. For Catholicism is, in a paradox, a bigger thing than the faith. It is a kind of nationality one is stuck with for ever. Or, rather, a supranationality that makes one despise small patriotisms. A lapsed Catholic feels he has a right to sneer at devout Anglicans and Presbyterians. In Stephen Dedalus's words, he has rejected a logical absurdity, and he can feel nothing but contempt for an illogical one. Again, the Catholic Church, since it preaches a philosophy as well as a theology, leaves the renegade with certain convictions that he does not have to square with religious belief. In the Augustinian–Pelagian controversy which, in one form or another, still rages, he is on the side of St Augustine. He accepts the doctrine of original sin because history shows this to be more realistic than the liberal, or Pelagian, image of humanity, as at best, good, at worst neutral. He rejects determinism and accepts free will. So did the British heretic Pelagius, but he posited a *liberum arbitrium* unqualified by the inherited taint of evil. In the moral sphere, the lapsed Catholic will tend to maintain that we are totally responsible for our actions and can blame neither environment nor a genetic endowment when we do wrong. We can, of course, blame original sin, but it is a primary human duty to recognise its prompting and regard it as an inalienable heritage, like the capacity for speech. The lapsed Catholic is neither an optimist nor a pessimist. He is a realist and very wary of utopian politicians.

In old age I look back on various attempts to cancel my apostasy and become reconciled to the Church again. This is because I have found no metaphysical substitute for it. Marxism will not do, nor will the kind of sceptical humanism that Montaigne taught. I know of no other organisation that can both explain evil and, theoretically at least, brandish arms against it. The Church has let its children down too often to be regarded as a good mother, but it is the only mother we have. During the time of my cutting the cord, or untying the apron strings, she increasingly took on the role of an unsympathetic stepmother. She had her grotesque counterpart at Number 2 Leabrook Road, with her sign of the cross and 'Glory be to God' when it thundered. There, I knew, was a woman destined for heaven.

My father said 'When you snuff it you're finished with,' and Winston Churchill, more elegantly, spoke of an eternity of black velvet. I clung to a homemade eschatology. It was not really eccentric, this belief in the immortality of the soul, since J. W. Dunne, with his serial universe, propounded it pseudo-scientifically. He spoke of psycho-neural parallelism, with a dissolution of part of the brain finding a kind of spiritual correspondence in the death of its psychic counterpart, but no possibility of the destruction of the ego, since that had no physical location. But what did the immortal ego do with itself? This was never made clear. In my adolescent view it contemplated beauty. You could demolish the beautiful, but not its essence. I started, but did not finish, a bad ode to a landscape:

> Sweet scene,
> What though men tear
> And blast your living green?
> I have small care:
> It is enough that you should once have been.

You built up your eternal datum of beauty out of the transiently beautiful. Beethoven's symphonies were a witness to the undying beauty they imitated. I could imagine a sort of Ninth Symphony going on for ever in the other world, immensely complex but, by a mystical paradox, also intensely simple. Then I saw that this symphony might be God, the Ninth listening to itself, and I drove the image away with an attack of migraine.

I was a bad poet, and my badness was confirmed by my

winning first prize in a free verse competition organised by the
Manchester Lyric Club. It was a prize of three authographed books
– *Songs of a Sourdough*, by Robert W. Service, *Song of a Sailorman*,
by Eden Phillpotts, and the song of somebody else by somebody
else. I sent a sonnet to the *Sunday Times*, which sent it back:

> Calm lies our harbour, while the maiden day
>   Leans forth her arms to night and bids it go,
>   Smiling, and waits to wake with gentlest glow
> Quayside and sea, and tall gaunt ships that sway.
> I wait no longer now: wide lies the way,
>   Unsure, uncharted. Only this I know:
>   That sea has dubious currents, tides that flow
> Frustrating all the havened ancients say . . .

I wrote that when my examination results appeared. I had passed,
though I had gained no scholarship. Nobody else had passed, but
Br Martin had probably won his bet. I saw myself as having
completed my education, though I felt uneducated enough, and
again looking for a job. But all I knew was more Latin than
before, as well as an ability to compare the imagery of Hopkins
with that of the Book of Job. I knew most of Hopkins by heart,
and still do. When Lord Alfred Douglas, a rather worse sonneteer
than myself, wrote to the *Sunday Times* complaining that Hopkins
did not scan, I was able to submit a letter explaining sprung
rhythm to the pederastic fool. In other words, I was less qualified
for a job than I had been a year earier.

But Br Martin was stern with my father. He called him in,
gave him a glass of Cork gin and water, and said it would be a
sin against the Holy Ghost if I did not go to a university. He was
convinced, he said, that another year of work for the Higher
School Certificate would secure me at least a Corporation scholarship. It was a matter of my gaining three distinctions. I already
had three passes. It was in the logic of things that I should do
better. He seemed to leave out of account that the set books would
be different. Still, even if I had to study Tacitus instead of Pliny, I
was bound to know more Latin after another year. My father
submitted, my stepmother was mystified. I went back to school.

IT WAS NOT the same as it had been before. The oak table had been removed, and pinewood desks had been installed. Br Martin was taking Sixth Form education seriously. I was among raw boys from an Upper Fifth of strangers, including a fat lout named Beasley who was called Kong. I wanted to rebel, and the only subversive act I could think of was an insistence that I take Music at the advanced level and not History. This was not a reflection on L. W. Dever's teaching. I felt I knew music well enough not to have to work hard at it. There were three scores to study – Haydn's *Creation*, Schubert's 'Trout' Quintet, and Brahm's Second Symphony. There was reduction of a few orchestral bars to a piano version, basic musical history, the setting of a poem, elementary harmony. There was immense doubt about my proposal in the high echelons – they knew nothing of my musical attainments; there was nobody to instruct me – but I had my way. As public proof of my ability, I composed a Prelude and Fugue in D minor in the style of Bach. Bach was a challenge but also a comfort. He was, some said, the very voice of Lutheranism; he was even called the fifth evangelist. Playing him, I felt revolt against Rome in my very fingers. Callaghan played my Bachian composition at a school concert. It was a sort of double defiance.

It was still 1934, and Germany was more than Luther and Bach and a defected enemy. On July 25 Dollfuss was murdered by Austrian Nazis. On August 2 Hindenburg died and Hitler became dictator. We were not, as Protestant schools were, removed from the events. For there came to us a good Catholic boy from Munich called Böll (no relation to Heinrich). He was a cropped caricature but not aggressive. He was polite and highly pacific. But he was forced into fighting on two fronts. One was represented by the blackshirt Dowd, who thought highly of Hitler, while Böll considered him an atheistic clown whom a German Catholic Pilgrimage of Grace would soon demolish. The other front was embodied in a French lad named Schmitt, who came from Alsace and had family and even ancestral cause against Germany. But Schmitt also detested Dowd, because Schmitt was given to a Catholic version of communism. It was very curious to see these three together. Böll would half-heartedly punch at Schmitt or Dowd, and then these two would punch at each other. Tired, they would then punch at Böll, who retreated, settling his glasses on his nose and speaking regretful English in the regretful cadences of German.

Böll gave us false comfort about the Nazi menace. He was

more concerned about the wreckage of my soul than that of his country. He regretted that I did not go to the *Abendmahl* (a word I had learned from trying to translate Schoenberg's *Pierrot Lunaire*) and warned me of hell. *Die Hölle*, with its fluting vowel and clear L, did not sound too bad. But it was the same hell as the one in Manchester and Dublin, frying away with the same sizzle in distant Bavaria. Catholic meant universal. I had not just quitted the Holy Name; I had resigned from the universe. Walking Rusholme with Böll, I began to feel atrocious pains in my bowels like Martin Luther himself. Böll, with heavy acuity, stated that I had permitted a *Teufel* in my *Eingeweide* to *wohnen*, and the *Eingeweide* were anatomically very close to the *Geschlechtsteile* or genitals, and it was the devil of sex that had persuaded me to give up religion, so that I could sin freely and pretend it was no sin. This ought to have been true, but it was not. Lust had gone the way of faith, and if I had read *The Golden Bough* I would have seen the anthropological connection. I was a chaste schismatic, I did not drink at all, and much of what I ate came up again. I was kind, humble, industrious. I was a candidate for the heaven I had wantonly barred from myself.

I organised the Sixth Form Christmas dinner, which brought the oak table back in (Turkey Tennyson, Gravy Browning), and cursed my hypocrisy, thrusting, like Graham Greene's Scobie to be, the head of the divine child into the straw clotted with cowdung. My father attended his one mass of the year, the midnight one on Christmas Eve, and insisted I go with him. He was very drunk, but so were many males in the congregation. At the elevation he handed me a ten shilling note, my Christmas present. I thought the gesture in very bad taste and, as if to confirm that, a drunk three rows in front was sick all over his pew. At home, the days of the great family feast were over. My stepmother cooked a turkey no bigger than a capon for the three of us, and the Christmas pudding came from a shop. On Boxing Day my father and my stepmother quarrelled under the holly. She reviled what she called the flab of his heavy beer intake, and he called her an ignorant fat old cow. She said that this was the end, let the lawyers be called in, and she went to the kitchen with, she said, the intention of shoving her head in the gas oven, though, on a reflex, she had a box of matches in her fist. I said something I did not understand and still do not: 'You're too old to make decisions.' It calmed them down like a cantrip. My father went out for a two-mile walk to the nearest pub. Bitterly he realised how suburban we had become. I went up to my room and wrote my first modern poem:

> My father, his wife,
> Too old to make decisions,
> Yet plotted revisions
> Of their life.
> Nor could this hope be
> More vain, for
> It was left to me
> To show them the oven door.

It was unhopkinsian. To write like Hopkins meant having faith in something, even if it were only the communism of the Terrible Three we were hearing about. Br Andrew had a friend at Manchester Grammar School who had as friend in his turn the poet Cecil Day Lewis, later to be Poet Laureate. He, one of those Three, the others being W. H. Auden and Stephen Spender, was to give a talk on poetry to the Sixth Form of MGS, a far more august body than our own: they took two solid years over the Higher School Certificate and got scholarships to Balliol and similar places. Br Andrew took me, in January cold, to hear Mr Day Lewis.

He was a handsome man, though not so handsome as he was to become when he jettisoned communism and took to Thomas Hardy. He recited some of his verse, which had Hopkinsian compounds like 'brown-of-dawning-skinned' but was also ten-dentiously leftist with lines like 'Come on, this is where you get off, / Sue with her suckling, Cyril with his cough ... Old John Braddlum and Terence the toff.' These personages were, one presumed, to be left behind when the great bus rolled to the leftist utopia. I, an over-forward guest, asked him to recite one of his sonnets. He said he had not written any sonnets. I said oh yes he had and began to deliver from memory:

> Nearing again the legendary isle
>   Where sirens sang and mariners were skinned,
> We wonder now what was there to beguile
>   That such stout fellows left their bones behind ...

That was one in the eye for the MGS Sixth and fine propaganda for the Xaverian College. I added that Hopkinsians ought to master the Petrarchan form and not be content with the Shake-spearean compromise. I also, to my astonishment, averred that the communist cause was no substitute for Hopkins's Catholicism and that the effect of some of Auden's sprung rhythm with lavish head-rhyme was like the dangling of a puppet Hopkins as a drunken *défroqué*. How clever we are when we are seventeen going on eighteen. But there I was, not clever at all, standing up for Catholicism before Protestants when I had ceased to be a Catholic. I saw dimly that it was mostly a social or class gesture, the proclaiming of immemorial rights to dispossessing upstarts. It was chip-on-the-shoulder stuff. I would not be going to Balliol.

I would not, it seemed, be going anywhere. I sat my ex-aminations and gained distinction marks in English Literature and Music but only a subsidiary rating in Latin. This astonished Br Catejan, who was convinced that one of my two papers had been mislaid by the examiner. He was probably right, but nobody did anything about it. I would not be getting a State Scholarship, nor even a Corporation one. I would have to start looking for a job again. I could offer, despite the examination result, more Latin than before, and a detailed knowledge of the Tennysonian lyric. I had read, at last, Joyce's *Ulysses*, which L. W. Dever had brought back from illiberal Nazi Germany in the two-volume Odyssey Press edition. At the time this was a grave disrecommendation in many spheres. James Douglas had denounced it, along with the rest of modern literature, in the *Sunday Express*, and occasionally spilled over into the *Daily Express* with the occasional bark against poor dead Lawrence and living Joyce, whom a just God was striking blind, and the banality of Eliot ('The moon shone bright on Mrs Porter') and Pound ('Lhude sing Goddamn'). Douglas was a fine negative educator. I had some hope, through a drinking reporter pal of my father's, of at least being interviewed for a lowly job on the *Daily Express*, on whose towering offices in central Manchester I had written a sort of poem:

> Steel, stone and glass
> Daily express
> The power of the press.
> A Union Jack
> Brays like an ass
> Beaverbrook's brash
> Patriotic excess . . .

Unfortunately I knew no shorthand. My stepsister Agnes knew Pitman's well and agreed to teach me, but I got no further than the symbols for the plosives. Anyway, I was considered insufficiently pushing, too aesthetically dreamy, for a reporter's job.

I began, with some fear, to wonder what formal education was about. It seemed to disqualify one for any post other than that of the formal educator, who was dedicated to spinning a wheel that had no place in the commercial or industrial machine. Education fed what was left of the soul when religion was removed. I was literate, but I could not write a commercial letter. I knew no commercial Spanish. I was living inside myself and, without the strong support of the Church, was developing self-doubt and a certain timidity. I wandered lonely as a cloud and was pale for weariness. I applied for a job as an assistant horoscopist at a pound a week. This was with a shady firm headed by a woman with fine teeth. There were subscribers who, for an annual fee payable in advance, were sent a weekly report on the conjunctions of the heavenly bodies which was to guide them in their daily affairs. I did well, I thought, in the interview (my teeth were as good as hers), confiding that, as we all knew, astrology was a load of nonsense but one had to take advantage of the suckers. This was not what the fine-toothed woman wanted to hear, as I discovered a week later in a letter which did not offer me the job and had much of the tone of Fr Myerscough on heresy. I delivered parcels for Wilson's.

Then my father decided I was to become a civil servant. Specifically I was to sit for the annual Customs and Excise examination, which was highly competitive. There was a correspondence college that offered tuition in the subjects needed, and it guaranteed a return of the fees if the candidate failed. My father, with surprising innocence, saw no catch in this, but the catch was that one had to complete the course to qualify for the remission. The college ensured that one did not complete the course: it was still sending its lessons and model answers while the examination was being held. I now commenced one of the worst periods of my life: a period of gross humiliation. I had to study chemistry without a laboratory, geography from an illiterate textbook, what was called workshop mathematics, and subjects I already knew, including Latin. I had to start Latin from the beginning again, in order to satisfy the conditions of the course. I thought I knew something of English literature, but the

Customs and Excise authorities had a different conception of what English literature was. I should have known this. Had they not burned *Ulysses* at Folkestone?

Before the course of instruction began, my father took my stepmother and myself on a trip to London. In those days, for a Mancunian to visit the capital was an exercise in condescension. London was a day behind Manchester in the arts, in commercial cunning, in economic philosophy. True, it had the monarch and the government and was gratuitously big. It had more history than Manchester, but history was no more than a tourist frippery. When foreigners came to Manchester, they came to learn, not to feed ravens and snap beefeaters. Sometimes they learned too well, but that was not Manchester's fault. Manchester was generous, and London was not. London had some of the quality of Chorlton-cum-Hardy. It was also a long way away, for a Manchester Catholic much further than Rome or Lourdes. Distance is always a subjective property. You got the train at London Road Station (now called Piccadilly), had a good lunch in the dining car, though it was flavoured with the smoke of the engine, and were ready for tea when you arrived at Euston. Still you had made a long journey. The distance was that between the Mancunian and Londinian temperaments.

We stayed at the Strand Palace Hotel, where, to my chagrin, we were fed with dinners too big to eat, though our stomachs were capacious before the Second World War, and they expected seven courses – hors d'oeuvres (which my stepmother called horse dubs), soup, fish, entrée, poultry, pudding, savoury. It was humiliating for a Mancunian to send back plates half-touched to a London kitchen. Halfway through the second dinner my stepmother howled with pain and had to be assisted to her and my father's room. It was not her stomach, though that was a regular candidate for sudden torment; it was her mouth. A week or so before she had a molar removed by Harry Pratt, the Princess Road dentist. The doctor who was summoned found that fragments of the root were embedded in the gum and setting up inflammation. My stepmother had to enter a nursing home for their digging out. She had confidence in this doctor because he was a Jew. She referred to him ever afterwards as the Jew doctor, and always with approval. My father and I were alone in London.

My father had been drinking less and had lost weight. He was also quite the dandy, a credit to Manchester among the overdressed cosmopolitans in the Strand Palace bar. He also, by God, knew his London. How he had come to know it I did not know, but he whirled me about the prescribed sights, and on buses too, no taxi nonsense, and out to Richmond and Hampton Court. He was as voluble as a professional guide and could direct even a Londoner to Pentonville Road or Camden High Street. His chatter behind me on a Green Line bus, pointing out this or that, became a bore. But we were closer now than we had ever been, chiefly because I had passed my eighteenth birthday and could accompany him to pubs. L. W. Dever was to teach me to drink like an Irish Liverpudlian, but my father was teaching me to drink like a gentleman. There were not many of these lessons, however, because I had to be sent back to Manchester to report to an anxious family on the condition of my stepmother. I took the train from Euston and read through T. S. Eliot's *Collected Poems 1909–35*, which I had bought in Charing Cross Road. The entire volume failed to last the journey. Eliot had not written much from 1909 on. I took music manuscript paper from my suitcase and sketched settings of the songs in *Sweeney Agonistes*. I recorded these settings in Milan in 1981. Then I closed my eyes and muttered 'Polyphiloprogenitive' to myself, and 'Superfetation of *to en*'.

My stepmother was released from the expensive nursing home and had a new topic of conversation – pain relieved, the incompetence of Harry Pratt, the brilliance of the Jew doctor. She and I spent the day together, all day, every day, I with my lessons from the correspondence college, she with her topic of conversation. I split into several persons – the polite but inattentive listener, the unwilling student, the composer, the rabid reader of books unknowable to excisemen. I had occasional improbable images of myself, capped and uniformed, facing the spray of the Port of London in an excise cutter flying the flag. Then I turned to Burton's *Anatomy of Melancholy* or Doughty's *Arabia Deserta*. I had pocket money, but I did not smoke or drink or go out with women. The drinking came later. I was spending my cash on volumes of the Everyman Library. I taught myself Greek and translated the pseudo-Homeric odes:

> Sing to me, Muse, of Hermes's son,
> Twin-horned, with goatish hooves that run
> Aglint through the Arcadian groves,
> With dancing nymphs: the dance he loves.

I also found the epitaph for Margites: 'Him the gods had made neither a digger nor a ploughman, not otherwise wise in aught, for he failed in every art.' That would do for myself.

But the wide reading was a torment as well as a relief, since I had been taught that the function of the aesthetic disposition of words was to summon mental images, and that these images should be visual. Something had gone wrong with my brain: the only image that appeared in it was of an alleyway off Lincroft Street with, superposed on this, a ghostly cinema slide of George V, which appeared when the National Anthem was played at the end of a show. If I tried to envisage Arcadian groves or the Bay of Naples, all I saw was that grim double picture of no meaning. Was I going mad? The only way I could learn the information in L. Dudley Stamp's geography book was to process it into verse pastiches – in the style of Herrick for the exports of Czechoslovakia, Donne for Chicago, George Herbert for the export wool figures of Queensland. I was not being helped towards factual lucidity by reading the *Work in Progress* pamphlets from Faber and Faber. There would be no examination questions on the dream paronomasia of *Haveth Childers Everywhere*.

I decided to compose a symphony, and I bought quires of thirty-stave scoring paper from Boosey and Hawkes. The avant-garde spirit had deserted me. In 1934, Holst, Elgar and Delius had died, and I felt a devotion to them. My musical taste was becoming insular. I had heard William Walton's *Belshazzar's Feast* and First Symphony and understood that, after three decades of screeching discords, modified concords were back in as well as soaring Elgarian melodic lines. Vaughan Williams's Fourth Symphony in F minor was grinding enough, but it was *appliqué* discord. The reality in it was all too tonal, and the international stance was mere histrionics. I found myself stuck in the British idiom of the 1930s, and I have never really become unstuck. The scores I studied were of Holst's *Planets* and Elgar's First Symphony, whose first performance my father claimed to have heard at a Hallé concert in 1908. Elgar would teach me symphonic structure, Holst the use of a large orchestra. Actually, a large orchestra was easier to score for than a small one: with four each of woodwind you could keep a four-note chord within the one family and did not need the laborious ingenuity of distributing it among tone colours that were not quite homogeneous. Eight horns in unison would ride over the ensemble more authoritatively than four, and could spread themselves across the diapaison in a three-octave chord very rich and hair-raising. And then there was all the percussion – two men on kettledrums, three or four on xylophone, glockenspiel, celesta, big drum, cymbals, tambourine, whip and tubular bells. And two harps – the least audible instruments of the sonic army and the most fiddling to write for. I could make the orchestra even bigger than the one in *The Planets* or *Ein Heldenleben*. There was no worry about expense, since no musical society was ever likely to perform the work.

The writing of a three-hundred-page musical work is more laborious than the merely literary person is able to appreciate. You can spend four hours scoring a passage which, in fast tempo, may take only a few seconds to perform. The ring finger of my right hand is permanently deformed with the strain of writing that one work alone. It was a highly juvenile work, and the Luftwaffe, in the name of Beethoven, to say nothing of Wagner, was probably right to destroy it in 1941. But wherein did the juvenility lie? Not in the themes: themes are not the product of either a callow or a mature imagination. Elgar dug out boyhood melodies for his late work; the *idée fixe* of the *Symphonie Fantastique* was a tune from the *enfance de Berlioz*. We produce the best themes in our youth, but we need maturity for their proper handling. The value of this composition for me was the indulgence it granted to my auditory imagination while my visual fancy lay starved and probably innutrible. A desire to avoid the labour to an end unrealisable in performance led me eventually to prose composition, which I have always seen as an analogue to symphonic writing. The lyric poem is not enough: it is an étude or prelude or entr'acte. The short story stops as soon as it starts – a symphonic exposition with no development section, no recapitulation, no coda. An expository prose work is not an expression of the imagination. The epic poem no longer exists. We are left with the novel, the only literary genre for failed symphonists.

It was a long time before I attempted a novel. The urge to compose some great orchestral work continued, against all the odds. But that megalophonia was, as I should have realised, already out of date. The big orchestra was an Edwardian folly. Stravinsky's *Le Sacre du Printemps* was the last of the sonic supersplurges, and it was as much a parody of pretension as an act of self-indulgence – the Russian primitive in Straussian plush.

If I had known anything of the career of Havergal Brian at that time, I would have been warned off my ambitions. For Brian committed millions of notes to scoring paper and then committed that paper to a drawer. There was no hope of hearing them, and perhaps no desire to expose a musical mind he must have known to be mediocre to the hard Sophoclean light. The writing of melodies unheard is less stoically heroic than it appears. In the 1960s I contributed money to the funding of a performance of Havergal Brian's huge 'Gothic' Symphony, and, like so many, was desperately disappointed and even embarrassed by this display of second-rate musical thinking dressed up with bass oboes and basset horns. The work read far better than it sounded. There are perhaps, after all, no mute inglorious Beethovens.

I had to wait until 1975 for the performance of one of my large orchestral works – the Third Symphony in C – and, as I had by that time made some reputation as a novelist, I did not pin every hope on this public revelation of a musical gift which, for lack of encouragement, remained in a great deal of doubt. What I learned from that performance – inevitably, perhaps, an American one – was that my auditory imagination functioned very adequately. Everything was precisely as I had foreheard it in my head: not a note had to be changed. Whether there was enough musical nutriment in those notes to keep an audience attentive for forty minutes was another matter. But the listeners in Iowa City were at least polite.

I look back upon the period of composing my first symphony (in E major; the labour of copying those four sharps over and over was very exhausting) with shame rather than pride. This was no life for a young man: fatiguing study of repulsive subjects for an examination I had no hope of passing; relief through musical composition and intensive self-education in literature and philosophy; an eschewal of all youthful vice – no sex, no smoking, no drinking. No wonder I suffered from migraine. I saw none of my school coevals; they were going their own way. I knew no girls save my cousins. My stepmother picked her teeth with old tram tickets, brought up the wind without inhibition, braised beef and boiled spuds, invoked her childhood, railed at my father. My father was home most evenings now. Dr Sneddon had warned him off the draught Bass and he had a frame-shaking cough. It was the family cough that had recently done for my Uncle Jimmy. My father listened to the BBC while being railed at, or else read public library copies of Pett Ridge, Marie Corelli and Hall Caine. I gave him *Ulysses* to read, but he found it mostly unintelligible or, where briefly intelligible, wholly disgusting.

The major events of my life, or our lives, were external and dynastic. In January 1936 Stuart Hibbard, chief announcer of the BBC and in an invisible dinner jacket for the occasion, told us that the life of King George V was drawing peacefully to its close. The Prince of Wales became King Edward VIII, 'the bloody monarch' to his brothers. There was the odour of coming disruption when Germany repudiated the Locarno Treaty and remilitarised the Rhineland, Italian troops occupied Addis Ababa, and civil war broke out in Spain. Over European disruption swayed the harbinger of a British constitutional crisis, the Baltimore divorcee Mrs Simpson. The press was quiet about this, but the kids in the Manchester streets were not. Long before Christmas they carolled:

> Hark the herald angels sing
> Mrs Simpson's pinched our king.

Young as I was, I began to see that there was little trust in my elders. In December 1936 the king abdicated because he was in love, the Archbishop of Canterbury showed himself to be a hypocritical old fool, Stanley Baldwin was a ditherer, the new king had a stutter which His Grace kindly forewarned us of, Hitler and Mussolini and General Franco were villains, and my father considered contemporary literature a disgrace. It was time for me to start getting drunk.

There used to be fine old pubs in central Manchester, suitable for getting drunk in: the Luftwaffe did for most of them and, while its hand was in, for the score of my Symphony in E Major as well, which I had left in the keeping of one of the pub pianists. I would visit these pubs with L. W. Dever, who merely drank while I got drunk. You, or I, could get drunk on half a crown in those days: five pints of strong bitter beer, at sixpence a pint in the best room, would send me staggering through the slum streets. There were loose women around in those pubs, seductive in artificial silk stockings and the odour of June, which was also used for spraying cinemas. With one of these, and for the sum of tenpence, I engaged in erotic play in an alley, broke and spattered prematurely, was derided. Sex remained a problem. It was dirty or impersonal or both, and wholly physical. There was a girl at Blackpool, not Amy, who whispered to me during a bout of kissing: 'Are you sure it's not just like physical?' She needed an assurance I could give only hypocritically. I now needed that same assurance for myself. I needed the engagement of the entire female complex, which notionally contained an intellect. Could one go to bed with a woman and discuss John Donne and Jeremy Taylor with her? No such woman had come my way. Naked limbs, the scent of something more chic than June, the stockings real silk, an animal response to stimulation of the nerves modified, spiritualised even, with an apt quotation from *Paradise Lost* or a theme hummed out of the Ninth Symphony? On my lonely walks I had stood at the corner of Lime Grove and watched women students come out of their university union. Swots, all of them, books under their arms and odour-trapping hair there too, which film stars did not have. No seduction in them, a prolongation of schoolgirl life, sex sublimated into Anglo-Saxon verbs or notes on French diplomacy in North Africa. And yet it was in the university that I would have to look for the sexual consummation I was after. The alternative, very Irish, was to pretend that sex did not exist and to drink.

On the night of the coronation of King George VI I was found by a policeman, snoring in my vomit, on Wilmslow Road. He hoisted me in a fireman's lift, carried me to Leabrook Road, dumped me on the doorstep, rang the bell, strode off. My father came down in his nightshirt, opened up, called to my stepmother 'The little bugger's come home bottled', and let me crawl indoors to snore my bout out on the mat. Even he should have seen my frustration.

I sat for the Customs and Excise examination with thousands of others and, as soon as I had puzzled over the English Literature paper, knew there was no hope. This, in fact, was the one paper I totally failed. Give the ingredients of a rattling good yarn, with reference to either *Redgauntlet*, *The Four Feathers*, *The Thirty-Nine Steps* or *Sard Harker*. Write an appreciation of either Sir John Squire or Sir Henry Newbolt. State the required elements of an effective spy story, referring to work by W. Somerset Maugham or E. Phillips Oppenheim. What does Sexton Blake owe to Sherlock Holmes? Outline the plot of *The Forsyte Saga*. Write a brief account of the work of any two of the following: Hugh Walpole, H. de Vere Stacpoole, 'Sapper', Pearl S. Buck, Bret Harte, Nat Gould. My father would have made a better showing than I. There was, then, a whole sub-world of sub-literature suitable for excisemen, though it seemed to exclude

novels and poems about smuggling. I have ever since that examination felt respect as well as fear for men of the *Zoll, douane*
and *dogana*. I went home to find that the latest lesson from the
correspondence college had arrived. When the results came out a
candidate with the name Dainty, which suggested suitcase
rummaging in white gloves, had swept the board. I was Number
1,579 in order of merit. There was nothing for me now but to go
to Manchester University.

It was not too expensive – about thirty-five pounds an academic year – and my father would be able to claim an income tax
rebate in respect of my studentship (an advantage unavailable
with that rascally correspondence college). I wished to study for
a degree in music, but my lack of a qualification in physics shut
that door. I would have to join the Honours School of English
Language and Literature, which would lead nowhere. For that
matter, in the big world of graduate competition a Manchester
degree, however good, could never hope to prevail against one,
however bad, from Oxford or Cambridge. That was made very
clear to me by Br Martin, Br Andrew and L. W. Dever. Add an
education at the Xaverian College to one's curriculum vitae, and
one was at a hopeless disadvantage in a domain run by Protestant
snobbery. This was no cynical view: it was hard realism.

On July 7, 1937 – the day of the 'China incident', when the
yellow devils of Nippon added their gongs to the growing European cacophony – I went on a lone holiday to Scarborough. I
had saved two pounds of pocket money by giving up the booze,
and I had been given a box of one hundred cigarettes by the
Carreras tobacco firm. These cigarettes, named Carreras, were
not selling well, according to my father, because customers did
not know how to pronounce the name. I pointed this out to the
firm in a flowery letter, suggesting that they employ some such
slogan as 'None so rare as Carreras', which made the pronunciation clear. The gift was an expression of their gratitude, though
they dropped the brand before they could use the slogan. Starting
to smoke again, I thought I might as well resume drinking as
well. I had also sold a song to a Manchester comedian. The song
was called 'Cabbage Face' and was for use in a mock music lesson
in a pantomime. The refrain-title was a spelling out of the notes
that made up the melody, such as it was:

C A B B A G E
F A C E: Cabbage Face.

If we were in Paris, you
Might be called *mon petit choux*,
But you're in a different place,
So I call you Cabbage Face.

I got thirty shillings for that, copyright sold outright. I went to
Scarborough well-equipped with high-grade condoms.

THREE

I WENT TO my, and my father's, regular barber and he, before deploring my dandruff, said: 'So you're going to Owen's now?' Manchester University was still known as Owen's College to some. The name went back to the days when Liverpool, Leeds and Manchester each contributed a college to the Victorian University of the English North: those great cities were not considered important enough for a university each. Now Owen's College had become the Victoria University of Manchester, and in October 1937 I became a first-year student at it. At that period its reputation was not great. Jodrell Bank did not come into existence until 1957, just in time for the plotting of the track of the first Sputnik, and it was only hindsight that acknowledged its History Department to be the most distinguished in Europe, with L. B. Namier at its head and A. J. P. Taylor a mere junior lecturer. Ordinary Mancunians accepted that medical practitioners required training, but they mostly believed that was done at the Manchester Royal Infirmary opposite, or nearly. The more humane studies made little sense to them, and they wondered what these blackened Gothic buildings were for. They knew about students, a rowdy lot who erupted in fancy dress all over the city at Shrovetide for Rag Week and published the *Rag Rag*, an obscene magazine regularly banned and sold covertly at high prices in the Stock Exchange. But they did not know what those students were doing for the rest of the year, except boozing and fornicating. They knew nothing of the professors, not even Chaim Weizmann, the Zionist leader and eventual President of Israel, who gave the British government a new technique for the production of acetone in exchange for the promise of a free Jewish state. If they knew nothing of Professor H. B. Charlton, head of the English Department, they could be excused. I had never heard of him either.

The English Department was at the end of Lime Grove and

housed in a small building which had once accommodated a
troupe of lady dancers called the Tiller Girls. This, considering
my poor mother's trade, made me feel at home. Professor
Charlton had much of the temperament of a blustering father, as
well as a thirst for beer, and, like my own father, despised modern
literature. Literature for him came to a full close with Robert
Browning, whose works were offered as a subject for special
study, the others being Elizabethan Drama and the Nineteenth-
Century Novel. A single Victorian poet who had gone rather
out of fashion was thus considered commensurate with a vast
field of bewildering attainment. Professor Charlton was also a
Shakespeare specialist and had published *Shakespearean Comedy*, a
work which complemented A. C. Bradley's *Shakespearean Tragedy* and was quite as démodé. Charlton was an embarrassment to
the younger literary specialists, such as Frank Raymond Leavis,
only forty-two at the time, whose embassy at Manchester was
run by Dr Lionel Charles Knights, author of the anti-Bradleyan
How Many Children Had Lady Macbeth? and the near-Marxist
Drama and Society in the Age of Jonson. Between the *Scrutiny* and
Bradleyan extremes lay J. D. Jump, who was not yet sure where
he stood, and a Professor Wright, whom age and probable shell
shock had rendered confused.

The linguistic side of the English Department was no mere
casual acknowledgment of a tiresome truth – that without language you could not have a literature. It was full-bloodedly
philological in the German manner and seemed to despise aesthetic values. *Beowulf* and *The Owl and the Nightingale* were there
to exhibit objective verities which could not be gainsaid by any
amount of the contentious cleverness which was supposed to ani-
mate literary seminars. Sound-changes were facts and you had
better believe them. Manchester was in the north and it looked
north to the Teutonic realities. If you wished to specialise in
linguistic studies, it was wise for you to take Part I of the degree
examination at the University of Reykjavik. There you would
certainly know you were in the north. The study of Old Norse
and Old Icelandic took you all but nominally outside the English
Department. *Beowulf* itself might be the great English epic, but
you had better remember that it was composed in Jutland. The
god of Professor Florence Harmer was a Dane – the great Otto
Jespersen, who knew far more about the English language than
any native speaker of it. A constant phrase in her lectures was
'When I had breakfast with Professor Jespersen'. One morning,

suffering from a cough, she brought in pectoral syrup in a tea cup. 'That,' gloomily said one of my fellow students, 'is the authentic cup she drank tea from when breakfasting with Professor Jespersen.'

The basis of our linguistic enquiries was the still-young science of phonetics, which, as I had seen already when learning French at the Xaverian College, was always in danger of becoming a mere paper study: I mean, it seemed enough to some that the symbols of the International Phonetic Alphabet should be known without too rigorous a concern with their sonic referents. You could mispronounce the French *u* in *tu*, but you did not pronounce it any better if you got to know it as /y/ in the IPA. There were not many phonetics laboratories around in those days, and the phonetics laboratory we all carry on our shoulders was shamefully neglected: there was something ungenteel about fiddling physically with tongue positions and the spreading and rounding of the lips. And yet the story of the English language depended to a very great extent on the behaviour of the English mouth. Dr G. L. Brook, a distinguished Germanic philologist, spoke to us of i-mutation and the Great Vowel Shift, but he said little of the organic truths which underlay these phenomena.

And if he could not or would not elucidate the mystery of why, as opposed to how, Anglo-Saxon changed into Middle and later into Modern English, this may have been because the world of philology was not yet ready for the theory that English was not a language at all but a mere creole, a sort of pidgin response to Danish invaders on one side and Norman invaders on the other. In other words, Anglo-Saxon did not change into Modern English. Anglo-Saxon disappeared, together with its battery of genders and conjugations and noun-cases, during a period of human confusion. As for the mystery of the Great Vowel Shift, whereby *mūs* became *mouse* and *moon* ceased to be pronounced as if it were Dutch, the answer lay, if we had only known it, in the instability of the tongue when trying to phonate long vowels. There were wonders here, but they were not disclosed to us. A university education was concerned with damping the sense of wonder. One of the books we were recommended as light reading was *The Romance of Words*, by H. L. Weekley, but the title was considered something of an embarrassment, since it suggested enthusiasm of an amateurish kind. That Weekley was the man cuckolded by D. H. Lawrence was not then generally known; if we had known it, the knowledge might have cancelled the minor value of the book: the whiff of human nature it brought in would have been deemed improper for scholarship.

Dr Brook was, as I noted in a diary at the time, 'pated and teethed like a troll' – certainly Nordic, as befitted his specialisation, but not really human. It was rumoured that he had been a co-respondent in a divorce case, but there was no certain knowledge of a private life behind the philology. Of Professor E. V. Gordon, head of the English Language sub-department, we knew only that he had an Icelandic wife, suggesting a linguistic match rather than a romantic one, and that he had worked with J. R. R. Tolkien, who published *The Hobbit* in 1937 but was not yet the stepfather of a counter-culture. The fruit of collaboration was one of the most beautiful books ever published by the Manchester University Press or, indeed, any other scholarly house – a superbly printed and bound edition of *Sir Gawain and the Green Knight*, the handling of which was a profound physical pleasure. I had met Professor Gordon at my enrolment, and he had been astonished to learn that I had been studying a little Anglo-Saxon on my own. I was over twenty, I pointed out, had been in a kind of enforced leisure, was becoming conscious of the dual nature of English, knew Latin and French but nothing of the northern inheritance, had a natural curiosity to know at least a little. He looked at me with watery eyes, seeing promising material he would grab when I came to seniority; but he died within the year.

English students were mostly women, girls really, who expected a university course to be all burbling over the beauties of Keats and Shelley. They were disabused, and some of them cried over the knottiness of Anglo-Saxon. They had not thought it was going to be like that. The women sat on the left of the lecture-rooms, and the men on the other side of the aisle. This was chilling, but there was little comeliness or sexual promise over there, nothing to make one anxious to jump the divide. I, already a man, sat with clever Sixth Form boys who knew nothing of Joyce or Eliot, who gabbled their seminar papers in raw Lancashire and thought a phrase like 'Shakespeare shows here a strong sense of beauty' was a reasonable judgment. But there were three who had passed beyond boyhood and knew at least that Eliot and Joyce existed. These were Reginald Bate, from Shropshire; Denis Crowther Gaunt, from Warrington; and Douglas Rankine Mason, from Chester. I was a dayman, and so was Gaunt, catching early and late trains to and from Central Station. Mason was in lodgings with, he boasted, a drunken landlady; Bate was in Hulme Hall. The collegiate system did not exist at Manchester, but there were halls of residence, some of them religious foundations, set in parks of wet greens. These encouraged the prolongation of the life of school, with apple-pie beds and rags in the showers. At Hulme Hall Bate was of course called Master Bate.

I would come in for such lectures as I attended on the bus from Fallowfield. A great old man would sometimes travel on that same bus, the philosopher Professor Samuel Alexander from Melbourne, author of *Space, Time and Deity* and *Beauty and Other Forms of Value*. He was already honoured in life with an Epstein bust in the Arts Building on Lime Grove, a point of meeting ('Sammy's bust') for lovers. I do not know how his reputation stands in the post-Wittgenstein age, but at a time when metaphysics was still considered a branch of literature he was revered for the grace of his style and the plausibility of his vitalist speculations. The world arose out of a swirl of undifferentiated substance that froze into point-instants; creative evolution produced God. It was Bergsonian stuff. Its propounder had a wet nose and a dirty beard. He got off the bus with difficulty.

I would go to the Arts Building for my Intermediate courses in French, Latin and European History. I was never a good student; a native laziness still revolts against the learning of facts and vocabulary. A. J. P. Taylor lectured to a hundred or so of us and earned my enmity by scoffing at James Joyce's *Work in Progress*. He wrote on the blackboard ambidextrously. On my first term paper, which was awarded a fail mark, he wrote 'Bright ideas insufficient to conceal lack of knowledge'. I did no better in French. In Latin classes a simpering fair-haired lecturer reserved to me the task of translating lyrics from Fred Astaire musicals into Ciceronian prose. 'You say tomatoes and I say tomahtoes . . .' *Dico ego 'pomum', dicis tu 'phomum'*, with the help of Catullus.

Across the street from the Arts Building was the refectory, and next to it the cafeteria. In the refectory one was served a fair lunch for tenpence; in the cafeteria you served yourself for a penny less. One day on the refectory menu I read 'Fried God in batter'. A Japanese student reverently ordered this: anything was possible to the British. Other foreign students ordered bleef lissoles and glirred hossages. We were a cosmopolitan lot dietetically homogenised. There was no alcohol, but there was talk of a bar coming to the Men's Union. In the Men's Union you could eat beans on toast in the subterranean coffee bar, play billiards, go to debates in the lunch hour, listen to filth from medical students. Medical students confirmed that a university was an establishment of adult education. Some of them were positively ancient. A certain Jack Rothwell had made a lifelong occupation of failing his Second MB. Rents from a row of slum houses kept him going. He was the Union Treasurer. Eventually, approaching the statutory age of retirement but still a medical student, he absconded with the funds. This had always been expected.

Mason, Gaunt and I took to lunching in the public bar of the College Arms, on the other side of Oxford Road. We got bread, cheese and pickled onions for threepence and a pint of best bitter beer for fivepence. Then we smoked our pipes. There was a regular old man, chinny and in glasses, who would say: 'Bloody intellectuals. Let us down in the first war and they'll do the bloody same in the one that's coming. Fucking students of fucking nothing but betrayal. Mean, too. Stand us a bleeding pint.' But we were not rich; we had to watch the pence. Another old man wept over his wife, who had died of mortification of the womb. A local prostitute would come in to call a mild drinker of mild a fucking rotten bastard. Mason, Gaunt and I liked this environment, but we knew we should be lunching with decent girl undergraduates and plotting their seduction. We were not getting any sex at all.

In our literature seminars we were closer to silk or lisle stockings and the odd whiff of scent: the girls could not, in so small a huddle, flee across an aisle. Trixie Brayshaw, plump and blonde, looked promising. Marjorie Bottomley, more austerely blonde, with pink-framed spectacles, seemed unattainable. Pat Wilson, of a darker gold, with exquisitely shaped legs in gunmetal silk and clothes from one of the higher department stores, was well beyond us. These girls offered a sort of diluted and highly sexless companionship. It was not enough. Michael Callaghan of the Xaverian College was courting a blonde girl named Dorothy Fitzmaurice, who was remotely related to Pat Wilson. A Christmas party was held at the Fitzmaurice house, and I stayed the night in the same bed as Callaghan and a Fitzmaurice son. Dorothy Fitzmaurice gave me her teddy bear for additional bed-company. Gaunt said, when I told him: 'Sleeping with that teddy bear is the nearest you'll ever get to sleeping with Pat Wilson.' This was true. She disdained those of her own academic year and eventually became engaged to Len Halliday, a poet already a graduate. Perhaps, after all, there was something incestuous in mooning after someone of our own year and our own school. Reginald Bate saw that early. This Shropshire lad began to court a red-haired chemistry student in her second year. That led to genuine exogamy.

Literature is all, or mostly, about sex, but the girls in our seminars were natural disinfectants of it. In the first term my tutor was J. D. Jump, unsure of himself and his accent. When he spoke of 'the tragedy of blood' I saw, with my new phonetic knowledge, that final vowel flash out as an inverted *m* with a wiggly line through it – the unrounded mid-back phoneme centralised, typical of Lancashire. The same thing had to happen with the vowel of 'love' in 'love poetry', which comic-ruralised what the girls disinfected. But we were not much into literary love at that time. We were concerned with the function of the poetry of the poetic drama. I wrote an essay which set forth the notion that the drama was there for the poetry, not the other way round. A generation of dramatic emotion led to the setting up of what I called 'lyric point-instants' (Alexandrian language), and these were the justification of the drama – eternal poetic truths not stated nakedly but in the context of an emotional situation which explained them. Jump returned my essay with a pencilled 'Very interesting' and a whole page of further comment, which he had laboriously erased. He was not sure of himself.

L. C. Knights, who wrote for *Scrutiny*, was sufficiently sure of himself, backed up by Leavisian revaluation and the success of I. A. Richards's practical criticism. When I transferred to his seminar in my second term, I had already read some of his *Scrutiny* essays and part of his *Drama and Society in the Age of Jonson*. I approved the dryness of the style, the leftist sociological approach to the Elizabethan theatre, and the evidence that the canon of English literature which he and his school adhered to was the one I had discovered alone while my stepmother picked her teeth and belched. I mean, not Tennyson and Browning, not Keats and Shelley, but Blake, Hopkins, Donne, Marvell. The Leavis crowd had learned much from T. S. Eliot, but, while I knew *The Waste Land* by heart, I had not yet read his *Selected Essays*. I had, however, read William Empson's *Seven Types of Ambiguity*, and when Knights handed out his cyclostyled texts – name of author undisclosed, in the I. A. Richards manner, to ensure innocence of response – I had an idea what he would be after. He would be after verbal irony, connotatory resonance, form as content – in other words, what were the words doing?

I could not help recognising some of the texts – a chunk of the 'Proteus' episode in *Ulysses*, part of Pound's *Hugh Selwyn Mauberley*, the second page of Lawrence's *The Rainbow* – and feeling superior to those who did not. The girls mostly found Joyce formless and ill-written and Lawrence over-sensuous and even disgusting. Pound was horrid, what with his 'old bitch gone in the teeth'. Some of the men in the group found him un-patriotic, which was a fair prophecy. Knights could only convince those who, like myself, were prepared to be convinced that here was honest writing, the words charged with meaning. What he was perhaps not wholly aware of, though I think I was, was that he was moved by certain political considerations which he confused with literary judgments. Supposing that Pound had written in that same terse charged style in approval of the First World War? Was the literary taste that Knights was trying to impart merely an index of a certain moral or political approach? The Spanish Civil War was on, and Knights was painting jam jars to sell as flower vases to help the Republican cause. He kept quiet about Eliot's Anglicanism. He was, of course, entirely right about the maturity of the ironic content of Marvell's *To His Coy Mistress* and the inflated balderdash of Churchill's rhetoric in *The World Crisis*, but he seemed to be in danger of having to submit to the Marxist philosophy, which denied the existence of pure aesthetic values and made its literary judgments in terms of political orthodoxy. Ben Jonson and Philip Massinger mirrored economic change in the Jacobean era; even the cult of melancholy, in *Hamlet*, John Ford and Robert Burton, was a response to in-flation. This was healthier than Bradley and H. B. Charlton, but it had its own elements of morbidity. What did Dr Knights think of the religious ecstasy of Hopkins's 'The Windhover'? The ecstasy was irrelevant; the evidence of a divided psychological state ('buckle' in Empson's seventh type of ambiguity) was the poem's true content. The dedication 'to Christ Our Lord' had to take on a subjective signification: Christ was the objective cor-relative of a state of mind. I had enough Catholicism left in me to wish to argue about ontology, but that took us beyond liter-ature. Literature was words on the page.

Old extra-literary certainties were bidden dissolve. Hamlet and Ophelia were not real people. It was impertinent to demand what Hamlet was studying at Wittenberg. G. Wilson Knight was asking us to consider Shakespeare's characters as vast poetic symbols. As I wrote in a mocking poem of the time (whose real subject was the sexlessness of the women in the first-year English classes):

> Now we know that Shakespeare's
>   Figures ape no realities –
> Cognate rather with Blake's powers
>   And principalities.

Professor Charlton, meanwhile, denied the validity of any new approach to Shakespeare. He gave us a series of lectures without notes, marching up and down in heavy boots, telling us that King Lear was as real as we were – more real, since he was a man and we were still, whatever we liked to call ourselves, mere boys and girls. Did we know of Benedetto Croce? No, we didn't. Why, when he was our age he knew all about Benedetto Croce. What had gone wrong with the world? 'Moved on,' Gaunt muttered. Not that Gaunt altogether approved of Dr Knights. He mocked his accent. Knights pronounced 'fault' as 'folte', and so, Gaunt observed with his new-found knowledge of sound-combinations, with all back low vowels before dark l plus consonant. Pass the solte. Gaunt gave out Knights's prose with Knights's tonalities: 'Most readers of the *Henry IV* plays regard the historical segments as so much dry bread to be bitten through before they come to the [slight pause] meatah Falstaff.'

I lost touch totally with my university teachers after graduation, but I met L. C. Knights again in Washington, DC, in 1976. There was an international conference which mystically combined celebration of two centuries of American independence and the three hundred and sixtieth anniversary of Shakespeare's death (the wheel had come full circle, every degree of it). Alistair Cooke (a fellow-Mancunian), my Argentine namesake, and myself had been chosen to deliver the major addresses. Dr Knights and other scholars were merely in charge of specialist seminars. I do not think that Knights was altogether pleased to see me when we turned up at the same dinner party in Georgetown. I had made some sort of name as a writer, in the sense that certain participants at the conference knew who I was. Knights was known to the scholars but not to the hostesses. I think he resented this. I became chilled by an awareness of the gulf fixed between the imaginative writer and the scholar. Dame Helen Gardner was there too, tweet-tweeting, and I was expected to bow down to her. The gulf was a very British one; it did not exist in the healthier American climate of scholarship. I expected Knights at least to express modified pleasure at my having made a career in literature – after all, it was the aim of his tuition to promote devotion to the art – but he was cold and somewhat glum. I tried to defreeze the atmosphere by saying: 'There's a phrase of yours I've always remembered, Dr Knights. "Most readers of the *Henry IV* plays . . . the [slight pause] meatah Falstaff."' He walked away. I had unconsciously put on Gaunt's voice of parody. He did not turn up to my public discourse. Nor, of course, did Dame Helen Gardner.

The wheel came full circle in another way at this conference. The Argentine Embassy gave a cocktail party for Borges, and there were evident secret service men milling like fire ants. When Borges and I spoke in English they closed in for possible words of disaffection. I quoted the first line of Caedmon's Hymn: *'Nu we sculan herian heofonrices weard . . .'* Delighted, Borges responded with *'Metodes mihte ond his modgethonc.'* And so we continued to the end of the poem in linear antiphony. The snoopers were bewildered: what was this foreign tongue – Albanian, Upper Borogrovian? My courses with G. L. Brook had not been wasted. Nor, for that matter, though it seemed hard to persuade L. C. Knights of this, had my exposure to the *Scrutiny* ethos. If Knights had not taught at Manchester I would have been lost. I can still hear the dispiriting boots of Charlton, the banality of his peroration: 'Well, there's your Shakespeare. You've got him in your books: read him.' The term 'disinspiration' ought to exist.

Charlton took over one of our seminars when Knights, ill, was away. He opened an anthology arbitrarily and lit on one of the final sonnets of Gerard Manley Hopkins, the one with the sestet beginning 'I am gall, I am heartburn'. He had great fun with this, to the joy of the girls, who were much on his reactionary wavelength, alluding to the absurdity of using 'stomach trouble' as a metaphor for spiritual distress, typical of these modernist upstarts. I pointed out, as calmly as I could, that Hopkins had died in the same year as Browning. 'Oh, I don't think you can be right there, check your facts.' 1844–1889, I asserted. He discovered, by referring to the contents pages, that this was true, but he grumbled about it as at a dirty trick of my perpetration. He bore no real ill-will, however; he merely got Professor Wright to divert the class in literary history with sneers at Hopkins that should meet my hot response, and then to disconcert me with questions like 'What is the meaning of "a broth of goldfish flue"?' I could usually give the right answer, and the good-natured persecution stopped. But I, twenty years old and too knowledgeable, was marked.

THERE WERE HARD workers and skimpers, and I was one of the latter. Those who saw hard work as the way to a good degree concentrated on the English language, meaning often Old Norse and Old Icelandic; such were scared of the independence of judgment demanded by the study of literature. You could not go far wrong if you knew your Anglo-Saxon irregular verbs and the main phonological differences between the Mercian and Northumbrian dialects. To deliver a view of the Spenserian vowel music demanded some kind of intuitive faculty. You could tell from the start who the language specialists were going to be – girls mostly, with holes in their cardigans, unwashed hair, toddling back to their halls of residence with *Beowulf* under their arms. There were other aspects of university life than study, and these they virtuously ignored. Theatre, for instance, the Stage Society. Gaunt, Mason and I were keen on the drama. It might, apart from its primary values, be a way of holding a girl in your arms. We all got on to the committee, whose chairman was a law student of outstanding brilliance and pedantry named Frank Shepherd. Committee meetings he saw as ends in themselves. Wrangles about committee procedure precluded any possibility of actually agreeing to put on a play. Plays were, however, sometimes put on in the Round House at Ancoats, the centre of the university's slum settlement. These were usually one-acters like *The Monkey's Paw* and *The House with the Twisty Windows*. But Gaunt, who worshipped Noël Coward, insisted on playing the lead in *Fumed Oak*.

There was never any hope of Gaunt's taking a romantic role. His nose was too big, far bigger than John Gielgud's. He had done character parts with the repertory company in Warrington; he could do a fair imitation of Elsie Knights. His real ambition was to direct, which in those days was termed produce. Douglas Mason was the romantic type, with fair hair that he shampooed weekly with an egg. So was Valentine Riley, a law student of epicene looks. My forte was middle-aged parts, considered ap-

propriate since I was older than the others: either henpecked
husbands (*Fumed Oak* should have been for me) or lecherous
Ruritanian colonels. There was also Ronnie Majdalany, a swarthy
medical student who could do heavy roles. Among the women
was Jean Buckingham, a senior student of great blonde beauty,
with a sister who looked like Jean Harlow. Of them I wrote:

> Jean is ox-eyed,
> Her sister peroxide.

There was also Rosalie Williams, who could tap-dance and did
so at the annual rag show in the Gaumont Cinema, but who was
to end up as a professional actress with Joan Littlewood and also,
in what must be termed advanced middle age, as a character
actress on television.

I wanted *The Ascent of F6* to be put on. I had seen it with L.
W. Dever at the Princess Theatre, and considered it was the kind
of play a university drama group should be undertaking, not,
God help us, *The Monkey's Paw*. It happened that there was a
woman of considerable force, glamour and elegance named Renée
Gill who was, independently of myself, ambitious to produce the
Auden – Isherwood play. Her beauty was marred by a gutter accent
and vocabulary. She was not a member of the university, but her
fiancé was, a Romanian postgraduate student of law named
André Eminescu, no relation to the poet. He seemed to spend all
his spare time in the cafeteria reading *Timpul* (a Dacian corruption
of *tempus illud*, so the classical specialists told us), instead of
courting fiery, and indeed flame-haired, Renée Gill. She said
repeatedly that she was going to shove his fucking *Timpuls* up his
dirty Romanian jaxy, but he remained suave. Lancashire women
have more of the Latin temperament than the Latins, as Sicilian
men who have married into Lancashire will confirm. Renée Gill
was a flame in the cafeteria and would be more so in the theatre.

Her aim was to take charge of the Stage Society or, which
amounted to the same thing, draw all its members away into a
troupe of her own. As the Stage Society spent all its time on
committee wrangling, some of us would have been glad to follow
her, but there was the question of her lack of university status.
This did not seem to worry her: the drama came first. The social
structure of the university was, anyway, a very loose one. The
cafeteria, which was the centre of its social life, was free to all to
enter. No uniformed Cerberus barred the way in. Even the two

unions had open doors. When the bar of the Men's Union was, in my second year, inaugurated, regular extramural drinkers appeared in it, unrebuked and not even unwelcome. The university as an open society: discuss. Michael Callaghan used the union as his poste restante, though he paid no membership dues. There was no difficulty in Renée Gill's taking charge of intramural dramatic talent.

But Frank Shepherd, pillar of the law, could at least keep her off the committee, which, since the committee met in a committee room, meant off university premises. She could scream about the power and beauty of *The Ascent of F6* in that open bazaar which was the cafeteria, but she was not admitted to legalistic rebukes and points of order. It was a small miracle that the Stage Society was able, after months of hot argument, to agree on the prospect of a major production. The play was to be James Elroy Flecker's *Hassan*, which I remembered well from my days of sexual initiation with the WEA widow, and Gaunt was to produce it. Mason was to play the poet Ishak, Rosalie Williams Yasmin, Ronnie Majdalany Hassan. I was to write the music. Indeed, I wrote some of the music while points of order kept coming up. It was on a point of order, or committee ethics, that Gaunt was expelled from the production. He had bought two copies of *Hassan* and stuck their pages into a large loose-leaf book, making a production copy. He charged his purchases to the Stage Society. This was ruled by Frank Shepherd as irregular, since he had not consulted the committee first, and Gaunt was condemned in round judicial language. The production came to nothing. No production ever came to anything, except pieces like *The Monkey's Paw* for the poor of Ancoats. Renée Gill achieved the presentation of a play called *Dr Allen G.P.*, written by a local physician, in which some of us took part, enlivening the dialogue with our own jokes, but *The Ascent of F6* was never produced, at least not on the stage.

The Stage Society did not need exhaustive committee meetings in order to launch play-readings in one or other of the unions. Thus I was able to produce *The Ascent of F6* in a shortened form, and also the second part of *Murder in the Cathedral* for the History Society: it was in the chorus of women of Canterbury that I met my future wife. But our major achievement was a dramatisation of Eliot's *The Waste Land*, produced by Gaunt. D. G. Bridson, the brilliant North Regional drama producer, had presented his own version on radio, but ours, I think, was better. I composed jazz settings, with help from Wagner, of the lines of the Thames daughters, and performed a piano montage of *Le Sacre du Printemps, Tristan, Parsifal, Götterdämmerung*. None of the faculty came to hear: the gap persisted.

To the shame of the university, the development of non-commercial drama in Manchester had to be left to Joan Littlewood, who came to the city in my second year. She took a room over a shop on Oxford Road, with no furniture except a mattress, invited me over to discuss drama, and announced that the theatre had the duty of promoting social revolution. I could not agree: the drama was bigger than that, art could not be either (I was remembering my James Joyce) didactic or pornographic. The task of the theatre was to arouse static emotions, whatever those were. Purgation had to be effected within the structure itself, not in social acts stimulated by that structure. One should leave the theatre in calm of mind, all passion spent. This was pretentious talk. Joan Littlewood, a charming dark woman with gap-teeth like the Wife of Bath, was proposing harder work at Ancoats than we in the Stage Society had undertaken. Douglas Mason and I had appeared in a three-acter by Geoffrey Whitworth, so bad that I have forgotten its name. We had gone to the first night in a state of high frivolity, leaving a note on the table of the junior English seminar:

> To Ancoats we have gone,
> Every mother's son.
> We'll be drunk when we arrive:
> Let copulation thrive.

To Joan Littlewood the theatre was, at least, more than titillation. A seriousness of political motivation induced a rigorous concern with theatrical technique. When she put on, in the Round House, the first of her Living Newspapers, we pococurantists were moved and ashamed. *Fumed Oak*, quotha. *Hassan*, sprayed with June, forsooth.

There was no doubt about the strength of her technique and the thoroughness of its modernity. She had absorbed Brecht and Stanislavsky. A ramp thrust out from the side of the proscenium, and on it paraded workers out of *Metropolis*, some of them pressed local unemployed and their wives, many of them with their false teeth out. They sang angrily to the main theme of the first movement of William Walton's First Symphony:

March, men of the activist committees.
March, come from your stricken towns and cities.

She presented enormities like the 1935 Anglo-German naval agreement in lateral form, gossip spraying out of frank but anaemic love-making between members of the ruling class. Hitler and Mussolini pranced in a ballet as good as *The Green Table*. The lighting plot was complex and oiled like machinery. Amplified gramophone records swelled in on split-second cues. All the actors were amateurs, but Joan Littlewood had drilled them to the screaming limit. She herself demonstrated, in her own various performances, what the new theatre was about. The backbone of her organisation was a university one – Rosalie Williams, Vivian Daniels, Gerry Raffles: Raffles stayed with her till his death as business manager of the Theatre Royal, Stratford. What became a fiery East London institution had Manchester roots.

Kenneth Tynan wrote of Joan Littlewood's *Oh What a Lovely War* that it made one want to rush out of the theatre and cut the collective throat of the British establishment. That was precisely what one felt after those early Manchester productions. She stimulated us to a desire for revolutionary action, and even the Ancoats streets outside the Round House were drawn into the message: one emerged into slums of a squalor now rarely seen and wanted to tear them down with one's bare hands. The question Gaunt, Mason and I asked each other was, however: is this what the theatre is really about? We were Aristotelians, like Stephen Dedalus, and believed in tragic or comic catharsis. But I remembered the article on fugue in Grove's *Dictionary of Music and Musicians*: fugue was not a form; fugue was a method. Perhaps the same might be true of drama. Bernard Shaw thought so. There was didactic theatre as well as Aristotelian theatre; there was probably pornographic theatre as well, though we did not know where it was. All were equally legitimate. That, though, was a conclusion we wanted to avoid.

But it was becoming hard to think of pure art. Politics had got into all of us. There was a war on in Spain, and some of us felt guilty about not joining the International Brigade. There was undoubtedly a bigger war preparing itself in Europe, and that was going to absorb the lot of us. We calmed our cowardice about Spain with the reflection that we had better get our degrees before becoming cannon fodder. We could not afford the luxury of time off now for fighting the battles of international labour. National labour was not doing much about it, and we did not see the unemployed crying out to join their communist or anarchist brothers in Catalonia. But the communist women students of Manchester University told us where our duty lay, and we lowered our eyes over our cups of milky coffee. Noreen Lowe, for instance, who wrote poems with lines like 'Bombs burst over Barcelona' and read the *Daily Worker*. Everybody seemed to be reading the *Daily Worker*. L. C. Knights, who must have been horrified by its prose, excused himself by pointing to the excellence of its racing tips.

The Communist Society was by far the biggest of the university political groups, but I never belonged to it. My Catholic upbringing had left me with a conviction that a wholly materialist interpretation of history was false. If I had read Karl Marx more attentively than I was willing to, I would have realised that Marx thought so too, what with his knowing much Shelley and Shakespeare by heart and reciting Dante to his daughters on the way back to Soho from a picnic on Hampstead Heath. Few of our communists had read much of *Das Kapital*; they preferred to get their theory from the works of Lenin, in twelve volumes. Or, in the true communist manner, they accepted what the leader of the British communists told them to believe. There was an engineering student named Jack Allenson who worshipped Harry Pollitt and sang an eschatological song about Pollitt dying and becoming commissar for Soviet Hell. I seem to remember Allenson carrying his twelve volumes of the works of Lenin about with him, like Marley's ghost encumbered with cash boxes. Allenson called God Fred. He was in a Blakean situation without knowing it, since he had not read Blake. Hell was the eternal dynamic delight of the workers; heaven was a bloodless structure of the capitalists. It was hard to break away from the old mythology.

There were communist parties, some of which I attended because I was after a Latvian girl named Zozafin Wulfson. She was the only female communist who had any allure; the others eschewed it as a capitalist trap. At these parties we paid for our own beer and sang songs like

> I'll sing you one-oh,
> Red flies the banner-oh.
> What is your one-oh?
> One is worker's unity and ever more shall be so.

And so on, with 'two two the opposites, interpenetrating though' and 'six for the Tolpuddle Martyrs' and, finally and inevitably, 'twelve for the works of Lenin'. Knocking at the door for entrance to one of these parties, I would sometimes facetiously say: 'Open up – it's de Ogay Payoo.' I would be called a fascist for whom there was hope of conversion, but I was not a fascist. There was a Fascist Society, and a Miss Wray in our English first year was its secretary: she gave me a poster to put up in the Men's Union, but I crumpled it. I was not really anything but a renegade Catholic liberal humanist with tendencies to anarchism. Auden and Spender and Day Lewis, who had not proved notably quick to fight for Spain, struck me as naive; so, for different reasons, did T. S. Eliot. There was no answer to the world's problems in communism, and no personal salvation in Anglicanism. The solutions probably lay with renegade Catholic liberal humanism. I do not think, nearly fifty years after, I have much changed my position.

Temperamentally incapable of political activism, even for the liberal cause, barred by procedural paralysis from dramatic creativity, I took to university journalism. The university magazine was called *The Serpent*, known as The Snake to its editorial staff. Its name came from the university badge, which showed Vergil's serpent rearing skywards, with Vergil's *arduus ad solem* as motto. The editorship had just been relinquished by Lance Godwin, who was entering hard postgraduate work, and it was taken over by Cedric Hirson, a medical student who was in some strange phase of his studies which granted him ample free time. You needed this to edit *The Serpent*. The two assistant editors were to be myself and a near namesake – John A. Wilson. In university society we became John A. and John B., with no need of the surname. John A.'s briefcase asserted its initial, however, with W.W.W.W. His father's name was William Wilberforce Witherspoon Wilson, or some such eccentric combination, and this was his briefcase passed down. John A. had studied medicine but was changing his subject. His cafeteria talk gave no hint of any strong desire to specialise. He was merely well read in many fields and he wrote poetry. His girl friend was a classics student of statuesque beauty unmarred by the slight Lancashire accent she did not seem to wish to lose. With her the accent was ennobled. Dressed for a role in Euripides, she was, as I said in a review, 'coolly and beautifully Grecian'. She loved him more than he her.

Cedric Hirson had all the self-confidence of a Manchester Jew. I met him during the war when he was a Medical Corps captain,

and he admitted to brash arrogance which a comparative humility
of rank had made him lose. The war exacted humility from a lot
of us. Hirson as editor was far from humble. Few Manchester
Jews of wealthy background were. The Jews had sustained the
artistic glory of the city and helped its commercial advance. Two
of the great Manchester Jewish names were represented at the
university in two attractive girls – Mary Behrens and Nan
Zimmerman. Hirson itself was a considerable name. The other
journalistic manager of the university was a Jew of less patrician
origin – Gerry Wolfson, who inaugurated a weekly paper called
The News Bulletin. He was, and remained, a communist. The
downtrodden, not the Jews, were his people.

The Serpent had its own office, complete with telephone, in
the top floor of the Men's Union building. It was next to the
Joint Common Room, where members of both unions lolled on
couches, were served tea and crumpets and, in the dark during
dances, made love. An invitation to a girl to meet a man in JCR
never sounded innocent. *The Serpent* office was, because of this
contiguity, itself a place of intersexual contact, and tea was served
there too, by a pale-haired boy in a white jacket named Leslie.
When the key to the office was mislaid, which was frequently,
the only way into it was through its window, which necessitated
a near-leap from a JCR window over a dizzying gap four storeys
high. This was regarded as a test of journalistic courage.

The final bold journalistic act of Lance Godwin had been the
publication of a six-page supplement of his poems with Eliotian
notes. He wrote under the pseudonym of Walter Blent, and heavy
type announced the Blent Poems. Godwin was, I think, a good
poet, one of a university group whose other members were Ian
Stuart Black and Len Halliday ('Lucius Tombs'). Unlike the Terrible Three headed by Auden, they scorned political affiliation
and tried to synthesise a romantic approach to love with modernist
rhythms and lexis. I set one of Godwin's poems to music. It was
about the tropical Lancashire summer:

> The rattle basket dry
> Hung in the summer dust
> Over the parched rye
> Swinging
> A cantonelle
> With withered bell
> For spring.

It ended: 'A violin / Dances our brittle maidens in.' There were in *The Serpent* rather too many invocations of Rupert Brooke or brash exercises in headrime from students into whom Anglo-Saxon had been hammered. In one of my novels, *The Kingdom of the Wicked*, I hand over to Nero the first line of one of these latter, about Hannibal: 'Proud with his pachyderms piling the perilous passes'. Godwin's poetic instincts seemed to me to be right, but nostalgia perhaps gets in the way of an objective judgment.

Our first act in the new regime of *The Serpent* was to mock Godwin's pretension with what we called 'The Upjohn Poems'. These were of the order of 'A phthisical cat / On a bicycle sat / And winked at the waning moon', followed by obscure pseudo-notes. But we were serious too. I at last saw a poem of my own in print:

> You being the gate
> Where the army went through,
> Would you renew
> The triumph and have them decorate
> The arch and stone again?
> Surely those flowers are withered, the army
> Now on a distant plain.
>
> But some morning when you are washing up,
> Or some afternoon, making a cup
> Of tea, possibly you will see
> The heavens opening and a lot
> Of saints singing with bells swinging.
> But then again, possibly not.

I have never quite understood this poem. In my novel *Enderby* I ascribe it to the dyspeptic poet who is, despite what the critics say, not myself, though he is the author of some of my poems as well as his own. To him it is the voice of the Muse departing and counselling suicide. To me I suppose it was any young man rejecting the mother who had produced and sustained him to the point of his finding an arrogant freedom. But I had no mother. I had in mind, probably, a generalised situation for which it was my poetic duty to provide the words. The poem was headed 'To Tirzah'. Tirzah, I think, was a character in Blake's prophetic books who stood for the physically maternal. I do not propose checking on this. Blake once made me drunk and now I elect to be sober.

Books were sent to us for review. The reviews in university magazines are not unimportant: they are read by young people whose transient speciality is reading books. There was a book by a man named Cannon about moral disarmament, and the title for my review was 'Cannon Balls'. This aroused doubt when it appeared in proof. We had to be careful. It was changed to 'Cannonade'. When Laura Riding's *Collected Poems* appeared I published a review which pleased the author, who wrote a long letter to the editor demurring only at my description of her poetic persona as resembling one of the 'great-breasted females in William Blake'. She was encouraged to visit the university to lecture, with Robert Graves tagging along in worshipful silence. She was not great-breasted; she looked shrivelled and bowed and she limped. None of us knew that she had thrown herself out of a window, crying 'Goodbye, chaps' to Graves and his rival lover, and had damaged her spine. She talked for fifteen minutes on what she called 'The Story of Poetry' and refused questions on the grounds that these were bound to indicate a lack of understanding of her doctrine. But she dealt out more wisdom on a couch before the fire, while Graves smoked, threw his fag-ends at that fire and always missed.

Shortly afterwards Graves's own *Collected Poems* appeared, and these I attacked with undergraduate viciousness, finding the mature Graves inferior to the immature Auden. The poet sent a letter of counter-attack, accusing me of being not merely illiterate but analphabetic. A supporting letter from Laura Riding demanded that Graves's letter be published in *The Serpent*: she had made an opposed stipulation with regard to her own encomium of my taste and intelligence. In my review of Graves I referred to his missing his target with his cigarette-ends, and said that this was a fair analogue of his poetic technique. Graves angrily riposted that nobody had offered him an ashtray, that stupidity and discourtesy made appropriate bedfellows, and signed off with 'Who cares, anyway? Certainly not yours etc.' This was my first contact with the small-mindedness of the literary great.

Not that I was much concerned with literature except as a subject for academic study. I had no ambition to write for an extramural public: composing music was a different matter. When I entered literature seriously, much later in life, it was through music. I wanted to write an opera and so started by writing my own libretto. This was too long, so I turned it into a play. Nobody wished to produce the play, so I turned it into a novella. I was proposing an opera in my first year at the university, and Douglas Mason, who had genuine ambitions as a poet, collaborated with me on the libretto, which was about Copernicus. But in those days it was hard to draw the line between Brechtian epic drama and opera: what was *Mahagonny*, what was *Der Dreigroschenoper*? We ended up with a kind of *Singspiel*, parachronic in that Copernicus preached the noumenon of a heliocentric universe to a modern world satisfied with mere phenomena. One of the numbers was a tango:

> One kind of love
> Slakes its sorrow in the sunlight;
> One kind of love
> Melts its music in the moonlight . . .

The piano score of that tango is still around. I was told of a performance of it on BBC Radio Three in October 1985. The opera itself aborted as it had to. There was not the time for labouring at orchestral scores.

I did not wish to be known as a poet or critic or short-story writer. But I did not object to being known as a good journalist. If *The Serpent* needed a theatre notice or book review or short story I would provide it. If a page needed to be filled with a few lines of verse I would provide those too. I liked clattering at the office typewriter against deadlines; I liked the floor to be billowing in snaky galleys which had to be corrected with the right professional symbols. When my short story 'Grief' was awarded five guineas as the best piece of undergraduate writing of the year, with Harold Nicolson adjudicating, I was pleased about the money but embarrassed by the assumption that literature was my chosen vocation. I still wanted to be a great composer.

That *The Serpent* did not concern itself with music criticism – and this in a city where music was life, at least for the Jews, Germans and Italians – reflected Cedric Hirson's own prejudices. I wanted to go to concerts free and write about them, but concerts to Hirson were nugatory nougat. Music said nothing about the historical process we were living through. Did drama? Yes: even Euripides put on by the Classical Society. I attended Euripides in a translation by Lady Barlow and sneered at 'Barlow's mighty line'. I was publicly slapped by one of the actresses in the cafeteria. This had recently happened to the Dean of Fleet Street, Hannan Swaffer; I felt important. But I felt too, when I failed Latin General twice, that Professor Semple, who sponsored the Euripides production, was being vindictive, like Robert Graves though with more power to hurt. Journalism was dangerous.

Journalism became highly dangerous when the *Rag Rag* came out. The university had the tradition of helping to fund the Manchester hospitals by organising a Shrovetide carnival, or rag, and this was preceded by weeks of going round the town selling the *Rag Rag*. It was a male venture that was expected to skate about the black hole of obscenity, and a committee was convened in the Men's Union early in the year to discuss, over beer, its content. The editor was Gerry Wolfson, and I was on the committee. The content was to be not all dirt, but what dirt there had to be must be presented with delicate ambiguity. The public expected mild obscenity, but it was quick to be disgusted. On the back page of one issue there was the drawing of the backside of an elephant, with the legend 'That's another big job done'. This was banned by the Manchester Watch Committee, and copies were sold at a high price on the steps of the Stock Exchange. I contributed a drawing of a pawnbroker's shop door, with three brass balls prominent and the comment 'Superman'. We got away with this, but only just. In the age of magazines with names like *Shit*, *Wank* and *Fuck*, the equivocal management of dirt in the late thirites must seem pitiable. It was the way things were, and perhaps that way, which entailed scabrous ingenuity, was better than the gross freedom to present copulation and defecation. Some of the humour was childish, like the free offer of a picture of Eddie Cantor which turned out to be of a decanter. An acrostic required more skill, like, on the first page:

> From the faubourgs of Manchester,
> Under bridges, through the drains,
> Comes (ah, hear the branches stir)
> Keening of the southbound trains.
>
> Copies of our rag arrive,
> Up and down the vendors run.
> Nab your copies – four or five.
> That's the spirit – oh, well done!

I could, implausibly, have pleaded coincidence, but nobody spotted the foulness.

In the Men's Union, at noon on the eve of Shrove Tuesday, the rag debate was held. The motion was a mere concession to form; the vote also, since there was nothing to vote on. The two sides vied for foulness. I had to propose, in my second year, that a man loves a woman for her beauty. The opposition declared that a woman loves a man for *his* beauty (in the sense of 'that's a beauty, that is'). The audience was rowdy and equipped with cardboard farters; heckling was coarse and irrelevant; the medical students howled filthy obstetrics. It was university life at its worst. The debate ended with the debagging of a foreigner or suspected homosexual. The medicals chose badly one year – a Siamese with a withered leg. At my debate a fifth-columnist opened the door to let the Women's Union in. They carried a banner – 'Excelsior – or, We're Curious'. They pelted us with old eggs and green refuse. They were manhandled and their clothes ripped. I fought for Zozafin Wulfson, whose breasts were being forcibly exposed. It was not amusing. But it was, in the view of the town, what the gown was all about.

In the evening there was the Rag Ball, to which one came in fancy dress. The doors between the unions were now legitimately opened, and dull girl swots appeared in the glamour of gipsy skirts or no skirts at all. There were three bands and celebrity guests like Pat Kirkwood and even Gracie Fields, who was an honorary MA. It was glamorous and drunken and erotic. It ended with bacon and eggs at five in the morning. Then came the great day of the rag procession. How energetic we all were.

Each university school had a float provided by a local brewery. In my first year the English Department decorated and manned its float to represent Prison Reform. The men were convicts in old pyjamas arrow-painted; the girls wore very little as wardresses of reform; they sat on our knees and we embraced them and stroked their silk thighs; they waved empty champagne bottles to the Manchester air. How repressed and susceptible all we men were. We chased these girls on Ash Wednesday, moaning at the size of our erections, but they had become prim and skirted again. For them there was a great divide between reality and theatre. We had to sustain the show of the erotic all the way to the centre of Manchester, while other floats presented fairyland or Hollywood or Hawaii or the Roaring Twenties (remoter then

than they are now) or Hitler's Germany as seen with comic lack
of foresight by Jewish students of Economics and Modern History, or Mussolini in an Abyssinian cooking pot. A medical float
showed a frightful operation with hacksaws and garden shears
and the message GIVE US YOUR MONEY: WE KNOW YOU'VE GOT
PILES. Money was thrown at us from the crammed cheering
and booing pavements, thousands of pennies that stung. They
warmed half-nakedness in that February cold as nettles warmed
the legs of Roman legionaries near Hadrian's Wall. The crawling
wagons finally parked off Piccadilly and we got off to roam the
streets and offices and restaurants and pubs in our costumes, rattling collecting-boxes, jumped on and off buses free, quipping with
growing fatigue. As the cold evening came on, the police telephones were jammed with complaints: a broken saxophone, confidential files thrown through windows, typists' knickers removed,
cars overturned. Pub curates were weary with the swabbing of
student vomit. The festive day ended with a dance at Shorrocks's, at
which an Indian doctor named Soni bit and knifed and John B.
sang 'Sweet Sue' through the band microphone. Our dancing
partners were nurses from the Royal Infirmary and they carried
tooth paste in their handbags as a contraceptive. Raw infirmary
alcohol was tasted and drove men mad. The university women
were, wisely, back in their halls of residence. Ash Wednesday
had early lectures and crapula and retching on to Sweet's *Anglo-
Saxon Reader*. Those were the happiest days of our lives.

Some of us, at this season of bacchanalia, engaged in a little raw
sex in alleyways or kissed respectable women in the streets, but few
had got nearer to a regular erotic relationship with a fellow-student.
Indeed, Bate, Mason, Gaunt and I had the possibility of such a
relationship defused by some of the girls themselves. A message
came through Mason to the effect that it was time the more
personable men of the English first year realised that there were
personable women there, and that there should be an effort made
towards effecting sodality. This meant lunching together and using
first names. There was to be no question of pairing off. When my
twenty-first birthday arrived on February 25, 1938, an eightsome
of us had dinner at a restaurant in Piccadilly at three and sixpence
a head with six bottles of Sauternes at one and sixpence each. It
was a dinner of the regular prewar amplitude – with entrée,
poultry and a remove – and when I gave the waitress a tip of half
a crown she gasped 'Oh, thank you, sir.' Then we went in two
taxis to the Opera House to see Noël Coward's *Operette*. Noël

Coward was Gaunt's king and also Manchester's. Coward approved of Manchester, of the French restaurant at the Midland Hotel, of quiet assignations which London could not gossip about, of rock-hard Manchester taste which only genuine wit, pathos and melody could pierce. Manchester called Coward the Master before London did. Gaunt went backstage to pay his respects, and the Master said: 'Any relation to John of?' Gaunt went to see *Operette* again and was gleeful at being in on running repairs. It was not a good show, and Coward knew it. He added new verses to 'The Stately Homes of England':

> A manuscript of Chaucer contains a dirty joke,
> A fragment of a saucer that bloody Mary broke . . .

So my second term ended and my father prepared for death.

MY FATHER HAD grown thinner and he coughed much of the time. He went to the shop on Princess Road every morning and was brought back by Jack Tollitt in the car in time for lunch and an exhausted coughing afternoon in his armchair trying to read Pett Ridge. In the cold spring of 1938 he tried to sow some seeds in the garden, and the wind, unbroken by trees, cut him to the bone. He was only in his fifties but he began to look like a very old man. My stepmother tried to feed him strange mixtures but he rejected them. He took to his bed with what seemed to be pleurisy. His breathing was hard, and I kept hearing it as the rhythm of the variations by William Byrd on

> The leaves be green,
>   The nuts be brown,
> They hang so high
>   They will not fall down.

It was not the rhythm of the prize poem I was trying to write on the Bliss of Solitude. The local doctor I brought in, a stranger called Dr Hawkes, pronounced that the patient had pleuro-pneumonia and little could be done. The strain on the heart was great and would get greater. The heart was weak anyway. Dr Hawkes had some notion that the only thing to do was to give subcutaneous injections of adrenalin to stimulate a heart that soon would no longer respond to stimulation. The injections were left to me and I performed them clumsily. I sat by my father, who maintained a total alertness and cursed his dyspnoea – orthopnoea really, since he could only breathe sitting up – like some exterior demon. 'You'll get over it,' I soothed. 'Only by bloody dying,' he said. 'You'd better get the priest.'

The man who had said that when you snuffed it you were finished with was now taking death seriously in the Catholic manner. There might be an eternity and the screws of endless agony turned by a vindictive God. It was to be the usual deathbed repentance. I went looking for a priest in Fallowfield. This was the land of lobelias and tennis flannels and there were few churches, Catholic or other. I found one priest who refused to come since we were not in his parish. I found another who inveighed, much in the manner of Mr Eliot in *The Rock*, against feeble Catholics who used the Church for baptisms and marriages but not for regular attendance; he seemed to treat my request for the last rites for my father as a sort of frivolity. He left it to his ageing curate to indulge. This was an Irishman far gone in alcoholism, both the cause and the result of his failure to achieve a rectory. He tottered home with me muttering, dropping his bag twice. Quite in the style of an Evelyn Waugh graduate of Maynooth, he comforted my father with 'Dere dere, fella, it's a lovely death you'll be makin', I'm sure, glory be to God.' So my father was confessed of his poor little villainies, coughed out the host and had it reinserted, and then had the orifices of his body sealed with oil and grace. Like Gerontius, he was ready for the journey. The priest was fortified with whisky for his walk back in the spring chill. The Wilsons, Dwyers, Kemps and Tollitts began to arrive and congest the bedroom. 'How much bloody longer?' groangasped my father. And then: 'What does bloody God think he's bloody playing at?' It was thought that he ought to have the priest again, but he said he would prefer a pint of draught Bass. Then he told me to be good to my mother, meaning my stepmother, and expired horribly. I had seen death in films, but it had always been noiseless and hygienic. This was gross and loud. All knelt except me, who knew my *Ulysses* too well. All remained kneeling for the collapse of the excretory system and the filling of the room with a stench that had to be termed diabolic. Perhaps the Cathars were right and the flesh and the devil were one.

The husk with its collapsed sphincters was buried in Moston

Cemetery, and the mourners proceeded to the upper room of a restaurant for the funeral feast of ham and salad and fancy cakes. Why is it always ham? There is a cannibalistic touch, I think, pig's flesh being closest to human and the curing of it rich with resonance. Jack Tollitt went round the table with two other Johns, Haig and Walker, splashing hearty dollops into strong tea. Many a mourner had caught his own death in a hillside cemetery on a Manchester day of early spring. Nothing like whisky. The funeral party grew cheerful and even merry. My father's favourite jokes were recalled to set the table on a sad roar. They were innocently obscene with no sex in them. My Uncle Jack remembered the epitaph his brother had, not altogether facetiously, wanted carved:

> Under the stone poor old Joe lies,
> Nobody laughs and nobody cries.
> Where he has gone and how he now fares
> Nobody knows and nobody sodding well cares.

But on his grave there was only JOSEPH WILSON 1883–1938. I quoted the pseudo-Homeric lines for Margites. Neither a digger nor a ploughman. For he failed in every art. Was that true? He had had strong wrists to engage a keyboard but thrown the gift away. He had had a hard head at book-keeping. But there had been a good deal of the shiftless Irish in him, a love of drink and empty conviviality, balanced by accessions of ramrod Britishry, hair well trimmed, shoes well polished. The final test of attainment would be the reading of his will. But he died intestate. He had nothing to leave except his wardrobe, a brace of initialled bowling woods, racegoer's binoculars, a Parker pen. These were seized by other members of the joint families. I got nothing and I wanted nothing. He was out of my life and I could get on with my own. I wrote some verses that I neither finished nor published:

> Anciently the man who showed
> Hate to this father with the sword
> Was bundled into a coarse sack
> With a screaming ape to claw his back
> And the squawking talk of a parrot to mock
> Time's terror of air-and-light's lack
> Black
> And the writhing litheness of a snake,
> Then he was swirled into the sea.

But that was all balls and talk,
Nowadays we have changed all that,
Into a cleaner light to walk
And wipe that mire off on the mat.
So when I saw his end was near
My brain was freer
And scrawled a cancellation then
Of all the accidents of birth,
And I had a better right to the earth
And knew myself more of a man,
Shedding the last squamour of the old skin.

But it is not so easy to write off a father as a mere instrument of generation. There was plenty of him in me, even in the shaving mirror. Parricide, the Roman punishment for which I seemed to know all about, was partial suicide. Why, anyway, should I want to kill my father? He had better grounds for wanting to kill me, who had survived, crowing in my cot, a loved wife and daughter. He had commuted filicide into genial neglect. I had no Oedipal motive for either resentment or eventual guilt. Yet the guilt that now took possession was morbid and excessive. I dreamt about my father. He stalked my bedroom in his nightshirt; his head sprouted on its walls, multiply, like, as I wrote in a story about this guilt and those nightmares, 'squeezed comedones in acne'. The final dream about him was grotesque. He was wandering, still in his nightshirt, in a library that contained only bound volumes of *Punch*. Whimpering, he searched for something in volume after volume. Eventually he seemed to find what he wanted, grinned ghastlily, belched in a kind of drinker's triumph, then disappeared. He reappeared months afterwards in the flesh at a Hallé concert, during the final movement of Beethoven's *Eroica*. He wore his bowler hat. He nodded at me as to show satisfaction that I was still listening to music, then he vanished. I have had too much experience with revenants to scoff at the living traces the dead leave behind. Ghosts walk, no doubt about it. Hearing those final variations again on the radio a short time after, I saw my father's head, bowlerless, embronzed into that of a being of myth. Prometheus, of course: that was what Beethoven was doing too – getting a living man out of the stream of history he oppressed by converting him into mythology.

Something drove me to write a comic ballade to Prometheus. I was walking the streets of Manchester at night with a cigarette in my mouth but nothing to light it with. The lines came:

> Father of fire who, with bold simony,
>   Didst steal the seed, cached high on Olympus,
> Now in my need relive that felony
>   And lean down to my praying, piteous.
>   Be thou again as brave and bounteous
> As when thou first didst bring that art of heat
>   To nations bestial still and barbarous,
> And fetch a match to light my cigarette.

There was my father, proffering a flaring Swan Vesta. He had become both myth and comedy. He was out of the way. Whether he had anything to do with a curious and debilitating ailment that now struck me I do not know. The ailment is known technically as spermatorrhoea, emission after emission of seed during the night, in my case with no accompanying visions of fat women (who would all, if they had appeared, have been allomorphs of my stepmother). The seed passes, anyway, without erection or orgasm. It was perhaps the voiding of my father as donor of the seed that had become myself; it was perhaps a kind of mimesis of the father as Prometheus. It was more likely sexual repression. Awake, though, I had things other than sex to worry about. When my father had been alive he had provided nominal protection in a ménage where he was a mere employee. Now I was unprotected and had to live on my stepmother's charity. Some of the insurance money collected on my father's death could go to the completion of my education, but that too was a favour. I was totally orphaned.

My stepmother gave up tenancy of the house in Fallowfield and moved, with me, back to Princess Road in Moss Side. The shop, with M. Wilson above its window in gilt, was now at Number 47, in the corner of Raby Street. The premises were more commodious than those at Number 21, and there was a bedroom for my stepmother. For me there was a bed in the bedroom of my nephew Dan, then eleven, but this bedroom, at the top of the shop, was also a billiard-room, for Jack Tollitt was fond of the sport. If I went to bed early it was to the click of the snooker balls or to the plop of darts, for there was a dart-board as well. Jack Tollitt had a right to such solace, since he was now in charge of the business and had heavy responsibilities. He also had my stepmother watching his conduct of it, the poor widow-woman as she now called herself, conscious of the fragility of life and the solidity of money. Jack Tollitt ought to have given her full satisfaction, for he was distressingly energetic, disdained paid assistance, and even turned Sunday into a day of intense labour – the earliest possible mass, and then the hum and the knock of the vacuum cleaner in all possible corners, followed by a late cold lunch. I grew frightened of him.

I was frightened frequently in the night by the sleepwalking of my nephew Dan and the simultaneous nightmares of my niece Sheila. She would shriek and occasionally laugh; he would turn on all the lights of the house and deal out, on the dining-table, four full hands for a game of whist. Then he would put out the lights and go back to bed. He woke rested and always looked well nourished, though he would eat nothing but mashed potatoes. He, the genuine son with genuine mother and father and grandmother, enshrined the hopes of the family, though he did badly at school. I, the orphaned wraith on the periphery, was one of the dangerously and uselessly clever, of age but still at studies which had no clearly defined purpose in the real world, begging for pocket money when I should have been earning a wage. Money was becoming a problem. My stepmother, doling out my weekly four shillings one Monday morning, uttered unforgettable words: 'We thought you going to the university would be a grace and a blessing, but 'tis turned out to be a curse and a ruin.' This had something to do with my being crapulous on the Sunday morning and neglecting to go to mass. Religion, an aspect of and halo over secular efficiency, was back in my life.

One way of obtaining money was the invention of examinations I alleged I had to take, all of which required an enrolment fee – Intermediate Morphology, Applied Pornology and so on. But I never had enough for my regular week-end booze-ups, and, in the massive storehouse of cellophaned cigarette packets over which I lived, or at least slept, I was expected to pay for the odd twenty Player's. Thus some of my pocket money went back to the shop, registering the usual small profit on a retail sale. I envied the affluence of fellow-students, who began the day with a fresh packet of Kensitas (plus four for your friends) and thought nothing of spending sixpence on the latest Penguin.

Jack Tollitt was sometimes kind to me, especially when I had spent a Saturday delivering parcels of fumables to small shops or had collected an order of cut plug from the tobacco depot run by

O'Mahoney's. He would take me for the occasional Saturday or even Sunday night out to one of the refined boozers called roadhouses which were a feature of the thirties. He even considered it a good idea to take me to the dinners and dances which were an aspect of both business and religion. There were Catholic business affairs and secular business affairs, and, in the company of scented, bare-shouldered ladies, it was obligatory for the men to wear white tie and tails. So I was kitted out for all of seven guineas by the local tailor Bradford and his son. Bradford had lost his wife and taken to going to spiritualistic séances to evoke her spirit through a Red Indian control. His dead wife seemed to have little to say, but he heard a good deal about the world beyond from Julius Caesar, whom that world called Brighteyes, and Octavius Caesar, who was known as Tivvy. He talked much about these encounters while a tail suit was erected on to me. I was glad when the task was finished. I looked, they all said, well in it, being six feet tall and lithely slim. I would, it was said further, have no difficulty in picking up a good Catholic girl at one of the sodality or confraternity or Catholic commercial dances. So that was what it was all about. Michael Callaghan, now affianced to Dorothy Fitzmaurice, was in on it too. He had made friends with Agnes and Jack Tollitt and helped to establish the myth of my being clever but misguided. I too needed a Catholic fiancée, preferably one from a good Manchester Irish business family.

But I possessed as well as this need a certain minor onomastic magic. I was the son of my dead father, namely a Wilson. Jack Tollitt ran Wilson's, but the world had to know that the name was familially attached to one very much among the living. My stepmother was still really a Byrne and a Dwyer; I was genuinely Wilsonic; I recalled my father, known and respected in the world of tobacco. I was at the university, and this signified that the firm Wilson's had status. When the tobacconists of Manchester revolted against Kensitas and a great meeting of protest was organised by the Raleigh Club, I was present within the locked doors, ready at the rollcall to cry 'J. B. Wilson of Wilson's'.

I mentioned above the morning packet of Kensitas (plus four for your friends) bought by the richer of my fellow-students. The brand of cigarette no longer exists, but it was popular in the late thirties. A creature of the firm Wix, it had a suave butler on the packet and in the advertisements, presenting an open packet on a silver tray and saying 'Your Kensitas cigarettes, sir.' The shilling packet of twenty had a smaller packet attached to it, and this contained the four for your friends. Thus, you got twenty-four cigarettes for the price of twenty. The Wix generosity did not apply to the packet of ten, and this is what caused the trouble and instigated the great meeting of protest. For Messrs Wix insisted that wholesale and retail suppliers take tens as well as twenties plus four, and in the proportion that applied to other brands. Now a packet of ten Kensitas provided as good a smoke as Gold Flake, Black Cat, Senior Service or Player's, but nobody was prepared to buy one when, for double the price, he could get those extra four for his friends, meaning himself. The Wix benison had the effect of making smokers doubt the virtue of the tobacco, which was a pity: such generosity had to have a catch in it. The other catch, which hit hard small merchants who could not sell their tens, met so fiery a protest that Kensitas cigarettes were unanimously boycotted. Eventually the brand disappeared. Wix had not thought hard enough. The poor man who could afford only sixpence was subsidising the rich man with a shilling. I made my own little speech of denunciation at that assembly of the Raleigh Club. I had every right, being Wilson of Wilson's.

But I could still hardly afford to smoke. God knew how I would ever be able to afford to take a girl out. Poor as I was, however, I still insisted on the Friday night booze-up, with Gaunt and Mason and two men from the English second year named Ian McColl and Harry Green. Green and McColl fascinated me. They were coarse, rejecting totally the grace of civilisation, but the English language and its literature were their life. McColl was so soaked in Anglo-Saxon that it was a natural instinct for him to avoid Latinisms and Hellenisms even in colloquial speech. He was quite prepared, like the poet Barnes, to call an omnibus a folkwain or a telephone a fartalker. He knew German but hated the Nazis, who, after all, were only disinfecting their language of exoticisms in McColl's own manner. He and Green knew there was a war coming, and they did regular infantry drill with the university Officer Training Corps. They were both killed in France in 1940, following the tradition of First World War subalterns, and this they were perhaps prepared to foresee. They never spoke of a future; they were fixed in a present of which the literary past was a part. McColl composed orally an endless saga about two lecherous boozers called Filthfroth and Brothelbreath with lines like

> Wight then wendeth to pisshouse whitewashéd,
> Pulleth out prick, full featly pisseth.

Green, outside a pub in the Shambles called The White Horse, exclaimed at the ancient rune, which the Normans replaced with a digraph, in the definite article. In some arty antique signs, like those outside county town teashops, that rune appears as a Y, but it did not here. 'Christ,' Green cried, 'they've got a proper fucking thorn.' Green's hero was not to be found in academia. He was the RSM of the OTC, who once delivered this monologue: 'In the fucking regimental colours of the British fucking army there's fucking black, fucking red, fucking yellow, and all the fucking colours on the fucking snooker table except fucking pink. And now this fucker here says that he's seen fucking heliotrope. Christ strike me fucking what he says.' Both Green and McColl accepted the *Scrutiny* literary canon, but they were ahead of it, rather than behind, in exalting Kipling, Burns and A. E. Housman. Ale, lad, ale's the stuff to drink, for fellows whom it hurts to think. Mithridates, he died old. McColl felt there was a literary future for the *Shropshire Lad* technique if it could be deprissified:

> And I have walked no way I looked
> But multitudinously puked
> Into the gutter, legs outstretched,
> Holding my sconce low as I retched.

'Multitudinously', a blatant Latinism, he excused since it was being vomited up or out.

The Luftwaffe destroyed the Shambles, where the oldest pubs of Manchester stood, and where we swilled our fivepenny pints and I earned free ones by playing the piano. I partially solved my money problems by being paid ten shillings to play regularly at the Black Horse on Friday and Saturday evenings. It pleased McColl and Green that the Black Horse should be known to its patrons as the Cuddy. Cuddy was the familiar form of Cuthbert, and Cuthbert was the name given to the donkey in mediaeval bestiaries. A black horse might be in order for cavaliers, but a donkey was for the common drinker. They might have drunk longer in the Cuddy on my subsidies if they had not been inspired to linguistic excesses – loud recitations from *Beowulf* or the latest lines of the Filthfroth and Brothelbreath saga. Get your bloody pals out of here, this is a respectable pub this is.

But the weekend pianism would not have lasted long anyway. My father, a suffering pastmaster of the craft, had warned me of its hazards. The pianist was usually despised, especially by the casual pub-singers he had to accompany. He would ask them what key they proposed singing in, and they would reply: 'We've only got one bloody key to our 'ouse.' He would symphonise in one key and they would come in in another. They would invariably pitch themselves too high, break down, and blame it all on the pianist. The north-west was full of amateur singers, and pub-song, however inept, was usually respected. 'Best of order. The singer's on his feet.' But if the pianist took a couple of minutes off to gulp at one of his donated pints, he would be told: ''Ere, you, get on wi't' bloody job, that's what yer paid for.' If the instrument was out of tune and produced sour chords, that again was the fault of the player. Coarse voices were admired, efficient accompaniments were not noticed. The pianist's ignorance of very arcane songs or very new songs was condemned. An interlude of Chopin brought howls of anger. I was sacked when I showed off by playing the 'Jupiter' movement from the full score of Holst's *The Planets*. There was a narrow code of musical decency. I did not take up semi-professional pub-playing again until after the war, when I needed the week-end thirty-five shillings to supplement my salary as a training college lecturer. It is hard work and ill-regarded, and it requires uncommon tolerance and skill. A large memorised repertoire is needed and an ability to improvise accompaniments to songs one has not heard before. Few of the great professional concert players could do the job.

In the spring and summer of 1938 Gaunt, Mason and I remained womanless. Boozing with Green and McColl and quipping with whores and curlered stout-soused loose wives should, we recognised, not be the only release from study. We were now friendly enough with the girls of our own year, but these had insisted on a sisterly relationship which could be broken only with tears or screams of rape. We drooled, as though they were film stars, over women close to graduation – Esmé Stokes and Jean Buckingham and a fur-coated siren named Audrey Lightbowne. We played poker with segments of their unattainable bodies as stakes. Mason said, in a fantasy that the Nazis were to make real, though not out of love, that he would like a lampshade made of the skin of Esmé Stokes. He fought me in the junior seminar when I improvised a sneering rhyme:

> Everyone pokes
> Esmé Stokes,
> Uncouth blokes

> Who belch beery jokes,
> And an acneous lout who smokes
> Woodbines while he –

This was the life of frustration lived by normally sexed educated young males of the thirties. We needed anaphrodisiacs, a weekly dose of quinine in our tea. How the homosexuals got on we did not know. There did not seem to be many of them about.

What Manchester University needed, but what seemed reserved to the older seats of learning, was a touch of the epicene exquisite, the flavour of wealthy and cultivated decadence summed up in Waugh's Anthony Blanche. John A. Wilson's pastiches of Ronald Firbank in *The Serpent* represented a yearning for what the smoky industrial north-west could never provide: we were too grimly utilitarian for perverse chic. At a corner table of the cafeteria regularly sat characters who breathed a sort of insouciant leisure, medical women who wilfully failed the various stages of the MB, drank and smoked heavily, took mild drugs, had lovers, followed *Work in Progress*, read John Dos Passos, reminisced about escapades in Cap d'Ail and Munich, but whose bit of money manifestly came from a cotton broker father. We lacked the civilising force of aristocratic land. There were no aristocrats other than the Manchester Jews. Our foreigners were mostly Germans like Oskar Bünemann, Klaus Pickard and Karl Prauschnitz, the odd Armenian or Russian, hard-working research chemists who specialised in new techniques of industrial dyeing. We needed the air of a sybaritic world, but that was alien to our fog and blunt vowels.

As for homosexuality, Gaunt, Mason and I only felt its full blast in the thespian form. When a travelling Shakespeare company came to the Princes Theatre, we volunteered for walk-on parts and were greeted by an ageing queer who played John of Gaunt and Polonius. 'Everything off,' he cried, 'drop all your stitches,' and we stood shivering as for a medical examination while he appraised our gooseflesh. He dressed us as if we were babies, inserting a final lecherous hand to adjust the sit of our ballocks. In the intervals he, with horrible energy, leapt on to a pretty ephebe in the Law School whose name was Clement Forbes, so innocent that he wondered what the display of fierce affection was all about. One night of *Richard II* was enough for most of us, but Gaunt, whose love of the theatre was inordinate, insisted on appearing in *Hamlet* and even tossed a coin for the privilege of being one of the bearers of Ophelia's bier. He was at the head and had a constant view of the girl's cleavage. We in our free seats watched his codpiece sturdily fill. A black cat walked on the stage during that scene, and Gaunt had the wit to improvise blank verse sturdily intoned:

> Alas, poor puss, in nature's weeds of woe,
> What living prey thinkst thou to pounce on here,
> Where only death hath claws and ravening teeth?

The cat walked off at leisure, though to no applause. In the wings afterwards Gaunt was bitterly hit by a revived Polonius. He maintained his love of the theatre.

At the end of the academic year I passed my English papers but failed in French and Modern European History at the intermediate level. I could take these again in September, but I had a conviction that I would never pass in history so long as A. J. P. Taylor was there. Fortunately he left, beginning his long elevation, and a man named Bolsover took his place. He accepted the bright ideas and lack of knowledge of my second attempt at the examination, and I passed. I passed in French too, probably because Colin Smith, who was in charge of the oral part, was an amateur violoncellist and found my knowledge of French musical terms adequate. I was glad to be rid of French. It has never been my preferred foreign language.

Rid of it? I have spent the last twelve years living on French-speaking territory, but I have constantly resisted trying to speak it well or, indeed, speaking it at all. I occasionally give lectures in French and appear on French television, but always as though masochistically probing a sore tooth. I know how the French phonemic system operates, and I can phonate the perverse front rounded vowels adequately, but I will not learn the patterns of intonation. To speak French well one has to convert oneself into a temporary Frenchman, and this I refuse to do. I deploy a large and sometimes arcane vocabulary in the service of a display of John Bullishness. This happens especially when I have to appear on radio or television with French writers. I resent their exquisiteness, their proclaimed friability, their writhing at the agonies of producing art. I resent their incestuousness, their assumption that only the Parisian audience counts, their devotion to ephemeral literary theories and doubtful masters like Barthes and Derrida. The language itself I can accept and even revere in its written form, but I am aware that it is tainted with disease. It calls itself the major form of post-imperial Latin, but spoken French is trying to turn itself into an agglutinative lingo like Eskimo. I object to Christ being turned into Chri. There is something profoundly wrong with a language that changes *aqua* into *eau*. I sympathise with the Robert Graves of *Goodbye to All That*, who found his good French a discardable frippery and his bad German a part of his flesh and bone. My own German is atrocious, but I taste ancestral roots and fungi in the language. I married a Latin but I could never become one myself. In exile I sustain a Nordic patriotism.

Gaunt's and my devotion to English was permitted fulfilment: we were to stay in the Honours School. But Mason was ejected and told to take an Ordinary Arts degree. Nobody, in the view of Gaunt and myself, had a more exquisite sense of the genius of English than Mason. He wrote sensitive poetry. He had even entered a prize poem on the Bliss of Solitude, far too Poundian for the judges. Now he was to be a sort of one-eyed king of the blind. Gaunt pinned to the English School notice board a parody of Eliot's Fire Sermon, with 'O Lord thou chuckest me out'. This had to be explained to Professor Charlton, who despised and hence did not read Eliot, as he irritably tore it down. But something bigger than a departmental decision seemed likely, in September 1938, to chuck us all out. Hitler had taken Austria in March; the Munich agreement did not deceive us. There were too many knowledgeable Germans in the *Hauptstadt* that was Manchester, along with a growing number of refugee German and Austrian Jews, for us to think, as we were settling into the new academic year, that it was really peace in our time.

The first issue of *The Serpent* in that year was realistic and bitter. Cedric Hirson contributed a Dos Passos pastiche which ended with 'Peace in our time. But there's not much time when you're seventy.' Neville Chamberlain was to reach that age in 1939: to us he was very old and therefore very stupid. I published a poem entitled 'September 1938':

> There arose those winning life between two wars,
> Born out of one, doomed food for the other,
> Flood roars ever in the ears.
> Sloth-lovers hardly, hardly fighters,
> Resentment spent against stone, long beaten out of
> Mind resigned to the new:
> Useless to queue for respirators.

Besides, what worse chaos to come back to:
Home, limbs heavy with mud and work,
To sleep
To sweep out of a house days deep in dirt.
Knowing finally man would limbs, loins, face
Efface utterly, leaving regent in his place
Engines rusting to world's end, heirs to warfare
Fonctionnant d'une manière automatique.

The last line came from *Un Coeur Simple*. The image of machines
fighting each other came from H. G. Wells's film *Things to Come*.
This, which we had all seen some years previously, impressed us
as true prophecy. Wells's long war began at Christmas 1940. In
the book on which the film was based the *casus belli* was the
Polish corridor, the immediate incitement to hostilities a Polish
Jew's trying to remove a fragment of walnut from his teeth and
an SS man interpreting this is as a slight to the swastika. We
trusted Wells more than Chamberlain. Even the British state
seemed impressed by his promise of immediate poison gas: an
issue of respirators was the first chilling image of the film, done
in panic with clamorous crowds, and a more calmly bureaucratic
issue was the first feature of the new age that was on us. The tone
of the poem reflected, I believe, the sentiment of a lot of my
contemporaries. War was undoubtedly coming, and it would be
a repetition of the ramp of twenty years back, with the old killing
the young. It would be one capitalistic system fighting another,
said our communists. It would not be a struggle for socialist justice
like the war in Spain.

Two days after my twenty-second birthday Great Britain recognised General Franco's government. On March 16 Hitler annexed
Bohemia and Moravia and proclaimed a German protectorate.
On March 22 Lithuania ceded Memel to Germany. On March 28
Germany began a heavy anti-Polish press campaign. On April 1
the Spanish war ended. On April 7 Italy seized Albania. It was
hard, in the spring of 1939, to concentrate on Eliotian dissociation
of sensibility and linguisitic phenomena like i-mutation. But the
prevernal rag was untouched by worries about the future. The
Rag Rag appeared and was duly suppressed. On the float of the
English School we presented fairyland, with myself as the fairy
queen. That I should take on this role was the idea of Basil Hol-
gate, a sophisticate from Manchester Grammar School: I still do
not know why I was thought fitting. When the procession came

to an end, and, bruised with hurled pennies, we rattled our collecting-boxes round the town in our cold costumes, my false
breasts were much mauled by lewdly laughing women. I was
unmoved and did not in reciprocity finger real ones. I was
sexually fulfilled. I was even in love.

At the beginning of the year the English Department held a
party for freshmen and freshwomen, and I tried to seduce one or
two of the callow girls straight out of school. Our contemporary
women were firmly fixed as sisters, and our seniors were remote
stars; these new girls smelt of cheap perfume and approachability.
I spoke unwisely to Michael Callaghan, now an established
teacher, of a particular girl in whom I saw promise. Protestant?
Oh yes, Protestant. A new attempt was made to fix me up with a
good Irish Catholic girl, and Christmas was all parties at good
Catholic homes. Callaghan and I played piano duets for dancing
– 'Two Sleepy People', 'Music Maestro Please', 'Blue Orchids',
'Someday My Prince Will Come' (said Snow White, changing
hands for the fifth time, a common quip of the season) – and lay
in chaste embraces with good Irish Catholic girls all night after
midnight mass. But Protestantism was lurking ready to grab me,
and not among the freshwomen of the English School. There
was an Anglo-Welsh girl from Blackwood in Monmouthshire,
who had just joined the degree course in Politics, Economics and
Modern History. Her I was to marry and remain married to till,
in 1968, death did us part. She had seen me perform as a Ruritanian captain in a play put on at the pan-universitarian Freshers'
Reception. She had, she later said improbably, been attracted.

Her name was Llewela Isherwood Jones. Her father was an
English Jones, her mother a Welsh one. On the English side there
was a connection with the Bradshaws of Marple Hall in Cheshire
and also, through that, with Lady Charlotte Isherwood. Of
Christopher Isherwood, who appears as Bradshaw in *Mr Norris
Changes Trains*, neither the Jones father nor daughter had heard.
She was unliterary, a fact confirmed by her liking for Mary
Webb; he a chemist who had studied under Chaim Weizmann at
Manchester. He had, unusually for a man without a medical
degree, been commissioned as a sanitary officer in the Royal
Army Medical Corps during the Great War, had served in Pal-
estine under Allenby, had drunk a glass of lemonade with Law-
rence of Arabia, and had invented a field incinerator widely used
in the Near East. He was now the headmaster of Bedwellty
Grammar School near Tredegar. Married to a Jones whose

Welshness had rubbed off on to his own Bolton identity, he had been accepted by the ambiguous Welsh of Monmouthshire or Gwent, too close to England to be incorrupt, with an educational system that came under the Saeson. His accent was strongly Bolton, and his degree was extraterritorial, but he was adopted by the Welsh as a suitable Anglo-Welsh educator. He had done well in a country given to jobbery and canvassing ('No Canvassing' at the head of an advertisement for a Welsh appointment in the *Times Educational Supplement* probably means its opposite) by attaining his post on merit. He had an M.Sc. degree and was locally known as Eddie Jones Science.

That, as a headmaster, he had his limitations was shown by the fact that his daughter was attending his own old university in the one department of arts that did not require Latin. Latin was taught so badly at his school that it was assumed that no candidate for the subject at Lower or Higher School Certificate level would ever pass. It did not seem to matter much at the University of Wales, where Welsh was more important than the tongue of the ancient coloniser, but in England it was severely restrictive. Llewela Isherwood Jones was taking her multiple subject for somewhat negative reasons. She worked hard and did well. She had no conception of the temperamental disaffinity for a subject which made me so imperfect a student. There was the work, and the work had to be done. Moreover, Bedwellty Grammar School must not be let down, nor, especially, her reputation as its best scholar. She had been head girl too, the kind of nepotic appointment approved in Wales. Her heart was always in that school. She was convinced that she had learnt more from her history master Britten than distinguished professors like L. B. Namier could ever teach. She had, as I was slow to realise, a strong fixation on her father.

She was a tall athletic girl, blonde and blue-eyed, with a superbly developed body. She had played tennis and hockey for the county and swum for Wales. She danced, as the song said, divinely. She was only eighteen, a girl, and I, twenty-two, was a man. I had not expected to fall for a Nordic Celtic young sun goddess; my ideal woman had always been darkly Mediterranean, somewhat older than myself, skilled in murky sexual arts, the Shulamite, the Queen of Sheba. But Llewela Jones knew all about sex. She had been seduced at fourteen by a man named Rhys Evans, and only recently had she brought the affair with this man to an end. He had written a long letter to her, urging her, with Welsh fire, to come back to him, and recounting with remembered ecstasy the various details of the furtive sexual life they had enjoyed on summer evenings on the hillsides of Gwent. Her mother, Florence Jones, a gipsy-like Silurian but, oddly, a member of the Church of England, had opened this letter first and played holy hell with her. There was for Llewela Jones a powerful guilt to be packed in her trunk when leaving for Manchester. It was not guilt about sex. It was guilt about sex with Rhys Evans. She was very ready to wipe out sex with Rhys Evans through sex with me.

Her father knew nothing of this torrid affair. He was not Welsh, and he was, even for a Boltonian, cool about sex. He had spent his wedding night in the stiff shirt in which he had been married. When his wife complained that the English were not loving, it was clear what her Welsh corpuscles were really saying. She had been much courted by ardent men of her own race, some of whom reappeared to embarrass her when she had become Mrs Jones Science and a lady of position ('Well, Mrs Jones as I must now call you, here you are seeing me again, as admiring as ever and, you will be thinking, as ugly as ever'), but she had been won by a Lancastrian of intriguing coolness. Coolness went along with innocence. It is a father's innocence that endears him to a daughter. He cannot easily conceive of his little girl's rolling with knickers removed on the hillside grass when she is only fourteen. Llewela Jones's mother had suspicions when she did not have knowledge; when she acquired knowledge she flourished a large moral weapon.

The trouble was that there was another daughter, elder, born during the Great War, a consolation in the father's enforced absence, better loved, highly moral, a teacher recently married to another teacher in Willesden, both members of the Peace Pledge Union. The teacher she had married was a good Welshman, and a kind of sexual coolness in him was to be interpreted not as a failure to live up to the erotic fieriness of Wales but as a fruit of Nonconformist moral rigour. This daughter had maintained her virginity for a time after marriage, while the younger one had lost her hymen to strenuous games and pony-riding. Those pursuits were clearly unwomanly, and there was probably a moral judgment to be made on such casual defloration. The elder daughter was all that a daughter should be, unathletic, affectionate, bringing tales of her husband's lawful but brutish advances to her mother. To her mother she had written affecting

verses, copied out in pseudo-Celtic script by the husband, had
framed and glazed these herself and hung them on the wall of her
father and mother's bedroom:

> As the flowers need the sunshine,
>   Need its warm and cheering ray,
> So our hearts cry for the gladness
>   That love scatters on life's way.
>
> God is love, our Lord has taught us,
>   And I know this to be true.
> God is love itself reflected,
>   Gentle mother dear, in you.

This daughter's name was Hazel. An Irishman had once said to
Mrs Jones: 'You had the names of all the blessed angels and saints
to choose from, but you had to call her after a bloody nut.' That
was the sort of thing an Irishman could be expected to say. The
Irish, to the Welsh, were dirty and deceitful and took low wages.
That her younger daughter had become attached to a kind of
Irish Catholic would confirm to Mrs Jones that she was a bad lot.
Llewela Jones had lost her mother's love and felt guilty about it.
When her mother eventually died she would suffer the Freudian
trauma of believing she had killed her.

Llewela is the feminine form of Llewelyn. It has noble leonine
connotations, but to the students of Manchester it was a joke.
The English always have trouble with the Welsh unvoiced lateral
unless, like me, they have studied phonetics. Eddie Jones Science
still made Llanelly rhyme with belly and was not well understood
by Welsh railway clerks when booking a fare thither. Llewela
solved the problem for the Sais by borrowing the masculine
termination and calling herself Lynne. It was as Lynne that, in
the early days of the first term of 1939, she sent jointly with a
Welsh friend named Margaret Williams an invitation to Douglas
Mason and myself to partner them to the Ashburne dance. Both
girls were residents of Ashburne Hall, a noble structure with luxuri-
ant wet parkland around it in Rusholme. Mason, a son of Chester,
did not much care for the Welsh, and he was unwilling to go. I
was indifferent. We did not reply. Gaunt was jealous. He had
directed Lynne in a play reading and then taken her to the cinema.
It was only right that we should not reply. Women, even when
only eighteen, were treacherous creatures.

Then, when the dance was over, other partners having apparently been found without difficulty, I met a flood of Welsh wrath in the cafeteria. Lynne Jones tore into me for discourtesy, rightly so, and, on behalf of Margaret Williams, into Douglas Mason for, rightly so, the same property. We bowed to the anger, of a vehemence we had not previously met. It was rather charming anger, voluble and musical, with sharp elocutionist's consonants and round Cymric vowels. We offered to take them to the cinema, though it was not at the time clear who was to sit with whom. When we went to the Gaumont on Oxford Street to see Hitchcock's *The Lady Vanishes* and Sacha Guitry's *Roman d'un Tricheur*, the situation was clarified radiantly. I now had a girl friend. More, I had a mistress.

There was, for a time, an arctic chill generated by Gaunt and Mason. I had let down a solid confraternity partly sustained by sexual repression. I had grabbed, or been grabbed by, a girl whom Gaunt had fancied. Mason had his chance with Margaret Williams, a pretty, dark girl from Blaenavon, but the Roman fort of Chester had long been dedicated to keeping the Welsh in their place. He told me I was the triple pillar of the world transformed into a strumpet's fool or stool (the reading had never been clear) and then went mooning after Hilda Price, a student of history. She would not at first yield, and he went drinking alone in the Shambles, mooning on to fascicles of examination paper: 'Hilda, I long for your slender body.' Gaunt took a pale, Mimi-like girl named Winnie Ronchetti to a dance or two and then made her cry in a taxi. He settled at length on a handsome and witty girl named Joan Frampton in first-year English. Eventually they married and, as I write, are still married. Mason did not marry Hilda Price, but that was the fault of the war, which threw her into the arms of John A. Wilson. These two married and are still married. Fidelity was an extracurricular subject some of us mastered.

With Lynne there was no long courtship leading to physical conquest. Consummation came almost immediately after our trip to the Gaumont and was guaranteed by the sort of fondling that was mandatory in the back row. I was invited to tea in her room at Ashburne Hall and was fed hardboiled eggs and Kunzle cakes sent from home. Then we made love. It was dangerous in a hall of residence where men visitors were permitted rarely and the door was supposed to be left unlocked. Discovery, even suspicion, could lead to dismissal from hall for her, perhaps from the univer-

sity for both of us. There were watchful spinster tutors around
and fellow-students repressed and catty. We made love in the
snow and rain in parks and gardens, urgently and fearfully.
Contraception was a financial problem. Condoms cost dear, so
did pessaries. Pessaries, anyway, were not to be trusted. There
was a myth about at least one pessary in a packet's being neutered
as a sop to the Archbishop of Canterbury. Coitus interruptus,
which every young man thinks he can manage, leads to gin and
hot baths and nail-biting waiting for the salvatory flag. The *News
Bulletin* knew what was going on. After a harmless poem –
'J.B.W.,/Girls, won't trouble you./He's the fella for Llewela'–
came the indiscreet 'French without tears. Or, All's Llwell that
Ends Llwell'.

Her view of sex was both sane and perilous. It was something
you got out of the way so as to concentrate on the human essence
of a relationship. It was pleasant, exciting, natural, necessary, and
the mystery and fear that surrounded it had best be ripped off as
soon as possible. She discounted the irrational features of the
sexual urge, those that surge up in jealousy and sharpen knives.
Sex was not love. The statement 'I love you' had to come from a
conviction unattached to desire. When the blood burns, how
prodigally the soul lends the tongue vows. There is much panting
of 'I love you' when pants come down. It is better said over a
postcoital cigarette. I said it first in French, as many young Englishmen cautiously do, while we were travelling on a brewer's
dray to sell the *Rag Rag* in Cheetham Hill. She said: 'And now in
English.' I said it in English, as if in a film, but found the world
three-dimensional enough. The next stage was engagement.
When I won the short story prize of five guineas I bought a ring.
She said: 'Now take me to a pub and put it on that finger there.'
Men never know the right finger. Even officiating priests have to
count the phases of the Gloria from the thumb on, arriving at the
ring finger with the Amen. Women, from the age of four, always
know the right finger. I said: 'The pubs aren't open yet.' That
was somehow my fault: I ought to have arranged for the pubs to
be open. I was learning about women's irrationality and am still
learning, though irrationality only means contempt for irrational
laws. The pubs ought to have been open; the pubs always ought
to be open.

It was not a secret enagagement, except in both our houses.
The jeweller sent the certificate of guarantee to my home address,
however, though I had told him to send it to the Men's Union.

Thus my step-family found out about a hole-in-the corner affidation. My fiancée – it all had to come out – was Welsh, meaning dirty and treacherous, also Protestant, meaning treacherous and dirty. I had met nice Irish Catholic girls – Edna O'Farrell, Assumpta Costello, Kathleen Fitzpatrick, Mary Reilly, Noreen MacKinnon – and here I was choosing, or being chosen by, an infidel foreigner. There was sad recrimination.

To Lynne the fact of engagement meant a kind of sexual passacaglia. That is, there was to be a strong ground bass of unassailable love and free variations of philandering above it. She did not understand the image: she was not musical. Putting it without metaphor, she said that she and I knew where we stood with each other, and this gave us both, though especially her, licence to exercise curiosity elsewhere and widely. Whatever love was in her room at Ashburne Hall, it was not to be thought of as two people locked in a cell of conventional fidelity. There were plenty of attractive people around and it would be a shame and a waste not to find out what they were like with their clothes off. She sustained this attitude throughout a long marriage. In the manner of Molly Bloom, whose monologue was the only part of *Ulysses* she was ever to read, she wanted to compare bowstrings. The removal of her engagement ring was a signal of availability; I, wearing no ring, was to be available all the time, meaning whenever she said so. This was a kind of madness but also an odd sort of sanity. She agreed with H. G. Wells, who had presented himself at the beginning of the century as a free soul and a free body ready and willing for the enjoyment of hearty sexual exercise with all comers. Like Wells, she discounted the dangers of possessiveness. Sexual fulfilment does strange things, especially with women. It generates a fierce proprietoral sense, which is sometimes called love. With Lynne sex was altogether too casual. She could give it without getting anything out of it. *Ça vous donne tant de plaisir et moi si peu de peine* was one of her favourite aphorisms. The Dionysiac ecstasy had never possessed her.

We went to the formal dances of the University Unions and the halls of residence, tailed, ballgowned, sometimes together, sometimes with other partners. The other partners did not understand the nature of our engagement: they assumed it had been broken off; they sometimes believed that their own allure had been the cause of its being broken off. I learned more about women, having found the one I was to marry, than had ever been possible before. My old hunger for dark girls was appeased.

It was an absurd situation. When, as happened on at least two occasions, the engagement was genuinely broken, it was because of gratuitous intrigue and one shocking incursion of lesbianism. Lynne went down with German measles, and I was told by Gwendolen Hadfield, one of her fellow-residents of Ashburne Hall, that it was Lynne's especial wish that I not go to visit her. The ailment was mild but infectious, and she did not want me to be infected. This seemed reasonable, though uncharacteristic, so I stayed away. On Lynne's recovery I was surprised to have the engagement ring thrown publicly in my face. Miserable back in her room, she was violently consoled by Gwendolen Hadfield, who said that men did not understand love but here was one woman who did. Then everything became clear. Among the Iagos who would disrupt love for the sake of disruption was a blond German violinist whom I sometimes accompanied in Beethoven sonatas: he spun so plausible a story of a covert infidelity that Lynne was conducting with a Jewish bookseller that I was revolted. This time I broke off the engagement. Then Lynne and I brooded naked over the perfidy of friends and she became briefly pregnant.

Love does not of itself produce good love poetry. The feeling which produced the following was stronger than the imaginative impulse:

> Well, my Eurydice, that was pain enough,
>   Having only your name to call on in the night.
> Both day and night were long enough.
>   Now I lead you laboriously back to the light.
>
> Hell played at forfeits. On a swivel of the head
>   Rested your return. As one might stab a pin
> Idly at a fly for its irrelevant end,
>   The world was plunged in original sin.
>
> That was not in the pattern of our lives,
>   Whose miraculous fabric has for every strand
> Accounted. Wantonly the destroyer unweaves,
>   Just as he hides time's secret in his hand.
>
> But it is true I should have been destined then,
>   Climbing alone back to the light, to have met
> The deserved logical end. The tree that has been
>   Fruitful only stays to be fruitful yet.

> The undergrowth of laws that sees no light —
> This I believe in as much as anything.
> Hell would have seen you no Prosperpina
> Nor sent you back to wither up the spring.

A fruitful tree, indeed. Love and art are not compatible. They may even be antagonistic. Lynne often tested me with the sort of question that Orwell was to put in the mouth of deceitful O'Brien. Would I give up all for love? Would I give up music for love? Was love more important than being rich and famous? She remembered my answers, as women always will. Like God, women prefer love to art. They will accept art as a means of their own beautification or as a testimony to their power. I bitterly, during one of our tiffs, wrote lines which could be true for others if not for me:

> All the ore that waiting lay
> For the later working I melted before its time
> To make you ornaments for a day.
> And all else too I drew out: there is no more.
> For between man and man at the last
> There rests at least shame.

Lynne did not permit me to work at string quartets or piano sonatas, since music meant nothing to her. I could, however, write popular songs and try to sell them. No money in art, and we needed money. So, with Klaus Pickard's help, I wrote a song which found its way into Nazi Germany:

> *Ich nehm' ein' Zigarett'*
> *Und ich fühl' du liebst mich nicht mehr,*
> *Und ich weiss es ist aus,*
> *Und da macht mein Herz so schwer . . .*

With songs in English I had little luck. I have always been better appreciated by foreigners. A song beginning '*Muchisimas gracias — tan fàcil decir*' was much heard on the radio in Franco's Spain. I received no royalties.

LYNNE'S DOCTRINE OF free love applied only in Manchester. Back home in Blackwood during the Easter vacation she lived chastely, avoiding predatory Rhys Evans. I myself cached her engagement ring, lest her mother find it. An under-age affiancement would need the approval of her father as well, and this she would not get. I was not even permitted to send love letters, at least not openly: her mother would be up early with the paper knife. I had to turn myself into a fictitious friend named Sylvia, a student of literature who sent her copies of Eliot, Pound and the young Auden. Accompanying letters would retail university gossip and casually mention the sickness of John B. for some girl or other. But hidden between gummed end-papers of *Murder in the Cathedral* or *Look, Stranger!* or *The Dog Beneath the Skin* would be what Lynne called a 'real letter', meaning a few passionate paragraphs. Few, because love letters are hard to write. They evade physical particularities because, in cold ink, these embarrass with their impertinence; the rest is all transcendental nonsense like watered Goethe. But I made it clear that I loved her, meaning wanted her there and then, could not wait for the new term to begin.

In the new term she and I were publicly rebuked for kissing in a common room where faculty and students took tea, though at separate tables. A chemistry professor delivered the rebuke and then had me into his office for a moral lecture; his qualifications in chemistry gave him some authority over the glandular secretions of the young. Professor Charlton delivered warnings: I was not attending to my work and crucial Part One was coming up. Professor Gordon was dead and Professor Semple complained that I was not concentrating on my Livy and Ausonius for the pivotal General Latin examination (without a pass in an extraneous subject at the General level an honours degree could not be awarded). I did not see what Professor Gordon's death had to do with me, but Professor Charlton had a confused Browningian mind. I was shaken by the interview and had to be consoled with embraces in the Joint Common Room. There a new student appeared called Cooper the Snooper to denounce fornication and even hit out at it with a rolled copy of the *Church Times*. When summer came Lynne passed all her examinations; I scraped through English Honours Part One and failed General Latin. In the month of examinations Great Britain signed a defensive agreement with Turkey and, after a reflective pause, France did too. Italy and Germany formed a pact and, in London, Britain affirmed support of Polish independence. Also James Joyce's *Finnegans Wake* appeared and I bought it.

I got the money for buying it by inventing the need for a fee for an examination in Advanced Semantics. It was an expensive book – all of twenty-one shillings. It caused a brief rupture between Lynne and myself: for that sum I could have bought her a bracelet and two or three seven-course dinners. The book looked like nonsense anyway. She had no time for either of my preferred authors – Joyce and Hopkins. Up to the time of her death she would chant the name Gerard Manley Hopkins to the derisive tune of 'Johnny's got a zero'. She had given me a copy of *The House in Dormer Forest* by Mary Webb as a birthday present, but she had overcome her devotion to that writer in a way that Stanley Baldwin never did; she had not, however, yet learnt to embrace modernism. At a performance of *Paid On Both Sides* or *Out of the Picture* she would start a coughing fit and have to walk out. The same bout prevented her hearing any of my music beyond the first few measures. Anyway, *Finnegans Wake* looked like nonsense and sounded like somebody drunk in a Manchester Irish snug.

This, unfortunately, was also the view of Cedric Hirson, still editing *The Serpent*. I wrote a lengthy review of *Finnegans Wake*, claiming, with some justice, to understand it, but Hirson would not permit publication. He alleged that the book was of little interest to any but the mad, that it would not last, that it was politic to ignore it. This was, as nearly half a century of slow but thorough scholarly penetration of the work has shown, a grave journalistic error. There were no serious reviews of *Finnegans Wake* in the professional press: the notice of it given by Malcolm Muggeridge, still extant, was a disgracefully smug confession of incompetence to tackle it. Another Wilson, the one in America, published 'The Dream of H. C. Earwicker' in 1939 and reprinted it after in *The Wound and the Bow*. My review, rejected, was at least as perceptive as his, though it was shorter. Published in *The Serpent*, it might have survived in one of the toothcomb critical symposia. It was a missed scoop for *The Serpent*. The book impressed Lynne only because the apparent typing chimpanzees had put me into it as 'J. B. W. Ashburner'. It knew of the burning glands I took to Ashburne Hall.

In the summer vacation it was arranged that Lynne and myself go abroad together. Her story to her mother was that she was to walk over Europe with Margaret Williams. But her mother contacted the mother of Margaret Williams to see if this was true, and the mother said it was certainly a splendid idea. So

Margaret Williams and Lynne, in shorts and with rucksacks, were seen off at Newport station. When I arrived at Parkeston Quay I was surprised to find two girls instead of one. Was I being offered troilism? No, it was to be a sexless trip, three friends, one of whom happened to be male, tramping the roads of Europe and getting chastely into single sleeping bags at day's end. Women are strange, even at the age of eighteen and a half. They can turn themselves into nuns at the drop of a coif. I had to watch four exquisite Welsh legs striding over Belgium, France and Holland, as well as the half-revealed haunches above, and growl down sir down to my inflamed sensibilities. The libidinous Europeans would see the innocent trip differently: lucky Englishman to be copulating over the continent with two girls whose sexual readiness was confirmed by their long, bare brown limbs.

There was to be more than sexual austerity on this trip. On the train from Manchester Central to Harwich I had taken, alone in the first-class dining-car, a dinner of hors d'oeuvres, oxtail soup, poached turbot, saddle of mutton, cabinet pudding and a half-bottle of Médoc, ending with a choice cigar. Damn it, I was on holiday. I cannot remember where the money came from: I think I must have disavowed my Protestant engagement and said I wished to kiss the Pope's toe. I know that I had been collecting Roman guidebooks from somebody who had spent time with a *puttana* and her little dog off the Via Veneto. When I proudly told Lynne of my dinner on the boat across to Zeebrugge she attacked me as a spendthrift sybarite. We were to see the world cheaply, living off long loaves and inches of local sausage. I had got off on the wrong foot.

So we got our feet queasily off the boat at dawn and walked. Bad boys on bicycles circled round the girls' bare legs and, hooting, tried to grasp them. I had to buy a walking-stick to fend them off, shouting *méchant* and *salaud*. My prospective month's holiday was to be filled with the duty of protecting personable Welsh girls from the attentions of dirty foreigners. At least I had had that dinner. We walked. We walked to Bruges, where we saw a Memling exhibition, to Ghent, where we ate fried horse, to Antwerp, where we danced. The austerity was being relaxed a little. The girls brought crushproof frocks out of their rucksacks and I a pair of grey flannel trousers, and we went to a dance-hall which had taxi-dancers. A taxi-driver, mistaking the term, had entered there as if it were an occupational club, and sat bewildered. Everybody knew there was a war coming. *'Chamberlain a vendu l'Europe,'* we were told, and that innocent statesman was traduced as *J'aime Berlin.* The band played 'The Umbrella Man' and the dancers jeered. A drunken Belgian youth toasted the day when he and I would fight together the Boche. Peace in our time? I peace on his peace. The Germans had already sent their vanguard into the Low Countries, in the shape of holidaying *Hitlerjugend.* We met some of these tough cropped blond boys in youth hostels. They disdained to sleep in the dormitories and camped out toughly in the grounds. They yelped patriotic songs. I remembered something my father had once said, to the effect that the intonation of German always excited a kind of pity in him: there was a childish deprived tone that suggested patient regret at incomprehensible bad treatment. I now heard what he meant. I played the piano in one hostel and a decent Fleming past youth asked for *le Palais Glide.* The Palais Glide was a lined up dance of simple steps to the tune of 'Ten Pretty Girls' or 'Horsey horsey'. Flemings joined Lynne and Margaret to prance it noisily. Hitler youth came in to denounce it and drown it with *'Unsre Fahne flattert uns voran'.* Lynne slapped a blond sneerer. A pre-emptive strike, sort of. The war was only two months off.

Some scenes from one's past hug the mind with the force of a profound symbol impossible to read. I persuaded Lynne to make love among the trees on a hot evening. I had been too long repressed; this was joyful, ecstatic. At the beginning of orgasm a nightingale started to warble. A second or two after a *Hitlerjugend* song quelled it:

> *Wir marschieren für Hitler durch Nacht und durch Rot,*
> *Mit der Fahne der Jugend für Freiheit und Brot . . .*

The nightingale probably tried to mediate between biology and politics. I instinctively said: *'Eine Nachtigall'.* But this was Walloon territory and it was properly *un rossignol.* Of course, Hans Sachs towards the end of *Die Meistersinger* hailing the nightingale's song as the signal for national rebirth had got into my head. But orgasm passed and the loud youth anthem grew louder and the nightingale could no longer be heard. This complex of forces needed to be put into a poem. But I could not write the poem.

On the road to Liège two kind Germans gave us a lift in their Mercedes-Benz. They were cultivated men who spoke fine English. They had just returned from America and knew all the latest

American songs. One of them sang 'Three little fishes in an itty bitty pool':

> Swim, said the mamma fishy, swim if you can,
> And they swam and they swam right over the dam . . .

They both sang: 'What goes up must come down, and baby you've been flying too high'. To such men, humorous and cosmopolitan, it seemed one could say rude things about Hitler. One could not. One could at least perhaps argue rationally about the inadvisability of basing a political system on mystical racialism and the cult of a personality. One could not. The car stopped and we were politely told to get out. There were clearly Germans who were schizoid. They could embrace Anglo-American culture from Jefferson and John Locke down to the song about the mammy fishy, but they could still believe that Jewish blood was demonstrably different from Aryan. They could accept the term 'Aryan' as a legitimate racial denominator while knowing from their philological studies that it could only apply to a group of languages. They believed that a barking bigoted failed architect was a divine avatar. Their brains were split.

In a Luxembourg night club an elegant lady looked at my Celto-Lancastrian nose and said clearly: '*Il est juif sans doute.*' Holidaying or vanguard Germans at a neighbouring table turned with interest. To deny that I was a Jew would have seemed an endorsement of Nazi antisemitism. So I said: '*Oui, comme Jésus Christ.*' There followed a very amiable discussion in bad French with the Germans. It was about what precisely a Jew was. It seemed I was acceptable as a Jew on Luxembourgeois territory – for the time being, anyway. As a Jew in Germany I would have to suffer expropriation and, perhaps, eventually, liquidation. A Jew therefore, I suggested, had to be defined in terms of the national ethos into which he was deemed an intruder. Ah, no, not altogether, I was told. There was such a thing as Jewishness. Take the music of Mendelssohn: you can hear Jewishness in every note. The night club trio was taking a break, so I went to the piano and played part of the second movement of Elgar's Symphony No. 2 in E flat. 'That,' I then said, 'is from the Reformation Symphony by Mendelssohn. Where is the Jewishness?' It stuck out a mile, they shuddered; there was a certain unteutonic oleaginousness or *Schmierigkeit*. I then told them who the composer was, and they said that he must be a Jew and that they did not like this English Jewish cheating, especially when Jewish England was *das Land ohne Musik*. Finally it was affirmed, on the evidence of Hitler's Christologists, that Jesus Christ was the son of a Hittite woman and a Roman legionary. Before leaving I told them that the English equivalent of *heil* was sod and had them crying: 'Sod Hitler'. It was a small triumph. It was a dirty experience.

We did not go far into France. We slept in our bags under a bright moon near the Maginot Line and wondered about those fortifications stretching from Switzerland to Luxembourg. There had to be a profound statesman's secret the common people were too stupid to share in that sudden cessation at the Belgian border. Perhaps half of the schizoid German mind respected gentlemanly conventions and would consider outflanking not to be cricket. For some reason we slept uneasily. I heard tanks in my sleep and they turned out to be thunder. We woke soaked. We walked to soaked Montmédy and soaked Sédan and saw a France which has since disappeared – open drains that stank, a fuddled curé irritably hitting at flies as he took his tenth balloon of red. We ate a meal served with French pride – canned sardines, undergrilled horse-meat, a slice of dry cake. The rain poured, the gutters over-flowed, the flies buzzed. We were told that there was an autobus to get us to a train to get us back into Belgium, but we spent hours slapping flies that stung our bare legs and no autobus appeared. It turned out that the autobus had been coming and going regularly and we had been too Britishly stupid to notice: the autobus was a broken down Peugeot four-seater driven by a haughty lady. *'Vous vous êtes trompés, n'est-ce pas?'* she haughtily said. The phrase has stuck in my brain like a bar of detestable music. It seemed to sum up the know-all France we would perhaps soon be fighting to deliver.

We walked and hitched north into Holland. Near Utrecht I fell into a Dutch ditch, head over heels, bathed totally, rucksack and all, in foul slimy water. A kind Dutch gentleman who lived alone near by was sympathetic and allowed us to wash and half-dry everything in his cellar. My new copy of *Les Fleurs du Mal* sat in the sun with my socks and two shirts. He was a learned gentleman who spoke reasonable English. We were served weak tea and two biscuits each. He could not know that we were desperately hungry. He fed us with his admiration for German philosophy, his Hegelian belief that God was to be manifested in the State, his detestation of Dutch decadence, his hope for a radiant pan-

Teutonic future in which the English, if they were good, could join. With my clothes not yet dry, we had to raise our tepid tea in a toast to Aryan Europe. Then Lynne's Celtic blood rose and flooded and she said what bloody nonsense. I was glad now to be able to agree that it was bloody nonsense. We bundled the still-wet clothes and *Fleurs du Mal* together and left with no thanks for the six biscuits.

We ended our holiday in Knokke on the Belgian coast. We had just enough money to pay for three nights with a family that took in boarders. There was one bedroom, one double bed. We lay in total chastity like sardines in it. Lynne was in the middle. On the third night, one of exceptional heat, she got outside the bedclothes while Margaret Williams and I still lay beneath them. In that sense only may I be said to have got between the sheets with Margaret Williams. We danced at the Kursaal to 'Let Me Whisper I Love You'. I bought several strings of rosary beads to take home. These, in default of the Pope's blessing, I blessed myself. I tried out a few phrases of Italian. I was bronzed enough, though the sun shone less harshly over the Low Countries than the Eternal City. I was living lies, but so was most of Europe. We took the steamer to Harwich from Zeebrugge. Lynne and I kissed our passionate farewell on Parkeston Quay. We went to our respective homes, preparing our lies.

On July 10 Chamberlain had reaffirmed the British pledge to Poland. On August 23 von Ribbentrop was triumphant over the German–Soviet pact. On that same day I received a letter from John A. Wilson. He had been teaching English in a summer school in the Black Forest and, though that school would assume that all its English teachers were to be called John Wilson, I was welcome to take over his job. On August 28 Holland mobilised and I was on my way to Antwerp. On August 31 the British fleet mobilised and I was on my way back from Antwerp. On September 1 the Germans invaded Poland, and England and France mobilised their armies. On September 2 compulsory military service for all men aged eighteen to forty-one was decreed. My stepmother was distraught, though not on my behalf. It was my duty, indeed my destiny, to put on khaki at once and, after a brief phase of fulfilling what had always been in me, namely the manners of drunken and fornicating soldiery, go off to be killed. It was Jack Tollitt, well within the call-up zone, she was worried about, or rather his duty to the poor widow-woman M. Wilson. He was to go to the authorities at once and inform them that he had a business to look after, a delicate wife, two delicate children and a more than delicate mother-in-law who had a business for him to look after. Fighting the war was for those who had nothing better to do. Then, after more than twenty years of estrangement, my stepmother's brother Jim Byrne appeared, with a delectable double-jointed daughter who was engaged to the failed *fascista* Adolf Corradi. The cause of the estrangement had been long forgotten, as such causes frequently are; it is the need to be estranged that is important. Jim Byrne came like a messenger from the gods to announce that there would be no war. The British did not want to fight the Germans; it was the Americans who were our worst enemies. This briefly comforted my stepmother. Having done his duty, Jim Byrne disappeared, never to reappear.

September 3, 1939 was a beautiful late summer Sunday. I wrote bad verses about it:

> The night before last was Saturday night.
>   The cinema crowds were excited.
> The newsboys yelled 'Special!' with all their might,
> Some said: 'It's going to be war all right!'
>   The pimpled boys were delighted.
>
> Yesterday morning, after mass,
>   Chamberlain spoke on the wireless.
> Jack Tollitt was screaming of poison gas:
> 'Seal all the windows!' And while I was
>   Tired from the start, he was tireless.
>
> And then I went quietly to my room,
>   Avoiding stepmother, stepsister,
> And in my head a cloud of gloom
> Dripped dew on my individual doom
>   And an endless nightmare vista.
>
> I had never seen it so dark before:
>   The streets had invisible craters.
> Talk in the pub was about the war.
> I drank until I thought no more
>   Of democracy and dictators.
>
> I drank until I thought no more
>   Of Hitler's lust for dominion.
> And so I said when a drink-soaked bore
> Complacently turned and asked me for
>   My own considered opinion:

'The king is only a cinema slide.
  The soldier puts cunt before country.
Last night two drunks were run over and died,
A neurotic attempted suicide,
  And a girl was raped in an entry.'

An entry being a back alley. The stencilled effigy of the king on
the screen signalling the National Anthem and ragged attention
at the end of a film show. Jack Tollitt had indeed been shouting
that we were at once to be gassed and had ordered the household
to seal the window-frames with putty. The poem may be indifferent, but it was composed on the second day of war and records a
tired cynicism many of my generation felt. We did not think
that we, the young, were to repeat the sacrifice to a gerontocracy
which was the myth, still only emerging, that turned the First
World War into tragic theatre. We had all seen H. G. Wells's
film (Jack Tollitt, with his screams about gas, had certainly seen
it), and we knew that this new war would be all about bomb-
ing civilians. Picasso's *Guernica* had been on exhibition in Manchester, and it was all the war art anyone needed. It was the
damnable waste of time in prospect that wearied us.

I was determined to get my BA Honours, and the authorities
more than agreed. I took my statutory medical examination with
young miners who were ashamed of their subcutaneous coal-
dust. The examining doctor was the one who had me squirt
adrenalin into my dying father. I was A1 except for my myopia,
first-rate cannonfodder, but the tribunal in charge of call-up
postponement said that they did not want the flower of Britain's
youth rushing into khaki. There was not enough khaki, anyway,
and the small standing army, augmented by the territorials, was
about as much as the existing machinery could accommodate.
The situation as presented in Evelyn Waugh's *Men at Arms* applied
to potential rank and file as well as to Oxford gentlemen like
Guy Crouchback. What could be sickening about that novel, if
the nausea were not mitigated by comic irony, is the assumption
that a certain segment of British society was, on the grounds that
it had an income from land, an Oxbridge education, and friends
among the ruling class, specially qualified to lead those with none
of those irrelevant advantages. Kingsley Amis, reviewing *Men at
Arms*, was right to ask what was wrong with Guy Crouchbank's
enlisting as a private in the Pioneer Corps if he were so keen to do
his duty. Hore-Belisha's army reforms, which assumed that the

gift of leadership was something to be learned by anyone who could learn it, and not a paracletic bestowal on gentlemen graduates, were considered to be Jewish impertinence. We at Manchester University knew we were not gentlemen. We foresaw ourselves as private soldiers lucky to get a stripe. All, of course, except those like Green and McColl who had done officer training, something Guy Crouchback had not thought of doing. Green reported the first words of his hero the OTC RSM on the outbreak. 'You mark my fucking words, lads, it'll be the same in this fucking war as in the last fucking lot. VD, and a fucking lot of it. I wouldn't fuck a woman without a fucking FL not even if she was my own fucking sister.' The emphasis was right. There was to be a lot of fornication in that war.

Evelyn Waugh was right, in his *Put Out More Flags*, to point to the peculiarly dreamlike atmosphere of that first war winter. It was cosy. There was no shortage of Player's cigarettes, real cream cakes and whisky at twelve shillings and sixpence the bottle. There was a black-out, but this on moonless nights was a call to erotic adventure. The black-out became fearful only when it was compounded with Manchester industrial fog. I remember my walking Lynne home from the university to Ashburne Hall in the early evening of a winter day when the fog struck. Total black, Stygian, the two of us embraced and unable to move, excised from time-space while I improvised a story about a utopia in which cigarettes grew on trees and fountains ran iced gin and lime juice. And then the fog cleared, but not the black-out. I heard a man on a bus say: 'Now you know what it was like in the old-fashioned days when there was no bloody lights at all. The dark ages.'

Gaunt and Mason found academic work difficult. Gaunt especially found the writing of a thesis difficult. There was a new university offering prompted by the war: if you had passed Part One in your honours school you could be awarded a BA in ordinary arts. Gaunt grasped this and became a sudden graduate. He proposed converting his BA thesis into an MA one when, if, the war should one day be over. He joined the Royal Army Medical Corps. I, having failed General Latin, could not be granted this concession. I refused to enter the services degreeless. Mason had no such objection: he enlisted in the Royal Army Signal Corps. Men in the fancy dress of officer's uniform, on whom service with the OTC had imposed immediate mobilisation, came back to take examinations or even complete courses.

Their issue pistols rested on the desk with Pliny or Company
Law.

University life went on, though not much in the evenings. On
September 6 the Luftwaffe had raided British soil. It would
undoubtedly strike Trafford Park before the first winter was over,
and it would do so at night. Stray bombs would fall on the
university, and it would not be seemly to be destroyed in full
evening dress and spill blood on French chalk. The Rag Ball
started at four in the afternoon and ended at ten in the evening,
but the clocks were put forward to simulate deep night. Klaus
Pickard and I arranged a Weimar-style cabaret at 5 p.m. We had a
glamorous American girl student now, named Frances Colon
('Why poke the fire?' asked the News Bulletin's column 'Slightly
Scented'. 'All we need is a little coal on') who sang a dismal song
I wrote called 'Black-out Blues':

> Nothing's in sight now –
> I've got those black-out blues.
> Show me a light now –
> I've got those black-out blues.

War optimism was reserved to refectory waitresses, who said
'The boys of the bulldog breed will win through'. The greater
cynicism was reserved to the university communists.

Indeed, I was told by Gerry Wolfson that what was needed
was a play that would forecast what was undoubtedly soon to
happen. The Nazis would be overthrown by the German
communists, but the war would continue. Churchill (this was
just after he had formed his National Government) would give
speeches about an evil to be combated, and the new communist
evil would be indistinguishable from the old Nazi one. This
play was to be the work of a syndicate or collective or committee. It came to nothing save a few lines from an Audenesque
chorus:

> Weigh guns against butter, he said,
> But how can you spread
> Guns on bread?

Still, Wolfson, with Orwellian insight, was making out of his
own cynicism the conditions for the permanent war of *Nineteen
Eighty-Four*, down to a kind of oratory which could accommodate

a change of enemy without even breaking the syntax. But it required at that time a profound devotion to Soviet communism to be able to distinguish one kind of predator from another. On September 29, two days after the capitulation of Warsaw, Germany and Russia set about partitioning Poland. On November 30 Russia attacked Finland, and we were exhorted to think of Finland as the fascist enemy. On December 14 Russia rejected the offer of the League of Nations to mediate in the Russo-Finnish war and was expelled from the League of Nations. Therefore the League of Nations was fascist. There was plenty of doublethink around the communist tables of the university cafeteria.

On December 18 the *Admiral Graf Spee* scuttled herself, bayed about by the British cruisers *Exeter*, *Ajax* and *Achilles*, in the entrance to Montevideo harbour. This was what war was about, and to hell with ideology. In a pub at Christmas a sailor stood to sing, to the tune of one of the first of the popular Latin-American songs of the time:

> South of the border,
>   Down Montevideo way,
> The German pocket battleship
>   *Admiral Graf Spee*
> Knew that she was done for
>   And so had to stay
> South of the border . . .

It was artless, but it was better than 'We're Going to Hang Out the Washing on the Siegfried Line', whose tune the Germans were quick to take over and nazify, and 'Run Adolf Run' and Tommy Handley's, the first daring BBC venture of the war, 'Who is this man who looks like Charlie Chaplin?' The real songs of the war were *'Boa Noite'* and 'Down Argentina Way' and 'Brazil', fruits of America's good neighbour policy. My 'Blackout Blues' got nowhere. The communists were content to go on with 'I'll sing you one-oh. Red flies the banner-oh'.

At home, Jack Tollitt had put us all on a war basis, complete with nine o'clock curfew. Against this I revolted. I took to keeping out of his way. I would leave the premises by the yarddoor to avoid meeting him in the shop. Having become an Air Raid Precautions warden, he was a pedant about black-outs. He arranged for the whole family, except myself, to sleep in bunks in the cellar. I was permitted to take over the matrimonial bed on the second floor. Having made himself essential to the neighbourhood as a helmeted warden, he made arrangements to be employed in munitions – 'Front Line Work', as the badges of the munitions-makers proclaimed, as well as well-paid and not over-arduous – and to contrive, to my stepmother's relief, to run M. Wilson's at the same time. He had, as I have said, vast energy. I was determined to leave home as soon as possible.

An anti-intellectual who knew my weak spots, Jack Tollitt swore that the Anglo-Irish traitor Lord Haw-Haw was James Joyce, when the rest of the world knew he was William Joyce. Ezra Pound's treachery had somehow rubbed off on to his fellow-modernist. Listening to the German radio was a kind of masochistic obligation for the entire family. It hedged less and was more forthright than the BBC, which seemed to dither. There was a German radio programme addressed nightly to British workers, and this spoke reasonable sense, and in strong language full of 'bloody' and 'bugger', about Britain's shameful class-divisions. Lord Haw-Haw presided over dramatic dialogues in which a stupid Englishman of the upper-class discussed with an intellectual Nazi such topics as the writings of Freud. 'Good as the Pink Un, what?' said the Englishman over coffee and brandy in Dublin or Zürich or Lisbon, while the intellectual Nazi was fluent in his denunciation of degrading Jewish pornology. Once we had Schoenberg ('a bit noisy, what?') and the intellectual Nazi demonstrated the neurotic Jewish excesses of the twelve-tone system. This side of the war was great fun.

There did not seem to be much of another side to it, however, not in the first winter and spring. I went to the university daily, with my gas-mask case full of books. I fire-watched with Klaus Pickard, which meant a night of waiting for something to happen in the seething retorts of his laboratory. I attended lectures, and none of my lecturers forced a connection between the war and *Pearl* or *Sir Gawain and the Green Knight*. The war was deemed irrelevant to scholarship. It was a politician's matter, and politicians were notoriously unscholarly. Well, whatever the Nazis might say, as well as, eventually, George Steiner ('Hitler heard inside his native tongue the latent hysteria, the confusion, the quality of hypnotic trance. He plunged unerringly into the undergrowth of language, into those zones of darkness and outcry which are the infancy of articulate speech . . . A language in which one can write a *Horst Wessel Lied* is ready to give hell a native

tongue') language seemed blessedly neutral. Fronting and breaking went on in Anglo-Saxon regardless of the antichrist Danes.
But what was literature now saying to us who had just read the
first of the wartime white papers – 'The treatment of German
nationals by the Nazis'? Tennyson and Browning seemed smug;
it was no virtue in Jane Austen to leave out the Napoleonic war;
who, in this time of atrocities, cared about the virtue of Rich-
ardson's housemaid? The Elizabethans and Jacobeans were different: their language was beleaguered and given to violence. I was
specialising in Christopher Marlowe and was writing a thesis on
Doctor Faustus. This had a lot to say about my own condition
while the Nazi bombers were droning in to demolish Trafford
Park. Death might be near ('enter devils with fireworks') and the
hell the renegade Catholic had scoffed at as a fable might be all
too real.

My view of *Doctor Faustus* was that, like *Hamlet*, it tapped an
old channel of faith and a new one of scepticism. Though L. C.
Knights had stressed the unsoundness of the Bradley approach to
dramatic character, there was something in my unscholarly mind
which could not help seeing Prince Hamlet attending Dr Faustus's
lectures in Wittenburg. Obviously this is material for a Tom
Stoppard play, and D. J. Enright, in his long Faust poem, has
fingered a connective string. If Hamlet has learnt scepticism at
Wittenberg in Faustus's lectures, he has left the university too
soon, called by his father's funeral, to see the foundering of that
scepticism. Spirits can be brought back from the dead, and hell is
not a fable. Nor is purgatory, and here is the ghost of Hamlet's
father to affirm old Catholic doctrine which Wittenberg has
forgone. Hamlet's inaction is due to disbelief in ghosts. If he
thinks he sees a ghost then he is mad. If his father's murder had
taken place after the end of term, with Faustus's Helen already
raised, then there would have been no delay about revenge. (I
take it, incidentally, that Hamlet comes home about halfway
through the spring term. The air bites too shrewdly for the
summer one, and there is talk of Christmas as being so remote as
to be mythical. This is the unsound way in which my mind
works.) I naturally kept silence about the *Faustus–Hamlet* connection, except to say that there are no other plays of the period
that deal with eschatology.

I had known Goethe's *Faust* long before Marlowe's, because
of Gounod, Berlioz and Busoni, and it seemed to me necessary to
make the sort of comparisons more appropriate to the Compara-

tive Literature courses that at that time did not exist. Goethe's
Faust was much in my mind because of the war and Steinerian
talk about Germany fulfilling its Faustian *Schicksal*, also because I
had been discussing *Faust* with members of the *Freie Deutsche
Jugend*. This was a body of mostly young Jewish refugees from
Germany, whom university students were supposed to help with
English classes, singsongs in which 'Clementine' and 'It's a Long
Way to Tipperary' were sung with guttural sorrow, dances, hikes,
and metaphysical discussions. They were a haughty lot who found
Manchester inferior to Hamburg and Munich. Our soldiers were
sloppier than the *Wehrmacht*, the uniforms of our police baggier
than those of the SS, our cuisine was poor and our weather
atrocious. As rejected citizens of the *Reich*, they still assumed certain master-race prerogatives, such as jumping bus queues and
railing at harassed waitresses. They expected coffee in pubs and
made sour faces at our thin beer. They helped the cause of antisemitism immeasurably.

Still, some of them condescended to discuss *Faust* and *Doctor
Faustus* with me, sneering at my bad German accent and naturally
finding Goethe greater than Marlowe. When I cited Goethe's
admiration for *Doctor Faustus* out of Eckermann, they were
sceptical and assumed I had misread the passage in question. They
were profoundly positivist and considered Faustus's fears of
damnation very childish. Hell, they said, did not exist. Did, I
asked, evil? Evil – *Übel? Verbrechen? Unglück?* A bad man was an
evil man. People were bad, like Hitler, but there was, they said,
no such thing as ultimate or theological evil. They were innocent,
but we were all innocent then. We were living in the presence of
evil and did not yet know it. They assumed that Marlowe's *Doctor
Faustus* was a mediaeval work and that Marlowe himself was a
Catholic. This was not subtle enough, but it corroborated my
own suspicion about Marlowe, the pederastic atheist with mouth
of gold and morning in his eyes. He was Catholic all right. If
he was a spy, he was a spy for Philip of Spain. Walsingham's
men found out about this and had him killed in a tavern at Dept-
ford.

Doctor Faustus as symbolic autobiography was the theme of
my thesis. Marlowe wanted to be a Renaissance man but Catholicism held him back. Tamburlaine gains power through conquest, Barrabas the Jew of Malta through capitalistic enterprise,
Faustus through knowledge. But there is only one kind of knowledge worth having, and that is knowledge of ultimate reality.

Faustus wants hell. In his *Seven Types of Ambiguity*, the dangerous bible that many of us carried around, Empson suggests that the weak negatives of 'Ugly hell gape not, come not Lucifer' indicate a desire for hell to gape and Lucifer to come. 'I'll burn my books' – there was Nazi Germany. Book-burning was both a feeble gesture of repentance come too late, also a longing to get to the fire. I was a young man and probably misguided. I should not have written: 'Faustus, like Nazi Germany, desires hell as the final reality.' One does not write literary theses out of one's uneasy soul.

Writing about *Doctor Faustus* out of uneasy nerves was imposed upon me by the times. While the rest of the family slept in the cellar, I pecked at the office typewriter, a hundred pages of double-space foolscap, smoking heavily in a room without air that smelt, because of all the Swan Vesta cartons around, like a pine forest. Then the Luftwaffe trundled overhead on its way to Trafford Park. A bomb load was spilled a mile or two off. 'Ugly hell, gape not.' The earth shook. 'One drop would save my soul, half a drop.' I prayed and was ashamed of praying.

I submitted my thesis and sat my final examinations in a glass-roofed gymnasium, a perfect target for the Luftwaffe as agent of the annihilation of callow Manchester scholarship. Next to me sat Oliver Corbett, writing on Sophocles in first lieutenant's service dress, pistol next to the inkwell. While I was translating a passage from *The Dream of the Rood* the bombers droned over on a daring daylight raid. The anti-aircraft guns started up. I saw, with rare insight, that it was more important to translate *The Dream of the Rood* than to be engaged in a war. It would be vaguely noble to die with one's pen poised over a note about Mercian i-mutation. We were, to borrow from Dorothy L. Sayers's *Gaudy Night*, protecting Mansoul.

I summed up the season in verse:

Summer surprises, the sun imprisons us,
The pen slithers in the examinee's fingers,
Colliding lips of lovers slide on sweat
When, blind, they inherit their tactile world.

Spectacles mist, hand veins show blue, the urge to undress
Breeds desire in unexpected places, barrage balloons
Soar silver in silver ether. Lying on grass,
We watch them, docile monsters, unwind to the zenith.

> Drops of that flood out of France, with mud and work
> Stained, loll in the trams, drinking their cigarettes,
> Their presence defiling the flannels and summer frocks,
> The hunters to hound security, spoil the summer.

That must have been written in early June, after the Dunkirk
evacuation. It contradicts the high-flown nonsense about Mansoul. I should have been with that exhausted lot, spewed out of
France. When, on June 5, Hitler screamed on the radio his
proclamation of a war of total annihilation against his enemies,
he no longer sounded like *Beowulf*. The war was coming now,
though not yet close enough. When, on June 14, Margaret Williams announced that the Germans were in Paris, Lynne jumped
for joy, literally. It was the wrong approach. It was an exciting
bit of fiction about the Germans entering Paris. It was also the
right approach, that of protecting the importance of *Beowulf* and,
for Lynne, of surplus value. I wiped out the war and was
summoned to a *viva voce*.

Whether this was to decide between a first and a top second I
have never discovered. Knights and Charlton were there and a
number of anonymous but undoubtedly famous academics from
another world. I blustered, as young men will; I was ignorant
and arrogant. My eccentric interpretation of *Doctor Faustus* was
dismissed. A great bald academic said: 'Let us descend from these
lofty heights of profitless speculation and –' Then his chair fell to
pieces and he to the floor. Apt for the comic scenes of *Doctor
Faustus*, this caused academic laughter which boded me no good.
'Why do you say Fowstus and Dr Knights says Fawstus?' I
interpret the digraph phonetically and he historically. How? In
some Elizabethan texts Doctor Faustus is folk-etymologised to
Doctor Foster. 'What gives you the authority to contradict Mr
Eliot by denying that the Elizabethans got their five-act division
from Seneca?' There is no act division in Seneca. Eliot made a
mistake. He was always a bad Latinist. 'In the juvescence of the
year' is a disgrace. It should be 'juvenescence'. That pleased
Charlton, but nobody there liked Charlton. 'You mention here
something about a folk Hamlet that persists in Lancashire mythology.' Yes, Lancashire people say 'I'll play 'Amlet with thee,
lad,' referring to Amloth the proto-Hamlet and meaning that
they will go violently mad. And so on. There was a big crowd
waiting outside, as on the verdict of a star chamber trial. I got a
top second but I had failed General Latin again. 'Let it go,' said

Charlton, who disliked the classicist Semple. 'There's a war on. You've got your degree.'

So now I was ready for call-up, Private Wilson BA (Hons). But there was no great willingness to call me up. Lynne had taken her Part One but refused to go home. She was in love with someone, she wrote, and this someone was going into the forces, and she was going to stay in Manchester until he did. Her mother wrote: All right, bring him along too. So we travelled together to Newport and then took the local train to Blackwood. It was a different world, in which my speech was alien and considered comic. English then, are you? Come down here to be civilised, is it? A drunk on the train cried out against the war, saying that the nations were like plentyns fighting for loshins, isn't it. The girls were creamy-skinned and crammed with sex. The law of the English did not seem to run here. Trains stopped between stations to accommodate valley folk clambering up the sidings. The last bus crawled spectacularly overloaded. Pubs closed all day Sunday, meaning that they stayed open longer than on weekdays but you entered by the back door. At three in the morning on Monday I was still accompanying the local policeman on the piano: he had a fine tenor voice. The post office had a kettle on the boil always ready to steam open the mail. The postman knew your news before you did. Dylan Thomas's portrait of a Welsh town in *Under Milk Wood*, taken as whimsical fantasy by the non-South Welsh, is all too much hard truth.

My prospective father-in-law did not much care for my being an Irish Lancastrian, but I matched his Boltonian with my Harpurhey and asked if I could wed his lass. Not yet, of course, get engaged first. His lip trembled but he said yes. You'll have to buy her a ring. Got one 'ere, I said, pulling it out of the pocket of the dressing-gown I had borrowed from him. So there we were, Llewela and I, officially affianced. We had to visit outlying flanks of the Welsh Jones family to announce the news and for me to submit myself to the scrutiny of Tredegar and remote farms with outlandish names. Certain patriarchs knew no English. One had only once seen an Englishman before, a travelling inspector of the Ministry of Agriculture who had been granted accommodation but stayed up too late drinking home-brewed beer. None had known how to send him to bed because of the language difficulty, but a lad who had worked in an Anglo-Welsh magnate's kennels came up with the formula 'Cwtch, you bugger'.

Lynne's, or Llewela's, mother was swarthy and bright-eyed. She took to me as one orphaned, deprived, too thin, and fed me on nourishing Welsh dishes – roast leg of lamb with potch (mashed swedes and potatoes), brandy broth (stewed beef and chicken seasoned with Gilbey's port and, the crowning touch before serving, a half-tumbler of Martell's three-star). The invasion scare had begun, and we were told that the ringing of church and chapel bells would be the signal to dig out purloined Great War guns and stowed harquebuses. Lying in my bed in the spare room, I converted a sudden attack of tintinnus into external jangling and woke the household. But there was no invasion, though there was much discussion in the local pub as to how to respond to one. Bloody government let us down again, isn't it, the bloody 'Ome Guard armed with broom bloody 'andles. A man named Twm Black Lion had once met a German. Educated he was, and spoke like a gentleman. What's the difference, I say, man, between the bloody Germans and the bloody Sais? Foreigners both is what I say, isn't it, as soon have one as the bloody other. Somebody had heard that the Germans considered the Welsh to be one of the lost tribes of Israel and they would be done in like the bloody Jews. This led to reminiscences of one Enoch Davies who went mad and swore he had been born in Bethlehem. Scholar he was, mind, read and write the bugger could. In the winter he wore brown paper under his shirt to cwtch his chest. Biblical face he had too, but all the real Welsh had biblical faces. I also had a biblical face and so was not quite one of the Sais. Marrying a Welsh girl, is it? Go further and fare bloody worse, mind.

Llewela, as I had to call her here, damped natural ardour in deference to her bright-eyed mother, who spoke meaningfully of the good moral life. Our goodnight kisses were cool pecks. But we wandered into the woods of Cefn Fforest and made love while the birds, possible narks of the chapel, twittered and looked on. Emerging from a covert, hastily eased, twigs and bracken on our clothes, we met Rhys Evans the former lover, sleek-haired, moustached, bulky, a rugger-player. He was entering the woods with a new mistress, dumpy but exuding raw sex, whose name I learned later was Nest. There could not well be a fight in these circumstances, but Rhys Evans murmured to me: 'I'll get you, don't worry. And I shan't be on my own, you'll see.' It was clearly time for me to get out of Blackwood. As for Llewela, she brooded over a glass of hot orange in the Blackwood Café. She had unreasonably expected to find a Rhys Evans who had taken to his bed in the anguish of lost love. There he was with Nest, deemed hot. Just like a woman, I thought. Can't bear to see a man go. This man went back to Manchester, but he had arranged to go back anyway. There might be call-up papers waiting for me. Soon armed military police might appear in Blackwood. Taking you off we are, see. Bloody deserter you are, man, isn't it?

But there were no call-up papers waiting. Harold Buxton, the manager of the Oxford Cinema on Oxford Street, a kind of friend of the family, told me he had a friend named Squadron-Leader Hargreaves, in charge of Royal Air Force recruiting in the city, and he arranged an interview for me. I was grateful. I was now very anxious to get into His Majesty's Forces, which would really be getting a job. I needed a job; I was no longer a student but one of the unemployed. I went to see Squadron-Leader Hargreaves in the company of Michael Callaghan. Callaghan, who had started to specialise in physical training, was eagerly snapped up and was soon in blue. I was not wanted. I had nothing to give. I was not permitted to go out and trade honourably in death. I had to wait with the rest of the Manchester civilians for death to come in the form of air raids. On September 7 London sustained heavy damage from the Luftwaffe, but Trafford Park, and its appendage the city, was not forgotten. Refusing to shelter, I missed braining from skidding shrapnel. The Battle of Britain was, according to the records, over by September 15 (1,753 German aircraft destroyed, 915 RAF), but the Luftwaffe still droned to the north-west. In October Lynne was back in Manchester, ready for the new term. The skies were quieter. Then my stepmother died.

It was one of my duties to take her an early morning cup of tea. She would raise herself blearily and absorb the tea as a plant absorbs rain after a long drought, then, from a toothless mouth, make noises that meant she wanted a refill. Taking the exhausted cup down this bright wartime morning, I heard a crash of a falling bedside lamp and the thud of a falling body. She had suffered a heart attack, and rolled out of her bed. The priest was called before the doctor: there might be enough life still to justify Extreme Unction. The priest, a young, wiry athlete from Roscommon, gave her artificial respiration, but the spark of breath would not take. She was beyond the last sacrament. I was looked at wonderingly: I had administered a cup of something; I was friendly with German chemists. Too many people read too many detective stories. The death certificate was signed and the funeral was arranged. The will was also read: I, of course, received nothing, but the problem was to arise of dividing the estate, which meant a flourishing but indivisible shop, between two daughters. I was out of it, more an outsider than I had ever been. While my stepmother had been alive a tenuous link with my father held; now it would be all charity. The war, in a way, was a blessing. It would enforce a kind of pay-earning independence. But the war machine, despite my begging letters, still refused to call me up.

That day I learned something of the large egoism of which women are capable. ('It began with Eve, that delusion of uniqueness' – a line I inserted into my 1971 translation of *Cyrano de Bergerac*.) I had arranged to have lunch with Lynne in a small restaurant in Rusholme. I was inevitably late and was railed at solidly. I made my excuses: my stepmother had just died. All right, that was a sort of mitigation, but who comes first? She was not invited to the funeral, and that was seen as an affront. I showed her my stepmother's identity card, which I had taken from her purse. We could, with that and my own, book into a hotel as a married couple. That was ghoulish, which it was; in-excusable, and I could not and cannot excuse it. The war was getting at us. Our nerves were on edge. There was a year of war behind us, and what had it meant? A shameful evacuation from Dunkirk, twisted into a glorious victory; the so-called Battle of Britain, which was the virtual annihilation of London's East End. Silly songs like 'The King is Still in London' and 'Mr Brown of London Town'. Even sex was going wrong: too many parties at which everybody was enjoined to strip to the waist or take what they could find in the dark. My stepmother's funeral and the ham and whisky tea that followed felt more like normality. I yearned towards the army which did not want me.

But I found work. In the *Manchester Evening News* a garage proprietor advertised for a tutor for his young son, mornings only, thirty-five shillings a week. I wrote, not forgetting to add BA Honours to my signature, and got the job. Thirty-five shillings was reasonable money in those days, with beer still fivepence a pint and a packet of Player's only a shilling. The three-and-sixpenny dinner of too many courses was still available at the Piccadilly restaurants. When I told my step-relatives of the job there was talk of 'coming to some arrangement'. That meant

I was to be a lodger. I looked for a room on Ducie Avenue, a decaying street of once handsome Georgian residences behind the university. I found a large one with a double bed for five shillings a week. The landlady was a Mrs Hacey, who drank stout and fried her own chips, which were admirable and given free. I moved out and in, taking a shirt or so, the poems of Hopkins and *Finnegans Wake* in my rucksack. I was independent at last.

The boy I tutored in English and mathematics was a bright lad of eleven who had been ill, as I had once been, with cardiac rheumatism and had missed too much schooling. I was meeting surprising affluence. I had always assumed that garage men were oil-soaked tea-slurping illiterates dwelling in back kitchens, but here was a fine house with central heating and a cocktail cabinet. The room where I tutored had a white Syrie Maugham grand piano which nobody played. The tutoring was not arduous, since the boy refused to work and preferred to show me his skill in tap-dancing. He asked me how much his dad was paying me and then said 'Chicken feed'. He began to augment my wages with money he had cached up the chimney of the fireless grate. He liked garage work and was cheerily efficient with petrol pumps and chamois rag. He was tipped, and he saved his tips. Every day he would hand me a mound of half-crowns with an air of adult munificence. When my calling-up papers at last came to the Men's Union and I told him the lessons must cease (though they had never really started), he offered to take my girl friend and myself for a Midland Hotel blow-out, vintage champagne and all, but I foresaw his rebuking the sommelier and so demurred. He gave me instead a paper bag filled with notes and large silver, all (I counted townwards on the bus) of twenty-five pounds. I was ending my civilian life well off.

Lynne started her final year by, as was permitted to senior women students, moving out of her hall of residence into approved university diggings. Mrs Hacey's lodging house was not on the approved list, but Lynne moved into my double bed for a bacchanalian, or pseudo-marital, fortnight. Mrs Hacey, who was like Samuel Butler's Mrs Jupp, approved. It was a fine big bed for raunging and rollicking, she said. Take it while you can get it, like my old man used to say. Poor bugger, he snuffed it young, of an inseck in his head. I'll have some lovely hot chips ready in a jiff. So, well fed, often drunk, smoking like, as Mrs Hacey put it, a chimbley, making fierce love without constraint, I enjoyed the last days of a dangling man and prepared to join the war.

FOUR

I HAD RECEIVED a cordial notice of induction into His Majesty's Army, together with a note of welcome from the monarch himself, whose photograph on shiny paper showed an uneasily smiling field marshal. Presumably he made a quick change of fancy dress for the other arms. It was for him that I was to fight, or rather not fight, since I was to enter the Royal Army Medical Corps and try to save life rather than take it. The call-up authorities had made a wise choice on my behalf. They must have known of my antipathy to even the simplest of engines, and even perhaps of the tendency of all engines in my presence to grow shy, confused, inefficient, even self-destructive. I had given up trying to drive cars, use cigarette lighters, or wind up toy trains. A rifle in my hands would probably refuse to fire. I was to be a noncombatant, but not out of the conviction that animated Quakers or Oxford Groupers.

I also received a one-way third-class ticket to Eskbank outside Edinburgh. I had never had a one-way ticket before. There was no cosy promise of a return home, not that I had any home. I did not even have a next of kin, except for a fiancée. This term, always a dubious one since the acute accent proclaimed it to be a foreign loanword, was not permitted in the forces, and my next of kin was reduced to a friend. I travelled up with Hopkins and Joyce in my rucksack but little else, not even a change of shirt. I assumed that His Majesty was at once to kit me out fully, down to a new packet of razor blades. It was October 17, 1940, the war had been going for over a year, His Majesty was now fully organised, and on October 18 or at latest 19 I would be a fully equipped soldier. I already had my number – 7388026 – and, for mnemonic purposes, had converted it into a tune on the Chinese principle of notation. 1 is the first note of the diatonic scale and 8 the last. A zero is a crotchet rest. 7388026 made a catchy little theme, and I improvised a rhapsody on it as I went north.

The compartment remained empty all the way except for another recruit for Eskbank. He was small, simian and silent. I kept offering him Chesterfield cigarettes, and he docked these after the first two puffs and stowed them, in the manner of a poor student of St Mary's, Strawberry Hill. He had something on his mind, and I discovered what it was when I offered him my *Manchester Guardian*. He was illiterate, and he was ashamed of it. 'I haven't learnt to read yet' was the way he put it, and he seemed to think that the disability would be harmful. In a way it already was, for he could make no sense of the station signs, and at Huddersfield and Leeds he asked me if we were there yet. When we got to Edinburgh and had to look for the local train he clung to me whimpering. He had a small cardboard attaché case, and this earned the scorn of the lance-corporal who was waiting for us at Eskbank station. 'You're in the fucking army now,' he said, 'not frigging about on a fucking mannequin parade with a little fucking attaché case.' *Attaché, fiancée* – it was the acute accent again. My companion said 'I haven't learnt to read yet,' which he seemed ready to offer as an excuse for any delinquency.

The lance-corporal's bad language struck me as factitious. He was plump and moustached and had very clean fingernails, probably a car salesman in his former life. He was acting. We were all acting, the whole hundredfold intake of us. We sang 'Roll Out the Barrel' when we were put into line and marched off up the hill. We were acting good-humoured prisoners of war putting a brave face on it all the way to the *Kriegsgefangenenlager*. We were marched through the Scottish twilight to Newbattle Abbey, responded with acting glee to 'Keep those, them fucking heads up' as we entered the gate, and then came to rest in a kind of grim ballroom with minstrel's gallery untenanted, antlered trophies of the chase all around, a bland nude stone goddess or two. A man with three stripes and a crown surveyed us with pity he kindly tried to hide. 'That,' I said to myself, 'must be a sergeant-major.' It was a civilian error and I was soon ashamed of it. Here was a staff-sergeant. (I was interested to note in the television version of Waugh's *Brideshead Revisited* that the same error was made, with less excuse.) All the recruits looked both sick and defiant. We were a long way from home and nobody believed the war would be over by the Christmas before next. We were issued with pint mugs, mess tins, and knife, fork and spoon in canvas holdalls. We were given the first of many foul army meals – cooling stew and duff with custard – and then allotted to companies. I was put into B Company and marched off with a mess-tin-clanking bunch to a wooden hut in the company lines. We could not see a thing. The hut was glacial and lighted forlornly by what we were later to designate as a Transit Depot bulb – the dimmest possible wattage painted red, so faint that it would not disturb sleepers in a place where transience was on a twenty-four-hour basis. There were no beds. But there were the kapok mattress segments called biscuits and a mound of dirty blankets. Some of the recruits knelt to pray before retiring, presumably for strength.

The recruit next to me was a German Jew named Judah Apfelbaum, or Joe Appletree, who did not pray. Instead he railed at the hut corporal about the cold and filth and lack of amenity. 'I vash my teeth before sleep, but vhere is vashing place, you tell me that.' There was no washing place, only a row of cold-water taps half a mile off. The corporal replied, reasonably, that we were all in the same fucking boat. Apfelbaum then scrutinised me and said 'Vat your name?' I told him. 'Mr Vilson,' he offered, 'you are not vell. You are veak, I can see. You vill not be able to stand it. You and me vill valk out of here tomorrow unless they make things better.' He seemed to regard the training depot as a bad hotel we could exchange for another. But he was right to rail, as we saw next day.

After all, the headquarters of the RAMC was in the charge of doctors in uniform, it was dedicated to the promotion of health and hygiene, the healing of wounds and diseases, but it did not offer its trainees even the chance to be clean, let alone kempt. The day began in the dark with a blind cold water shave, a night breakfast with porridge in one mess tin and a fishcake in the other, and a solitary cold tap outside the mess hall for the rinsing of utensils, so that our knives and forks lay, like guns, in cold grease. Then came the dawn revelation of where we were to void. There was a muddy slope, just off the vertical, with field latrines at the top and no Army Form Blank. The slope was called 'Ill 60. Willed constipation became a necessity. There would have been no objection to living rough if only svelte officers had not given harangues about the *corpore sano* of the corps motto. The *mens sana*, it was presumed, would be difficult to promote.

I offer the facts of the next month or so as raw history, the situation of an army that had been at war for over a year. For five weeks I worked and slept in the same unwashed shirt, pathetically ennobled by a college tie, marched and drilled in sports jacket and torn baggy flannels, saw the shoes drop off my feet (I had come deliberately ill shod because I expected boots), did not bath, became of necessity chronically constipated, grew sick of my own odour. My stepbrother-in-law Jack Tollitt had faced air raids with steel helmet and service respirator. The corporal doing PAD duty at Newbattle Abbey (Passive Air Defence) blew his warning whistle with a field service cloth cap on and a boxed civilian gas mask hanging from his shoulder by a string. We helped to summon the Luftwaffe by carrying rubbish to the incinerator (which Judah Apfelbaum called the insinuator) before dawn. The garbage bucket contained the ashes of the hut stove as well as inflammable garbage. Every black morning duos could be seen bearing huge flaming fires to the dump. This seemed no way to run an army.

The men of my hut tried to preserve a civilised *mens sana* by maintaining urbane good manners with each other. The honorific Mr was always used, to the disgust of the NCOs. 'Who told you that?' – 'Mr Wilson, corporal.' – 'There's no fucking misters here below the rank of second-lieutenant, get that into your thick skull.' The uncouth enemy was the whole phalanx of warrant and non-commissioned officers. The commissioned were too remote to generate an attitude. But anger at their unprofessionalism rose one night when one of our number, Mr Whateley, went down with pneumonia. There was no doubt about the diagnosis: some of the recruits were well-trained St John's Ambulance men. We asked for immediate medical examination but could not get it. We asked for an ambulance; we compromised by begging for a stretcher. Eventually he had to be carried bodily to the distant bulk of Newbattle Abbey. We did not see him again, and we were forbidden to ask for a report on his condition. We became bloody-minded.

Bloody-mindedness ought to be the natural condition of soldiers. Never in the whole history of human conflict, as Winston Churchill ought to have said, have so many been buggered about by so few. Soldiers love the official enemy, seeing the mirror image of their own buggerings about in men they have no desire to kill. They learn hate from their own side. I still lie awake at night plotting vengeance on Corporal Newlands, a little Glasgow lout who, in allusion to my overgrown hair, a barber not yet being available, called me 'Currrrly'. He was one of the physical training instructors who, for a fancied insolence, made me run, to his jeers of 'Peck yer fuckin' feet up', three times round the square with arms held high. PT was always a torment. 'Soon,' said a writhing, evidently neurotic officer at the outset, 'you men will be thoroughly fit' (aye, fit to fucking drop), but it did no good with its silly games and false jocularity ('Come on, lads – one more for the King and Queen'), its naked shivering in a December dawn. I still hear the misery of its massed coughing.

There were a number of Glasgow toughs, one-eyed through Gorbals slashing, among the NCOs. These had probably been chosen to deal with the brutal Polyphemoi in the ranks. They spoke the same language, unintelligible to anybody else. The rankers wrote and read no language. I had never before realised how much British illiteracy there was. The roster of company duties had to be read out to them. I tried it once, but they growled in fierce rage: 'Put some fucker on to read as can fucking read.' The literate Glasgow toughs were CQMS McGonagall and Sergeant Dempsey. McGonagall said to me, pointing to the metal laurelled crowns on his forearms, 'What do you think these are, lad? Fucking glow-worms?' I said: 'Evidently not.' He said: 'You'll say *sir* when you speak to me.' I said: 'My father instructed me to say *sir* only to himself and to God Almighty. You are neither.' It was good to see him dance with rage. Still, I smelt high danger. I said: 'Dr Samuel Johnson called everybody sir as a mark of common respect. He said it even to a foul-mouthed bargee. So I will submit to calling you sir, sir. My poor father will turn in his grave.' He had me marked. Sergeant Dempsey had me marked. My accent grew unprecedentedly posh. I declared verbal war on the bastards. I was going to be very bloody-minded.

But not yet. There were six weeks of recruit training to undergo: the time for real bloody-mindedness would come when I went on to full-time fatigues and suffered the long wait for posting. In the meantime I was marched to classes in anatomy and first aid, mere attendance at which would qualify me as a Nursing Orderly Class 3. Sergeants were in charge of the instruction. Officers, who presumably knew more about the science of medicine than sergeants who, not knowing how to pronounce 'corpuscle', spoke of the white buggers and the red bastards, never looked in. One of our sergeants was an Edinburgh homosexual in his element with pawing and squeezing the more handsome recruits to show where the liver lay. I knew little of anatomy, except for the structure of the vocal organs. When this instructor referred to the hanging grape of the velum as the uvulva I was able to put him right. 'You're thinking of a different organ altogether. But, knowing you, I think perhaps you're not.' He knew what I was getting at. He too had me marked.

Being marked meant being picked on for extra duties, such as unloading a truck that had suddenly appeared with an unexpected benison of equipment as one was about to ascend 'Ill 60. Having boasted I could play the piano, I was regularly detailed for the shifting of wretched old uprights for ENSA concerts. The great thing was to run when stripes or glow-worms loomed. One was not thought the worse of for that. The men most admired were those who could walk the barracks all day in fatigue dress carrying a broom and doing nothing. Idleness and theft were accounted virtues when allied with quiet skill. Malingering with style was approved. An image of the army began to emerge – not the unfaithful and sluttish bride of Evelyn Waugh's marriage, but a loose animal organism essentially torpid, in which movement was mostly knee-jerks or the responses of Pavlovian conditioning. It was not, after all, all that frightening. Authority expressed itself in bluster. It was all a large performance, apt for the theatricality of the British soul.

We become habituated to anything. Partly kitted out, marched to a bathhouse and back, learning what we could get away with, we became a kind of soldiers. We had no caps FS, only steel helmets; we had no gaiters. We had service respirators, and I invented an elastic device for fixing these at the alert which, though efficient, was regarded as a heresy. It was an army of string and webbing. The Thomas's splint, which was the crown of our instruction, was a neolithic masterpiece of tapes and granny knots. The bureaucracy was endearingly amateurish. The same F. L. Wilson kept appearing on company details although its owner had long been posted. As this Wilson never turned up, another Wilson, namely myself, had to be charged with dereliction of duty, one Pte Wilson being as good as another. I enjoyed being brought before the company commander, a sort of unhappy GP, to explain my absence from retreat parade. 'You admit you are Wilson?' – 'Yes, but not F. L.' – 'You are the only Wilson in B Company. It was your duty to assume a typing error and obey an obvious order.' – 'It is not my duty to assume that my superiors make errors. Almost by definition they are incapable of errors.' – 'You will say *sir*.' – 'Sir.' – 'All right. Dismissed.' F. L. Wilson was still on company orders the following week. Then he became an unperson.

Having no issue of caps FS, which were called cunt caps partly because of their shape and partly because they made you look a cunt, some of us bought peaked caps, which were known as cheese-cutters. There was a sort of unwritten law at Newbattle Abbey that only members of the depot staff should wear these. Officially they went only with service dress; unofficially they vaguely denoted the authority of a trained private soldier. Greater love for the army hath no man than that he should expend part of his weekly seventeen shillings and sixpence on making himself smart. Some, including myself, bought the twopenny lanyards which only the Royal Engineers were supposed to loop beneath their epaulettes. We were learning soldier's pride. We took pride in yelling 'Sah!' and responding like clockwork to orders. We proudly went out, smart soldiers, to the tea parties given by the kind ladies of Eskbank. We took tea on Princess Street in Edinburgh, and kind ladies would not let us pay for our poached eggs on haddock and our shortbread. The old life, only six weeks back, was alien. I had to remind myself that I had a loved fiancée or friend. There were too many Eskbank lassies ready for what were known as meat injections.

At Christmas discipline relaxed, and sergeants dripped soup down our necks in the hollied mess hall. The RSM, a fearful monster on the square, grew first jolly then tearful and said he loved us like sons. We thought we might conceivably learn to love the Corps. 'You are,' said the QMS of B Company, 'fucking gentlemen, and don't you fucking forget it. You are not fucking infantry, drooling over the stabbing of a bayonet in the enemy's fucking goolies. Next week you are going to show how much you are fucking gentlemen, because the new latrines will be ready. No more going for a crap up 'Ill 60. You will be able to have a decent gentlemanly crap in proper fucking surroundings and I want to see no scrabblings of shitty fingers on the walls. Shit like fucking gentlemen.' The RAMC band appeared at this time, and we assumed it was to celebrate the opening of the latrines, but it was only to give resonance to the complex ritual of a commanding officer's parade. The regimental march was by Ralph Vaughan Williams, an old RAMC man, who had typically resurrected a folk song called 'Pretty Joan'. The words we sang to it were 'We're browned off, we're browned off, we're always fucking well browned off.' This meant we were fed up. We were too, chronically, as well as fucked up and far from home. We were all these things in the liturgical sense of all being miserable sinners.

I suppose it was a kind of military devotion that turned me into a bugler and a piper. I knew how a bugle worked: you evoked a segment of the harmonic series by varying lip-pressure on the metal embouchure. I was permitted occasionally to blow lights out and reveille. Blowing the latter one morning over the deep and unrousable dark, I reflected that the harmonic series was a fact of nature, and that the atonalists had tried to separate music from nature, which was a grave sin. I studied the chanter under the pipe-major and graduated to the whole bag of barbarous Celtic tricks. I tried to imagine a Schoenbergian accompaniment to 'The Flowers of the Forest'. Nothing was more moving than the wail of that lament in the freezing Eskbank dusk. You could not, unless you were pacifist, Viennese, and neurotic, wish to get away from the harmonic series and the diatonic scale. Bagpipe music was simple and heroic, limited in range and restricted to the key of A major; the skill lay in the management of grace notes. With other pipers, some of them earnest, bespectacled and clerkly, I skirled behind the big drum on the Sunday march to mass, desperately afraid of slipping on the icy hill. ('Some day,' I vowed, 'I will live where there is no ice.' I fulfilled the vow.) Once I skirled and slipped and fell, and the pipes squealed for me like a dying pig. They had been insulted.

Piping my way to mass, attending mass, piping back from mass, I had resumed religious practices I thought I had done with for ever. But the army is roughly concerned with soul as well as body, though it neglects the elements in between. On joining up, Douglas Mason had declared himself an Intellectual Hedonist and been asked what the fucking hell that was. Spiritual apportionment had once been simple in the army – 'RCs this side, C of E that, fancy buggers in the middle', the fancy buggers being free thinkers, Jews and atheists. Now it was subtler, and Judaism and the United Board of Protestant reformists were no longer the domains of fancy buggers. Still, choice was limited, and it was only just that I should be an RC. I was not, whatever else I was doing, wearing khaki on behalf of His Majesty's Protestantism; I was in the war to support the European Catholic tradition, which unfortunately had to accommodate most of the one-eyed thugs from the Gorbals. It was a pity that the Catholic padre was a Maynooth man who, jingling the coins in his pocket, told us that God had sent the war as a kind of moral test and we would need Christ's grace to get through it without our noses dropping off. It was a pity too that the Church of England padre was a civilised reading man of rare intelligence, the one outpost of humanism in a barbaric morass. I proposed using the obligations of Catholicism to counter the army ethos – demanding fish on Fridays and the right to confess when I wanted to and go off to mass alone for urgent special intentions. Unfortunately the Church conceded too much and played along with the army. Friday was no longer a day of abstinence, and there were no more holidays of obligation. All I could do was to strike out at the NCO bigots who cried: 'Come on, you fucking RCs or arseholes, get fell in for midnight mass at three in the afternoon, lucky fucking lot, getting fucking privileges while the rest has to fucking work.' That, of course, was on Christmas Eve, and he had a drop taken, but I was not going to let him get away with it. I demanded that he apologise for his intolerant foulness or take the consequences. He apologised. This was regarded as a small victory for the oppressed rank and file, RC, C of E, or fancy buggers.

I was marked, and battle was engaged when training was over and the time came for living in fatigue dress while awaiting posting. It was an opportunity to see what soft-armed intellectuals could do when confronted with labourer's labour. It was like the Chinese Cultural Revolution. I stood in the pounding rain with a bank manager, a senior librarian, and an anthropologist with a Durham MA under a towering heap of human faeces, the final spoils of supersessed 'Ill 60. Near by was a truck on to which it had to be loaded entire by winter sundown. 'Well,' said Pte T. F. Barton the antropologist, 'we've reached rock bottom, gentlemen. There's a kind of joy in it. No feasible punishment awaits us if we down tools. We cannot be demoted. We cannot even be put on fatigues, since we're on fatigues already. We could be sent to the military prison known as the glasshouse, where, I understand, the sergeant warders are Dickensianly brutal and even speak Dickensian English, saying 'werry' for 'very'. That might be interesting, but I don't think it will happen. I suggest that we inform that RASC driver, snug and dry in his cabin and reading what looks like a trashy Penguin, that work is temporarily suspended because of the inclement weather.' The driver asked no greater authority than Barton's weary scholarly voice and took his trashy

Penguin back to the transport park. The mound of faeces stood till it fermented. Then it was bulldozed into Scottish earth. This was one way of coping with the impossible.

I would make use of my ordered visits to the Quartermaster's Store, armed with indents and chits, to telephone B Company in a fatigued patrician voice and berate the Company Commander for a failure to send in the obligatory BF752 on time. This would cause panic, since none knew what a BF752 was. It was pleasant to be sirred by the Company Commander and apologised to abjectly by CQMS McGonagall. Only once did I dare impersonate the Commanding Officer of the depot, a numinous entity seen of no one, to congratulate B Company on the brutality of its discipline. The sirring sounded a little doubtful; I was probably going too far.

I went into physical action only twice. The first occasion was during the obligatory hour of the wearing of one's respirator, when, snouted and anonymous, I was detailed to scrub the floor of the Navy, Army and Air Force Institute, known as the NAAFI. Two civilians laughed at the scrubbing monster and roughly exhorted him to put some beef into it. I assumed that these were the NAAFI manager and sub-manager but did not realise that they carried the honorary rank of sergeant. I joyfully arose and emptied my bucket of filthy water on to their trousers. What had I to lose? They could not find out who I was by ordering me to remove my respirator. They were very angry and abusive. The second occasion was when I was on perimeter guard duty with a Gorbals delinquent. Being non-combatants, we were allowed only gnarled oak clubs as weapons. The thug drooled over his truncheon and almost kissed it, long deprived as he was of the means of violence. We were to watch for the return of a certain Corporal McKay from the boozer and do the bastard. I had nothing against this NCO since I did not know him. But the Gorbals man gave a long unintelligible recital of wrongs, real or fancied. 'Yon's the fucker,' he growled as we breathed smoke in the bushes. 'Ye gae the first, mon.' I had always suspected that Gorbals thugs were cowards. I took a half-hearted swing and knocked off the corporal's cap FS. He was very drunk. I apologised and said that I thought he was someone else. He accepted the apology and reeled to his quarters. The Gorbals villain said: 'Ye did wrang. Yon's nae the bastard.' After that I stayed pacific.

The only physical harm I was responsible for during my stay

was unwilled, the consequence of obeying orders. I was doubtful of their propriety and told the ordering corporal so. He said: 'Get on with the bleeding job.' From the front portal of Newbattle Abbey stretched a long corridor which I was told to swab with hot water though no soap. The portal was ever open, the temperature was below zero, and icy winds howled in. As soon as I swabbed, my hot water cooled and then froze. A seven-foot-tall warrant officer marched in, ignored my warning, and then measured his length. He recovered, none the worse, and swore at me. I reminded him of my warning. I gave no further warnings; I merely watched from now on in a horror of fascination. A fat major fell heavily. An officer of the Auxiliary Territorial Service broke a hip. I went off to the NAAFI for char and a wad, my eleven o'clock right, and did not return. The casualty reports were heavy. I genuinely regretted this, since all my victims were faceless neutrals.

My posting came through on a day of deep snow with a metal sky. I was to proceed by rail to a field ambulance in Northumberland. I assumed that a field ambulance was a motor vehicle and protested that I could not drive. But no, the B Company sergeant informed me as he handed over my travel warrant, a field ambulance was a medical unit that operated in the field: it did not skulk with scarlet majors at the base. It had three companies. The 189 Field Ambulance had, at this season, dispersed its companies widely through snowy Northumberland; all I would know till the spring arrived was HQ Company, a congeries of useless odds and sods to which I was well suited. The CQMS, his glow-worms dull in the snowlight, growled: 'Too much fucking chat, lad. Get out. We've got fucking work to do,' meaning heating one's fat arse at the stove and slurping char. I was glad to be able to say, nothing to lose after all: 'You have no gift of leadership, sir. This is a momentous day for me, since I am being posted. You ought to make some decent gesture of farewell to a departing member of your flock. Sir.' He said: 'A soldier's farewell. Now fuck off.' I said: 'Allow me to deliver a solemn valedictory anathema, sir. May your remaining testicle shrivel and your useless prick drop off at the root. May you wake crapulous from the regular excess of intake of booze you consider the due of your rank, and whose consequences visible are a nasal luminosity more scintillant than your fucking glow-worms, and contemplate with despair the abysmal depths of your incapacity to lead. A failure, sir, that's what you are. Now put me on a fucking B252.' He roared from the stove raising his drained mug in threat. I got out. It was a small triumph.

So I trudged, as in retreat, the snowy road to Eskbank station, cap FS, at last issued, on head cropped by a Sweeney Todd formerly employed at Strangeways Prison in Manchester. I had given away my cheese-cutter, forbidden in the field. I was in an overcoat that reached to my ankles as if I were in the cavalry, baggy battledress ungaitered, kitbag containing dirty underwear and Hopkins and Joyce hoisted, dealing frozen breath to the frozen air. Ahead of me, bound on the same posting, was a man I was soon to call Mr Nesbit, the ugliest man I had ever seen. His face had been through a mangle and then been hydraulically squashed. He was toothless. Being toothless did not impair one's capacity to eat army food, which was mostly overcooked slop with the bones removed. Nesbit belched painfully, but so did we all. The army's first aim was to implement chronic dyspepsia and dry up the bowels. Nesbit was a heavy smoker lacking wind, bloody-minded to the limit, coarse, ignorant, whose West Hartlepool dialect sounded like a prose edition of *The Dream of the Rood*, except for the spit of evident blasphemy. But he and I were drawn together, refugees from Newbattle Abbey, whipped to new territory we feared. We yearned for our hutmates and filthy blankets on the floor, even for 'Ill 60. We shared a compartment to Newcastle, changed for Morpeth deep in snow, and there awaited transport. It was a long time coming, but it came. It was a small truck with a drunken poet sprawled in the back, an Eskimo-haired private excused boots. He announced himself as the unit poet and recited a few lines of mock-Augustan verse to prove it:

> The odour of a gracious age still lingers,
> Though soldiers daub the walls with shitty fingers,
> And bully, stewed, replaces the roast ox.
> Milady's ghost, in red to hunt the fox,
> Is also red to hear the *fucks* and *cunts*,
> A language militant that frights, affronts.
> Though proper to a drunken squirearchy,
> 'Tis wrong for an enkhakied peasantry.

He had also written the unit song. He sang it:

> When we find Hitler,

He'll be in an awful mess.
We'll get a stretcher party
To jog him to the CRS.
And the 189 Field Ambulance
Will always do the trick:
Around his balls a tourniquet
And a Thomas's on his prick.

A Thomas's, then, had a genuine application in the field: it was not just a training depot fantasy. But what was a CRS? A Camp Reception Station. There was a whole new vocabulary to learn. G1098, for instance. He made jazzy riffs out of this, warbling:

G1098, G1098, G1098,
And the driver said: 'Bugger it.'

To the tune of 'Make All My Dreams Realities', he sang:

Make all my men fatalities.
Slowly and clumsily, throw them into ambulances.

I saw what he meant about the odour of a gracious age when we skidded to headquarters, a fine Georgian mansion with a cyclorama of hills and a wide park heavily under snow. 'Cheviot Hall,' the poet announced with pride. And then he said coldly: 'You are not wanted here, you know. We are a band of brothers. You are intruders. You will find out.' He nodded direly and limped, excused boots, off. I found out almost at once from the regimental sergeant-major who greeted Nesbit and myself. He was pained by Nesbit's ugliness and, as it were, had him shovelled up at once and removed. To me he spoke in low tones, as though in a conspiracy to keep my known crimes away from public hearing. I did not at first take him for an RSM: his cloth coat of arms on the forearms was so dim as to look like dirt; he wore battledress and a cap FS, was in no wise like the resplendent roarer of the square at Newbattle Abbey. I assumed he was a large and specially privileged private soldier, and I spoke to him as such. He said: 'I tell you, this is the end. We were all pals when we formed in Luton in peacetime, and now they send in sods like you.' I said I was quite willing to be posted away again. He said: 'You're not the worst of my problems. They put Colonel Winters in the loony bin and now we've got this outsider. He thinks I'm a cunt and I think he's a bastard. So watch it, boy.' This made little sense.

I found out about Colonel Winters later. He had a loaded pistol and a drawerful of buckshee ammo, contrary to the Geneva Convention, and was always threatening to shoot people. Apparently he had winged a staff sergeant, since posted, and been declared deolali tap or plain doolally. The new colonel, Frankel, was considered too sane and hence boring and was much resented. I was resented on a smaller scale and stowed into the kitchen as a pan scrubber, though dragged out periodically for PT, toboggan-riding down the snowy hill, and the loading of G1098 stores. I did not object to kitchen fatigues. The only enjoyable day I had had at Newbattle Abbey had been devoted to field cooking, for which I disclosed a talent. The sergeant cook at Cheviot Hall was a former sea cook whom everyone called Jack. He enjoyed throwing plates at the wall. He and I ate rump steak most days for dinner, while the rest had what the ration truck brought in.

Headquarters Company was queer; queer too in the colloquial sense, which was why it did not welcome intruders, especially ugly ones like Nesbit. We slept in what had formerly been servants' quarters, beyond the green baize, four or five to a room. There were many whisperings and rustlings in the night, as well as rhythmical thuds at a distance. There were tears and re-conciliations. Only outsiders like myself called NCOs by their rank. One fair-haired boy had a complete set of false teeth. He would take these out sometimes in the evenings and advertise a gamarouche for sixpence. There was an upright piano, and this I played. The music, the provision of an outsider, was at first resented, but later I became a brief musical hero. For a unit dance was organised, and the dance band from Morpeth did not turn up because of the snow. So I saved the situation by playing for five solid hours and was given much beer. 'Well done, Wilson boy,' they said. They called everybody boy, even the RSM who, at one point in the dance, silently wept on to the piano lid.

But it was a temporary heroism and a very transitory gratitude. The next morning I was brutally put on to the loading of G1098 stores while the more privileged nursed their hangovers. Cra-pulous though I was, I learned, almost for the first time, to laugh in the army. For the sergeant in charge of the store-loading, which was a kind of rehearsal for going into action, got the loading wrong and ordered us to unload. A private, not an outsider but one of the chums for some reason in disfavour, said, with his-

trionic satisfaction: 'Oh, nice work.' It expressed soldier's habituation to fuck-ups, an assumption enshrined in the SNAFU
acronym, a quiet delight that the army was not letting the men
down by disclosing a long-concealed efficiency. My laugh meant
that I was at last a sort of soldier. Then we all went for medical
inspections, more frequent in a field ambulance than in the
fighting units. The lieutenant who conducted mine was a man of
fierce squat handsomeness called Mr Empson. He said: 'Wilson,
for a pianist, your fingernails are a disgrace.' He did not like my
prepuce, which he considered too tight. He wished me to be
circumcised. Until my eventual posting abroad he was to reappear
in new contexts, remembering, urging, a frustrated *modin* or
mohil.

In February 1941 I was permitted to go on what was termed
privilege leave, to emphasise that it was a gift and no right. I
travelled in full equipment, with back and side packs and respirator at the alert, at last a soldier, unexpired portion of the
day's ration in my haversack and my water bottle a quarter full
of whisky. This kind of victualling was necessary: the train from
Newcastle to Manchester expended a day and a night in getting
there, perpetually rerouted to avoid smashed segments of the
permanent way and blitzed marshalling yards. The fellow-
privates who sat opposite doled out comforting army philosophy:
'Never mind, lads, it'll soon be Christmas' and 'Put another pea
in the pot and hang the expense' and 'Roll on death and let's
have a go at the angels' and (of RSMs and CSMs) 'There's many
a big spud that's rotten'. I was becoming aware of the vast
patience of the rank and file, a temporary sanctity too good for
the God who made the world.

I was going to Manchester to see my next of kin, my fiancée
or friend. She was working on her thesis – French policy in
Morocco from 1912 to 1914 – and lodging with a Mr and Mrs
Nixon in Rusholme. Warned of my coming, Lynne had written
to me, they were fitting out the front parlour as my bedroom.
These were university-approved diggings, and there was to be no
funny business on the lines approved by Mrs Hacey, who had
loved to listen to the raunging and rollicking of the unmarried
young. It was, I gathered, to be a sexless leave. Whether it had
been a sexless term and a half for Lynne I was not able to judge. I
had left her in the keeping of two Old Xaverians, students of her
own year, named Rowland Harper and Bernard Bruce Brown.
They were not sexless, far from it: the one loved a girl named

Malise and the other a certain Winifred Tupling who once said
to him: 'Poor boy, you have got it badly, haven't you?' But they
were loyal, reliable; they were Old Xaverians.

Lynne was appalled to see me shorn and in ill-fitting battledress.
I must get a commission right away and look like Siegfried
Sassoon. It was the sartorial aspect of my rank that shocked her.
Most women ambitious for their conscripted men primarily
objected to their failure to look like Wilfrid Owen, secondarily
to being seen in public places with swaddies to whom the world
offered the stock response of contempt. It let the women down.
Many a man has been lashed upward by his wife or friend. The
colonel's lady and Judy O'Grady may be what Kipling says they
are, but women know the value of skin and, even more, what
covers it. I had a leave of being trounced for not putting in for an
officers' selection board. I refused: my duty was to stay with my
own kind. And the money? I had not much thought of the
money. I had bed and board, such as they were, and half a crown
a day, enough for twenty fags and three pints of bitter. I was,
except for the bizarre interlude of the garage boy's tutorship,
better off than I had ever been. Lynne spoke of marriage after
her graduation: she did not much care for the prospect of marrying a private soldier. Where was my ambition? Like a regular
soldier or a politician (and she had studied politics; she was even
specialising in a deep and narrow phase of French diplomacy),
she thought of the war as a continuing aspect of life, not a brief
bad dream to be endured. The war was already summoning her to
the rank of assistant principal in some ministry or other. Well then,
I said happily, there is the money. This was the wrong response.

The university's Rag Ball occurred towards the end of this
leave, and I was made to go to it dressed as an Arab sheikh. This
was more becoming than private's khaki, but it was thin theatrical
costumier's stuff and I caught cold in it while waiting for a bus. I
was interested to note that one tall fair stripling went to the
dance as an SS *Obergruppenführer*, complete with swastika bras-
sard. He walked the daytime street in this outfit and few took
any notice: it is hard to impress Mancunians. When I got back to
the Rusholme diggings I went down with shivering and a high
fever. A civilian doctor said I was unfit to return to my unit. I
sent his certificate to the 189 Field Ambulance and received a
month's ration coupons by return. So they wanted me to stay
away for a month, did they? I took that extended leave to the
limit and went back to Morpeth much refreshed. The day after I

left, the military police arrived at Mr and Mrs Nixon's house to arrest me as a deserter.

It was my unit that was deserting *me*. I got to Morpeth and waited for the regular daily truck that called there. It did not come. In a pub I was told that the 189 Field Ambulance had moved, none knew where. I almost began to cry. But in a chintzy café I met a camp-follower, one of the girls who did so much to disrupt service security. She knew where the unit was: she even gave me the orderly room telephone number. So I telephoned. The chief clerk seemed disappointed that I was still at large. I should be in the glasshouse and crossed off the unit's strength. Transport was sent for me. Headquarters Company was in a larger country house than before. The RSM soft-footed towards me like a butler. 'Back then, are you?' he greeted. 'We thought we'd got rid of you. That ugly bugger's been posted, anyway.' He meant Mr Nesbit.

The 189 Field Ambulance did not get rid of me until the spring brought a shift of the entire formation. The headquarters of the 54th Division settled in Cheltenham, and the field ambulance, sundered in the winter, came together as an entity in Andoversford. Again there was a fine mansion, but not for the housing of the troops. We went into huts. A bugler was needed to sound over the camp, and I volunteered. I did more: I composed company calls but, as the harmonic series is limited, it was not easy to tell them apart. I did more again: fifes were indented for and I formed a fife band. I tried to please, but I could not. I was not one of the boys. But I was not the only one who was not one of the boys. There was an Oxford Grouper who prayed for me nightly, seemed smilingly to invite my persecution, and left pamphlets on my bed. But he was harmless, whereas I had a copy of *Finnegans Wake*, generally supposed to be a code book. My inefficiency on parade was interpreted as deliberate disruption: no one could have a BA degree and be naturally so stupid. A private had just been promoted to lance-corporal, and he was eager to show off his efficiency with the disposition of the canvas on a three-ton truck. This could be unfastened and turned into tents. A high wind blew, I unfastened too many of the rope stays, and the detail watched the canvas blow far away full-bellied. I felt sorry for that lance-corporal: he was ambitious and said sir far too often. A major went away on a gas course and came back enthusiastic. A gas squad was formed and I was put into it. I idly unstoppered a demonstration canister of phosgene.

There was, true, a disruptive force inside me, but I tried to fight against it. The Germans had to be beaten sometime, though nobody was sure quite when, and all this stretcher drill and these thirty-mile route marches were profoundly necessary. I wanted to be a good soldier, and the first step towards a declaration of serious intent would be to let myself be circumcised by Mr Empson. But I stuck to my prepuce.

The Entertainments Section of the division canvassed the units for a trained musician able to arrange and orchestrate. The RSM sobbed with relief when he put my name in. I was, if accepted, to remain on the nominal strength of the field ambulance but to anticipate an indefinite detachment. I was accepted.

IDLE TROOPS REQUIRE entertainment. There was never such idleness as in the Home Forces at that time. They were bored with excessive repetition of drill movements, naming of parts, lectures on syphilis, exhortations about security and the danger of camp-followers. Their evenings were filled with booze and fights. Occasionally a local teacher would give a lecture on beetles, with lantern slides, or a travelling officer would give a reassuring account of Germany's shortage of oil. Lighter diversion was provided by ENSA groups, graded according to star status. The big names rarely appeared, and I was considered lucky, in more than five years of army service, to see Cicely Courtneidge in a theatre in Gibraltar. The troops saw fifth-rate pierrot shows with ancient tenors who trilled 'I'll Walk Beside You', wrinkled soubrettes who creaked as they cavorted, and comedians who were coarse but not funny. John Priestland, the general officer commanding the 54th Division, was wise to order the formation of an army concert party and dance band for the exclusive entertainment of his own troops. It was as much war work as skulking in the quartermaster's store. It was strenuous, enlivened with acrimony, but it was not dull. The group I joined was called the Jaypees, after Priestland's initials which, white on red, formed the divisional flash. The group was part of headquarters, was fed and paid by whatever local unit could be bullied into accepting supernumerary personnel, and was billeted together outside the reach of reveille bugles. It worked late and it rose late. I reported for duty at Moreton-in-the-Marsh, where it was lodged in a loft above a government egg-packing station.

I met for the moment only its commanding officer, a lieutenant of the First Berkshires named Bill Elliott, handsome, dark, pipe-smoking, like an Elstree actor performing the role of an army officer. He was a genuine soldier, however, a territorial infantryman who had worked in peacetime for Lyons the caterers and had been responsible for staff entertainment. He had volunteered for the post of Divisional Entertainments Officer and come down a notch in rank, but he was sitting pretty in a civilian billet with his wife Sybil and a golden retriever, away from mud and regimental duties. His troupe was, unusually, on a brief route march that day. It came back while I was being greeted, and achieved a shambling halt. Its sergeant eventually got it into line facing the same way and made it fall out. It at once began to quarrel with itself and with its sergeant. This sergeant was Harry Walkling of the First Hertfordshires, a saxophonist high in rank but low in the musical hierarchy. He played tenor, but Ted Norman, a First Berks private and a clever Jew from Bethnal Green, led with his alto and ran the band.

The band was a small one, but, as I was to discover, loud. There was another First Herts man, Bill Brian the trumpeter; a pianist from the RASC, Ted Wright; a drummer who had professionally been known as Styx Williams and had signed on, also in the RASC, apparently under that sobriquet; finally, a double bassist who also played the piano accordion, Dick Nutting from the Royal Engineers. Another RASC man, Bob Morgan, was a violinist who had played with the pit band at the Coventry Hippodrome but was not permitted to play with this one, which disdained bowed strings. He was a kind of gipsy fiddler billed as the Great Romano. These were the musicians. The concert party proper, which got on very uneasily with the band, was headed by a First Berks corporal named Pat Glover, an eccentric dancer and comedian. Bill Clufton, from the RAOC, also danced, sometimes eccentrically. He spoke posh, but this was discovered, when his mother came to visit, to be no mere professional veneer: he was of 'good family' and used Edwardian clubman's locutions probably learned from his father. The chief comedian was Douglas Close, known as Charlie Close, Charlie (Chase, Chaplin) having the right comic connotations. Then there was Paul Anderson of the RASC, a German whose family, on settling in England and wanting to be onomastically absorbed in it, had chosen a diversity of names. His father was Ableman, his mother Carruthers, and his sister Elsie Fairbanks, which pointed back to

Feuerbach. Then there was Ted Willis, Elliott's batman, who worked the lights and was also a comedian. There were too many comedians. Paul Anderson, known as Andy ('Charlie and Andy – in trouble again!') called himself a light one, or feed. He also delivered affecting monologues of his own composition. Another RASC man, a driver, sang 'Call, Call, Vienna Mine' and 'Macushla' in a subdued tenor. He was Jack Varney, a Yorkshireman whose behaviour varied with the phases of the moon: at full moon he had to be watched. There was another member of the troupe excused parades, since she was a civilian. Her name was Babs Farrell, and she had been hired through a theatrical agency. There seemed to be no suitable talent to be detached from the ATS. Babs was paid an Equity wage.

I groaned as I sensed a repetition of the field ambulance's mistrust. Whose job was I after? It was made clear by Mr Elliott that I was there to rescore the company's concert repertoire, to devise some show band numbers, and to assist Willis with the lights. The musicians sniffed round me like dogs. What confidence I had was highly qualified. I had scored for symphony orchestra but knew nothing of saxophones and trap drum parts. But there was something that Bill Brian had wanted for years – an arrangement of a song that Louis Armstrong had sung called 'If We Never Meet Again'. He had heard it on an American record not distributed in Britain; nor was there any sheet music of it on Charing Cross Road. He sang it to me and I notated it. Then I arranged it. I missed the midday meal as an earnest of my desire to please. In the afternoon the arrangement was completed and the band and myself shambled to the church hall where rehearsals took place. The number was played, and Bill Brian put down his trumpet to take the vocal. The band was pleased; the song was numbered 97 and put into the band library. I was accepted.

These numbers were important to the band, since some of them constituted an inner code unintelligible to the non-musicians. For instance, the arrangement of Rimsky-Korsakov's *Chanson Hindoue* known as 'Song of India' began with a phrase punctuated by two loud quavers which suggested the dismissive insult 'ballocks'. This duplet also occurs in the last movement of William Walton's First Symphony, and Constant Lambert had been well known for shouting 'Ballocks' when it appeared. This was the kind of gratuitous information the band did not want: it prized its illusion of originality. The number of 'Song of India'

was 62, and the number became a synonym for 'ballocks'. Ted
Norman had once used it to a brigadier, then saying sorry, he had
been thinking of his father's age. 'Thanks for the Memory' (15)
and 'I Know Why' (27) and 'Let's Have Another One' (53) also
served the coded vocabulary. Number 100 stood for a telephone.
Band parts of new numbers came regularly from Charing Cross
Road, but it was thought that the century required something
special and non-commercial. I had always wanted to be the
composer of Debussy's *Prélude à L'Après-Midi d'un Faune*: now
was my chance. I gave the band a simplified version of it called
'An Afternoon on the Phone', keeping to Debussy's key sequences
and not easing matters for instruments used to playing in flats. So
Bill Brian, muted, had to sinuate the opening flute passage in
what for him was now F sharp major. But the D flat vision of
Venus became an easy E flat vision for Bill and Harry Walkling,
and a B flat one for Ted Norman. It was good to see soldiers
clodhopping round with local girls in flowery dresses to the
strains of that refined impressionism. Number 100 proved as
acceptable as any other quickstep. It was the beat that counted.

My first evening with the Jaypees was a working one. The
band got into black trousers, bow ties and white bum-freezers,
and the concert party reserved its changes till it arrived at the
infantry unit where it was to perform. Theatrical baskets, spot
lights, Styx's drum kit and xylophone, Dick Nutting's double
bass were loaded according to a kind of G1098 formula on to a
three-ton truck, and we sat where we could on a trip into the
Gloucestershire wilds. We arrived at the battalion we were to
entertain, or rather its nearest village hall, and I was instructed by
Willis on the operation of my light – changes of coloured jellies,
black-out cues, spotting and flooding. He then went among the
troops noting in ink on the back of his hand the names of unpopular officers and eccentric other ranks: these he would in-
corporate into the first sketch, 'The New Recruit', where he
borrowed Harry Walkling's striped jacket to turn himself into a
recruiting sergeant. The band, spotlighted but not much listened
to, played three numbers, then the curtain rose for an opening
pierrot chorus whose words I could not hear, followed by Varney
in tails singing 'Macushla', then on to the comedy. The comedy
was harmless, of the order of 'Do you put manure on your
rhubarb?' – 'Yes.' – 'Funny, we put custard on ours.' The dancing
was eccentric – Pat Glover in drag, he and Bill Clufton as Tut
and Tut Tut, the advance party from the Middle East, cavorting

to the *Ballet Egyptien* in metal brassières clashed to the music. The Great Romano fiddled Monti's *Czardas*. Babs, lovely and pink-lighted, sang 'I Ain't Got Nobody' in her off-the-shoulder gown. The troops mooned at her. Ted Wright the pianist mooned at her too. He was in love with Babs.

The piano did most of the work while the band sat idle. There were just no band-parts for anything except 'Call, Call, Vienna Mine'. I got down next day to the labour of orchestrating everything, tarting up the opening chorus with a discordant fanfare and cunning wisps of counterpoint, getting the *Ballet Egyptien* off the keyboard and on to bass, saxophones and drums, getting an open-air brass-blare into the accompaniment to Styx's xylophone solo 'On the Track'. I improved things a little. I appeared on the stage only to be comically shot down in the closing sketch. Willis and I learned a great deal about antique electrical wiring. Later we were to set Guildford Town Hall on fire. But I was increasingly being called on as a pianist. Ted Wright was a competent reader of notes, but he could not improvise and he could do nothing from memory: he even carried the National Anthem in his pocket. The band was not satisfied with him. Some nights there were concerts and other nights there were dances, and Bill Brian and Ted Norman had had jazz experience which they wanted to use at these latter – free improvisations on 'Blue Skies' and 'The Darktown Strutters' Ball', not slavish adhesion to Tin Pan Alley printed notes. Gradually Ted Wright was eased out of dance work. He was glad of this: dance band nights were nights when the concert party was free, except sometimes to collect money at the door, and the courting of Babs could proceed in a parlour, not in a three-ton truck or backstage. And so I played the jazz he could not.

It was strange to be in the army and not have to rise at reveille. It was strange to be a soldier and yet be wearing a kind of evening dress. The only war wounds I was sustaining were bleeding fingers from pounding the bass of congas. We were real soldiers only on pay parades, when we had to salute as we clutched our pittance. We made our own tea and boiled our own eggs for breakfast. After all, we were billeted over an egg-packing station and Ted Norman was courting one of the egg-packers. Eggs had to be expendable and were frequently expended when the official stamp of the British lion came down on them. The egg history, or oography, of the war is an unwritten story in itself.

Poland had been occupied since 1939, but the civilian egg ration was mostly Polish. The eggs were always bad but, being part of the food ration, always accepted: hope that there would some day be a good one persisted beyond victory. The British eggs with their Marketing Board stamp started fresh but, in the interests of democratic distribution, had to be sold stale: no farmer's wife could put her hand under a hen and serve a new-laid breakfast. Eggs, like human beings, had to be processed, bureaucratised. But we in Moreton-in-the-Marsh got official rejects, straight that morning from Gloucestershire hens. For dinner we got army slop.

We travelled widely and worked hard. We deserved our mornings in bed. When the division moved from Gloucestershire down to the Home Counties we should properly have returned to our units for a kind of Bethlehem census, but we stuck together. We developed the ferocity of artists and trade union members. If we had not joined Equity or the Musicians' Union we would have provoked strikes among the civilian entertainers of the land. When General J.P. laid on a divisional exercise, Redland versus Whiteland, we were employed as fifth columnists. Our disruption of some corners of the battle was efficient and earned praise. We had the steely relaxedness of a commando unit of pals. I had a home and I was composing verse as well as music. In the spring of 1942 I wrote this:

> Time becomes war and long logic
> On buried premises. Spring supervenes
> With the circle as badge, which, pun and profundity,
> Vast, appears line and logical,
> But, small, shows travel returning . . .
>
> Here in barracks is intake of birds,
> The sun holds early his orderly room,
> The pale company clerk is uneasy
> As spring brings odour of other springs.
> The truckdriver sings, free of the road.
> The load of winter and war becomes
> Embarrassing as a younger self.
> War disintegrates into words.

By then we were in barracks in Suffolk, shouting '62' to the orderly sergeant who tried to drag us out of them fucking

wanking pits. When his aubade turned into poetry we knew we
had beaten him:

> Rise and shine, rise and shine,
> You've had your time, I'll have mine.
> Hands off your cocks, pull on your socks,
> Orderly room's at nine.

Sometimes he would add the cadenza 'Shit, shave, shampoo, and
piss buckets out of the window'. We stayed under the blankets.
We had had a hard night. We had had a hard winter.

My little poem means what it says. The war had become a
nominal permanency, a mess of words for company notice boards
and War Office publications, the disregarded premise of our being
in the army. The reality bigger than the soldier's day summed up
in the sounding of last post was the procession of the seasons.
The East Anglian winter had been mud frozen and then briefly
thawed to freeze again, knife winds, the chilled huddling in our
three-ton truck to travel to the entertaining of this battalion or
that, a gun emplacement, a detachment of sappers or gunners,
pioneers who, being Central Europeans, knew more about music
than we did. On Christmas Day the band played for the troops'
dinner and we gnawed on what leftovers we could find. And we
planned a new show with original songs and monologues, something sophisticated. We did this with some doubt. How much
sophistication could the troops take? I had become discouraged
by the lack of musicality of the British army. In the town of Eye
our band had to compete with a local one which was considered
superior to ours. This band, all six pieces of it, played in unison
like an Arab ensemble. The pianist had only two chords. The
blunt simplicity pleased the local dancers. And here was I with
my special reduction of the *Rhapsody in Blue* and a proposed
contrapuntal opening chorus. In any case, the limitations of being
a mere entertainer were oppressing me: I was hungering after my
own kind. I was becoming morose and slow: I did not have the
quick egoism of these stage people, and the fist-fights bored me. I
was being reminded that I was, dreadful word, an intellectual.

I have to apologise for using the term 'intellectual' at all in a
British context. The French have intellectuals – in Paris there is
even a *Club des Intellectuels* – but they do not exist in Great Britain.
Let me say instead the educated and soft-spoken. There were
plenty of these in the services and they mostly had low rank.

They were not used. It was perhaps good for his soul for a BA or Ph.D to rake clinker and clean latrines, but it was a ghastly waste. Linguistic skills were ignored, as also the cerebral ingenuity that could have transformed army intelligence (which, as Aldous Huxley's Spandrell reminded us, stood in contradistinction to animal and human). The naval officer who misled the Nazis by planting false information on a corpse was decorated, gratefully promoted, and made money out of his book *The Man Who Never Was*. Thousands of us could have shown similar ingenuity but never got the chance. The regular army regarded its conscript educated as the enemy, barrack room lawyer stuff, feared articulacy and tried to humiliate it. I remember cleaning out the latrines at Newbattle Abbey and being asked by a visiting general what I had done in civilian life. I told him and he said: 'At last you're doing something useful.'

The division of the forces which had obtained during the previous war had wasted its educated men in a different way, sending them to be killed in Flanders at the head of untrained platoons, but there was an implied philosophy that the educated led and the uneducated were led by them. There was no such disposition in the Second World War. The ranks were full of the educated, bored and disaffected. Civilian intellectuals like Arthur Koestler (the term is appropriate for him) despised them without realising it. He wrote an open letter to a typical army reading man in what he called 'the thoughtful corporal belt', saying: 'Read for pleasure, man, and ignore Joyce and Péguy.' Even George Orwell seemed to believe that Ingsoc would be the creation of disaffected civilian intellectuals – dons and BBC producers who had been denied political power. There was a far greater danger of revolution bursting in the forces: the nearest they came to fomenting one was seen in the 1945 landslide victory for the Labour Party. The weapon of political education was thoughtlessly put into the hands of educated sergeants. I left the Entertainments Section of the 54th Division to become one myself.

War Office publications addressed to junior officers were aware of bombs smouldering in barrack rooms and warned of them. 'There will be men in your platoon whose education and manner of speaking will impose on their less well-endowed fellows. Such men will think that they should themselves be commissioned and will try to undermine your authority. They must be dealt with sympathetically but firmly.' It was not true that the educated

thought they had a right to a commission, though their
womenfolk invariably did. Few of them would have survived
the assault courses and agility tests of the officer's training school.
But they were available for employment in fields where they
could have pricked professional torpor. Torpor was a property of
the regular army, aware that there was a war on but resentful of
it when it did not lead to automatic promotion. That war did
not necessarily have to be won, though most assumed it would
not be lost. The civilian conscripts wanted that war to be fought
well and quickly so that real life would be resumed as soon as
possible. The attitude of the professional NCO was: 'What does
it matter how long it lasts so long as there's plenty of fags, wallop
and crumpet?' Educated privates wanted to hear Debussy on the
barrack room radio (there was a scornful *Punch* cartoon showing
just this) but the regulars, it was said, had their own BBC – beer,
bacca and cunt.

The musicians, comics and dancers of the concert party were
only partially my own kind – more my mother's kind – but I
should have been grateful for the chance to play with harmony
and counterpoint at an elementary level, toughen my fingers at
the keyboard, and practise Mendelssohn's Violin Concerto with
the Great Romano. It seemed to me, however, that there was a
bigger job to do in the army – that of preparing its conscripts for
a postwar life of greater cultural and political awareness. The
army had been bemused into thinking so too, and the old Corps
of Army Schoolmasters had become the Army Educational
Corps. The task of its old sergeants – contemptuously called
'Schoolie' in the mess – had been the giving of elementary instruction to enlisted boys and nursing NCOs through the Army
Certificate examinations which they had to pass if they were to
be promoted. These sergeants, whose sole soldierly quality had
been a capacity for heavy liquor, had never been oppressively
cultivated. They could cope with the three R's and discuss the
editorials of the *Daily Mail*. Now they were to be augmented by
intakes of men with degrees, higher journalists and BBC producers, secondary schoolmasters and even dons. These were to
have their own recognisability: the first thing they did not look
like was soldiers.

I applied in early 1942 for transfer to the Army Educational
Corps, attended an interview, was told I was too young and had
no instructional experience, but apparently impressed through
eagerness. Some of the concert party scoffed at the prospect of

my being enstriped and granted authority. I did not, said Paul Anderson, have 'enough personality'. If by that, I retorted stung, you mean a stage persona, you're probably right. Education is not cavorting and milking easy laughs. If by that you mean stage jealousy and the picking of fights over missed cues and upstaging, you're probably right again. My tendency to bring a kind of gentlemanly weariness to the factitious urgencies of show business was generating mockery. The musicians had grown sick of my providing atonal surprises in my impoverished solo passages: they were far from ready for progressive jazz. Historically speaking, it was something to have jazz at all in a country whose popular music had been maudlin waltzes and novelty numbers like 'Never Be Cruel to a Vegitubel'. They listened open-mouthed to American records of Count Basie's 'The World is Mad' or 'Big Noise from Winnetka' or 'Blues of Israel'. This latter, I told them, was a crib of the coda of the slow movement of Tchaikovsky's Fifth. That was something I should not have known: it was disloyal to jazz. There was too much sly cribbing even in commercial numbers like 'These are the Things I Love', which used both a Tchaikovsky romance and Sibelius's *Valse Triste*. Popular music was a battening sub-art and I was growing sick of it.

The town of Eye, not far from John Skelton's rectory of Diss, was, anyway, a place for profound depression in a leaden winter. Suffolk seemed rich only in massive untenanted churches reared on wool and beetfields. We seemed to live on beetroot ('My beloved beet,' wrote Robert Herrick, but he had probably had some meat to go with it), and the YMCA canteen specialised in beetroot sandwiches and weak tea. The troops seemed duller and coarser than ever, seeking out crumpet in the chill evenings and sometimes finding it. I wrote a poem about them:

> Nymphs and satyrs, come away.
> Faunus, laughing from the hill,
> Rips the blanket of the day
> From old paunched and dirty Will.

> Each projector rears its snout,
> Truffling the blackened scene,
> Till the *Wille's* lights gush out
> *Vorstellungen* on a screen.

> Doxies blench to silverwhite,
> All their trappings of the sport,

Lax and scattered, in this light,
  Merge and lock to smooth and taut.

See, the rockets shoot afar!
  Ah, the screen was tautest then.
Traffic the parabola
  When the sticks reel down again.

This is over-scornful and over-serious. I was invoking Schopenhauer and Spengler to describe fumblings in cold beetfields.
There was nobody to whom I could show the verses with a hope
of their being understood except a local frustrated rector who
played Ravel. Anderson's poetic taste was limited to his sentimental monologues about the Auxiliary Fire Service in the
London blitz. Having written the poem, I had to put on a gipsy
costume to play with Bob Morgan in the officers' mess, our faces
stained with potassium permanganate solution which seemed
likely to stay for ever. There Mr Empson reappeared to advise
me to have my prepuce snipped off. He told the mess about it,
and I cursed him for unprofessional conduct. Since I was a gipsy,
he took no disciplinary action. But I was becoming bloody-
minded again. It was time for me to move on.

I can date the last poem I wrote in Eye with total exactitude:

Now earth turns her heavy body about
  An hour before reveille, the matchstriking hour.
Soon frost will leave the flat drab fields of beet
  And blue smile over the networks of barbed wire.

Cold will not wound the sentry at the gate,
  Beating his sides and cursing for release,
Nor breakfast mean a journey through the night,
  Boots marching raggedly on morning ice.

Now comes to mind the sainted birdbishop
  Who, despite Singapore, still keeps his feast,
When girls performed their love rites before sleep
  And magic snared the one they wanted most.

It went on to say:

Dearest, you shall not lack a protecting arm
  To hold you from the spring gales from the sea . . .

Lynne was the dearest addressed. We had married in Bournemouth in January 1942. The army was paying her a small marriage allowance, to which part of my own pay contributed. I was
poor. This was another reason for wanting to join the Army
Educational Corps.

Lynne had achieved a degree no better than my own and then
spent a month's holiday with the concert party, to the disgust of
Babs. Mr Elliott had attempted a routine seduction, but the rest
of the troupe was wary. She was from another world, and the
womanly bossiness she had a right to exert on me, but no right
to apply to my comrades, was considered a gesture of class
superiority. She was too ready, much to my embarrassment, to
tell officers in saloon bars that I, meaning she, was properly of
their social status and get them to deplore, to their own embarrassment, my lack of ambition. She then entered the Board of
Trade as an assistant principal, settled in digs in Bournemouth,
where the department was evacuated from blitzed London, and
organised the 'Make Do and Mend' campaign. Then she was put
to battling with the unions over the allocation of clothing
coupons to the workers. She favoured the smaller unions, like
the one that tried to protect the rights of chimney sweeps. Her
Welsh fire was considered useful. She could counter the blustering
of union representatives with womanly bossiness. She was kept
busy. On my leaves to Bournemouth I saw little of her. My
honeymoon was a single lovely afternoon. I held her briefly from
the spring gales from the sea. Then I was summoned to the Army
Educational Corps depot in Wakefield to sew on three stripes
and undergo a brief course in instructional technique. The course
was not impressive.

I was impressed, however, even overawed, by the intellectual
quality of some of my fellow recruits to the Corps. Men of great
academic distinction had been clearing parade grounds of scraps
of paper and specialising in the disposal of kitchen swill. Much of
the course consisted of physical training and football and what
was called roadwork. Masters of Arts and Doctors of Philosophy
then went into an overheated hut to hear a lecture on how to
keep the men awake. The fatigued new sergeants unkindly
dropped off and were warned that if it happened again they
would be returned to their units. The commandant gave the same
lecture at the end that he gave at the beginning. The RSM swore
and said we had to stop thinking of ourselves as fucking high-

brows. The civilian servants, old army lags, told us quietly that the whole bloody thing was a sham and that our real job was to bring some human comfort to the men. Nobody else would do it: the officers, even the chaplains, were a dead bloody loss. Much of this comfort they foresaw as writing letters home for illiterates and reading to them the letters they received. This was a partially accurate forecast. A line from one such letter from home has long been burned into my brain: 'That shavin-stick you lef behind has bin a good usban to me.' As for burning illiteracy out of the army, that was thought presumptuous.

On this course I heard a Welshman declare that before the war he had been red but now he was fucking purple. The general view of such radicals was that the class structure of the civilian world was duplicated so grotesquely in the services that it would be our duty to take advantage of it and show clearly the necessity for a classless society. Where the civilian servants thought of us as lowly welfare officers, the Welshman saw us as political commissars or polkoms, much esteemed in the Red Army, propagandists in orthodox Marxism and editors of wall newspapers. Our patriotism, unlike theirs, was to be given to a world that existed only *in potentia*. The superstructure of army discipline, directed to the waging of a war that at that time looked hopeful only because the Americans had entered it, must be cynically sustained, but underneath a new race of political revolutionaries would be bred. I saw the point but thought the programme hopeless. I wanted something infra-political – an awareness of a world bigger than that of mere subsistence, a concern with culture and civilisation. Get the bastards to think rationally, to examine prejudice in the glare of reason, to read, look at pictures, listen to music. This was bourgeois, according to my Welshman: his fingers flew to his holster when he heard the word 'culture'. The holster was real: we were a pistol-carrying corps.

The army already had a centralised scheme whereby the men were taught, and encouraged to discuss, the reasons for the war, its conduct, the nature of the enemy. Under W. E. Williams, a civilian eventually ennobled, the Army Bureau of Current Affairs issued pamphlets intended for the ingurgitation of officers and their regurgitation as lectures or group discussions. It was not the task of the Army Educational Corps to help here: unit officers were considered intelligent enough to be able to take in the facts of an ABCA pamphlet and process them into an enlightening discourse. This rarely happened. Most officers dutifully recited the pamphlets as if they were Army Council Instructions; the men did not understand and they were bored. Some unit commanders refused to allow their men to be contaminated by current affairs. 'I'm having no socialism in my battalion,' cried more than one colonel. This cry grew louder when the British Way and Purpose scheme was introduced, for this was clearly political. It was harmless enough politics, for it presented the British Constitution as a fact of nature and it assumed that the British Empire would be with us for a long time.

I exchanged my RAMC badge, with its Aesculapian snake, for one that showed an open book with nothing in it. I was then posted to the Emergency Medical section of one of the great lunatic asylums of the world at Winwick, near Warrington. I was back in Lancashire. I changed trains at Manchester and thought it a good idea to visit 47 Princess Road on the way. I wished to make peace with the step-relatives I had so rudely walked out on. I was also short of money. Peace was made and a few shillings were advanced. I then travelled to Winwick and found the hospital deserted by its army personnel. It was Saturday and everybody went home for the weekend. No quarters had been allotted to me. I had better report on Monday morning. So I went back to 47 Princess Road, saw *Citizen Kane* in the evening with my nephew Dan, and slept, as before, next to the billiard table. It was a weird way of being in the war.

A MILITARY HOSPITAL was as much an army establishment as a barracks, with sick troops lying to attention for the morning inspection, matrons of the VAD carrying the rank of major, and no let-up in spit and polish even for the dying. The Emergency Medical Section of a civilian hospital was rather different. Certain wards were allocated to sick servicemen of all arms, the medical staff was civilian, and there was a minimal RAMC attachment of a CQMS, who preferred to be called a sergeant-major, a sergeant clerk, and a few orderlies of the excused-boots variety, all under a military registrar of field rank who came from the infantry. I was marched in on the Monday morning to the military registrar's office and promptly fell heavily on the over-polished oilcloth. It was no place for army boots. It was no place for army rations either, for I had taken breakfast in the senior warders' mess and been fitted out with tiny pots of margarine and mar-

malade on the scale which oppressed civilians. I was marched in
and out by CQMS Backhouse, a Liverpool veteran in bright-
buttoned service dress who had told me this was a cushy billet
and to keep my nose clean. He meant that there was plenty of
sex on offer among the nurses, some of whom were temporary
and frivolous, but that the amenity must not be abused. I had
been given a genuine bed in a genuine bedroom, though with
bars on the window, and there was a harmlessly gibbering lunatic
to make the one and polish the other. The first thing I saw from
the window was a large wardrobe walking down the garden
path. This was one of the regular thefts tolerated in the institution.
I was given a pass key like the senior warders and made to assume
that my status was much like theirs. It did not seem to be an
enviable status. Close daily contact for many years with mental
patients had rendered most of these abnormal in speech and behaviour. They could be violent, irrational and incoherent. Sanity was best sought among the sick troops. Their grouses were
rational and their comportment human.

Many of the inmates of the asylum were sufferers from GPI or
general paralysis of the insane, the final stage of syphilis. They
gawped, shambled and mumbled, though occasionally they
cursed the universe loudly. They were permitted to see films on
Wednesday afternoons so long as these were of a sedative nature.
But it was hard to know what a sedative film was. *Pride and
Prejudice* caused a riot and had to be stopped at the point where
Darcy said: 'Miss Bennet, I admire and love you.' Some of the
patients had perverse talents engendered by their disease. I was
introduced to a human comptometer who could, from a slobbering idiot mouth, announce immediately and accurately the
product of a hard long multiplication. Another could give the
day of the week for any date in history. I tried him on June 16,
1904, and he came out at once with 'A Tursday'. There was a
morose hulk of a man who had taught himself to play violent
rhapsodies on the piano. These were atonal but coherent and
embodied distorted memories of classical themes, as though
picked up by a starling. It was like listening to a summary of
human history ending with doomsday. There was a sort of poet
who had written with a pencil stub a sort of Blakean prophetic
book full of characters like Eveson and Grimsthorpe. He was
temporarily lucid when I met him and was concentrating on
epitaphs. He had just written one on the head of the asylum
orchestra:

To write your epitaph it is a pleasure.
You were a liar in full measure.

One or two of the patients were voluble and plausible. I listened
for an hour to an account of inventive achievement which
included an alphabet without digraphs and a smokeless boiler.
Then came: 'In 1931 I was made a sir but I said no to further
honours.'

My first task was to go the rounds of the service wards with a
Dr Nussbaumer and his entourage, which was big enough for
royalty. He would vaguely prescribe 'education' for convalescents
who needed to be jolted out of apathy. I did not trust him. He
seemed to regard the provision of all these sick troops, whom
war was making expendable, as a heaven-sent chance for experiment: see how far you could go with a particular line of
treatment and, if it killed your patient, try again. I grew suspicious
when I was conducted to a civilian ward where an infant with a
grotesquely enlarged skull was being artificially kept alive, presumably to see how far the enlargement could go. 'Hydro-
cephalus,' announced Dr Nussbaumer. 'Note the wide anterior
fontanelle and the bones separated at the sutures. Note the
prominence of the veins in the scalp and listen to the crackpot
note of this percussion,' tapping with a pencil. 'The famous
Cardinal, who died in Guy's, had a head circumference of thirty-
three inches. In Paris there is a hydrocephalic skull measuring
thirty-nine. This child is three months old and has twenty-nine
inches already.' He seemed to wish to beat the Paris record. Why
an army sergeant should be in on this sordid epiphany was not
made clear. Perhaps the bigger audience the better. 'We can do a
lot here,' he said, 'but not everything. Give us time.'

I had left the Royal Army Medical Corps only to be inducted
back into it. An ATS sergeant was admitted and died of no clear
cause. There had to be an autopsy, conducted by civilian mechanics but witnessed by two of the military personnel. This had
to mean myself and CQMS Backhouse, since the other soft-
footed soldiers were squeamish. So he and I stood while the
whistling practitioner ripped off the poor girl's scalp, trepanned,
eviscerated, handled kidneys and liver like a family butcher and
wrote down the weights of the organs on a dart-player's slate. It
was a salutary experience, the more salutary as it was repeated.
The body was nothing, then – a mess of meat, a few jugs of
blood and a tangle of entrails; the war was teaching the cheapness

of human flesh. And the soul? 'Handled thousands of the buggers,' said the sawyer, intermitting his singing, 'and never seen a soul yet. Quick to get out, a soul is. Escapes through the intercranial fissures.'

It was not long before I saw a corpse for which I felt a certain responsibility. On a fine spring afternoon I took a small group of men in convalescent blue into the grounds for a discussion on the progress of the war. Few of the men could see why it was being fought. We came in because of bloody Poland. Bugger Poland. Us coming in because of Poland has meant these so-called Free Poles shoving their poles into our wives and daughters. The Jews? Bugger the Jews. Why fight for the Jews? Rubbing their hands and making money while we lot gets the shit at half a dollar a day. It was a depressing session. And when this is bloody over it'll be the same as it was after the last lot. The buggers what stayed home will have the jobs and us sods go begging. A certain Corporal Hardwick spoke sensibly, much in the tone of Cecil Day Lewis's poem about defending the bad against the worse. I dismissed the group and Corporal Hardwick walked off on his own. He walked, I discovered afterwards, down to the railway line and laid his head on it. The Manchester-Liverpool express severed his skull neatly. When the body was brought in, CQMS Backhouse, probably rightly, took the opportunity of pointing out the location of the hippocampal sulcus and the lingual gyrus. Young Butterworth, a highly neurotic clerk, went off to vomit. There was an enquiry as to how far I had helped to exacerbate a known depression. I began then to doubt the value of army education.

I was given by Dr Nussbaumer a chance to exercise therapy in a field I knew a little about. One of the depressed soldiery was a man who suffered from sigmatismus, an inability to pronounce the s-phoneme. He said he came from Kidderminter, where as a child he had suffered from a gattric tomach, which he blamed for the speech defect. I worked towards an s by getting him to substitute the unvoiced palatal sh for it, so that he came from Kidderminshter and had had a gashtric shtomach. This made him sound drunk. He resisted the treatment, however. He wanted his sigmatismus, a badge of life's ill treatment. There was also a man with a cleft palate who had been fitted with an obturator. The nasality of his speech continued. Feydeau's cruel farce in which the closing of the palatal fissure immediately quells nasality is wrong: a cleft palate sufferer gets out of the habit of lowering and raising the velum. The patient has to be taught to yawn consciously and deliberately, thus restoring mobility to the soft palate and its hanging grape. Then, with practice, he ceases to say 'Hning a hnong of hnixpenhn'. My patient, like the asigmatic one, resisted cure. Any small distinction, however harmful, is precious to a man. Besides, he thought his cleft palate might get him out of the army.

I was given a young subaltern who had sustained brain damage and suffered from total dyslexia. I had to teach the technique of reading and writing from scratch to the cerebral hemisphere which knew nothing about it. I began to see clearly how arbitrary our graphemes are. It was possible to relate a capital B to a bum or bottom, but remove a cheek for the lower-case letter and the patient was lost. A small g looked like a pair of glasses and an S, small or large, like a snake, but it was almost impossible to attach phonemic significance to the vowel letters. The Hebrew or Arabic alphabet might have been easier. But in time memory flashed across from the injured hemisphere to the sound one, and the reading gift came back through a long slow mist.

In a month or so I had a visit from the Western Command Education Officer and his deputy. The deputy was George Edward Cecil Wigg, eventually to be a Labour MP, the Paymaster General, Chairman of the Horse Race Betting Levy Board, and a life peer. He and his master made it clear that therapy was no part of my duties, whether occupational or speech. Occupational therapy was woodwork and soft-toy making, and it became legitimate education only when practised by fit men on gunsites. Speech therapy was not a specialisation that officially existed in the army. What that was truly educative was I then doing? I told them of discussion groups, omitting mention of the corporal's suicide and the opinion that it was all tomfoolery. I chaired a weekly lecture arranged by the Extra-Mural Department of Liverpool University, to which even profoundly crippled and moribund patients were whipped. On Friday afternoons we had a programme of army training films. That, said these two, is not education. But, I protested, one of the films was *Next of Kin*, and artistic and well-sculpted narrative about the dangers of poor security. That, they said, was instruction or entertainment or both, but it did not fit into the slot of true education. I had formed a dance orchestra, I said, with myself on piano, the physical training sergeant on trumpet, and a clerk (neurotic Butterworth) on drums. That was far from being education, and so had been my show *Hospital Blues*, in which I performed the *Warsaw Concerto*. That was certainly not education. The *Warsaw Concerto* not education, when its big theme was based on four notes of solmisation in *King Lear*? There is no call, said Lieutenant Wigg, to be either truculent or facetious.

What, then, precisely was Army Education? It was things to see, like wall newspapers and information rooms, it was soft-toy making, so long as this was not occupational therapy. It was lectures about the sempiternality of the British Empire. Could, I asked, it be language-teaching? I had a rather successful evening class in German, at which many nurses attended and which usually ended in a recital of German songs. My job was not to teach nurses. But, I said, if I organised a Brains Trust in which the major question was whether platonic love was possible on a desert island, and the room was crammed with nurses, was I to throw the nurses out? Questions like that were not educational. I began to feel the old military hopelessness. It was becoming clear even to naive me that what was wanted was a lying report for forwarding to the War Office, amalgamated with other reports and boiled down to statistics which should impress. When I mentioned the number of weekly educational sessions held, I fancied I saw Lieutenant Wigg's pencil hovering over the possibility of falsifying the figure. I remembered something I had heard from the education sergeant at Peninsular Barracks in Warrington: 'I gave four lectures, sir.' – 'I suggest you gave forty.'

I reported as what I thought a major coup a lecture given on Nazi war aims, very well attended and enthusiastically received. It was different from most such lectures in that it had been delivered by a genuine Nazi, or at least a serving officer in the Luftwaffe. He had been taken prisoner, developed some baffling ailment in camp, and been sent to Winwick, where he messed with British officers and had no fear of being shot if he escaped. He did not seem to wish to escape. He was taken regularly, in uniform too, to the Swan, a refined hotel and roadhouse a mile or so away. He spoke admirable English, was a fine specimen of Nordic manhood, and was extremely popular with the brother officers who were his official enemies. The talk he gave was lucid and well argued. He spoke of the need to homogenise the German population to secure unity of culture, the obstacle which the Jews and Slavs represented to such an aim, the essential cultural brotherhood of the Germans and Anglo-Saxons, the Aryan future, the wastefulness of war. It was only when a Jewish lance-corporal spat at him that he disclosed the darker side of the Nazi destiny. When I told my two visitors of this genuine piece of education they grew restive and spoke of the danger of MI5 finding out. I felt, as often before, that I was marked.

I was sent, with other sergeants and an ancient warrant officer class one, on a woodwork course. This was in a school in Chester, and the instructor was a civilian teacher who said: 'Slow and sweet, slow and sweet – that's the song of the saw.' I feared that I, along with the others, was to be turned into a cigarette-box-and-soft-toy-man on a gunsite. There had been altogether too much talk about soft toys, and there had even been a great conference in Warrington to which a handsome WO I had rushed on his motor cycle from his gunsite and, accoutred like a Martian still, had spoken of soft toys as an aspect of the war effort. At the Chester course there were no soft toys. I made a small box with ill-fitting mortise and tenon joints which had to be secured with glue and brown varnish. I also bound a book. First, of course, catch your book, a paperback which had to be ennobled with cloth boards and fresh stitching. That, the summer of 1942, was a strange time for Penguins. There was a novel by Constance Holme called *Crump Folk Going Home* which nobody wished to buy; there was very little else. I ended by buying yet another copy of Tawney's *Religion and the Rise of Capitalism*, without which, as Lynne had wittily said, no household was complete. It turned into a wretched hardback. My fears about being converted into a practical man were allayed. My report said: 'Not a strong student. Seemed nervous of the tools and of the work in general.'

Then I was sent, with the entire instructorate of Western Command, to a day's session in Chester to hear about what was called 'Second Front German'. A civilian with the manner of a con-man spoke of how the complex German language could be reduced, for the benefit of occupying forces, to a simple pidgin or sabir. You removed all the grammar, dismantled the accidence, made all the nouns masculine (I saw a learned-looking sergeant shudder at the prospect of *der Fräulein*), and took advantage of Anglo-German cognates in the learning of a minimal vocabulary. You could equip an ignorant swaddy with enough German in a week to enable him to cope with Goethe's people. The scheme was rejected and the man cried. 'What can I do now? I have invested time and ingenuity in this work. Must it all be wasted?'

The Western Command Education Officer suggested that he try another command. A Welsh sergeant muttered that he ought to join the fucking army. Then sergeants and warrant officers went to get drunk together, boast, lie, grow depressed.

There was a feeling around that Army Education was not the only unproductive sideshow. The whole of the British army, if not the navy and the RAF, was a sideshow. The Yanks were coming, the Yanks had come. They were to take over the war this side, while the Russians got on with it on the other. In the Far East the British were out of it, all dying of beri-beri in Changi. Sick American officers appeared at Winwick, and I persuaded a colonel to talk to the men. He had little to say about American war aims, which he did not well understand, and I had to translate him into British English. He was much less of a success than the Luftwaffe man, who had left with nurses' tears and affectionate pommellings from brother enemy officers. The general impression was that the real enemy had arrived.

The extra-mural people of Liverpool University sent a smiling civilian along to explain all about our American allies. He made the mistake of mentioning in his exordium the admirable tea of welcome he had just been given, which earned boos from the ill-fed audience in hospital blue. I had never been able to understand the hospitality delivered by Winwick to visiting lecturers. It was entirely a civilian bestowal. I travelled to Warrington station in a chauffeured Daimler, picked up the lecturer, took him in to a spread of inexplicable opulence, with pre-war veal and pork pies, boiled ham, tongue, salad with hard-boiled eggs, pastries of a creamy or feathery delicacy. I had to warn the visitors against expressing public satisfaction with this treatment, but they would never learn. After the lecture they would be escorted back to Warrington station with a dram inside them. One of my tasks was to ensure that they did not miss the last train which, waffling or locked into discussion, they were sometimes likely to do. The propagandist for America missed his because he was nearly torn to pieces by vigorous invalids and had to be washed and sewn. The car had to drive him all the way to Liverpool, and it ran out of petrol on the way back.

He spoke too much of the admirable treatment that the American people accorded their brave boys – the ice-cream parlours on battleships, the smartness of the uniforms, the proposed GI Bill of Rights, above all the pay, which he spelt too explicitly out. There were growls when it was disclosed, chapter and verse, horse's mouth, just what a private first class was getting. No wonder they could get half-slewed in our pubs, better off than a fucking British officer; no wonder the bloody tarts pulled their drawers down for them. Heard of the new utility knickers? One yank and they're off. The point the lecturer was, perhaps justly, making was that a democracy ought to look after its fighting men. The British had not, never, and it's no good you soldiers and sailors moaning. When you were civilians you had your chance to force government into better treatment of the khaki custodians of British civilisation. You did not take that chance; now you are rightly suffering. This started the riot. Was this Army Education?

That disparity of treatment between the allies caused more trouble than history, and for that matter literature, drama and film, has cared to record. There was a large American Air Force base at Padgate, near Warrington, and evening Warrington was full of GIs with jingling pockets and loosened ties and collars. The collar and tie were themselves a reminder to British other ranks of how low they had sunk: they were a hold on to civilian freedom and gentility; the coarse khaki battle blouse buttoned to the British chin and chafed the neck. But it was the wild American spending that caused the real trouble. Our men sat gloomily over their halves of washy bitter while the GIs cleared out the exiguous spirit stock and, well fed, sneered at a rationed and beleaguered people. Meanwhile the Warrington girls clung to them, cats on heat, already skilled in the phonemes and idioms of every state in the Union. 'Where you going, Lucy?' I heard one fourteen-year-old yell at another. 'Going to get shagged by the Yanks.' Shagged they were, and not always discreetly in the dark. Indiscreet, a drunken top sergeant announced in a public bar: 'This country is OK. If your beer was as cheap as your women it would be worth living in.' Then the fight started.

Warrington felt like occupied territory. Smokeless British troops scrambled for the largesse of packs of Lucky Strike and Chesterfields thrown from issue cartons. But the odd educated pfc stood at the bar uneasily apart from his fellows, aware that he was in the country of Charles Dickens and that Stratford-on-Avon was a brief train ride away. With some of these I discussed Emily Dickinson and Walt Whitman. There was no such thing as the unity of a nation. The two significant entities were the cultivated and the ignorant. Ignorance was at its most frightening in a British government which, as Mass Observation had tried to point out before embarking in its remedial programme, knew nothing of the common man and woman. Railway station propaganda like 'Your Patience, Your Courage, Your Perseverance Will Bring Us Victory' spoke out of the ruling unconscious in millions of posters. 'Be Like Dad, Keep Mum' caused a riot among working wives. And nobody up there had ever thought for one minute of the impact of GI wealth on tommy poverty. Pay should have been equal and the greater value of the American war effort expressed in Stateside bank deposits.

It was no good drawing a discussion group together out of the idle wards and asking what we should discuss. There was only one subject: why do the Yanks get more money than what we do? There was a powerful subtext of sexual jealousy here. The women of Britain had been awakened by an exotic erotic *élan* highly disturbing to their menfolk. It was not just the Americans, it was the Free Czechs and the Canadians and the Poles. Rightly is they fucking well called Poles. What the sick men of Winwick saw of the Poles corroborated a dubiety that went back to September 1939. Why fight for the bastards? Men who loved to hear the *Warsaw Concerto*, which was like classical, never thought as how I'd get to like that sort of rubbish, hated the intolerant haughtiness of such Polish patients as gloomed Slavically in the wards. A Polish flight-sergeant said to me that I was to get him cigarettes. I will not. You will, your rank is lower than mine. I will not. I will report you. Carry on, matey. You will call me what I am, I am superior to you. The antisemitism of the Poles made their British comrades ardent prosemites. God works in a mysterious way.

My career at Winwick was far from successful. During the glorious summer of 1942 I spent too much time in the bushes with complaisant nurses. The Irish nurses clung to their virtue, but the British ones went the way of their newly awakened race. Good clean heterosexual exercise was nature's response to illness, injury, death, and the twisted eros of the mental patients. In the lavatory at the end of the corridor where I slept lurked a humpbacked rouged and lipsticked lunatic who called himself Mary. He barbered but he was also openly buggered. There was a vast mortuary crammed with unwanted mental cadavers which smelt like a cheese factory. Army Education confirmed the cadavers, with an imperial flag stuck into them. Sex was the answer, but the sex was found out. The Military Registrar tripped over my spread bare legs in the bushes. But it was Major Lalkaka who did for me.

Major Lalkaka was a handsome Brahmin who went the rounds
of the units lecturing on India, its wrongs, its wretchedness, its
shining unimperial future. He was a brilliant lecturer, but he was
more haughty than any Pole. He kept his distance from the
untouchables. While he was telling my emblued men about the
sufferings of the great mother of Aryanism, a jabber and scuffle
of mental patients was suddenly to be heard outside the hall where
he lectured. He demanded that I quell the noise. He sat down like
a god and proposed intermitting his wisdom till silence be
restored. He had a right to absolute silence as a British field officer
and a Brahmin. I went out and was embroiled in the screamers
and tearers. There was no warder about; the restoration of order
was not my proper responsibility. I dealt a faint slap and was in
danger. I escaped back to Major Lalkaka. But he had gone to
complain of the intolerability of his situation; never in his army
career, to say nothing of Brahmin civvy street, had he met such
inefficiency and lack of control. All this was taken with a sprinkle
of Cerebos at Western Command, which had put Major Lalkaka
on to peripatesis to get rid of him, but the Military Registrar had
found a pretext for a demand for my posting. The posting came
at a very awkward time.

Lynne, my wife, had secured her own posting. She was filling
an assistant principal's vacancy at the Board of Trade office in
Manchester. My summer had been one of dalliance, the autumn
brought married life of a sort. Lynne had got rooms in Rusholme,
and I would sneak off to these after the day's work in Winwick,
sneaking back by the early workmen's train. I had no pass, and
there was always the danger of being accosted by military policemen at Central Station; with them, mere lance-corporal's, rank
could not be pulled. I was lucky, but I had also learned how to
run. I had also learned how to augment Lynne's civilian rations
by filching canned meat from the hospital stores and buying
illegal eggs and even chickens at a Winwick farm. The evenings
and weekends were blissful but furtive, but they were also tiring.
I was getting my full share of legitimate love but not enough
sleep. Only Christmas, with its two full days off, granted by
custom not regulations, was restful. It was also the time of our
Catholic marriage. We needed sheets for our bed and had no
coupons to buy them. Nor, for that matter, money. The Tollitts
of 47 Princess Road had a large number of spare sheets, but they
were wary of letting them be spread on a bed that was only
marital according to secular law. A Catholic marriage would

secure the issue of sheets. The last Sunday of Advent saw our quiet evening wedding after Benediction. The priest had put the Catholic angle to Lynne, but she had riposted with a Church of England staunchness. The children of the marriage would, the priest said, have to be baptised into the Catholic faith. Oh no, they would not; her Anglican father and mother would break their hearts. So it was the worst kind of mixed marriage, though Lynne approved of the ceremony, which enjoined no Miltonic obedience from the woman. We had a pre-war Christmas dinner at the Tollitts'. The lavishness of food and drink was obscene, but, in those days of cigarette shortage, a tobacconist could get anything. We walked home to Rusholme with our sheets.

ON NEW YEAR'S Day 1943 I was posted to the Infantry Training Centre at Peninsular Barracks, Warrington. This was properly the depot of the South Lancashire Regiment, and the band was still there. But it was primarily now an ecumenical congeries of all the British regiments, which sat uneasily together. There was a conflict of regimental customs and even rates of march. The RSM wearily walked the parade ground with his pace-stick. The fore-and-aft cap badges of the Gloucesters confronted Scots bonnets; cockneys in the Welsh Fusiliers flaunted black nine-pointed back flashes. The process of dismantling regional loyalties was on: infantry was a stew in which the meats of proud battle history were reduced to a neutered fibre. Men came in from civilian life to be turned into basic infantry with six weeks' training. Many of them had been in occupations which they had thought reserved; some of them had been earning twenty pounds a week in munitions and making a secondary industry of manufacturing cigarette lighters. They were disaffected, and one of my tasks seemed to be to calm them down with a weekly lecture which said in effect: Bugger it, lads, I know how you feel, but it'll soon be over with the help of your flabby right arms and we'll get back, God and that bloody swine Churchill willing, to a better life than before. This was officially known as the British Way and Purpose. The official content was more elevating.

Here was the army with a vengeance: grim barracks, salutable parade ground, prepuce-probing medical officers, barking regimental sergeant-major, dithering Anglican chaplain, aloof colonel, disdainful second-in-command, watchful guardroom, a strict control of passes. There would be no sly sleeping out here. As one of the odds and sods that made up Headquarters Company, I formed up before its commander, Major Behrens of the great Manchester Jewish family, and asked for a permanent pass to comfort a wife made hysterical by the London blitz. Nothing doing, sergeant. But, as always with the army, one could get away with most things, the more outrageous, because unbelievable, the better. It was possible to visit the company office in the evenings, steal pass-forms and sign them oneself – J. Joyce, E. Pound, E. M. Forster, Lieut for Major – and take also a sheet or two of ration coupons. There was no check on such things. Early rising had been a problem in illegal absences from Winwick: the establishment was small, if late for duty one was missed. Now that I was at vast anonymous Peninsular Barracks, it was less dangerous if sleep and love occluded the noise of the alarm clock and one woke at ten. I would stroll past the guardroom near noon, books borrowed from Lynne under my arm, coming back to lunch in the sergeants' mess from some vague bookish duty.

But my heart stopped one such day. I had been granted a small office in the administrative block, and there, at noon, I found a chit summoning me to an interview with the CO at eight that very morning. I went to the orderly room to make implausible excuses for not attending: the wind from the window had blown the chit into a dusty corner; only now had I seen it. The orderly room sergeant went vicariously pale and arranged another interview for the morrow. I was marched in by the RSM and awaited the worst. The CO said: 'I'm sorry I missed you yesterday morning, Wilson.' (His name too was Wilson, but it was a better family, somewhere in Wiltshire.) 'I seem to have had another engagement. My apologies.' He then read out an angry report about the comportment of sergeants of the Army Educational Corps: filthy greasy clothing, uncut hair, shambling gait, sloppy saluting when saluting at all. 'Very nasty all that, Wilson. It looks as if we have to turn you into soldiers. It says something here about the allotment of part-time regimental duties to lick you into shape. From now on you are, under Captain Lansdowne, concerned with Intelligence.'

The army at that time knew little about Intelligence. The Intelligence Corps had only just been formed. In it professors of Russian and Albanian with lance-corporal's rank obeyed the orders of public school officers with a little French. But the linguistic side of Intelligence was not then much regarded –

E. Phillips Oppenheim stuff for real spies like Willie Maugham.
Intelligence was the identification of German aircraft, lectures on
the German army, map-reading. I did not object to lecturing on
the German army; for good measure I added the Japanese one.
Map-reading was simple enough, except that cartography rarely
seemed to bear much relation to real terrain. 'Well, the map's
wrong, then' is not an invention of Evelyn Waugh. I did not
seriously object to Intelligence except when it conflicted with my
evening marital life. I was leased out to the Home Guard, usually
in the back room of a pub where hospitality was in order, and
they deeply appreciated talks on the German soldier whom they
would never see. Meanwhile my wife, in the manner of women,
chafed. Women, even in the Auxiliary Territorial Service, saw
no relation between the army and real life.

A sergeant was posted to Peninsular Barracks with no defined
duties. He had been sick and Y-listed and lost his regiment. I
handed my Intelligence duties over to him. Captain Lansdowne
did not seem to see any difference. He called him Wilson though
his name was Williams. I had freed myself of regimental duties
without the wearisome toil of going through channels. I could
get on undistracted with the British Way and Purpose. When
Colonel Wilson was ordered to construct an information room,
he summoned me for its implementation, but whether in an
Intelligence or educational capacity was not clear. It was all one,
anyway. The walls were covered with maps for the following of
the Pantelleria landings, and from the ceiling dangled models of
Stukas and Blenheim bombers ecumenically mingled. I put some
reproductions of modern sculpture on a special board, but these
were torn down as distracting. I made a wall newspaper with a
flaunting banner – PENINSULA – but never changed its content.
The Pantelleria landings went on for ever; nobody noticed.

Colonel Wilson would have been happy to forbid Army Education, which of course was pure socialism, but he was under War
Office orders to have the men instructed in current affairs and
the British Way and Purpose. The men had in particular to be
apprised of the revolutionary nature of the Beveridge Plan, focus
of postwar hopes, symbol of the coalition government's liberalism. Beveridge had set his own scheme forth with some imagination. Nobody can now remember offhand what the Five
Giants were that had to be trounced: most people break down
after Ignorance, Squalor and Poverty. What was vaguely inspir-
ing was the proposition of a unitary mode of slaying them – five,

like the little tailor, with one blow. A single payment, a single stamp on a single card, and all aspects of social welfare were accounted for from the sperm to the worm or, as some put it, from the erection to the resurrection. The men to whom I lectured on the plan with a rather rare enthusiasm were not convinced. The only beverage we want is beer and tea that isn't NAAFI gnat-piss. They had centuries of disillusionment behind them.

I was supposed to give basic political education to platoons, but it saved time to orate to companies. I could get bigger laughs that way and deliver the kind of rhetoric that obviated the need for close reasoning. The sound went down better than the sense. Some of the arguments for the British Way and Purpose as presented in pamphlets and wall-sheets were not convincing to working men who had been union officials or had read Tom Paine. The British Empire, it was generally agreed, was a bloody racket. Despite the official impartiality of British justice, everybody knew that there was one law for the rich. The House of Lords was an anachronism. I devised a talk which owed nothing to the prescribed material. This was about what I called Civilisation. Civilisation was committed to promoting a hedonism which took for granted basic subsistence – jobs, housing, food and drink – and intensified the human capacity for pleasure. The more subtle kinds of pleasure had to be taught – music, literature, the joys of foreign travel, even gastronomy – and that was where education came in. The men were no more convinced than they were with Beveridge. Why should we have to understand what a lot of foreigners is jabbering about? Classical music, except perhaps for the *Warsaw Concerto*, is like tomcats fighting. Books gets you thinking, and thinking never did the working man any good. I was often appalled by the election of ignorance. I am less appalled now.

I sank humbly to a level about which there was no argument when the illiterates came in, along with the ill-nourished. There was an intake so shockingly thin and unmuscular that the training time and the rations had to be doubled. The bottom of the barrel was being reached – young men brought up on bread and scrape whose teeth had to be drawn and to whom (long after the drawing) dentures were issued. Many of them had missed school and could not even follow the *Jane* cartoons in the *Daily Mirror*. It was decreed that after a dozen sessions with the AEC NCO they should be equipped with enough literacy to take down a telephone message and read company orders. Unfortunately the

announcement that they should attend my instruction in the
evenings was posted on the company notice boards, which,
naturally, they could not read. 'Illiterates will report at 1800
hours . . .' This was army ineptitude worth prizing.

Eventually I got my gipsies, Cypriots, Irish and gormless
Anglo-Saxons. The only way to get the alphabet into them, upper-
and lower-case, was by associating the shape of the letters with
experiences so basic they could hardly be forgotten. I considered
at that time contributing an article to the journal *Army Education*
on the Scatological as a Teaching Aid. A was for Arse, but why
was it for Arse? The upper-case A could, with some twisting, be
made to look like a lavatory seat. But why did the small one bear
so little resemblance to its big brother? It was no good talking of
the twin heritage from Rome and Greece. At least the lower-case
letter had an arse-like rounding. B, of course, was all right, a
palpable bottom: for *b* a cheek had been cut off. The small *g*, as
with my Winwick officer, was acceptable as a pair of glasses
(damn it, one could not be scatological all the time), but the big
G baffled. Soon, however, my illiterates could, tongues protruding at the side, write BAG and GAB. Such words never
appeared on company orders. They could even manage ABCA,
which did occasionally appear, but ABCA sessions were not for
them. I fretted. I did not get far. The War Office eventually
produced its primers for illiterates – 'Well, said Sam, it is good to
eat a good plate of cold beef and a piece of dry bread' – but too
late for me. My illiterates departed able, just about, to write A
BAT IN A BAG, but they could not read company orders.

I fretted, but the other sergeant instructors, whose tasks were
simpler, throve. Some of them were enriched by their platoons.
'Well, lads,' the platoon lance-corporal would say at the end of
the course, 'you've had a bloody good corporal and not too
bad of a sergeant, so how about a bit of a whip-round?' Thirty
half-crowns every six weeks, divided proportionately as to rank,
was a fair gift. Some sergeants collected a single cigarette every
day from each member of the platoon. Bribery to be kept off the
charge sheet was acceptable. It was not a bad life. It was not a
bad mess. An old schoolfellow of my wife's, Sergeant Margaret
Lewis, was in charge of the catering. Beer flowed. I played the
piano. There was one sergeant mad on Bach's choral prelude
'Sheep May Safely Graze'. The RSM would call, in those synthetic patrician accents peculiar to the rank: 'Enough of that,
Schoolie. We will have "Pale Hands I Loved". *Real* music.' My

one real cultural achievement was, with the aid of a CSM, to have the first cellist of the London Philharmonic Orchestra removed from his intake back to his art. This was a fiddle entailing a falsified medical report. The CSM and I felt rewarded when we heard on the radio the cello solo in the *Lac des Cygnes* Adagio. That's him. Switch off that rubbish, Schoolie, and let us have 'Pale Hands I Loved'.

If the RSM called me Schoolie or, on more formal occasions, School Sarnt, my equals called me Tug. I slept in a hut with sergeant specialists – PT, pioneer-watchmender, weapon training experts. I was educated into the Kipling world. Here the British Empire was sweat and charpoys and mistri wallahs, not the lost cause of the British Way and Purpose. The sergeant who slept on the bunk above me swore he had met Kipling, a little bloke with thick glasses who sneezed all the time up in the 'ills. He was not to be believed though he was old. He was one of the tolerated ancients too far gone in alcoholism for duties, a feature of many a wartime barracks. He had delirium tremens and spoke to a regimental bishti who could have been Gunga Din. He wet his blankets every night, and the whiskified urine dripped on to me gently. He would not, he said, exchange them blankets for the finest sheets in the Raffles in Singapore. The aroma of them blankets was like memory, a record of his life. At length, as was expected, he fell out of his bunk and broke something internal and complicated. He went to his rest.

On my leaves, both official and filched, I was touching the borders of the literary life. Lynne and I clearly saw that what my fellow sergeants called pissin' off 'ome most evenings was doing me no good and not helping her status in the Board of Trade. She was neglecting her duty to deprive the smaller trade unions of coupons for overalls and give in to the bigger unions, which demanded allowances for Sunday suits as well as dungarees, valuable war work. We were both becoming neurotically guilty about our mornings of heavy sleep after nights of love. She could not dissemble her lateness for work; I would not be able to for ever: one of these noons the Educational Department of the War Office would be waiting for me, having arrived on the night train. Lynne received rebukes: she was not good enough for Manchester; she would have to be transferred to London, where slackness was in order. Government departments, no longer scared of the Luftwaffe, were saying goodbye to the sea breezes and palms and Palm Court trios and returning to the capital. It was with sad relief that we heard of her transfer in the summer of 1943. She went, and I spent the evenings on pub crawls with my sergeant buddies. No more pissin' off 'ome, except at weekends. She wrote that she had taken a room almost opposite Baron's Court tube station. That was where I was to go on furlough.

When I went on my first weekend leave (signed Ford Madox Ford, Capt for Lt Col), I saw that I would have to be more careful than in easy-going Manchester. For in London there was a larger ration of military police, who would waylay guilty-looking soldiers at the top or bottom of Underground escalators and perhaps be experts in pass forgery. A name like Ford Madox Ford would arouse suspicion because of its implausibility. The thing to do on seeing MPs hovering was to go boldly up and ask about train times, requesting politely also that they stand to attention when addressing an NCO of superior rank. I was only once caught out, and that was by a brigadier who protested about my failure to salute him. I replied that I believed such courtesies had been dispensed with at railway termini. Not so, he said. He asked to see my pass, which I had foolishly allowed to be signed by Cyril Connolly, 2nd Lt for Capt. He accosted me by a railway bookstall which had copies of *Horizon*. He made a note about 2nd Lieut Connolly. If I heard no more, it was because, in that autumn of 1943, the Infantry Training Centre at Peninsular Barracks was being disbanded and papers were being burnt.

In London I was surprised to see a Lynne more of the world than previously. She was as elegant as clothes rationing permitted, witty and sought after by a man known as Charlie Parly, the name given to the Parliamentary Secretary of the Board of Trade, and a great frequenter of pubs. The provincial Lynne had never much cared for pubs, fretting over her small sherry and anxious to be gone while I ordered my third pint. Now she was downing gin paid for by men from Price Waterhouse and senior officials of the Board of Trade in smart bars like the Captain's Cabin where my three stripes were not welcome. There was one official called Cecil, of Eton and Balliol background, who had a boil on his bottom. Someone said: 'Hello, Cecil old boy, how's the BOT?' – 'A little better, thank you,' he replied. He was married to Lady Cora something and recounted dialogues with her full of 'Well, I said, Cora old girl –' This was distinguished company. Then Lynne was suddenly transferred to the Ministry of War Transport, and the company she kept became large, diverse, and shady. It also became literary.

It became literary chiefly through Archie Currie, who had worked with Chesterton on *G.K.'s Weekly* and wrote for *Punch* as A.C.C. He had something to do with the Merchant Navy Supply Association and also with the Dutch refugee family firm of Schats Davits, which had a monopoly of endaviting lifeboats. Through him Lynne and I became acquainted with the drunken literati of Fitzrovia. She was friendly also with the whole of the Scotland Yard Special Branch, which she met in St Stephen's Dive in Westminster. And then there was Norman Ray, chief crime reporter of the *News of the World*, knowing whom meant knowing all the pubs and clubs of Fleet Street. I did not see how the Ministry of War Transport connected with crime, but Lynne was enquiring into something that may have been criminal – the loss of a floating harbour, a prototype of Mulberry, which had been reported as seen, successively, off Montevideo, Cape Town, and Hobart, probably with pirates aboard. The government contract for this had also disappeared, though it was found eventually stuffed inside a cushion a bony executive officer had imported into his comfortless bureau.

My leaves, official and filched, became continuous hard-drinking sessions with a little love at closing-time. Most of the drinking took place on what has become known as the Julian Maclaren-Ross circuit. Maclaren-Ross may well have earned immortality as the X. Trapnel of Anthony Powell's *A Dance to the Music of Time*, but his *Memoirs of the Forties* remains a valuable record of the underside of the war, and many a non-reading man in Peninsular Barracks had read a story or two of his in *Lilliput* or *Penguin New Writing*. He was the only writer of that time who, in a brisk no-nonsense style that owed something to Hemingway, was able to show with fearless accuracy the fucked-up condition of the private soldier. In 1943, after a court-martial and a period in the glasshouse, he was discharged from the army and worked with Dylan Thomas in one of the innumerable documentary film units that used ex-RAF men to portray the wasted patience of the Home Guard, or ex-gunners to glorify the RAF. Maclaren-Ross, with his teddy bear overcoat and silver-knobbed cane, an Oscar Wilde with less talent but no homosexuality, became a symbol of wartime London Bohemia. He had his regular post at the end of the bar in the Wheatsheaf, Rathbone Place, propped up against the wooden settle on which sat Mrs Stewart, an old lady who did crosswords and drank Guinness and, though poor, was too proud to accept help with the one or treats of the other.

The Wheatsheaf was the most popular of the pubs on the circuit. One came from Oxford Street to Rathbone Place and first met the Black Horse, too funereal to be convivial, and then the Bricklayers Arms, set back on Gresse Street, quiet, small and a good pace for assignations. It was known as the Burglars or the Burglars Rest, because of a notorious break-in for the drinking up of the stock and a sloshed sleep after. The Marquess of Granby, at the corner of Rathbone Place, was run by homosexuals. Paul, the bearded homosexual pianist, wore little gold earrings and said: 'My dear, this boogie-woogie makes me wet my knickers. I prefer something more *raffiné*,' meaning 'You are my Heart's Delight'. The Duke of York, past the passage known as Jekyll and Hyde Alley, had as landlord Major Alf Klein, an irritable but sometimes generous man whose whisky intake was formidable and, by the late fifties, had done for him. I saw him give the pub piano to Cyril Clarke, a drunken musicologist: 'Go on, take the bloody thing away.'

It was in the Duke of York that I had evidence of Lynne's courage, a quality she never lost except in the dentist's surgery. A razor gang, Pirelli's mob, came in and nearly cleared the bar. Major Klein retreated in good order. The mob leader, cherubically fair and probably of Venetian origin, ordered pints of bitter from the cowed bald barman with no intention of paying. The beer he poured on the floor before throwing the glasses at the walls or grinningly threatening such customers as were left with the jagged butts. Lynne said: 'What a pity to waste good beer.' The little mobster, with his gorillas behind him, leered: 'You want to drink it then?' He ordered the drawing of pint after pint. These were for Lynne. I tried to help. 'You keep out of it, soldier.' She downed three pints without a golden hair's turning. 'You're a good kid, you are. If you're ever in trouble with those bastards of O'Flaherty's or the Maltese mob you just call on Pirelli.' Then he threw insolent fivers on to the counter and led his thugs out. Lynne's courage owed something to innocence. She could not take the Pirelli gang seriously: it was just something out of *Brighton Rock*.

No mobsters entered the Wheatsheaf: there was no room. To get to the gentlemen's toilet one had to fight through a highly literary mob and climb stairs thronged with small poets and their girl friends. From the toilet I could always hear Lynne's crisp consonants ringing clearly. She had a remarkably well-placed voice: it was a great asset with the loud Special Branch as it had been with bullying trade union secretaries. She rarely had to raise it. She would be arguing with Sister Ann the respectable prostitute, or Nina Hamnett the painter, or Dylan Thomas or John Heath-Stubbs, John Large, John Singer, Noel Sircar, other writers, some remembered, most forgotten. The Wheatsheaf saloon bar was a hall of transient fame. Much was expected of John Singer, the Commercial Road poet who had published a volume called *The Fury of the Living*, from which I recall only an epigram on C. E. M. Joad, the giggling bearded philosopher of the BBC Brains Trust:

> The indefatigable Joad
> Ingeniously contrives
> A neat solution in advance
> At which he then arrives.

John Large, the Canadian poet with the pork-pie hat, survives, as far as I know, only in translation in an Indonesian anthology I once used in Malaya. He ended, like many London bohemians, as an unemployable literary journalist who sold his review copies without reading them, getting the core of the content from the blurb on the jacket. Noel Sircar, a Eurasian who worked at the India Office, had a literary future before him put paid to by a near-lethal mugging. His *A Boyhood in India* was a small masterpiece. Bob Pocock, the BBC producer, was fascinated by him and called his Soho epic, a parody of Eliot, 'Mr Sircar's Saturday Circus'. He would also sing 'I dream of Sircar with the light brown tool'. Sircar was the man arrested and called a spiv by the police because, after closing-time, he looked for William Hazlitt's grave in the churchyard of St Mary's, Soho. He was always after, as he put it, 'a bit of C', and would ty to discomfit literary ladies with 'I'd like to fuck you. I wouldn't half shove it in.' When his approaches were reciprocated he would turn tail.

Dylan Thomas's sexual appetite was much exaggerated, especially in the United States. During my absence abroad Lynne technically committed adultery with him a few times, but to go to bed with Dylan was to offer little more than maternal comfort. He was usually too soused to perform and, when not soused, he foresaw his morning guilt and was inhibited. All he really wanted was female warmth and a protective cuddle. He never grew up, and his verse is bogged in his Swansea childhood. He had in common with Maclaren-Ross a genuine concern with literary

craftsmanship, reflected in his instance by innumerable neat drafts
– a single change of word would entail an entire recopying – and
in Maclaren-Ross's by the exquisite smallness of his calligraphy.
Archie Currie said to him one evening: 'Julian, how beautifully
you write.' Maclaren-Ross took the compliment in its deeper
sense and was wounded when he saw it referred only to his pen-
manship. His ego was large; Dylan's was non-existent. Maclaren-
Ross was handsome and knew it; Dylan was ashamed of his body.
Maclaren-Ross's capacity for drink was bottomless: it was an
aspect of his Scottish blood. Dylan, being Welsh, could not take
as much alcohol as the world thought. I remember him in the
bar at Richmond station beginning the day with several pints of
orange squash: that was to shock his stomach and keep it quiescent
when the real drinking began.

It is, of course, pointless to compare the two men at all: Dylan's
reputation has suffered since his death but he remains a major
poet; Maclaren-Ross was a short-story writer with a very minor
talent, though it was a talent wartime England needed. It is the
Soho ambience which minor and major shared that draws one
into thinking of a literary school. There was no school, although
Tambimuttu, the Ceylonese poetaster who edited *Poetry London*,
thought he was presiding over one. If there was a unified literary
movement in the forties, it was only in the sense of poets and
poetlings moving together from the Wheatsheaf, which closed at
ten-thirty, to the Highlander in Dean Street, which followed different licensing laws and stayed open till eleven, and then moving
to the Coffee An' afterwards. The name of that establishment has
been garbled into the Café Ann. There was no visible name (the
black-out was on, anyway, and one never went there during the
day), but the point seemed to be that you could get coffee an'
something else – a horse steak or a salami sandwich. Army deserters or call-up dodgers who had no ration book could, in Soho,
gorge on a variety of unrationed foodstuffs – local pigeons and
sparrows, Italian delicatessen, totters' nags dead of old age. The
King of Poland, in his long red cloak, would dub anyone knight
who would pay for his dish of horse. Meanwhile the small writers
in drab civvies, unfit for conscription or dishonourably discharged, kept alive the civilisation the rest of us notionally
defended.

Dylan Thomas was the one big name, but George Orwell,
known chiefly as a competent journalist who had had his larynx
weakened by a Spanish bullet, sometimes appeared in the

Wheatsheaf or the Fitzroy Tavern to down a silent half. He stood on the edge of a company of film workers one evening to listen distractedly to Gilbert Wood, a petulant painter mentioned scornfully though not by name in Maclaren-Ross's *Memoirs*. Wood specialised in daubing pictures to deck film interiors. He was terrified by even the mention of rats and, inevitably in his presence, rats would sooner or later gnaw into the conversation. He had been put to work on the décor of a film called *Death of a Rat* and wondered if he dared resign. I believe that Orwell picked up the idea of Winston Smith's phobia from Gilbert Wood. When, much later, I told Wood that I had eaten stewed rat, he fainted.

I had no real right to mingle with the literary crew. I had not published either prose or verse and did not wish to, still considering myself to be a composer. There were not many musicians around on that Soho circuit: such composers as had work would be busy scoring the background slush for a film; the players would be playing. I took around my recently completed piano sonata, looking for some fellow-musician who would offer an opinion, but I found none. The writers, many of whom were film workers, felt capable of judging Wood's décor, but the gap between the sphere-born harmonious sisters was as wide then as it is now. Dylan could play a Scriabin study in F sharp major on the piano of somebody's flat after closing-time, but he had learnt it by being shown where to put his fingers; my score appealed in its calligraphy to both Dylan and Maclaren-Ross, but it was Arabic to them. It was out of a desire to be known as some kind of intelligible artist to the Soho literati, and also on the urging of a highbrow recruit at Peninsular Barracks who said he was a friend of Cyril Connolly's, that I sent verse and prose to *Horizon*. I received no reply. The prose, I thought, was not bad. It was a story based on the experience of Bernard B. Brown, the old Xaverian who was now in the navy. A man who has been to the cinema in a drunken stupor wakes the next day in the belief that he has seen the greatest film ever made – the story of humanity at length and in a variety of styles, from *cinema vérité* through comedy and melodrama to animated drawings. It turns out that he went to a news cinema.

It was in the summer of 1943 that Lynne and I were married for the third time. Her family had acquiesced in the engagement but been dubious about her marrying a poor private or a less poor sergeant. But we both had the feeling that I was not

much longer for the Home Forces, and that before I was posted
overseas we ought to regularise our situation at the Blackwood
end. I wrote to Lynne's father asking if we might now get wed,
and he said aye. He said more: there would be a full-scale do in
Blackwood with both the Lancashire and Tredegar families
invited: arrangements were already under weigh. Frightened, we
sent a telegram: 'Married today home tomorrow'. Lynne caught
shingles on this, her third honeymoon, and was untouchable. In
the pubs there was commiseration from the sex-loving Welsh.

In the autumn the Primary Training Centre was dissolved: either
the army now had enough infantry or they could get no more.
I had odd visions of the Soho crew on parade, Tambimuttu as
right marker, and then folded them all back into their nobler role
of keeping civilisation alive. The dissolution came at the right
time, because I could see trouble ahead. This was over my refusal
to salute the lieutenant quartermaster. He demanded salutes and I
told him why I would not give them. I had entered his office
during his absence to speak to a Czech ATS clerk who wanted to
improve her English. The quartermaster had returned and rudely
ordered me out. He was a ranker and exhibiting ranker's
grossness; it was not, I told him, the way for an officer to behave.
I was a sergeant: I was not 'you'; nor was I to be ordered to
bugger off. If he wanted the courtesy of a salute he must show
courtesy himself. The affair was ready to be taken to Lieutenant-
Colonel Wilson when my posting came. It was a sort of ghostly
return to Winwick – an EMS hospital, this time in Liverpool,
complete with RAMC CQMS, sergeant clerk, excused-boots
orderlies. The Military Registrar, a friend of the man at Winwick,
was harsh with me. He had some notion that I had been posted
to him in disgrace, though there was no evidence of this in my
dossier. His friend may have spoken to him of the Major Lalkaka
débâcle or tripping over my bared legs in the bushes: the name
had stuck. I started off at a disadvantage.

The hospital was at Walton, but I had a number of subsidiary
establishments to visit, one of them a sort of hideaway for military
sufferers from venereal diseases. The Liverpool people were of
very large generosity and laid on an admirable variety show and
a black-market spread for these vanquished in love's lists. They
did not know why they were in hospital blue; they assumed they
had been stricken in battle. The head of the charitable group
gave an eloquent speech about these poor lads who had suffered
for England, meaning Liverpool, and the poor lads took it all in

with leering complacency, each cuddling a female companion who had, so to speak, been served with the meat pies and jelly and blancmange. I had to warn each of these good-hearted girls against slipping off for a bit of that there before I escorted the gonorrhoeal louts back to their lonely beds. The general view was that there was more than one way of becoming a war casualty, but hands were now knocked away from under skirts.

The view of Liverpudlians that they are a race apart is well-founded. There is the unanalysable genetic mixture of a great port and also Welsh from the south and Irish a jump across from Dublin. The speech is distinctive. 'All got your furs, love?' cried the tram conductresses, who kept warm with a bit of moth-eaten fare. The energy is immense and explains the gratuitous violence. The fighting O'Sullivans were introduced to me as a family that had a fight before they went to bed. One of them were a lad who liked to fight with 'is 'ead, but once he got it torn with his opponent's fish 'ooks. Terrible, terrible. Generosity could lead to violence. If I asked a direction I would soon have a crowd around me giving contradictory instructions. I would leave a fight behind and have to ask again. The amount of free love available in wartime Liverpool was terrifying; the nurses at Walton should have been tired off duty but were rabid for dalliance. There were also a lot of fierce amateur musicians around. One of them, a civilian doctor at Walton, invited me to discuss Schoenberg while he was on duty. The duty consisted of cutting up hundreds of dead babies with scissors, newly born or still in the foetal stage. One of these corpses squirted a secretion at him full in the mouth that was talking of crab canons. The little cadavers were the fruits of casual Liverpool love, of which there was a Thoreauvian plethora. This doctor had just been involved in the practical joke of serving stewed human placenta in the staff dining room. It was a tough life, and there were nightly German fireworks over the docks. Of all the British cities that deserve the curative attention of a central government Liverpool comes first. The Bootle Beatles were taken too seriously, but, in their modest way, they exempli-fied the combative energy of the great decayed port. Guilt pricked me when I began to feel a larger loyalty to it than to Manchester.

I used to go, weak at the knees, to the home of an amateur violinist whom I accompanied. I wrote out the top lines of many popular songs for him, formed a trio with a corporal on drums, organised a dance and earned the Military Registrar's favour. I wanted to get to London at weekends and needed that favour.

294   *Little Wilson and Big God*

The violinist very generously allowed me to pretend I was sleeping at his address, working on music with him while awake. Telephone calls would come from the suspicious CQMS, a fat bad soldier who talked of charpoys and tack wallahs but had never moved further than New Brighton. Yes, I was there all right, working away and not to be disturbed. This kind fiddler was a good Catholic who hated lies. He once said to me that God had put people like Yehudi Menuhin on earth to warn lesser musicians of the perils of vanity. When I told Yehudi this forty years later he was much impressed.

In November 1943 I received notice of my posting overseas. I had expected it. I went on embarkation leave the day after coming back off a cheating furlough. I had bought one of the new battle berets which did not fall off like the despised cap FS and, in a new battledress issued to a sergeant since discharged dead at Walton, marched soldierly from Barons Court Underground to 122 Barons Court Road. I was to report at the end of my leave to the monstrous Transit Depot at Marylebone. This extended the leave somewhat and might have extended it indefinitely. The RSM at the depot cried loudly to his clerk that he did not want any of these Army Educational Corps geezers on his premises: let the erudite sods sleep out. I went to him joyfully and said I had a London address. Stay there then, sarnt, glad to be rid of you, but don't forget to report to your course at 0900 hours. I scurried away with my kit. Only on the tube train did I wonder what was all this about a course. Clearly there were two lots of AEC personnel – one summoned to London for some mad conference on Second Front Albanian, the other condemned to transportation. I did the right thing. I got off at the next stop and went back to Marylebone. Trying it on, weren't you, sarnt? Here you are and here you bloody well stay till that boat 'oots for you in the 'arbour. Fuck you, sarnt-major. Say that again, sarnt, and you'll find yourself on a 252. But he knew there could be no real discipline in this grey limbo. Why, even lance-corporals shouted at us to get in line with our fucking mess-tins. A master gunner confided that my destination, encoded as P, was to be Gibraltar.

So it was goodbye to Soho. Julian Maclaren-Ross, in his clear patrician accents, told the Wheatsheaf saloon bar that a convoy would be steaming to the Mediterranean in a day or so: were there any German agents disguised as contributors to *Poetry London* at all interested? There was only one presumed agent regularly drinking in that pub, and this was Barry O'Mara.

Nobody knew whose side he was on, but it did not matter. He was well liked, and he was besotted with a foul harridan he called a peerless English rose. It was sad saying goodbye to the heart of culture; unspeakably sad saying goodbye to my wife. We looked to the future and employed no let or hindrance in bed. I took a slow train to Avonmouth and embarked.

WE WERE A draft of five, replacing time-expired sergeants who, having had two years of Gibraltar, had presumably had enough. There was Harry Stephens, a Welsh sociologist with the eyes of a mystic; there was Ben Thomas, a Welsh mathematician known in his home town of Emlyn as Ben Maths, who looked like an egg perched on a battledress; there was a morose Lancashire woodwork expert called Albert Parker; there was Jimmy Wilkinson, a teacher of French who had written his MA thesis on the influence of Plutarch's Lives on La Fontaine; there was myself, who, to my surprise, was being sent out as a specialist in German. Everyone was politically very far left except myself, who stuck to my home-made brand of Liberalism. Wilkinson believed that the British Revolution could not be much longer delayed: he had seen, though nobody else had, swaddies saluting with a clenched fist and, by God, officers of the junior sort grimly clenching back. The time for discussion was over and, taking the British Way and Purpose to lonely Scottish gunsites, he had refused to discuss. He had said: 'Gentlemen, I give you the facts, no more. There is a House of Lords. There is a House of Commons. Comment, if you wish.' If someone said: 'The House of Lords is a load of anachronistic shit,' he would reply: 'That's a point.' If someone said: 'Get rid of the king and install Joe Stalin,' he would reply: 'That also is a point.' When someone said: 'Sergeant, you're a bloody idiot,' he replied: 'I will not gainsay that that is certainly a point.' He had become known, he said proudly, as That's-a-point Wilkinson. The long knives were coming out, he affirmed; do not be surprised if there are British bombs planted in the engine-room. He was referring to the transport aboard which we lugged, bawled at in the dark, our kit.

It was a long sick voyage. We had to get to the Mediterranean by lurching to the middle of the Atlantic and then back to the Bay of Biscay. When the OC Troops discovered my pianistic skills he wanted me to be posted to the ship. He was a musician himself and impressed by my musical memory. A ship's concert was arranged, there was no sheet music, and I accompanied everything out of that faculty I have since lost. A vast woman major of the RAMC, an ophthalmologist, performed with a small dark captain the dungeon scene from Flecker's *Hassan* and I underscored it out of *Tristan und Isolde*. Then I was sick on the keyboard. Everybody was sick, though not on the keyboard. There was one giant of an AEC sergeant, not in our draft, whose speciality was Mediterranean history. He had not seen the Mediterranean before, and he was sick when it arrived. He was being posted circuitously to the Falklands and had been equipped with both tropical and polar gear. When we were not sick we were constipated. Sick or constipated, Sergeant Wilkinson waved his arms at the ocean, as though conducting a super-Straussian orchestra from which the theme of revolution would, in the trombones and tubas, shout out. There were Gibraltarian dockyard maties aboard, going home after visiting their evacuated families, and these, said Wilkinson, had received revolutionary orders from a house on Great Smith Street, just behind the Colonial Office. There was a Brains Trust chaired by the Gibraltar garrison Anglican chaplain. Nobody but he knew what dialectical materialism was, but he refused to define it except in emotional circumlocutions. Wilkinson nodded to us all: everything was working out as he had expected. Then he stood and told the audience a long dull story about a talking horse.

There was not much sex available on this ship, except for lipsticked members of the Women's Royal Naval Service, who wagged their haunches on deck in dapper bellbottoms and went below to inflame only the commissioned. But one jolly blonde Wren, not of good family, who opened the concert as Venus trying to still the waves from which she had sprung, was friendly and permitted cuddles between bouts of marine nausea. On the Rock, we were told, there would be no women. All had been evacuated to zones of safety like Belfast and Greater London. There had once been regulated brothels in Gibraltar, but a pious Lieutenant-Governor's wife had had these abolished, forcing men over the border into La Linea, there to pick up gon, gleet and syph. 'You'll have to wank, lads,' said a sergeant sadly. We arrived on Christmas Eve. The OC Troops wished us all to remain on board till Boxing Day, so that I could play the piano for carol singing. But he was overridden by garrison orders. Infantry and artillery and engineer drafts minced down the gangplank in heavy boots.

Our tiny draft waited for instructions. None came. Perhaps we were not wanted, perhaps we could go home?

Eventually a small truck arrived for us, decorated with the garrison flash of a tower and a key. A warrant officer class one, hatchet-faced and saturnine, accosted us with no greeting. 'Two of you for the First Herts,' he said, 'and three for the Engineers. This is no longer a two-year station, so you'd better go with somebody you can stand the sight of.' Stephens and I opted for the First Herts up at Moorish Castle. It was disconcerting to meet a fellow-instructor so unfriendly. This WO I, whose name was Crump, was conscious of his rank, but rank back in the Home Forces had meant nothing: to be promoted to glow-worms or fighting cats meant more money but no more power or responsibility. Here it was going to be different. Crump's grimness contradicted the mild air and the festive show of lights. The war was very much on here, but Gibraltar from the air had to look like neutral Spain. We all knew we were not going to get on with Crump, who demanded to be called either Mr Crump or sir. Behind Crump stood the great Rock, grim as Crump but much bigger.

This Rock made Gibraltar impregnable. It was tunnelled, both by nature and by the Royal Engineers, and the tunnels were crammed with provisions against an endless siege. When the Germans were defeated these provisions were broken open and found to be mostly putrid. In December 1943 it was very important not to allow the Rock to be taken by the Germans, who, taking it, would control the Mediterranean and probably win the war. Nobody knew how the cat would jump in Spain. General Franco was neutral now, but he might soon permit the Germans to trundle through La Linea and crash the frontier. It was necessary for the British to maintain relations of a cool friendliness with the Spanish authorities, and even to welcome the annual farce of a pretence that Gibraltar was really governed from Andalusia, laying on a parade for the putative boss from Algeciras. The Gibraltar garrison was large, with a full infantry brigade, gunsites from Windmill Hill to Willis's Farm, and tunnelling companies of the Royal Engineers. A battalion of Liverpool Scottish, mostly cockneys in kilts, was stationed at Buena Vista; the First Hertfordshires were up the hill which Stephens and I now ascended.

The first man I met was Bill Brian the trumpeter, who was on guard duty. In the sergeants' mess was Harry Walkling, now the drum major. I spent my first evening getting seasonally drunk with the band. Then I lurched off to high-set quarters I was to share with Stephens and a brigade staff-sergeant. There was going to be a lot of climbing on this damned Rock. I awoke queasy and with unripe banana colic to hear singing. That, said the staff-sergeant, was the Poles. They sang their national song every morning. The words the staff-sergeant put to it were:

> Oh, tell us, Joe, what's your intention?
> See how we shake with apprehension.

Stephens and I now attempted to march down the hill that led to the Garrison Education Office. We were prevented by snarling apes that were celebrating Christmas morning with an unwonted enmity to the human element. They were guarding the ramp or stairway that took one from the Moorish Castle to the town. We marched back to barracks and proposed going down by the endless steps that led to the Casemates. There were apes there too, including the senior Scruffy: somebody seemed to have got them drunk. On Winston Churchill's insistence, the Rock apes had to be encouraged to flourish. There was an old Spanish superstition, perhaps implanted by the Nazis, that when the apes left, the British would leave too. So the apes had to be fed and their breeding blessed, and there was even a sergeant i/c Rock Apes. Having fought with Scruffy, Stephens and I were late for our Christmas morning welcome from the Garrison Education Officer. We were rebuked. There were no seasonal greetings. We were merely told what we had to do.

Our officer was Captain W. P. Meldrum, soon to be gazetted Major. He had a slight look of T. S. Eliot, but there was even less of the poetic about him than there was in the poet. Stephens and I were to travel the height and width of the Rock, take boats to Detached Mole and back, visit the lucky units at sea level, and deliver the British Way and Purpose according to a plan devised by Mr Crump there. We were not to be the free agents we had been back home: we were mere limbs controlled by a centre. Did Mr Crump perhaps prepare our talks for us? I unwisely asked. No, he provided the title and indicated the subject-matter. In the evenings, said Meldrum, I, Sergeant Wilson, would teach various subjects in Nissen huts. German, of course, is your speciality. Oh no, it is not. Oh yes it is, it says so here. Finally Meldrum said that we were all to be issued with bicycles. For travelling up the Rock? No, for use at sea level. I refused to be issued with one, I said; I had never ridden a bicycle in my life and I was not going to start now. Oh yes you are. Oh no I'm not. I asked for a motor-cycle or, preferably, a ride in a car from the garrison transport pool. It was a bad start. And this was Christmas morning.

My early novels are full of the names Meldrum and Crump, attached to the more detestable of my minor characters. I think somewhere I have a Crump-Meldrum or Meldrum-Crump of special detestability. WO Crump and Captain-soon-to-be-Major Meldrum were perhaps not in themselves detestable. They believed in Army Education as a vehicle for their own ambitions, and they spread a lot of it over the Rock. Meldrum got his promotion and, in the New Year Honours list of 1945, appeared with an OBE. This popularly stands for Other Buggers' Efforts, whereas the lesser award, MBE, means My Bloody Effort. Crump, whose qualifications were appropriate to a primary school teacher, was soon commissioned and rose himself to field rank. They did no educating themselves, but they laid on the whip to the men in the field, or on the Rock. They granted little leisure. They earned resentment; it was their ambition, fulfilled through a quantitative approach, which made them admired. They imposed a six-day week with no interludes of free time; Sunday was grudgingly granted as an interlude perhaps necessary for the washing of underclothes and khaki drill. For me Sunday was devoted to the reading of German. I was replacing a man with high qualifications in the subject. Wilkinson, who had thought himself sent out to teach French, found himself teaching Spanish. More, he was made to contribute daily to the *Gibraltar Chronicle* a breezy feature called *Mejor Su Español*. Later I was ordered to teach Spanish, also French, also Russian. It was just a matter of ordering. You were in the army, and you obeyed orders to teach Intermediate Sanskrit or Advanced Internal Combustion Engine Maintenance. I was ordered to teach piano-playing and four-part harmony; I even eventually was given two RAF men who wanted to learn orchestration. These I did not mind. It was the assumption, never dismantled, that I was a German expert which drove me mad.

There were three hours of classes in the evenings. These were voluntary and began in fine style with hordes of men eager for self-improvement at the army's expense. Once they had been issued with primers, many considered that they could learn the subject well enough on their own. This diminished the size of a class, as also did the waning of enthusiasm. At the end it was possible to arrive at a Nissen hut for a class in Maltese or Turkish and find no students present. Naturally one ticked the names of the absent in the register and preserved the fiction that the class was flourishing. The registers, as so often in organised education, were the reality, the instruction the shadow. A lance-corporal with a Ph.D., who had written a little book on the influence of Hegel on McTaggart, looked after the registers and prepared the statistics that were sent to the War Office. These, presumably, got into official records which nobody read.

In 1944 the evacuated females began to return. There were a great number of pert and pretty and over-scented Gibraltarian girls, and they required education. The nuns and Christian Brothers who looked after the schools had scuttled off, resentful of possible German air raids on Irish neutrals, and they had not yet returned. So it was left to the army to invite these girls to evening classes and thus augment the statistics. I was ordered to teach them French. They giggled and would not learn. Some of them left after the filling in of the register. The class was an alibi: they wanted to giggle at boys in the main square which was called the Martello or Hammer. Those who stayed were a torment with their brown bosoms and cheap perfume. I was repressed; we were all repressed; repression showed clearly when the time came for the wearing of khaki shorts. I committed a terrible crime one dark evening at the back of a Nissen hut in the Alameda Gardens. I grabbed a girl and hungrily kissed her. She yielded briefly then loudly screamed. This was the brutality of the colonial oppressors. Other girls came and pounded at me. I drooped, I nearly wept, I was ashamed. I was also resentful. I feared official complaints at gubernatorial level from the girl's parents. I feared a headline in the *Gibraltar Chronicle*. Fortunately she said nothing. She needed the alibi of the class. She wanted to give her kisses to a boy called Gomez or Holgado.

But when one of my classes lost its khaki component entirely and I was left only with perfumed gigglers, I rebelled. I cancelled the class and told Major Meldrum why. I was not here, I said, to provide colonial education: that was the job of colonial officials not military instructors. He saw the diminution of his statistics and ordered me to teach civilians. I replied that I did not think he could give that kind of order. I was prepared to fight this out at a higher level. Resentment at doing work proper to civilian functionaries was exacerbated by an income tax demand I had just received. Civilian functionaries did not get such demands: Gibraltar was a free port and a tax-free colony: not even the Lieutenant-Governor paid income tax. Meldrum, a cunning compromiser, said I could have no objection to holding a class of civilians if the primary students were military. This was true. The class I had cancelled was reconvened, and Mr Crump sat in the front row doing office paperwork.

It was clear that I would never get promotion from Major Meldrum. There was a vacancy for WO II, and, though I was his senior in service, Ben Thomas received the crowns. I shrugged, for I did not desperately need the money. Nor did Ben Thomas. He was a teacher in civilian life, and his local education authority was paying his full salary. It might have been a decent gesture to grant the promotion to either Stephens or myself, who had had no tenured employment before call-up and were both married, but Meldrum seemed to me to have little justice in his inventory. Nor any compassion.

There is no resonance in the term 'compassionate leave', for which I was now driven to apply. That was in the April of 1944. I received a letter from Sonia Brownwell, later to become Sonia Orwell, who was an occasional drinking friend of Lynne's. The letter was about Lynne, and Lynne was too ill to write it herself. Lynne had been working late at the Ministry of War Transport on the scales of victualling for the small craft of Operation Overlord. Leaving the office at midnight she had been set upon by four men who, though in civilian dress, were evidently GI deserters. Their accents were southern. The attack was not sexual but in the service of robbery. The four snatched her handbag and one of them tried to pull off her tight gold wedding ring. He was prepared to break or even cut the finger. Lynne screamed to no response of help. Her screams were stilled by blows. She remembered being kicked before losing consciousness. She was pregnant and she aborted. She was sick now with perpetual bleeding glossed as dysmenorrhoea. If I had been concerned about not receiving letters from her, here was the reason. My response need not be described. I went at once to Meldrum and demanded home leave. He would not grant it. So, I said, it is more important to keep up this farce of Army Education than to fly to the bedside of a desperately sick wife? That is how the army sees it. God fuck the army. You're a bad officer, sir. I demand a posting. You will not get it. I already have one posting on my hands. This was Wilkinson's. You will do nothing? Nothing. I failed to salute as I left and was called back.

There were, for the next few days, reports from various units about my failure to preside over British Way and Purpose parades. I was spending the time drinking heavily in low bars on Main Street. It was unfortunate that at this time a ship from Italy unloaded American troops on their way home. I got into fights, though I was not responsible for the American corpse that was later found on Line Wall Road. The Americans did not behave well. The British rarely behaved well either, but the Americans behaved worse. They offered dollars to respectable Gibraltarians for the loan of their wives. They expressed contempt for the limey cocksuckers. They drank, they vomited. They were ferried like the dead back to their ship by black Charons. They disclosed, as the more ignorant British did, a total misunderstanding of a colonial situation. They despised the colonisers and the colonised. The susceptibilities of foreigners were a joke. They spilled money. Only the blacks showed any dignity. Many of us went through a bad phase of Americanophobia. I considered I had better reason for it than any. It was an American who put me right.

He was a captain whom I found wandering late on Main Street, a provost officer charged with getting the drunks on to the ferries. He had done his work and needed a drink. The bars were closed, but I knew a small club run by a Gibraltarian named Frank or, because of the reputed size of his organ of benevolence, *El Burro*. Frank let the captain and myself in, and we drank. The captain, who was of Hispanic origin and was named Baroja (the *jota* palatised), spoke reasonable Spanish. He also spoke civilised English. He had read philosophy and theology, and what he had learned from the war was a confirmation of the existence of theological evil – evil for its own sake, evil as *summum bonum*. The United States, he said, had, after the death of the New England theocracies, embraced a positivist or meliorist doctrine which denied the existence of evil. Soon they would come back to a realisation of its reality. These were prophetic words. As for what had happened to my wife, this had to be accepted as an evil enactment which had to have enactors of some nationality or other. It could have been Poles or French Canadians. The American aspect of the matter was accidental and unimportant. 'You're looking for an easy target of hate,' he said. 'It's easier to blame a nation than to blame the human endowment. Your wife's a war casualty, but the whole of life is war. In the meantime,' he said, 'if you want anything done about that major of yours, it can easily be arranged. We've got two days more for ship refitting. I can get a party to thump him as he goes to his quarters. You just tell me where they are, that's all.' It would have been easy, yes – a major with AEC flashes, the only one on the Rock. But I let it go. It is often enough for a thing to be possible. Its realisation can be an unnecessary bore. I climbed to Moorish Castle feeling better.

I began to receive letters from Lynne. The bleeding continued, and she was being dilated and curetted by a distinguished though aged gynaecologist. The haemorrhage, which was steady though not copious, had to be balanced by a large liquid intake. This meant drinking beer in pints, which were not permitted to ladies in most pubs – not even in the Duke of York, where pints had been forced upon her by a mobster. I wrote loving and commiseratory letters back, larded with curses. These curses, I discovered later, were neatly excised by the censor. The work of deleting 'fuck' with a razor blade must have been laborious, but the intercepting enemy would, it was presumed, read too much into it – a signal of British despair.

THE TROOPS I tramped Gibraltar to regale with the British Way and Purpose were not desperate, but they were certainly fed up, fucked up, and far from home. They astutely recognised that the war was no longer a concern of the British. It had been handed over to the Americans and the Russians, and the defence of the Rock belonged to an outworn strategy. A thing still rankled among the longer-settled orange-suckers, as members of the garrison were called by the visiting Royal Navy. A garrison notice had stated that much American money was, as it were, symbolically invested in Gibraltar. A great American insurance company used the Rock as an emblem of impregnability, and if the Rock fell to the enemy the company would be ruined. So it was the duty of the Gibraltar garrison to defend that segment of American finance. The cynicism of the troops was profound. The chief symbols of their alienation were the men who were leading them to victory – Field-Marshal Montgomery and Prime Minister Churchill.

Montgomery was primarily hated as a puritan who made his men run ten miles before breakfast and denounced smoking and drinking. There were too many unit commanders who transmitted this doctrine of austerity, in accents not too remote from Montgomery's own, to men who did not have ten miles to run, except into Spain, and who were stationed in a smoker's paradise. In Gibraltar it was sinful not to smoke. Cigarettes were duty-free, plentiful, and of a variety forgotten in wartime Britain. I became an eighty-a-day man. Drink was a different matter. Beer came from Britain in barrels, some of them filched by the Docks Operating Group, and it alternated between Tetley's, a very acceptable brew, and Simmonds's, which was an emetic with a court-martial in every cask. Large drunkenness was intermittent, depending on the arrival of the ships. But, to men deprived of women, smoking and drinking were the sole comforts, and that bastard Montgomery would, given a chance, take those comforts away. There would, without them, be only the solace of the army cuisine, which was non-existent. All the rations came in the dehydrated form instigated by the Americans, so that every meal was of something reconstituted – mince, onions, eggs, watery mash. Little was bought from Spain, which had, after a debilitating war, nothing to export except sherry, which only the officers drank. True, there were bananas and sour Sevilles sold by cackling Andalusian crones, but these were a marginal item of diet. After a *corrida* in Algeciras, a slice or two of tough bull might appear in a Gibraltar restaurant. Grinning *bonitos* or ray stinking of menstrual ammonia would come from the fishermen on Catalan Bay, but very rarely. The cooks had become experts in reconstitution, and army slop mocked the possession of teeth.

So Montgomerian austerity was highly unpopular, and Churchill, who stood for its opposite, was unpopular for profounder reasons. He was a warmonger whose qualified approval of the Russian destruction of the Nazi gangsters he excoriated with his dentures out would soon turn to open belligerence. The men foresaw that he would, after the victory over the Germans which the Americans would ensure, defer demobilisation as long as possible, so that the Red menace might think twice before engulfing liberated Europe. From the professional angle, both Montgomery and Churchill had, respectively, military efficiency and political righteousness as their aims, and their programmes were praiseworthy. But conscripted troops are primarily human beings who resent being converted into disposable counters – not only Evelyn Waugh's Brigadier Ritchie-Hook spoke dreamily of expending men like chips – and their humanity was outraged by the inhumanity of their leaders. They were not fighting-fit war machines, Montgomerian reductions; they were not the faceless khaki pieces of a great game of Ludo; they were civilians in temporary fancy dress who could not take war as army professionalism nor as the continuation of diplomacy by non-pacific means. They worried about home, and they wanted to get back there.

Looking once at Colonel Nasser on television, I saw him accept his glass of iced water from a white-coated *fellah* without offering thanks. That, I thought, is bad statesmanship: never ignore the common man, especially on television. Churchill's great pride was not to ignore him, but his techniques of democratic bonhomie were ham-fisted. It was his custom when inspecting Home Forces troops to go down the line grinning with a big cigar. The cigar, intended to endear, did not do so. The men were usually starved of tobacco and enraged by the Cuban aroma. Churchill would ingratiatingly use obscenities that would have shocked Montgomery, but the men saw that it was all an act. They heard in his Edwardian twang (as Orwell called it) not the voice of equality but that of a ruling class more deeply entrenched than that represented by their haw-haw officers. Some of the Royal Engineers on the Rock were peacetime bricklayers. A few had met Churchill, who had an amateur interest in bricks. He would tell some foul joke about cropping your headers and knocking the facework over, well-seasoned with fucks and bloodies. The bricklayers heard the worst note of condescension: the unhandy attempt to use their idiom, never getting it quite right.

My duty as a purveyor of the British Way and Purpose was to uphold an inveterate political system kindly being modified in the direction of a philosophy of state welfare. I had to make a negative war (defend the bad against the worse) appear positive. War itself was turning into a metaphor: we were enacting the charade of a struggle to turn Britain into a democracy. Equality of rights was one of the shibboleths. Lecturing on the postwar national health service that was envisaged, I stated, rightly I think, that all men were the same with their clothes off, and that not even a full general had his rank tattooed on his backside. The officers present at the lecture walked out and reported me for insubordination. The British Way and Purpose material on the future of education seemed to emphasise the necessity of a loss in prestige for the public schools, as also for the older universities. An Old Etonian gunner officer rose to protest the necessity of elitism and was howled down by his own men. Again, I was an agent of insubordination.

I had to turn myself into a mere vague voice of the Utopia that is nowhere. The men needed that voice – the articulacy they could not themselves attain in the service of disaffection. I should have been very happy to hand over to the experts who produced pamphlets on instructional technique the task of presenting a golden future to the Docks Operating Group. These men were very difficult to handle. They staged mutinies. They stole lavishly from the goods they unloaded and sold them on the black market. Their muscularity was complemented by profound ignorance. When I visited them in their dark cavern facing the Casemates square, I had to be locked in by their sergeants, Daniel among the snappers and growlers. The first task was to quieten them, and not through the regular military technique of demanding quiet, which did not work. The thing to do was to grab some docker arbitrarily from the front row and talk to him with whispering earnestness, thus inducing the listening silence of the curious. With this gained, I would cry: 'Gentlemen!' That provoked large howls of derision. I would follow with 'Those of you who can read may have seen the word over public urinals. I use the word with that meaning.' While they were thinking that over, I would try and introduce the prescribed topic – the future of the British Empire, Our American Allies, Our Russian Allies, the Housing of the Future, Health Services in a Democracy. There was no means of prevailing against the rage of this mob. The dockers were enraged at being in the army at all. They had overestimated their importance as overpaid civilians. They were enraged at low pay and army discipline, which they refused to understand. They were enraged, so far as I was concerned, by a compulsory hour of civic education.

It had been one of the tasks of the old trade unions to educate their members. The unions now had the sole task of holding the country to ransom. Even the *Daily Mirror* published a cartoon in which striking miners or dockers, I forget which, raised their banners over the bodies of the slain in khaki or blue. The caption was: 'Your fighting comrades thank you.' The conscripted dockworkers had no sense of solidarity with these comrades. Their ignorance was astounding. They would be as well satisfied with living under Hitler as under Churchill. Hitler was right to kill the Sheenies. The original inhabitants of America were the Negroes, and the Yanks had dispossessed them. Pay for the workers could easily be raised: it was merely a matter of printing more money. Their nicking of bales and packages could (this was subtle) be excused on the grounds that the flow of stolen goods encouraged trade. All our glorious allies, it was alleged, had been sent to East London for the sole purpose of seducing the dockers' wives. ''Ad this letter from her,' cried a docker named Jack (poor ole Jack, let Jack 'ave a bleedin word), 'sayin' as 'ow she's fuckin orf with this 'ere Yank and says she 'opes as there is no 'ard feelin's. God curse both of the bastards. An nickin' three gross of nylon stockin's for 'er an all.' I unwisely ended that session by shouting 'You don't need me. What you need is a drink.' The dockers at once battered open the locked door and bore me with them to the Universal Café on Main Street, newly open at noon. They were generous. They stood me drinks they paid for from thick wads. They called the waiters Spanish bastards and hooted at the orchestra.

I had composed one Sunday, in the intervals of reading Hemingway's *Fiesta* in German, a setting of a song by Lorca – *La niña del bello rostro* – for a singer named Merita, who had a two months' contract with the Universal or UV. She sang this with a gorgeous Moorish wail. When, seeing me surrounded by dockers, she struck it up, she was at once howled down and asked for 'Yours' and 'Johnny Pedlar'. It was then that I went mad and hit out. It was action unworthy of my rank. The military police were called in, and the dockers fought them. I quietly left. Word of this did not reach Major Meldrum but news of the abandonment of the lecture did. I was severely rebuked. I said the dockers were ineducable. If Mr Crump smirking there thought differently let him have a go. Nonsense: nobody was ineducable. How, I said, about those Italian prisoners up on Windmill Hill?

My being sent up weekly to these was rather more farcical than being locked in the dockers' den. The Italian prisoners of war could not easily escape from Gibraltar, which was a prison anyway, and they were given fatigues to do in the open. When they did wrong they became doubly prisoners. I was sent up to harangue them on the British Way and Purpose, which was not really appropriate. Moreover, they knew few words of English. *Siggy, fuckifucky* and *porapi* sufficed them. *Porapi* was a deformation of the Andalusian *porapis*, which was a deformation of the Rock locution *poor as piss*. Nor was I qualified to tell them of the Italian Way and Purpose in Italian. After all, I had been sent out here as a German expert. My first visit was a silent

smoking of illegal cigarettes I handed round. For my second I
wished to read aloud from *I Promessi Sposi*, very popular in the
sergeants' messes of the Rock as *The Betrothed*, which had been
overproduced by Penguin. But the only Italian text I could find
was a *Divina Commedia* in the Garrison Officers' Library to which
I had no official access. I read from Dante haltingly and through
smoke. I was rebuked by Major Meldrum first for the smoke and
next for not teaching the British Way and Purpose. Dante, he
said, whatever it was, was not the British Way and Purpose. It
used to be, I cried hotly, the bloody European Way and Purpose
until the bloody English permitted a stupid randy monarch to
introduce what was called the Reformation.

This outburst I later found interesting. I had assumed that I
had freed myself from the nets of Catholicism, but here I was
speaking out for Catholic Europe. Of course, I was *in* Catholic
Europe, despite the bobbies in British helmets and the insistence
of the Gibraltarians that they were, though mostly Genoese with
a Spanish admixture, really a kind of brown Englishmen. They
were Catholic, when they were not Jews, and held baroque
processions on feast days. The women went to mass in mantillas.
They spoke monophthongal English without nuances. When asked
in English classes to write a sentence illustrating 'Too many cooks
spoil the broth', they would write: 'In the kitchen there were too
many cooks. Because there were too many cooks the broth was
not good.' They were a kind of Iberians who feared Iberia. They
preferred British-style brown bobbies to Franco's *policia*. But they
were of my own kind. They made the sign of the cross and heard
the bell of the Angelus. I was drawn to the women with crosses
hanging from their delectable necks. The Protestant Lynne was
sick and far. I was in warm garlicky unreformed Christendom.
My unconscious knew this, however much my conscious mind
dealt with the British (Protestant) Way and Purpose. And, as for
God, there was God towering high overhead, the mists of the
Levant on his brow.

I walked all over God, bearing the official Pelagian message. I
got to know every inch of him, on foot, on a motor cycle that
overheated when mounting and freewheeled down, in the occasional car from the garrison pool. I tramped out to the units on
Catalan Bay and took a boat to the gunners on Detached Mole.
Coming back on a boat, one foot on the gunwale and the other
on the slippery quay, I fell into the oily water and, coming up,
cracked my head on the boat's bottom. The Spanish boatmen

hauled me aboard and were more concerned about my wrist-watch than my life. They were poor men much exercised about other people's possessions. When they found that the *reloj* was waterproof they were relieved. I myself, spitting oil, was not relieved of the rest of the day's duties: the show had to go on. The show went on in the summer heat that bounced back from the Rock, in the rains, in the season of the Levant. The Levant was a wind from Africa that, in times well remembered by the older inhabitants, had brought skyloads of frogs and lizards to rain down on Main Street. In my time it mostly brought tooth-ache and migraine and profound depression.

But who were we to be depressed and self-pitying? We were out of the war. It was something remote to be followed on maps or seen, in a stench of oranges, at the cinema. On June 4, 1944, allied forces entered Rome. On June 6 an invasion fleet of 4,000 ships victualled on a scale determined by my wife sailed for Europe. On June 7 the Japanese thrust outside Imphal was defeated. On June 12 the first V-1 bombs fell on England and the Docks Operating Group belatedly declared war on Hitler. The Russians took Minsk. The Western allies took Caen. The Ameri-cans took Guam. Warsaw rose. Myitkyina fell. Paris was liber-ated. Marseilles was taken. Rumania surrendered. Holland was entered. The first V-2 bombs fell on England. On December 16 the Germans began their last western offensive in the Ardennes and spoiled the Christmas of the Rock garrison. But the war seemed to be coming to an end in Europe, and the strategy of Army Education entered an expansive phase. The future would soon be upon us and we were not quite ready for it. Education had to be vocational as well as inspirational. The men must be taught trades. Plumbers and commercial artists had to be given three hasty stripes and inducted into the corps. Major Meldrum was flanked by two new staff officers class III. The cadre of five that had sailed from Avonmouth in late 1943 was swamped and sardonically watched the new men take over.

Sergeant Wilkinson was no longer with us. His conflict with Major Meldrum had been long and obscure. Its opposed themes were Meldrum's 'You will obey orders' and Wilkinson's 'All I want, sir, is a fair crack of the whip', which nobody, perhaps not even Wilkinson, well understood. Wilkinson took ship and, it was believed, had been stripped of his stripes, returned to his old infantry battalion, and sent out to fight in Burma. We were not allowed to forget that the Nips, dirty little fighters, would still be

waiting for us when the Jerries had gone under. The threat of the
Japs was as good as the threat of a court-martial. Wilkinson and
Crump went home on the same boat, Crump to glory, Wilkinson
to disgrace and, Meldrum perhaps hoped, death. Ben Thomas
had to be promoted to WO I. It was taken for granted that
Meldrum would import a ready-made WO II to complete the
establishment. This he did, a moustached and double-chinned
bluffer to whom Ben took a great dislike. Welsh enmities are
highly irrational, even doglike. Ben would come back to billets
from the Welsh Club in Irishtown, drunk on Scotch whisky, and
fight this new man. This new man, whose name was Frank
Barton, would not wish to fight back. He preferred the weapons
of intrigue. Ben would get himself into trouble on odd visits to
Spain or be sent to shore insensible from a shipboard bout with
petty officers or be found drunk and bleeding outside the Rock
Hotel, which, out of bounds to Other Ranks, he had attempted
to enter. These escapades did not affect his mathematics. WO II
Barton would report them, nevertheless, to the major, just as he
would report that Sergeant Stephens and I were still in bed. There
came a time, very much a signal of the war's end, when WO I's
were permitted to wear a collar and tie with their battledress, just
like commissioned officers, and Barton bitterly resented this. He
went to the medical officer and complained that the battledress
collar chafed his sensitive neck: he too was permitted to open his
buttons on to a shirt and tie. 'We'll stop this nonsense and collaborate,' he said to Ben, collars and ties confronting each other.
The next week WO II's were, sore neck or not, promoted to the
same gentility as their senior brothers. Barton was aware of a
damp victory.

Sergeant Stephens had, like myself, tramped the Rock to bring
enlightenment to the troops. Stephens was an experienced WEA
lecturer who had the gift of the *hwyl*. He maintained, like a good
professional, a high technical standard in the service of what he
knew was army nonsense, but he at length grew dispirited and
morose. News of the death of his new-born daughter came
through. She had been christened Lynn, not after my wife but
after an admired film actress named Lynn Bari: still, in that time
of superstition and buzz-bombs, the news was ominous to me. To
Stephens it was wretched enough to drive him to a demand
for compassionate leave which, naturally, Meldrum refused. The
dead could not be made undead, said Meldrum, with infuriating
reasonableness, the distraught wife would get over it. Stephens

succumbed to the squalor that, on that overcrowded and bug-ridden Rock, always lay lurking to trap the unwary. He ceased to wash his khaki drill. He grew tired of trying to keep the bugs at bay by the weekly burning of his iron cot in kerosene. The bugs lay nightly waiting for him in the bed crevices. In phalanxes they marched across the ceiling. Let them take possession of the world.

He and I still messed with the First Herts, clean soldiers who fought the bugs and prevailed. To me these decent unlettered infantrymen were sanity. They were hospitable to the naval petty officers and held gala nights for them in the sergeants' mess. Their RSM held on to decency by refusing to allow the petty officers to recite dirty monologues. 'No, gentlemen, not in my mess.' There were Saturday sessions of tombola. There was the band, from whose bandmaster I learned how to score for that strange stringless combination. I wrote a march. I wrote a retreat number for flutes and drums. Harry Walkling, with his four inverted stripes, was superb as drum major. He twirled his baton at the end of the Ceremony of the Keys, during which the garrison was symbolically locked against the enemy. He had swank, panache. And then the First Herts departed to fight, and the First Dorsets took over. Stephens and I now became old sweats learned in Rock lore, advisers on comportment. The Dorsets' band was slacker than the First Herts'. The new drum major did not throw his baton in the air. The NCOs were ancient and complained of the killing climb up the Casemates steps. Stephens and I grew old with them.

I made one last effort to free myself from Major Meldrum. He had appointed me editor of a magazine he wished to call *Gibraltar Education*. I preferred the title *Vista*, and a First Herts sergeant designed a superb cover for it. I envisaged sharp articles, scintillating book reviews, Eliotian poetry, Maclaren-Ross short stories. The project ended up as a kind of school magazine. Meldrum rejected my article on Hölderlin, of whom he had never heard, Private Chomutoc's brilliant survey of the work of Kafka, of whom he had never heard, and replaced these and other intellectual treats with pedestrian progress reports and dull forecasts of quantitative glory. Still, on the strength of this thwarted appointment, I applied eagerly for the post of editor of the magazine called *The Rock*, openly advertised in garrison orders. Meldrum, who had driven me into being qualified for it, opposed my appointment, and one of the journalistic Cudlipps got the job. From then on I bowed to circumstance and, along with the Germans, ceased to fight.

It was 1945. In January US forces landed on Luzon, Warsaw was captured by the Russians, and the Burma road was reopened. In February the Yalta Conference sold half of Europe to the Russians and Dresden was bombed. In March the allies took Cologne. In April the Russians invaded Vienna and the Americans Okinawa. Roosevelt died. The Americans and Russians linked up in Germany. In May the German armies in Italy surrendered, Berlin was taken by the Russians, Rangoon was captured by the British, the German forces in north-west Germany, Holland and Denmark surrendered, and (the 8th) the end of the European war was declared. Gibraltar, like the other democracies, celebrated VE Day. Major Meldrum conceded that the troops would prefer to get drunk rather than hear about the British Way and Purpose, and he even cancelled the evening classes.

I CELEBRATED VE Day by going to jail. It was a Spanish jail, so there was no true disgrace in it, but it made me unavailable for the British Way and Purpose for a day or so. My crime had been to uphold the democratic philosophy in a bar in La Linea and, outside this bar, declare to the Spanish citizens that Generalissimo Franco was, among other things, a foul *cabròn*. Members of the *Guardia Civil* heard this and dragged me to a dirty lock-up. They did this with apologies: heads of state, whatever we privately think of them, must not be publicly traduced. I shared a cell with a very fat Andalusian whose crime was not political but was not otherwise clear. He was on the best of terms with his jailors, and his little daughter, whom he kissed with tears presumably because of her referred disgrace, brought him cheese, sausage, black bread, and a flask of fortified wine. These he divided with me. The little jail, adjunct of a police station, served no food except a morning mug of coffee, tepid and sugarless. The fat man, after his meal, sang flamenco – 'My mother-in-law is dead – long live gaiety' – and then snored. I expected to appear before a magistrate, but the Falange believed in rough justice: lie in the straw with the rats and think things over. Having congratulated me on our victory in the west, the police accepted my remaining pesetas and waved me off.

One had to wear civilian clothes to cross the frontier. I had none of my own and had borrowed some when I could stand VE Day in Gibraltar no longer. It was damnably depressing. Barrels of Simmonds's beer, hidden against the event, were rolled into the Alameda Gardens, and soldiers and sailors got drunk together before they fought, fought before they passed out. Ben Thomas and I, visiting mess after mess, were afflicted with the same Celtic fantasy: we could smell the corpses of the slain burning on the north wind. The war was over, but at what a cost. In the sergeants' mess of the First Tunnelling Company we saw an unburnt corpse being carried drunkenly out: it was of a veteran Irish staff-sergeant who had had the last of his nightly colloquies with leprechauns. His liver had long collapsed and now his celebrating heart had given up. I climbed on the billiard-table and delivered an all-purpose funeral oration. I was thrown out. Spain was a refuge.

Goering, questioned before his trial about Germany's biggest mistake in the conduct of the war, said that Hitler had been foolish in not marching through Spain and taking Gibraltar. It had obviously been thought about. Shortly after Germany's defeat the Ferdinand and Isabella Plan was discovered, and the translation of it into English was handed over to young Tom Frank, a British gunner on the Rock who was a German national. I helped to gorblimey it into official English. The Intelligence officer who commissioned the work was honoured and promoted; Tom Frank remained an undecorated gunner, but I soon had him teaching elementary German in the Educational Corps. The captured document was, in the Teutonic manner, pedantically detailed, and it even said who would ride with whom in the triumphal procession through Main Street or *Hauptstrasse*. The point is that Spain was always a potential menace, and that was why there were so many of us sucking sour oranges. One of the great jokes of infantry marches as far as Four Corners and back was to pretend to be about to cross the frontier and, at the last moment, smartly about turn. But the troops on the whole felt rather friendly towards Spain. The girls there slept with them, though for money, while the Gibraltar girls were aloof and had money enough, thank you, of their own. The Spaniards were real Iberians and the Gibraltarians merely imitation ones. There was the sense of a full-blooded culture beating in Adalusia, while the Rock scorpions had only the culture of trade, bankbooks, and London matric. The Gibraltarians produced no art, yet they

despised their cousins over the border as ignorant serfs who lacked
the benefits of britannicisation. The poor workmen of Gibraltar
were daily Spaniards who drank impotable water from the yard
taps and ate a crisp substance lacking nutrition and called fried
air. Every Gibraltar enterprise, including Army Education, had
its ill-paid *hombre*, and *hombre* was a term of contempt.

To visit La Linea in the forties was to feel glum at the aftermath
of a wasteful war, with whining widows skulking behind the
carious façade of the Centre of Culture and Rest. The streets
were potholed and the drains stank, and ragged urchins howled
for *peniques*. The town was full of mantillaed prostitutes for the
servicing of the British troops, and not all were habituated to the
trade: there were too many young women whose husbands had
been killed or imprisoned or had taken to the hills and corkwoods
in defiance of the regime: they needed the pesetas for which they
hired themselves out. The army, if not the Lieutenant-Governor's
lady, recognised the need for carnal relief. Not only did it issue
condoms, it provided a little pocket inside the fly of the service
trousers for storing them, the pocket FL. It issued tubes of
prophylactic ointment and had built a kind of venerean bus shelter
with running water for the laving of the penis, midway between
the Spanish frontier and the North Shore airfield.

Carnal relief was not and never will be enough. It is shameful
to engage in a simulacrum of love for money, and I still feel
shame at having carried an urgency over the border to discharge
in a wretched room smelling of garlic and cheap scent. And yet I
have learned to associate garlic with the erotic and to feel excited
in retrospect at the sound of Andalusian Spanish in the mouth of
a girl. The Gibraltarians reeked of garlic too and spoke the same
dialect, but their women were respectable and wanted marriage
with a decent soldier of acceptable rank and a future in civvy
street. The men of Gibraltar, with the right exogamic instinct,
sought their wives in Spain and turned them into Gibraltarians.
So I, a well-spoken sergeant, was invited to tea to meet musky
daughters and take them to the cinema afterwards. It was assumed
that I was unmarried. Perhaps the news had been passed from
Major Meldrum to the front office that I was a widower, a matter
of confusing Stephens's dead Lynn with my injured homonym or
near. One invitation came from an Irish police sergeant with
crossed swords above his stripes to show he was a physical training
instructor: he was known as *el tio con los sabres*. His daughter was
a pretty Hibernico-Spaniard whom I had taught. I grew worried

at the third invitation and brought my injured wife into the talk. I was kicked out at once as a philanderer, muscles under the sabres. My ineligibility was passed on, and there was no more tea in tiny flats on Castle Steps or Hampton Ramp.

With these Gibraltarian families one could speak English, except, sometimes, with the mother. I knew enough Spanish to converse over the border, but with most of the troops there was only the lingua franca of jigajig. The more decent of them wanted a better rapport; they even felt there was a sort of indecency in imposing the English tongue, as well as an English body, on those poor girls. In other words, there was a motivation behind the Spanish classes held on the Rock, but there was a big difference between the Spanish of Hugo's primer and the local dialect, which turned *España* into *Epaña* and confused *ll* and *y*, so that *calle* was *caye* and *yo* became *llo*. A music hall artist from Madrid was booed in a Gibraltar theatre because he pronounced *facil* as *fathil*. It was the problem of teaching uneducated men how to grapple not just with dialectal subtleties but with the whole strange corpus of a foreign tongue that led me in a particular pedagogic direction. It was to produce eventually a book called *Language Made Plain*.

As Army Education expanded, specialist departments grew. The emphasis was on the practical – plumbing, woodwork, commercial art – and the more humane subjects became a sideshow, but I was encouraged to create a department of languages. Men who thought a London school certificate might be useful needed a language, and while Spanish, the contiguous one, kept in the lead, there was a call for French, German, Russian and even Dutch. Skilled linguists began to emerge from the rank and file, private soldiers who had suffered six years' waste. One man, the son of an operatic impresario, had mastery of five tongues, including Russian. My old French tutor at Manchester University, Colin Smith, a lance-corporal in Intelligence (hardly a single Spanish speaker had been sent to Gibraltar) was only one of the French experts. I even found teachers in Hungarian and Finnish, though there was no one for them to teach. But the whole project of trying to bring ordinary uncultivated Englishmen into Europe through at least a smattering of one of the European tongues did not have much success. Nobody in British education had ever thought much about language teaching.

The army produced a number of moderately useful primers, all about a couple of soldiers called Bill and Jock who happened to find themselves in France or Germany or Russia. The Forces Education Broadcasts of the BBC were a help. I remember one highly dramatic broadcast in which Bill and Jock were taught the difference between separable and inseparable particles in German. 'You have plenty of these good English cigarettes,' coos a German tout. 'You ought to advertise.' Jock says: '*Nein. Wir anzeigen nicht.*' Old Professor Muller hears him and says: '*Ach, nein,* Jock. It must be *wir zeigen nicht an.* Let us take a beer in this hostelry *Zum Tiefen Keller* and I will teach you.' Few of our German language students in Gibraltar got as far as that. Most were bogged down in the basic principle of gender. They just could not see why one word had to be masculine and another feminine and, in German, yet another neuter. One student puzzled over *das Pferd* and asked Tom Frank if all the horses were castrated in Germany. My approach was as gross as the one I had used with my illiterates when teaching the alphabet. I would say that some cultures were so obsessed with sex that sex entered into things that had no sex. Thus, a pencil was like a prick and hence was properly *el lapiz* or *le crayon.* Water was rightly feminine: you could dip your wick in it. Discussing this technique – prick-words and cunt-words – in the Army Education office, I disgusted a high Anglican clerk who spoke like a bishop. He asked for transfer and told the major why. This, naturally, did me no good.

But, as in marital sex, language teaching can know no limitations of propriety. Any device can serve if it drives home a linguistic truth. Even the kind of abstruse knowledge that most language primers abhor may be used. To relate the pronunciation of Chaucer's English to that of Italian or Spanish at least, if only historically, naturalises the exotic. To demonstrate that Old English had genders until, around 1066, Englishmen were forced to turn their language into a creole in order to cope with the Danish and Norman invasions, can, again, relate one phase of English to its European sisters. But, at the level and with the material my language department had for its work, there was no way out of the true problem. Not even erotic motivation is enough: a man will only learn a foreign language when his life, or livelihood, depends on it. I was to see this very clearly when I went to Malaya.

More important, anyway, than anything the Army Education Scheme could offer was the business of getting the residual war over, Churchill out, and home. In preparation for the general election of summer 1945, we began to receive propaganda from rival parliamentary candidates. The only address I had was that of my wife's parents, and so I was in the constituency of Bedwellty in Monmouthshire or Gwent. The Labour candidate was a dodderer named Sir Charles Edwards, certain of being returned; the Conservative was an army officer whose brochure began 'Mr Churchill asks you to vote for Captain Threlfall'. There again was the fissure in British society. Nobody seemed to realise that the election was powered by a negative purpose, at least in the services – getting Churchill out. Churchill did not realise it himself. He wept at a defeat he did not foresee. When the troops of Gibraltar went in July 1945 to the polling booths (and here was a sight unprecedented: drawn bayonets guarding the ballot boxes), the vote was almost totally for Labour. Some historians have seen the Labour victory as a triumph for ABCA and the British Way and Purpose: not so. There was nothing political in it other than a vague wash of utopianism. The men wanted to get home, and Churchill wanted them to stay put. As simple as that.

As for getting home, it was going to be a slow business whoever was in power. The War Office issued a pamphlet outlining the release scheme. More important than the words was a numerical chart. There were two coordinates – age and length of service – and these met in a numbered release group. It was the task of unit officers to explain the scheme and dole out the numbers, but I unofficially took on the job myself, using British Way and Purpose sessions for the purpose and getting more attention than ever before in my instructional career. Of course, the release numbers were unattached to any calendar date: 25 got out of the army before 26, but nobody knew when this would be. My own number was 30, and I was not to be released until May 1946, The state was high-minded about not wanting to flood the market with the demobbed: gently does it. The men were not convinced.

The men heard about the Labour landslide on July 26, 1945, with 'The Red Flag' sung in the House of Commons and Mrs Bessie Braddock MP bouncing her fat in the Speaker's chair to inaugurate a new era. Two weeks later, nuzzling oranges or picking the pips out of pomegranates, they saw on the cinema screen the devastation of Hiroshima. This awed them: the nature of the new era had changed overnight. Nothing in ABCA or BWP had prepared them for this. Ben Thomas Maths now revealed himself as a physicist. I can still hear his Welsh voice speaking a stressless English in which emphasis was provided by obscenity, explaining it all with the aid of a blackboard: 'If the material is pure fucking uranium then the neutrons enter other fucking nuclei, making more fucking fissions and more released fucking neutrons. Then you get a branching chain of nuclear fission and so much fucking energy that in theory, in theory mind, there is no reason why the whole 'orld should not dissolve into heat, light and fucking sound.' So the world war was really over, and the bloody-minded would no longer have the Nips, dirty little fighters, dangled at them like poisonous puppets. In the weekly meeting in the Education Office I lighted a cigarette without permission and gave Major Meldrum a sour grin.

The growth in the AEC establishment had been so rapid that I did not know some of the personnel. There was a plumber WO II with dust on his crowns who greeted the new era without aitches, and there was a WO II of very vague qualifications and a Birmingham accent whose promotion had to be regarded as a marital necessity. I heard him as an RE sapper announcing that he was the man who had fulfilled every soldier's ambition, that of fucking the RSM. He had in fact married a WO I of the ATS and now, only a notch lower (that would soon be put right), he could fuck her with a better grace. There were other new instructors who looked like East End wide boys (I fancy there was one who taught hairdressing). My own recommendations for induction had mostly been overruled – our lance-corporal expert on Hegel and McTaggert, an MA in English, a Royal College of Music teacher of counterpoint – but not even Major Meldrum could deny that Sergeant Tom Frank, being German, knew German. Meanwhile a huge Command library was being shelved by corporal librarians – a Chinese dictionary, a three-volume guide to Florentine incunabula, other works which it became a pious duty to steal – and trombones and xylophones which no one would ever play were being locked into storerooms.

Major Meldrum, of his kindness, now proposed sending on Army Education courses in the United Kingdom such of the older personnel as had high release group numbers. These courses would entitle them to a month's disembarkation leave: the course was a mere disregardable pretext. He was rewarding his pets, and I was not among them. He regarded 27 as a high release number. With joy I allowed him to make arrangements for the sailing dates of the lucky ones, and then I threw the little bomb of my own 30. He was embarrassed. He said: Are you sure that is your number? I replied: Naturally, we are all capable of error, but here is one error I am unlikely to make. He was speedily on the telephone. I was to get leave, without the appendage of a course, before Christmas. First, though, I had to do a week's weapon training.

I suppose that that was as good a time as any to start handling weapons. The shooting match was over, so I had to learn to shoot. The logic of the army was, and probably still is, of a profoundly mystical nature. That AEC instructors were also combatants had been made clear on the Gibraltar victory parade, when three of us had marched with pistols in our holsters. It was realised just before this event that the AEC had no regimental march, so it was suggested by the bandmaster of the Dorsets that I speedily harmonise and orchestrate 'Lillibulero'. But that, with the dwarfs' work-song from *Snow White* as trio, had just been pre-empted by the Royal Electrical and Mechanical Engineers. So I arranged 'An Apple for the Teacher', a song made popular by Bing Crosby. Some obscure machinery in the higher command made a connection between marching armed AEC sergeants and weapon training, and here I was, firing at the butts with Sten gun and Bren, getting a marksman's score with the latter. This presumably qualified me to shoot up my wife's lovers on leave. There was a lot of that going on.

I SAILED WITH other leave-men on an old French tub with a Chinese crew. There were no bunks or hammocks, so we slept on the decks of saloons stripped down to function while rats jumped and played about us. There were a lot of rats, encouraged to breed by the Chinese cooks, and these seemed to be our main item of diet. At least, the corpses in the savoury stews we were served were too small to be those of rabbits. We shrugged and chewed. They would be clean rats anyway, well nourished on soya flour, none of your sewer horrors. We could also eat the hands of bananas that some men had shouldered aboard as gifts for their families. The three-week voyage (the engines kept breaking down) over-ripened the fruit: it would reach port as mush and had best be eaten. A pity. The generous men had cleaned out the fruit-shops. The one book on Gibraltar that most reading troops on the Rock knew had been written by a civilian, and it began: 'It is good to sit outside the Rock Hotel and watch the drab tommies sweating up the hill.' It ended with the author's sending one solitary banana home to his son. The drab tommies were not like that. As well as bananas they proposed smuggling small birds and animals into England – a marmoset, chirping canaries, a chameleon. These poor creatures all died on the voyage and were tearfully committed to the deep before the Chinese cooks could get hold of them.

There was a small ship's library and, bafflingly, this contained three copies of Rex Warner's novel *The Aerodrome*. I had not had the time for keeping up with contemporary literature on the Rock, but I knew that the great influence on writers like Warner and William Sansom was Franz Kafka. Kafka was hard to get hold of, but the British allegorists were a way into him. It had not been, for me, a very literary war. I clung to my *Finnegans Wake*, determined to get to the bottom of it (or should I say the inverted delta of it?) and *Ulysses* had a new meaning, since its heroine was a daughter of Calpe. Joyce had got his Gibraltar right without visiting it, and some of my Gibraltarian friends were surprised at references to people they had known – Mrs Opisso, for instance, whose son objected to Molly Bloom's derision of the name. But Joyce had got Molly all wrong and had probably mistaken the rank of her father. Brian Tweedy, represented as a major, would not have fathered a girl who spoke pure Dublin. Even as a sergeant-major (his probable appointment) married to a Spanish woman (again unlikely: he would probably have married a Gibraltarian) he would have come home daily to hear his little girl lisping Spanish, which Molly seems to have learned from Hugo's primer. That last chapter of *Ulysses* is based on a brilliant bluff. What is curious is the fact that Joyce the traveller never showed any desire to visit the Rock.

There was little literature, apart from the stories of Julian Maclaren-Ross, which spoke directly to the soldier. The war novels were to come later, and they were to come mainly from America. The books I was reading at war's end were of a pacific nature – Eliot's *Four Quartets*, at last completed, Auden's *New Year Letter* and Cyril Connolly's *The Unquiet Grave*. Even Waugh's *Brideshead Revisited*, which the soldier-author had gained an extended leave to write, was a gross exercise in nostalgia. There was no imaginative reconstruction of the puzzled life of the other ranks. A certain amount of writing had been done on the Rock, and the magazine *The Rock* had even published a supplement called *Poetry Gibraltar*. This was of low content, but

Tambimuttu had (I sent home a copy) been excited by the title. I had trounced the mean quality of the verse in an article and gained enemies. But I seemed to justify my attitude by winning the Governor's Poetry Prize of a guinea or so (soon drunk up). The judge was Christopher Hassall, Ivor Novello's lyrist ('Shine through my dreams and once again / Slowly and secretly / Whisper your love to me'), who found that my work evoked more than it said. My poem was, is:

> Useless to hope to hold off
> The unavoidable happening
> With that frail barricade
> Of week, day or hour
> Which melts as it is made,
> For time himself will bring
> You in his high-powered car,
> Rushing on to it,
> Whether you will or not.
>
> So, shaking hands with the grim
> Satisfactory argument,
> The consolation of bone
> Resigned to the event,
> Making a friend of him,
> He, in an access of love,
> Renders his narrow acres
> Golden and wide enough.
>
> And this last margin of leaving
> Is sheltered from the rude
> Indiscreet tugging of winds.
> For parting, a point in time,
> Cannot have magnitude
> And cannot cast shadows about
> The final kiss and final
> Tight pressure of hands.

The last lines will not bear too close a logical scrutiny. Major Meldrum did not seem pleased with the award. It implied that his sergeants were more intelligent than his warrant officers. But perhaps creativity had nothing to do with intelligence.

We landed at Greenock, and those of us whose destination was South Wales were bundled together in a camp before being

marched to the train for Newport. Thus I became a kind of
honorary Welshman: 'Where 'oo goin' then, Taff? Blackwood, is
it? Never 'eard of the bloody place, fair play.' And then, when I
had handed over my nylon stockings and bottle of whisky and
unpacked my cigarettes (short as hell in Wales as elsewhere), my
wife and I could take a shy look at each other. I was thin. She
had plumped out: that would be the prescribed heavy liquid
intake, meaning beer by the pint. The bleeding continued. Sex?
The shyness of a two-year separation was bad enough; here was a
physical barrier to be confronted with both frustration and relief.
On the bedroom wall, temporarily hiding the framed ode to her
mother, Hazel, Lynne's sister, had pinned a coy welcome back to
the marital act: two ill-drawn corpses in tentacular embrace. This
was a splendid anaphrodisiac. For Lynne sex had already been
made cold and hence dirty. The explorations of the eminent
gynaecologist ('One finger professionally, gentlemen; two fingers
socially') had mechanically excited. We lay back to back, and I
caught a whiff of garlic and an Andalusian cackle. I should not
have come home. It was not just a matter of the problems of the
brief renewal of marriage. I had forgotten how cold a British
November could be; I did not like the Welsh children following
me with 'Got any gum, chum?'; I had not liked the pub near the
bus-stop in Newport, with its printed notice 'No whisky, brandy,
gin or stout. You put 'em in, you get 'em out'; I did not like the
post-victory cynicism under the dirty fog. I had had the feeling,
a sergeant in uniform with kitbag and full equipment, of being
derided in the streets. It's Tommy this and Tommy that and
Tommy go away. Soldiers belonged to the pre-atomic age. The
next morning I put on the pre-war civilian clothes that had been
sent from 47 Princess Road. I also put on an overcoat. We were,
Lynne said, to start on our travels.

We were about to travel to visit the man who loved her.
Whether she loved him in return was not yet certain. I was to
spend my leave being measured against him so that she could
make up her mind. I had suspected something like this. The British Way and Purpose had done nothing to deal with the fundamental British problem of marital readjustment after long
separation: that was at least as compelling as the Health Service
and the 1943 Education Act. Photographs of private soldiers who
had shot their wives and their wives' Polish and American lovers
had already been appearing on the front page of the *Daily Mirror*.
What went on in the ranks of the cultivated was subtler and pre-

sented no easy solution, but we were all starting to learn that love was only a durable fire if the man was there to fill the coal scuttle.

Travel? Hotels? Money? I did not have much, I was still only a sergeant. But Lynne was still with the Ministry of War Transport, though with little to do and gladly sent on a month's leave. She still had her flat on Barons Court Road. She also had a white mouse named Fitzroy which was to travel with us. It had been a comfort to her during the time of the V-2s, as also its black companion Cornwallis, which had disappeared. The mouse travelled in a cage in a military sidepack. Whose was the sidepack? Herbert had given it to her. So Herbert was in the army? Herbert was a major. More, he was a major in the Army Educational Corps. He was Major Williams, a Welshman from Tredegar and by way of being a remote cousin. She had met him at a party in London. He had given her dinner and taken her to a talk given by the poet Louis MacNeice. Then to the cinema to see Olivier's *Henry V* and to dinner again. Later he had declared love. Had they slept together? That was a question not to be asked. Not even by a lawful husband? Sleeping with people, she said, was obviously difficult. We were travelling in a cold train, exceptionally dirty, to Shrewsbury. Shrewsbury was the headquarters of Mid-West District, where Herbert was Deputy District Education Officer. Soon he was to move to the AEC Depot at Blackheath as Chief Instructor. He had done well, and with no better qualifications than myself. My rank still rankled.

We stayed at the Blue Posts in Shrewsbury. The manager took me on one side after registering. He wanted to ask a blunt question, he said. Was I in the forces? Yes, still. Did I wet the bed? There was a new world of frankness or insolence opening up. There were, the manager said, too many servicemen coming back wetting beds. Something to do with nerves or something. No, I did not wet the bed. Good. Sorry, but I had to ask. We put the mouse Fitzroy, trundling his exercise wheel, into the wardrobe of the chill room. Then we went to meet Major Williams in the saloon bar of the Loggerheads.

He was not prepossessing: older than myself, nearly bald, bespectacled, with a variety of facial tics. He winked involuntarily and that, I was to learn, had earned him a number of unsought conquests. He bit at flies, like Harold Foreman of the Xaverian. He had a voice of great charm. After six halves of bitter he told me he was in love with my wife. I replied in the manner of Coco in *The Mikado*. Lynne, standing by the fireplace with her two halves in lieu of an unpermitted pint, looked at me in disgust: I had been expected to make some highly possessive avowal. But I was not ready for that. Then a wing-commander walked in and ordered Lynne to get away from the fire. I thought at first he was pulling rank, but he was expressing the new spirit of socialism. 'We're in charge now,' he said, straddling the fireplace. 'The time for you people is all over.'

The trouble with Herbert Williams was that I liked the man. He liked me too. We had a common background of humane studies. We both knew Latin, which Lynne did not, and could quote Catullus and Seneca at each other. He had a good tenor laugh. One could play music on the triangle, as in the Scherzo of Liszt's E flat Piano Concerto. The three of us were a *Gestalt*. This happens not infrequently in love struggles: the lover is not merely a foil to the husband and wife, he is a kind of a sounding-board, complement, completion, solvent of marital boredom. But there was an older and grimmer ethos poking me in the shoulder – whispers of cuckoldry, sneers about the *Hausfreund* and the complaisant husband. I had not expected my leave to be that kind of marital comedy. I lay awake wondering about it, listening to Fitzroy treadling his mill. It was not the future yet. The future would begin sometime in 1946. I had to end my leave not so much with the conquest of a rival as an assurance to my wife that I cared enough to fight, or rather that I was worthy of an opponent with whom I had not yet properly engaged. Women love to be fought over, but the more cultivated woman prefers the fight to be, as on the stage, a witty logomachy. Herbert Williams knew all about logomachies, having taken his degree in classics. He raised the big question when we all got to London: who was to sleep with her? That was gross. He was clearly biting his nails in his officer's bedroom at Eltham Palace, Blackheath, entertaining visions of Lynne and myself rolling over each other in the top floor flat on Barons Court Road. But we were chaste enough, had to be: the dysmenorrhoea was flooding and she had to be fed with Sir Charles Dodd's synthetic oestrogen known as stilboestrol. But that she and her major had been sleeping together I had no doubt. There were more kinds of sexual congress than the one grudgingly permitted by the Catholic Church.

The coarse soldier's dream was unfulfilled. Get up them stairs. Your battledress is wet. Yes, she was in the bath when I got home. It was best to be drunk most of the time, in the Rathbone Place pubs which (Julian Maclaren-Ross at his accustomed corner,

Mrs Stewart doing her nightly crossword, a fatter Dylan reciting 'The Green Eye of the Little Yellow God') breathed the comfort of continuity. Best to flop into bed incapable. I would be glad to be back sucking oranges. London was big and dirty and rude and full of civilians who had done well out of the war. There had, during that war, been a unified spirit, a civic soul, which the ham-fisted government had tried to personify in a character called Billy Brown of London Town. He had been a cartoon figure in tube trains: 'So let's all move along, says Billy. To block the entrance up is silly.' To which the pencilled reply had been: 'You may be right without a doubt, But how the hell do I get out?' Billy Brown, in City bowler and striped trousers, was no more. The new Londoner was the spiv, the wide boy, with a corner in nylons or battered cans of condensed milk. There was no heat, and I had grown used to the sun. I wanted to get back.

At the terminal in Liverpool from which I was to sail, I read WELCOME HOME LADS AND A MERRY XMAS. I was to spend my third Christmas in Gibraltar. Some who should were not to. A number of the leave-men had gone missing. That was to be expected. I was put in charge of ten men of the draft and lost one of them. The bloody war was over, wasn't it? Yes, it was, an abominable interlude that upset regular military routine. Now, even for conscripts, real soldiering could begin. An earnest of this on the ship was compulsory PT. Peace was a terrible softener to them what had not soldiered proper. There were three very young AEC sergeants on the boat, replacements or augmentations, and one of them was a very Nordic ballet dancer named Reg Hanson. I was absolutely sure that his skill had not specifically been indented for. Bricklaying, yes, but not ballet. The ship was large and crammed with troops as for a south European invasion. There was a cinema, and we were paraded to watch Danny Kaye and the Goldwyn Girls. 'Fucking lovely they are,' said a wistful sergeant whose leave must have been as frustrated as my own. At night the ship blazed over the Bay of Biscay. Men neurasthenically responded with 'Put them bloody lights out' before realising that the bad days were all over and worse days were beginning. There is nothing like a war for bringing both drama and dramaturgy into dull lives. The drama is substance, the dramaturgy a shape. Life had grown shapeless. The leave-men had had a foretaste of the future and did not like it. When the Rock loomed in Christmas sunlight the new boys sang Cole Porter's 'Don't Fence Me In.' Those returning yearned towards it as to a mother.

My companions of the draft of 1943 had all gone home, with the exception of Wilkinson, who had apparently gone to his death among the snakes and leeches. WO II Barton was now a WO I. There was another WO I, a Liverpudlian named Fazackerley, who had arrived as a sergeant and shot up during my absence. He stuttered and hence could not instruct. His place was the front office, though his left-handed scrawl was unreadable. There seemed to be little for me to do. I was, to Major Meldrum, an embarrassing reminder of the primitive days of educational *bricolage*. He did not want to see me. He did not want to see anybody except the two SO III's who executed his orders. One of these was a wet-toothed former gunner who said 'Get your finger out' and 'How many bods on the register?' and 'Put them in the picture.' The other was a willowy sapper named Captain Taylor, an intellectual Methodist who called his underlings by their Christian names. He ordered me to supervise the unloading by swarthy *hombres* of a new cargo of textbooks on Sinology and Campanography. I let the men go off during the lunch hour. They did not come back and I was blamed. Captain Taylor said: 'I've a good mind to put you on a charge. Don't you see how I hate enforcing discipline, but you leave me no alternative. And please wipe that truculent scowl off your face.'

'What precisely would the punishment be if I were put on this charge? Sir.'

'A severe reprimand. Entered on your crime sheet. It would do you no good in civilian life, you know.'

So there it was. Our peacetime careers were to represent no new start. The army was to pursue us.

I said: 'And if I report to Eltham Palace that the only work you can find for me to do is the supervision of Spanish *obreros*?'

'You have no such right. And you will not be insolent. Oh, John, John, can't you see that you force me into an attitude that is totally contrary to my nature? Apologise for your dereliction of duty and we will say no more about it.'

'*Peccavi. Mea culpa, mea culpa, mea maxima culpa.* Sir.' To call him *Domine*, the bloody fool, would have been going too far. I was glad, though, that he had called up Eltham Palace from my memory of leave. My wife's lover was a power at Eltham Palace. I might, with luck, frustrate the future career of the regular officer Meldrum.

Among the unladed gifts from the War Office was a huge wad of thirty-stave scoring paper. I set up a table for myself in

the Command library and began to compose a symphony in A
minor. A petty officer appeared with a cello in a ship's carpenter's
coffin. I dropped the symphony and started to write a cello concerto. I wrote an orchestral overture called *Gibraltar*. I wrote a
choral setting of Wilfred Owen's 'Anthem for Doomed Youth'.
All this, I told the snooping officers, was legitimate work: why
else had so much scoring paper been travelling the high seas? I
was left alone. I was left alone to organise musical appreciation
on the Rock. I built up huge weekly audiences for gramophone
concerts at the YMCA. I revivified the Gibraltar Musical Society.
I became a free agent of the arts. I covered the walls of the AEC
physics laboratory with a mural representing the story of organic
life. I became film critic for the *Gibraltar Chronicle*.

The *Gibraltar Chronicle*, founded in 1707, was the oldest daily
newspaper in Europe. The technology of its production was primitive – a flat-bed press in a damp cellar – but, thanks to the literacy
of its army staff, it was a superior production to the *Daily Mirror*.
If I used words like 'orotundity' in my copy or referred to Martha
Raye's 'pectoral and buccal amplitude' no blue pencil intervened.
What I wrote was printed entire. I had a free pass to the four
cinemas of Gibraltar, and the best, the Naval by the Calpe United
football stadium, often had European premières. Gibraltar, then,
was no cinematic backwater, and what I was practising was
serious, if unpaid, journalism. But it was a temptation to encode
messages of insult to the staff officers of the AEC. The acrostic
remains the best cryptogram. I achieved the following in a notice
of a Frank Sinatra film: 'Mellifluous, emitting long-drawn
roulades, undoubtedly magical is Sinatra, a fine unassuming
comedian, kicker in nobody's goal, fool (ostensibly) of love.' This
made so little sense that any intelligent reader would naturally
look for a hidden message. Only a sick bay attendant at North
Shore wrote in objecting to the obscenity. Major Meldrum was
unknown to him.

The irony of my terminal situation on the Rock was that it
was my free activities that gained Meldrum the reputation for
cultural energy and educational achievement. What many could
not understand was why a mere sergeant was scintillating when
dull warrant officers taught elementary arithmetic or stuttered on
the telephone. It must have been galling for Meldrum to receive
blunt reports of the low quality of the British Way and Purpose
sessions from the units of the Rock and a demand that someone of
my expertise and experience be sent to harangue them. It was

better in the old days, they said. They did not much care for
these youngsters of the egalitarian future, in whom mediocrity
was to be accounted a democratic virtue. The Pay Corps refused
to have any educational sessions at all unless they could have me.
Meldrum, embarrassed, called me in and asked if I would accept
promotion. I replied that such acceptance would seem to condone
his policy and his evaluation of merit. 'It would mean more
money,' he said feebly. It was, in fact, his best argument. I
unpicked my stripes and became a warrant officer. It meant more
money.

I received letters from Lynne reporting that, according to the
gynaecologists, what her condition needed was domestic calm in
a good climate. 'Why not a year or so in Gibraltar? You could
get a civilian job there and married quarters, and we could visit
Spain and North Africa and drink sherry and eat grilled swordfish
and lounge in the sun.' She was telling me all about it. Come to
sunny Gibraltar where you already are. I visited Mr Withers, an
epicene with a goatee at the British Council, but he said that my
school and university were against me. I approached Dr Soames,
the head of civilian education, and he thought that there might
be a vacancy for a promoter of higher studies. Wait. And then
Captain Taylor decided to organise what he called a Speaker's
Eisteddfod. There would be political speeches, speeches for the
prosecution and the defence of imaginary criminals, so long as
the crimes were not obscene, recitations of prose and verse.
Anybody could enter. He said coyly that he had heard I was
conducting an affair with a Spanish lady, and I was the obvious
expert for the choosing of poems for the Spanish verse-speaking
section.

This affair with the Spanish lady was providing me with the
friendly sexual relief I could get neither at home nor in the
brothels of La Linea. The lady was less a lady than a singing
artiste from Granada who had a three months' contract to perform
at the Universal Café or UV. Her name was Conchita, she was
ten years older than myself, maturely beautiful, especially when
dressed to sing '*Epaña, nuetra madre*' in national costume. She had a
room in a boarding house and a desire to learn English. We sat
on the bed for the conduct of our lessons. She tried to offer me
hard-earned *libras* and *chelines*, but I would not accept them.
Friendship, I said. Ah yes, *amistad, intimidad*. That *intimidad*,
with its *News of the World* overtones, led to our using the bed not
for instruction in English. I had a mistress, at least until the ter-

mination of her contract. Sex was the warm world of garlic, the newsvendors calling *Calpense* (the local Spanish language paper) in the lazy afternoon, her and my pleasant Catholic guilt. She did not turn me into an expert on Spanish poetry. Rather, she learned about Spanish poetry for the first time when, in naked languor, she listened to my reading from the *Oxford Book of Spanish Verse* – Lorca, Gongora, St John of the Cross. She loved Lorca's '*La Casada Infiel*'. This I submitted to Captain Taylor, also '*En una Noche Oscura*'. The poems were set.

Unfortunately Gibraltarian schoolchildren were permitted to enter the Speaker's Eisteddfod, and these were taught by Irish Christian Brothers who were appalled by my choice of poems. Severe letters were sent to the civilian head of education and Major Meldrum. Lorca's poem, glorifying adultery, was disgusting; moreover, the man was a communist. The poem by San Juan de la Cruz, though mystical in intent, was understood by the ignorant as a celebration of physical love. To invite innocent schoolchildren to be soiled by Lorca's filth (communist filth) and a distressingly carnal mystical effusion, even from a saint, was probably to commit the sin against the Holy Ghost. The person who had chosen these poems was a sinner and should, if justice were to be done, not be permitted to defile the Irish Catholic Rock further. 'A future here?' cried Dr Soames. 'You thought you had a future here?'

Captain Taylor was permitted early repatriation in order to be interviewed for the headship of a Methodist college. I sought the same privilege to take the examination for the post of interpreter at the International Labour Office in Montreal. Nothing doing. There would be plenty of good jobs going for men who had served under Major W. P. Meldrum, OBE. That officer naturally foresaw a good job going in a wider territory than Gibraltar for himself. Little did he know that Major Herbert Williams was already at work frustrating his ambition. I completed my tour on the Rock if not gloriously then loudly. An artificer sergeant of the REME built for the YMCA a record-player of an unprecedently blasting kind, and eardrums were shattered with Beethoven's Ninth Symphony. Part of the Rock fell down. Conchita's contract came to an end and she went back to Granada. On Franco's radio I heard her sing my song '*Muchísimas Gracias*'. Release group 30 packed its kitbags and strapped contraband wristwatches all up its forearms. I spent my last evening in La Linea, with the Birmingham WO II scuttling after me crying: 'Don't do it. Think of your wife. You'll get a dose.' The ship hooted in. One May morning we boarded. We sailed. The Rock sank, englutted to soft chords, raising not a bubble.

'A very popular line this in peacetime,' appraised a gunner who had worked for Cook's. Goanese stewards played the first bars of 'In the Mood' on their dinner carillons. Everybody looked north with hope and dread. Tom Frank sang '*Sous les Toits de Paris*' in German:

> *In Paris, in Paris*
> *Sind die Mädels so süss*
> *Dann sie flüstern:*
> '*Monsieur, ich bin dein.*'

A Scottish sergeant worried about the glass eye which the army had issued him. He had lost the real one on the North Shore firing range. The army issue did not fit well: it fell on to his dinner plate and rested among the mashed potatoes like an Arab delicacy. A stout RASC private kept saying: 'A job? Me? What does the likes of me want with a job? One thing the army taught me is how to nick. I look forward to a life of nicking.' Another private daily tapped the badges of rank on my forearms. 'Them'll soon be off, major. Then you'll be no better than what I am.' We landed at London docks, and the first thing we saw ashore was a poster of an agonised widow over the slogan 'Keep Death Off the Roads'. Someone had scratched this out and substituted 'She Voted Labour'. We were all sent to the Demobilisation Centre at Aldershot. The whole procedure of discharge was gummed up when Tom Frank announced himself to be a German. It was assumed that everyone was British and that it had been the Germans we had been fighting. If you were British you could start getting money, a post office savings book, and a demob suit. If you were a German you were supposed to be over there receiving allied rehabilitation. 'Say you're British,' pleaded a carpet-slippered major. 'Just for the sake of getting this lot over.' But Tom Frank would not deny that he was of the race that had produced Beethoven and Goethe. We were slowed up.

So there, at length, it was. I was free and had an ill-made demob suit of a deplorable sick green colour to prove it. I had entered the army at the age of twenty-three and was now twenty-nine, approaching early middle age. It had been an inglorious war for me, a great deal of time wasted, and I had learned nothing. I had brought home with me the score of a violoncello concerto which eventually I would convert into a violin concerto for Yehudi Menuhin, and also an enhanced knowledge of the possible meaning of *Finnegans Wake*. This seemed insufficient capital for a civilian career. But first I had to thread through the maze of a baffling demobilisation leave.

LYNNE HAD CHANGED. The first thing I noticed about her flat on Barons Court Road was a double platoon of encrusted empty milk bottles. Her Welsh cleanliness seemed to have deserted her. She was plumper, drinking hard. She welcomed me, and a pair of size three Spanish shoes, not as a husband but as an addition to her male entourage. I arrived at her flat to find it empty of people, but soon people arrived whom I did not know. There was an out-of-work film actor named Wilf, who wanted to make a film about what happened in history to the treacherous thirty pieces of silver, with himself playing Judas. There was Dylan Thomas, fag stuck to blistered lower lip, afternoon-club-drunk. There was Eddie Williams, younger brother of Herbert Williams, manager of Grindlays Bank in Calcutta, home on leave. There was Lynne, pretty rather than beautiful with her plumpness, pert and swearing. I sat while a bottle of Kümmel was uncorked, an outsider, the uniform a joke, my rank an obscene joke, Dylan singing, fag on lip, 'Kiss me goodnight, sergeant-major, sergeant-major, be a mother to me'. Later Wilf was to say: 'When I first met you, there was a bloody sergeant-major around, what the fuck was he doing there?' We all went out to dinner in Soho, Eddie Williams paying, I handing round the Gibraltar cigars, Dylan warned twice by the management.

At night Lynne and I lay, me embarrassed, in her narrow bed. She was not embarrassed. She dealt briskly with my engorgement. The next morning I stayed in the flat, ostensibly to read *Animal Farm*, actually to disencrust the milk bottles under the cold water tap. She went out early. She had resigned from the Ministry of War Transport but had many things, unspecified, to do. Then she was to have lunch with Sonia Brownwell. We could not foresee any connection between that lovely blonde girl, later to be ravaged through drink, and my reading of *Animal Farm*. *Animal Farm* and the milk bottles had their own connection – the hopelessness of trying to cleanse sordor, the fatuity of utopias. The British utopia was, without bricks let alone straw, in the making. I wished I was back in Gibraltar. I even began a love letter to Conchita in Granada.

In the evening we were in the Dean Street pubs. There were three Williams brothers – Jim, the youngest, a medical officer just home from West Africa; Eddie, the bank manager, M.Sc. of Jesus College; Herbert, the major with the white mouse Fitzroy in his left breast battledress pocket. I now saw that there was a love triangle from which I was excluded. It was Herbert versus Eddie. Eddie wished to marry Lynne and take her back to India, warmer and fuller of amenities than my Gibraltar; Herbert wanted to thwart this. There was brief fraternal punching in the French House, the peeping white mouse carefully avoided. I stood with my half of bitter watching, fascinated. Then Eddie announced that we were all going to stay in a house in Henley-on-Thames, there to see the regatta and work out, in Welsh calm, this first problem of the peace. Eddie was small and plump but masterful. He was the manager of a great bank in a great Oriental city. Of the two, from Lynne's angle, I should have thought Herbert, who opposed classics to Eddie's mathematics, was the more congenial figure, despite the tics. Leaving the pub, he involuntarily winked at a prostitute. She, encouraged, followed. Discouraged, she called 'Fucking bastard'.

The house Eddie had rented for a month in Henley was stockbroker's baronial in a garden crammed with tiny frogs. He had not rented it entirely from his own pocket: a Grindlays manager from Poonah, also on leave, was splitting the cost. His name was George Tagg, and he had picked up a temporary mistress, a failed film actress named Gwen, much given to suicide attempts. She was a woman of great classical beauty who swore terribly. Female swearing seemed to be one of the attributes of the peace. A sly lad who boasted of how he had kept out of the services through pleading a gastric stomach delivered black market goods daily. Gwen and George Tagg shared the master bedroom. Lynne and I were permitted twin beds in a smaller room. Eddie slept chastely alone pending the great decision. Herbert came from Blackheath at weekends to try to resolve it. The situation was absurd besides, I suppose, immoral. But we had just emerged from a great war and moral standards were in a state of shock. Lynne wept nightly, using my arms for comfort. She did not know where she was. I knew where I was, and that was not in Gibraltar, with its processions in honour of the Sacred Heart and the mosquelike Anglican cathedral built by the Royal Engineers.

I had money. I could draw three pounds daily from any post office, a lot of money then, though not to Eddie Williams. I could go up to London alone to see *Caesar and Cleopatra*, that misguided conversion of a minor comedy into a Cecil B. De Mille epic which absorbed all the layabouts of London into its crowd scenes. I could, while there, see about jobs at the Labour Exchange. As I feared, there were no jobs. I had to apologise for having been in the army and failed to get myself qualified. Wing-commanders were moving into automobile sales rooms, though there were few automobiles to sell and a pitiable petrol ration. A demobbed warrant officer with an arts degree and no professional training did not even have wizard-prang glamour. In the factories, I gathered, there were many opportunities. A Ministry of Labour spokesman, with a genuine proletarian accent, had been sent to us in Gibraltar to tell us of industry crying out for workers. He had a story about two men he had triumphantly rehabilitated. One had lost his left arm and the other his right, and they had been set to work on a stamping press as a single operative though with a full wage each. Get into the factories, he counselled us. He as good as told our Ph.D. lance-corporal that he had nothing to lose but his aitches. As for the future of education, we were warned to beware of the airy-fairy. We had a Labour government now, grease-stained and armed with spanners, and education meant being down to earth. As for teachers, they had very weak trade unions and could not expect much of a future.

I was vaguely concerned about my own lack of a future, especi-ally as Lynne had reviled me about my inglorious army career and my failure to get her to the sun and the grilled swordfish. One night she even inveighed against both of us. 'We're cheap,' she said, 'cheap,' meaning that she had not been to Girton and I to Jesus College (which, as I reasonably pointed out, was reserved to Welshmen anyway). She meant also that she had been brought through her Ministry work in touch with men who had been to Eton and married Lady Cora Something. I felt she had a right to be taken by P and O first class to India by Eddie Williams and live a memsahib's life. That was why I did not fight much. But if anybody wanted a divorce, on what grounds could it be obtained, and how soon? Divorce judges were weeping about the huge number of service divorce writs, but these at least had been filed on the reasonable ground of adultery or desertion. I, clinging to my Catholic scruples, would never seek divorce; Lynne could not easily charge me with adultery or cruelty. 'You tried to rape me,' she said, 'when you came on leave.' That was untrue, a woman's half-dream half-nightmare. She admitted it was untrue: she had merely wished to hear what it sounded like. I watched the two Williams brothers quarrel for the possession of my wife, and approved the melodious stichomythia. It seemed to me that I was watching a play whose author I had at some time met in a London pub.

Meanwhile the Henley regatta was on, and it was hard to believe that there had ever been a war. Elderly military men trotted along the towpath crying 'Well rowed, I say.' John Betjeman was there preparing his poem about ATS without their hats calling Cheerio and Cheeribye. There was gin in the pubs. In the restaurant of the great hotel I ordered rabbit pie and wondered that it contained nothing but breast of chicken. It seemed like a breath-drawing interim before the harsh sumptuary laws by which, which it had not been during the war, bread was rationed and was one of the statutory three courses in restaurants, potatoes too were rationed (the wartime slogan had been 'Go easy on bread, eat potatoes instead'), whalemeat and canned snoek were staples, tough workers in pubs queued for lemonade, and the Welfare State was being painfully constructed. The tables of the great houses groaned with game while port was brought dusty from the cellar. The common people had a weekly smear of margarine and a slice or two of corned beef. The gap had not been narrowed much. When the Labour government announced its African groundnut scheme (the first great disaster of the peace), it was making an assumption that the British would never eat butter again and would spread their rationed bread with processed monkey nuts. War austerity became peace austerity, which was more austere, but caviare and pâté de foie gras were unrationed.

There was a writer already working on a novel which should present the ultimate austerity, whose properties he took from the years of the British peace. This was Orwell, whom I saw briefly at the Mandrake Club, which specialised in dubious gin flavoured with cloves and a large number of chessboards. It was run by a man named Boris. I had brought back with me from Gibraltar a number of tins of Victory cigarettes, which were a very briefly maintained army ration and were quite unsmokable. But I paid taxi fares with them. Orwell's noncommittal eye took in the tin I had on my table at the Mandrake, which became the Chestnut Tree Café, but did not accept a cigarette, preferring to roll his own. But his description of the Victory cigarettes in *Nineteen*

Eighty-Four is accurate, and his Victory gin is Boris's. Odd members of the club sat in dark corners doing chess problems. Occasionally there were chess tournaments. I was beaten in one of these by a refugee German master who handicapped himself with a German queen (queen removed and replaced with a rook). Meanwhile the saccharine water with its clove flavouring went round like a medicine, to become one of the tastes of Orwell's totalitarian future. The physical reality of his prophecy is, for me, set firmly in the forties, though it makes me shudder to remember that I pondered over chess moves in the Chestnut Tree Café. Orwell's power to ensour things was considerable. The song sung from the telescreen in that gin shop of the doomed goes 'Underneath the spreading chestnut tree I sold you and you sold me'. Orwell took it from a harmless boy scout ditty which George VI, in his capacity as scoutmaster, had made popular. We had watched and heard him leading it, fag in mouth, on the newsreels. The term Orwellian is wrongly applied to the future. It was the miserable forties that were Orwellian.

The Henley idyll, with its altercations and heavy drinking, came to an end. I had still not found a job. Lynne and Eddie Williams arranged to spend a kind of proleptic honeymoon in Eastbourne. What was to be done with me? Herbert Williams found a solution, perhaps to ease his own conscience. He had served in Shrewsbury under a certain Tony Scriven, now a lieutenant-colonel, who was running a Mid-West District School of Education near Wolverhampton. The two-week courses for potential sergeant-instructors of the AEC were, at that time, in the hands of the Workers' Educational Association, which Tony Scriven did not trust. It was all, he said, Marxist propaganda. He proposed courses in educational technique and subjects like Political Economy and International Affairs which should have a neutral, or right-wing, bias. He was an old soldier, risen from the ranks, loyal to the Crown and the Empire, with a German wife he had whipped to a like loyalty. So I was told. I had to travel to Brinsford Lodge, near Coven, and see whether he considered me eligible for running neutral or right-wing courses.

I travelled, and in Wolverhampton I saw the dark dwarfish *Urvolk* whom the invading Celts had driven from the fields to the smelting of iron. They were now making automobiles and bicycles, but they were still dark dwarfs. At Coven I learned that it had been rich in witches, and perhaps still was. At Brinsford Lodge, which I had expected to be a decayed mansion, I found what many supposed to be the pattern of the future – namely, a concentration camp of prefabricated huts, protected from flat uninhabited country by barbed wire. It had been built by the Ministry of Supply and housed both workers and functionaries of that branch of government, who took buses daily and came back to dine in an Ingsoc cafeteria. Lieutenant-Colonel Scriven had taken over one of the larger buildings and converted it into a centre of education. Students and instructors had cells in sleeping blocks. There was a dance hall that was also a theatre, and there was a club that followed pub licensing laws. Scriven had come from Shrewsbury to appraise me and to show me, with disguised disgust, the Marxist drivel that was being fed to the troops.

Scriven was a man of dark ferocity in perpetual pain from a back broken in action. He had, being a forceful infantry instructor, been turned into an army schoolmaster and later commissioned. One had to assume that his high rank reflected high academic qualifications, but it was difficult to be sure. He believed that university lectures were never less than two hours in length and he could not safely be contradicted. His Cockney lack of grammar had to be taken as normative, though his German grammar was good. He had a display of what were termed, in bold lettering, AUDAL AIDS. I had never met the term before and wondered, though not aloud, what it meant. He listened scornfully to a quite sensible account, from a dark, pretty WEA girl whose northern accent reminded me of that old WEA initiation, of the progress of nineteenth-century socialism. 'Balls,' he muttered and then 'Dangerous balls.' I sensed that he was not a man to be contradicted or even engaged in friendly dialectic. He said over tea and muffins: 'You're okay if Bill says so.' Bill was Herbert Williams. 'You'll have to come under Birmingham University Extra-Mural for appointment and pay, but don't forget the army's boss. Oh Jesus, this bloody pain in my bloody back.' I was sympathetic. A car came to take him back to Shrewsbury. I was to wait for something in writing.

The WEA course had come to an end, and only the dark pretty girl I had heard lecture was left behind. The rest, three gingerish men and a sloppy woman in beads, had gone off in a car. They had been very critical of T. S. Eliot and doubtful if good reactionary art was possible. The girl, Bridget, stayed the night with me in my cell in the male block. The wheel had come round again, except that she was teaching me nothing except the immeasurable gratitude of one who holds a pliant and eager girl's body in his arms. Well, there still seemed to be plenty of sex around, and it might last sometime into that phase of the peace termed normality if the Labour government did not ban it. Two could play at the fornication game. I had no doubt now that Lynne's coyness about sex was unconnected with her dysmenorrhoea. With some she was not coy.

But now I had nowhere to go except Eastbourne, where she was. I knew what hotel she was at, a good one apt for a nabob, and I would enjoy the drama of confrontation, perhaps in the double bedroom in the middle of the night. And then, on the train whose bright lights still looked like treason, I thought I would wait till the following morning, confrontation after a free breakfast, and spend the night, as if waiting for a dawn train, in Eastbourne railway station. But the station closed down after my train's arrival, and I was cast out on to the streets. I found a pub that provided bed and breakfast and woke up the landlady, a mature handsome woman named Mrs Brewster. She seemed ready to give more than a bed, but that may have been an inflamed illusion. She had a husband, Harley, a light sleeper. I slept late and did not engage the world till opening time. And at opening time Lynne and her nabob walked in, surprised but not guilty. They were already well known in this pub. 'Look, Harley,' Lynne cried to the landlord, 'my brother. You bad boy, why didn't you telephone that you were coming?' So my role was fixed for me: my wife's brother, Eddie Williams my (bad word in Hindi) brother-in-law. I let my brother-in-law buy me a drink.

I heard ancestral voices accusing me of being nowt but a bloody cookold, my wife one for 'oorin and t'bloody broosh. This was certainly no way to begin the peace. Later Harley Brewster, and his wife concurred, said that I ought to get married, choosing a girl as good as my sister. I let the farce continue for a week. A telephone call came for Eddie from Grindlays Bank in London, which, having deposited fifty pounds, I was using as a poste restante. A cable for him, urgent, recalling him from leave. Also a telegram for me, saying that I had got the job. Five hundred pounds a year and a lodging allowance. Start next Monday.

FIVE

My wife and I, like so many of the luckier couples whose relationship survived the war, found ourselves, as the autumn of 1946 arrived, reunited but physically separated. That was the first of the two phases of marital renewal during the peace. The second phase, that of building a hearth, was endlessly delayed by shortage of money and of rentable properties. The dream of owning a home was regarded as indecently capitalistic in the age of the Groundnut Scheme. So I lived in my cell at Brinsford Lodge with a four-day break between courses, and I travelled on these breaks to wherever Lynne happened to be. Eddie Williams had persuaded her to give up her flat on Barons Court Road, too small and squalid for a nabob's prospective wife, also unnecessary when he could hire houses in Henley and Richmond. Now he had been called back to Calcutta because of the sudden death of his deputy manager, and talk of marriage was reserved to air mail letters. Then the talk ceased and Eddie became engaged to the daughter of a judge. His brother Herbert sardonically found a job for Lynne on the staff of a new educational magazine published by the Turnstile Press. Its editor, a lecherous Scot who often harangued officers' courses at Eltham Palace, had her writing articles which I rewrote, adding inlays of style, attempted her seduction, and disappeared without paying for her work or her hotels. Lynne accepted that it was less trouble to be a more or less faithful wife to me than to be a shuttlecock between the Williams brothers. Our marriage was reconsummated. The world was still a dirty place like Gibraltar, and one of us gave crab-lice to the other. In a hotel bedroom we shaved off each other's pubic hairs. What better symbol of the renewal of intimacy?

At the Mid-West School of Education I had two colleagues – John Pilgrim, a High Anglican son of Braintree in Essex, courtly and learned, and the Indian Harvey Day, bearded, vegetarian, a journalist. Pilgrim was appointed instructor in educational technique; Harvey Day and I had to conduct such subject courses at Lieutenant-Colonel Scriven considered desirable – International Affairs, European History, Musical Appreciation, Drama, Politics. There was the assumption of the ignorant that the educated were educated in everything: back to the army again. Harvey Day did, in fact, know everything, being a journalist. He had two suitcases under his bed, both crammed with indexed newspaper cuttings. He rejected no newspaper commission and could, when called upon, lecture on any subject from St Thomas Aquinas to the Therapeutic Employment of Music in Private Zoos. He was indifferently interested in everything, wrote on the Wonder of the Human Eye for *Everybody's Weekly*, Disease and Politics for *The General Practitioner*, and Albinism for *The Rabbit-Breeder's Gazette*. His lectures were popular because they specialised in anecdote: from them you learned that St Thomas Aquinas was so fat that a lunette had to be cut out of his dining table, though you were told little of the content of the *Summa Theologica*. Lieutenant-Colonel Scriven was not much concerned about the content of anything, except that in a political course Karl Marx must not be mentioned, and that in a literary one *Ulysses* must be denounced. Scriven insisted that his civilian instructors be treated chummily by their army pupils and called by their first names. He himself, however, had to be addressed as sir.

I was saddened to see the quality of the private soldiers of both sexes who were sent to us for instruction and then induction as full sergeants into the Army Educational Corps. They knew nothing, except for the odd eccentric who knew too much, and, on posting as instructors, could do little. One sergeant I visited at a Military Hospital had an unused instruction room which he kept highly polished against Scriven's rare visits. That, he considered, was as much as could be done. The new era of the national service soldier had started, in which reading meant comic papers like *Beano* and the height of serious music was the Bach–Gounod *Ave Maria*. If service instructors had been available for the kind of compact fodder Harvey Day and I fed the students we would not have been there, but the days of enstriped and pipped dons were over. Being civilians, we had only the authority of our knowledge, such as it was; having no rank and being called by our first names we were faintly despised as belonging to no hierarchy and being in *faute de mieux* posts which smelt of impermanency.

To both Pilgrim and myself, old soldiers, it was as though we had not quite been demobbed.

God did not strike this peace, as he did the previous one, with a great murderous epidemic, but he inaugurated 1947 with the worst winter in history. Brinsford Lodge became a starved gulag until toboggans were imported for dragging supplies over five miles of snow. There was no fuel for heating. Industry, we heard, had broken down all over the country, and the trains were not running. The black-out returned. By St Valentine's Day, with a disastrous coal crisis and the prospect of a slow industrial recovery when the thaw arrived, if it ever did, there was a demand for vigorous governmental leadership and talk of the replacement of Prime Minister Attlee by Foreign Minister Ernest Bevin, who was, however, dying of angina pectoris. There was a great deal of rage about. I had been composing a *Sanctus* for a mass, but now I tore it up. Longing for sun and oranges, I decided to fall in love with the ATS sergeant who was attached to the school. She was London Jewish, but still a remote daughter of the Mediterranean. I had met attractive enough ATS girls during my army service, but there had always seemed to be a hint of incest in the prospect of a relationship. Now I was no longer wearing khaki and could, with little guilt, strip my sergeant of her uniform and disclose the woman beneath. Her cell, or mine, became a nut of sexual riot.

Very occasionally in our lives we are set upon by Dionysus. We go erotically mad and damn the consequences. That this should happen to me and to her in a wretched winter in the wilds of Staffordshire in an army school and a Ministry of Supply concentration camp was one of the improbabilities that make life interesting and dangerous. It is hard to keep such liaisons quiet. John Pilgrim had a High Anglican distaste for fornication, coupled with an East Anglian coolness, and Harvey Day, who was devoted to his Eurasian wife but was no prude, considered that we were being indiscreet. Lieutenant-Colonel Scriven, who was appalled by the reputation of *Ulysses*, would not countenance an affair of this kind but was too self-centred to notice the odours of heat. This was the only heat that prevailed in that winter. Then the spring came, and the summer, and my sergeant ended her service. The liaison, wholly civilian, continued in the gloomy station hotel of Wolverhampton at weekends. It cost money. I had little money. I had a wife to support.

Cats will leap on the knees of cat-haters. It was through going with a Jewish girl that I learned the extent of British antisemitism. It was not of the ideological Nazi kind but the public bar stupidity of 'them with long noses' and 'blame it all on the bleedin' Jews'. Wherever we went her presence, though unnoticed, called it forth. I could hit out, but I could not become a Jew. I longed for diatribes against the Catholics and occasionally got them, which made me feel better. The sense of being cut off from the main stream of British life, inhibited during the war, was returning. Catholic or Jew made little difference so long as one was not Protestant. The real religion, hence the real culture, lay somewhere east.

I should have married this girl, but, though I had good enough grounds, I could not now seek divorce. Moreover, her Judaism was reinforcing my Catholicism and making the notion untenable. And my wife was turning herself into my poor wife, sick, lonely, neglected. Guilt, guilt, and then the leap of the hungry dark forces in a hotel bedroom smelling of breadcrumbs. There is no poetry for such transports, except perhaps in the Song of Solomon. Physical appetite is no mere metaphor. And it raged in Wolverhampton, centre of rayon, paint, rubber and heavy and light engineering. It was permanently frustrated, though it never really came to an end, when Lieutenant-Colonel Scriven's instructional scheme began to collapse.

It began to collapse when he transferred it to an army camp, the headquarters of the Army Ordnance Corps at Nesscliff, near Shrewsbury. John Pilgrim found a permanent job as a county organiser of further education, and Scriven fired Harvey Day. This was because Harvey Day complained, justly, to the Extra-Mural Department of Birmingham University of the frivolity of army education and the ignorance of its officers. I found myself alone, a long-haired civilian among cropped soldiers, teaching educational technique, until an ageing adjunct was brought in by Scriven, a homosexual who came with a boy who stole everything of his and mine that he could find and then departed. An honorary officer, I dined in the officers' mess and learned, without the trouble of taking a commission, what the high army life was like. And I desperately applied for posts of a less transitional nature. Eventually I obtained one. I was appointed Lecturer in Speech and Drama at an Emergency Training College in Bamber Bridge, near Preston, Lancashire. The term 'emergency' implied impermanence, but less so than being under Lieutenant-Colonel

Scriven. The college was housed in a former US army camp. Students dwelt in single rooms in blocks, and at the end of each block there was a tiny apartment for a lecturer and his family, its rent paid for by the duties of block tutor. Lynne and I, married for six years, were now able to set up home for the first time. Real meals and our own bedsheets. These were what our marriage needed. After a brief riot in London with, respectively, her lovers and my mistress, we settled to fidelity and the comforts of the domestic life.

The Emergency Training Scheme of which I became a part was set up by the Ministry of Education to provide teachers quickly and cheaply for schools that were responding to a rising birth rate. It was a very sensible scheme, drawing as it did on ex-servicemen who had already shown some instructional talent in the forces and felt they had a teaching vocation. These were given a year's intensive training in such basic subjects as were taught in primary schools, and also permitted to specialise on a more academic level if they showed aptitude for secondary school work. Thus, I found myself teaching the history of European drama as a so-called special subject, the techniques of drama production at a subsidiary level, and the art of speech as an aspect of basic instructional training. The men were mature and many had suffered. They had seen the world and did not take kindly to a geography course taught by a man who knew it only from books. They could not be disciplined in the manner of schoolboys. Most had wives; the rest found mistresses they imported for occasional nights into their bedroom-studies. These had to be flushed out with gentle words. There had to be some kind of order, especially as the principal of the college was an Evangelical lay-preacher. I was younger than some of my students and certainly had enjoyed lower service rank than many of them. One had been a brigadier. If I was to prevail over them it was through the virtue of knowledge.

Speech is the basic concern of the teacher. If he cannot be understood and, more important, if he cannot be heard, he cannot teach. He requires the vocal training of the actor. He has to learn to breathe from the diaphragm and he has to learn how to 'place' his voice. That I must put the term in quotation marks is an indication that the nature of voice production is not well understood. Why are some singers better than others? Why can some actors (though, I think, few of the new school) whisper and yet be clearly heard at the back of the gallery? There are voices that are miracles and cannot be explained. But one of the secrets of the voice, at least in speech, lies in the trickery of the imagination. One gathers it into the front of the mouth and hurls it. One breathes properly. One articulates sharply. Most American actors, who belong to a traditon which equates vocal virility with pushing the sounds to the back of the throat, fail to project well in a theatre. They fear that following the British stage tradition of forward placing will emasculate their pitch. They honestly believe that the British stage voice is higher-pitched, hence more effeminate, than the American, when it is merely projected from the front of the mouth.

In my classes there were men with a variety of regional accents. The question was whether to recommend, rather than enforce, the adoption of the neutral south-eastern accent which too many of them associated with privilege. Ahm prahd of mah weh of speekin'. It were good enough fer me dad. Yes, but was it in order to take a northern accent to a southern school? It was best for me to be scientific and teach a course in general phonetics, showing how speech-sounds were made and how they could be unambiguously notated. There was no trouble with the consonants. With the vowels and dipthongs the *Pygmalion* class element began to enter. There was a sound that south-eastern speakers used in 'love' and a sound that they used in 'bull'. In Lancashire and Yorkshire the two sounds were levelled under an intermediate one shown, in the International Phonetic Alphabet, as an inverted *m*. What were these northerners going to do in a Croydon or Hounslow school – impose their compromise phoneme as a norm? Free fights nearly began with consideration of the *ah* in south-eastern 'bath', the real badge of vocal privilege. The thing to do was get some of these students acting, using dialectology as a conscious tool: the standard speech of the BBC was merely one of the dialects.

I became professionally interested in dialectology and, at weekends, Lynne and I would walk through the Lancashire countryside from village to village and, in the pubs, I would notate dialectal variations in the old-fashioned Henry Sweet, or Henry Higgins, manner. I did not realise that phonetics was now a matter of laboratory spectrograms and was, anyway, dying as a discipline. Phonemic opposition was coming in from the Prague school, and a phone – a speech-sound in isolation – was of little interest to the new linguists. In the nineteen-fifties the death of the hegemony of cultivated speech would be announced. The

normative would be done for, and Hamlet speak like a Northumbrian.

I produced a complete *Hamlet*, cutting not one line from the
First Folio version, and presenting it in two halves on two nights.
I also produced *Murder in the Cathedral*, with Lynne leading a
chorus of men of Canterbury, and *The Ascent of F6*, with Lynne
in a side box as Mrs A. The educative aspect of these productions
was the *bricolage* – the making do with little or nothing. Monks'
habits could be improvised out of blankets, mediaeval jerkins out
of ordinary jackets turned inside out, a mountain could be made
out of someone's nicked piece of parachute silk. *Hamlet* could be
done in modern dress, with preserved army uniforms and fascist
brassards. The college president observed these productions carefully, ears keen for the obscene and even the doubtful. He allowed
a student's production of *Titus Andronicus* to get to the line-learn-
ing stage, thinking Shakespeare to be probably harmless, but then
he was shocked to discover rape and cannibalism and mutilation.
He was a pious man. He required me to contribute to the religious
life of the college, so I delivered a fiery sermon on hell. Before
the sermon he had me on my knees and prayed over this, God's
temporary servant.

One of the interesting aspects of my educational career in Great
Britain was the steady diminution of salary. This was because of
the various scales that operated. I dropped a hundred pounds a
year when I left Scriven for Bamber Bridge, and was to drop
further when I got permanent employment in a grammar school.
This had something to do with the differences of the Pelham and
Burnham scales. Poor enough at Bamber Bridge, I took to
earning extra money by playing the piano at weekends in the
Black Bull. This was not considered decorous, but, apart from
free beer and thirty-five shillings, I was interested in the village
community, which was of a kind that perhaps no longer
exists.

Bamber Bridge called itself 'the Brigg' and was given to extreme local patriotism. There was a bus conductor nicknamed
Laddie who would ask riders on the Ribble Line: 'Art tha a
Brigg lad? If tha art, tha needn't pay.' The South Lancashire
dialect persisted and was not always intelligible, even to a
Mancunian like myself. I had never heard my grandfather speak,
but here he was, resurrected. When Lynne, entering the Black
Bull from heavy rain, was asked 'Art witshet?' she did not realise
that the question was 'Art thou wet-shod?' Standard English of a

kind was reserved to song. There was a lot of song in the seven
pubs and in the British Legion, for this was the North-West of
England, the cradle of British popular entertainment, with Blackpool not far away. It was also a region which the Reformation
had barely touched. Nearby Preston was etymologically Priest's
Town. Country pubs had statues of the Sacred Heart or the
Virgin Mary in the saloon bar, and there was much swearing 'by
t'mass'.

The village was self-sufficient. It had its cooperative stores, its
fish and chip shop, its British Legion concert room, where aspirants tried out their acts before seeking bigger worlds. The bigger
world of Preston, Leyland and Blackpool was a brief train or bus
ride away. Modern history had touched the Brigg only with the
arrival of American troops, who had set up the camp which was
now a college, though still named 't'Camp'. The American past
was still alive in the painted notices that it would have been
irreverent to remove. I remember delivering a Stanley Holloway
monologue which began:

> There's a place in t'Brigg called t'College.
>   It's the camp where the Yanks used to be.
> You can tell by the way they spell CENTER,
>   With the R comin' after the E.

In 1943 there had been the Battle of Bamber Bridge, well remembered, though it never got into the official chronicles of the
war. Black soldiers had barricaded the camp against the whites
and trained machine guns on to them. The Brigg was totally
black in sentiment. When the US military authorities had
demanded that the pubs impose a colour bar, the landlords had
responded with 'Black Troops Only'.

It was a community given to endogamy. The name Bamber
predominated. When I asked a little girl what was the name of
her dog she replied: 'Laddie Bamber', with the rising intonation
that indicated surprise at my stupidity in not already knowing.
The surprise-lift in speech patterns was invariable when information was requested. 'Where's Bamber the butcher?' – 'Over
thur,' with the rise of a full octave. Every aspect of the village
was known totally to its inhabitants, and the same knowledge
was expected of strangers. Adultery went on and was known if
not condoned. Scandal was dourly propagated. Lynne and I were
friendly with a railway stoker named Harry Chapburn, who used

to give me the reduced-fare tickets which were his due in the trade, and which I needed when I went on interviews for permanent jobs. One Saturday evening in the Black Bull, when I was pounding the piano, Lynne and Harry Chapburn entered together. This was a great moment for the scandal-lovers, and the untrue story went around long after that I had struck up 'Jealous Heart' (or 'Jeller Sart'), a popular song of the time. The village had its siren – a near-foreigner from Leyland named Jenny Dewhurst – and its cuckolds. It would have been easy to over-romanticise the earthy life, with its mad mothers on local farms, its jealous fights, its Saturday wives placid over Guinness while their men, collar-studded if not collared, threw darts in the public bar. It was the kind of life, though given an urban bias, later to be processed into the television series *Coronation Street*. The villagers probably now watch this, in preference to living their own lives.

This was the reality, rarely visited by the lecturers of Bamber Bridge Training College, though the students took some of it in. Such college life as was offered – the whist drive, the Sunday evening undenominational service – Lynne and I avoided. The social life of marriage was best conducted in pubs. Its more intimate side went well in the tiny flat, though its sounds penetrated through the thin walls to the student quarters. Rows were listened to judicially by these students, the married among whom knew all about rows. The students would sometimes join in the family life, bringing hares for jugging or farm eggs for frying. It was not a bad life. Lynne had got over her ailment and had been restored to the slim blonde beauty of her student days. Her mother had sent us the family piano. We bought a Siamese cat and had a border collie bitch wished upon us. We were to avoid, on doctor's orders, the making of a human family. We had, for the moment, family enough in the mature students we had to look after. We were settled, also unsettled. I reached thirty without finding a permanent post. Every Friday the *Times Educational Supplement* was delivered, and I read only the back pages, which advertised jobs.

The work of answering advertisements was a profession in itself. University posts demanded eight copies of one's *curriculum vitae*, which meant importing a typewriter and a primitive copying machine. I travelled for interviews and always came home defeated. Army service had conferred no real experience: teaching army students was not considered much of a qualification. I had to compete with men who had been reserved into teaching and had become MAs. I went to London to take the examination for Licentiate of the Royal Academy of Music (Drama) and the Associateship of the Royal College of Music (Composition). I failed the practical tests less through incompetence than through truculence. In the music examination I did not at first recognise the chord of the Neapolitan sixth and had Dr Herbert Howells railing at me with 'Come, come, don't you eat ice cream?', an infantile rebuke. In the drama-teaching test I was given a group of female students who bitchily conspired to make me lose my temper, infallible sign of a lack of teaching talent. Two years of instruction of tough adults, with no new paper qualifications, were not fitting me for anything. I was lucky to be given the post of English master at Banbury Grammar School.

One ought not to whine in retrospect, and it is enough to say that the post-war years were not easy for anyone not protected by a strong trade union. The teaching profession was insulted by inadequate scales of pay, and the strike weapon was considered not merely undignified but treacherous. One's students came first: it would have been an immoral act to neglect them, especially as the O and A levels approached. The unwillingness of teachers to fight left them in a situation derided by the other professions. Moreover, a teacher could not assume that a suitable post would be available on his home ground, if he had one. A school job meant new roots and the problem of buying accommodation, since council houses were not to be rented to strangers. Lynne and I borrowed from her father enough money to make a down payment on a £1,300 labourer's cottage, on which an £800 mortgage was granted. My annual salary, when tax and national insurance had been deducted, was not much over £350. It was necessary to moonlight in order to live. This meant, for both of us, evening classes and vacation tutorship for children destined for the public schools Common Entrance. Our drinking, when we had time for it, was limited to draught cider; our smoking was, by an agreement we trespassed, down to ten daily Woodbines each.

Lynne's only luxury, her Dior original, was her Siamese cat Lalage. This, a seal-pointed queen of the Wychdale breed, was exclusively devoted to her mistress, insisted on sleeping in the middle of the bed, and regularly tried to evict me from it with brutal claws. She tolerated me only when on heat, when she recognised the male principle. She howled like a fiend for a mate but viciously drove away suitors. She died old, on the borders of Siam, still a virgin. The border collie bitch, Suky, was prolific, always chose to mate with the ugliest male she could find, and produced large litters thrice yearly. These were grotesque in appearance but of great intelligence and vigour. They were given away as rewards for good work to the younger pupils of Banbury Grammar School. There were times, especially in spring when the may appeared, when the life of an Oxfordshire village with, like Bamber Bridge, seven pubs was idyllic enough. Long country walks with a dog. Cider in the midst of a Midlands dialect. Little money, but money was not everything.

The village was Adderbury, with its fine church in the perpendicular style. This had a carillon which, every three hours, played a tune appropriate to the day of the week. On Sunday we had 'O Worship the King' and on Saturday 'Home Sweet Home'. On Monday there was 'Hard Times Come Again No More' and on Friday, the day for pay packets, 'See the Conquering Hero Comes'. This was Protestant territory and, drunk on cider, I would sometimes inveigh against the reformist theft of a Catholic church. Lynne's view was always that the English Church sustained a continuity from the time of the Anglo-Saxon conversion, and that its Catholic phase was no more remarkable than its High Anglican. She denied the historicity of the papal claim to supremacy over the Christian world, calling on her school studies to question, even from a Catholic angle, the authority of Rome when perhaps Avignon had better authority. She remembered her sixth form history but had forgotten most of what L. B. Namier had taught her. She was not a scholar. She evinced no literary taste, and left it to me to choose novels for her at the public library. She was, however, devoted to Jane Austen, whom I have never been able to read with pleasure. I prefer Johnson's *Rasselas* to *Persuasion*.

I perhaps seem to be giving evidence of marital incompatibility. I have not declared love for a long time, and I had better declare it now. I loved her, and we sustained reciprocal love for thirty years. I wish love could be defined. As marriage advances the physical element loses the excitement it always possesses with a stranger: it becomes comfort, release, an occasional signal of assumed affection. It even creeps out of marriage, barely noticed. Marriage is built on a common past, a closed culture, a community of myths. A shared line of poetry can evoke a whole swathe of experience. The conversation of a married couple is built out of codes. When I played the piano in a pub and Lynne considered that I had played too much, she would say simply: 'Mary.' It was enough. The mystified others would not know that she was referring to Mr Bennet in *Pride and Prejudice* telling his daughter that she had delighted them sufficiently. Lynne would catechise me about the Bennet daughters, and, like a television adapter, I would always leave one out. Such a catechism, and the sharing of the *Daily Telegraph* crossword, will keep a marital evening going. Communicaton is of the fundamental Malinowskian sort, purely phatic. But each word and even grunt is laden with a shared past.

Marriages break because a new sexual excitement is adjudged more important than the small closed civilisation that has been steadily built over the years. Such a collapse is sometimes implausibly justified by a fancied weariness of codes that have gone on too long. Or there are mannerisms which irritate in a marriage far more than in a mere friendship. One's irritation, which could modulate into anger if one let it, is hard to explain. At Bamber Bridge Training College I produced a stage version of Nigel Balchin's novel *Lord, I Was Afraid* (a very good and original novel in dramatic form, unaccountably forgotten). Among the characters was a Pamela whom Lynne referred to consistently as Pam. Why should I see red at that? She would ask me to read aloud to her Kipling's 'Tomlinson', and I would dread the moment when she joined in the chorus 'Not in Berkeley Square'. What lies under the rage aroused by such trivialities? Lynne's own subdued rage at my composing music, which she did not understand, was always expressed in an uncontrollable cough when it was performed. She would leave the hall or room, coughing, and hence hear little more than the opening bars.

In the village of Adderbury we more or less eschewed physical infidelity, which she never considered important unless one saw it in action: then the knife would be justified by a whole culture of jealousy. There was not much opportunity for adultery, anyway, and I was the one to commit it spectaculary if discreetly with a fellow member of staff. It was, I suppose, a means of imparting a sting to the honey of the four-year idyll. Time itself was melting, and I could have stayed on in that tiny labourer's cottage in a village which took little account of time until impoverished retirement. That time meant nothing was made clear to me in the Red Lion, where the village postman remarked that there had been rare goings on when the old Earl were alive. He gave a vivid account of the Earl's activities. These were proved accurate when I checked on the life of John Wilmot, Earl of Rochester (1647–80), the local nobleman he was referring to. When I came back on a visit after three years in Malaya, the postman said: 'Hello, Mr Wilson, you been on your holidyes?'

The landlord of this pub, Ted Arden, was from Stratford-on-Avon. He was of the family of Shakespeare's mother, though he made no capital out of this, and he had inherited a fiddle-browed Shakespearian head which was clearly an Arden endowment. I put him eventually into the novel *The Right to an Answer*, though transferring him and his pub to Leicestershire, and made him more Shakespearian than he was. But it was he, in his aitchless ungrammatical Warwickshire, who told me of the Stratford tradition that Shakespeare had an affair with a black woman and this resulted in his nose dropping off. 'That's what yer get,' he would say, 'by buggerin' off to London and neglectin' the wife of yer bosom.' The wife of his own bosom, who was a social cut above him, blonde, boyish, exophthalmic, slim as a Toledo blade in toreador pants, he visibly adored and called 'me ole duck'.

Banbury, the town to which I travelled every day, had an ancient reputation for puritanism. Here a man hanged his cat on Monday for killing of a mouse on Sunday. Shakespeare has a Puritan called a 'Banbury cheese' in *The Merry Wives of Windsor*, and the cheese itself had maintained its flavour. There were also Banbury cakes, which Leopold Bloom feeds to the Dublin sea-gulls. The Banbury cross of the nursery rhyme had been restored by the Victorians. Inevitably there was a couture boutique called The Fine Lady. The Grammar School, which served a large rural area, was a little aloof from the town, socially and topographically. At that time of educational reform grammar schools, which had been founded to teach Latin grammar, were in disrepute. Secondary modern schools and technical schools were to be considered as, if not more, important. The elitism of the public school was to be allowed to continue for a time, if only because so many socialists sent their sons to Eton, but the grammar school was to confer no social advantage on its pupils. Theoretically at least the path to a university could branch out of a secondary modern school. The egalitarian philosophy of the postwar era may have been accepted, cynically I believe, by members of the Labour Party, but parents and teachers alike knew the truth: that the road to the smaller distinctions – the greater ones being reserved to Harrow and Rugby – began in the grammar school.

Banbury Grammar School was mixed, and I was back to the Gibraltar situation of teaching girls as well as boys. These girls were gym-slipped, which most men know to be erotic but the staider women who look after schoolgirls not. Young breasts bud and burgeon, and the girls are aware of it. A mixed school is a dangerous place for susceptible male teachers. The conduct of an adulterous affair was one way of avoiding mischief. I was set to teaching phonetics in the junior school and various varieties of English in the higher forms, with the pleasure of near-adult literary instruction in the Sixth, where the girls were wholly nubile. The school was streamed into A, B and N, N standing for Normal. It was thus normal to be a slut or a lout. In the lower A stream I could ask the question: 'Why don't we place a centralisation diacritic on a schwa?', to which the answer was chorused: 'Because schwa is already a central vowel.' On Friday afternoons I would read aloud to 3A from Evelyn Waugh's *Decline and Fall*, Ray Bradbury's *The Silver Locusts* and Orwell's *Nineteen Eighty-Four*. 'Sir, does Julia become an unperson?' asked a wide-eyed girl, tremulous. These children could write an acceptable pastiche of Joycean interior monologue.

The staff was a good staff, all gowned except for the PT man, a grizzled ex-sailor who would talk of that play that has Bottom in it, and Derek Rolls, too handsome to require a degree. It was a staff with brilliant side-talents which produced brilliant children. Kenneth Tryon, who taught German and French, was a remarkable portrait painter whose daughter Valerie became a notable pianist. For her I composed a sonata and a bagatelle. Maurice Draper, the chemist, made tonic water for which no one could afford gin, painted exquisitely, and played the flute. His Eurasian wife made superb curries. Kenneth Carrdus, who ran the English department, was another skilled flautist, percussionist as well, admirable producer of Gilbert and Sullivan. The headmaster, Dr Rose, led a family of violinists and had founded a string orchestra. For this I composed a *Partita* which was played in the Town Hall. The women teachers were charming, sufficiently worldly, and knew all about the problems of pubescent girls. Who could not but be happy in such an environment? The talk was cultured, but the culture we needed could be nothing but talk. Who could afford to buy books and gramophone records and trips to the Stratford and London theatres? Some of the pupils could.

Whining is, I say, out of order, but I retain the right of protest that men and women of this calibre should not be appreciated by either a Tory or a Labour government. Here was the backbone of bourgeois culture, disregarded and even reviled. The provincial grammar school gave the community its plays, concerts, even operas, as well as its better citizens. It produced few delinquents. One N stream boy I taught, remarkably versed in the Old Testament, tried to break into Lloyd's Bank, but he was exceptional and there was even a certain nobility in his project. In the B stream there were occasional flurries of sexual passion but no known pregnancies. The A stream sent young men and women to the better universities with, if I had it, a very fair literary equipment. When, in the middle fifties, the Watch Committee of Banbury complained of the BBC TV adaptation of *Nineteen Eighty-Four*, too violent for children to see, some of my children could yawn and say they knew the work already. The Lower Sixth, under my guidance, formed an Emotional Engineering Committee and published a long poem in the style of *The Waste Land* entitled *Sonata in H*, which dealt with the H-bomb apocalypse we all feared. But to the new world that was being forged, deutero-Elizabethan, all this culture meant little.

My private attempts to add to the musical culture of Great Britain were consistently thwarted. My *Passacaglia for Orchestra* was rejected by the BBC, and to have partitas and sonatas privately performed was little consolation. The danger of becoming settled at a provincial grammar school lay in habituation to the satisfaction of local achievements – well-produced plays which London never heard about, speech and drama festivals which London actors condescended to judge. The provinces were not yet ready to rage at London condescension or neglect. I left England before the angry young men erupted. Lynne grew impatient at my spending money on scoring paper and inking crotchets when I should have been applying for jobs or, with equal lack of hope, attempting to break into the literary world. With great daring I sent a volume of poems to Faber and Faber. Mr Eliot himself returned them, regretting that I was not yet ready for publication but marking three poems that he liked. One of them was this:

> 'Prudence prudence,' the pigeons call,
>   'Serpents lurk in the gilded meadow.
> An eye is embossed on the garden wall:
>   The running tap casts a static shadow.'

'Caution caution,' the rooks proclaim,
   'The dear departed, the weeping widow
Will meet in you in the core of flame:
   The running tap casts a static shadow.'

'Act! Act!' the ducks give voice,
   'Enjoy the widow in the meadow.
Drain the sacrament of choice:
   The running tap casts a static shadow.'

I still do not know what the poem means, except that it was
perhaps telling me to get out of Banbury. But who was the
widow?

At least I published in the *Banbury Guardian*, covering agricultural shows at a penny a line and being told I was 'badly left'
when I failed to turn up for an exhibition of tractors. I was
allowed to write the notices of performances of *Messiah* and *Quiet
Wedding* and learned the first rule of provincial journalism:
mention everybody's name. 'Mrs Dalziel and her assistant Mrs
Fortescue provided refreshments with their usual efficiency' had
to replace some sharp but helpful critical point. Provincial
journalism was all about having one's name in the papers. But
the *Banbury Guardian* had, to its regret, to publish two poems of
mine when I won its gold medal for verse. There was an old
endowment embarrassing to the borough philistines; there had
been some eccentric and wealthy lover of literature hidden away
in a country mansion who financed the award in his will. What
readers of the *Banbury Guardian* made of this sonnet was never
recorded:

A dream, yes, but for everyone the same.
   The mind that wove it never dropped a stitch:
   The absolute was anybody's pitch,
For, when a note was struck, we knew its name.
That dark aborted any urge to tame
   Waters that day might prove to be a ditch
   But then was endless growling ocean, rich
In fish and heroes till the dredgers came.

'*Wachet auf!*' A fretful dunghill cock
   Flinted the noisy beacon through the shires.
A martin's nest clogged the cathedral clock,
   But it was morning: birds could not be liars.

A key cleft rusty age in lock and lock,
        Men shivered by a hundred kitchen fires.

The Vicar of Banbury, a man with a nose like a piece of cuttlefish bone stuck in a budgerigar's cage, a great drinker in the White Lion (one of the few hotels in the world that were awarded a crown, higher than four stars), who had the ugliest church in all England, seemed to guess that the poem was getting at the Reformation. My Catholicism was not easy to quell. The Vicar of Adderbury worried about it. He said to me: 'I mean, there's the question of your dying. Where in God's name do you think you're going to be buried?' But it was a very imperfect Catholicism, a mere rough bludgeon for knocking the Protestant Midlands. In the early fifties a group of Jesuits learned in Vedanta were trying to spiritualise the Church and make it acceptable to subtle Hindus, but the Pope countered that with the gross materialism of the dogma of the Virgin Mary's physical assumption into heaven. My Catholicism was somewhere in the past, perhaps contemporary with the building of Adder-bury church.

Lynne had been tolerant of both my dithering Catholicism and my music. She had bought me a second-hand guitar and a more than second-hand acoustic HMV gramophone. At that time long-playing records were replacing the old brittle discs, and Banbury's music shop was selling off its superseded stock very cheaply. I wasted much time searching for the sundered instalments of Elgar's symphonies. But not so much time as trying to compose a symphony of my own. Lynne gave me a sort of ultimatum. I was to stake everything on a single great work. If that failed I was to assume that music was a failed vocation and whatever future I had lay in literature. A great work? This meant an opera. I was, Lynne said, to write my own libretto, which, being nothing but words, she would at least be able to understand and even judge. Now, there is nothing in the world more difficult than writing a libretto. Most of the failed operas fail because of this. The problem is less one of language than of plot. The plot must be appropriate to a short story, but the effect of its mus-icalisation must be rather that of a Jamesian novel. I doubted my ability to compose a tragic opera, but I thought I might achieve something in which myth carried a Verdian weight and yet was excused by comedy. I found a plot that seemed possible in Burton's *Anatomy of Melancholy*. It comes in Part 3, Section 2,

Member I, Subsection I, immediately after the story of the Lamia
from which Keats made a poem:

> One more I will relate out of Florilegus, *ad annum* 1058, an
> honest historian of our nation, because he telleth it so con-
> fidently, as a thing in those days talked of all over Europe. A
> young gentleman of Rome, the same day that he was
> married, after dinner with his bride and his friends went a-
> walking into the fields, and towards evening to the tennis-
> court to recreate himself; whilst he played, he put his ring
> upon the finger of Venus's statue, which was thereby, made
> in brass; after he had sufficiently played, and now made an
> end of his sport, he came to fetch his ring, but Venus had
> bowed her finger in, and he could not get it off; whereupon,
> loath to make his company tarry, at the present there left it,
> intending to fetch it the next day or at some more convenient
> time, went thence to supper, and so to bed. In the night,
> when he should come to perform those nuptial rites, Venus
> steps between him and his wife (unseen or felt of her), and
> told him that she was his wife, that he had betrothed himself
> unto her by that ring which he put upon her finger: she
> troubled him for some following nights. He, not knowing
> how to help himself, made his moan to one Palumbus, a
> learned magician in those days, who gave him a letter, and
> bid him at such a time of the night, in such a cross-way, at
> the town's end, where old Saturn would pass by with his
> associates in procession, as commonly he did, deliver that
> script with his own hand to Saturn himself; the young man,
> of a bold spirit, accordingly did it; and when the old fiend
> had read it, he called Venus to him, who rode before him,
> and commanded her to deliver his ring, which forthwith she
> did, and so the gentleman was freed.

A delightful little story, and one that I did not realise had
already been used, though taken not from Florilegus or Burton
direct but from F. Anstey, in Kurt Weill's Broadway musical
One Touch of Venus. I had the notion of giving the tale a contemporary setting and providing a more telling dénouement than
Florilegus's with an exorcism ceremony. This would be performed by a Church of England vicar very improbably using the
Rituale Romanum and failing. He would dramatically doubt the
power of the Reformed Church to deal with demons and be told

that Venus was no demon but a saint. Mediterranean Christianity had absorbed the classical past and, through the acknowledgment of Venus's benignity, the bridegroom would be released from his contract only to enter a bigger one, in which a pagan goddess was permitted to bless a Christian marriage. The work was to be called *The Eve of Saint Venus*, which is the title given to the Loeb translation of the *Pervigilium Veneris*. Alternatively it was to be called *The Gods in the Garden* or, after Falstaff, *Gods Have Hot Backs*. All the gods were to be present, and they would provide the chorus.

The libretto grew too long. I grew too interested in it. It had a wholly unsettable monologue for the Vicar:

What has the Church been to most of us, even me?
A suit kept clean for ceremonial occasions.
Part of the gentle English pattern, where, in retrospect,
The winter has never been really so rough,
The summer never a fire. The whole land
Is a sort of drawing-room furnished in taste,
Covered in pink cretonne. God, we liked to think,
Presided genially over the cricket club
And the darts tournament.
But the dust could never be disturbed, and the ancient lawn
Never be mined by moles. The comforting
Shibboleths were enough – the simple magic
Of baptism, syrup for the sick, and the noble
Stock responses of the prayers for the dead.
But now we travel to a fiery land
Where the beasts have talons and the birds secrete
Venom. What can I do now, what can I do?
I approached this problem bubbling like a child
With a show-off hobby. My gun was a toy gun:
It could never really frighten a burglar.
Well, the burglars are in, are in. And I
Tremble, impotent, at the top of the stair.
There are two ways to take, but they're both unfamiliar
To an old man who has no maps and knows only
A lane leafy in summer, with the distant bells,
And the gargoyles waiting, ready to grin a greeting
For me to grin back to with a sort of love.
But let it not be said that an old man lacks courage.
Let the bishop stop sipping port in his run-down palace,

Let the dean pause at the ruridecanal conference,
Let the curate take his eyes off the ball for a moment,
And look at me now. Forty years in the Church,
The morganatic gift of a syphilitic monarch,
Too old and too weak for the waterless trek in the desert,
The sweating mass in the jungle, the care of the poor
In the scorpion-crawling abbey. But not too old
For the renunciation of everything
That meant everything. I am not worthy.
Domine, non sum dignus.

And then, dear dear, he tears off his clerical collar. Try setting all that to music.

Monstrously long for a libretto, it was even too long for a play. The Adderbury Actors I had formed, few of them living in Adderbury, had put on *Juno and the Paycock*, but they could not be asked to cope with a comedy that turned into theology, crammed with the *Rituale Romanum* and *De Rerum Natura* and the *Pervigilium Veneris*, all in the original Latin. It was a derivative play, full of echoes of *The Cocktail Party* ('the waterless trek in the desert' and so on) and parodic Christopher Fry, who was just going out of fashion. I turned the aborted affair into a novella and filed it away. I did not consider that publishers would consider it publishable, at least not yet. In 1964, a vaguely daring year (Shakespeare's quatercentenary; the opening of the BBC's second television channel), a publisher published it with illustrations to make up the weight. Then amateur dramatic societies in Connecticut, Düsseldorf, and Alaska turned it back into a play. Bruce Montgomery, the film composer who wrote detective stories as Edmund Crispin, wanted to make an opera of it, but he was losing hope and energy. In 1953 I deafened myself to the vocal and orchestral possibilities latent in Florilegus and, accepting Lynne's ultimatum, gave up music.

But in that year it seemed at least possible to sit down in the boxlike study-second-bedroom, look out at the night-scented stocks shamming dead in sunlight, see the new litter of nine gleefully escaping from the coal-shed, and consider an artistic creation of some bulk. I had tried hard to better myself and travelled for interviews at colleges which had already filled their vacancies but gone through the charade of placing the posts on the open market. One college sincerely offered me a lectureship, but only on condition that I taught Laban dance as well as phonetics. I had to say no, but I beat my breast about it until I pictured myself teaching Laban dance. I seemed likely to stay on at Banbury Grammar School until I was sixty-five, with lowered artistic sights, poor, vaguely discontented (as the song says), bullying myself into believing that I was happy. I was becoming psychic at that time, performed as Professor Sosostris the chiromancer at garden fêtes, and saw no mark of change in my own hand.

The whole ambience seemed charged with kindly ghosts telling us both to stay where we were. The cottage we lived in had previously been owned, piped, electrified and redecorated by a man whose wife was schizophrenic and needed country quiet. On her second day in the house she had taken a knife to herself and bled to death. We feared her violent ghost, but she had left only her kindlier residue. Sometimes, when we opened the door that led to the stairwell, a scent of violets would gush down. The cupboard we used for crockery, totally empty when we began to charge it, bestowed a shilling of 1745 two years later and, the year after that, a telescopic toasting fork of the same century. The ghosts who flitted on the upstairs residential corridor of the Red Lion were benevolent, even the male ectoplasm in striped pyjamas who left the toilet as I went in. No spirits screamed; many nodded at me, as at one who would eventually join them in eternal Oxfordshire. Only once was I aware of the malevolence of a revenant, and that was in a pub in a neighbouring village, where I felt myself being strangled and had to rush out. A man had, in fact, been strangled there a century before.

Stay, then, was our decision (we ignored that it was an enforced one) in 1953. It was a hopeful year. On May 29 Hillary and Sherpa Tenzing reached the summit of Everest. On June 2 Elizabeth II's coronation was televised. How could the country be going to pot when we were all neo-Elizabethans? On July 13 the British steel industry was denationalised. On July 27 the Korean armistice was signed. On September 26 sugar, after fourteen years, went off the ration. December was the warmest December for twenty years, and Christmas Day was like spring. Why, then, the sourness of some verses I wrote then?

> Here ruined farmers, in new hacking-coats,
> Pour Scotch and ram fat bacon down their throats;
> And children, obdurately red and flaxen,

Proclaim the crass inbreeding of the Saxon.
Observe the maidens who, with brawny arms,
Gush the seductive fragrance of the farms.
They feel the body should be mainly meat,
That ankles have no function and that feet,
Disdaining shape and glorying in size,
Should shout a curious kinship to the thighs.
But lest with so much weight the streets should rock,
The dessicated matrons of good stock
(Though not for soup) tune their patrician reeds
In shops which specialise in tasteless tweeds,
Then hog the pavements with their barking spouses
Before they seek their deathwatch-rotting houses,
Where flies die in the port and rabbit, stewed,
Provides for dog and man a basic food.
. . . The manor gates are down, the past is dead.
American police patrol instead,
Save there, where feudalism's greasy scraps
Still touch the villagers who touch their caps
To soap king's lady or to upstart lord
Who licked the party's boots or swelled its hoard,
Trimming like mad or clinging like a louse
To be translated to the Upper House,
Whence now he comes to dogmatise and hector,
Sway the church sycophants and hound the rector.

It is, was, the sourness of the dispossessed. The Aluminium Works
was where the money was made; the loveliest Queen Anne house
in Adderbury was let to a US Army Chemical Warfare noncom
whose name, in cartoon lettering, blared from the gate: TOP
RANDY SCHULZ; the lord of the manor was a political peer;
the bourdon of an emancipated Anglo-Saxon peasantry and a
decayed gentry oppressed. Somehow I had to get out, or merely
on.

IN THE WINTER of 1953, stricken with mumps but not emasculated, I wrote a brief novel on a typewriter borrowed from
the office of a builder who had designs on my wife. I had
already foreseen, from my work on the impossible opera libretto, that writing a novel would be easier labour than composing

a symphony. In a symphony many strands conjoined, in the same instant, to make a statement; in a novel all you had was a single line of monody. The ease with which dialogue could be written seemed grossly unfair. This was not art as I had known it. It seemed cheating not to be able to give the reader chords and counterpoint. It was like pretending that there could be such a thing as a concerto for unaccompanied flute. My notion of giving the reader his money's worth was to throw difficult words and neologisms at him, to make the syntax involuted. Anything, in fact, to give the impression of a musicalisation of prose. I saw that that was what Joyce had really been trying to do in *Finnegans Wake* – clotting words into chords, presenting several stories simultaneously in an effect of counterpoint. I was not trying to emulate *Finnegans Wake* – which had closed gates rather than opened them – but I felt that *Ulysses* had still plenty to teach to a musician who was turning to fiction. Any single episode of that work presents counterpoint of a baroque intricacy – what with a book of the Odyssey finding a modern parallel, enforcing a symbolism and a style, while an organ of the body presides, as well as an art or a science, and there is a predominant colour as well, prob- ably, as a Domenican letter.

I did not wish to go so far, but I approved the groundbass of a myth for the novel I wanted to write. The novel was to be about the later days of my service in Gibraltar, and, as Joyce had made the *Odyssey* the substructure of his novel, so the *Aeneid* would be the underpinning of mine. My hero, a failed musician like myself, would be Sergeant Richard Ennis. Ennis was close enough to Aeneas. He would have a pious duty to help build, through edu- cation, a new world, and this piety would be partially learned from his father, an old-fashioned utopian socialist dead in an air raid. The name Ennis would be appropriate also in a non- Vergilian context, since Ennis comes from a Celtic root meaning an island, and Ennis would be a kind of Celtic Catholic tempera- mentally isolated from his Protestant fellows. He would have a friend, a *fidus Achates* named Agate, a homosexual ballet dancer, but he himself would be powerfully heterosexual enough to be deflected from the founding of a new world by a liaison with a dark widow like Dido of Carthage.

In 1969, at the University of Chapel Hill in North Carolina, I attended, with a curiosity that overcame embarrassment, a lecture on this novel given by a brilliant young professor named Tom

Stumpf. Stumpf pointed out what I had not previously noticed –
that the name R. ENNIS spells SINNER backwards. This was a
shock to me, reminding me that one is often less in control of
one's work than one thinks. I had had to fight all the way through
the writing of the novel against the introduction of themes like
guilt and sin – to which the Catholic in me instinctively turns –
and here I was planting such themes, in poor disguise, in the very
name of my hero. Stumpf's analysis of the novel was just. It was,
he said, about authority, the factitious kinds represented by art or
military organisation, the real kind represented by the Rock or
the Church or God. But all I had attempted to write was a realistic
comic novel about service life with a cunningly disguised mythic
under-score. The title itself would imply a lack of solidity in the
intention. *A Vision of Battlements* will do well enough for the
Gibraltar skyline as observed from the sea, but I took the phrase
from a book called *The Illustrated Family Doctor*, where the following was said of migraine: 'Warning of an attack may be given
by tingling sensations in the limbs, impairment of vision, flashing
lights, a vision of battlements, noises in the ears, mental depression
or other phenomena.' In other words, the agony of the subjective.

Ennis is not in the AEC but the AVCC – the non-existent
Army Vocational and Cultural Corps. He facetiously fills out the
initials on page 1 to 'Arma Virumque Cano Corps', thus pointing
a little too obviously to the Vergilian undertext, instead of letting
the reader find it out for himself. Soon he is in bed with a young
Gibraltarian widow named Concepción, whose name is all too
appropriate, since she conceives a child by Ennis. She was married
to a young Gibraltarian called Pepe who, improbably for one of
his breed, fought for the Spanish Loyalist cause and got killed.
She is being wooed by a fat businessman named Barasi (anagram
of Dido's suitor's name, Iarbas). Him she will marry when she
discovers she is pregnant, and she will go to live in the hell that is
La Linea. Ennis wishes to marry her but cannot, being married
already to a fair-haired patrician Englishwoman named Laurel.
He meets a version of Laurel on the Rock, a Wren named Lavinia,
and has to battle with a PT warrant officer instructor for her
favours. This man's name cannot be Turnus but Turner is near
enough. Ennis is responsible for his death through falling from the
highest point on the Rock, Willis's Farm, and he is sent home to
find that his wife has left him. He has plenty of cause for guilt.
He should be at his work of founding the new world, but he is not

sure whether this is the mere visionary battlements of the music he is trying to compose, or the utopia of the British Way and Purpose.

The officer who gives him his orders, as from high Olympus, is not Major W. P. Meldrum, which would have carried realism too far, but a version of Colonel Scriven, renamed Muir after the Scottish educator who educated my wife. Thus does the strategy of the fiction-maker operate. People are always looking for photographs of real-life personages in fiction, and the law of libel encourages them to do so. In fact it is hard for the novelist to transfer real life to his structures: it is much easier to create characters out of nothing, or to make them composites of the known and the invented. Ennis is certainly not John Burgess Wilson, though he has all his faults and some of his disregarded talent. Concepción I should have loved to know. She tries hard to be a furious Dido but fails. Ennis does his best to follow the path of Aeneas, but the signposts are ambiguous. On VE Day the funeral games are reduced to a race between taxicabs. Ennis's fortune-telling Sybil is Mrs Carraway, a Queen's Army schoolmistress. The Vergilian references are all too, so to speak, *appliqué*. 'Here's the Hampton Court maze, where we got lost on our honeymoon . . . And here's the last photograph my dear son had taken . . . died in training. He was just getting his wings. My husband, you see, had been in the Flying Corps.' If anyone recognises Daedalus and Icarus here, how far does it help the story?

James Joyce said that his Homeric parallels were a mere bridge for marching his eighteen episodes over: once they were across, the structure could be blown skyhigh. This was disingenuous. Joyce recognised that his real need was to thicken the text, orchestrate it, introduce complex harmony and counterpoint to satisfy his own deep quasi-musical need and, presumably, the need of readers of similar temperament for whom narrative simplicity was too monodic to be acceptable. Joyce required the device of myth not because myth would say more about modern life, either through mockery or elevation to a plane of genuine heroism, but because myth justified textual inspissation. This was pretty much my own situation with *A Vision of Battlements*. If Joyce laboured to the point of physical agony over his huge construct, I merely enjoyed erecting my much smaller one. I completed it in six weeks, kept no carbon copy, and then entrusted it to the mails and to Messrs William Heinemann. I chose Heinemann because, at that time, I greatly admired the novels of Graham Greene, and

Heinemann was Greene's publisher. I had little hope of its immediate acceptance. I forgot about it, took out my music manuscript paper, and wrote a dozen easy pieces for solo violin. Lynne did not object: this was not really art. *The Young Fiddler's Tune Book*, as the little collection was called, went to Messrs Curwen, who very nearly accepted it. Then, in the new year of 1954, a letter came from Roland Gant at Heinemann requesting a visit from me to discuss my novel.

This was an awkward situation. I was in debt to the grocer and overdrawn at the bank. I could not afford a return train ticket from Banbury to London. But, three days after the receipt of the letter from Gant, a letter came from the Colonial Office. I was summoned to an interview at Great Smith Street, and a return rail voucher was enclosed. So, after all, I was able to get to London. What I did not understand was why the Colonial Office wished to see me. I was still on the Army Z Reserve. Perhaps some cunning arrangement between the War Office and the Secretary of State for the Colonies was enforcing the filling of posts in the White Man's Grave through the device of conscription. I racked my skull for other explanations. I had been applying for various jobs overseas, though none, as I thought, in the dwindling British colonial empire. I had tried to become a lecturer in a Church of England mission college in East Africa and even become involved in a long mystical exchange of letters which continued long after the post was filled. 'What precisely (do not be afraid to bare your inmost soul on this matter) is the intimate relationship you enjoy with the personality of Jesus Christ?' I had applied for a small headship on the island of Sark. In our innocence Lynne and I had entertained visions of running with our dog Suky over the yellow sands, she furnishing the tiny community with all the puppies it could possibly desire. We did not realise that only the Dame of Sark was permitted to own a bitch.

I presented myself at the Colonial Office on a freezing January day, and was interviewed by high functionaries about a post for which I could not remember having applied. 'About this lectureship in Kota Bharu Training College,' they began. Lectureship? Kota whatever it is? I know nothing about it. But you applied. Oh no I did not. Oh yes you did. I was shown my letter of application. I could tell from the efficiency of the typing and the cold clarity of the phraseology that I had written and sent off this letter when I was tight on draught cider. I had evidently come home from the Red Lion one Saturday night, made the application in a trance, posted it, then gone to bed to forget all about it. I could not deny that that was my signature and this the somewhat old-fashioned typeface of my borrowed Edwardian Oliver. Why, a man who turned out to be the Chief Education Officer of the Federation of Malaya wished to know, did I think I had been summoned for this interview if I denied having requested it? I thought, I said, that it was about a post in the Channel Islands. They all gaped. What gave me to believe that the administration of the Channel Islands was the responsibility of the Secretary of State for the Colonies? The whole colonial system, I improvised, was based on a number of empirical anomalies – condominia, protectorates, trucial states and so on. The gaping did not abate. These functionaries, I foresaw, were going to dine out on this. Could, the chairman asked, the interview proceed on the assumption that I had applied for a three-year contract to teach spoken English in a multiracial teachers' training college in the sultanate of Kelantan? Ah no, I said. If I am to be offered a colonial post I require this to be a permanency. I have had enough of temporary appointments. Would I then wish to be considered for a permanent and pensionable post in some educational establishment, not yet to be specified, in the Federation of Malaya? Yes, I would, but not till the end of the current academic year. I had a feeling (after all, I was now to take a tube train to Messrs Heinemann) that something might happen this year which would change my life without my having to sweat in shorts among leeches and hamadryads. My 'yes' was meant to sound unequivocal, but I was silently qualifying it. I went to see Roland Gant.

Roland Gant told me that he had liked reading *A Vision of Battlements*, and so had his assistant, the poet James Michie. It was, he said, funny. I had not, in fact, intended it to be funny, but I assumed the right posture of modesty on this revelation that I was a coming comic novelist. Unfortunately, Gant then said, it did not seem possible to publish the work as a first novel: it had too much of the quality of a second novel. Would I now go home and write a genuine first novel and submit it to Messrs William Heinemann? Certainly, I said. I treated myself to a cup of British Railways tea and then took the train back to the Midlands. The world was certainly changing.

The first novel, properly my second, that I now began to write was about life in a provincial grammar school. Gant had neither praised nor condemned the mythic substructure of *A Vision of Battlements*: he had merely not seemed to notice it. I felt it would be in order to apply myth once more to a realistic novel, and I chose the fourfold matrix of Wagner's *Ring of the Nibelungs*. This was not altogether arbitrary. The hierarchy of gods, heroes and dwarfs found a parallel in a grammar school. The gods had their specialisations, just like teachers. If Loge was the god of fire, Lodge could be the name of a chemistry master. A Miss Fry could be a sort of Freia, her golden apples her pert little breasts thrusting at her gold-weave jumper. Wotan could be Woolton, the headmaster. The possibilities were interesting. The most malignant of the dwarfs could be a spotty little demon named Albert Rich, close enough to Alberich. The golden ring stolen from the Rhine daughters could be something dangerous like a schoolgirl's diary, crammed with sexual fantasies involving members of the staff. Possession of this would confer power. It was not possible to find an easy parallel for Fafner the dragon or *Wurm*, except in an ambitious deputy headmaster who would use the diary to topple his principal Woolton. The name Gardner – that of a detestable Banbury shop owner – would do, with its Fafner suffix and its palinlogue of *drag* from *dragon*. And Siegfried? Perhaps an heroic teacher of German having an affair with a brown-haired mathematics mistress named Hilda.

The realism overcame the symbolism. This usually happens when the novelist possesses, which Joyce did not, a genuine narrative urge. It requires a perverse devotion to sheer form to hold up action while the symbols sound. The perverseness is most spectacularly visible in the 'Oxen of the Sun' episode of *Ulysses*, where the meeting of Bloom and Stephen, immensely important to the narration, is occluded by a series of literary parodies which serve the representation of the growth of the embryo in the womb. Could anything be more demented and yet more admirable? In describing the adulterous act of my hero Howarth-Siegfried and Hilda on a school excursion to Paris I tried to go further than Joyce by hiding the shameful deed in a kind of reversed history of French prose style, with the Strasbourg Oath collapsing into Latin at the moment of climax. This had nothing to do with the Ring of the Nibelungs: it was sheer literary self-indulgence.

But the main theme that began to emerge as I wrote was totally unwagnerian: the Catholic guilt already present in *A Vision of Battlements* was permitted to bloom rankly in the new work. It was the real meaning of the title *The Worm and the Ring*. Christopher Howarth the hero is no true Siegfried. He is a renegade Catholic married to a devout daughter of the Church who, suffering from Lynne's ailment of dysmenorrhoea, forbids marital sex. They have a son who may be regarded as the imaginary fulfilment of Lynne's own thwarted pregnancy. While Howarth is fornicating with Hilda in the school library, instead of patrolling the playground as master on duty, the son climbs on to a roof to retrieve a ball that has been thrown there, falls on to spiked railings (like the Alec Mitchell of my youth) and dies in agony. The father's guilt is so extreme as to be near-comic. He crawls like a worm; he has betrayed not merely the ring of marriage but the twin golden rounds of social and religious responsibility. He escapes in shame from the scene of his sin and becomes a salesman for Italian wine.

At the time of writing the novel I had been undergoing a phase of Catholic guilt which had, in part, been promoted by Graham Greene's *The Heart of the Matter*. My apostasy had never been perfect. I am still capable of moaning and breast-beating at my defection from, as I recognise, the only system that makes spiritual and intellectual sense. But I see that the novel, an essentially comic and Protestant art-form, is no place for the naked posturing of religious guilt. When I sent the typescript of *The Worm and the Ring* to Roland Gant, I foresaw the kind of response I would get with fair accuracy. Gant was 'cross'. My novel was a mess and I probably was too. Heinemann would certainly not publish it. If I was going to write a publishable novel at all I had better cleanse myself of Catholic guilt. I had told Gant that it was likely I would be going to Malaya. A very good thing too, he opined. It would be better for me to get away from Catholicism and learn that there were other religions in the world, not all of them guilt-laden. Islamicised brownskins would do me no harm. Out of Malaya a publishable novel might emerge. I dreamed of a Singapore *Ulysses* but then cast the image away. Neither Joyce nor the Catholic Church had so far done me much good.

Arrangements for leaving England and sailing to Malaya proved complicated. Selling the cottage and its furniture was no problem, but there was the question of the household pets. Could they go with us? The collie bitch Suky, I thought, certainly not: the tropics would be lethal for a long-haired dog with a chill border-country ancestry. Our Siamese cat Lalage would be doing no more than going home: no kitchen fire was ever too hot for her. Lynne's devotion to this creature, which sustained a consistent hate for me, seemed morbid but was probably not. She had a capacity for rapport with animals, wild or tame, which I have never seen equalled. She would weep over dead birds and tend sick ones. She would dry out bumble bees caught in a shower. Her love of the animal kingdom was matched by a country girl's knowledge of plants and flowers that was practical as well as aesthetic. During the bad time of the postwar cigarette shortage she would dry out Honesty and Old Man's Tobacco and roll acceptable smokes. Leaving behind temperate flora and fauna to embrace the grosser tropical varieties caused her more pain than I at first realised. Leaving Lalage behind was impossible. But the P and O ships that had the monopoly of transportation to the colonies would not take animals. I very nearly had to cancel the contract I had signed and send back the tropical kit allowance.

It was easy enough, apart from the problem of Lalage, to have grave doubts about the advisability of going to Malaya. There was a war on there, called a *dzarurat* or emergency, and we were to be sent to the royal town of Kuala Kangsar in the state of Perak, where the Chinese communist terrorists were at their most active. In the England of the summer of 1954 the consequences of our own war were dimming out. Meat was coming off the ration. We were still too poor to afford T-bone steaks, but, by dint of waiting patiently and not indulging in union activism, we had seen the Burnham scale of teachers' pay improve somewhat. Moreover, I had given a successful course in Modern English Literature for the WEA, and I had been offered good money for similar courses under the aegis of extra-mural Oxford. In time we would be able to afford a television set, if not a car. We had even taken a week's holiday in Wimereux near Boulogne, and Lynne had, I learned later, copulated in the Manche with a young man called Emile Sollers. We had more or less got over one war and here we were perversely proposing to live with another. Lynne wept much at the prospect of leaving England, which was now virtually forced upon her by a solution to the problem of transporting Lalage. For Archie Currie, still with Schats Davits, knew all about the Far Eastern runs of the Rotterdam Lloyd line. If we sailed on the *Willem Ruys*, and not the *Carthage* or *Cathay* or *Corfu*, we could take our cat. The Colonial Office demurred at the eccentricity of our choice (a Dutch line was more expensive than a British one) but eventually gave in.

I kitted myself out with white ducks and tuxedo at one of the shops in Soho that specialised in cooks' and waiters' gear. I drew two months' salary from the Oxfordshire education authority at

the beginning of the school summer vacation. We drank antici-
patory gin pahits in the Red Lion as we taught each other the
rudiments of Malay. This language was a revelation. It had
learned something that the more conservative tongues of the
Indo-European sisterhood did not wish to learn – that properties
like gender and word inflection were a needless luxury, that the
strength of a language lay in semantic subtleties and not syntactic
complexities, that the rigid taxonomy of 'parts of speech' meant
nothing. The Malay language, and later the Chinese, changed not
just my attitude to communication in general but the whole shape
of my mind.

Our few crated possessions – books, the HMV table gramophone with its records that would turn into saucers with the heat,
a picture by Gilbert Wood, my second-hand guitar – went to
Southampton. We scrubbed out an empty cottage. We travelled
to the ship with our three suitcases and our Siamese cat loudly on
heat in a basket. We had reserved first-class seats on the train, but
these had been taken by second-class undislodgeable louts and we
had to stand in the corridor. The hotel manageress at Southampton would not accept our crying cat, so we wandered the
rainy town till we found a kind of dosshouse that was used to
loud noises. We dined on half-cooked sausages and cool chips.
We had expected to leave England in a little glow of muted
monied glory, but it was not to be. England did not care whether
we left her or not. We were glad to board the *Willem Ruys* and
enter foreign territory.

THERE WERE SOME aspects of the voyage that looked forward to a
better life – drinking champagne in the first-class dining saloon,
myself in white tuxedo, Lynne in a backless evening gown, while
the ship's little orchestra played a piece I had composed for it –
Middeloceann. But the bulk of our time was spent in rowing with
the ship's officials about *de kat*. Lalage was not permitted in our
cabin. She was to be tied to a table leg in the cabin of the bo'sun.
She could be untied for a brief period of comforting caresses on a
secluded part of the promenade deck, but the ship's siren would
madden her and she would dig all her claws into me. She ended
in a cage between decks, howling to invisible heaven and frightening the Indonesian crew. A *kuching Siam*, I soothed, not an *afrit*.
The Malays were said to be fond of cats; there was even a town

called Kuching in Borneo. But these Malays had never heard a *kuching Siam* on heat before. They were ignorant and brutal Malays, the sweepings of the Indonesian ports, and they were scolded and even swiped by neighing Dutchmen. Three nights out they emptied a vat of boiling water on to the head of an unpopular steward. If these represented the Malays of Malaya, we were not sure that we wanted to go there: let us leave the ship at Colombo and find our way back. But these were Indonesian Malays, and the colonising Dutch had never treated them properly. Indeed, the Dutch colonial record was a bad one. The British had done rather better.

We spent such time as could be spared from soothing Lalage in her cage in very heavy drinking. The barmen had Martian names – Teo and Toon – and were expert in powerful cocktails. Lynne and I, who had drunk draught cider and weak bitter beer, were now confirmed gin addicts. It was the beginning of the end for one of us. We were trouncing livers that were going to suffer anyway from lack of Vitamin B, and we were subscribing to the fallacy that tropical sweat disposes of alcohol before it can get to the liver. A woman's liver, anyway, is smaller than a man's and suffers more from Vitamin B deficiency. Lynne began the digging of her grave on board the *Willem Ruys*. This became another source of guilt. Should a man take his wife to the tropics? Was it my fault that, bored, frustrated, this wife, like so many others, developed anorexia and alcoholism?

I began to shed Catholic guilt, making room for a privier variety, when we reached Port Said. For there I saw the trade name SHELL in two Arabic letters – *shin* and *lam* – and knew I had reached the territory of Allah. Malay in Malaya, if not in Indonesia, used both Romic and Arabic letters – the latter called *Jawi*, or Oriental – and I had to master that Semitic alphabet in order to pass examinations and jump the efficiency bar. Writing Arabic script changes a man. It moves from right to left, from back page to front, and it is sparing of vowel symbols. It goes in for calligraphic flourishes that suggest Arabian Nights sybaritism. The beauty of a copy of the Koran lies as much in the outward form as in the inner meaning. Even to write COCA-COLA or GUINNESS is to indulge in a small creative act like the playing of the flute. The beauty and power of Mohamed's own script did not impress Lynne. Nor, for that matter, did the Malay language when she had learned the hundred or so words suitable for kitchen instructions. I was disappointed. She did not seem disposed to take the East seriously. As the ship left the West behind she brooded too much on the past. She wept over our dog Suky. Suky had been given to a farming family and would help with the rounding up of sheep. She never gave us a backward glance, ready to resume lavish pupping as soon as she had found a mate ugly enough. Lynne wept over her father and mother, whom she was convinced she would never see again. She was half right.

As we entered a zone of heat more furious than anything I had known in Gibraltar, I felt I was approaching a world I could live in. I sweated and was happy to sweat. Where there ain't no ten commandments and a man can raise a thirst. That summed it up. My repressive Catholic heritage was a very small and eccentric item in the inventory of the world's religions. I would sweat and drink gin pahits and taste the varied sexual resources of the East. I resented my wife, as all men going East have to. The memsahibs ruined the Empire through failing to understand India. I envied the single men going to rubber estates. I was being unjust and treacherous and storing material for massive guilt. As we approached Singapore Lynne lay exhausted on her bunk. Drink, heat, chagrin? When we arrived and I dealt with the importation documents for our cat and supervised the transfer of our crates to Malayan Railways she still lay exhausted, unable to disembark. She tottered eventually to a taxi and a bed in the Raffles Hotel. There I brought in a Eurasian doctor who diagnosed exhaustion and prescribed rest. I had to telephone Kuala Kangsar and arrange a postponement of our journey north. I resented my wife. I wandered Singapore and was enchanted. I picked up a Chinese prostitute on Bugis Street. We went to a filthy *hôtel de passe* full of the noise of hawking and spitting, termed by the cynical the call of the East. I entered her and entered the territory. Two days later Lynne was fit enough to leave, and we took the night train to Ipoh.

SIX

THE FEDERATION OF Malaya, or *Persekutan Tanah Melayu*, was not quite a British colonial possession. There were three crown colonies – Penang, Malacca and Singapore – which were under direct British rule, and a number of territories under Islamic monarchs with a British adviser. These were Perak, Selangor, Pahang, Johore, Kedah, Kelantan and Trengganu, which were ruled by sultans; Perlis, under a mere raja; and Negri Sembilan (which means ninth state), where a system of matriarchal government and a law called the *adat perpateh* prevailed. By 1957 all these territories, including the three crown Straits Settlements, were to be granted total independence. This was an answer to the communist claim that Malaya was under permanent foreign capitalist domination which had to be fought to the death. The British Labour government had had some weird notion of dividing up an independent Malaya along gridlines resembling a street plan of Manhattan, but the ancient tradition of river sultanates won, with some states bigger than others, all to come under an elective king whose seat would be in the federal capital Kuala Lumpur, meaning Muddy Estuary but interpreted by André Gide, impressed by the sexual laxness of the city, as '*Kouala l'impure*'. When I arrived in Malaya in late August 1954, the great Malay cry, slogan of the United Malay Nationalist Organisation, was *Merdeka*. This means freedom. Some Chinese cynics heard it as *muntega*, or butter, which they alleged would be more useful than freedom. The Chinese and Indians, who did the work of the Federation while the Malays watched the coconuts fall, feared independence, which would put power entirely into the hands of the Malays, a very xenophobic lot.

Lynne and I arrived in the early morning at Ipoh, with luggage and howling Siamese, ate bacon and eggs in the station restaurant, then took the slow train to Kuala Kangsar. There we were met by

Jimmy Howell, principal of the Malay College and a Welsh-speaking Welshman. The Malay College was where I was to teach English. It was known as the Eton of the East, and it was reserved entirely to Malays who, since they were going to rule the Federation, needed all the education they could get. The medium of instruction was English, and there were examinations to be taken in the major subjects of the regular Western curriculum, except that History would be Malay History, the foreign language would be Malay, and there would be a test in Koranic studies. The teachers were a mixed lot – British expatriate, Chinese, Malay, Tamil, Eurasian – with a monoglot *haji* to teach the correct mode of the wailing of the word of the prophet. After a day or two at the house of Jimmy Howell, whose Chinese cook Ah Hun searched our luggage before we left to ensure that we were stealing nothing of his master's, Lynne and I were put into King's Pavilion, formerly the residence of the British Adviser to the state of Perak but now the preparatory school of the College.

Kuala Kangsar is a town built at the junction of the rivers Perak and Kangsar (*kuala* means not only an estuary but also a point where a river meets a tributary). It is the royal town of the state of Perak, though not so big or important as Ipoh or Taiping, and in it the Sultan has his palace or *istana*. It was in Perak, which means silver, that tin was first mined and the first rubber trees were planted. There was, and perhaps still is, a tradition among the more chauvinistic of the Malays that rubber had been planted in prehistoric times, when Al-Iskander the Great was ruling Malaya with the help of his tutor Aristotle, and that the British had made themselves rich through its theft and exploitation. Not true. The rubber came from Brazil by way of Kew Gardens and was wholly a British enterprise. The tappers were Tamil, as the tin-dredgers were Chinese. The Malays stayed in their *kampongs* and watched the coconuts fall or ate durian in the season of durians.

Not far from Kuala Kangsar, on the road to the tin-town of Ipoh, was the village called Sungai Siput (meaning Snail River), reputed to be the headquarters of the Chinese communist terrorists. These terrorists were certainly more active in the state of Perak than in, say, the maritime province of Kelantan, because of the great number of rubber estates there abutting on the jungle. They would come out of the jungle, steal supplies, terrorise the Chinese and Indian workers, and garotte or shoot the white planters. All this in the name of human freedom. Their arms were mostly left over from the time when they were fighting the Japanese. Perak was full of troops of the Malay Regiment, which had its quota of British conscripts, and questing planes and helicopters hummed over the jungle. The atmosphere was war-like. Car trips to Ipoh could be dangerous. The mems in their flowery dresses went to do their shopping in armoured vehicles. Planters laid their heavy service revolvers in the beer-slop of the Idris Club. This was named for a former sultan of Perak, Idris being the Koranic equivalent of Enoch. The sultan who reigned during the time of the Emergency was Yusof.

Yusof was also the name of the cook boy who came to work for us. He was homosexual but far from effeminate. He had been in and out of the hands of the police for various small thefts, and police medical examinations disclosed a *zakar* or *hak* or *pesawat* or *jantan* or *kalam* or *'urat* or *butoh* or *ayok-ayutan* and a pair of *buah pelir* or *buah peler* or *kelepir* or *bodek* or *telor* (there is no end to the number of Malay terms for the genitals) bigger than any in Kuala Kangsar. He could shift a piano single-handed. He dyed his hair with henna and muscularly minced. The advances he made to me were politely repelled, but he demanded a kind of earnest of an intimate relationship between us – a studio wedding photograph of the two of us, me in Palm Beach suit and *songkok* or Malay velvet cap, him in bridal dress adorned with frangipani. When I would not yield to this he exacted various acts of revenge – thefts of money and of underpants, finally the lacing of my gin with an aphrodisiac bought in the market. The aphrodisiac proved to be an emetic. He had picked up cooking in the kitchen of the Malay Regiment officers' mess, and he served us nauseating dishes with cold sculpted potatoes, parodies of some dream of the *haute cuisine anglaise*. Lynne taught him simpler recipes – stew of *kambing* (goat or mutton: one could never be sure) and even lobscouse, which was eventually adopted in the town as a dish believed to be native Malay. He would ruin these with fistfuls of carraway seeds. Eventually we lived on his curries, which, being Malay, were mild but not bad. If he stole from me, he made up for this by stealing from the store cupboards of the preparatory school mess – tinned peaches and polished rice. When he set the table he would place with the salt cellar and the Worcester sauce a tin of furniture polish. He could not read.

When he was given money for marketing he would spend some of it on a small animal – an ailing mouse-deer or *pelandok*, a twittering yellow bird in a bamboo cage. He adored Lalage but

Lalage mistrusted his big brown feet. Lalage became the nucleus of a whole domestic zoo. Yusof brought in, with the help of a friend, a huge turtle that slept in the bath at night but, during the day, clanked around the house, knocking its shell against the wall. We were also given a *musang* or polecat which stank to heaven and ate two *katis* of bananas every day. The polecat was named Farouche and the turtle Bucephalus. Two rhesus monkeys, male and female, were also imported, but these swung on the ceiling fans and were destructive. All over the walls cheeped *chichaks* or house lizards, hunting or copulating loudly. Black scorpions clung to the bedroom walls and greeted one on waking with twitching tails an inch or so over one's head.

Our *amah* or cleaning and laundering girl was named Mas, which means gold. She was very small, less than five feet, and of mixed origin – Sumatran, Siamese, a touch of China. She spoke a little English – 'Yusof a bit cracked, tuan,' she would say, rightly – but was fluent in all the tongues of the peninsula. Her father called himself Mr Raja and was reputed to have committed incest with her – *sumbang*, a terrible crime – but was immune from any criminal charge because the Sultan owed him money. He looked wholly Tamil. Mas had been married at the age of twelve. This was unusually young, but the occupying Japanese had had the delicacy not to send married women to their brothels. Mas's one son, born when she was thirteen, was a burly policeman who looked ten years older than his mother.

I gained the impression from Mas, and from other Malays, real or pseudo, that the Japanese occupation had been easy on the sons of the soil but very tough on the Chinese. This, naturally, pleased the sons of the soil, who had been allowed to turn to Mecca in the west at sunrise on condition that they turned to the east first and who, apart from the brothelisation of the unmarried girls, had been treated with reasonable courtesy. Yusof Tajuddin, one of my colleagues at the Malay College, had learned Japanese so well that he won an elocution contest open to native Nipponese as well as to the occupied. The learning of Japanese did nobody anything but good, since the Japanese were going to take over the East, if not the world, commercially when their more aggressive imperialism failed. Yusof Tajuddin had rather liked the Japanese, a clean and logical people. The Japanese had been impressed with the colonial system they took over. To the Malays the return of the British had not meant liberation from an oppressive regime but the mere replacement of a set of yellow foreigners by white ones. It was the Chinese, aggressive in business, murderous in the jungle, who were the real enemy.

Yusof Tajuddin may have liked the Japanese, and Mas have tolerated them, but both shuddered at memories of what King's Pavilion had been during the occupation. 'This not good place, mem,' Mas used to say. Yusof Tajuddin, in his impeccable RP English, was more explicit. King's Pavilion had been used as a centre of torture and interrogation. Dried blood, irremovable with any amount of Vim, stained the floor of the main bathroom, through whose open channels much blood had flowed. Yusof Tajuddin explained the peculiar chill of the bathroom, otherwise inexplicable in a house with few fans on which the sun beat, in psychic terms: the frozen hands of death clutched it still and would clutch it for ever. A Scottish engineer of intense scepticism entered the bathroom on our invitation and came out shuddering. In the raintrees and banyans at sunset, Yusof the cook alleged, the voices of the tortured and executed could be heard complaining. Lynne and I could not hear these voices, but we knew Yusof to be superstitious in the manner of his race. He found *hantu-hantu* (or *hantu 2*) everywhere. I do not know the etymology of the word, which means ghost, but have often wondered whether there is some ancient connection, through Sanskrit, with *haunt*. For Yusof everything was haunted. His middle finger, or *jari hantu*, was haunted and must be careful about what it touched. He had seen a *hantu bangkit*, a sheeted ghost risen from the grave that, prevented from walking by its winding sheet, had rolled towards Yusof with evil intent. He had seen the *hantu belian* or tiger ghost. There was a kitchen ghost, disguised as a mat, that sometimes reared itself at him and made him smash the crockery. There were gnomes in the soil, *hantu tanah*, and the owl, or *burong hantu*, was a literal ghost-bird that stared at him and made him scream in his sleep. He knew all the *hantu-hantu* or *hantu 2*. The voices in the banyans were nothing compared with the visible ghosts with trailing entrails or the spectral huntsman (*hantu pemburu*), but they were there. We had better believe it.

There were good ghostly reasons for not wishing to stay in King's Pavilion, but the real causes for our dissatisfaction with the place were more mundane. It was beautiful enough, an ample structure of the Victorian age, and the view from its verandahs was sumptuous. It looked down on great trees and gardens tended by thin Tamils drunk on *todi* or palm wine; beyond was the confluence of rivers; beyond again the jungle and the mountains. But the gorgeousness of the vista was in-adequate payment for the responsibility imposed on us. We inhabited what was in effect a huge flat cut off, but not cut off enough, from the classrooms and dormitories of the prepa-ratory school. At the beginning of the school year weeping Malay boys would arrive with their mothers and fathers, who would stay a night with them and try to stay more, and pre-pare to be turned into sophisticated collegians. They knew no English, and this had to be taught to them in a two-year course by a Mr Mahalingam and a Mrs Vivekananda. They were taught weird vowels and doubtful accentuations. Mrs Viveka-nanda made them sing 'Old Blick Jooooh' and Mr Mahalingam did not correct them when they turned *bullock cart* into *bulokar*. When lessons were over they made much noise and pissed from their balcony into the inner court, visible while Lynne and I ate lunch. If I railed at them they ran away. If I entered their screaming dormitory they would drag out their prayer mats and howl towards Mecca, knowing that their religious de-votions rendered them untouchable by the infidel. They called me *Puteh*, or white, and also *Mat Salleh*, or Holy Joe. The other teachers of the Malay College could go to quiet houses on Bukit Chandan, meaning Sandalwood Hill, when their work was over. Lynne and I had to cope with noise and responsibility.

It was literally a responsibility for life and death. The garden was full of snakes, of which Malaya has a large variety, and a king cobra with a growing family was much around King's Pavi-lion during my tenure. Scorpions would get into the boys' shoes or beds and sting them bitterly. Hygiene was a problem, for the water supply was erratic and sometimes totally failed. Because of some fault in the meter, the Water Department recorded an excessive use of water in a dry time when, in fact, there was no water at all. My complaints and counter-complaints were rebuffed. I groaned in my stomach: I had the reputation of being bloody-minded; it was the army all over again. Moreover, a linguistic burden was being imposed upon me which I could not, in my first few months, easily sustain. I had to harangue these young boys in good idiomatic Malay and, though I was learning the language fast, I was not able to learn it fast enough.

Colonial functionaries had to learn the major language of their territory at a formidable level. A kitchen jargon, good enough for wives, with bad grammar and a master-race pronunciation, was usually preferred by the natives, who did not believe it was possible for a foreigner with a white skin to learn their tongue. Colonial civil servants had to disconcert these natives with a linguistic mastery, including a control of many registers, equal to, or greater than, their own. In Malaya there were many languages, but Malay was considered, for political reasons, to be the obligatory specialisation. You could, if you were mad enough, learn Hakka or Cantonese or Kuo-Yü or Tamil or Hindi or Urdu, but you had to take examinations in Malay. You had to take the Standard One examination in your first year and the Standard Two before the end of your first three-year tour. If you failed, an efficiency bar was invoked, and you were not entitled to annual pay increments. There had been an Englishman posted to Malay College who had opted to specialise in Chinese (Kuo-Yü, the national language which few Malayan Chinese spoke but which their children learned at school), and the political pressures of Malayaphonia had not yet begun to apply. He learned Chinese well and could write three thousand characters, but he was punished for his eccentricity. He was posted to Kelantan as headmaster of a Malay school in a district where there were few Chinese. This story was told to me by Jimmy Howell with relish, but I was appalled at that vindictiveness. Howell himself had failed again and again to pass his Standard Two Malay, but the efficiency bar had not been invoked. He, like too many expatriates, did not take language-learning seriously enough. During the war he had had the chance to learn Japanese, and he had been sent on a course with fine amenities, including recording apparatus. He had used this apparatus for recording popular songs. I did not think this funny.

I was given, at the expense of the Federation, instruction in Malay spoken and written (Rumi and Jawi) from a *munshi* named Syed Omar. Syed signifies descent from the Prophet, improbable in a Malay but an accepted fiction, and a Syed had to be called *tuan*. Malays who had no prophetic blood or had not been to Mecca to become hajis were usually addressed as *enche*. Tuan Syed Omar instructed me well and sometimes rapped my knuckles with a ruler. He taught me how to address sultans and rajas, with whom one conversed in a register unavailable to the common sort. The common sort ate, or *makan*, but princes *santap*. Rice-planters and fisherfolk slept, or *tidor*, but their rulers *beradu*. The root of *beradu* signified a singing contest of handmaidens in which the winner went to bed with her lord. There was a very large princely vocabulary and it had to be learned. I also had to read the *Hikayat Abdullah*, the autobiography of the *munshi* of Sir Stamford Raffles, and take in the political wrangles and court gossip of a newspaper printed in Jawi. These lessons took place on the verandah of King's Pavilion while mosquitoes zoomed and struck and flying beetles boomed, copulated, shed their winds and died. I passed my Standard One at distinction level after three months of instruction. This did not make me popular among my fellow-expatriates. I went on to pass my Standard Two in less than a year, a Federation record. This made me hated. Before leaving Malaya I took the optional Standard Three examination, all hard Arabic and Sanskrit loanwords and scrawled Jawi, which conferred a bonus. This made me worse hated, but I did not care.

There was always an amateurishness in colonial administration, and even in technical specialisation, which was deemed desirable by the British, who have never trusted professionalism. Sir Frank Swettenham, one of the founder Malayan administrators, laid down succinctly the qualities desirable in a new recruit to the service – good at games, not so good at studies, unmarried and amoral enough to employ a sleeping dictionary, not too matey otherwise with the natives, clubbable. He might have added something about artistic taste, or lack of it, but that, like a fear of intellectualism, is probably implied in the first two items. If I had hoped to find intellectual companionship among my white colleagues it was because I expected a transferral of the grammar school atmosphere to a college celebrating fifty years of academic glory. But there was little glory, except on the rugger and hockey fields. Jimmy Howell announced with satisfaction at a staff meeting the installation of a hundred stout locks for the library bookcases. 'One for each book,' I unwisely said. The extra-curricular lives of the teachers reflected the lack of academic ambition in the school itself. They had their long-playing record-players and their shelves of book club novels, golf clubs in the hallway and stengahs on the tray. They took trips to Ipoh to shop at Whiteways and take a bit of decent *makan* in the Ipoh Club (*ikan tinggeri belle meunière*). They had their decent little cars.

Lynne and I had never learned to drive, an aspect of our long poverty, and I was not sure that I wanted a car. Few of my non-expatriate colleagues had them, and to whizz around the little royal town in a Ford or Austin was to emphasise the gulf between the privileged whites and the poor blacks, browns and yellows. Not that the coloured were necessarily without cars: there were rich Chinese and a Sultan with a whole polished fleet of Buicks and Daimlers. But the Malays trudged on big brown bare feet or took trishaws. I walked and soaked my shirt in the damnable humidity: this, and my growing mastery of the Malay language, placed me too close to the natives for the comfort of my colleagues. I also carried on a quiet love affair with one of the natives, a girl named Rahimah who worked as a waitress in a Chinese coffee shop. She was very small and very pretty and she was a divorcée. Muslim divorce was too easy, and there were far too many of these cast-off girls about. I was deeply sorry for Rahimah, who had a small wage, scant tips, and a small son named Mat to look after (Mat being the Malay short form of Mohamed). I gave her what money I could, and we made love in her tiny cell that smelt of curry and Himalayan Bouquet while Mat was at the junior Koran school.

I had better say a little now about love-making in the East. With Malays there were certain restrictions on the amatory forms, laid down by Islam, so that only the posture of Venus observed was officially permitted. Islamic women were supposed to be passive houris. The demands of Islamic wives for frequent sexual congress did not indicate true sensual appetite: they were a test of the fidelity of their husbands. A Malay female body, musky, shapely, golden-brown, was always a delight. Malay women rarely ran to fat, which was reserved to the wives of the Chinese towkays and was an index of prosperity. Malay women kept their figures after childbirth through a kind of ritual roasting over an open fire, tightly wrapped in greased winding-sheets. They walked proudly in *sarongs* and *bajus* (little shaped coats), their glossy hair permanently waved, their heels high. They were seductive as few white women are. Lying with Rahimah I regretted my own whiteness: a white skin was an eccentricity and looked like a disease. Simple though Malay sex was, it had an abundant vocabulary. To copulate was *jamah* or *berjima* or *juma'at* or *bersatu* (literally to become one), or *sa-tuboh*, *asmara*, *beranchok* (this term was peculiar to Perak), *ayut*, *ayok*, and much much more. There was even a special term for sexual congress after the forty-day birth taboo – *pechah kepala barut* – and there were two for the boy's initiation after circumcision – *menyepoh tua*, with someone older, *menyepoh muda*, with someone younger. The orgasm was dignified with an Arabic loanword, *shahuat*, or colloquially called *rumah sudah ratip* – literally, 'the structure has gone into an ecstatic trance', *ratip* or *ratib* being properly the term for the transport produced by the constant repetition of the holy name *Allah*. Where the Western term for experiencing orgasm is, in whatever language, 'to come', the Malay mind, using *keluar*, thinks of going out, leaving the body, floating on air.

My experience with Chinese girls was mostly, alas, commercial. Prostitutes, or dance-hall girls, knew all the postures, were thin, live, lithe, sinuous, but disappointingly uninvolved in the act. Kuala Kangsar, like other Eastern towns, was full of Chinese women who went around in sexual sororities, aware, in their age-old wisdom, that only a woman can give a woman satisfaction, and that multiple congress is more ecstatic than dual. In one Malayan school I knew, the sole Chinese woman teacher seduced the white teaching wives, broke up all their marriages, and induced a male and a female suicide. Chinese men, so Chinese women seemed to believe, were not useful in bed. They deemed it sufficient to have a long-lasting erection, and there were Chinese medicines around, usually with a high lead content, which ruined the prostate but contrived a hard and unproductive rod. I knew a Chinese businessman of eighty in Kuala Kangsar who had married a wife of eighteen, a sign of prosperity unmatched by marital prowess until he filled his system with lead. He died smiling on an erection.

The few Thailand women I met in northern Malaya called the sexual act *kedunkading*, with a resonant stress on the last syllable, enjoyed congress as a laughing game and experienced quick and happy orgasms with little help from the male. It was the Indian women who, as one would expect from the serious Sanskrit amatory manuals, disclosed most knowledge of the techniques of inducing transport, for themselves and for their partners, of renewing desire more times than the frame seemed capable of supporting, of relating enjoyment to strenuous athletics, and leaving the male body a worn-out rag tenuously clinging to a spiritualised sensorium open-eyed in heaven. I had sexual encounters with Tamil women blacker than Africans, including a girl who could not have been older than twelve, but none with Bengalis or Punjabis. Whatever her race, the Eastern partner's allure was always augmented by the ambience of spice from the spice-shops, the rankness of the drains, the intense heat of the day, the miracle of transitory coolness at sundown, with the coppersmith birds hammering away at tree-trunks and the fever-bird emitting its segment of a scale – sometimes three notes, sometimes four. Sex in the West is too cold, too unaromatic. It is only fair to say that Orientals, especially, for some reason, Sikhs, have found ecstasies in Bayswater unprocurable in the lands of spice.

I wrote a novel some years ago which presents a whole lifetime of homosexuality and, in American bookshops, found its way to the shelf specialising in 'gay' literature. For all that, I have never had homosexual proclivities, and I do not well understand what causes the inversion, which goes against biology. There seemed, in my time in Malaya, very few British expatriates drawn to brown male bodies. Islam does not approve of sodomy, despite its prevalence in the desert and in the lands of the Moghrab, and my cook Yusof seemed to be a rare and notorious exception to the sexual current of Kuala Kangsar. He was sometimes called benignly a *limau nipis*, or thin-skinned lime, which is one of the few terms the Malays have for catamite, or a member of the *kaum nabi Lot*, the tribe of the prophet Lot, which is a libel on the one straight man of the Cities of the Plain, but his disposition was merely mused upon as an interesting deviation. In the dormitories of the Malay College there was little amatory thumping around. I was surrounded in the Federation by a vigorous fleshly normality. Only the Sikhs, feeling themselves to be an exclusive warlike brotherhood, grunted against each other with turbans awry and beards wagging. The land pullulated with brown and yellow children tumbling into the monsoon drains. There was no danger of its going dry through unwillingness to breed.

There was enough commercial sex around in the towns of Malaya, but there was a certain discretion of display. The secondary exploitation of it, in stage shows or blatant underwear advertisements, was mostly abhorrent to the Eastern mind, though there was a famous Chinese striptease performer named Rose Chan who drew crowds of towkays panting under their binoculars. It was the white woman who was expected to be shameless and provocative. Marilyn Monroe and Jane Russell were to be seen in Cinemascope, and there was a full-page advertisement for *The Barefoot Contessa* in the *Straits Times* presenting Ava Gardner as 'the most beautiful animal in the world'. Some of my students pinned this page to the wall above their beds. The crinolined or embustled mems of the old days had been untouchable, but things were changing in the new age of democracy and equality. All Kuala Kangsar was on fire when a French film called *Ah! Les Belles Bacchantes* was shown. In it French women exhibited pert little bosoms and men of all races united in groans of lust.

The Frenchwoman, or *perempuan Peranchis*, stood for lasciviousness, and the town of Kota Bharu on the East Coast was known, pathetically, as the Paris of the East because of the sexual licence that was believed to prevail there. There was a Frenchwoman in Kuala Kangsar, but she was a very austere doctor of medicine in a white coat. There was only one woman who, not behaving like the traditional English mem in the East and possessing the blonde beauty of a film star, was taken to be erotic in the French manner, and that was my wife.

If I had been quietly learning about Eastern sex, while pretending to be running a literary and debating society in the Malay College, the two of us had, almost from the start, been learning about Eastern society in less specific ways and out in the open. This meant drinking Tiger and Anchor beer in Chinese *kedais* and talking to the natives. We had hoped to find among the Malayans properties like ancient Oriental wisdom and a lack of the racial snobbery which made the *orang puteh* or white man so detestable. But we found that the Chinese, Malays and Indians were no wiser and just as much given to racial prejudice. The Malays called us *lintah puteh* or white leeches, the Chinese *ketam bersepit* or pincered crabs (in allusion to their chopsticks), and the Tamil *taik Adam* or Adam's shit. They were highly conscious of gradations of colour, and the blacker you were the closer you were to the primordial slime. Yusof Tajuddin was an *orang pekan* or Penang man with mixed Malay and Tamil blood and was very dark. His lighter-coloured Malay brethren called him *Raja Hitam*, the black raja, and he had seemed to try to save himself from total negritude by marrying a Malay woman so fair as to be called 'Teh or Puteh. There was an ambivalence in the native attitude to whiteness. The white man was detestable, but the skin of the beloved was praised as being close to *thalji* or snow, a purely poetic image probably of Persian origin: no Malayan had ever seen snow, except in the film *Holiday Inn*, whose song 'White Christmas' was much crooned by Malay College students through the college microphone. There used to be a false doctrine disseminated among American univerity students that the symbolism of colours was reversed in Africa and Asia, so that white meant evil and black good, but, in Malaya at least, black was bad because it was the colour of night when the *hantu 2* were busy. The day was white, honest and harmless.

Sadly, very sadly, a number of the Malay clerks, Chinese businessmen, Sikh railway officials and Tamil civil servants we drank with considered Lynne and myself of a breed inferior to the aloof club-frequenting whites because of our desire to be friendly with the natives. One Tamil who had recently learned the word *despicable* said to me: 'You know, Mr Wilson, you are despicable.' Why? 'Because you drink with us people who are known to the white man to be despicable.' Sadly too a Sikh policeman slipped off his sandal and, under the kedai table, began to stroke Lynne's shod white foot with his great bare brown one. She was of the new white approachable breed and, as American films made clear, had all the wantonness of Western women. This made Lynne cry and put herself into brief purdah, but soon she was carrying on a very intimate relationship with, if not a Sikh, certainly a Punjabi. Indeed, a Punjabi police corporal of the transport pool.

THERE WAS, BECAUSE of the Emergency or war, a new class of expatriate policeman around in Malaya. The police were as much engaged in the war as the army, and it was the police who were in charge of armoured transport. Policemen used to emergencies were brought out under contract, chiefly from Palestine, and they were made into lieutenants. The rank of police-lieutenant seemed to imply a degree of education and refinement, but most of the breed who appeared to drink deeply in the Idris Club were a brutal lot. They spoke a little debased Arabic and had learned ten words of Malay. A lieutenant of the Malay Regiment, whether white or brown, was more than a cut above any of these and he considered that they debased his own rank. But there was one police-lieutenant of mysterious origin who might have been Anglo-Indian but spoke English with an accent undoubtedly Midlands though hard to place. He was sallow-brown through the punishment of his liver. He was nearly seven feet high and was called Lofty. His real name was Donald D. Dunkeley. He had spent most of his working life, in what trade was never made clear, in India, and he spoke Hindi, Urdu and Punjabi with fluency and, I learned, an almost pedantic accuracy. He was in charge of police transport though he himself could hardly drive, and his constant companion was his corporal, Alladad Khan. Alladad Khan was moustached and neat and had married above himself. His wife, Hadijah Bibi, had a brother named Sardar Khan who had been to a police college in England and was of high rank in the Singapore police force. He was constantly used as a stick for beating Alladad Khan, whose wife accused him of lack of ambition and a taste for Western impurities like Tiger beer, bacon and eggs and kissing on the mouth. He was a Muslim like all his race but a bad one, something like a Malay.

Lofty Dunkeley knew that I had no car and had heard me in the club consider whether I ought to succumb to the white man's ethos and buy one. Lofty was rather anxious that I should buy a car for reasons of his own. There was an assistant rubber estate manager named Halliday who was due to be repatriated and anxious to sell his car so that he could settle his Singapore Cold Storage and club bar bills. Halliday desperately needed repatriation. His estate had known too many invasions from communist terrorists and two of his Tamil overseers had been garotted to the accompaniment of a song about the brotherhood of man. He himself had missed death from rifle shots too narrowly and too often, and he was a hard-drinking tangle of nerves. He wanted seventeen hundred Straits dollars or *ringgit* for his Austin A70 and Lofty, falsely or at least prematurely, said he had found a buyer, though the price would have to be brought down by a couple of hundred. A Straits dollar was worth two shillings and fourpence in those rational pre-decimal days, so that there were exactly nine to a guinea. Halliday, after hysterical drunken wrangling, agreed to let the car go for fifteen hundred bucks. Lofty then approached me over warm Tiger beer in the Double Lion kedai and announced a real bargain – a second-hand A70 like new for seventeen hundred dollars. I needed a car, meaning that he did, and he knew I did not drive, but he would provide Alladad Khan as a regular unpaid driver, punch out the bullet dents in the bodywork, and see to free oil and servicing (not petrol, though: far too bloody risky). And, I asked, what was in it for him, Lofty? Well, he said, he liked the odd drink, same as myself, and there were several little kedais on the dangerous road north which he frequently had to travel to inspect transport pools of the Police Circle. If he parked outside a kedai it was better to use a private car than a police vehicle. Too much bloody natter which would get back to his boss and, besides, if you used a police vehicle you had to have a bloody armed escort. The car he proposed that I buy was, he admitted, likely to get shot at, but duty was duty, we all had to take our bloody chance. When the car was not being parked outside kedais or being shot at I was welcome, with Alladad Khan at the wheel, to use it in any way I wished, whatever that meant. All this seemed a reasonable proposal, so I drew

seventeen hundred dollars from the bank and left the trans-
action to Lofty. He got the car for fourteen hundred dollars so
was able to pay off one or two bar bills of his own.

A very curious sodality now began. The four of us went around
in the A70, its bullet dents punched out, its body regularly
polished by Malay police underlings. The car had no spare wheel,
but Lofty was fatalistic about a tyre being shot at. The terrorists
lurking in the scrub at the sides of the road were likely to get all
four and then you were bloody done for. A short life and a beery
one. Lofty lived for Tiger and Anchor and, when I could afford
it, Carlsberg, which cost more but was better than the Singapore
brews. That car never took us any great distance. It would bring
Lofty and Alladad Khan from Police Transport to King's Pavilion, where Lofty drank our gin raw and our refrigerated beer
thawed out, since he could not abide anything cold. He was in
the East, he said, because it was warm. Cold beer was a sort of
anomaly. Alladad Khan learned to drink heavily too. After a
long tropical night of boozing they would wake from dry-
mouthed sleep on the two planter's chairs on the verandah and
start again. Alladad Khan would have an intentional tremor and
Lofty profound head-shakes. Lofty's regular pleasantry was: 'Who
am I nodding at? The same bugger you're bloody waving to.'
He would translate this into Urdu. He knew no Malay and used
Alladad Khan as an interpreter as well as a driver. Alladad Khan
called Lofty Lofferty and was rebuked: 'Let's have a bit more of
the Mister bloody Dunkeley.' Alladad Khan addressed me as *sahib*
and *munshi*, having a traditional Indian respect for a teacher. With
Lynne he fell in love.

Love. A damnable concept in Malay, which has about two
hundred words for the condition. The Sanskrit loanword is *berahi*
and the Arabic one *muhabbat*. 'To fall in love with' is *jatoh hati ka-
pada*, literally 'to allow one's liver to tumble on to or into or
towards somebody'. What Alladad Khan said to Lynne was: '*Saya*
love', *saya* meaning I. I did not know about this. I would go to
bed at midnight, leaving Lofty snoring on the verandah and
Lynne and Alladad Khan talking quietly in Malay under the
ceiling fan of the living-room. Friendship, I thought, East and
West making connection on a Platonic level. I found out later
that the connection was physical and conducted in the spare bedroom. Should I have been angry? My own infidelities were experimental, fired by a reasonable desire for knowledge; this was
the sort of thing that should bring in Alladad Khan's wife with a

sharpened kris and induce me to pay five dollars to a professional Malay assassin. But the discretion of Alladad Khan was exemplary, and women have an inborn gift of duplicity. Well, Lynne was at least penetrating or being penetrated by the exotic. She had talked much of wanting to go home, there was nothing for her in Malaya, but now she wanted to stay. This wanting to stay survived the end of the love affair with Alladad Khan. Both realised the impossibility of the relationship. Yusof walked one night in his sleep and was heard burbling about *hantu 2* outside the spare bedroom. If Yusof had awakened he would not have been slow to spread the scandal. He rather fancied Alladad Khan himself, but he had been rebuffed.

We could no longer stay in Malay College because of the deterioration of the relationship between myself and Jimmy Howell. He wanted me there in King's Pavilion, soothing little boys with nightmares and keeping them away from the haunts of the king cobra and its family, which was now growing up and puffing out angry hoods. I heard that there was a new two-storeyed house available on Bukit Chandan and told Jimmy Howell that I did not see why my wife and myself should not enjoy the amenities of other expatriate married couples. Damn it, even Mr Vivekananda and his lady had a decent semi-detached and an *orang kebun* tending a private garden of papaya trees and pepper bushes. Damn it, there was no peace in King's Pavilion even when the vacations came, for then the Chinese repair men got to work and used our lavatories insolently. But Jimmy Howell wanted me to be in charge of the welfare of the junior school and rebuked me for claiming a quiet domestic life off duty. Regretfully, I had to ask for a transfer. Until the transfer came through my principal and I had no word to address to each other. It was an unhappy situation.

In some ways I would be sorry to leave Malay College, for I liked the senior boys whom I taught, and felt that a rapport was growing. They appreciated my pedagogy. They were supposed to study Chaucer in Nevil Coghill's translation, but I had passages from the original cyclostyled and passed round. Mediaeval English seemed to them closer to Malay, at least in pronunciation, than the braying diphthongal modern instrument of colonial oppression. Not that there *was* any colonial oppression: the boys liked to believe there was and that coming independence was really liberation from a harsh yoke. They held to the myth of hating Mat Salleh, or Holy Joe, but they accepted his culture. They accepted it best in its American form, which represented a revolutionary rejection of colonialism and a refashioning of the autocratic ancient into the democratic modern. Even boys in the junior school would sign their little essays Ibrahim bin Yusof, *yanki kauboi*, or Mohamed bin Lot, *chicago ganster*. Everbody drank Coca-Cola, which transliterated beautifully into Jawi. It was preferred to orange crush, which they generally wrote in their essays on picnics as orang crush, suggesting violence and cannibalism. They regretted that their religion forbade the eating of hot dogs, which had *haram* pork in them. They listened with interest to my reading aloud of *The Sun Also Rises* or *The Killers*. They wanted to play baseball but had to make do with cricket. Into the British vacuum, due in 1957, America would inevitably step. Japan too. It was an anachronism to make them read *Essays of Elia* or the poems of Kipling, a writer who seemed to them unforgivably crude.

For these young men were delicate of perception, very courteous, and, though active enough at games, lacking in energy and far from robust. This had something to with the enervating climate, which knew no seasons except the brief interlude of the monsoon cutting into an endless summer. The hours of dawn and sunset never varied, and though there was damp there was never any invigorating chill. You could find this chill if you climbed to the Cameron Highlands, but that was a white man's preserve. My students were often tired and could not be driven too hard. Driving them too hard could result in the energetic, murderous but eventually suicidal onset of *amok*. Failure of sensitivity to their taboos could have the same effect. To touch them on the head was unpardonable; to order them to go out into the rain was a physical affront. The Malay response to a hurt or insult was a long silent period of brooding following by running *amok*. The *pengamok* would kill whoever he could in the expectation of being killed himself. There had been *pengamoks* at Malay College, driven to murder by British stupidity or harshness, but not in my time. An approach to *amok*, though in the town not the school, involved an Australian colleague named Morley. Morley had picked up a Malay injured in a car crash and driven him in his own car to the town hospital, where the man bled to death. The man's friend tried to kill Morley because of a purely, as it were, syntactical relationship with the dead man. This at least suggested a structure, but most *pengamoks* killed with a fine arbitrariness.

There were two other Eastern diseases, painful to see but

dangerous only to the sufferer. One was *latah*, defined in Wilk-inson's Malay–English Dictionary as 'a nervous paroxysmal disease aroused by suggestion and often taking the form of hysterical mimicry'. The aetiology is, I think, unknown. One Malay boy exhibited the symptoms when someone stupidly suggested to him that he was a bicycle: he pedalled himself to exhaustion, slept, foamed in spasm, and then woke to forget all about it. The other ailment, *shook jong*, had a similarly baffling cause but affected only the Chinese. A Chinese male would be convinced that his penis was retracting into his scrotum and try to hold it to his leg by sticking a sharp knife in. The metaphysical explanation had something to do with the force of the *yin* overcoming that of the *yang*. It could end in hysteria and death. I actually saw a Chinese so afflicted in Kuala Lumpur. He stole a superfine jeweller's knife and rammed it in, screaming, on the sunlit street. Laurence Dur-rell was very unwise to make a joke about this in his novel *Tunc*, suggesting that an amulet engrossed with an anagram of his title might drive it away. *Shook jong* is no joke. Nor is *latah*. Nor, God help us, is *amok*.

None of my boys, as I say, ran *amok*, but they could nurse deep resentments. They resented that one of their number, Mat bin Hassan, had been expelled for allegedly copulating with a student from a Malay girls' school in the grounds of Malay Col-lege. The belief of his fellows was that they had merely been kissing, an exotic importation from American films and not part of the Malay pattern of foreplay. The Malay kiss is made with the nose on the cheek of the beloved and is called a *chium*. To use the lips was exciting and possibly immoral, but it was not copulation. When my Fifth Form learned that I was to leave the college they assumed that I was doing so in disgust at the treatment of Mat bin Hassan, over whose summary expulsion I was alleged to have argued hotly with the principal. The form leader, Hussein bin Wahab, made an affecting speech, and then everybody stood to sing a song of farewell which Ahmad bin Aladdin had composed. I wish I could have understood the words, which were in an English whose stresses did not coincide with those of the music, the samba-like rhythm of which was gently struck on a desk-top. I gave Ahmad bin Aladdin my second-hand guitar. He wept. I wept. We all wept. *Tangis*, weeping. *Tangisi*, to weep. *Menangis*, a more telling form of the verb. Note the Welsh-type mutation. The term came to an end.

Lynne and I were to be sent to Kota Bharu on the East Coast,

not far from the Thai border. Kota Bharu means Newcastle. But
soon it appeared that we might have to leave Kuala Kangsar only
to go home to England. For I was given a medical examination
of some thoroughness, and there was a sizeable spot on one of
my lungs, according to the X-ray plate. If this were cancer or
tuberculosis my contract would be cancelled, since severe illness
was not permitted during the period of probation. We had sold
our cottage and our furniture and had nothing to go back to.
Lynne showed her habitual strength of character and worked out
a future. She would work, I would try to write. It was a kind of
rehearsal for what was to happen in 1959. Meanwhile we awaited
a more thorough examination of the X-ray plate than was possible in Kuala Kangsar. In Ipoh it was concluded that the spot on
the picture was fly-dirt. In relief we got drunk.

We got drunk at a party given at the Istana, or sultanic palace,
for visiting British MPs. We were invited, but Lofty Dunkeley
was not; nevertheless, untuxedoed, he insisted on going (all that
free booze). He did not know how to address His Highness Sultan
Yusof. He said '*Ada baik?*' to him, which means 'How's tricks?',
and then added his habitual little joke of 'motor *baik* or pedal
baik?' He also called the Sultan *lu*, which is the form of 'you'
used only to Chinese cooks. The Sultan was stony. The MPs
were ebullient. I asked Sir Robert Boothby how long he thought
the British would stay in Malaya. 'A thousand years,' he replied.
Another MP was amazed at the symmetry of the trees in the
jungle, which he took, in his brandy euphoria, to symbolise
somehow the well-organised British presence. He did not seem
to realise that he had been looking at a rubber estate. Some British
officers of the Malay Regiment told the MPs how they were
keeping the territory free for capitalist exploitation. 'There was
I,' kept saying a captain named Paddy O'Shaughnessy, 'on top of
the *gunong*, with me *senapang* under me arm.' Mountain, gun.
'"Another island free of terrorists," I reported.' He had so
reported of some twenty islands, none of which had previously
known the foot of man. To the Sultan he introduced himself as
'Paddy O'Shaughnessy, your honour, first to arroive and last to
leave. There's a nice little bottom,' giving an amorous tap to the
rump of the Sultan's latest wife. The Sultan was glazed. Father of
the Perak faithful, he had nevertheless to drink brandy on doctor's
orders.

Back at King's Pavilion, whence our goods had already been
shipped east, Alladad Khan *menangis*. Also Lynne. Also myself.

Lofty Dunkeley did not weep but got seriously drunk on *todi*. He had bought a farewell gallon of it from the Tamil drink-shop, forbidden to Europeans, but Lofty's continent of provenance remained, last as first, in doubt. *Todi* stank of vegetable decay and burning brown paper. You had to plug your nose while you drank it. It was rumoured to be rich in vitamins. It certainly got one drunk.

Lynne and I, and Lalage loud on elected heat in her basket, took an aircraft of Malayan Airways to Penang and awaited a flight thence across the spine of mountain and jungle to the East Coast. Yusof Tajuddin and his wife Puteh met us for a drink in the airport bar. Yusof spoke of the Malays of the state of Kelantan, of which Kota Bharu is the capital, with reproachful envy. 'Children of pleasure,' he termed them. The coast outside the town was known as the *Pantai Chinta Berahi*, usually translated as the Beach of Passionate Love but more accurately rendered as the Beach of Irregular Lust. He warned me to watch myself. I proposed watching myself, and Lynne also. Each of us had received an anonymous letter signed 'The Voice of the East', in which the sins of one were lovingly recounted to the other in babu English full of references to the holiness of even scandalous truth, 'precious jewel though embedded in head of toad', and the horrors of jealousy 'that is mocking the meat it is feeding on, sister (brother)'. Chastened and determined to be chaste, we boarded our plane, Lalage howling in insincere *chinta berahi*.

I was going to train students of all the races of the East at the teachers' training college that had been set up between Kota Bharu and its airport. It had been set up on one of the greatest termite colonies of the East. The termites were slow to eat up the Public Works Department huts and family residences. They found the college library easier fodder and chewed it up from within, leaving only the book spines on show. The staff of the college, with the exception of myself, did not belong to the Colonial Service. They had all come from a Malayan college in Kirby, Liverpool. The Federation education authority discovered that it was cheaper to bring over a handful of instructors from England than to send hundreds of Malayan students there. These instructors, together with their principal and vice-principal, had no obligation to learn Malay or burrow into the intricacies of a mixed Asiatic culture. They were on contract and had no stake in the history, past or future, of the territory.

The segment of the territory called Kelantan was as strange to the students as to their teachers. This was a very Malay state that went its own way and regarded the civilised west beyond the jungles and mountains as a foreign country. Penang? Kuala Lumpur? A corrupt island and a corrupter city, where there were too many Chinese and the air stank of pork. The Malay spoken in Kelantan was as different from the Malay of Johore (generally regarded as the standard form of the language) as Dutch from the Queen's English. It was unfortunate for me that I had at once to take my Standard Two Malay examination in Kota Bharu. There was no trouble with the papers, but for the oral test I was bidden converse with an ancient toothless Malay of the kampongs who said *hamba ta' 'seh* when a Kuala Kangsar man would have said *saya tidak mahu* (I do not wish to). I protested to the Mentri Besar or chief minister of the state, who was sitting in on the examination, and said, in English: 'Do you understand, sir?' He replied, in a starched Oxford accent, 'Not a word, old boy.' So a toothed and charming young woman was brought in who spoke the clear language of federal prostitution. I understood and passed.

The Mentri Besar, Tungku Hamsa, was a dwarf prince of the sultanic family who believed in Western progress so long as it did not go too far. The pleasure garden of the city, whose prostitutes were mostly discarded wives of the Sultan, he named the Biarritz Park. The train that went daily to Bangkok he called the *Sumpitan Mas* or Golden Blowpipe. This was blowpipe territory. Little men of the tribe of Temiars, the aboriginals or *orang asli* of the state, would emerge occasionally from the jungle to blow a painless lethal poison into the domestic animals of the kampongs and drag the corpses back to eat. These charming folk, who had only three integers in their counting – one, two, many – had charming superstitions: you were in for trouble if you laughed at a butterfly or combed your hair during a thunderstorm. They had no concept of God and would happily gorge on jungle pig. It was the aim of the Malay autocracy to gather them into reservations and forcibly convert them to Islam. This, as the British anthropologists pointed out, was the surest way to kill them.

The Malays of Kelantan, apart from speaking a dialect which was painful to learn, had an Islamic culture which no Iranian ayatollah would tolerate. The women of the faith scorned purdah and considered themselves to be superior to their menfolk. The wife would always walk proudly ahead and the husband trail behind. They were women of great grace and beauty and had few inhibitions about sex. That Islam was too blatantly a faith of male domination they recognised without, as yet, being able to reform it through reference to the Koran. For divorce, of which there was far too much in Kelantan, was assumed to be a purely male right, and that the holy book grants it to women too was insufficiently known. A man could rid himself of his wife by pronouncing the cantrip *talak* thrice before a witness. A woman could do the same thing if she had the shocking grounds of *nusus* – unwillingness or inability on the part of the husband to engage in the marital act – and recover the whole of the *mas kahwin* or dowry. The women of Kelantan needed elementary religious education which the *imams* and *muftis*, in the manner of priests, did not wish to impart to them. All they could do was rail and spit when wronged, or seek revenge through paying a dollar or so to the *orang kepak kechil* – men with little axes – and procuring the mutilation or demise (for five dollars) of the smug wrongdoer. When Sultan Ibrahim harangued the prostitutes of the Biarritz Park for selling the use of their bodies, they threw things at him, yelling that if it were not for such as he they would not have had to sink so low. He had the statutory four wives but changed them, one at a time, with a frequency that bewildered.

There was one Malay woman I came to know well – 'Che Isa, a superb creature of forty, who had married a Eurasian named Cyril. Isa is the Islamic name of Jesus, a rather effeminate prophet in the view of the Muslims, so that his name is given only to girls. 'Che Isa was of Bugis stock from the Celebes and was, like all of that race, capable of hard ferocity. Cyril was scared of her. When her voice rang clearly at a party – *'Mana Siril?'* (Where is Cyril?) – he trembled over his brandy ginger ale and flirtation with another man's wife. Isa spoke openly of Cyril's sexual insufficiency and, while her hand was in, that of Haji Latiff, a Malay of Afghan blood who had married an Arab named Sharifah, of the genuine line of the Prophet. Of them both she would say: *'Dia ta' boleh buat. Dia main-main sahajah'* (They can't fuck. They can only play about). Isa had a magnificent body and a rich temperament. Her mouth was not constructed on Malay lines, with the protruding teeth which forbid kissing. Her sexual appetite was enormous and her erotic inventory suggested Indian schooling. But, somehow or other, a good deal of Indian culture had got into Islamic Kelantan. At the Biarritz Park there was a nightly performance of the *wayang kulit*, an endlessly long shadow play which featured the Hindu gods and demons. The royal house of Kelantan was said to have descended from the white bull of

Shiva. There was an ancient fair-haired goddess of harvest, a *dewi* of whom such as my blonde wife could, in moments of Malay enthusiasm, be considered a reincarnation. Of all this mixed culture the staff of the Malayan Teachers' Training College knew nothing nor wished to know anything.

The principal and vice-principal met Lynne and myself at the airport or *tempat kapal terbang* (place of flying ships) and put us in a single room in a sort of barracky limbo. We had been in the Federation a whole year and still did not have a house. Lynne grew hysterical about this, foreshadowing a state of breakdown which was to lead to attempted suicide a year later. We had intended to bring Mas and Yusof with us from Kuala Kangsar, and it was a good thing we did not: there were no quarters for them and no house and kitchen to keep. Yusof, who had stolen an *ela* of silk from the bazaar, was anyway in the hands of the police, and Mr Raja, Mas's father, had made impossible conditions about his daughter's transportation east. Our A70 arrived and we engaged a driver, Mat bin Salleh. His main task was to take us to the sands of the China Sea, in which we swam. The Malay women of the nearby kampong were greatly interested in the anatomy of the *orang puteh*, whether *laki-laki* (male) or *perempuan*. They handled our genitals freely and were assured they were little different from the generality of the human race, meaning the Kelantan Malays. They watched us benevolently as we avoided water snakes, Portuguese men of war, and shoals of fishes that would nibble right through a swimming body. Their children asked for the gift of a *kupang*. A *kupang* was twelve and a half cents: a dollar to them was a piece of eight, as in America. As a *kupang*, like an American bit, had only an abstract existence, they had to be given two *kupangs*.

Eventually we were given a house. Mat bin Salleh was turned into a cook, and his wife, Maimunah binte Ibrahim, into an amah. Mat became a very good cook, since he had not come to us, like Yusof, with preconceived notions of the white man's cuisine. He learned to roast a *gigot* or make a Lancashire hotpot on basic principles taught by Lynne, and these to him had the remote technicality of gear changes. The house began to fill with cats, with Lalage as a seal-pointed virgin matriarch who controlled them rigorously. She underwent an imaginary pregnancy and permitted the kittens to suck at her dry teats. We ended with twenty-five cats, all of whom were to die of feline enteritis. The tropics are hard on small animals. We had also a rooster named Regulus who, with his harem, insisted on living in the house. Regulus challenged me to fight and perched on the tub when Lynne was bathing to crow against the perils of water. We had an otter or *anjing ayer* (water dog) that whistled like a train when it wanted food. It was killed by a snake. Snakes lurked for coolness among the pepper bushes and under the pomelo tree. They reared at the army of cats, which divided into sections to feint from the front and strike from the rear. The cats settled to eat the dead snakes like pigs lined up at a trough. I began to write my first published novel.

I HAD ENOUGH material for a novel. It was sufficient to write of Kuala Kangsar, which I rechristened Kuala Hantu, and of the state of Perak which contains it. Perak became Lanchap, which, as an adjective, means smooth and slippery but, as a verb, to masturbate. I remade the Malay College into a multiracial school and took a good deal of trouble over manufacturing a history for it. I needed Chinese in this school, and I especially needed a young Chinese communist who holds indoctrination sessions in a dormitory. The hero of the book, Victor Crabbe, is a teacher of European history whose syllabus contains a survey of the rise of Marxism. There is meant to be an implied irony in the presentation of Marxism as both a Western intellectual heresy and a source of Oriental terrorism. The young communist seems to the headmaster, Boothby, to be doing nothing more than conducting homework sessions and helping his fellows in their academic understanding of the doctrine of surplus value. So he fails to take Crabbe's unease seriously. He is a fool with whom Crabbe is forced to quarrel, and Crabbe, like his creator, has to leave his post and travel to new adventures in the Federation. He is not, however, to be identified with his creator. His name has its own irony, suggesting the past imperial triumphs of the British and, at the same time, a backward scuttling into the sand of failure and eventual death. He has a fair-haired wife who is unhappy, but she is not Lynne. Her name is Fenella, which comes from Scott's *Peveril of the Peak*, and she is a second wife clearly unsatisfactory when compared with her predecessor, who died in a car accident. Crabbe's first wife, who is not named but is probably May or Maya, an onomastic foreshadowing of Crabbe's husband-like love of Malaya, was dark and Mediterranean and possibly Jewish and was built on the Jewish sergeant of the ATS for whom I fell heavily in the late 1940s.

While I was writing this novel I could see clearly enough that it was the first panel of a triptych, and that the final panel would not disclose its entire content till Malaya achieved independence some two years hence. The title of the second novel is mentioned in the first: *The Enemy in the Blanket* or *musoh dalam selimut*, a term applied seriously to a traitor and jocularly to one's wife. The title of the first novel is *Time for a Tiger*, this being the slogan of Tiger beer, brewed by Fraser and Neave of Singapore. In the Chinese kedais of Malaya there was a rather handsome wooden clock with the slogan displayed on it. I wanted one of these clocks and wrote to Fraser and Neave to say that I was about to advertise their product in the title of a novel, and would they perhaps be willing to show gratitude by letting me have one. Their reply was cautious: they wanted to read the manuscript of the novel first. Stung, I inserted in the text a line of dialogue: 'Not Tiger, not Anchor. Make it Carlsberg. It costs a bit more, but it's a better beer.' When the novel appeared in 1956, I was presented with a two-dozen case of quart bottles of Carlsberg lager. Fraser and Neave did nothing. Not until 1970, when I was revisiting Singapore, did they write to me saying that I 'and your lady wife' were at liberty to drink freely and gratis of any of their brews while we were in the territory. But it was too late: I had become wholly a gin man.

The title was appropriate to one of the characters in the novel. I remade Donald D. Dunkeley as Nabby Adams and presented him pretty well as he was, except to solve his money problems and slake his unslakable thirst by giving him first prize in the Federation lottery. The name Nabby Adams turns him into the first of the Islamic prophets – *Nabi Adam* – or possibly Adam's son, whether Cain or Abel is not clear: he raises cain and is able enough at drinking. Alladad Khan is wholly there, as are other personages of Perak – the bald-headed beardless Sikh who spoke like an East End Jew and looked after the aborigines of the state; Lot the Water Department drunkard who said: 'The Koran forbid only what make men drunk. Me nothing make drunk so nothing to me is forbidden-*lah*'; my girl friend Rahimah; Yusof the cook, now Ibrahim, who tries to compel his master's love with an aphrodisiac. None of the staff of the Malay College appear there. The headmaster is not Jimmy Howell but a composite named for Sir Robert Boothby. Nevertheless, the white expatriates of Kuala Kangsar desperately wanted to see themselves in the novel and sought advice about libel from an Ipoh lawyer. There was no libel.

The novel was published and rather well reviewed. I had received an advance of fifty pounds, which was what first novels were usually paid at the beginning of the century. It retailed at thirteen shillings and sixpence, a price which confirms the ancient historicity of these memoirs. The writer of the blurb, unable to accept that Nabby Adams, with his illiterate obscenities and drunkenness, could really be a lieutenant, demoted him to sergeant, so that I was blamed by careless reviewers for inconsistency. Some reviewers, perhaps with justice, complained of the exotic richness of the vocabulary. I was in love with all the languages of the East and could not resist writing phrases like 'Victor Crabbe slept through the *bilal's bang* (inept Persian word for the faint unheeded call), would sleep till the *bangbang* (apt Javanese word) of the brontoid dawn brought him tea and bananas'. The book was sometimes compared unfavourably with the Eastern stories of Somerset Maugham, who was considered, and still is, the true fictional expert on Malaya. The fact is that Maugham knew little of the country outside the very bourgeois lives of the planters and the administrators. He certainly knew none of the languages. Nor did Joseph Conrad. When I stated, as a matter of plain fact, that I knew more Malay than Conrad, I was accused of conceit. Whether *Time for a Tiger* is a good or bad novel, its details of Malayan life are authentic. After Henri Fauconnier's *Malaisie* (which won the Prix Goncourt but is now forgotten in France), it remains the first novel to state what the life was really like. If it sold moderately well, and still sells a little, it was, is, because of the authenticity. I gained from its initial sale a very false impression of how my literary career would go. I thought I would be read as much when I wrote about England. But English readers think they know all about England. A desire for information is what frequently sends them to a novel (*Hotel, Airport, Il Nome della Rosa*) which retails information falsely but painlessly. *Time for a Tiger* went into its several printings not for the beauty of its prose or the vivacity of its characters: it gave painless information about a British territory which the British would soon be abandoning.

Having written one book, I wrote, with the encouragement of the publishers Longmans Green, another and very different one. The fact that the British would soon be leaving the Far East imposed a certain urgency in various pedagogic fields. There was, for instance, no phonetic description of the Malay language and there were no home-grown scholars of the subject. I worked on this, but with no hope of publication. What was urgently needed for publication, and not only in Malaya, was a study of English literature which took an exotic stance, presenting the culture of a Christian tradition and the climate of a northern country as in need of explication. The snow of *A Christmas Carol* was not poetic *thalji*: it was the stuff of the deep-freeze shredded and falling from the sky (Mat our cook would never believe this was possible). Marriage in Christian novels had none of the dissoluble frivolity of its Malay equivalent. Literature is not universal. Malays would laugh at Graham Greene's *The Heart of the Matter*, finding the dilemma of a man who commits suicide because he loves two women essentially comic. Shakespeare was usually acceptable, confirming the claim of his near-universality. I saw in a Borneo kampong a grainy presentation of Olivier's *Richard III*, which was taken to be a melodrama about twentieth-century England and whose costumes were so like the ceremonial ones of the Malays as to bring the story close to home, especially when sharp weapons lopped heads. But George Eliot and Jane Austen were hard going for even Malayans who used English as a second language. There was a need for the book I wrote, which looked at the history of our literature from an angle of tropical heat, with the ceiling fan spinning and the *bilal* calling the last *waktu* of the day and flying beetles bumbling on the verandah. This book was published in 1957, the only book ever to appear under the name John Burgess Wilson. It is, I think, still around.

I had another pedagogic ambition, which was to produce an anthology of modern English literature in Malay translation. I worked on the rendering of parts of *The Waste Land*, some of Pound's *Cantos*, and Aldous Huxley's *Ape and Essence* with a Malay who was properly an Achinese. He had served as a stoker in the British navy, was foul-mouthed in all companies which spoke English, and could down a bottle of Benedictine at a sitting. We did not get far with *The Waste Land*, which became *Tanah Tandus*. The first lines went:

> *Bulan April ia-lah bulan yang dzalim sa-kali*
> *Membawa bunga lilac daripada tanah mati*
> *Memchamporkan ingatan dengan hafsu . . .*

It would not work. Why, in the tropics, should *bulan April* be different from any other *bulan*? How could a *bulan* be *dzalim* or cruel? The attribution of a painful quality to a *bulan* forced the Malay mind to interpret the word as menstruation, which could and can be unpleasant. How could *thalji* or snow be *berlupa* or forgetful? What kind of *bunga* was a lilac? Only when the thunder began to speak in Sanskrit would *Tanah Tandus* make sense to the East, but we did not get as far as that. *The Waste Land* revealed itself, while the cats were chewing raw snake, as a very ingrown piece of literature which had nothing to say to a culture which had no word for spring and did not understand the myth of the grail.

Meanwhile there were the difficulties of teaching the teaching of English to my young Malays, Chinese, Indians and Eurasians. These were wholly charming and the girls were excessively seductive. They were crisply laundered and freshly shampooed, clear-eyed and smooth-skinned, and they exhibited exquisite limbs on the playing field. They were flirtatious in a manner that Europe was trying to forget. They bade me look forward to the monsoon season, when they would all be wearing sweaters. One girl of mixed blood dressed in all the Malayan costumes – one day a Chinese cheongsam slit to the thigh, the next a Tamil sari with exposed midriff, the next a Malay baju cut low on the bosom: a kind of serial nudity. The Chinese girls were the cleverest, and the Chinese young men cleverest of all. One of my specialist literature students, Ooi Boo Eng, has become a distinguished professor. Mustafa Ma, a Chinese Muslim, ran everything – the Islamic Society, the Chinese Society, the Chess Club, the student body itself. It was easy to see why the Malays feared the Chinese – such energy, such intelligence, such inborn capacity for rule. There were rumblings of political trouble ahead; there was also the major problem which would result from the imposition of the Malay language, or *Bahasa Negara* (tongue of the country) on a mixed nation with the right to call itself Malayan, eventually Malaysian, but with no obligation to regard Malay as the primary language of thought, discourse, government and law. The non-Malay Malayans had a stake in English as a second language. The Chinese and Indian lawyers are still clinging to it as an instrument of the courts. Malay, they feel, is not ready to assume the responsibilities of a major language. With its lack of a capacity for abstraction, typical of a tongue of fishermen and paddy-planters, it finds difficulty in coping with a world of high technology. Chinese does not. English certainly does not.

Though the English instructors of the Malayan Teachers' Training College were temporary expatriates, unobliged to hammer out a relationship between the native culture and the imposed one, they had a clearer view of what higher Malayan education required than the permanent officers of the colonial service. At the Malay College we used to receive occasional written exhortations from the Federation Education Officer in Kuala Lumpur about the necessity of teaching English well, but the stress was on a pedagogy suitable for speakers of English as a first language. When I asked Jimmy Howell what qualifications our federal chief had for this concern with the teaching of English, I got the reply: 'He writes a good letter, he gives a good lecture.' This was not enough. My two colleagues in Kota Bharu knew better. English as a second language has to be taught on an assumption of alien linguistic habits in the learner. A good number of our Malayan students spoke English in the home, but they would soon have to teach it from scratch to children who spoke only an Asiatic language – that was, if the Malay politicians accepted the need for English at all. Politicians are terrible people.

Chinese is a tonal language. I began to take private lessons in Kuo-Yü to learn what tonalism meant. I was helped a little by my musical background, but I never mastered totally those shifts of intonation which make the meaning of one monosyllable different from that of its six or seven homophones. With a language built entirely on monosyllables there is obviouly a vast limitation on the number of morphemes possible, and six or seven variations in tone provide parameters which make little sense to speakers of an Indo-European language. Conversely, Chinese learners of English assume that certain intonation patterns have lexical significance. There is, for instance, the 'catalogue tone' which automatically gets into a recitation of words meant to illustrate phonemic contrast – man men, cattle kettle, bad bed, and so on. The falling tone in each pair is taken by a Chinese pupil to have a certain semantic content. A teacher of English as a second language has to know about this and adjust his intonation accordingly.

The Americans, as usual, were ahead of the British in awareness of ESL (English as a Second Language) problems, and it was they who produced the books which enlightened as to principles and granted the material for teaching drills. Intensive drill was essential in the inculcation of new linguistic habits. Take, for instance, the 'question tag' which, in English, is highly eccentric. Welshmen,

Chinese, Malays and Indians alike would say 'You're going out, isn't it?' instead of 'You're going out, aren't you?' Only by drill could an automatic formulation – main verb made negative in tag – be secured. There was also the business of distinguishing between a phoneme and allophone, so that the *i* of *bit* was to be seen not as a variant of the *ea* in *beat* and the dark L of *fill* was not necessarily to be used, since the Welsh and the Northumbrians, who claimed English as a first language, ended *fill* as they began *lily*, with the clear L which serves most languages exclusively. Malayan students of English could make the grammatical errors which the British made with no rebuke. What they had to avoid was making the mistakes which tended to turn English into a dialect of their own tongues.

For there was no doubt that, especially with the Tamils, English was in danger of turning into a communication medium intelligible only to its Asiatic speakers. Tamil, a Dravidian tongue highly inflected and with a large Sanskrit vocabulary, was capable of taking over English and making it obey the rules, grammatical and phonemic, of a language considered older, better organised, richer. I heard Tamil government officials speak to each other in a rapid bubbling English of which I understood not one word. There was no danger of this kind of assimilation happening with the Chinese, who spoke mutually unintelligible dialects united only in the necessarily non-phonetic script, and broke their native Babel with ESL. This sometimes happened with Malays whose dialects were in gross conflict, but the Malay educational pundits proposed imposing the Johore dialect on the peninsula, taking over the role of the slow historical process which had made South-Eastern English the received tongue of an island of similar size and similar dialectal richness.

Every morning, having taken my tea with canned milk and a few golden bananas or *pisang mas*, bunched to look like a cricket glove, I would walk across the *padang* or field that separated our bungalow from the college premises. I would have to leap over a monsoon drain in which snakes basked and great puffing lizards. If I wore shorts the girls would give a wolverine whistle which they had learnt from American films. We all had to yield to American culture, and my lessons would sometimes consist of a close examination of an item in *Time* magazine, briskly dealing with the new phenomenon Elvis Presley or the Suez crisis as seen from an American angle. An extract from *The Times* would seem remote and parochial. If the Americans were teaching things to

South-East Asia, who would teach South-East Asia to the Americans? They would be embarking one of these days on a disastrous Asiatic adventure, and no American publisher would take my *Time for a Tiger*, which might have been enlightening. That some kinds of Asiatic communism (though not the kind fermenting in the Malayan jungle) might be nothing more than attempts at agrarian reform could not be made clear to the United States which, at this time, was in the grip of McCarthyism. Nevertheless, the Americans knew all about the technology, including the technology of language, which the East needed. What they did not know was the nature of the Eastern mentality.

Friday, the Muslim Sabbath, was my day for digging deeper into this mentality. At sundown, when the next day, *hari sabtu*, was beginning, Lynne and I would start a drinking and dancing evening with our Malay friends, who were Bugis or Afghan or Arabic but called themselves Malays, in the Biarritz Park. There would be Haji Latiff and his wife Sharifah, Isa and her husband Cyril (who had married into Islam and hence had become a Malay), Bangsir, who was half-Chinese, and his wife Normah. They were all steady drinkers of Dog's Head stout and brandy ginger ale and ready dancers of the *ronggeng*. They were unabashed that the most popular *ronggeng* tune of the time was *Rukun Islam*, which recounted the principles of the faith to a samba rhythm. My translation of the final verse ran:

> If you do not obey all these tenets
>> And pray to Allah day and night as well,
> Then some day you will find it all too late
>> for penance,
> And a house will await you in hell.

Hell – *naraka* – they did not take too seriously. *Arak*, which the Koran forbade, was not the same as beer or brandy. Pork was a different matter, but there was a Malay at the college very keen on ham and eggs. This was a gentle and permissive Islam, and there were times when I thought of being converted to it. Haji Latiff, who had made the trip to Mecca and married a descendant of the Prophet, hotly urged it. If I wished to stay on in Malaya after independence, which I thought sometimes I did, conversion was essential. He had my Islamic name ready for me – Yahya (which means John) with the patronymic bin Haji Latiff, to announce to the world who had recommended the conversion.

Lynne was to be Hadijah binte Abdullah, daughter of the slave of God. Perhaps, I thought, if I worshipped Allah the God of the Catholics would leave me alone.

He would not leave me alone. There was a French priest, Father Laforgue, in Kota Bharu, barely tolerated by the Islamic leaders, despite the counselling of religious tolerance in the Koran. He had served in China and been expelled by the communist regime, so here he was looking after the Chinese Catholics in Kelantan. There was a Mr Lee at the college, and Father Laforgue, assuming that he was Chinese, came to visit him. Mr Lee was far from Chinese. He was an elderly teacher of what he called art who spoke Lancashire English not easily intelligible to his students. He seemed to think he had been transferred to a suburb of Liverpool unnaturally hot, and he tried to grow cabbages in his garden. He had no servants, and he had bought a bicycle for his wife so that she could pedal seven miles into town to do the daily shopping. He considered the Catholic Church to be the Scarlet Woman, the more scarlet for having a French representative, and he sent Father Laforgue packing after giving him a glass of Ribena, for he kept no stronger drink. Father Laforgue came to see me, who lived next door. Lynne unkindly told him that I was a bad Catholic. Father Laforgue tried to work on my soul in French. I rebuffed him with talk of my wish to enter Islam. He prayed for me: Islam was the old enemy, not to be compared with watery Protestant substitutes for the true Catholic faith, and the dragon beginning to gnaw at my soul had to be strenuously fought. He was ejected from Kelantan fairly soon. A Chinese Catholic had become Muslim on marrying a Malay wife but, dying, repented of his apostasy and called in Father Laforgue to give him Extreme Unction. The Islamic authorities found out. Though the Chinese died in peace, Father Laforgue suffered summary eviction from his parish and lived in the neighbouring state of Trengganu with a poor Chinese family till the money came through for his repatriation. This turned me against Islam.

Allah and Jehovah could not coexist in Kelantan, and Nabi Isa provided merely a pretext for getting blind drunk on Christmas Day. But, despite rational Islam, magic flourished and demons could be summoned to harm one's enemies. Black magic, called *'ilmu panas*, literally hot magic, was not limited to the *pawangs* in the villages, with their charms and philtres. Lynne and I met a Tamil magician named Mr Pathan, who was a high officer in the Public Works Department. We met over glasses of lager in the interracial club of Kota Bharu, and he was greatly attracted to Lynne's blonde beauty. He himself was squat, black and ugly and he realised it. 'But,' he said, 'beauty is in the eye of the beholder', and he turned himself briefly into a handsome young man for Lynne's benefit. This shook Lynne very badly. He then tried to steal her away in his car by making me retire to vomit, though my stomach was sound that day and I had taken only two glasses of lager. Lynne tried to get away, but she was whisked off in his car. I recovered sufficiently to tell our driver Mat to follow fast. Mat knew his house, which was of a standard PWD pattern suitable for officers of Pathan's rank, no eldritch castle, and we arrived there to find Lynne sinking into a seducible trance. I absurdly recalled the black magic novels of Dennis Wheatley and told Pathan that I could see a Christian cross burning on his forehead. He merely chuckled. Mat and I grabbed Lynne, slapped her to recall her to normality, then took her home. I could swear that Pathan had no shadow.

Lynne grew very frightened of Pathan, who would turn up at our house when I was out teaching and propose innocent structural improvements to the premises. He tried his hypnotic tricks again, but she set the cock Regulus on to him. Regulus merely crowed. Lalage, who should have spit and clawed, recognised congenial evil and purred. I came home for lunch to find Pathan taking a friendly glass of water while Mat looked on from the kitchen door. A magician, I had read, should never receive hospitality: it put you somehow in his power. Pathan said he was there to offer hospitality, dinner at his house. He looked less black and squat, younger, handsomer. He desired, he said, only friendship. Those little tricks of his – nothing, he had thought we might be amused. In those days of sodality between the ruling whites and the ruled, soon to be self-ruling, browns and blacks, it would have been a major error to refuse such hospitality. Lynne and I, with large misgivings, accepted.

Pathan served a hot cold Madras curry. Malay calls hot of temperature *panas*, of taste *pedas*. This was *pedas* enough, and only the rice was moderately *panas*. The rice was served by a dribbling grinning boy who offered a fresh portion for every spoonful one ate, the while Pathan railed at him in Tamil. 'My eldest son,' he said, 'and a fool. Will you have some soda water with your whisky?' Please. 'But there is no soda water. The fool has neglected to buy it.' He cursed the boy, who visibly trembled, and threw him the car keys. He was, I gathered, to buy soda water. The nearest shop was some ten *batu* or milestones away. We heard the car take off with excessive speed and return five minutes later. The boy entered carrying soda water. I did not like any of this. We had here a zombie, certainly a kind of slave in a perpetual state of hypnosis. Lynne ate nothing: she was starting the first phase of the tropical anorexia which afflicts many white women after a year in the East. Pathan accused her of spurning a Tamil's hospitality. She denied this and began to cry. The zombie rushed up with a dishcloth for the tears. Pathan soothed her and announced that we were his friends. To us he meant no harm, he said, but to one of my colleagues he did. This was Abdul Aziz, a fat teacher of Malay, who was believed to have a debt-slave in his household. Debt-slavery was an ancient Malay custom which British law had not been able to liquidate. If a man died in debt his children discharged the debt in servitude. I did not like Abdul Aziz but I began to tremble for him.

I was surprised that Pathan was so open about what he proposed to do to Abdul Aziz. Probably he believed that, if we told others, we would not ourselves be believed. He had obtained, he said, a photograph of Abdul Aziz from the office that issued identity cards – which, in that time of the Emergency, everybody had to have. He had had an enlarged drawing of Abdul Aziz's fat face made from this photograph – he would show us the drawing if we wished – and he was sticking pins in the eyes on this drawing, to the accompaniment of debilitating cantrips, and shortly Abdul Aziz would go blind. Further calamities would follow – lockjaw, a falling out of teeth. Why this vindictiveness? Pathan was vague: something to do with one of his daughters and a son of Abdul Aziz. Pathan said toothily: 'My enemies – they should be aware of the sort of man they are enemies of. You, sir, are not my enemy, nor is your lady wife, though she scorns to eat the rice of a lowly Tamil. All I ask is your friendship.' That sounded like a threat. We were very glad to get away, and so was Mat, who had been sleeping with one eye open in the car.

I looked at Abdul Aziz carefully when I saw him in the staff room next day. He was as fat as ever but blinking and complaining of trouble with his eyes. 'And your teeth?' I asked. Strange I should ask: two of the back *gigi* had become inexplicably loose. I said that I had dined with a certain Mr Pathan: did the name mean anything? Abdul Aziz turned pale beneath his brown. The next day I saw him in earnest discourse, under a tree rich in *kelawar* or fruit-bats sleeping upside down, with a local haji. Three days later Abdul Aziz had departed – a matter of family trouble in Pahang. Could he thus distance himself from the hot magic of Pathan of the Public Works Department?

WE OURSELVES, A week or so later, were able to avoid Pathan. We were to go to Kuala Lumpur. The time had come to put our students into English language schools in the major towns of the Federation to give them, under the supervision of their instructors, a chance to try out their teaching abilities. When I had been at Bamber Bridge Training College we had had the same kind of supervised practice. Then I had had to visit grimy elementary schools in Bury, Bolton, Nelson and Colne. Kuala Lumpur would be very different – the shining capital of the Federation, full of drink and sin. The name of the city was not prepossessing though it was accurate – Muddy Estuary – and it tried, with its rarefied pleasures, to rise above its name. First, though, the students had to console themselves for a month's separation from each other by putting on a fancy dress ball. On the dance floor there would be, for libidinous instructors like myself, an opportunity to handle the delectable bodies of the girls.

One of the male Chinese students had turned himself into a tribal negro, near-naked and boot-polished all over, shaking a spear and crying Bonga bonga. Mustafa Ma, more dignified, was dressed in traditional mandarin costume, which was not properly fancy dress. Many of the girls dressed or undressed as American chorines. Lynne wore a sari and had had a silver nose ring fitted by a Bengali student of high caste. I covered myself with playing cards to represent the spirit of bridge. The sexual current was hot. In the grounds cunnilingus and fellation proceeded, chiefly among the Chinese students. The flashpoint is low in the tropics. Lynne and I took to Kuala Lumpur aching glands and an expectation of adventure.

We stayed in the Paramount Hotel on Batu Road. This was run by Chinese who did not object to a yowling Siamese cat on the premises: there was, God knew, noise enough. The Chinese can be very loud, and their shouts and firecrackers keep off evil spirits. I did not fear Pathan on Batu Road. I visited the schools in the mornings and in the afternoons and evenings Lynne and I drank. We drank too much and ate too little: anorexia was striking me who, in the manner of white men in the tropics, had

eaten heartily of Singapore Cold Storage frozen meat, only realising how tasteless it was on the day Mat had ritually slaughtered
and then roasted a young sheep, a gift of the Agricultural Department. In Kuala Lumpur I could take only Brand's chicken
essence wrapped in brandy. We made love in our narrow bed
among the *chichaks* and cockroaches, hearing a Chinese woman
in the next room sing all the songs of the day – 'Stranger in
Paradise', 'Let Me Go, Lover', 'The Yellow Rose of Texas'. But
my lovemaking was not good enough.

I was told it was not good enough. Of course, it never is after
fourteen years of marriage. It becomes cosy, friendly, and it relies
too much on routine. Lynne had been given, in Kuala Lumpur, a
new standard of lovemaking by a Eurasian we met in one of the
innumerable bars on Batu Road. He was short and had several
teeth missing, but he was outstanding in bed. No husband likes
to be told of his sexual shortcomings (that word takes fire in the
context), and I was told too brutally and drunkenly. The telling
did not kill love, which is above sex, but it killed desire. It sent
me lonely to bars where I met British soldiers, on local leave.
Some of these had their own sexual grievances, chiefly against
the Chinese prostitutes of the town, who charged too much and
gave too little, and I heard bitter encounters. 'You bloody Chinese
bitch, we're killing your lot in the bloody jungle.' – 'Go away,
you silly man, I not like you.' But one soldier, a half-Maori,
would talk only of a French writer he called Prowst. He loved
Prowst, and this love he assumed, uneducated as he was, to be
the mark of a debased taste. I put him right on that. Then I went
to eat alone, tuxedoed, in air-conditioned restaurants, where I
saw some of our senior lecturers, dirty old men that they were,
dining with some of our Chinese girl students. Then I met Father
Laforgue, without a parish and awaiting a posting, in his element
with rich Chinese who fed him snake wine (blood of snakes
slaughtered on the table) and roast duck. Then, in the Paradise
Cabaret, I remet Mek Hitam.

Mek is the Kelantan honorific for Miss or Inche (which serves
both sexes). Hitam means black, and Mek Hitam was, though
Malay, very dark. She had previously practised the trade of
prostitute or *perempuan jahat* (bad woman) in the Biarritz Park in
Kota Bharu, but ambition, or trouble with the Islamic authorities,
had led her to the capital. She gloried in her profession. I remembered the State Education Officer, Frank Jones, asking her
how many men she had slept with. She replied: '*Kalau semua*

*orang kerani dalam negeri mulai tulis nama-nama-nya dia tidak pernah
habis'* — if all the clerks of the state were to start to write down
their names they would never finish. I joined the list. It was not
right, somehow. I knew Mek Hitam too well, we were both of
the Kelantan family, it was like seeking consolation with an old
friend. And one does not look for reassurance about one's sexual
powers with a prostitute. I left Kuala Lumpur, after a month of
supervising teaching practice and tippling, bitter, low, and not
very well. My heart thumped, I felt the heat. Lynne coughed, and
there was something in the resonance of the cough that spoke of
a damaged liver. But she still had twelve years of life ahead of her.

I went back to the writing of my second published novel, *The
Enemy in the Blanket*. The setting was an imaginary Malay state
called Dahaga, which means thirst, with a capital named Kenching. *Kenching* means urine, *sakit kenching* means gonorrhoea.
The locale was only vaguely related to Kota Bharu in Kelantan,
but certain of the real-life inhabitants got into the story — 'Che
Isa, Haji Latiff, Bangsir. I was inventing more now, photograph-
ing less. The fictional state is in the hands of an upstart called the
Abang, or Big Brother, while the Sultan, hag-ridden and impotent, merely goes through the motions of rule. The Abang
seeks the seduction of Fenella Crabbe and, for his vast collection
of cars, the Abelard of Victor Crabbe. This car-greed was based
on reality: a sultan had given certain expatriates the choice between yielding their cars, when they were particularly fancied,
and being thrown out of the state. Sultans had more power than
was commonly realised: the British advised rather than controlled.
The Abang, aware that the days of usurpation are over with the
coming of a rigid federal constitution, takes his filched wealth to
Europe and Fenella goes with him. Crabbe, the headmaster of a
large school, is set upon by hatred of the British, black magic,
and fear of being arraigned on the capital charge of aiding the
communist terrorists. His cook, an ancient Chinese, has been
feeding Crabbe's rice to his terrorist son-in-law in the jungle.
Crabbe has also been conducting an affair with the nymphomaniacal wife of the State Education Officer. This comes close to
the reality of my own situation during a period of sexual estrangement for which, I had to feel, my wife was responsible.
The book ends with a Malay *pantun*:

> *Kalau tuan mudek ka-hulu,*
> *Charikan saya bunga kemoja.*

Kalau tuan mati dahulu,
Nantikan saya di-pintu shurga.

This means: if you, my lover, go up river, pluck me a frangipani flower; if you, my lover, die before I do, wait for me at the door of heaven. The prosodic technique is based on assonance. The first two lines relate to the last two chiefly in their sound, hardly at all in their content, except that frangipani, like cypress, is associated with graveyards. The poem is significant for Victor Crabbe in that, having lost a living wife, he tends to brood upon his dead one. His own death, which I knew had to come in the third panel of the projected trilogy, is foreshadowed, as is the death of the British Empire, whose last surviving pocket Malaya is. I was growing gloomy.

Lynne was growing worse than gloomy. Her sister Hazel had been writing to her about the impending death of their mother, who had cancer of the throat. She seemed to feel that Lynne was evading the daughterly responsibility of watching at the bedside and listening to the final croaks of moral objurgation addressed to the daughter who, though absent, was still in the mother's mind as one who had sinned sexually (she could not forget Rhys Evans and the fervent love letter) and had still to be forgiven. Lynne, according to Hazel, was enjoying the high life under the banyan trees and leaving heartbreak and the labour of nursing to one who was not so lucky. Lynne could have gone home – the Federation would have paid her air fare – but she could not come back unless she paid the return fare herself. We did not have enough money. Nor, if she waited for the end of my tour after helping to arrange her mother's funeral, would she have anywhere to stay. Lynne suffered from the extremes of guilt, some of which she passed on to me. In good Freudian fashion, she felt she was killing her mother. When news of the death came through by cable, we spent our bank balance on flowers to be sent through the agency of Singapore Cold Storage. Then Lynne, clothing herself in light black for the tropics, borrowed an Anglican prayer book and read through the service for the dead. I, a Catholic, was placed at a great distance during this ceremony.

She sustained the distance in our daily life. The nymphomaniacal wife who got into my novel entered the vacuum and, distraught and not too far from the conditon of *amok*, I yielded too easily. Life at home was hell, black with guilt or loud with hysteria, and the cats were dying from feline enteritis which the Tamils of the Veterinary Department were not skilled enough to cure. The garden was full of cats' gravestones. The son of Mat and Maimunah, Mohamed Noor, grew ill and was treated inadequately by the *bomoh* or medicine woman of the nearest kampong. He was near death from pyrexia of unknown origin, or *demam kepialu*, and only Western medicine saved him. When I was out teaching Lynne took an overdose of sleeping tablets after writing a farewell note: 'I can't stand it any longer. L.' I got home in time to make her vomit on mustard and water. Hazel wrote to tell her that their mother had tape-recorded a final message begging for morality and love, and Lynne, having no more sleeping tablets, merely drank herself into a stupor. Then she subdued the guilt before asking for a divorce. I asked her to think, wait: my three-year tour would soon be over. She drank more moderately. *Time for a Tiger* was published; she read it and laughed.

My tour was ending and there would be no further tour. The white expatriates could apply for short-term contracts with an independent Malayan government, and willingness to enter Islam would be a recommendation. One or two white officers had already done this: there was even a Haji Banks, expert in the Koran, living in Trengganu. My phase of being bemused by the possibility of becoming a Muslim with four wives (I had the permissible three already lined up) was fading. Lynne introduced, though not for long, the God of the Church of England into the household. The God of the Catholics, invoked by Father Laforgue, was still lurking behind the pepper bushes and the rain trees, a snake in an impaired Eden. Neither Lynne nor I was well. Enfeebled, she had been bitten by sand flies and caught dengue fever. I had occasional visits from a mild malaria. My heart thumped; neither of us could eat. Perhaps we needed to be back in the north. The Federal government could not give me a pension after so short a term of service, but it could give me a *selamat mas* or golden handshake. Soon a draft for a thousand pounds passed through the college office. Several Malays then came to the door asking for a loan. This, according to the books, is a cementing of Malay friendship: a demand for a loan which there is no intention of repaying. Haji Latiff asked for two hundred dollars and, when I refused, called me a white bastard. Lynne and I were not rich but we had a sizeable sum in the bank. The days of genuine near-poverty were over and would never return.

I started to write the third novel of my trilogy – *Beds in the East*. The title, prefigured in *The Enemy in the Blanket*, comes from *Antony and Cleopatra* – 'The beds i' the east are soft'. The pseudonym Anthony Burgess was taking on a certain solidity, but the character of the novelist had not yet subdued entirely the failed musician called John Burgess Wilson. The failed musician dug out some quires of thirty-stave music paper that had been mouldering with the shoes and clothes in that humid heat, and he composed a farewell gift for the Federation of Malaya – *Sinfoni Melayu*, a three-movement symphony which tried to combine the musical elements of the country into a synthetic language which called on native drums and xylophones as well as the instruments of the full Western orchestra. The last movement ended with a noble processional theme, rather Elgarian, representing independence. Then, over a drum roll and before the final chord in C major, the audience was to rise and shout '*Merdeka!*' The work was never to be played. It was never acknowledged by the Cultural Department to which I sent it. It would have been a hopeless undertaking: the Federation still has its military and police bands, but it has no strings. In *Beds in the East* I father it on a young Chinese composer of genius who, similarly, never hears it played. It was, for me, the last of several hopeless gestures to the end of an East–West rapprochement. East and West could meet in bed or over a gin pahit. East and West have finally met in high technology, colour television, electronic games. The books that I found on sale when I returned to Malaya briefly in 1980 were mostly the romances of Barbara Cartland. Kuala Lumpur has American hotels whose electric supply fails and leaves guests suffocating in the elevators; it has Mercedes for the Chinese and Lambrettas for the Malays; it has *Dallas* and *Dynasty*. But it does not have a symphony orchestra.

We put spending money in our pockets and purse by selling our refrigerator to a Sikh and our car to an enterprising group of Kelantan fishermen who would rush their catches to the market in it: they had had enough of relying on the Chinese both for ice and transport. Our poultry went to the kampong with Mat and Maimunah and a flourishing Mohamed Noor. Mat was given a *surat* or letter of recommendation extolling his skill in the British, Indian and Italian cuisines. This he passed on to his cousin of the same name, who had no cooking skills at all, and then settled to being a royal driver. Lalage, now old and forgetful, went to a visiting Siamese couple who took her back to Bangkok: it was satisfying to think that, after a full but virginal life, she would end her days on ancestral ground. I boxed our goods – a camphor-wood chest, cloisonné vases, Kelantan silver, such books as had not been eaten by termites – and forwarded them to Lynne's widower father in Leicester. I received air tickets – BOAC Britannia from Kuala Lumpur to London, with a night stop in Colombo and calls at the cities of the Middle East which, then as now, were all barbed wire and shifty brown soldiers. We would spend a few days in Rome and prepare for white skins among olive ones. What we were to do with the future was unsure. I could not, I thought, make a living out of writing. Few can. At the age of forty I was still unsettled. But, leaving Kota Bharu by Malayan Airways, I wept for Malaya and not for ourselves.

It was strange, in summer Rome, to feel rich. I was on terminal leave from August to Christmas, and Malayan pay went far in Europe. Both of us noted shamefully that we were not yet ready for Europe. We had absorbed, from expatriates less bohemian than ourselves, a kind of arrogance necessary for dealing with the Chinese that would not do in either Rome or London. The Chinese cheated and knew we knew it. They expected, cheerfully, to be rebuked for it. They got away in their bars with watering the gin and whisky, though they could not get away with watering the Pernod. They expected, as did the Indians, dramatic haggling. It was not right for Lynne to throw spaghetti at the manager of a Roman restaurant or scream over a bar account that seemed excessive. It was not appropriate, either, to do this in Malay. We threw our coins in the Trevi fountain but did not expect to return to the venal pagan city which eventually became my home. I drank a quart and a half of Frascati daily and heard my heart turning into a punchball. Lynne got through a regular bottle of Bosford's gin and wept or screamed over it. Soon she calmed down. But we saw that we had acquired suicidal habits in Malaya. We would maintain them, nevertheless, in England, until the fear of God was put into us by physicians. But for Lynne it grew too late. We flew to London and were appalled by the white faces.

The days of austerity were over. The British were tearing into beef and lapping up cream ices. We had forgotten the taste of fresh food, as also of draught bitter beer. We ate in Rule's and were shocked to see scampi cooked in butter. There was a new laxness about. The memory of wartime and postwar deprivation was still strong in me, to say nothing of the ascetic aspirations of Crippsian socialism, and I did not like this hedonistic Britain. Everybody had a television set, and a constant question in pubs, when Lynne and I apologised for our ignorance of the new world and explained our tropical truculence, was 'What kind of television do you have out there?' Damn it, there was not even a Malay word for television, though I was later to suggest *jauh-tengok* or *JT*. We had seen a little of BBC television before sailing, and that had been genteel and leisurely, but now there was a commercial channel full of banal urgencies. The British seemed to be giving nothing to the world but consuming much. There was a new cult of youth, and the young were being encouraged to do most of the consuming. I had heard of Teddy boys, and now I saw them on street corners and in coffee bars. They had originally called themselves Edwardian Strutters, and they wore a kind of costume which evoked a period of chauvinism and imperial expansion. This was a curious anachronism in an age when I and others were presiding over the collapse of the Empire. There was clearly a vague nostalgia for an old Britain which the new one contradicted. The collective aggression of the imperial epoch had transformed itself into a debased violence of which youth had the monopoly. The more articulate of the young were angry, and John Osborne was telling them why. It was anger at the consumerist vacuum which the young were themselves condoning.

Trevor Wilson, a Malayan Information Officer with whom I had dined in Kota Bharu, had given me some silk shirts, made in Kuala Lumpur, to take back to his friend Graham Greene. Greene had an apartment in the Albany, no longer decorated with the innumerable whisky miniatures which he had been collecting and was now to empty into the pages of *Our Man in Havana*. He was amiable and I signed a copy of *Time for a Tiger* for him. He took me to lunch at the Café Royal and, as it was Friday, we ate fish. Greene made it clear to me that he had achieved much and had reached a plateau where he could afford to take leisurely breath. He had not written the definitive Malayan novel which should match the definitive Vietnamese one entitled *The Quiet American*, and he did not seem to think that I would write it either. I was comic, there was frivolity in my book. He praised the other great Catholic, Evelyn Waugh, and considered *The Ordeal of Gilbert Pinfold*, which had just appeared, a masterpiece. My own Catholicism, being of the cradle variety, was suspect. I was evidently not to be taken as a professional novelist, rather as a colonial civil servant who had had the luck to find excellent fictional material in the course of his duties. I was an amateur. This was pretty much my own view of myself. I shook hands with Greene, whom I was not to see again till we were both settled on the Côte d'Azur, and went to look for a job.

The job-seeking was conducted from the suburb of Aylestone in Leicester, where Lynne's widower father was living. He was there because his dead wife had wanted to be near the preferred daughter Hazel, whose husband was headmaster of a local primary school. Hazel was ghoulishly anxious that Lynne should hear the final message of the mother, taped before, as she put it, 'her throat closed for ever'. Lynne refused to hear it and tried to drown her guilt in the local pubs. With the illogicality that is permitted to women, she blamed the Malayan venture, wholly my idea, for the guilt of absence from her dying mother's side. She was drawn closer to her father and further away from me. He had been subsisting on shop food; now, like a good wife, she cooked him Welsh and Lancashire dishes. She supervised the housework of the twice-weekly slattern who dripped cigarette ash on to the mats. Over gin in the Black Swan or Mucky Duck she extolled her father's brilliance as a headmaster and the depth and width of his scientific learning. I had, in comparison, done little. I was forty, had published a funny but superficial little book but faced two doubtful futures, the one literary, the other pedagogic.

True. It was back to the old days of answering advertisements in the *Times Educational Supplement* and attending interviews for posts which had already been quietly filled. That I had spent three years in colonial education was not to my advantage, rather the opposite: I was out of touch with the educational policy of the new Britain. I could not relate to the youth that was being fed on rock 'n' roll and skiffle and great disc-jockey names. I had specialised in the teaching of English as a second language; here, as I undoubtedly knew, English was a first one. But, I pointed out, Britain would soon be inundated with Asian immigrants who did not like liberation from the colonial yoke, and new techniques of instruction which I already knew would be needed. This was not believed. Heads were shaken. I had wasted six years in the army; now, changing khaki for tropical cotton, I had wasted another three. I was not wanted in Britain; I had better look elsewhere.

The British Council proposed sending me to a college in Peshawar to teach phonetics. There was, I was told with referred pride, a small phonetics laboratory in that college. I had doubts, which I did not express, about the value of a phonetics laboratory on the North-West Frontier. Having learned Malay and some Chinese, I did not relish having to forget them and learn new, Indic, languages. When the post of English instructor at the Sultan Omar Ali Saifuddin College in Brunei was announced as vacant by the Crown Agents for the Colonies, I applied and was accepted. It was a contractual job; it would last three years, at the end of which I, forty-three, would have to start looking for employment again. In Britain I would naturally be even worse qualified than I was now. I had visions of odd contractual posts in Iran and the Seychelles and an early death from snakebite or revolutionaries which would solve all problems. Best not to look too far ahead. There was a general belief that there would soon be an atomic war and that we would all expire to the music of skiffle. We were all in the same boat of a diminished future.

Lynne wept in the train to Southampton. Here we were again. I, rather, the cheap, the feckless, the futureless. 'Well,' I said, 'there's this,' showing her again an advance copy of *The Enemy in the Blanket* (price twenty-one shillings), the design on whose dust-jacket showed a Sikh pulling a white man and woman in a jinrickshaw. I, who had always looked up to publishers, was discovering that they could be as inept as authors. The reviewers would blame me, not the cover-designer, for that blatant display of ignorance. Never mind. Drink up and have another. We were in the dining-car, taking tea of miniature bottles of Booth's gin. It was a damnable chill English January; at least, like the rich, we were moving towards warmth. We embarked in foul drizzle – a homely P and O ship, nothing exotic to accommodate a Siamese cat. It was the *Carthage* or the *Canton* or the *Corfu*: they were all the same. We were travelling to Singapore again, by way of Port Said, Aden, Colombo, Penang. I unpacked my typewriter on to the dressing-table of our Bibby cabin and got on with the third panel of my Malayan trilogy. I also, always my custom on ships with a ship's trio, wrote a piece of music for the drunken violinist, pianist and drummer. It was a drunken ship. At the end of the evening's dancing the fiddler, now transformed into a saxo-phonist, would yell: 'Sod off to bed. You've had your lot.' This had to be accepted with the good grace of first-class passengers who knew that the ship's company knew that they had not paid for their first-class passages. The P and O line was a kind of adjunct to the old colonial system; the two deaths would come together. Stewards were cheeky and the meals, though elaborate, bad. But the bars never closed.

I was aware that I was not now, as I had been on the *Willem Ruys*, an anonymity in a white tuxedo. I was known to these colonial functionaries and businessmen of the East. I had written a novel which many of them had read. I was not Willie Maugham but I was an acceptable epigone. I could even be heard tapping away in my cabin, actually writing something, probably putting my fellow-passengers into highly paid fiction. They assumed, especially the colonial wives, that they were worthy of this transference, or at least the flightier wives tried to make themselves worthy, or at any rate memorable. It was assumed also that a writer should be a 'character', and perhaps his wife too. Lynne and I fulfilled all expectations by insulting the Egyptians at Port Said, on the very reasonable grounds that they had destroyed the de Lesseps statue. We had a fight in a Port Said shoe-shop, after one of the lecherous assistants, knowing that white women were more than approachable, had slid his hand up Lynne's left leg. We got fighting drunk in Aden. We sobered up at Penang, where we gave lunch on board to one of my former colleagues at Kota Bharu. She was a physical training instructress of intense Tamil beauty, Christian, convinced she was really white and that her darkness was a kind of hereditary sun-tan. She wished to marry an Englishman and could not, she affirmed, bear the touch of a black or brown or yellow skin. She had had white lovers who promised marriage and then went home to find a bride called Enid or Ethel. She had been transferred to Penang, where the search for a white husband went on. But those days were over. The East had to look after itself now, but in a sense it had been ruined for good by the glimpsed glamour of the West. There was no more beautiful girl in the world than this, our friend, but her beauty would grow to plainness and her marvellous body to fat without the fulfilment of her quest. She was a true victim of imperialism.

Lynne and I disembarked at Singapore and spent two nights at the Raffles Hotel. We had a good deal of shopping to do. The Crown Agents for the Colonies had put us in touch with an old Brunei hand on leave, and he had written us a helpful letter in which he said that the amenities of the state were primitive. There was a housing shortage, so we had better resign ourselves to the prospect of months in a Chinese hotel. There were few shops and there was certainly no Singapore Cold Storage. In the market one could buy rice, Chinese bread which was always well laced with sugar, and *ikan yu*, or young shark. There were no green vegetables but there were gross and bulbous tubers of no known name. There were no clothes and there was not even any crockery. There was no shortage of gin. Clanking with crockery, we boarded the dawn flight to Brunei Town, calling on the way at Kuching in Sarawak. Landing at Brunei Town, we nearly got back on board the aircraft. There had, we learned later, actually been a man who had done just that. His name was Walker and he had been known as Walkin Walkout.

BRUNEI IS A small sultanate set between Sarawak and British North Borneo, now called Sabah. Brunei means Borneo, a small maritime strip giving its name to the whole of that dreadful uncharted jungly island. It had been a very primitive territory, inhabited by fisherfolk who built their rickety houses over the Brunei river and fished through the ill-fitting floorboards. There were also planters of rice and sago. The people were Malay, descendants of pirates, and the sultanic family was said to have been founded by a mythical figure known as the *nakhoda ragam* or singing pirate skipper, who had sung loud songs of derision when his victims walked the plank. The Sultan of my time was Omar Ali Saifuddin, who gave his name to the school where I was to teach. The state had become suddenly rich with the discovery of oil, which was being exploited by men from Texas in the west of the territory, and the Sultan was trying to make up his mind, with British advice, as to what to do with the massive oil revenues that were pouring in. He built himself an *istana* in the form of an extensive motel, and, at the time of my arrival, an ornate mosque on the river was awaiting its ceremonial opening. The dome had been covered with gold leaf which, owing to the contraction and expansion of the structure with comparative cool and large heat, fell to the ground in flakes and splinters which were taken by the fisherfolk to be a gift from Allah. There was a single street of shops, run by Chinese, which sold long-playing records and old copies of the *Daily Mirror Weekly*. There were Tamil civil servants, Iban dog-catchers with blowpipes, Land Dyak sweepers,

Australian roadbuilders and water engineers, a British Adviser and his staff. The Malays, who were proved by the miraculous gush of petroleum to be God's chosen, were to do no work but subsist on lordly welfare handouts. They were also to be educated in the more useful technologies of the West, so that they could, especially if they were of the royal family, the better run the state when the British had been ejected. They were even to learn English, though not too much. The territory was crawling with gormless tungkus and rajas, princes of the blood.

The principal of the Sultan Omar Ali Saifuddin College, who met us at the airport, was a non-academic man named Lawrence Bradshaw who was armed with various talents. He could build boats and play all the stringed instruments. He spoke a very rapid if ungrammatical Malay which, being of the territory, was somewhat different from the standard dialect of Johore. Up in Malaya *kita* had meant we; here it meant you. *Pandai* did not mean clever, it meant obsessed with. A man, like the cook we were eventually to have, who was known to be *pandai perempuan*, was not necessarily clever with women. Bradshaw put us up in the OK Hotel, full of hawking and spitting and Turkish squat-toilets. God knew when we would get a house. We sat to a dinner of *mee* and plum-coloured sauce that tasted of mothballs. Lynne cried herself to sleep and I went grimly out looking for opium.

I had smoked occasional pellets in Kota Bharu, and, going to shop after shop, I revised the vocabulary of opium-taking. The Malays called the drug *apiun*, which was from the Arabic, and also, following the Chinese, *osai* or, when it was prepared for resmoking, *tengkoh*. There was even a table of weights – ten *hun* were one *chi*, and ten *chi* were one *tahil*. I found, at the back of a shop that sold crockery (old Brunei hand, indeed), two very old Chinese puffing gently. I was courteously offered a pipe and a heated pellet. I squatted and joined the smokers. I did not go into a De Quincey trance. I relaxed enough to see time not as an *a priori* Kantian category but as a very subjective and flexible dimension, pullable like latex. Later, abetted by an ailing liver, the bad visions would come. For the moment it was enough to shrug off the future and the responsibility of an unhappy wife. Opium is a fine drug. As laudanum it cures aches and once re-conciled, with a Sunday of dreams, the British proletariat to its damnable fate. The doctors resented it and lobbied for its proscription. They won, and the white poppy became a bad growth like deadly nightshade. The British worker lost his solace and took to football and beer. It is all a great pity.

The next day I went to the Omar Ali Saifuddin College and met my future colleagues. Two of them, a Chinese pair now married, had been my pupils in Kota Bharu: they tutted at what was evidently my degradation. There was a coarse big-breasted Australian girl who said things like 'better than a slap on the tits with a wet mackerel' as well as the mandatory 'good on ya'. Her I tried to lure into the ladies' toilet for five minutes of lechery, though not yet. There was a chubby Oxford giggler who had married a seven-foot Mongolian wife named Pui. She referred to herself often as 'poor Pui', chiefly in plaints about her cook's underdone rice. There was a Chinese woman, plain, pigtailed and with glasses, who exuded sex that proved to be exclusively lesbic. It was she who was to spread her cult and break up homes. An old and very brown Chinese named Po Soo Jin hummed and muttered to himself and seemed perpetually stoned, though he was to prove sexually very active. A burgher from Ceylon named Matthew Bastians taught Welshy English with the invariable question-tag 'isn't it?'.

My task, apart from teaching variable question-tags, was to instruct mixed racial groups in the history of the British Empire as far as its temporary shattering, prefiguring a permanent one, in the Second World War, with strong emphasis on the development of the United States. It was to be a study of rise, decline, and fall, with the seeds of decline already planted in the rise. I was also to teach a group of Malay young men the phonetics of their own language. These, destined to be teachers in monoglot state schools, knew no English, and my approach had to be from inside a language that was innocent of technical terms of any kind. The technical vocabulary of *pelajaran bunyi* (study of sounds), better termed *fonetik*, had to be constructed from scratch. So I burdened them with *fonem* and *alofon* and had great difficulty in conveying the highly sophisticated distinction between the two. What was a labial? Probably *bunyi bibir*. What, for God's sake, was an unvoiced labial? Perhaps *bunyi bibir dengan tiada suara*, a ghastly mouthful. Again, what numerical coefficient was to go with these new entities? Malay, like Chinese, is not satisfied with a simple one or two. There has to be an imaginative noun of number – *telor*, meaning egg, for round things like testicles, *biji*, meaning seed, for, bafflingly, eggs, *buah*, meaning fruit, for a big thing like a car or a house or the continent of Asia. I cut through the fanciful web of the coefficients and spoke of one plain phoneme – *suatu fonem*. After all, these speakers of a primitive language had to be brought into the modern age.

The mixed students, though courteous and amiable in the Asiatic manner, were all vaguely doped, as though slowly coming out of an opium trance. They lacked contact with a lively modern city like Singapore. They lacked even contact with the cinema. All they knew of the modern age was the flaring oil pipes of Seria, which one could reach only by jeep along the sand at low tide. The jungle was close, and there was a lot of it. Even the Chinese, brightest of the Orientals, lacked sharpness. As for the Brunei Malays, why should they study? This strange substance oil, denied to the Jews, granted lavishly to the children of Islam, was bringing in more money than the sons of the soil, meaning of the pirate-ridden waters, could ever hope to spend. Work had always been an alien substance to the Malays, into whose nets the eager fish homed, whose paddy yielded three crops a year, for whom bananas and coconuts fell, to say nothing of the foul-smelling intoxicating durian in the season of durians. Allah, with his draughts of oil, confirmed that the Malays should have Cadillacs as well as coconuts. I began to see my own desperation approach, though slowly, like a sampan on the horizon.

Lynne sobbed at the cheerful noise of hoicking in the OK Hotel and demanded a house. We were given a very strange flat of three floors, access to the two highest of which was by means of a fire escape. The bedroom was as open to visitors as the kitchen and living-room, and curious Ibans and Malays would climb the metal stairway to gawp at Lynne and myself attempting the act of love. There was no bathroom, but there was an outside *tong* filled with monsoon water in which we were intended to sluice, publicly, naked. It was not possible to obtain a servant. Entry to the state was restricted and you had to order your servant from overseas well in advance, filling in in quadruplicate a complex form to be returned to the International Labour Office. There were no shambling unemployed crying out for work. Lynne cooked on a charcoal stove but melted in the heat. After protests, we were moved to a genuine house, a tiny geometrical Public Works Department structure in which the water supply depended on the rains and the electrical current blazed, dimmed, died, reawoke, dimmed, died. The PWD furniture was full of termites, and the varnished arm of an armchair crumbled at the touch. Lynne continued weeping.

This little dwelling was one of four, attached one to the others, in a desolate spot on which the scrublands glowered and sand swirled in a hot wind. Across the road dwelt, in a house of his own building, a Malay named Azahari. He was a man of politics who led what had been known as the National Socialist Party until the evil omen of the name was explained to him. Now it was called the Party of Freedom. Azahari had a henchman named 'Che Gu' Salleh, who, as his honorific proclaimed, was a Malay schoolmaster. These two, and their followers, wished to make the growing oil-wealth serve a modern state, not a traditional sultanate with Allah being banged into one's ears all the time. Azahari would be a genial, essentially democratic, dictator, 'Che Gu' Salleh his Goebbels, and loyal party members would be policemen in exquisite uniforms, designed, perhaps, in Paris. The British were no real problem. They would go soon, but the Sultan proposed staying, sitting comfortably on oilwells. He would be permitted to leave, having tranquilly accepted the truth that hereditary rule was undemocratic (though Azahari's son, Tumbledown Dick to his Cromwell, seemed likely to be groomed for succession). I found Azahari's project unrealistic. He tried unsuccessfully to implement it shortly after I left. The Sultan refused to retire to the Côte d'Azur, and British troops were called in to quell Azahari's uprising. I found him hospitable. He had money derived from a printing works which, with botched type and many literals, produced Azahari's banned revolutionary pamphlets. There was always a welcome for the dwellers in the wretched hovels on which he looked out from his neat, though lavatoriless, palace. We were all white, and he needed white support. He wanted me to translate his *Mein Kampf* – *Perang Yang Akan Datang*, a good clanging title meaning The Coming Battle – into Macaulayan English.

We were all, I say, white, but we were poor white. Next door was an Australian road-builder living with, or perhaps married to, a girl of the Land Dyaks. Next door to this ménage was another mixed one – a British under-officer of Passport Control genuinely married to an Iban or Sea Dyak. The Sea Dyaks traditionally look down on the Land Dyaks, whom they consider to be descended from *mawas*, which the English call *orang utan*, a term properly only applied to real men of the forest. Between these two girls there was much enmity and scratching and hair-tearing. The fourth house housed, incredibly, two Italians from Piombino, father and son, Nando and Paolo Tasca. They had come from Tripoli to cut marble and fit it on the floor of the mosque. These two would fight each other over women and the pitiful wage that Nando paid Paolo. Sometimes, Nando would cry over Paolo's behaviour in the town and sob '*Tutto Brunei parla di te.*'

Nando Tasca would ship huge bales of marble to Singapore, where an Italian agent arranged their disposal with local build-ing contractors. Nando's view was that good Italian marble was wasted on the brown heathens of Brunei. On the more shadowy areas of the mosque floor he would have concrete poured and then make a marbly design with paint and a wire brush. 'These a people not a know,' he would say. 'They not a know a nothing.' Then Paolo broke the marble-cutting machine and none knew how to repair it. Fatherly fists flailed and, unfilially, Paolo struck back. Paolo would leave the hovel bruised and cry to the Brunei moon: '*Dormirò nel minareto!*' And he would climb the winding stairs to the summit of the minaret, where the loudspeaker had already been installed for the *bilal's* calling the people to prayer, and he would sing 'Stardust' to the sleeping town, the words changed to *polvere di marmo*, or cry his wrongs: 'My fader bloody bastard. *Proprio un fara-butto.*'

As there was already so much noise in this clutch of hovels, Lynne and I saw no harm in adding to it by holding furious parties for our native friends. These were furious for their own reasons – low pay, the disregarded small print in their contracts, snotty superiors – but they were ready to be furious also on our behalf. They were not natives of Brunei but of Sarawak – Minggu, who led a team of dogcatchers and supervised their euthanasia with blowpipes; little Joe, whose father had been the head-shrinker of his longhouse; the giant Paul, whose roots were Hawaiian; Jim, who was a mixture of Chinese, Welsh, Christian British North Bornean, Buginese and Sumatran and had worked as strong man for a Chinese secret society. Joe played trap drums and Paul the cornet and they were overjoyed to recruit me as pianist for gigs in private houses and on lawns. Their signature tune was called 'Sarawaki'. They did not know that this has been written in the thirties by the band leader Harry Roy on the occasion of his marriage to Princess Pearl, youngest and most flighty daughter of the White Rajah of Sarawak. They had converted this simple tune into a very native cantilena, and they believed it came from Sarawak prehistory.

At the first session in which I played I gave a speech. It was a birthday party, and I said: 'It is good to have something to celebrate in this unhappy place at this unhappy time.' These words were conveyed to the British Resident, who had me marched into his office for a military-style rocket. This official knew that I had served in Malaya, and he disclosed the chip-on-shoulder attitude of Sarawak functionaries to servants of the Federation. But he had not merely worked in Sarawak; he had been assistant to the last of the White Rajahs, the end of the line of hereditary Brookes, and this gave him a romantic *cachet*. The Labour Government of Great Britain, considering, like Azahari, that there was something unclean about this family rule, deposed the final Brooke and brought in a series of career officials who were suffering from the dismantling of the British Empire. Every appointee of this series was assassinated by the Ibans, who were devoted to the Brookes. The Rajah's methods of administering justice were idiosyncratic and sometimes took the form of six of the best on the bare Iban bottom, but he was known to be a fair man. The Maharanee's nymphomania was respected too. She had many party tricks, the best known of which was her standing on the residency billiard table, lifting her skirt to disclose no knickers, and then saying to the players: 'Come on, boys, pot the red.' There was never a dull moment with the daughters either. The removal of the Brookes and their replacement by dull men who followed the book of rules was too much for the cheerful simple hearts of both Land and Sea Dyaks. These officials were not decapitated, merely knifed. In my time the ruling official of Sarawak, who had authority over the expatriate officers of Brunei, was not, for some reason, considered a candidate for assassination. Perhaps the people of Sarawak were growing habituated to the new pedestrian status of being a Crown Colony. They would be part of the new congeries of states called Malaysia soon, anyway. One had to move with the times.

The British Resident rebuked me for words which were, at best, indiscreet, at worst inflammatory. But my next offence was more grave and led to a court case, as well as harsh admonitions, personally delivered from Sarawak. I completed the third part of my Malayan Trilogy and invited dogcatchers, PWD storemen, waterworks operatives and other low life to a party to celebrate. In the house next door, the Australian roadman gave a party for his muscled native workers, and much *samsu*, a black Chinese rice spirit with a high lead content, maddened them to ferocious song and fortissimo drumming on the party wall. My guests countersang and counterdrummed, and Nando Tasca and his son, who had declared a rare truce and were in bed early, were awakened by the noise and came out near-naked to protest. The son was absorbed into our party and the father into the other. The parties came to an end simultaneously at three in the morning, and opposed groups armed with empty bottles and knives confronted each other outside the contiguous front doors. Harsh words like *chelaka, puteh berlumor, vafnculo, pommy bastard* and *my fuckin' fader* rang in the Brunei night. It was Lynne, whose Welsh blood was hotter than any of the Mediterranean or the China Sea, who considered striking the first blow. At least she approached a stunted but powerful roadworker, whose Land Dyak brown was burnt to black, with an empty gin bottle. This was the signal for bottle butts to be smashed against the pebble-dash walls and raw sharp glass presented.

The fighting did not get further than the drawing of surface blood. Azahari's lights were on and his house had, except for a lavatory, all modern conveniences, including a telephone. He had called the police when the noise was transferred from the hovels to the street. He was a civilised man who accepted riot only as a device of political reform. The police in their Land Rover were slow to arrive. They had brought with them the wife or mistress of the Australian roadbuilder, who had been plying the trade of prostitute in the town. Prostitution was forbidden in this Muslim state, whose Islamic undername (which it shared with Perak) was *daru'l-ridzwan* or the Abode of Grace. The police had not wished to charge the girl, who was primitive and innocent, so had merely taken her services free in an empty cell and then brought her home. Names were taken but no arrests made. Brunei itself was a kind of prison, walled in by sea and jungle.

When the charge of riot was eventually heard in a court with an attap roof but no walls, the whole town assembled with children in arms. The magistrate was a gum-chewing Australian and the case was conducted in English. The police evidence was highly tendentious. 'In one house there was being quiet party. In other house was more noise. Tuan Wilson had given people much drink in OK Hotel. Then he bring back the people to drink more.' There were loud protests quietened by a gavel and the threat of *rotan semambu* or Malacca canes. The case came to

nothing. The magistrate picked somewhat arbitrarily on a
roadworker and Minggu the dogcatcher and made them shake
hands and vow perpetual *perdamaian* or peace. But Lynne was
now given the name of troublemaker. The Australians believed
she was the sister of Aneurin Bevan and dedicated to the promotion of unrest. They got out of her way when she appeared in a
bar called the Snowman, which had no ice. I was heavily rebuked
by the colonial chief of Sarawak, who flew from Kuching to
deliver his rebuke. I thought, with hope, that I might be repatriated, but I was to serve my three-year sentence without
remission. I had to behave: this was not Malaya.

The beneficial result of the fracas was our transference to a small
but detached bungalow with a garden. An Indian Muslim named
Ahmad appeared from nowhere and offered his services as cook and
houseboy. He had a fat wife who, when not eating, would act as
laundrywoman. How he had entered the state was not clear, but his
evidently illegal status was condoned by the authorities: Lynne and
I would no longer, it was hoped, be drinking on empty stomachs.
Ahmad, as if to announce to the world our devotion to gin,
decorated the front lawn tastefully with empty Gordon's, Booth's
and Tanqueray bottles. A goat was brought by a one-eyed Iban
who, for one Straits dollar a day, acted as our knifed bodyguard.
'Banyak musoh,' he said, many enemies. This goat gave no milk
but it cropped the back lawn. Other animals appeared. There was a
friendly renegade Sikh who had amassed a private zoo too large for
his personal attention: our bungalow, with its sizeable covered
courtyard, was to be an annexe. He brought a young hamadryad,
only about six feet long, which coiled about Lynne and exhibited
great devotion to her. When it amorously squeezed too hard it
would be slapped on the head with the admonition 'Naughty
snake'. It slept between us in the double bed, hissing its pleasure, and
would get up occasionally to eat the toads in the bathroom, which
themselves were there to eat the insects. The next acquisition was a
pair of rhesus monkeys, male and female, Mat and Aminah, dressed
in dirty Malay ceremonial costumes. They were chained to a
horizontal pole. Mat was jealous of me and, at my approach to feed
them their breakfast bananas, would hug Aminah in his arms and
fluently piss all over my white ducks. A couple of pye dogs, Horatio
and Ophelia, joined the menagerie, and a great number of cats.
Wire netting was erected behind the servants' quarters and hens and
a couple of cocks were imported. We would not starve.

There had always seemed to be a danger of starvation, since

one could not live for ever on young shark and rice. The lack of green vegetables made us white-tongued and costive. Constipation was the prevalent ailment among the expatriates. A Tamil clerk I knew used the day of rest, Friday, as the occasion for a kind of ritual purgation. He would drink a whole bottle of castor oil and arise on the working Saturday thin, pale, slow in his movements but clearly cathartised. I spent too much fruitless time in the toilet. Entering it one day I saw a middle-aged man on the seat, writing poetry. It was a brief hallucination but it led me to the creation of a character named Enderby.

I spent the afternoon writing. The teaching day began at dawn and ended at one o'clock. The rest of the time was free for games and siesta, meaning siesta, for the students did not care for games. They had no Welsh rugger-playing Jimmy Howell to lash them on to the field. There were always two cats taking their siesta or ziz on my PWD desk, and one of them would fretfully push with his haunches at the typewriter carriage. I wrote a novel called *Devil of a State*. I had thought of *Hell of a State* as a title, but hell is a strong word. The novel was, is, about Brunei, which is renamed Naraka, Malayo-Arabic for hell. Little invention was needed to contrive a large cast of unbelievable characters and a number of interwoven plots. Though completed in 1958, the work was not published until 1961 when, for what that was worth, it was made a choice of the Book Society. Heinemann, my publisher, was doubtful about publishing it: it might be libellous. I had to change its Borneo setting to an East African one. Heinemann was right to be timorous. In early 1958 *The Enemy in the Blanket* appeared, and this at once provoked a libel suit.

In the novel there is a British lawyer practising on the East Coast of Malaya and making little money. He marries a wealthy Malay widow in order to pay his debts and secure the appearance of prosperity which will help heal his wounded practice. Though brought up as a Catholic he has to enter Islam, despite the remonstrances of the local priest, who is French. The marriage turns out to be pure *naraka*, and the lawyer tries to get out of it by proposing that he and his wife sail to Mecca to become *hajis*. He has been in contact with an old comrade of the Royal Air Force who runs a small private airline in Jidda. Thence he intends to fly to Suez and thus escape a disastrous marriage and a failed Eastern career. We do not know what happens to him, but there are hints that he crashes and dies. Lynne and I had been friendly with

a white lawyer in Selangor, and I showed him the manuscript
of the novel, wishing to know whether there was, in his view,
any resemblance between himself and the fictional character. He
laughed the notion away. I should have secured in writing his
denial of libel, but I considered him a friend. When the novel
arrived in the few Malayan bookshops he was prompt to act.
The libel suit was announced on all the radio stations of South-
East Asia, but I first received notification of it in a letter from
Heinemann. I was severely disturbed. The plaintiff was asking for
a lot of money which, in the manner of the East, was augmented
in gossip and continued radio and newspaper reports.

I did not see how a writ could properly be served on me, who,
according to the legal advice I took, was living in a territory
outside the reach of the high court of Singapore, where the libel
claim was being made. Singapore was now an independent territory, but Heinemann, who maintained an agency there, had to
accept the jurisdiction of its courts and answer the charge through
a Singapore solicitor. I had to furnish my publisher with a prayer
that the charge be set aside, but I did not propose to act on my
own behalf. Unfortunately, while I was teaching one day, the
college messenger handed me papers which I thought to be instructions about the tightening of discipline or some such internal
matter. I signed distractedly and went on with my lesson about
the collapse of the British Empire. Then I discovered that I had
accepted the serving of a writ.

At the beginning of a libel suit papers are exchanged, and then
the case settles into a sleep disturbed, for the defendant, with
ghastly dreams of humiliation and financial ruin. *The Enemy in
the Blanket* was withdrawn from sale, and I had grave doubts
about the possibility of a literary future. I had received and corrected
page proofs of *Beds in the East* and given Heinemann an assurance
that the work contained nothing defamatory. But whether publication would take place remained unsure. I had been lectured by
the British Resident and his Sarawak superior on the theme of
irresponsibility; now similar lectures were delivered in airmail
letters by the chairman of Heinemann. I had hoped that, if I
could establish myself as a novelist, I might free myself from the
kind of bondage I suffered. My golden handshake from the Federation of Malaya had been invested in Imperial Chemicals and
the British Motor Corporation, but there would never be large
enough dividends to secure financial independence. We were
going through a bad time, and this made us drink more.

Lynne erupted in a snarling letter, while the hamadryad sympathetically hissed, to the plaintiff we had thought to be our friend, but his lawyer, a white East Coast settler who might, with equal injustice, have made a libel claim, joyfully filed this as a clinching proof of malicious intent. The laws of libel are unfair to novelists. Malice may be a strong card for the plaintiff to play, but it is nothing compared to the real weight of the charge – that identification of a loathsome fictional character with a real-life personage has been made by a number of 'responsible people', that that personage has been morally or professionally harmed, and that only an apology and a large sum of money can salve the hurt. An apology is out of order when no malice has been intended or, as frequently happens, the author has never even heard of the person allegedly injured. Publishers are too ready to accept, without argument, the gravitas of the charge, and to settle out of court. The author's work is pulped and his creative labour wasted. And he never knows when, in all innocence, he may be served with another writ for libel. No wonder some novelists write historical or science fiction. But even a reconstructed past or an imagined future can be unsafe. 'Responsible people' testify that Lambert Simnel is really Simnel Lambert, noted brain surgeon, or that Goshnorov of Planet X7 is a damaging portrait of Noshgorov, admired Soviet defector.

In what, in Europe, would have been the autumn of 1958, Lynne and I flew, with my colleague Po Soo Jin, to Kuching, capital of Sarawak, for the hope of a week's solace. The real object of Soo Jin's trip was to ease sexual frustration by visiting an Iban longhouse, where an injection of foreign seed was, following a sound exogamic instinct, considered beneficial to the tribe. Soo Jin persuaded me to travel with him along the coast to a longhouse long as a street, ill-smelling of old fish and fermented mice, considered a delicacy, where handsome near-naked elders bade us drink deep from a calabash of *tuak* and exquisite girls with exposed breasts giggled at the prospect of love in the long night from a couple of nameless foreigners, one yellower than the other. The lopping of heads and the skilled shrinking of them were no longer part of the culture of these beautiful animists, but there was a very old man who tended the historic heads that were affixed to the wall, crooning over a Japanese specimen whose pince-nez he polished and whose hair he smoothed with a home-made unction. Ancestral skulls rattled about, playthings for the children or components of a kind of xylophone. There was unintelligible song before the oil wicks were finger-and-thumbed out, and then we settled to public love and sleep. It was a soothing experience. The libel suit seemed far away. The Ibans waved us off with smiles of gratitude. We had invigorated their stock in exchange for a little broiled fish and a spoonful or so of fermented mouse. I sometimes think of the child I may have fathered, now grown to thirty and happy with love and a little fishing. I hope to have given something to the East.

Christmas came, and we wept over our corned beef for turkey and pudding. There was a little drinking session in the morning at the house of one of the state officials, and some of the children of expatriates attended. They were given orange squash essence diluted with the water kept in old gin bottles in the refrigerator, and they complained: 'It's not nice, mummy.' They were told to drink up and be quiet. It turned out that a full bottle of gin had got among the empties, and these children were made first drunk and then very ill. In the afternoon Lynne and I drove with our former neighbour, the white husband of the Iban, who had gone back to her tribe to have a baby, to the oil-town of Seria, where there was to be a fancy dress dance in the government rest house. We travelled along the sand of the shore in a Land Rover, since there was as yet no road, and we misjudged the table of the tides. We raced the incoming waves but lost. The differential was flooded and the waters rose. Crocodiles, which had adapted themselves to shore life in order to prey on monkeys, lazily considered swimming in across the *sungai* that joined the sea to examine us. The water had risen to our waists and was still rising. Lynne, always courageous, stripped and swam to the nearest kampong. Twenty men produced a rope and hauled us out. This sort of thing had happened before. We trudged through scrub and sharp *rumput* to Seria, only a mile or so off. The fancy dress dance had already started. The three of us won second prize as a party of castaways. This was no life for anyone.

The government of Brunei recognised that life was hard for white expatriates, and it granted six weeks of home leave annually, with first-class air passages both ways. We travelled by Malayan Airways to Singapore and then by Qantas to London. The State Treasurer of Brunei was at the Raffles Hotel, where we spent our overnight stop, and he shook his fist at me, though he proffered no action more aggressive. I had been invited, just before Christmas, to sing some Christmas carols, to my own piano accompaniment, on Radio Brunei, which was very short of programme material. I had put my own words to the traditional tunes, and one of the songs, to the melody of *Adeste Fideles*, went:

> Come, all ye crawlers,
> Psychosycophantic,
> Doff and defer to the State
> Treas-ur-er.
> Give him a parcel
> And then lick his arcel.
> Foregather at the Yacht Club,
> That snottier-than-snot club,
> Give pleasure to your treasure,
> The Treas-ur-er.

Lynne and I never visited the Yacht Club, which had, since there were no yachts, no concern with yachting. I did not love the State Treasurer greatly because he was chairman of the housing committee, by which I considered we had been unfairly treated. I had sung another joyous song which attacked what I regarded as Islamic hypocrisy:

> Muslims awake, salute another day
> Of gin, whisky, Dogshead stout.
> And B.G.A.
> Great is the law, the law the Prophet taught –
> Don't give the bloody thing another thought.
> You're seven hours late for lunch –
> Food is cold, of course.
> Don't fret: go out and get
> Your tenth divorce.

I hoped that these, and other seasonable slanders, would annoy. I even hoped to receive a letter while I was on leave, informing me that my contract had been terminated and that my crated possessions would follow by the next available transport. But no such letter came. The Mentri Besar, or Chief Minister of the state, was a humorous Malay who had little faith in the functionaries imported from Sarawak, and found that I was the only man who could appreciate his sarcastic hyperbole and respond to it in kind. 'What an excellent man is the British Resident, and how supremely beautiful is his lady wife. His efficiency is incredible, and his charm veritably devastates.' The Mentri Besar did not wish me to leave the state. Not yet, anyway.

In Leicester Lynne found that her father had just fulfilled a proposal he had intimated in a letter. There was a local widow of no education but a powerful thirst for stout, whom he appreciated for what he termed her good yeoman stock. He had talked of marriage, and now there was a new Mrs Jones in charge of the little house in Aylestone. There was no room for us, so we took a room in a private hotel in Bloomsbury, run by a middle-aged but still sexually vital Italian woman from Bermondsey and her ancient Swiss husband. ''Ow are you, my sweetee pie?' she would say, and he would sourly respond: 'I am de same. I do not shange,' and chuckle ominously. We turned the West End, with the help of drinking clubs, into a site of non-stop carousal. We were setting up trouble for ourselves.

Beds in the East appeared, and I appeared, for the first time, in a BBC radio book programme. I was called 'Mr Burgess' and saw that a new identity had been established. The reviews were mostly disdainful – here was a moderately amusing brief novel (price thirty shillings) about the rump of empire (and oh, how boring the Empire always was), a region Somerset Maugham made his own, so it ill behoved minor writers of fiction to try to usurp his place with their ill-conceived, and probably ill-informed, fantasies – but one or two remembered the earlier novels and commended the whole trilogy. Heinemann did not seem to be fearful of the possibility of further libel suits. None came. Nor did Heinemann take the existing libel suit too seriously. The publisher's lawyers appeared to foresee its outcome of a few months later – the setting aside of the charge in the Singapore high court, and the awarding of taxed costs against the plaintiff. The plaintiff, as I expected, had difficulty in paying.

But this, in the early English spring of 1959, lay in the future. Indeed, a whole new future, and a very tremulous one, lay in the future. We flew back to the hot wet dishrag atmosphere of Singapore, flavoured with cat-piss, and took the dawn flight to Brunei. We were met by our driver Aziz in our second-hand Oldsmobile, a gesture of efficiency which unnerved us. Aziz was a vague relative of the cook-houseboy Ahmad. In our absence other relatives had poured in, all unpestered by the immigration authorities, and these had overflowed from the servants' quarters into a kind of tented concentration camp on the back lawn. They had eaten the goat and killed, without eating, the snake, but there seemed to be more poultry than before. The rhesus monkey Mat richly micturated a greeting: he had thought he had got rid of me. The bitch Ophelia had seven puppies. Various cats had kittened. There was a *kuching hutan* or jungle cat snarling in the garage. There was plenty of livestock, including ourselves, for the servants to look after, but Ahmad himself had run away. His fat wife was tearful – '*Dia pandai perempuan, tuan*' (he's a damnable womaniser) – and assumed I would take her on as a mistress. Ahmad eventually returned and was bashed with a dustbin-lid.

It was an unhappy time and an unhappy place, but why? There were no terrorists in the jungle, the electricity and water fitfully functioned, and there was much to look forward to – a visit from the Duke of Edinburgh, the ceremonial opening of the mosque, a sumptuous garden party in the grounds of the istana. The general unhappiness seemed to spring from what I can only call a sense of uncreativity, a lack of stimulus, an awareness of mediocrity at the top. The Sultan was a grave withdrawn figure and a dismally good Muslim. We would have been happier if he had quarrelling Chinese mistresses or harmlessly crashed in one of his many Cadillacs. He seemed aware of malaise among the expatriates, and he summoned them all to the istana gardens, where they were seated at bridge tables and served warm orange crush. We wondered, while we waited for his appearance, if he was going to deliver a surprise appropriate to an Eastern prince – something from the Arabian Nights, mass beheadings, the New Zealand nurses and typists converted to a harem, munificent gifts, plank walking, first-class fares home and lavish pensions. But he spoke prepared Malay of a vagueness I had not thought possible in that earthy language. Written Malay uses graphemes like *maka* and *shahadan*, punctuation words without true meaning intended to be accepted as points of rest for the eye, never to be spoken, but the Sultan enunciated these solemnly and used locutions like *menunaikan muslihat di-ithbatkan tiada belum nyata* – to implement policies decided upon but not as yet clearly articulated. If his aim had been to induce a kind of tranquillising bafflement he had, after an hour of such gobbledygook, fulfilled that aim. We trooped away dazed. It was at least another hour before the Snowman and OK bars resumed their regular noise, eye-scratching, and passing out.

Brunei needed eccentrics. More, it needed eccentrics as human sacrifices. I, being a writer, had to be eccentric, and Lynne, being a Celt like Dylan Thomas or Brendan Behan or, indeed, Oscar Wilde, had to be a sacrificial eccentric. It was expected that we should clear bars by hurling chairs at windows or (that old business had not been forgotten, mythicised rather) smashing glasses in Australian faces. The Brunei police were usually waiting for us outside bars at closing-time, courteously, though at gunpoint, charging us with being drunk and disorderly and taking us to the station for questioning, rebuke, warning, but never a night in the cells. The real police persecution was reserved to our servants, especially our driver Aziz.

If Lynne was wilder than I was, sexually wild too, which was dangerous, it was because I was gaining some fulfilment out of writing my new novel. This was called *The Right to an Answer*, and it was based on a true story that Lynne had told me. She had known in wartime London a pair of married couples who had indulged in weekend spouse-swapping. This harmless-seeming diversion ended in the breaking up of two marriages. Mr A fell in love with Mrs B and they set up a ménage; but Mr B did not fall in love with Mrs A. Mr B committed suicide, an unusual act in wartime. It was a highly moral story, warning of the dangers of not taking marriage seriously enough. For a writer like Ford Madox Ford it might have provided material for another *The Good Soldier*; for me it was almost, but not quite, the stuff of comedy. I set the plot in an unnamed Midlands town like Leicester, imported into the Black Swan or Mucky Duck of Aylestone the landlord of the Red Lion in Adderbury, and had a great Midlands figure, William Shakespeare, warning from the grave of the dangers of impairing marital stability. For the first time I used a first person narrative, inventing a businessman named J. W. Denham who works for a British firm in the East. He comes home on leave to observe, with hypocritical disgust, the weekend routine of chortling adultery, and witnesses the horrible débâcle to which it leads. The book was also intended to be a sardonic study, as seen through the eyes of an outsider, of the mess of postwar England — all television, fornication, and a rising generation given to rock music and violence. Denham, though his life is fixed firmly overseas (in Japan, which I had, in my ignorance of the reality, to fabricate from books), is a dull Englishman — as the narrator of *The Good Soldier* is a dull American — who knows England, but there had to be another exotic character who comes to England with a complete ignorance of its *mores* and becomes involved innocently in the marital mess of the main plot. This was an invented Tamil from Ceylon named Mr

Raj. He was based on no one; he emerged from my unconscious fully armed and, against my will, he took over the
novel.

If the three books already published, and the one reluctantly
accepted, were to a large extent imaginative manipulations of
events and persons in my own Far Eastern life, *The Right to an
Answer* was almost entirely invention. That I could invent was
the final proof, to me, that I had not mistaken my vocation. The
vocation had come late, but, by the middle of 1959, it had already
yielded seven novels and a novella – rather more than E. M.
Forster had accomplished in his entire ninety-one years. Some
spark in a deep layer of my unconscious ignited a conviction, not
yet to be articulated, that I might make a living at the writer's
trade. This unvoiced conviction perhaps partially explains the
crucial event that was soon to happen.

Trouble arrived with the Duke of Edinburgh. I put on a tropical suit and a tie and supervised the lining of the road from the
airport with little brown children in their Friday best, all lan-
guidly waving union jacks. The Duke's car appeared and most of
them cheered; the more sophisticated cried 'Merdeka!' In the
afternoon there was a garden party on the lawn of the British
Residency, and the Duke, hands folded behind his back, went
smiling from group to group. Tug Wilson, a Cockney stores
functionary who had adopted a Buginese son ('I don't fuck his
arse, that's what they all fucking think, but I fucking don't') said:
'Served under you in the navy, sir. Jolly nice to see you again,
sir. Keep the flag flying, sir.' The Duke said: 'Good show. Jolly
good luck.' He then came up to the group which contained Lynne
and myself. Two New Zealand typists curtsied but Lynne looked
grim. The Duke said: 'Everything all right here? Everybody satisfied?' The typists said: 'Oh yes, thank you, sir.' But Lynne said:
'No, everything is not bloody well all right. The housing is
inadequate, they promise decent schooling for the kids of expatriates and provide nothing, and the whole administration is
fucking inefficient.' The British Resident and his staff, standing
behind His Royal Highness, heard all this with little joy. The
Duke, used to the strong language of the navy, seemed to like
this intrusion of truculence into the blandness. He asked for details
of administrative inefficiency, and Lynne was pleased to tick them
off. Favouritism on the housing committee, police persecution of
the innocent, bribery and jobbery. The Duke went off to be
curtsied to by a knot of Australian wives, followed by a glower-

ing escort. A bolt shot; it wouldn't be long now before enforced repatriation. We went home. I had better try to finish
my novel.

No action was taken. The Mentri Besar beamed when he met
me later in the street and said: 'What delightful people your
compatriots are. How they love honesty and clear speaking. Do
give my fondest regards to your lady wife.' As the day for the
ceremonial opening of the mosque drew nearer, the administration
had enough on its hands without having to prepare a writ of
exeant. The marble-cutting machine had been slow to be repaired,
the Tascas, *padre e figlio*, fought instead of beautifying the mosque,
Azahari's party had been indoctrinating whole gangs of workers
in the techniques of industrial action. But at length, in a time of
drought, with the brown frogs fighting the green frogs for the
possession of waterholes, all was ready, and dignitaries from sister
Islamic states began to arrive, as well as Far Eastern correspondents
of European journals, for an evening reception in the istana
gardens, a circumcision ceremony for the two youngest princes
of the blood, and the turning of the key in the ward of the most
expensive *masjid* of the Muslim world.

At the sultanic reception, with boy scouts opening bottles of
Moët et Chandon that had basked in the afternoon sun, Lynne
got spectacularly drunk and tried to fight one of the feebler visiting rajas. She was not invited to the *sunat* or *khatan* or *khitanat*, at
which two brave boys had their *kulups* snipped off by the *modin*
and grew pale as the blood dripped on to a banana leaf. There
were many who wished that they had not been invited, and they
were not impressed by the shrimp canapés. For the opening of
the mosque, at which bandsmen fainted in the heat while they
tried to play 'God Save the Queen' in fast galliard tempo, the
drought broke and Allah rained bountifully on to the ceremony.
We all went back to work.

I was teaching one morning when the end of my colonial
career was signalled. The class was Form Four, the subject the
Boston Tea Party; the fans were not working and it was
rumoured that a female cobra was looking for her young in the
corridor outside. At the end of the lesson I felt I had also come to
the end of my tether. A great deal of tension had been building
up – a dissatisfied wife, a libel action, Australians who called me
a pommy bastard, a disordered liver, dyspepsia and dyspnoea
which morning droplets of Axe oil did nothing to alleviate, a
very large measure of simple frustration. I had done my best; I

could do no more: let other agencies take over. I lay on the classroom floor and closed my eyes.

There was prompt action. The principal, Bradshaw, appeared, and he summoned strong Malays. I was taken to the local hospital. I felt well enough now but maintained my passivity: passivity from now on would be the answer to everything. I was placed in a two-bed first-class officer's cubicle where an old Chinese, clearly not a first-class officer, chirped cheerily like a hunting *chichak*. The white doctor who examined me, Glyn Griffiths, was a fellow-graduate of Manchester. He performed various tests with a neurological tray. He took X-ray photographs of my head. There were no facilities for a spinal tap. He discharged me but said I must go back to England, where they knew all about tropical diseases. He was convinced I had a tropical disease.

With natural perversity, I now objected to being sent home. If I was to be sent home, I conceded, it must be for the purpose of a medical examination only: I then wished to come back to Brunei. That lying down on the classroom floor had been an act of purgation or reconciliation or something. I was all right now. In the presence of the State Education Officer and his deputy, as in the presence of a pair of priests, I was prepared to say: '*Mea culpa, mea culpa, mea maxima culpa.*' I had done wrong, but now I would gird up my loins for cooperative and constructive labour to build a better Brunei. They shook sad heads. Pack your books, they said: you will not be coming back. I wondered if the administration had found the pretext for repatriation they had been looking for. I imagined the Duke of Edinburgh at a mild curry dinner saying to the British Resident: 'Good girl that, whoever she was, Welsh by the sound of her. Spoke out. Didn't give a damn. Misguided but fearless honesty. Good show. Don't take any action, okay?' And now, in my willed collapse, they had found what they needed. I said to the State Education Officer and his deputy: 'The Mentri Besar wants me here, you know. That means the Sultan does too.' They shook their heads even more. Get your things crated. But I refused. I had a novel to finish before I left. Let whoever wished to be rid of me see to the crating and forwarding and the payment of outstanding bills.

Lynne and I were sent off very speedily. Glyn Griffiths furnished me with a number of little typed slips requesting help and forbearance from airlines and hotel managers. I might collapse again or erupt into mindless aggression. Lynne was there as my nurse, but it was I who had to do the nursing. She kept collapsing in the public rooms of the Raffles Hotel. She collapsed at Singapore airport. When we were in flight she became very alert. Ice was forming on the pastel ceiling over her seat, a fire seemed to be starting beneath the carpet of the deck below it. The stewardess at first thought her complaint was part of a referred hallucination: she had received one of Glyn Griffiths's typed slips. But the engineer took it more seriously: he descended into the bowels of the aircraft and restored normality. I sustained my passive pose: *che sarebbe sarebbe*. At Colombo a hydraulic fault had to be remedied. At Bombay the starting-handle came away in the pilot's hand. On the long haul to London, having ceased to worry about myself, I worried about Lynne.

Old Far Eastern hands averred that the tropical zone was no place for white women. They ceased to eat, they drank, their livers were small and responded more than a man's to alcoholic abuse and a chronic shortage of Vitamin B. Their genetic economy became deranged and they were prone to nymphomania. I leave the confirmation of this to the experts in tropical medicine, or its explosion to the forces of women's liberation. Lynne's career in Malaya, but far more so in Brunei, had been marked by all these parameters of decay. But instead of sitting at home under the ceiling fan, reading *Bhowani Junction* or *Our Man in Havana*, occasionally bawling out the *kuki*, she had engaged the tropics with active and dangerous zest. She had embraced a monkey and been severely bitten and had to submit to daily anti-rabies injections, which promoted a convincing simulacrum of the disease itself. She had fallen on dirty ground and been treated for tetanus. She had been stricken by dengue or sand-fly fever and sometimes, usually in bars, went into shakes interpreted by the unkind as delirium tremens. She had, in Kuala Kangsar, briefly been unpaid headmistress of a vast privately run afternoon school, and the responsibility and work had brought on a nervous collapse. And then there was the matter of the guilt over her mother's death, which she knew to be irrational but could not, by taking thought, expunge. And yet there was something in her, as in me, which saw the tropics as normality and the temperate zones as the locale for suicidal dementia. White skins looked like disease, the brown skins of Asia – *hitam manis*, or sweet black – were what God had intended: Nabi Adam and Siti Hawa in the Garden of Eden had been black or brown, exchanging *chium-chium* or *chium* 2, not kisses. White culture had been erected on a chronic fight against the cold; tropical heat was the norm. I did not believe I was sick, but I foresaw a true trauma in the acts of readjustment to England, where *laba-laba* were only spiders and *kelip-kelip* or fireflies did not exist. If we had been ruined by the East, it was not, I thought, in any sense that a British doctor, pallid, treating pallid people for 'flu, would understand. But I was to be proved wrong.

We installed ourselves in a room in Bernard Street, Bloomsbury, in the private hotel of the Italian lady from Bermondsey. I had been instructed to report to Sir Alexander Abercrombie at the Hospital for Tropical Diseases, bearing an envelope that contained X-rays of my head and, I presumed, a confidential letter from Glyn Griffiths. The envelope was sealed with red wax, but Lynne tore it open. She would not show me the letter, but she read part of it out, saying at the end 'The bastard'. For it said, impertinently, 'His wife is a chronic alcoholic'. What was thought to be wrong with me Lynne did not say. I delayed reporting, and we drank for four days in August Soho, whence the poets, if not Pirelli's mob, had long departed. Julian Maclaren-Ross was no longer to be seen; Dylan Thomas had died in New York; George Orwell was dead of tuberculosis. Lynne and I both believed, perhaps wrongly, that the British government had been responsible for these two deaths – the Inland Revenue grabbing money Dylan had set aside for his son Llewelyn's school fees, Llewelyn's expulsion, Caitlin's bitter cable to New York, Dylan's terminal jag; the government's unwillingness to bend the rules of foreign exchange to get Orwell to a Swiss sanatorium. We were disposed to hate the British government: we had seen its colonial representatives at work and been appalled. And so I delayed contacting the knighted doctor who would initiate the diagnosis and prognosis of my disease. I did not believe I had a disease.

When I belatedly got to the Hospital for Tropical Diseases I was rebuked: I was still in the service, still under orders. But I was the only colonial officer there. The other patients were businessmen who had been bitten by strange fish and insects while implementing Britain's export drive; there was a concert pianist who had picked up a monstrous tapeworm in Brazil; a thin man who had not travelled further than Bognor Regis dithered in bed with a Caribbean infection. I had my faeces pincered in tiny pellets by a most elegant lady in white and put under a microscope. I was given a spinal tap, and cerebrospinal fluid as pure as gin was borne off for analysis. Then I was told to take a cab to the Neurological Institute in Bloomsbury. We had chosen our diggings well: Bernard Street was just round the corner.

I was placed in a huge ward full of neurological ailments. The man in the next bed had a face fixed in an *homme qui rit* rictus. 'We'll soon put that grin right,' said his doctor, who saw the face as merely another limb. Old men quivered in palsy. A patient in a bed opposite had been reduced to the mere fodder of apparatus like an octopus. He said to the staff nurse, 'Evenin',' staff,' but she did not respond. 'Fair drives you up the bleedin' wall, dunnit, don't say good mornin', good evenin', kiss my arse nor nuffin'.' This was not a first-class officer's ward. Dr Roger Bannister, well-known for having achieved the one-minute mile, came to me with a neurological tray. This was a device for testing olfactory responses. I smelt mint and said it was mint, lemon was lemon, decaying vegetable matter was what it was. My intelligence was superficially probed. Define 'spiral'. What is the difference between 'gay' and 'melancholy'? In those days there *was* a difference. 'Gáy', I said, was of French origin and 'melancholy' of Greek. That was a kind of obsessive wordman's answer and probably adjudged wrong. Take 7 away from 367 and continue the subtraction to the limit. The octopus man heard and was quicker than I was: '360 − 353 − 346 − 339' (all with theta-tismal *f*). 'Easy when you play darts, innit?' More of my spinal fluid was drawn off. I wanted to know why. Dr Bannister said it was to check on the protein content.

The next day, in my thigh-length Chinese dressing gown, all dragons, I was allowed to shuffle to the electroencephalogram department, where my brain waves marched in high troughs on a screen. In the afternoon I covertly dressed and went out. Lynne, as I had expected, was in a pub, or just emerging from one, for it was closing-time. Across from the pub in Coram Street was an illegal drinking club run by Jewish identical twins, Ralph and Leo. They took it in turn to answer police charges and do stretches. Here I met the Kettle Mob, which sold kettles or cheap watches to men on building sites. 'You'd better get back,' said Ralph to me, 'to vat bleedin' 'orse spittle, or we'll 'ave Roger in 'ere runnin' all over you wiv 'is spiked shoes.' It was the first day of a strange pattern of existence. In the morning I submitted to various tortures; in the afternoon I got drunk; in the evening I got into my hospital bed. I thought of running away, but where could I, or we, run to? I received a contract for *The Right to an Answer*. I received a letter from the Crown Agents for the

Colonies stating that my contract was terminated, and that the cost of my hospital charges and extraneous expenses were being met by the Sultan of Brunei. A note from the Hospital for Tropical Diseases stated that I was not, under any circumstances, to return to South-East Asia. A letter from the Mentri Besar of Brunei proposed a new contract under the terms of the state, not of the moribund colonial apparatus. Po Soo Jin wrote to say that the Chinese grocer to whom I owed money had grabbed my Oldsmobile in quittance, but certain Malays and Ibans had shoved the car into the Brunei River. The cook-houseboy Ahmad wrote on three air mail forms, like three volumes, a long plaint in bad Malay: I had cruelly abandoned him and what was he, with an eating wife and many relatives, to do? I sent him a hundred dollars and said he could keep the chickens.

The daily tortures were, I gathered, to divine what was wrong with my central nervous system. 'Nothing wrong,' I boldly said, 'except talent.' Dyes were plunged into my carotid arteries and X-ray photographs taken. I was inverted and my brain was pumped full of air. I was milked of cerebrospinal fluid and felt my vertebrae collapse like a house of cards. I began slowly to realise what disease was suspected. Did I ever have olfactory illusions? In moments of stress could I smell newly sharpened pencils? I remembered that George Gershwin, one day at the keyboard, had known such a smell and had shortly after died of a cerebral tumour.

Summer became autumn. I was transferred to another ward where I had only duties to perform, not probings to suffer. At dawn I went out and bought copies of the *Daily Mirror* for my wardmates, *The Times* for myself. Rioting in Singapore. Parangs and krises being wielded in Kuala Lumpur. Independence had not proved such a good thing after all. I composed an endless passacaglia for the concert pianist with the Brazilian tapeworm, but, I learned, he had died. I wrote a sonnet:

Augustus on a guinea sate in state,
    The sun no proper study but each shaft
    Of filtered light a column: classic craft
Abhorred the arc or arch. To circulate
(Language or blood) meant pipes, and pipes were straight.
    As loaves were gifts from Ceres when she laughed,
    Thyrsis was Jack. Caruso on a raft
Sought Johnjack's rational island, loath to wait

Till sun, neglected, took revenge, so that
   The pillars nodded, melted, and were seen
As Gothic shadows where a goddess sat.
   For, after all, that rational machine,
Granted to all men by the technocrat,
   Chopped logic and became his guillotine.

One of my doctors saw this and shook his head in gloom. It was perhaps, to him, the kind of rhymed nonsense that I had met in Winwick Asylum. It meant, I said, that the seeds of romanticism were contained in its opposite, classicism. He did not understand. 'What,' I asked, 'is my situation? I have been here a long time and have been told nothing.'

'Your situation is that you have had an excess of protein in your cerebrospinal fluid. We see from our later tests' (what later tests? There had been no later tests, except, perhaps, in my sleep) 'that the protein is steadily diminishing. The content is approaching normality.' (But what was normality? Spinal taps are no part of an orthodox medical overhaul.) 'You seem to have been suffering from some psychological distress' (he looked with renewed gloom at my sonnet, at my endless passacaglia) 'which rest and a normal life in a temperate climate will probably cure. You are to be discharged.'

Discharged into the ranks of the unemployed. There seemed to be something else at the back of this neurologist's mind (art as a kind of dementia? Keep away from art?) but, to me, he said no more. He had, I discovered, said something of a certain gravity to my wife. I packed my bag, dressed, and slept that night with Lynne in a double bed. In the night I woke and heard her weeping. I did not ask why; she had been weeping a lot these last years. The next morning we took a map of the South of England and blindly stuck a pin in it. The pin said we were to go to Hove. We went to Hove and its autumnal gales. I did not care much for it. It was full of ancient people who had come there to die. A little way up the coast was Brighton, which Graham Greene had turned into a fearful place full of razor gangs. Still, we had to rest somewhere until we had worked out the future. We found a furnished apartment and stocked it with gin and cheap white wine. I bought a typewriter. I would see if I could earn a little money by writing articles and short stories.

I wrote a short story based on one of the experiences of Ralph or Leo – the twins were interchangeable. Ralph or Leo had worked as a dining-car steward on British Railways. One Christmas Day he had served a fine dinner, much appreciated by the clientele, but he, and his fellow-stewards, were baffled to find that nobody left a tip. It turned out that a passenger with a plummy patrician voice had stood, while the stewards were collecting the coffee from the galley, and said to all: 'I think you'll agree that we've had a superb meal, and that the cook and the stewards deserve, on this festive occasion, a little more than the meagre gratuities to which they are accustomed. I suggest that you donate a pound apiece. I will collect the money and, on your behalf, take it to them in the kitchen with your compliments and best seasonal wishes.' Then he got off, pocket bulging, at the next stop. I called my story 'The Great Christmas Train Mystery' and wrote it in Cockney, full of tosheroons and clods. It was published in a magazine called *Argosy*, which has since disappeared, along with the tosheroon. At Christmas I received a letter from Heinemann saying that the libel suit had been quashed in the Singapore high court, but that the French publishers who had bought *Time for a Tiger* had decided to waive their right to it, as they had little confidence in my future as a writer.

This blunt shutting of my door into Europe depressed me. With Lynne, to whom the announcement of a closed future brought reverberations of a wider resonance, I sensed that there was some knowledge she possessed which she was unwilling to divulge to me. After Christmas 1959 she unlocked the little door. It was a relief to her: women do not like keeping secrets. She said: 'What they told me at the hospital was that you have an inoperable cerebral tumour. That's what Glyn Griffiths, the bastard, suspected also.'

'Inoperable? Tumour? I feel all right. The sea air is doing me good. You too.'

'They said that feeling all right has nothing to do with it. They give you, at the most, a year to live.'

'Nonsense.'

'That's what they say. They seem to know all about it.'

'I don't believe it, I can't.'

'That's what they say.'

'Nothing in writing?'

'Nothing. But they spoke out loud and clear. Well, no. They mumbled rather.'

'So you have to prepare for a widow's existence.'

'It looks like it.'

'You'll need money.' I did not really believe this prognosis. Death, like the quintessence of otherness, is for others. But if the prognosis was valid, then I had been granted something I had never had before: a whole year to live. I would not be run over by a bus tomorrow, nor knifed on the Brighton racetrack. I would not choke on a bone. If I fell in the wintry sea I would not drown. I had a whole year, a long time. In that year I had to earn for my prospective widow. No one would give me a job ('How long do you propose staying with us?' – 'A year. You see, I'm going to die at the end of it.' – 'No future in it, old boy'). I would have to turn myself into a professional writer. Work for the night is coming, the night in which God and little Wilson, now Burgess, would confront each other, if either existed. I sighed and put paper in the typewriter. 'I'd better start,' I said.

And I did.

Index

About The Author

The author of some fifty books including *A Clockwork Orange* and *Earthly Powers*, Anthony Burgess is widely recognized as one of the most important writers in the English-speaking world. Now his autobiography offers a richly detailed and unforgettable portrait of his first forty years, from his childhood in Manchester to the moment when, having been told he was dying of a brain tumor, he began seriously to write. Here is the account of his Catholic upbringing in Protestant England, an experience that Burgess feels has marked him for life—and from which he derives his title (his real name is John Burgess Wilson). Here is the story of his ambitions to become a composer, his infatuation with English poetry, and his attempt to win a scholarship to Oxford. Burgess also describes his years at Manchester University, his extraordinary and often strained marriage to his first wife, his experiences in World War II, as well as his prodigious appetite for foreign languages, and his stint as a teacher in the Far East. Written with a mixture of wit, insight, and stunning virtuosity, *Little Wilson and Big God* is funny, touching, outrageous, brilliant—and a major work by one of the foremost writers of our time.

Anthony Burgess lives in Italy, Switzerland and England.